G000300844

STREET ATLAS
Hertfordshire

Contents

III Key to map symbols

IV Key to map pages

VI Route planning

VIII Administrative and Postcode boundaries

1 Street maps

177 Index

   177 Abbreviations used in index

   177 Town and village index

   178 Index of hospitals, industrial estates, railway stations, schools, shopping centres, street names and universities

First published 1986 by

George Philip Ltd, a division of
Octopus Publishing Group Ltd
2-4 Heron Quays, London E14 4JP

Second colour edition 2000
Second impression 2001

ISBN 0-540-07681-3 (hardback)
ISBN 0-540-07682-1 (spiral)

Digital Data

The exceptionally high-quality mapping
found in this book is available as digital
data in TIFF format, which is easily
convertible to other bit-mapped (raster)
image formats.

The index is also available in digital form
as a standard database table. It contains
all the details found in the printed index
together with the National Grid reference
for the map square in which each entry
is named and feature codes for places
of interest in eight categories such as
education and health.

For further information and to discuss
your requirements, please contact
Philip's on 020 7531 8440 or
george.philip@philips-maps.co.uk

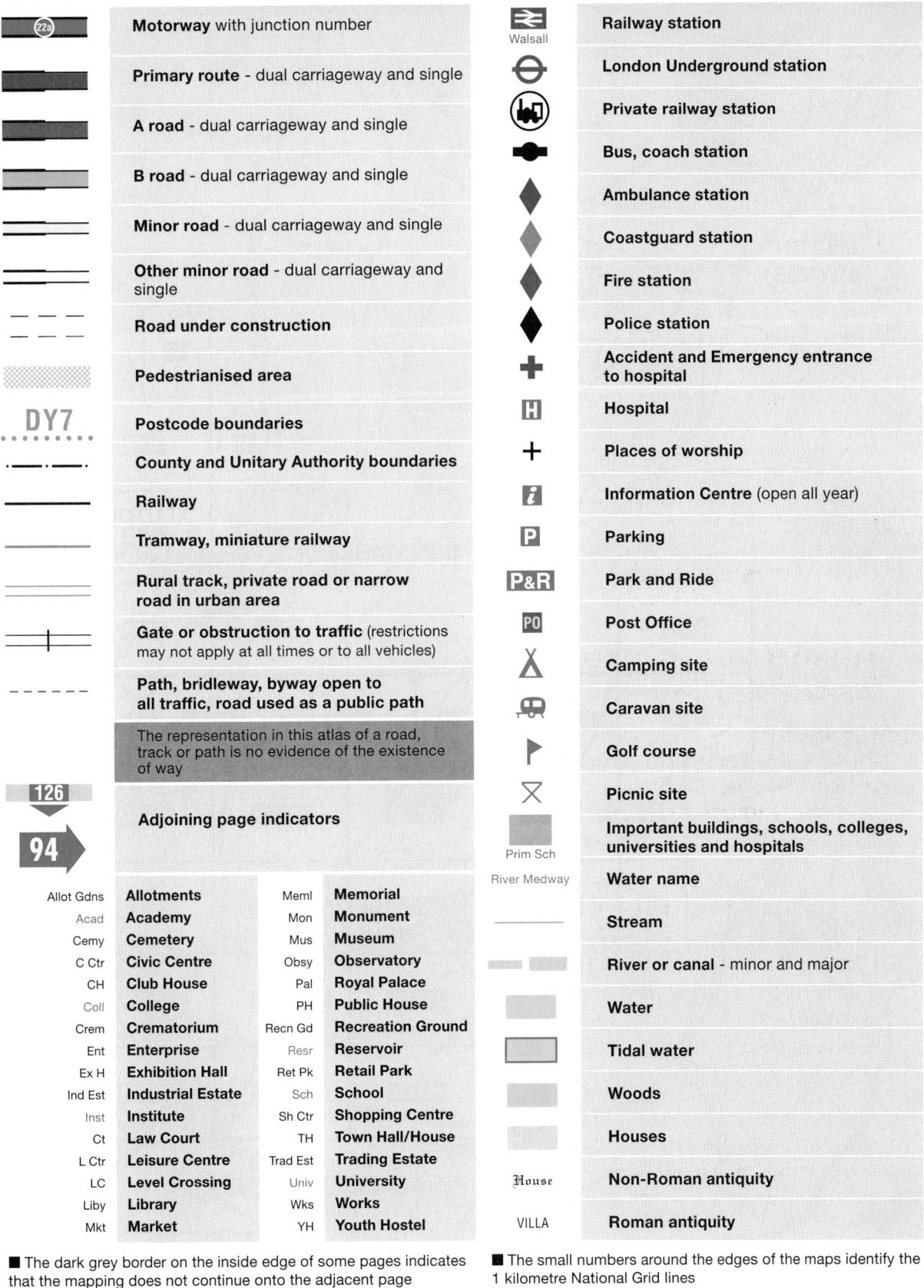

		Motorway with junction number
		Primary route - dual carriageway and single
		A road - dual carriageway and single
		B road - dual carriageway and single
		Minor road - dual carriageway and single
		Other minor road - dual carriageway and single
		Road under construction
		Pedestrianised area
DY7		Postcode boundaries
		County and Unitary Authority boundaries
		Railway
		Tramway, miniature railway
		Rural track, private road or narrow road in urban area
		Gate or obstruction to traffic (restrictions may not apply at all times or to all vehicles)
		Path, bridleway, byway open to all traffic, road used as a public path

The representation in this atlas of a road, track or path is no evidence of the existence of way

126
94

Adjoining page indicators

Allot Gdns	Allotments	Meml	Memorial
Acad	Academy	Mon	Monument
Cemy	Cemetery	Mus	Museum
C Ctr	Civic Centre	Obsy	Observatory
CH	Club House	Pal	Royal Palace
Coll	College	PH	Public House
Crem	Crematorium	Recn Gd	Recreation Ground
Ent	Enterprise	Resr	Reservoir
Ex H	Exhibition Hall	Ret Pk	Retail Park
Ind Est	Industrial Estate	Sch	School
Inst	Institute	Sh Ctr	Shopping Centre
Ct	Law Court	TH	Town Hall/House
L Ctr	Leisure Centre	Trad Est	Trading Estate
LC	Level Crossing	Univ	University
Liby	Library	Wks	Works
Mkt	Market	YH	Youth Hostel

Walsall	Railway station
	London Underground station
	Private railway station
	Bus, coach station
	Ambulance station
	Coastguard station
	Fire station
	Police station
	Accident and Emergency entrance to hospital
H	Hospital
	Places of worship
i	Information Centre (open all year)
P	Parking
P&R	Park and Ride
PO	Post Office
	Camping site
	Caravan site
	Golf course
	Picnic site
Prim Sch	Important buildings, schools, colleges, universities and hospitals
River Medway	Water name
	Stream
	River or canal - minor and major
	Water
	Tidal water
	Woods
	Houses
House	Non-Roman antiquity
VILLA	Roman antiquity

■ The dark grey border on the inside edge of some pages indicates that the mapping does not continue onto the adjacent page

■ The small numbers around the edges of the maps identify the 1 kilometre National Grid lines

The scale of the maps is 5.52 cm to 1 km
3¹/₂ inches to 1 mile 1: 18103

0		¹/₄		¹/₂		³/₄		1 mile
0	250 m	500 m	750 m	1 kilometre				

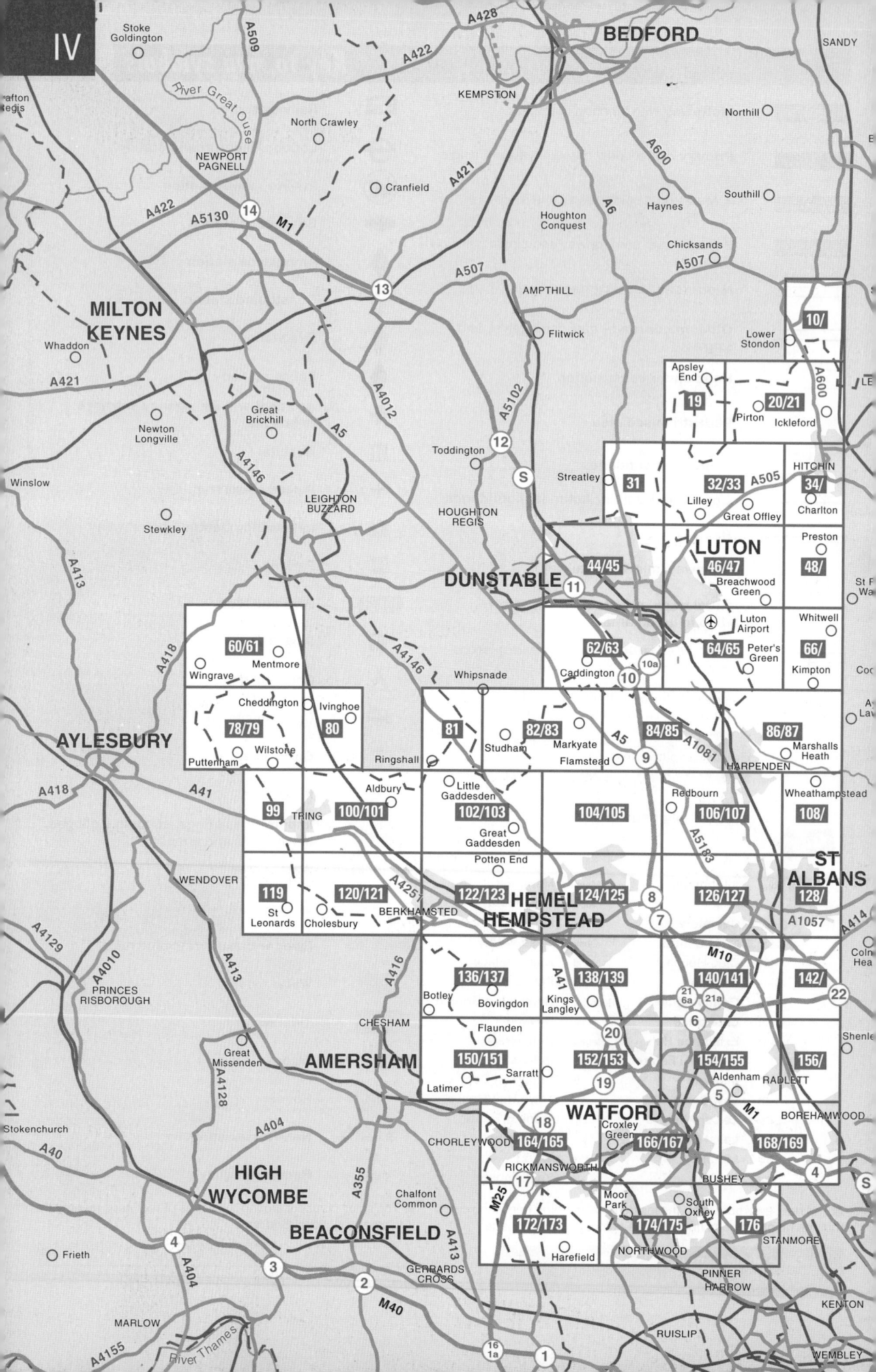

IV

Stoke Goldington
Whaddon
MILTON KEYNES
Newton Longville
Stewkley
Winslow
A413
AYLESBURY
A418
A41
PRINCES RISBOROUGH
HIGH WYCOMBE
Stokenchurch
A40
Frith
MARLOW
River Thames
A4155

NEWPORT PAGNELL
North Crawley
Cranfield
Great Brickhill
Wingrave
Mentmore
Cheddington
Ivinghoe
Puttenham
Wilstone
Ringshall
Aldbury
TRING
Cholesbury
BERKHAMSTED
WENDOVER
St Leonards
Great Missenden
CHESHAM
Botley
Bovingdon
Flaunden
AMERSHAM
Latimer
Sarratt
BEACONSFIELD
Chalfont Common
GERRARDS CROSS
M40

BEDFORD
KEMPSTON
Houghton Conquest
Flitwick
AMPTHILL
Toddington
LEIGHTON BUZZARD
HOUGHTON REGIS
DUNSTABLE
Whipsnade
Studham
Markyate
Flamstead
Little Gaddesden
Great Gaddesden
Potten End
HEMEL HEMPSTEAD
Kings Langley
Redbourn
ST ALBANS
Aldenham
RADLETT
WATFORD
Croxley Green
CHORLEYWOOD
RICKMANSWORTH
Moor Park
Harefield
NORTHWOOD
South Oxhey
BUSHEY
STANMORE
PINNER
HARROW
KENTON
BOREHAMWOOD
Shenle
RUISLIP
WEMBLEY

Northill
Haynes
Southill
Chicksands
Lower Stondon
Apsley End
Pirton
Ickleford
Streatley
Lilley
Great Offley
HITCHIN
Charlton
LUTON
Breachwood Green
Luton Airport
Peter's Green
Kimpton
Whitwell
Preston
Harpenden
Marshalls Heath
Wheathampstead

10/
19   20/21
31   32/33   A505   34/
46/47   48/
44/45
62/63   64/65   66/
84/85   86/87
60/61
78/79   80
81   82/83
99   100/101   102/103   104/105   106/107   108/
119   120/121   122/123   124/125   126/127   128/
136/137   138/139   140/141   142/
150/151   152/153   154/155   156/
164/165   166/167   168/169
172/173   174/175   176

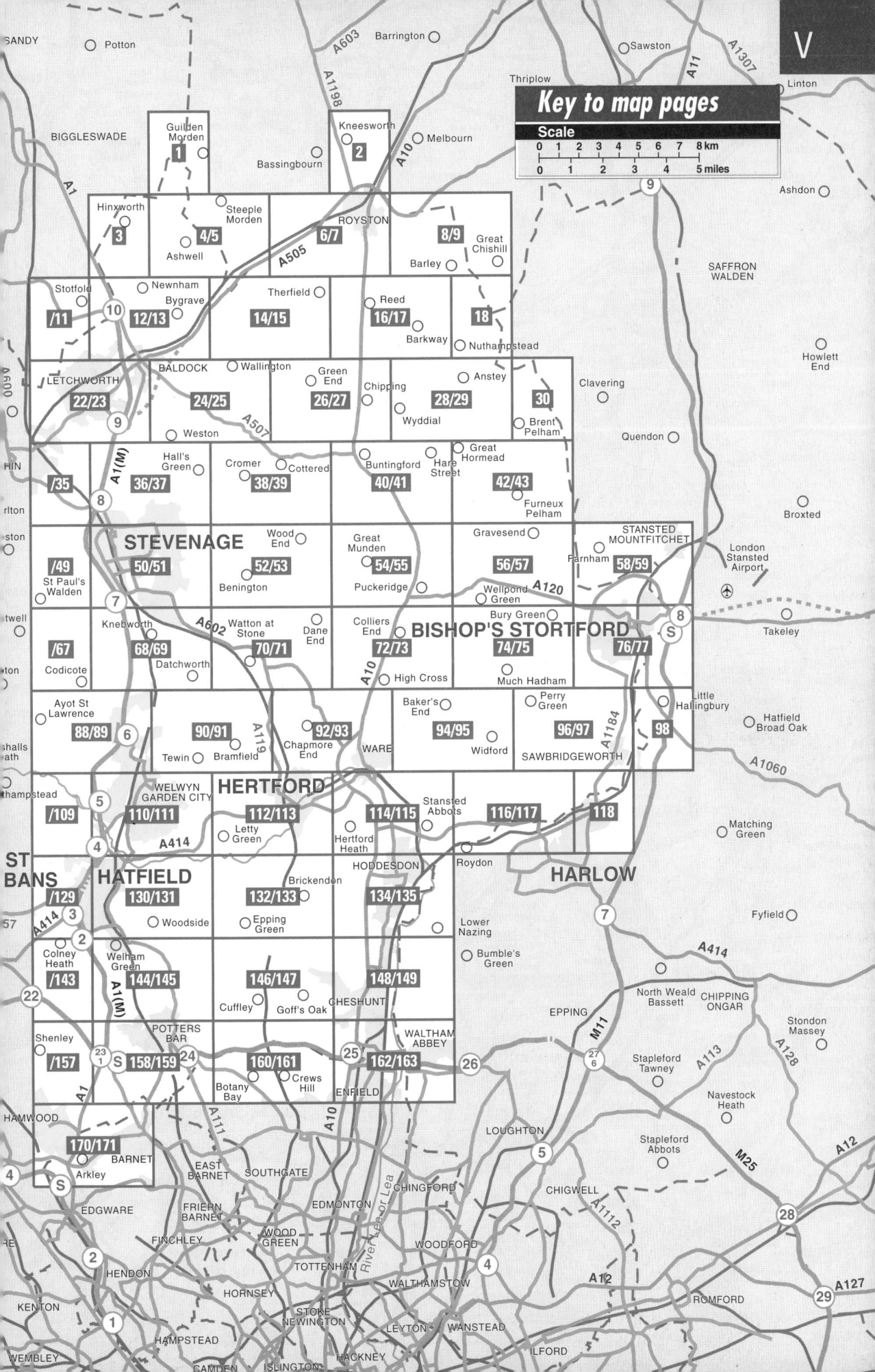

Key to map pages

Scale

0 1 2 3 4 5 6 7 8 km
0 1 2 3 4 5 miles

1 Guilden Morden
2 Kneesworth
3 Hinxworth
4/5 Ashwell / Steeple Morden
6/7 Royston
8/9 Great Chishill / Barley
/11 Stotfold
12/13 Newnham / Bygrave
14/15 Therfield
16/17 Reed
18 Barkway / Nuthampstead
22/23 Letchworth
24/25 Baldock / Wallington
26/27 Green End
28/29 Chipping / Anstey / Wyddial
30 Brent Pelham
/35
36/37 Hall's Green
38/39 Cromer / Cottered
40/41 Buntingford / Hare Street
42/43 Great Hormead / Furneux Pelham
/49 St Paul's Walden
50/51 STEVENAGE
52/53 Benington / Wood End
54/55 Great Munden / Puckeridge
56/57 Gravesend / Wellpond Green
58/59 Farnham / STANSTED MOUNTFITCHET
/67 Codicote
68/69 Knebworth / Datchworth
70/71 Watton at Stone
72/73 Dane End / Colliers End / High Cross
74/75 Bury Green / Much Hadham
76/77 BISHOP'S STORTFORD
88/89 Ayot St Lawrence
90/91 Tewin / Bramfield
92/93 Chapmore End
94/95 Baker's End / Widford / WARE
96/97 Perry Green / SAWBRIDGEWORTH
98 Little Hallingbury
/109
110/111 WELWYN GARDEN CITY
112/113 HERTFORD / Letty Green
114/115 Hertford Heath / Stansted Abbots
116/117
118
/129
130/131 HATFIELD
132/133 Brickendon
134/135 HODDESDON / Roydon
/143 Colney Heath
144/145 Welham Green
146/147 Cuffley / Goff's Oak
148/149 CHESHUNT
/157 Shenley
158/159 POTTERS BAR / Botany Bay / Crews Hill
160/161
162/163 ENFIELD / WALTHAM ABBEY
170/171 BARNET / Arkley

Route planning

Scale

0 1 2 3 4 5 6 7 8 km
0 1 2 3 4 5 miles

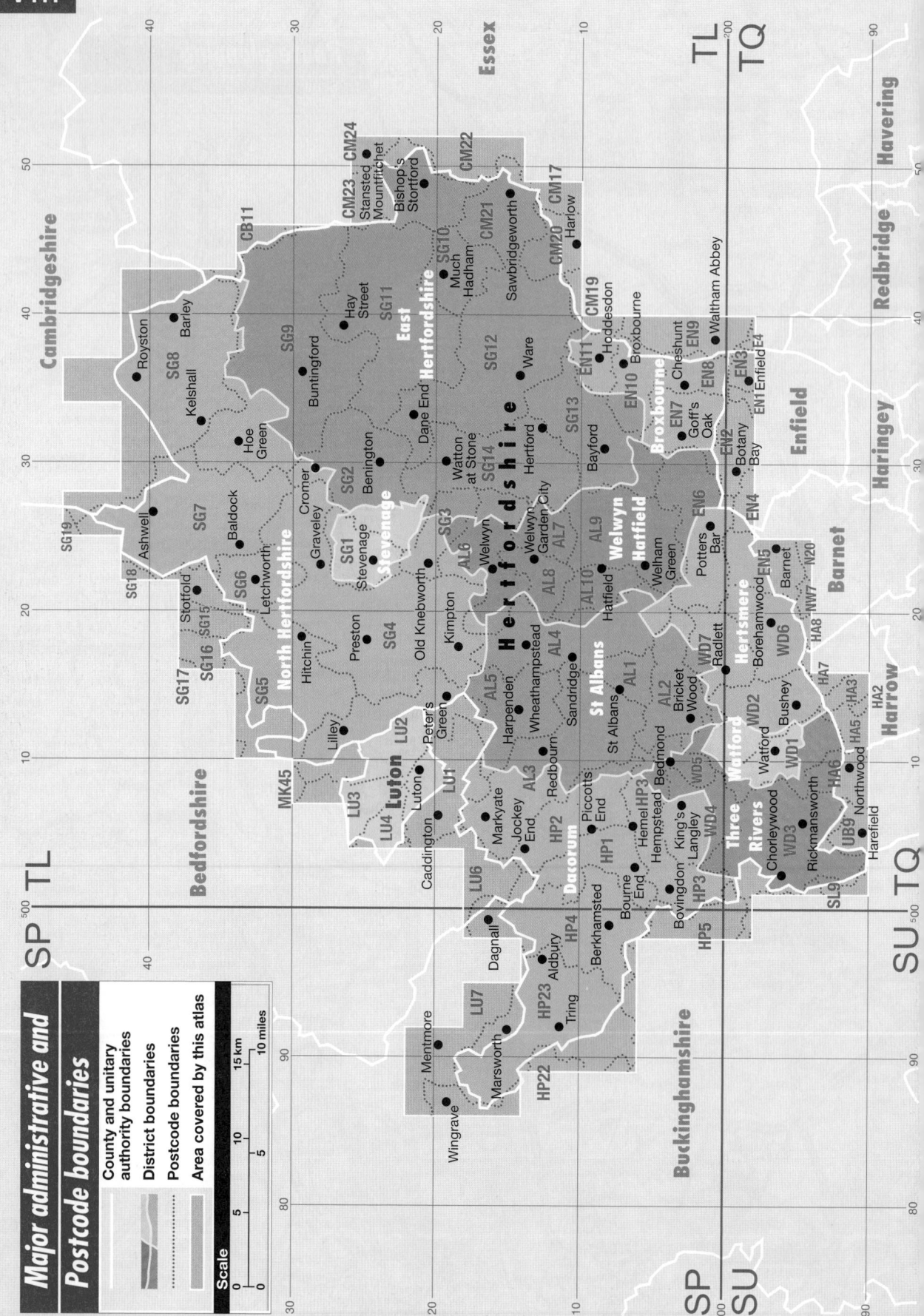

Major administrative and Postcode boundaries

County and unitary authority boundaries

District boundaries

Postcode boundaries

Area covered by this atlas

Scale

0   5   10   15 km

0   5   10 miles

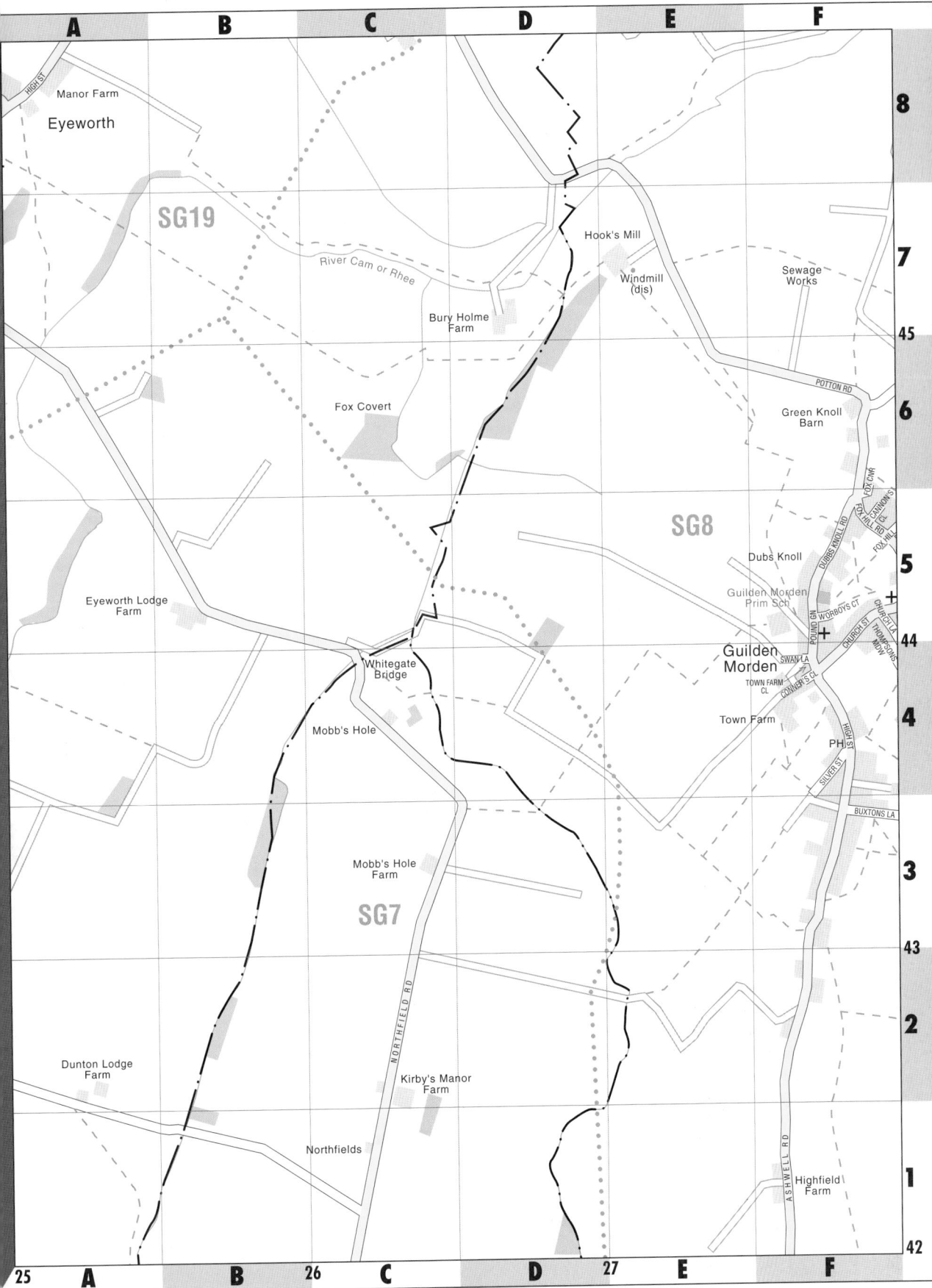

A B C D E F

8

Manor Farm

Eyeworth

SG19

Hook's Mill

River Cam or Rhee

7

Windmill (dis)

Sewage Works

45

Bury Holme Farm

Fox Covert

Green Knoll Barn

6

POTTON RD

FOX CLNR

DUBS KNOLL RD

CASHION'S

FOX HILL RD CL

FOX HILL

SG8

Dubs Knoll

5

Eyeworth Lodge Farm

Guilden Morden Prim Sch

WORBOYS CT

POUND GN

CHURCH LA

THOMPSONS MDW

44

Guilden Morden

SWAN LA

CHURCH ST

Whitegate Bridge

TOWN FARM CL

CONNER'S CL

Mobb's Hole

Town Farm

4

PH

HIGH ST

SILVER ST

BUXTONS LA

Mobb's Hole Farm

3

SG7

43

NORTHFIELD RD

2

Dunton Lodge Farm

Kirby's Manor Farm

Northfields

ASHWELL RD

Highfield Farm

1

42

25 A B 26 C D 27 E F

A **B** **C** **D** **E** **F**

Meldreth

Mettle Hill Farm

Mettle Hill

Dyer's Green

Ermine Farm

Frog Hall

Bassingbourn Barracks

OXFORD CL

Danger Area

Harcamlow Way

Resr

CHESTNUT LA

Danger Area

TOWER CL
ORCHARD CL
THE CAUSEWAY
NIGHTINGALE AVE
WELLINGTON PL
CANBERRA CL
PH
PH
SWINNELL CL

TOWER CL

Kneesworth

H
Kneesworth House

SG8

OLD NORTH RD

TUDOR CL
TUDOR CL

Beauval Farm

Harcamlow Way

Bury Farm

ASHWELL ST

Nurseries

A1198

A10

Highfield Farm

Sewage Works

Holland Hall

New Farm

WORDSWORTH
THACKERAY
ST PANCRAS HO
KEATS CL
BURNS RD
TENNYSON CL
1 SWINBURNE C
2 SCOTT CL
THOMAS
OWEN DR
BE JEMAN
MASEFIELD
TEASDALE CL
SPENSER
SHELLEY
SWIFT
COLERIDGE CL
KIPLING
LINDSAY AVE
KEATS CL
LARKIN
BLAKE CL
MELBOURN RD
HOUSMAN AVE
MILTON CL
OLD NORTH RD
Schs

A505

A1198

A505

34 35 36

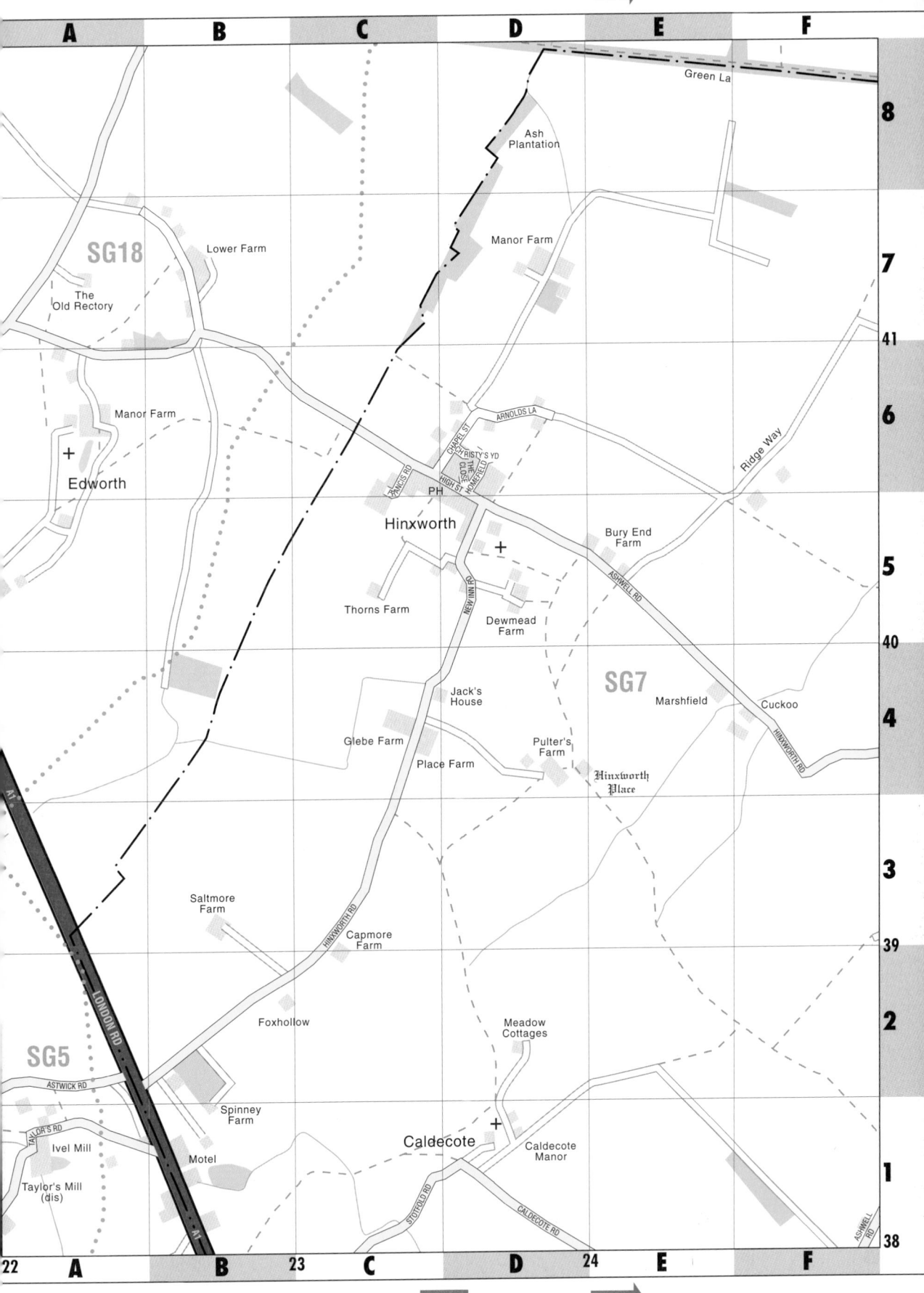

A | B | C | D | E | F

8

Green La

Ash
Plantation

SG18

Lower Farm

7

The
Old Rectory

Manor Farm

41

6

ARNOLDS LA

Manor Farm

CHAPEL ST

CHRISTY'S YD

+

Edworth

FRANCIS RD

HIGH ST

THE
CLOSE

MORFIELD

PH

Ridge Way

Hinxworth

Bury End
Farm

5

+

ASHWELL RD

NEW INN RD

Thorns Farm

Dewmead
Farm

40

SG7

4

Jack's
House

Marshfield

Cuckoo

HINXWORTH RD

Glebe Farm

Place Farm

Pulter's
Farm

Hinxworth
Place

3

A1

Saltmore
Farm

HINXWORTH RD

39

Capmore
Farm

LONDON RD

Foxhollow

Meadow
Cottages

2

SG5

ASTWICK RD

Spinney
Farm

TAYLOR'S RD

+

Ivel Mill

Caldecote

Caldecote
Manor

1

Motel

STOTFOLD RD

Taylor's Mill
(dis)

CALDECOTE RD

ASHWELL
RD

A1

38

22 | A | B | 23 | C | D | 24 | E | F

3
1

A B C D E F

8
7
41
6
5
40
4
3
39
2
1
38

25 A B 26 C D 27 E F

Green La
Ridge Way
Barrowsford Bridge
Northfield Rd
Cold Harbour
Ashwell Rd
SG8
Sewage Works
Common La
Bluegates Farm
River Rhee
Ashwell End
Bluegates Dairy
Elbrook House
SG7
Cemy
Baldwin's Corner
Ashwell Bury
Fordham Cl
Green La
Love's Farm
Love La
Rollys La
Gardiners La
Hill St
Springhead
Lucas La
Icknield Way Path
Quarry Hills Farm
Whittington Farm
Hinxworth Rd
Farrow's Farm
THE RICKYARD
Ashwell Village Mus
Bacons La
Church St
Swan St
ALMS LA
HODWELL
High St
Hotel
PH
Silver St
PO
Kingsland Way
Ashwell St
Station Rd
Ashridge Farm
Woodforde Cl
West End
Colbron Cl
Wills Rise
Back St
Bear La
Dixies Cl
Claybush Rd
Ashwell Prim Sch
Ashwell
Partridge Hill
Newnham Hill
Newnham Way
Claybush Hill
Arbury Banks
Icknield Way Path
Ash Hill
Ashwell Rd

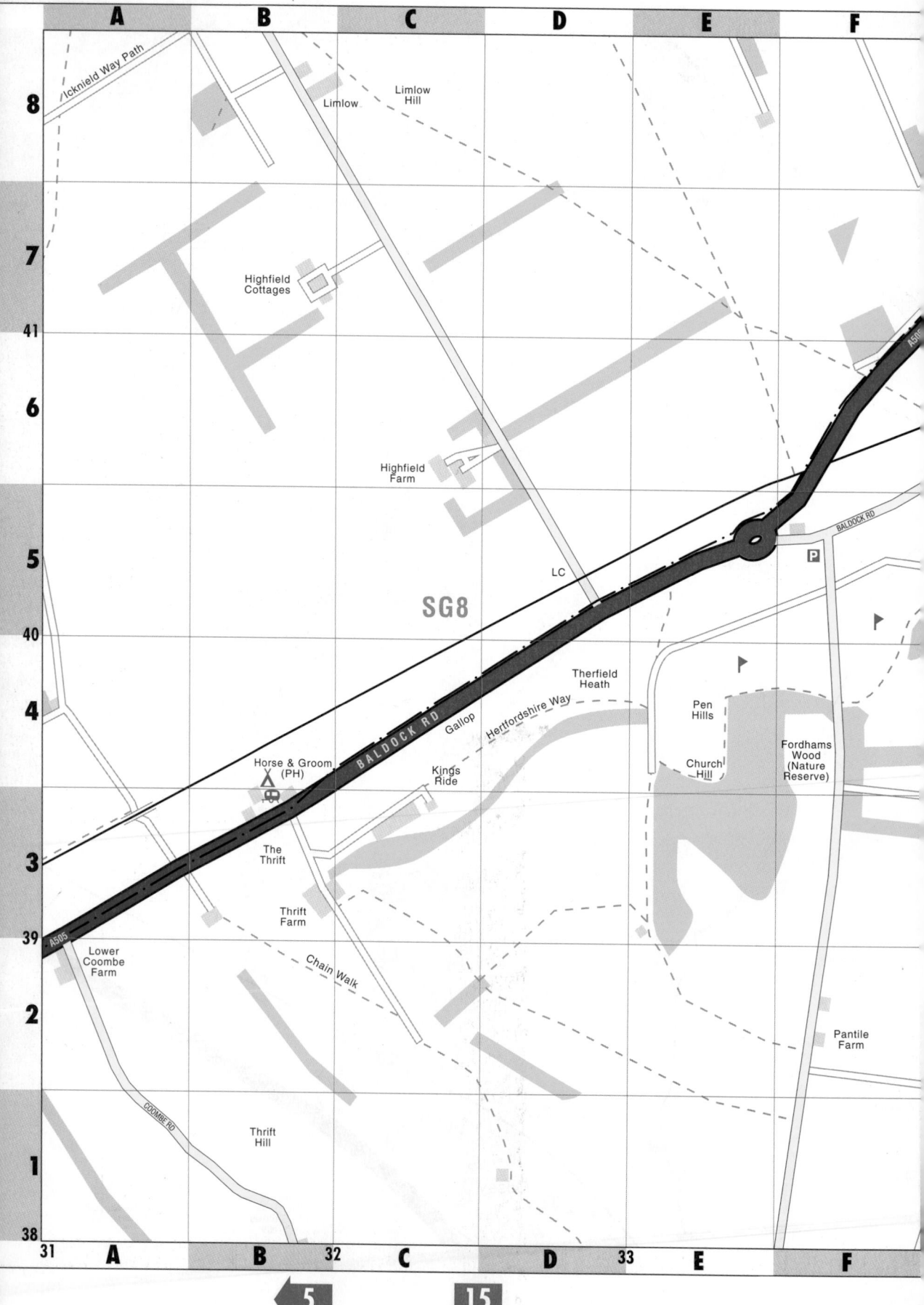

Icknield Way Path

Limlow

Limlow
Hill

8

A

B

C

D

E

F

7

Highfield
Cottages

41

6

Highfield
Farm

LC

5

SG8

P

BALDOCK RD

40

Therfield
Heath

4

Pen
Hills

Horse & Groom
(PH)

Gallop

Hertfordshire Way

Kings
Ride

Church
Hill

Fordhams
Wood
(Nature
Reserve)

3

The
Thrift

Thrift
Farm

A505

39

Lower
Coombe
Farm

Chain Walk

2

Pantile
Farm

COOMBE RD

Thrift
Hill

1

38

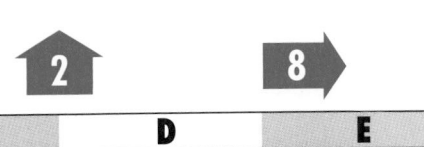

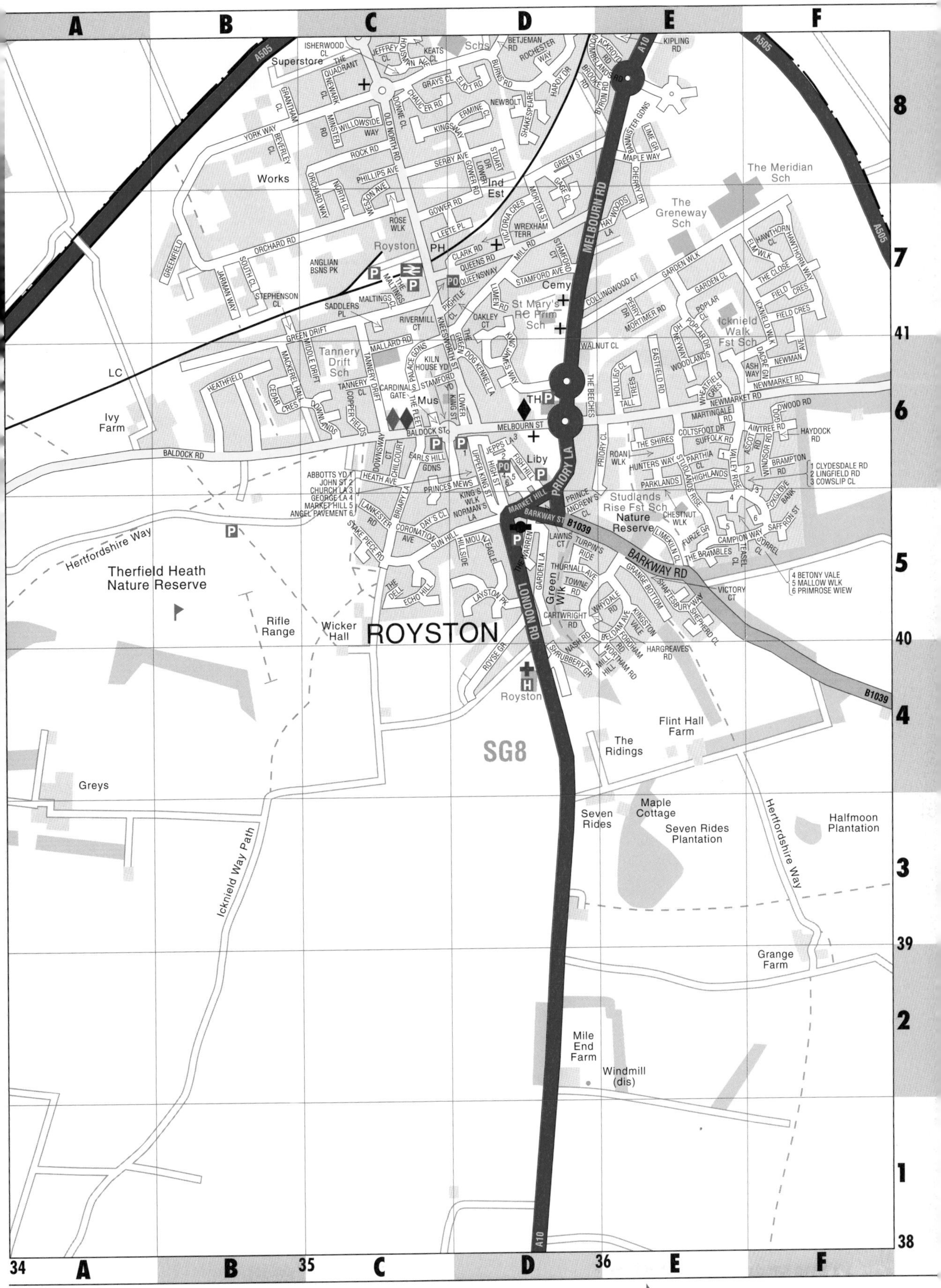

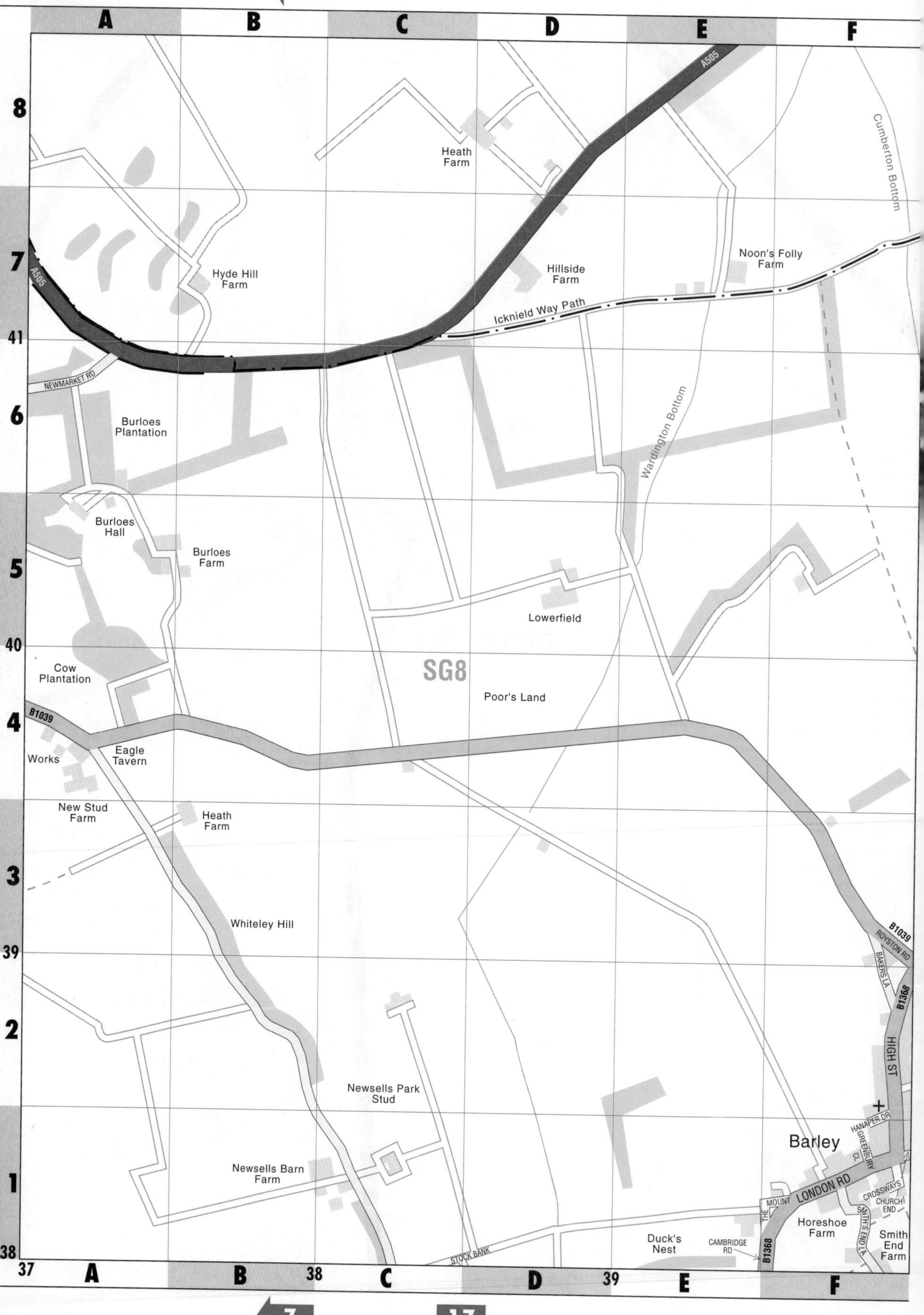

A B C D E F

8

7

41

6

5

40

4

3

39

2

1

38

37 A B 38 C D 39 E F

A505

Heath Farm

Hyde Hill Farm

Hillside Farm

Noon's Folly Farm

Icknield Way Path

A505

NEWMARKET RD

Burloes Plantation

Cumberton Bottom

Wardington Bottom

Burloes Hall

Burloes Farm

Lowerfield

SG8

Poor's Land

Cow Plantation

B1039

Works

Eagle Tavern

New Stud Farm

Heath Farm

Whiteley Hill

B1039

ROYSTON RD

BAKER'S LA

B1368

HIGH ST

Newsells Park Stud

Barley

HANAPER DR

GRETCHRY CL

Newsells Barn Farm

THE MOUNT

LONDON RD

CROSSWAYS

CHURCH END

SMITH'S END LA

Horeshoe Farm

Smith End Farm

Duck's Nest

CAMBRIDGE RD

B1368

STOCK BANK

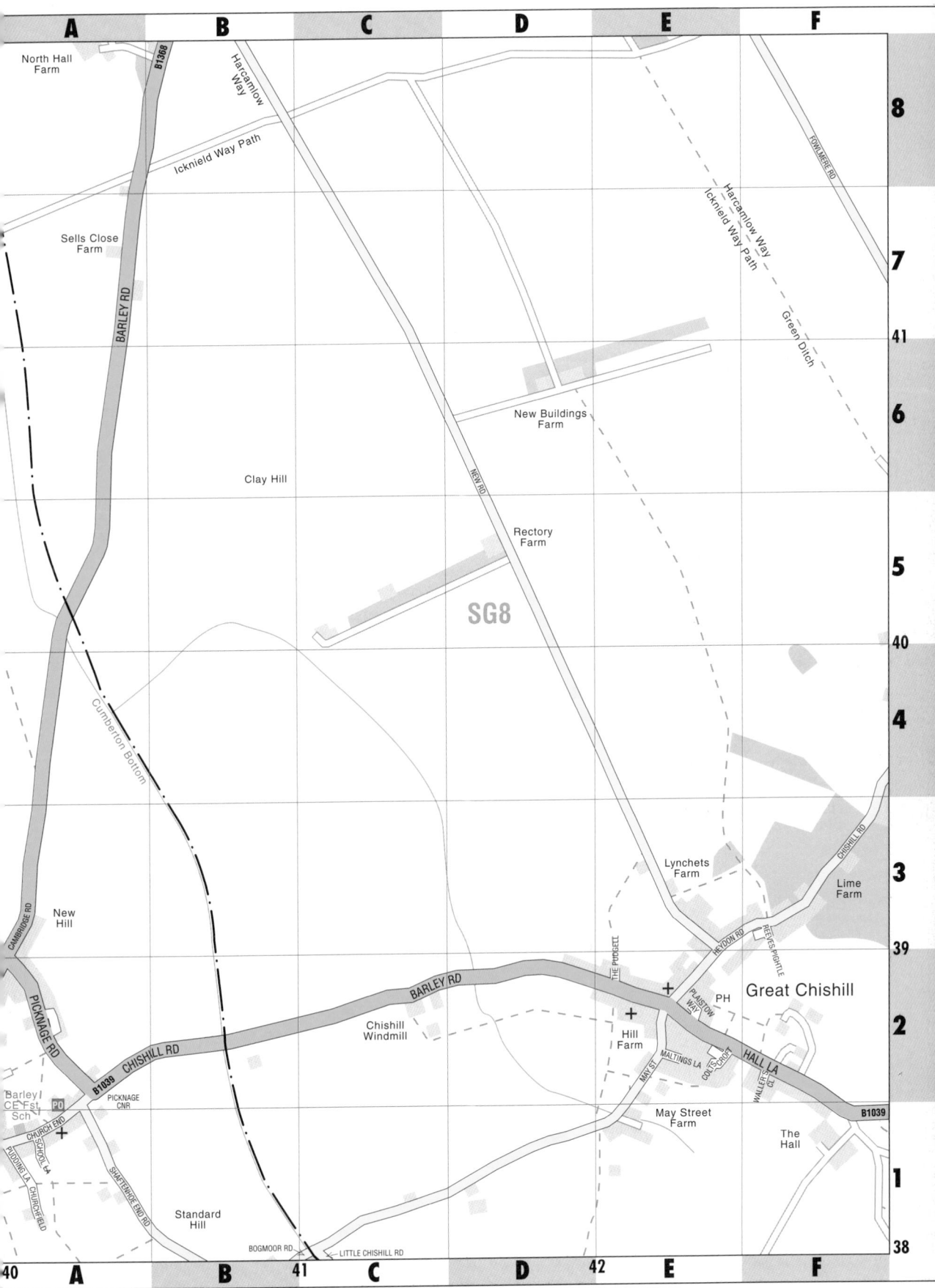

A B C D E F

8

7

41

6

North Hall Farm

Harcamlow Way

Icknield Way Path

B1368

BARLEY RD

Sells Close Farm

Harcamlow Way
Icknield Way Path

FOWLMERE RD

Green Ditch

Clay Hill

NEW RD

New Buildings Farm

5

40

Rectory Farm

SG8

Cumberton Bottom

4

New Hill

CAMBRIDGE RD

Lynchets Farm

CHISHILL RD

Lime Farm

3

39

PICKNAGE RD

BARLEY RD

THE PUDGETT

HEYDON RD

REEVES PIGHTLE

PLAISTOW WAY

PH

Great Chishill

2

Chishill Windmill

Hill Farm

MAY ST

MALTINGS LA

COLTS CROFT

WALLERS CL

HALL LA

B1039

Barley CE Fst Sch

PO

PICKNAGE CNR

CHURCH END

SCHOOL LA

May Street Farm

The Hall

1

PUDDING LA

CHURCHFIELD

SHAFTENOE END RD

Standard Hill

BOGMOOR RD

LITTLE CHISHILL RD

38

40 A B 41 C D 42 E F

A B C D E F

A507

NEW RD

THE GARDENS
ARLESEY RD
PARK
FARM
CL
A6001
PH
ARLESEY RD
A50

Henlow

Arlesey
Bridge

SG17

Old Manor
Farm

Cityfield
Farm

7

Westfield
Farm

Middlefield
Farm

37

Henlow Airfield

MIDDLEFIELD LA

HITCHIN RD

Middle
Water

6

Sewage
Works

SG16

River Hiz

Camp

Playing
Field

SG15

5

A600

Derwent
Lower
Sch
SPRECKLEY
CL

OWEN JONES CL
DAWSON CL
MORRIS CL
WEEDON CL

Laurels
Grove

MILL LA

36

WHITTLE CL

TEDDER AVE
FRANKS CL

WHITWORTH JONES AVE

Susans
Grove

KAREN
HO

OLDFIELD FARM RD
DERWENT RD
NENE RD
OLYMPUS RD

AVON CHASE

STRAW
PLAIT
WAY

Greyhound
Stadium

A6001

PO

AVON RD

Oldfield
Farm

4

STATION RD
ALTON RD

PH
PECKWORTH
IND EST

HENLOW IND EST

BURNELL AVE
THE
CRESCENT

OLDFIELD FARM RD

Lower
Stondon

ASTRAL CL

BOXTON AVE

Playing
Field

Lindas
Grove

Works

3

Cherry Tree
Nurseries

APPLECROFT
ORCHARD WAY
CHERRY TREES

BEDFORD RD

CHESTNUT AVE

NORTHERN AVE
WESTERN AVE
CENTRAL AVE
EASTERN AVE
SOUTHERN AVE

THE OVAL

Wr
Twr

PEAR TREE
CL

PLUM TREE RD

35

Old
Ramerick

2

Holwellbury
Farm

Holwell Bury
House

Holwellbury

Ramerick
Bottom

1

Ramerick
Nursery

A600

SG5

LC

34

16 A B 17 C D 18 E F

12 →

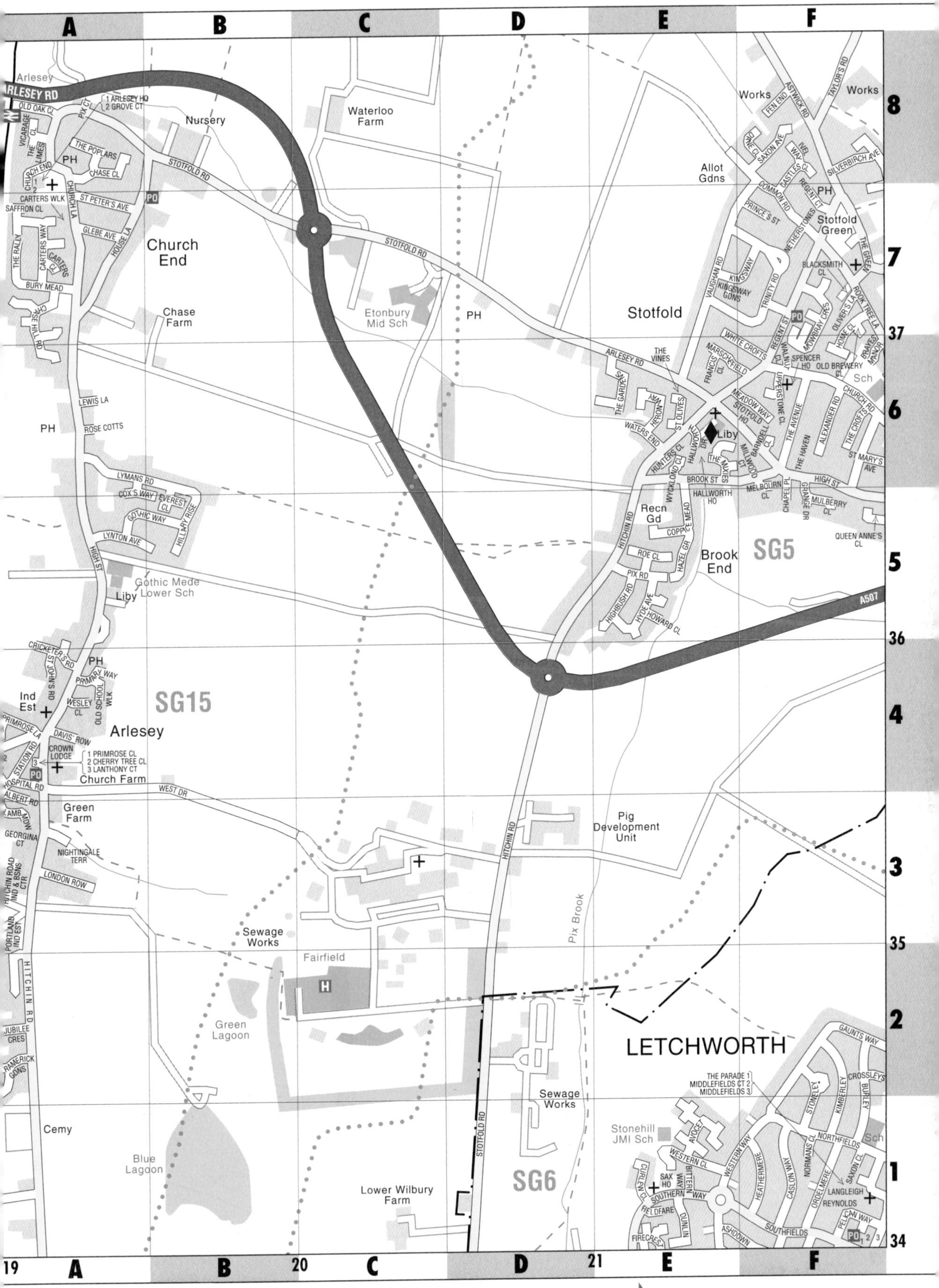

| A | B | C | D | E | F |

ARLESEY RD
Arlesey
Old Oak Cl
1 ARLESEY HO
2 GROVE CT
Nursery
Waterloo Farm
Works
Works
8

VICARAGE
THE POPLARS
PIX CT
CHURCH END
PH
CHASE CL
ST PETER'S AVE
CARTERS WLK
SAFFRON CL
GLEBE AVE
CARTERS WAY
HOUSE LA
CHURCH LA
STOTFOLD RD
PO
Church End

Allot Gdns
PEN HILL
ASTWICK RD
TAYLOR'S RD
SAXON AVE
CASTLES CL
REGENT CL
PH
SILVERBIRCH AVE

COMMON RD
PRINCE S ST
Stotfold Green

STOTFOLD RD
STOTFOLD RD
WETHERSTONES
Stotfold

CHASE HILL RD
THE RALLY
BURY MEAD
Chase Farm
Etonbury Mid Sch
PH
ARLESEY RD
THE VINES

7

37

KINGSWAY
KINGSWAY GDNS
VAUGHAN RD
TRINITY RD
WHITE CROFTS
SPENCER HO
MONYRAT CRES
OLIVER'S LA
HOME CL
BRAXLEY CL
OLD BREWERY
Sch
PO
REGENT ST

THE GARTELLS
LEWIS LA
ROSE COTTS
PH
WATERS END
FRANCIS CL
MARSCHFIELD
MEADOW WAY
STOTFOLD SHO
CHURCH RD
ALEXANDER RD
THE AVENUE
THE CROFTS RD

6

LYMANS RD
COX'S WAY
EVEREST CL
GOTHIC WAY
HILLARY RISE
LYNTON AVE
HIGH ST
Gothic Mede Liby Lower Sch

HUNTERS CL
HERON RD
NEW RD
ST OLIVES
HALLWORTH
WYCKLONG CL
THE MAZES
BROOK ST
HALLWORTH HO
Liby
Recn Gd
COPPICE MEAD
HAZEL GR
Brook End
MELBOURN CL
CHAPEL PL
GRANGE DR
HIGH ST
MULBERRY CL
ST MARY'S AVE
QUEEN ANNE'S CL
SG5

5

HITCHIN RD
ROE CL
PIX RD
HIGHBUSH RD
HYDE AVE
HOWARD CL
A507

36

CRICKETERS RD
ST JOHN'S RD
PH
PRIMARY WAY
WESLEY CL
OLD SCHOOL WLK
SG15
Ind Est
PRIMROSE LA
DAVIS ROW
CROWN LODGE
1 PRIMROSE CL
2 CHERRY TREE CL
3 LANTHONY CT
Arlesey
PO
Church Farm

4

HOSPITAL RD
STATION RD
ALBERT RD
AMB
GEORGINA CT
WEST DR
Green Farm
NIGHTINGALE TERR
LONDON ROW
HITCHIN RD
HITCHIN RD
Pig Development Unit

3

PORTLAND IND EST
HITCHIN ROAD IND & BSNS CTR
Sewage Works
Fairfield
H
Pix Brook

35

JUBILEE CRES
RIMERICK GDNS
HITCHIN RD
Green Lagoon

LETCHWORTH

2

GAUNTS WAY
STONELEY
KIMBERLEY
CROSSLEYS
BURLEY
THE PARADE 1
MIDDLEFIELDS CT 2
MIDDLEFIELDS 3
NORTHFIELDS
Sch

Cemy
Blue Lagoon
STOTFOLD RD
Lower Wilbury Farm
Sewage Works
SG6
Stonehill JMI Sch

CURLEW CL
SAX HO
WESTERN CL
WESTERN WAY
BITTERN WAY
DUNLIN
HEATHERMERE
CASTON WAY
NORMANS CL
DROLMERE
SAXON CL
WESTERN WAY
LANGLEIGH
REYNOLDS
PELICAN WAY
SOUTHERN WAY
FIELDFARE
SOUTHFIELDS
ASHDOWN
FIRECREST
PO
1

34

| A | B | C | D | E | F |

19   20   21

↓ 22   12 →

A   B   C   D   E   F

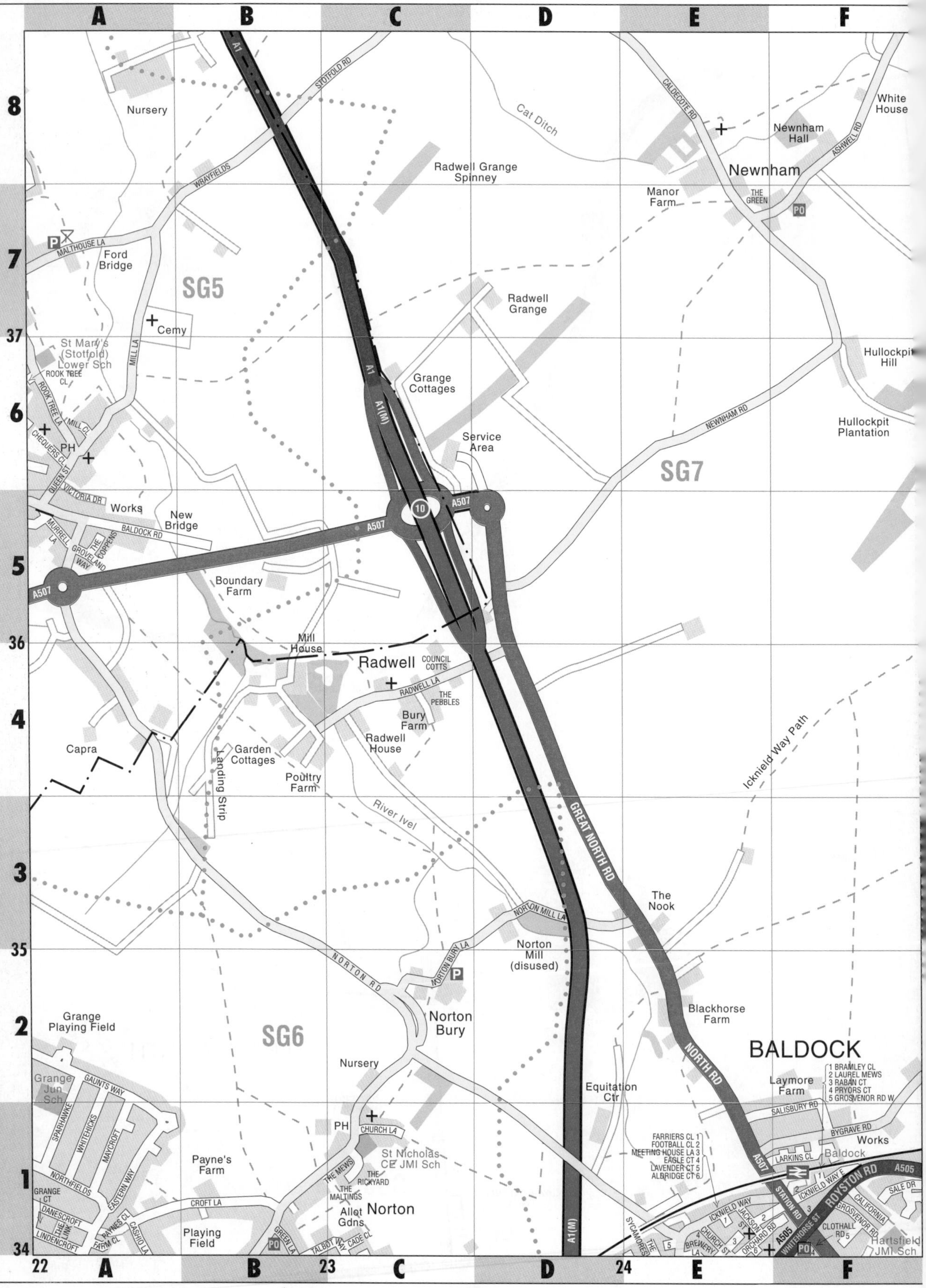

8

Nursery

White House

Cat Ditch

Radwell Grange Spinney

Newnham Hall

Newnham

THE GREEN

PO

Manor Farm

WRAYFIELDS

STOTFOLD RD

CALDECOTE RD

ASHWELL RD

7

P

Ford Bridge

MALTHOUSE LA

Radwell Grange

SG5

Hullockpit Hill

37

Cemy

St Mary's (Stotfold) Lower Sch

ROOK TREE CL

MILL LA

Grange Cottages

6

PH

CHEQUERS CL

ROOK TREE LA

MILL CL

Service Area

Hullockpit Plantation

NEWNHAM RD

SG7

Works

New Bridge

VICTORIA DR

MURRELL LA

GROVELAND WAY

BALDOCK RD

A507

10

A507

A1(M)

5

A507

Boundary Farm

36

Mill House

Radwell

COUNCIL COTTS

RADWELL LA

THE PEBBLES

4

Capra

Garden Cottages

Landing Strip

Bury Farm

Radwell House

Poultry Farm

Icknield Way Path

River Ivel

3

The Nook

GREAT NORTH RD

35

NORTON MILL LA

Norton Mill (disused)

NORTON RD

NORTON BURY LA

P

2

Grange Playing Field

SG6

Norton Bury

Nursery

Blackhorse Farm

NORTH RD

BALDOCK

Laymore Farm

SALISBURY RD

1 BRAMLEY CL
2 LAUREL MEWS
3 RABAN CT
4 PRYORS CT
5 GROSVENOR RD W

GAUNTS WAY

SPARROWHAWK

WHITEHICKS

MATCHCROFT

Grange Jun Sch

PH

CHURCH LA

Equitation Ctr

BYGRAVE RD

Works

Baldock

A505

1

Payne's Farm

St Nicholas CE JMI Sch

THE MEWS

THE MALTINGS

THE RICKYARD

FARRIERS CL 1
FOOTBALL CL 2
MEETING HOUSE LA 3
EAGLE CT 4
LAVENDER CT 5
ALBRIDGE CT 6

LARKINS CL

A507

ROYSTON RD

ROSVENOR RD

CALIFORNIA

SALE DR

EASTERN WAY

NORTHFIELDS

GRANGE CT

DANESCROFT

LINDENCROFT

PAYNES CL

CASHIO LA

CROFT LA

GREEN LA

ALBDT

CADE CL

Allot Gdns

Norton

PO

Playing Field

STATION RD

ICKNIELD WAY

JACKS

STYCAMORES

WHITEHORSE ST

ICKNIELD WAY

CHURCH

BREWERY

ORCHARD RD

Hartsfield JMI Sch

CLOTHALL RD

PO

A505

34

4
14

A   B   C   D   E   F

8

The Knoll

Cat Ditch

Pembroke
Farm

Pembroke
Cottages

7

37

Icknield Way Path

Gravelpit
Hill

Mitchell
Hill

Bygrave
Plantation

6

Sewage
Works

SG7

Manor
Farm

Park
Wood

Bygrave

Old
Rectory

5

Manor
House

36

ASHWELL RD

4

Red
Cottages

WEDON WAY

3

Bygrave
Common

35

The Firs

ROYSTON RD

2

BYGRAVE RD

Half Way
Farm

Warren
Farm

WALLINGTON RD

A505

Warehouses

ASHVILLE WAY

1

SALE DR

RHEE SPRING

BESENBERG

DIMMEL

LEVEN

CONSTANTINE

34

STANK ST

HURST CL

BUSH SPRING

IREDALE VIEW

RYE GDNS

BINGLEY

SAXON WAY

MERCHANTS WLK

YEOMANRY DR

WYNN CL

MALTINGS

CHAUNCY GDNS

HLEYN WAY

REPLE CL

DOWNLANDS

25   A   B   26   C   D   27   E   F   34

24
14

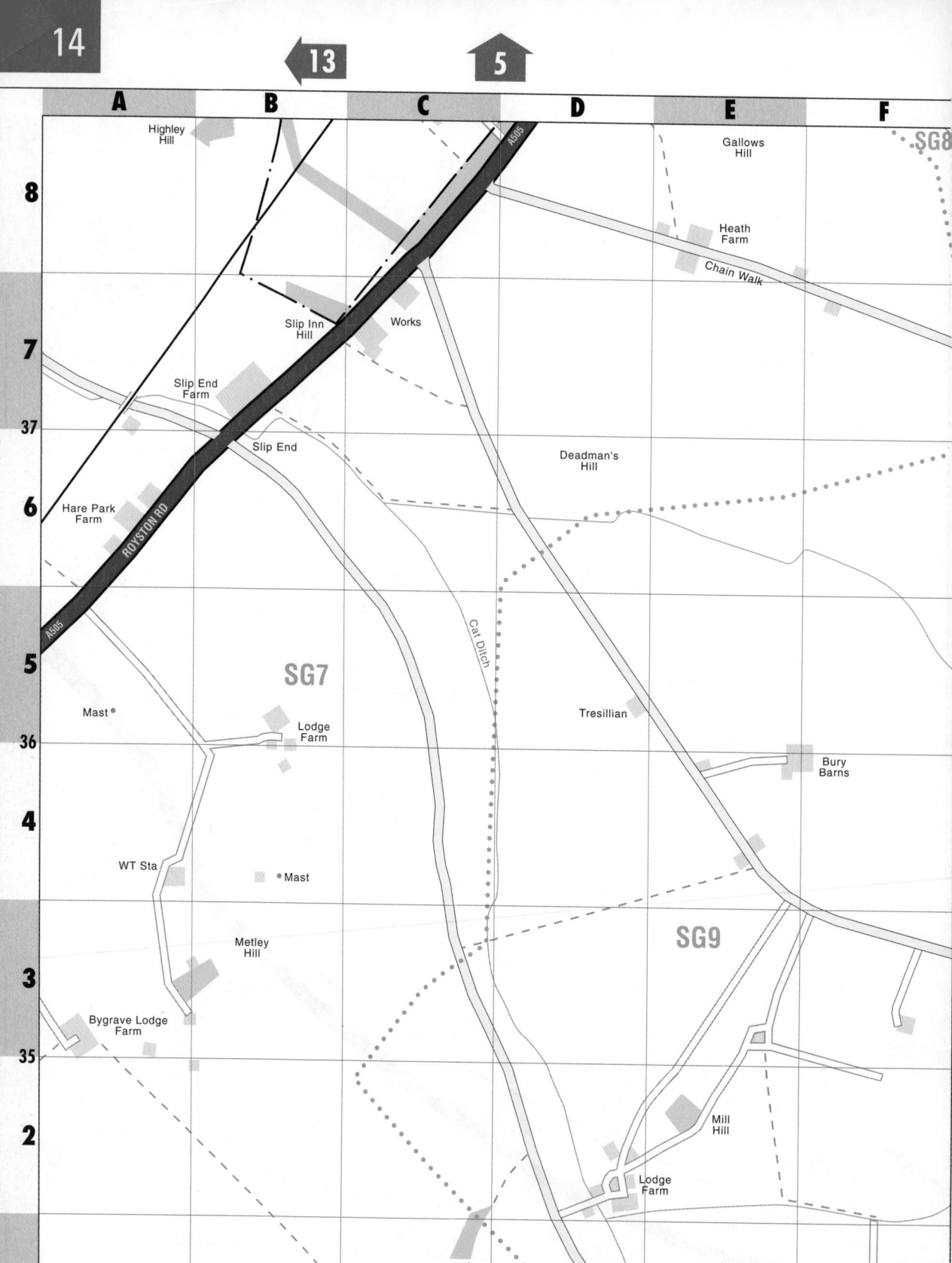

A   B   C   D   E   F

8

Coombe Farm

Chain Walk

Hertfordshire Way

COOMBE RD

Park Farm

MILL LA

Hill Farm

Slipes Wood

Therfield

Horseshoe Wood Farm

Mast

Wtr Twr

Tuthill Farm

TUTHILL CT

PEDLARS LA

THE CAUSEWAY

Therfield Fst Sch

The Fox & Duck (PH)

7

SG8

Hall

CHURCH LA

POLICE ROW

Hay Farm

37

Crouch Hill

Chain Walk

Stump Cross

North End

Recn Gd

ROOKS NEST LA

Mount Hill

Fox Hall

Hay Green

HOOPS LA

6

Grange Farm

Hagger's Farm

Hay Green Farm

Duck's Gn

Pott's Hill

Manor Farm

Kelshall

KELSHALL ST

Chain Walk

5

36

Rain Hill

Chain Walk

Hertfordshire Way

Kelshall La

4

Woodcotes

Wheat Hill

Lords Wood

3

Gannock Farm

SG9

Little Sark

35

Gannock Green

Philpott's Wood

Icknield Way Path

Hawkins Wood

2

Drift Way

Hertfordshire Way

Notley La

Chestnut Hill

Partridge Hall Farm

Park Lane

The Mount

Sandon Bury

PAYNE END

Notley Green

1

Sandon

DARK LA

RUSHDEN RD

PO

The Chequers (PH)

Sandon Jun Mix Inf Sch

Roe Wood

Icknield Way Path

Cock's Lodge

34

A B C D E F

8

7

37

6

Icknield Way Path

MEADOW WAY

HAYWOOD LA

Washingditch Green

River Rib

Mardleybury

Reed End

SG8

Mast

Hatchpen

Hertfordshire Way

THE JOINT

HOBBS HAYES

JACKSON'S LA

WILLOW CL

BLACKSMITH'S LA

CROW LA

5

36

Holborn Farm

Mast

Southview

Reed Fst Sch

CHURCH LA

HIGH ST

The Cabinet (PH)

Wisbridge Farm

Reed

4

ROOKS NEST LA

Dane End

Rooksnest Farm

Mast

DRIFTWAY

Queenbury

Reed Hall

Gannock Grove

3

35

Kelshall La

Chapel Green

River Rib

Reed Wood

2

Sewage Works

Brandish Wood

Hilly Wood

Southfield Grove

1

34

Slate Hall Farm

A10

SG9

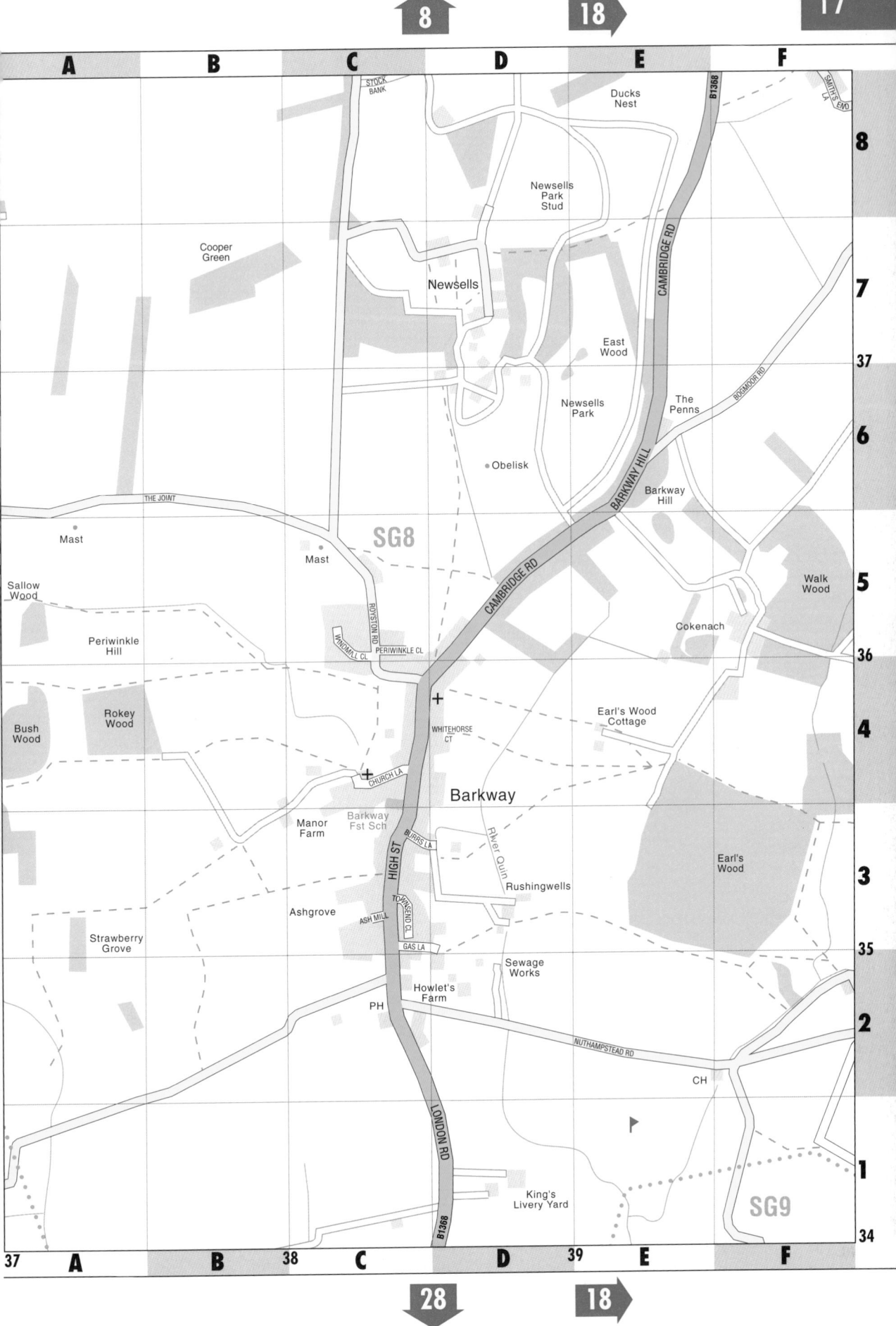

8
18

A B C D E F

8
7
37
6
5
36
4
3
35
2
1
34

STOCK
BANK

Ducks
Nest

B1368

SMITHS LA

Cooper
Green

Newsells
Park
Stud

Newsells

CAMBRIDGE RD

East
Wood

BOGMOOR RD

Newsells
Park

The
Penns

Obelisk

BARKWAY HILL

Barkway
Hill

THE JOINT

Mast

SG8

Walk
Wood

Sallow
Wood

Mast

Cokenach

Periwinkle
Hill

ROYSTON RD

WINDMILL CL

PERIWINKLE CL

Bush
Wood

Rokey
Wood

WHITEHORSE
CT

Earl's Wood
Cottage

CHURCH LA

Barkway

Manor
Farm

Barkway
Fst Sch

HIGH ST

BURRS LA

River Quin

Rushingwells

Earl's
Wood

Ashgrove

ASH MILL

TOWNSEND CL

GAS LA

Sewage
Works

Strawberry
Grove

Howlet's
Farm

PH

NUTHAMPSTEAD RD

CH

LONDON RD

B1368

King's
Livery Yard

SG9

37 A B 38 C D 39 E F 34

28
18

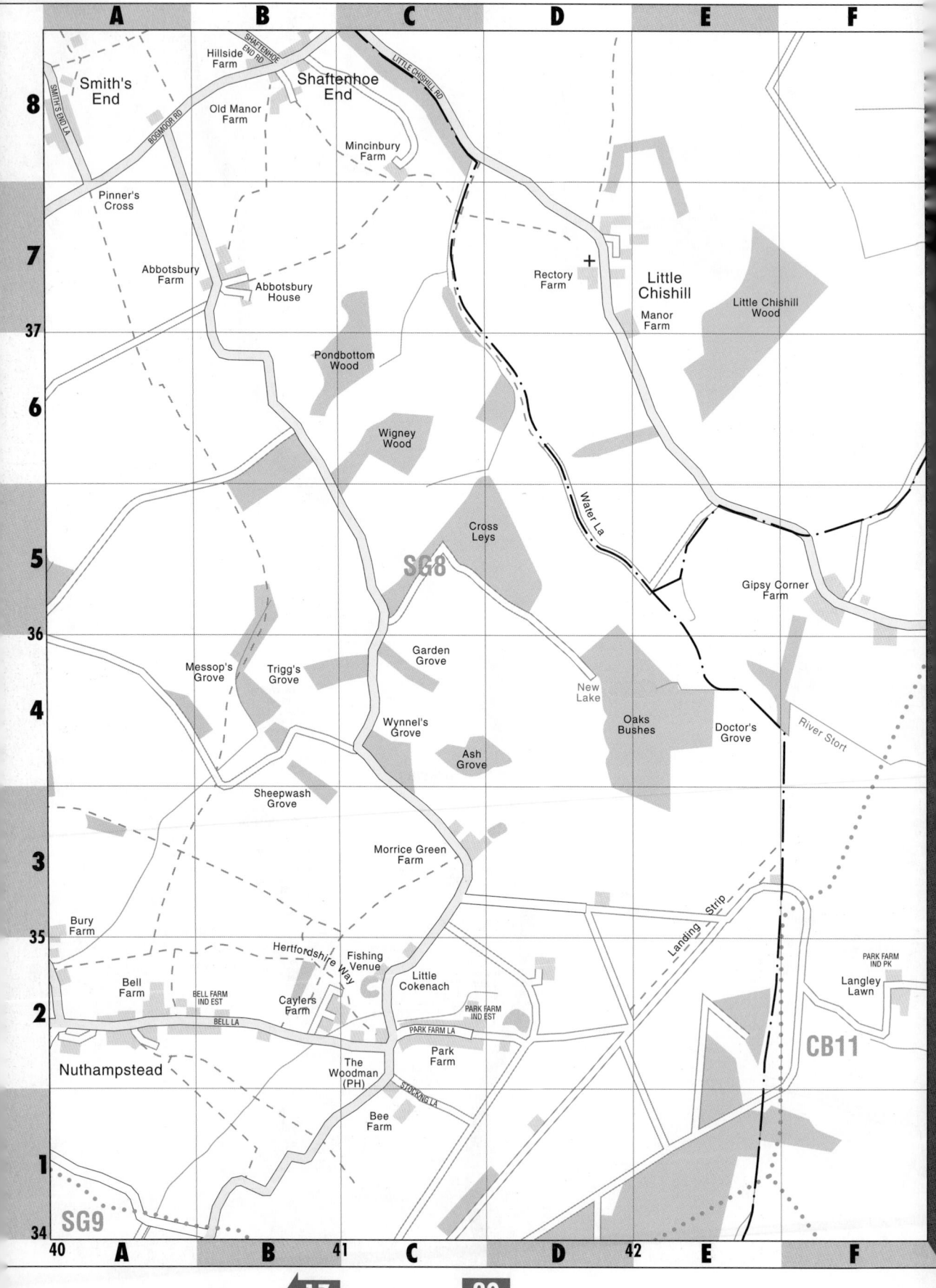

A   B   C   D   E   F

8   Smith's End

Hillside Farm
Shaftenhoe End

SMITH'S END LA
BOGSMOOR RD
SHAFTENHOE END RD
LITTLE CHISHILL RD

Old Manor Farm

Mincinbury Farm

Pinner's Cross

7   Abbotsbury Farm

Abbotsbury House

Rectory Farm

Little Chishill

Manor Farm

Little Chishill Wood

37

Pondbottom Wood

6   Wigney Wood

Water La

Cross Leys

5   SG8

Gipsy Corner Farm

36

Messop's Grove   Trigg's Grove

Garden Grove

New Lake

4   Wynnel's Grove

Ash Grove

Oaks Bushes

Doctor's Grove

River Stort

Sheepwash Grove

3   Morrice Green Farm

Landing Strip

Bury Farm

35

Hertfordshire Way

Fishing Venue

Little Cokenach

Park Farm IND EST

PARK FARM IND PK

Langley Lawn

Bell Farm

BELL FARM IND EST

Caylers Farm

2   BELL LA

PARK FARM LA

CB11

Nuthampstead

The Woodman (PH)

Park Farm

STOCKING LA

Bee Farm

1

SG9

34

40   A   B   41   C   D   42   E   F

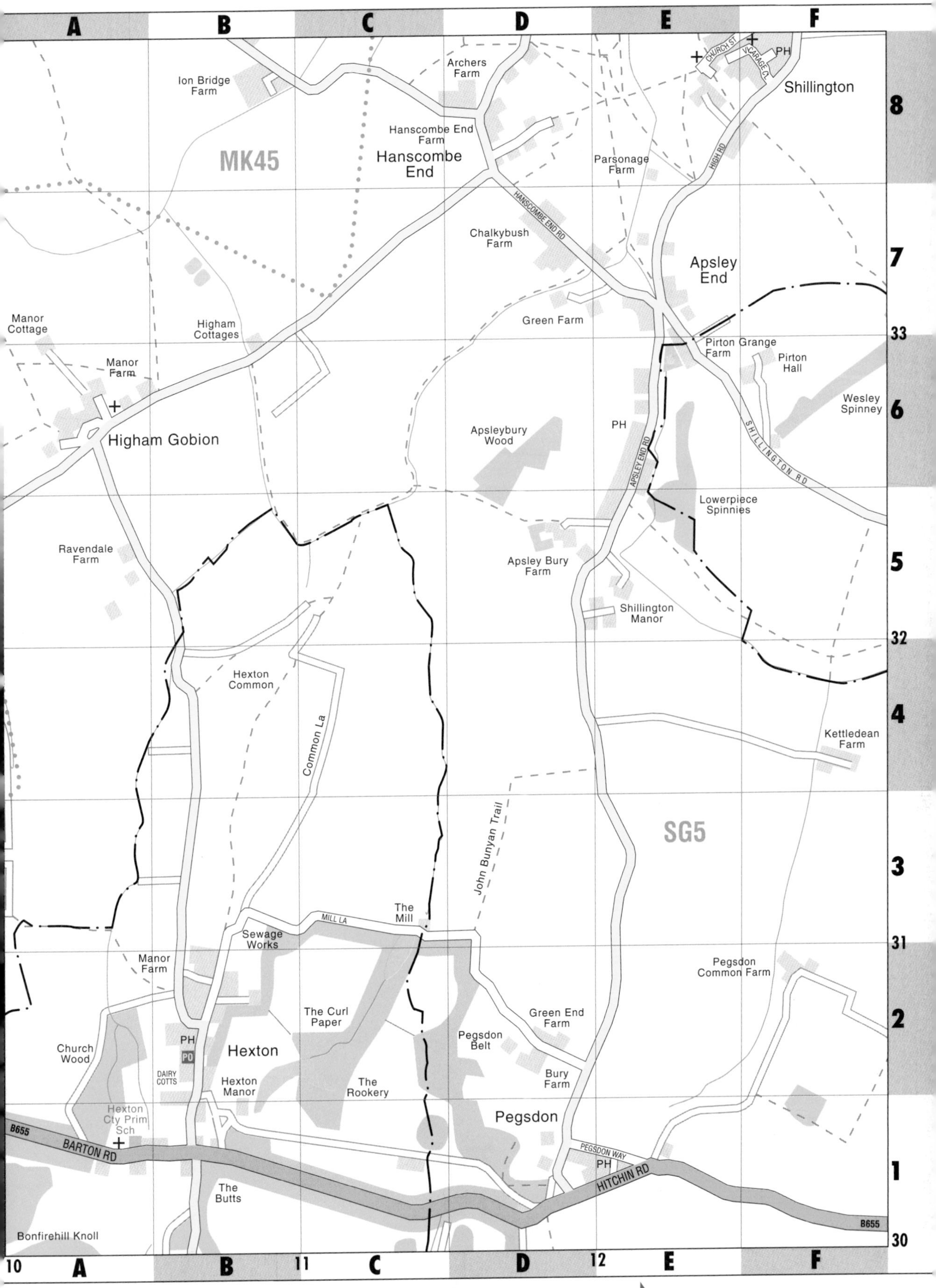

A   B   C   D   E   F

8

Ion Bridge
Farm

Archers
Farm

Shillington

CHURCH ST
VICARAGE CL
PH

MK45

Hanscombe End
Farm

Hanscombe
End

Parsonage
Farm

HIGH RD

7

Chalkybush
Farm

Apsley
End

33

Manor
Cottage

Higham
Cottages

Green Farm

Pirton Grange
Farm

Pirton
Hall

Manor
Farm

PH

Wesley
Spinney

6

HANSCOMBE END RD

Higham Gobion

Apsleybury
Wood

SHILLINGTON RD

APSLEY END RD

Lowerpiece
Spinnies

Ravendale
Farm

Apsley Bury
Farm

5

Shillington
Manor

32

Hexton
Common

Kettledean
Farm

4

Common La

SG5

3

John Bunyan Trail

Manor
Farm

The Mill

MILL LA

The
Mill

31

Sewage
Works

Pegsdon
Common Farm

The Curl
Paper

Green End
Farm

2

PH
PO

Hexton

Pegsdon
Belt

Church
Wood

DAIRY
COTTS

Hexton
Manor

The
Rookery

Bury
Farm

Hexton
Cty Prim
Sch

Pegsdon

B655

BARTON RD

PEGSDON WAY

PH

HITCHIN RD

1

The
Butts

B655

Bonfirehill Knoll

30

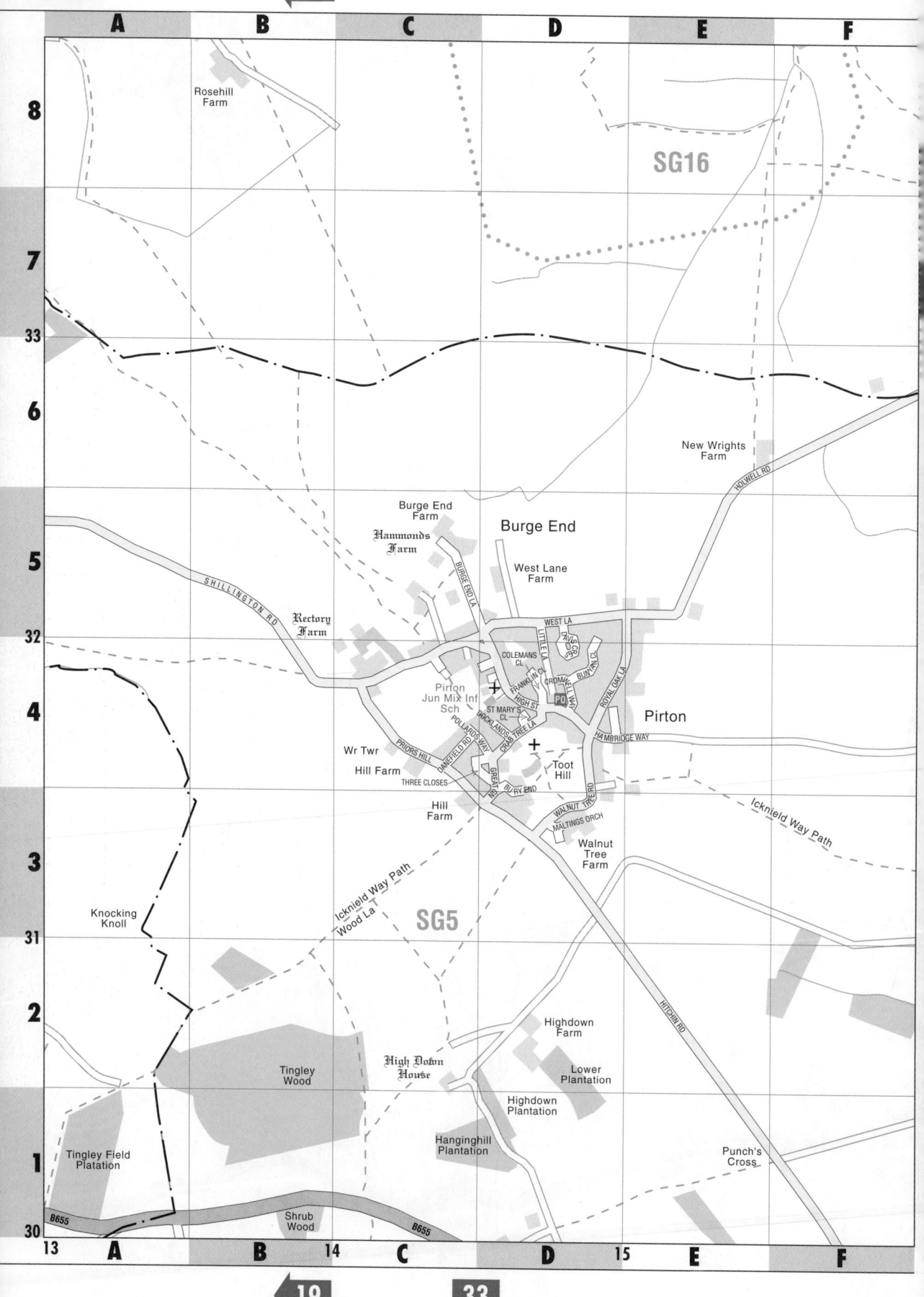

19

A B C D E F

8

SG16

7

33

6

New Wrights
Farm

HOLWELL RD

5

SHILLINGTON RD

Burge End
Farm

Hammonds
Farm

Burge End

West Lane
Farm

WEST LA

32

Rectory
Farm

BURGE END LA

LITTLE CL

COLEMANS
CL

FRANKLIN CL

HIGH ST

GRD LANE WAY

BUNYAN CL

ROYAL OAK LA

PO

Pirton

4

Pirton
Jun Mix Inf
Sch

ST MARY'S
CL

ROCKLANDS WAY

CRAB TREE LA

HAMBRIDGE WAY

Wr Twr

Hill Farm

PRIORS HILL

DANEFIELD RD

POLLARDS WAY

GREAT GN

BURY END

Toot
Hill

THREE CLOSES

Hill
Farm

WALNUT TREE RD

MALTINGS ORCH

Icknield Way Path

3

Walnut
Tree
Farm

Icknield Way Path
Wood La

SG5

HITCHIN RD

Knocking
Knoll

31

2

Highdown
Farm

Lower
Plantation

Tingley
Wood

High Down
House

Highdown
Plantation

Punch's
Cross

1

Tingley Field
Platation

Hanginghill
Plantation

30

B655

Shrub
Wood

B655

13 A B 14 C D 15 E F

19   33

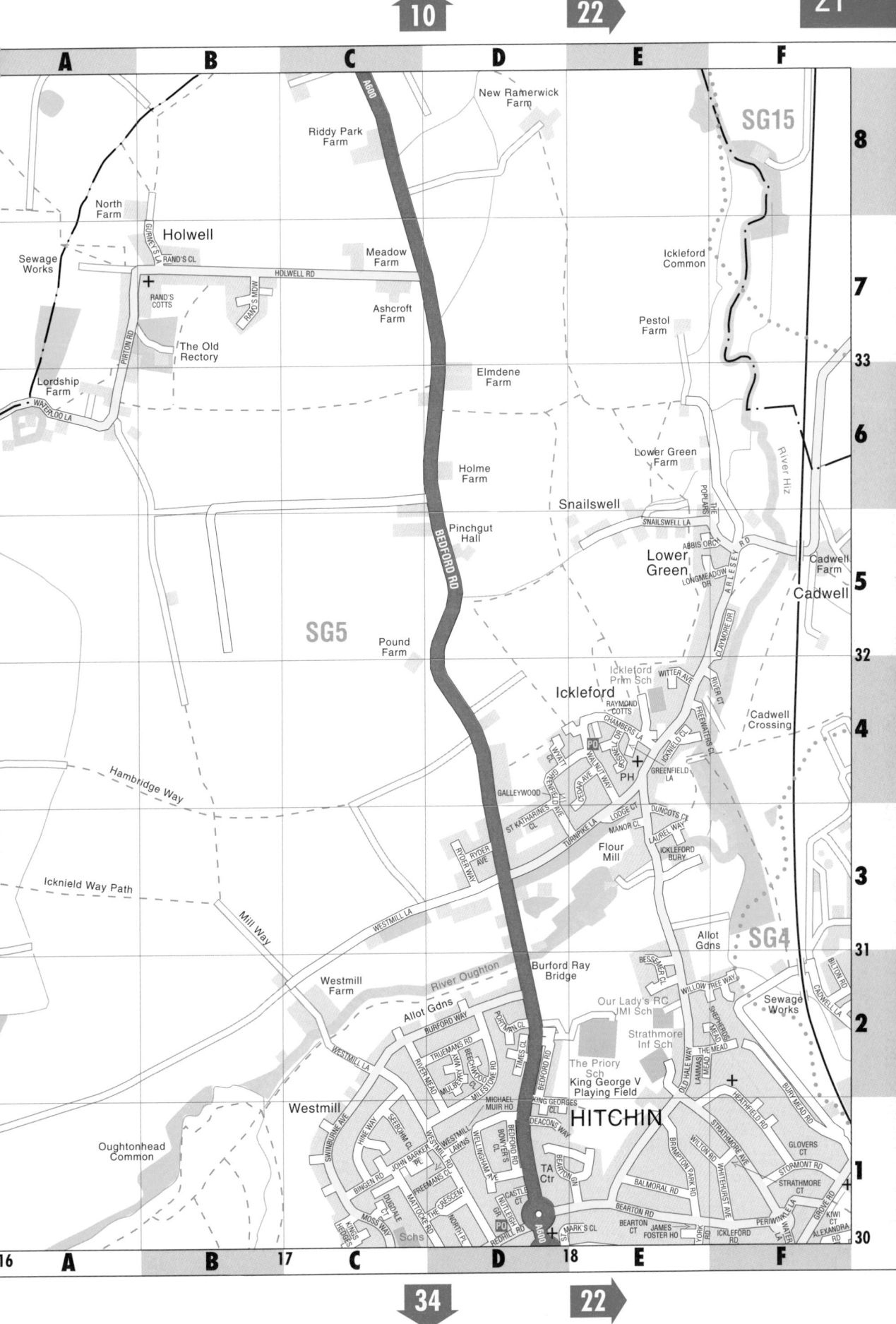

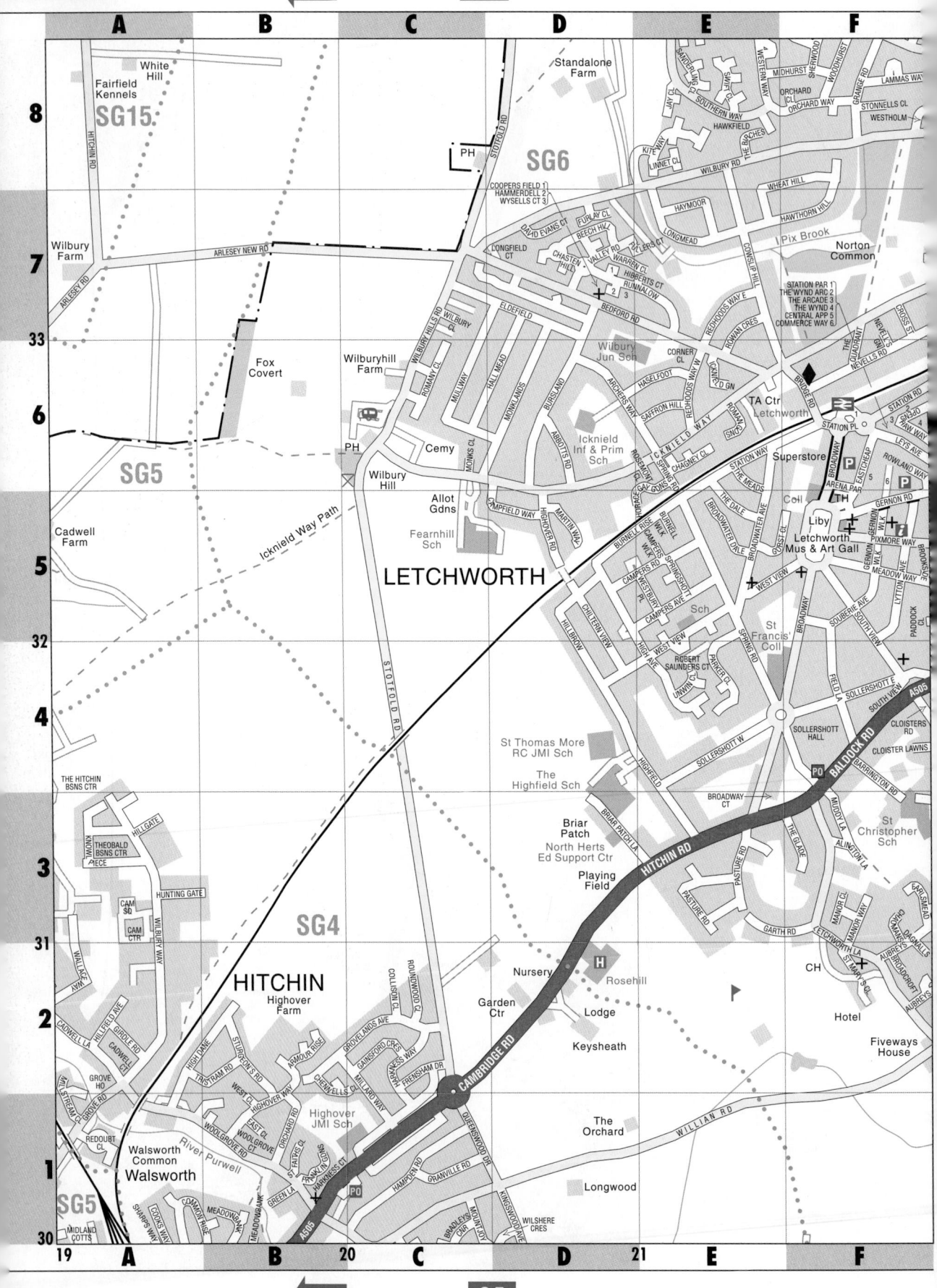

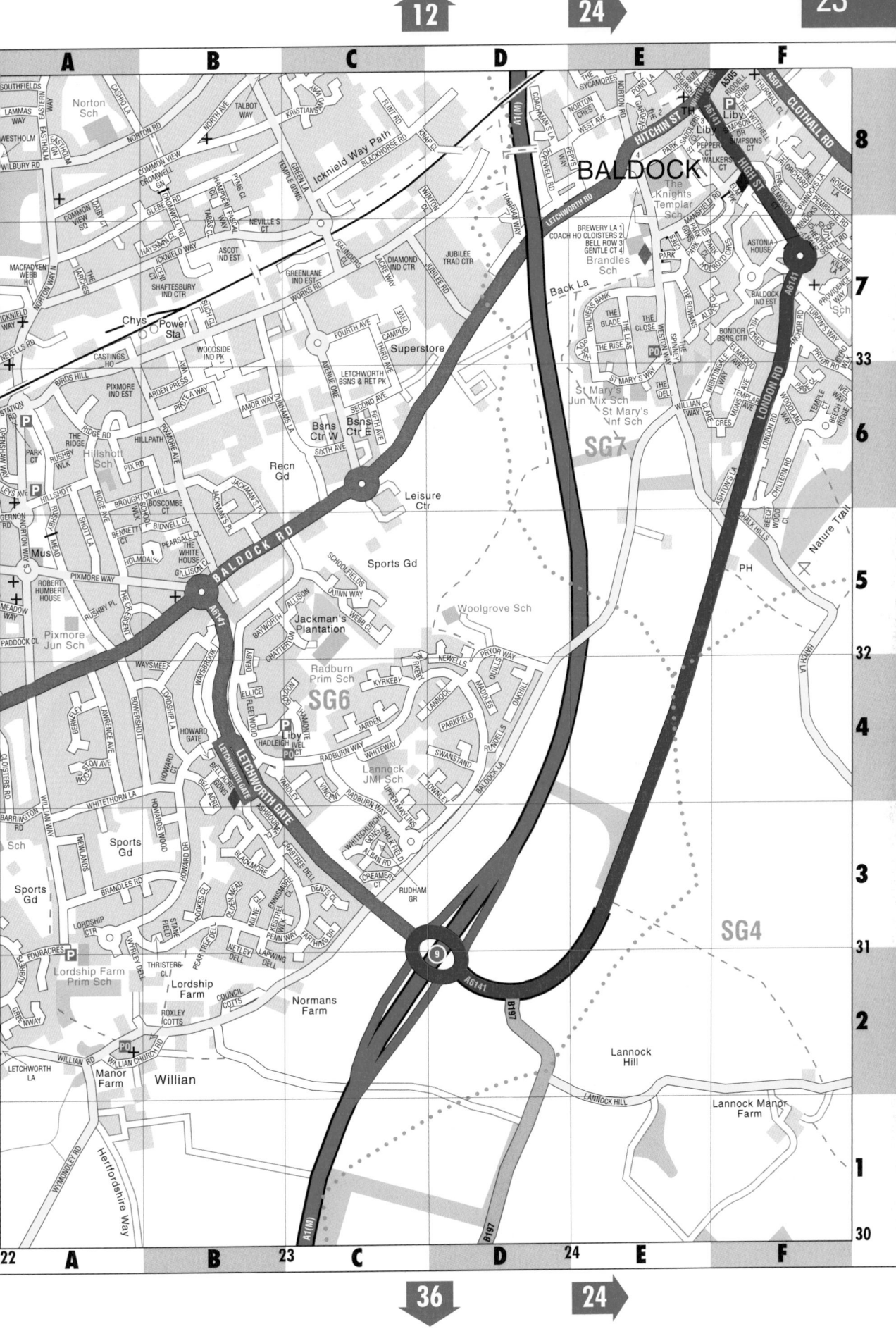

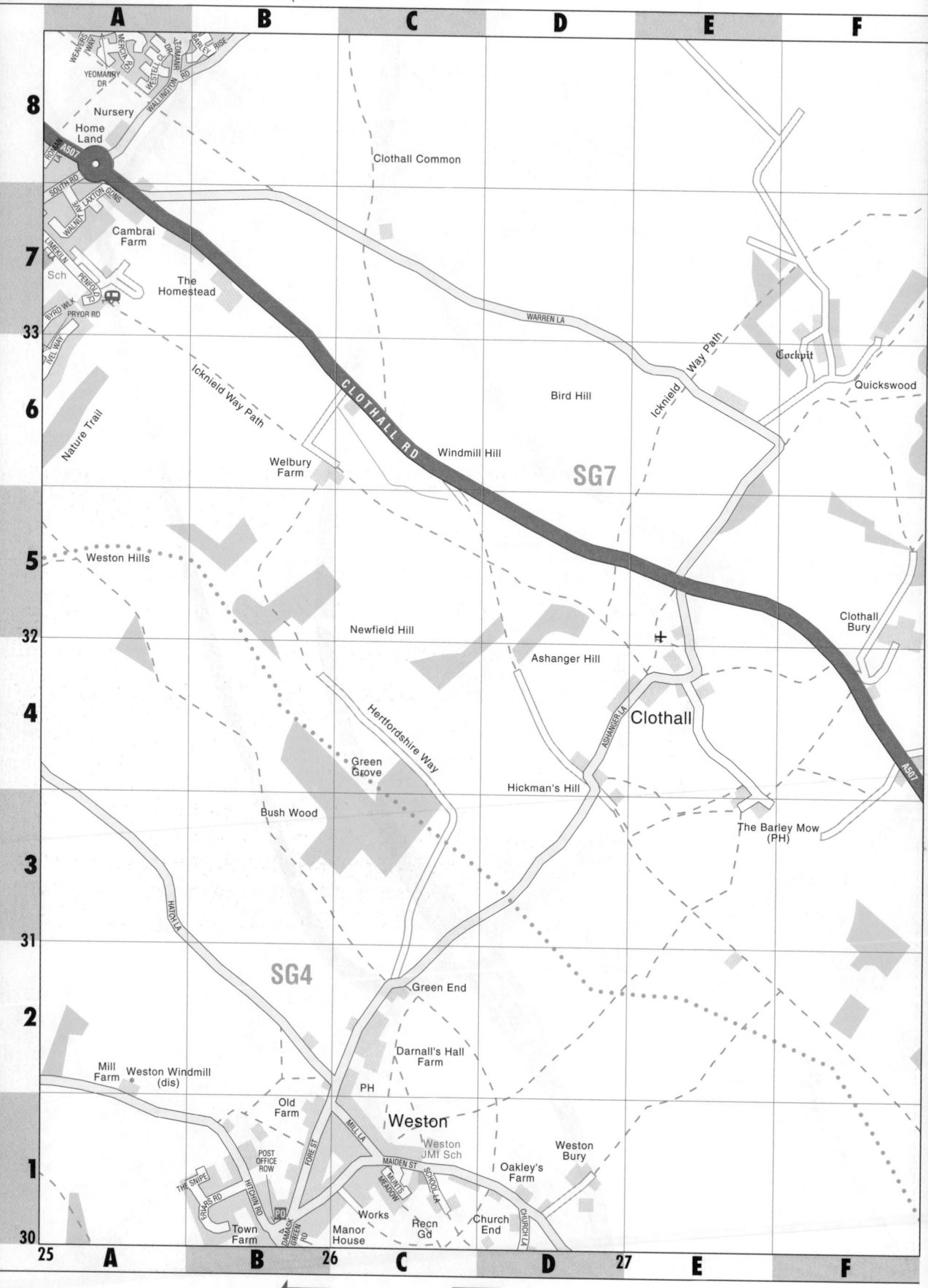

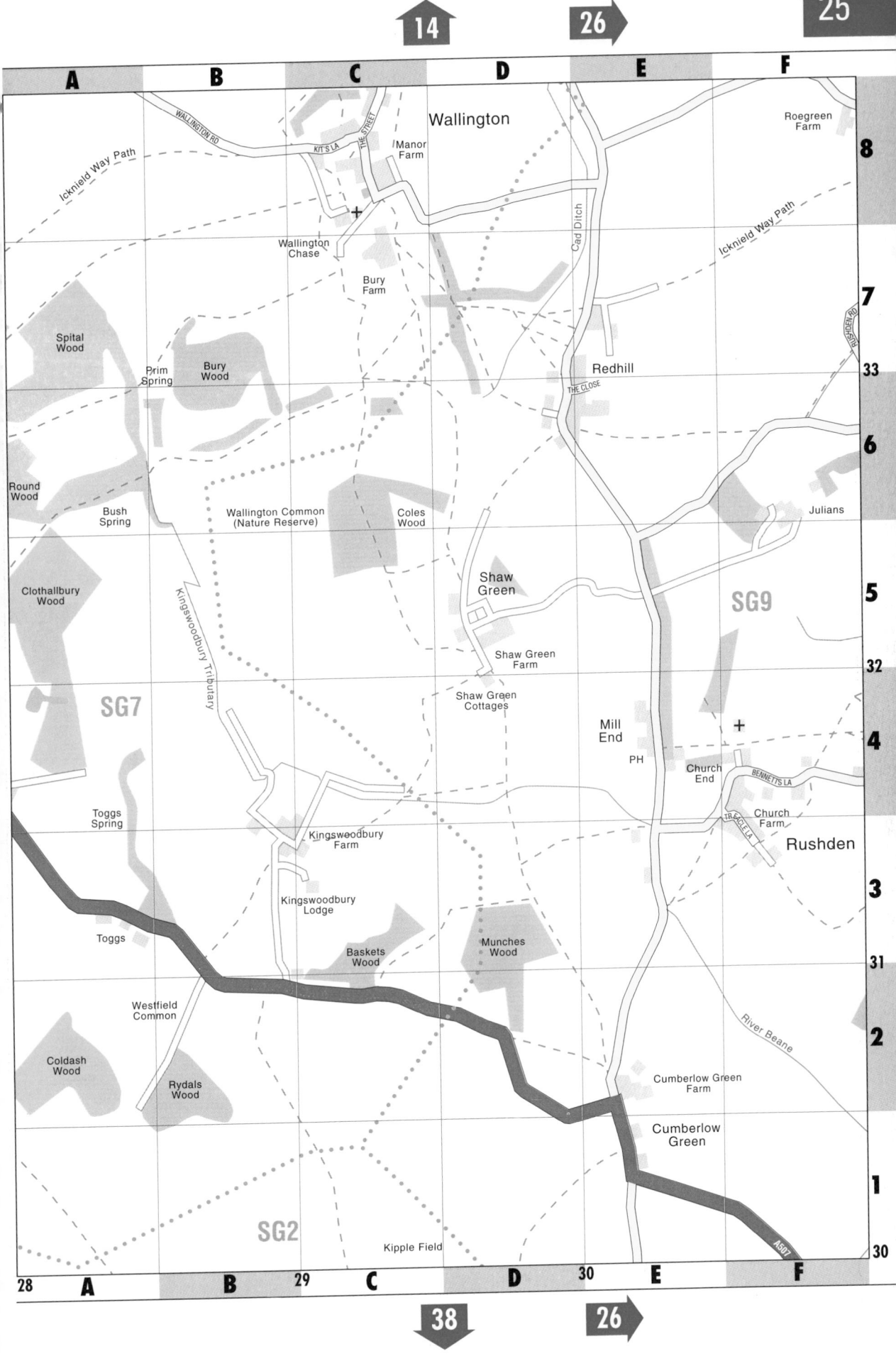

8
7
33
6
5
32
4
3
31
2
1
30

Wallington

WALLINGTON RD

KITS LA

THE STREET

Manor Farm

Icknield Way Path

Cad Ditch

Icknield Way Path

Roegreen Farm

Wallington Chase

Bury Farm

Redhill

RUSHDEN RD

THE CLOSE

Spital Wood

Prim Spring

Bury Wood

Round Wood

Bush Spring

Wallington Common (Nature Reserve)

Coles Wood

Julians

Clothallbury Wood

Kingswoodbury Tributary

Shaw Green

SG9

SG7

Shaw Green Farm

Shaw Green Cottages

Mill End

PH

Church End

BENNETTS LA

Toggs Spring

Kingswoodbury Farm

TREACLE LA

Church Farm

Rushden

Kingswoodbury Lodge

Toggs

Baskets Wood

Munches Wood

31

Westfield Common

River Beane

Coldash Wood

Rydals Wood

Cumberlow Green Farm

Cumberlow Green

SG2

A507

Kipple Field

28
A B 29 C D 30 E F 30

25
15

A B C D E F

8

Tichney Wood

Five House Farm

Icknield Way Path

SG8

Rockells Jersey Farm

Killogs Farm

Roe Green

West Wood

RUSHDEN RD

BECKFIELD LA

Green End

Green End Farm

7

Beckfield Farm

Chain Walk

Nursery

River Beane

33

Doebridge Farm

Friars La

Friars Grange

Bird's Nest Farm

Mill End

6

Offley Green

Friars Wood

Chain Walk

Wood Farm

Mill End Farm

5

Bachelor's Wood

Chain Walk

Lye End Farm

32

Little Manor Farm

Southern Green Farm

Whitehall

Burgess La

4

Southern Green

Broadfield Lodge Farm

SG9

Park Wood

Ellen Green

Middle Wood

Great Wood

Bush Wood

Chain Walk

Steward's Ley

3

Lodge Farm

Chapel Wood

31

Chain Walk

Hall Farm

Needle Spring

Broadfield Hall

2

Foxholes Wood

Boldero's Wood

Southfields Farm

Little Wood

1

Horneywood La

Throcking

30

Water Tower

COTTERED RD

Throcking Hall

31 A 32 B C 33 D E F

25
39

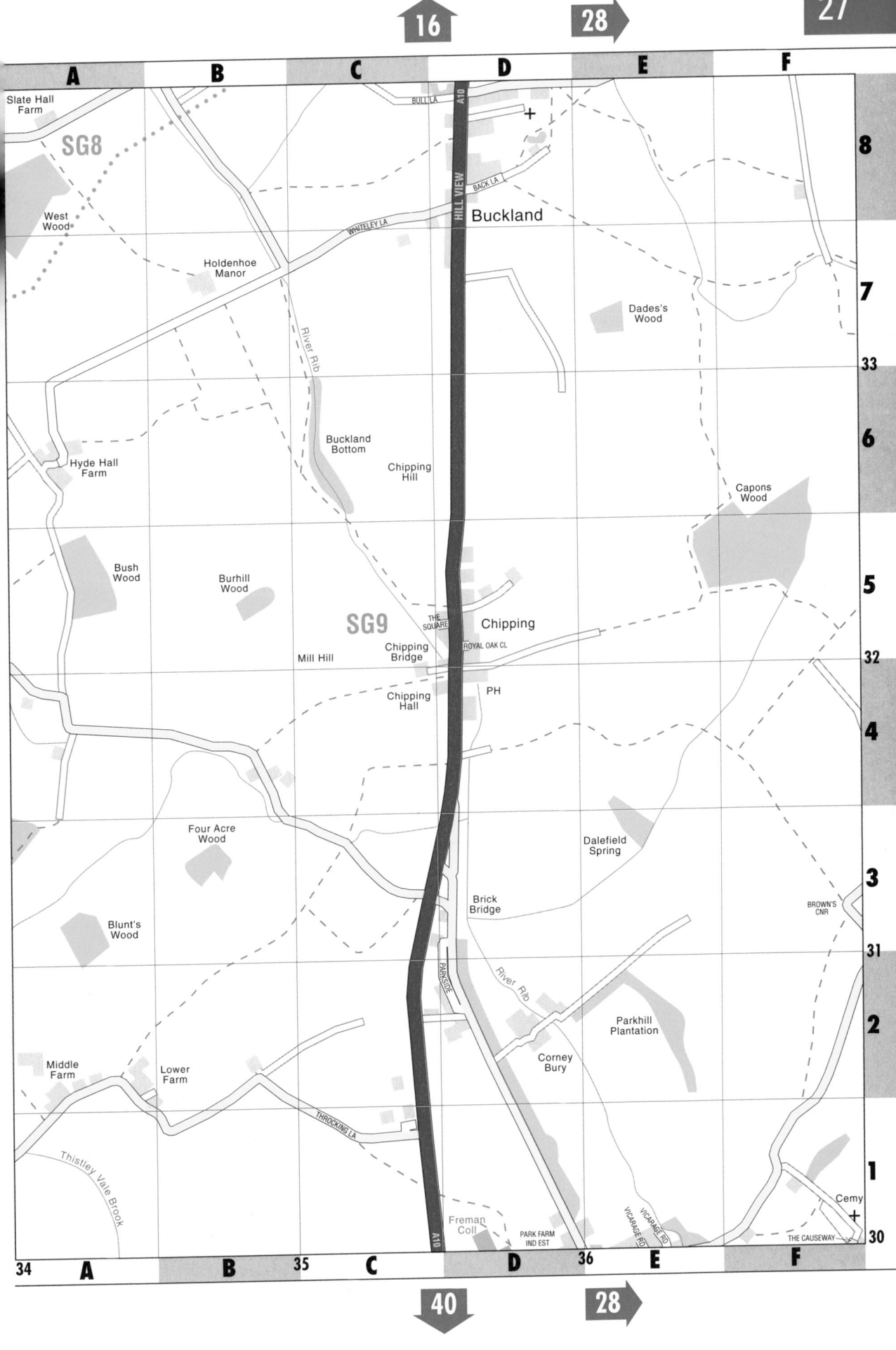

A B C D E F

8

7

33

6

5

32

4

3

31

2

1

30

Slate Hall Farm

SG8

West Wood

BULL LA

Buckland

HILL VIEW

A10

BACK LA

WHITELEY LA

Holdenhoe Manor

River Rib

Dades's Wood

Buckland Bottom

Chipping Hill

Hyde Hall Farm

Capons Wood

Bush Wood

Burhill Wood

SG9

THE SQUARE

Chipping

ROYAL OAK CL

Mill Hill

Chipping Bridge

Chipping Hall

PH

Four Acre Wood

Dalefield Spring

Blunt's Wood

Brick Bridge

BROWN'S CNR

PARKSIDE

River Rib

Parkhill Plantation

Middle Farm

Lower Farm

Corney Bury

THROCKING LA

Thistley Vale Brook

A10

Freman Coll

PARK FARM IND EST

VICARAGE RD

VICARAGE RD

Cemy

THE CAUSEWAY

34 A B 35 C D 36 E F

27
17

A B C D E F

SG8

North End Farm

LONDON RD B1368

8

Biggin Bridge

7

Biggin Manor

Northey Wood

River Quin

33

BIGGIN HILL

Cave Gate

6

Cave Bridge

Stapleton Bridge

Lincoln Hill

5

Forty Acre Plantation

Cavehall Plantation

32

Cherry Orchard Plantation

SG9

New Barns

Wyddial Hall

Fox Hill

4

Peartree Field Wood

Bushleys Grove

ROSE COTTS

SOUTHSIDE

Home Farm

Wyddial

Beauchamps

River Quin

Flint Cottages

3

MOLES LA

Silkmead Farm

31

Moles Farm

Beauchamp's Wood

2

Beauchamp's Plantation

Bradbury Farm

Works

1

B1368

30

37 A B 38 C D 39 E F

CB11

SG8

Scales Park

8

Bandons
Farm

Pain's End

White Hill

7

Northey
Wood

Two Acres
Farm

Cheapside

The Chequers
(PH)

MOAT SIDE

33

Anstey
Castle

Lower
Green

The Hale

6

Anstey

Meesden

Anstey
Fst Sch

Snow
End

The Fox
(PH)

Roger's La

LINCOLN
HILL

Daw's
End

Coltsfoot
Farm

Manor
Farm

5

SILVER ST

32

Anstey
Bury

River Ash

4

Hertfordshire Way

Puttock's
End

SG9

Mill
Mound

3

Brick House
Farm

31

2

B1038

Borley Green
Cottage

ANDERSON'S LA

Hormead
Hall

Three Acre
Wood

1

HALL LA

Black Ditch

HALL
COTTS

CONDUIT LA

HALF ACRE LA

Dane End
House

30

40   A   B   41   C   D   42   E   F

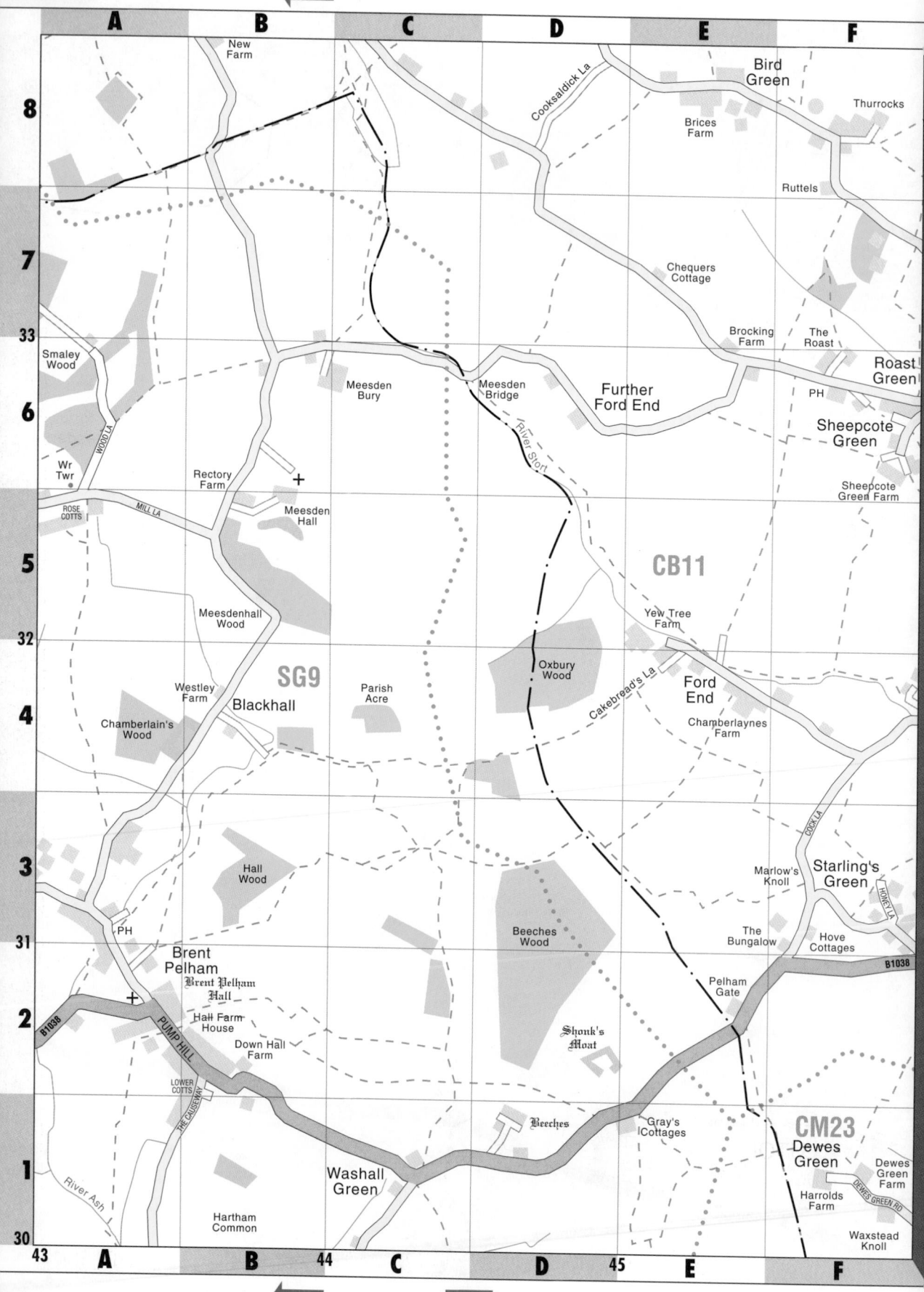

A   B   C   D   E   F

8

7

33

6

5

32

4

3

31

2

1

30

43   A   B   44   C   D   45   E   F

New Farm

Cooksaldick La

Bird Green

Brices Farm

Thurrocks

Ruttels

Chequers Cottage

Brocking Farm

The Roast

Roast Green

PH

Sheepcote Green

Smaley Wood

WOOD LA

Meesden Bury

Meesden Bridge

Further Ford End

Sheepcote Green Farm

Wr Twr

ROSE COTTS

MILL LA

Rectory Farm

Meesden Hall

River Stort

CB11

Meesdenhall Wood

Yew Tree Farm

Westley Farm

SG9

Blackhall

Parish Acre

Oxbury Wood

Cakebread's La

Ford End

Chamberlain's Wood

Chamberlaynes Farm

Hall Wood

Marlow's Knoll

Starling's Green

HOBE LA

PH

The Bungalow

Hove Cottages

COCK LA

Beeches Wood

Pelham Gate

B1038

Brent Pelham

Brent Pelham Hall

B1038

PUMP HILL

Hall Farm House

Down Hall Farm

Shonk's Moat

CM23

Dewes Green

LOWER COTTS

THE CAUSEWAY

Beeches

Gray's Cottages

Dewes Green Farm

DEWES GREEN RD

River Ash

Washall Green

Harrolds Farm

Hartham Common

Waxstead Knoll

A B C D E F

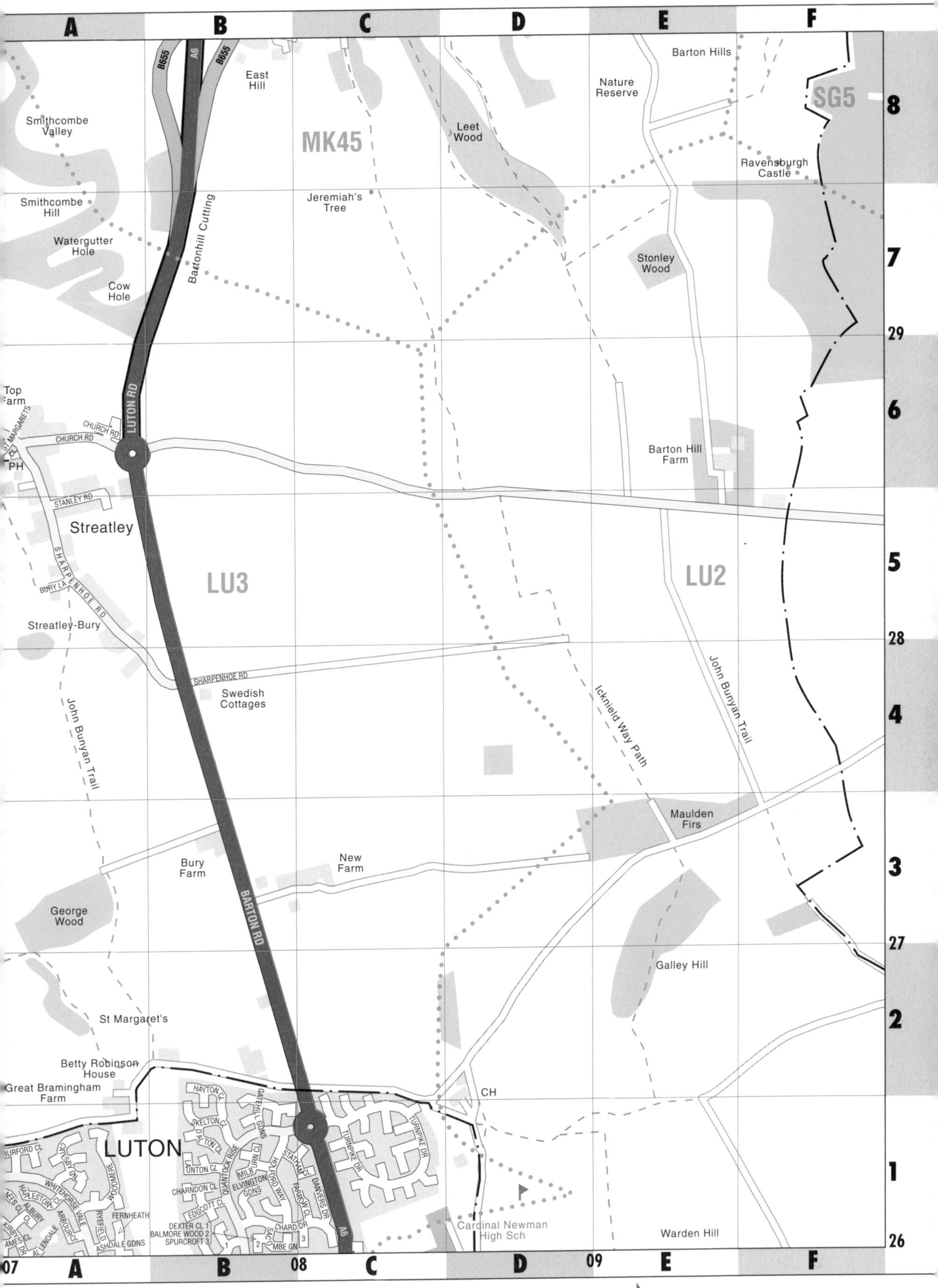

Smithcombe Valley

East Hill

MK45

Leet Wood

Barton Hills

Nature Reserve

SG5

8

Smithcombe Hill

Jeremiah's Tree

Ravensburgh Castle

Watergutter Hole

Stonley Wood

7

Cow Hole

Battonhill Cutting

29

Top Farm

LUTON RD

CHURCH RD
CHURCH RD

Barton Hill Farm

6

PH

STANLEY RD

Streatley

LU3

LU2

5

SHARPENHOE RD
BURY LA

Streatley-Bury

28

SHARPENHOE RD

Swedish Cottages

Icknield Way Path

John Bunyan Trail

4

John Bunyan Trail

Bury Farm

New Farm

Maulden Firs

3

BARTON RD

George Wood

27

Galley Hill

St Margaret's

2

Betty Robinson House

Great Bramingham Farm

CH

LUTON

Cardinal Newman High Sch

Warden Hill

1

26

07 A 08 B C 09 D E F

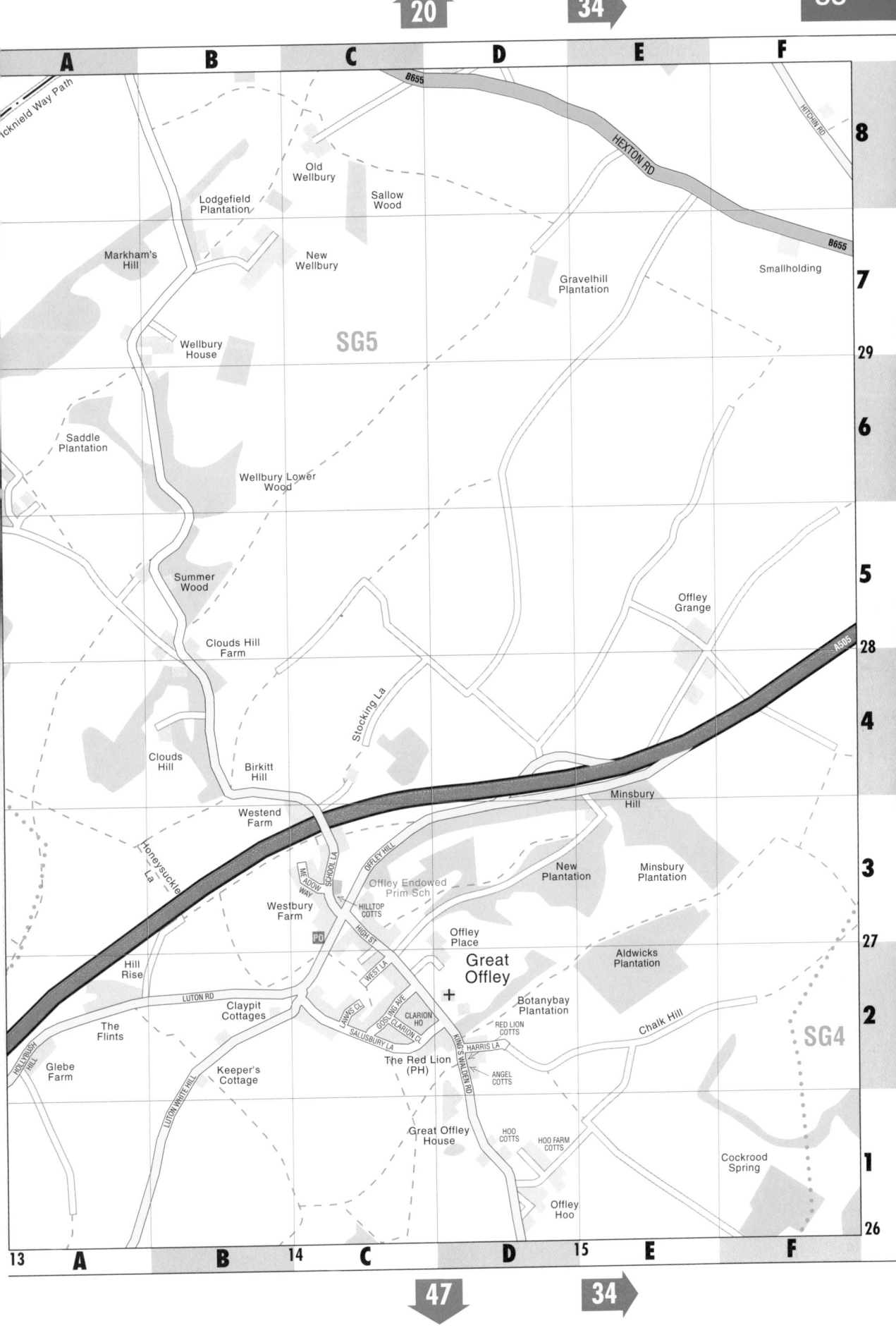

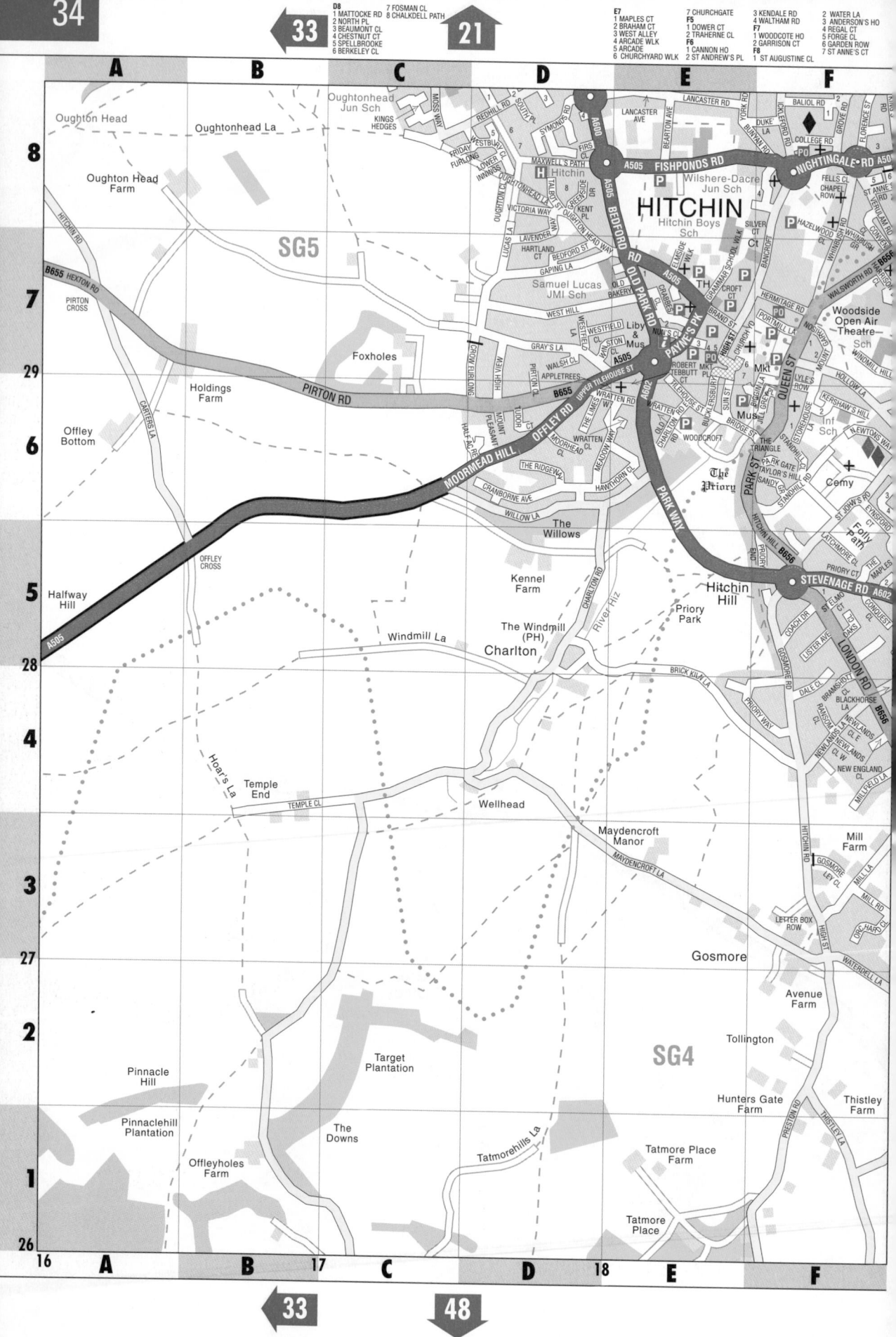

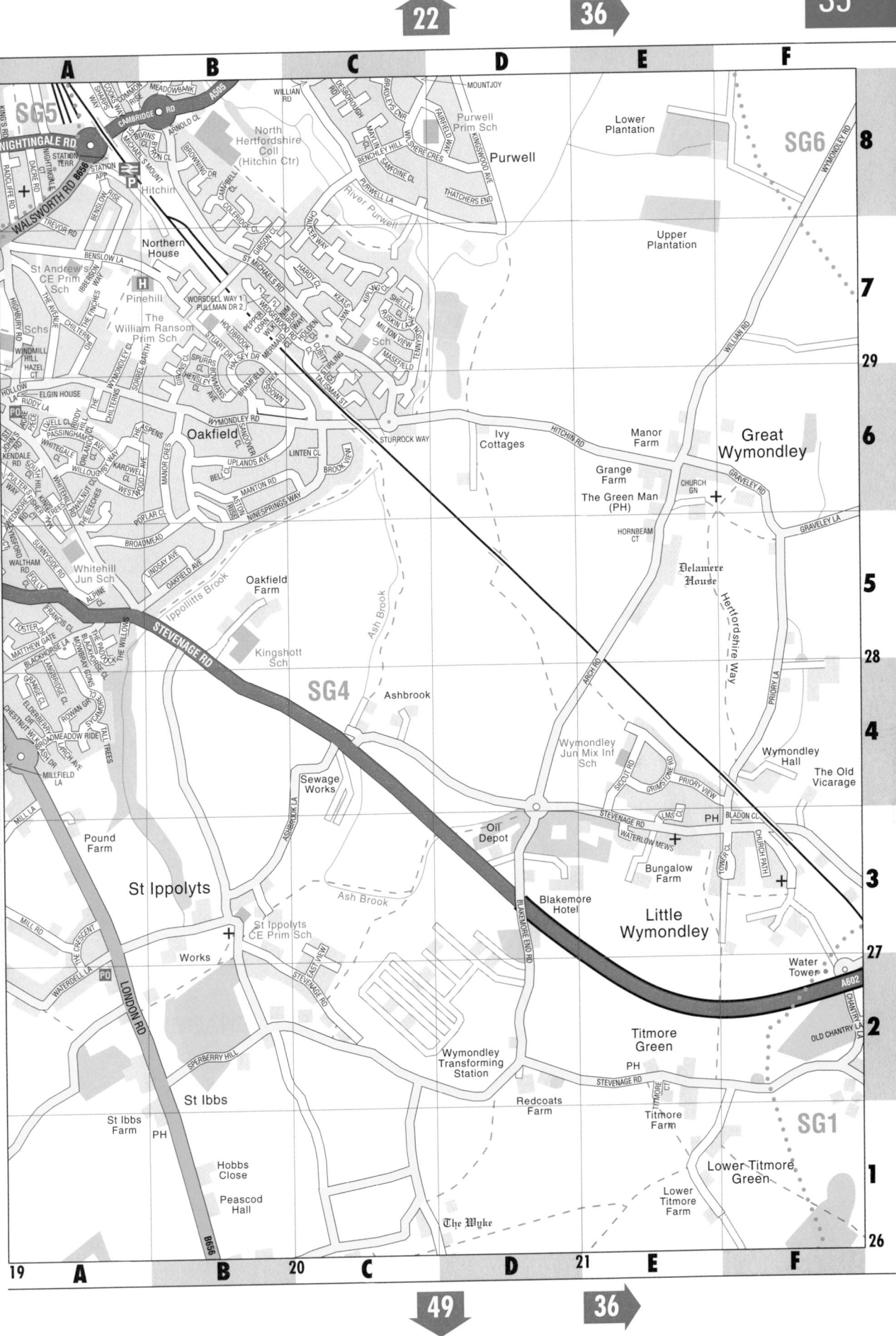

22   36

A   **B**   **C**   **D**   **E**   **F**

8

7

29

6

5

28

4

3

27

2

SG1

1

26

SG5

SG6

SG4

A   **B**   **C**   **D**   **E**   **F**

19   20   21

49   36

NIGHTINGALE RD

KING'S RD
RADCLIFFE RD
WALSWORTH RD
TREVOR RD
BENSLOW LA

North Hertfordshire Coll (Hitchin Ctr)

Hitchin

Northern House

St Andrew's CE Prim Sch

Pinehill

The William Ransom Prim Sch

Oakfield

WYMONDLEY RD

Whitehill Jun Sch

STEVENAGE RD

Oakfield Farm

Kingshott Sch

Ashbrook

SG4

Sewage Works

Pound Farm

St Ippolyts

St Ippolyts CE Prim Sch

Works

LONDON RD

St Ibbs

St Ibbs Farm PH

Hobbs Close

Peascod Hall

The Wyke

Ash Brook

Oil Depot

Blakemore Hotel

Wymondley Transforming Station

Redcoats Farm

Titmore Green
PH
STEVENAGE RD
Titmore Farm

Lower Titmore Green
Lower Titmore Farm

Wymondley Jun Mix Inf Sch

Little Wymondley
Bungalow Farm

Water Tower
A602

Purwell
Purwell Prim Sch
River Purwell

Lower Plantation

Upper Plantation

WILLIAN RD

Manor Farm

Grange Farm

The Green Man (PH)

HORNBEAM CT

Delamere House

Hertfordshire Way

Great Wymondley
CHURCH GN
GRAVELEY RD
GRAVELEY LA

Wymondley Hall
The Old Vicarage

PRIORY LA

ARCH RD

Ivy Cottages

HITCHIN RD

SG6

35
23

A B C D E F

8

7

29

6

5

28

4

3

27

2

1

26

22

WYMONDLEY RD

The Lodge

Roxley Court

SG6

Hertfordshire Way

A1(M)

B197

Jack's Hill Farm

CH

Jack's Hill

How Wood

Stonesley Wood

Graveley La

The Ranch

Mast

Landing Strip (Private)

SG4

The Beeches

Riding Sch

Manor Farm

MILKSEY LA

Graveley Hall Farm

CHURCH LA

Graveley Bury

Graveley

Ledge Side Plantation

Lodge

TURF LA

OAK LA

PONDSIDE

ASHWELL

ASHWELL COMM

HIGH ST

George & Dragon (PH)

Graveley Prim Sch

Hertfordshire Way

Chesfield Park

Ten Acre Plantation

Park Plantation

B197

GRAVELEY RD

MIDDLESBOROUGH CL

MANCHESTER CL

NEWCASTLE CL

ST ANDREWS DR

DAVIDS DR

ISLINGTON WAY

WESTON RD

STEVENAGE

B197

STEVENAGE RD

CHANTRY LA

A602

8

B197

A602

Corey's Mill

LISTER CL 1
ASTON CL 2
GRAVELEY CL 3
HOLWELL 4
ASHWELL 5
BYGRAVE 6
GOSMORE 7
FROGMORE HOUSE 8
EASTHALL HOUSE 9
DANE END HOUSE 10
CODICOTE HOUSE 11

SG1

Recn Gd

RIPON RD

Todd's Green

Superstore

HITCHIN RD

NORTH RD

UNDERWOOD RD

GRANBY RD

DALTRY RD

TURNER RD

EAGLES

ARNOLD CL

MORGAN CL

NEWBURY CL

LANCASTER CL 1
GLOUCESTER CL 2

GUILDFORD CL

IONA CL

CANTERBURY WAY

Lister
H

P

COREYS MILL LA

DALTRY CL

THURLOW CL

WOODFIELD RD

FOSTER RD

BOSWELL GDNS

CHANCELLORS RD

WILSON RD

MATHEW'S

Rooks Nest Farm

ST ALBANS WK

ST ALBANS TR

WESTON RD

NORMAN CT

YORK RD

STEVENAGE RD

CAISTER CL

CRESTONLANDS

INGLESIDE

CHESIRE RD

MUNDESLEY

SHERINGHAM AVE

CHAPMAN RD

FOVANT

ANSELL CT 2

KNOWLE

TARRANT

The Old Walled Garden

WHITMORE

TUDOR CL

BURYMEAD

RECTORY LA

NICHOLAS PL

CHESTNUT WLK

The Bury

Cemy

A1(M)

A602

FISHERS GN

Fishers Green

KESSINGLAND CL

ALDEBURGH CL

1 CRANBOURNE
2 CAVALIER

BAWDSEY RD

John Henry Newman RC Sch

B197

A1072

MARTINS WAY

GRACE WAY

BADER RD

TRUMPER RD

CONSTANTINE CL

WISDE RD

JESSOP RD

JESSOP RD

A1072

TRAFFORD CL

TRENT CL

Trotts Hill Prim Sch

A B C D E F

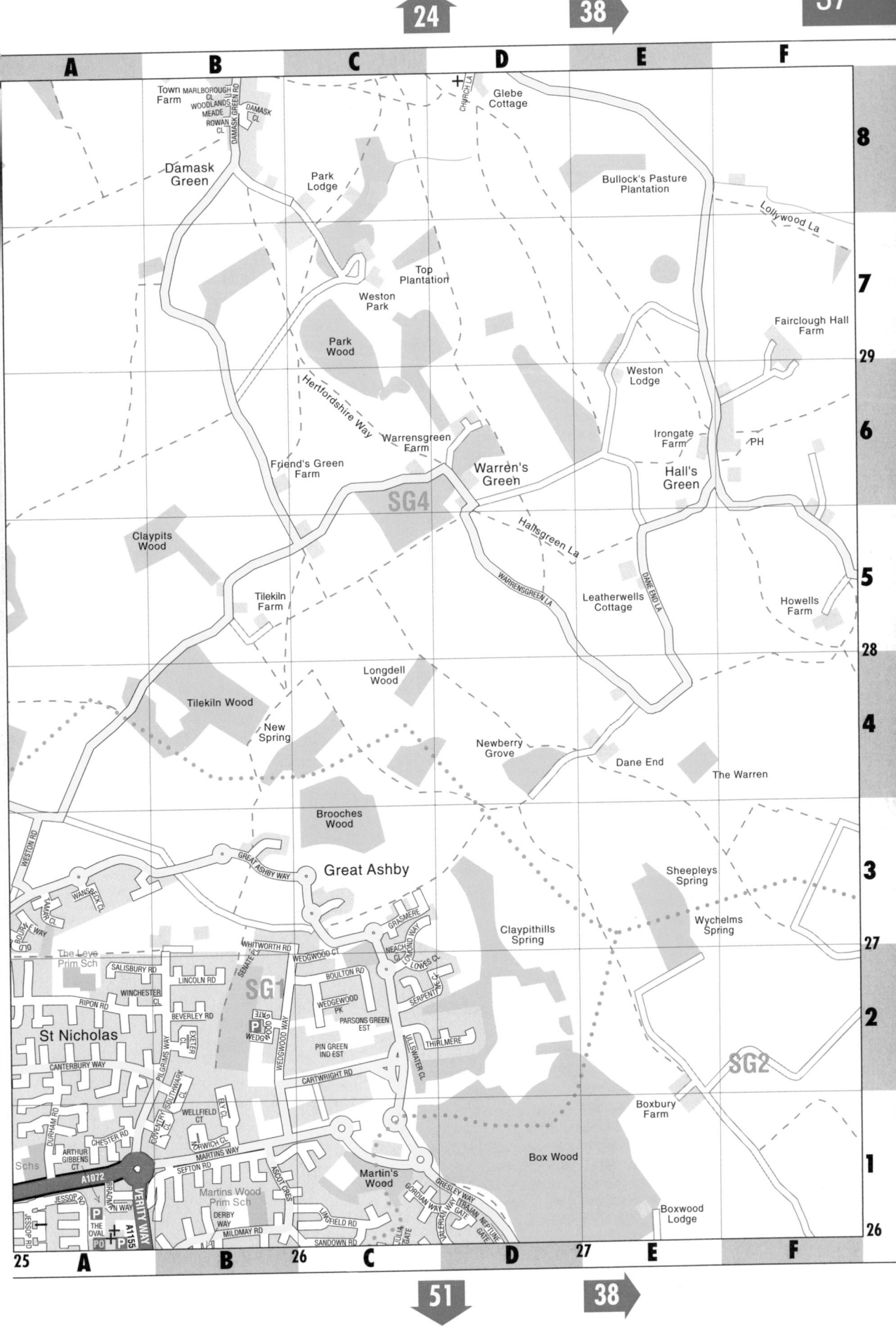

A   B   C   D   E   F

8

Town Farm
MARLBOROUGH CL
WOODLANDS
MEADE
ROWAN CL
DAMASK CL
DAMASK GREEN RD

CHURCH LA

Glebe Cottage

Bullock's Pasture Plantation

Lollywood La

Damask Green

Park Lodge

7

Top Plantation

Weston Park

Fairclough Hall Farm

29

Park Wood

Weston Lodge

6

Hertfordshire Way

Warrensgreen Farm

Irongate Farm

PH

Friend's Green Farm

Warren's Green

Hall's Green

SG4

Claypits Wood

Hallsgreen La

5

Tilekiln Farm

WARRENSGREEN LA

Leatherwells Cottage

DANE END LA

Howells Farm

28

Longdell Wood

4

Tilekiln Wood

New Spring

Newberry Grove

Dane End

The Warren

Brooches Wood

3

Great Ashby

GREAT ASHBY WAY

Sheepleys Spring

Claypithills Spring

Wychelms Spring

27

WESTON RD

WHITWORTH RD

WANSBECK CL
TAMAR CL

GRASMERE

NEACH
CL

GROUND WAY

SALISBURY RD

LINCOLN RD

WEDGWOOD CT

BOULTON RD

LOWES CL

SERPENTINE

SG1

GATE
P
WEDG

WINCHESTER CL

BEVERLEY RD

EXETER CL

WEDGEWOOD PK

WEDGWOOD WAY

PARSONS GREEN EST

THIRLMERE

2

RIPON RD

St Nicholas

The Leys Prim Sch

PILGRIMS WAY

SOUTHWARK CL

PIN GREEN IND EST

ULLSWATER CL

CANTERBURY WAY

CLARE

WELLFIELD CT

CARTWRIGHT RD

SG2

DURHAM RD

BOXBURY CL

CHESTER RD

NORWICH CL

Boxbury Farm

Box Wood

1

Schs

ARTHUR GIBBENS CT

A1072

VERITY WAY

SEFTON RD

MARTINS WAY

ASCOT CRES

Martin's Wood

LINGFIELD RD

GORDON WAY

BRESLEY WAY

TILBURY WAY
GATE

NEPTUNE
GATE

Martins Wood Prim Sch

DERBY WAY

MILDMAY RD

SANDOWN RD

JULIA
GATE

JESSOP RD

P

THE OVAL

A1155

P
PO

BRADMAN
WAY

DENBY WAY

Boxwood Lodge

26

25   A   B   26   C   D   27   E   F

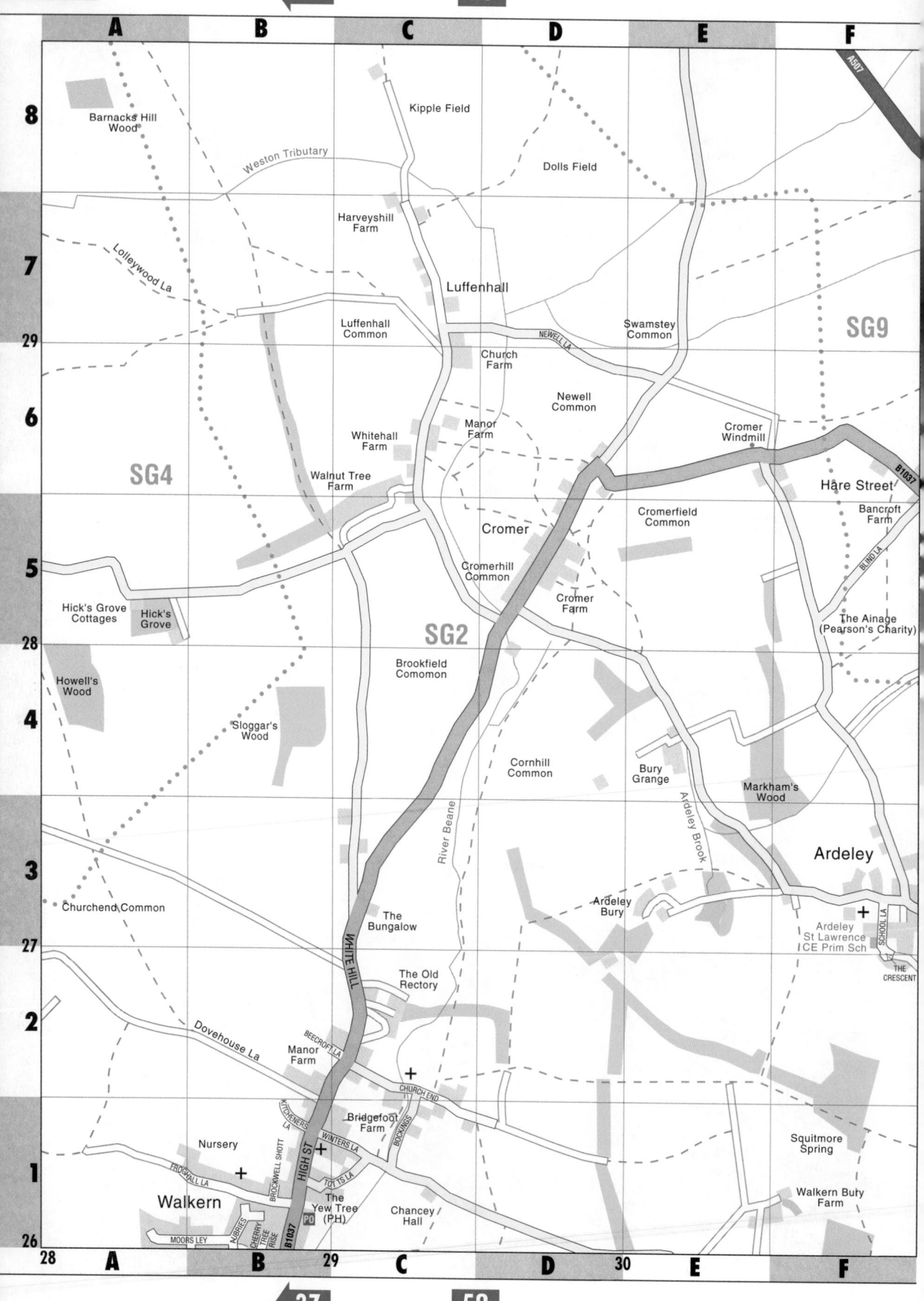

A   B   C   D   E   F

8

Barnacks Hill
Wood

Kipple Field

Weston Tributary

Dolls Field

7

Lolleywood La

Harveyshill
Farm

29

Luffenhall

Swamstey
Common

SG9

6

Luffenhall
Common

Church
Farm

Newell
Common

NEWELL LA

Cromer
Windmill

SG4

Whitehall
Farm

Manor
Farm

Walnut Tree
Farm

Cromerfield
Common

Hare Street

B1037

Bancroft
Farm

5

Cromer

Cromerhill
Common

Cromer
Farm

BLIND LA

The Ainage
(Pearson's Charity)

28

Hick's Grove
Cottages

Hick's
Grove

SG2

Brookfield
Comomon

4

Howell's
Wood

Sloggar's
Wood

Cornhill
Common

Bury
Grange

Markham's
Wood

Ardeley

3

Churchend Common

River Beane

Ardeley Brook

Ardeley
Bury

Ardeley
St Lawrence
CE Prim Sch

27

The
Bungalow

THE
CRESCENT

SCHOOL LA

2

Dovehouse La

Manor
Farm

BEECROFT LA

The Old
Rectory

CHURCH END

Squitmore
Spring

BROCKINGS

Nursery

WHITE HILL

Bridgefoot
Farm

WINTERS LA

Walkern Bury
Farm

1

FROGHALL LA

KITCHENERS LA

HIGH ST

TOT TS LA

BROCKWELL SHOTT

AUBRIES

Walkern

CHERRY TREE RISE

PO

B1037

The Yew Tree
(PH)

Chancey
Hall

26

MOORS LEY

28   A   B   29   C   D   30   E   F

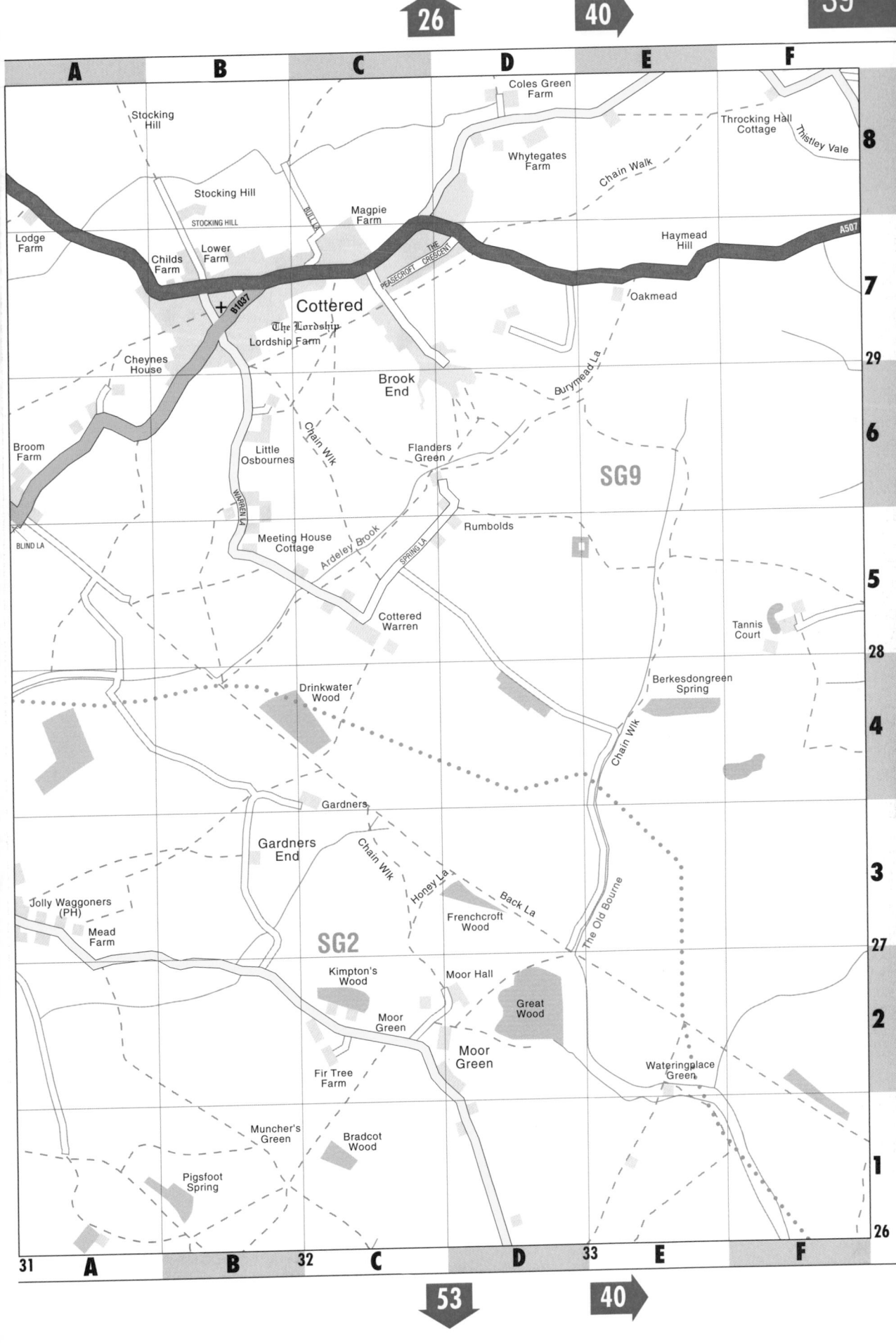

A   B   C   D   E   F

8
Stocking Hill
Stocking Hill
STOCKING HILL
Lodge Farm
Childs Farm
Lower Farm
Magpie Farm
Cottered
The Lordship
Lordship Farm
Cheynes House
Brook End
Broom Farm
Little Osbournes
Chain Wlk
Flanders Green
WARREN LA
BLIND LA
Meeting House Cottage
Ardeley Brook
SPRING LA
Rumbolds
Cottered Warren
Drinkwater Wood
Gardners
Gardners End
Chain Wlk
Honey La
Back La
Frenchcroft Wood
Jolly Waggoners (PH)
Mead Farm
SG2
Kimpton's Wood
Moor Hall
Moor Green
Great Wood
Moor Green
Fir Tree Farm
Muncher's Green
Bradcot Wood
Pigsfoot Spring

Coles Green Farm
Whytegates Farm
Chain Walk
Throcking Hall Cottage
Thistley Vale
A507
Haymead Hill
Oakmead
BULL LA
PEASECROFT
THE CRESCENT
Burymead La
SG9
Tannis Court
Berkesdongreen Spring
Chain Wlk
The Old Bourne
Wateringplace Green

29
7
6
5
28
4
3
27
2
1
26

31   A   B   32   C   D   33   E   F

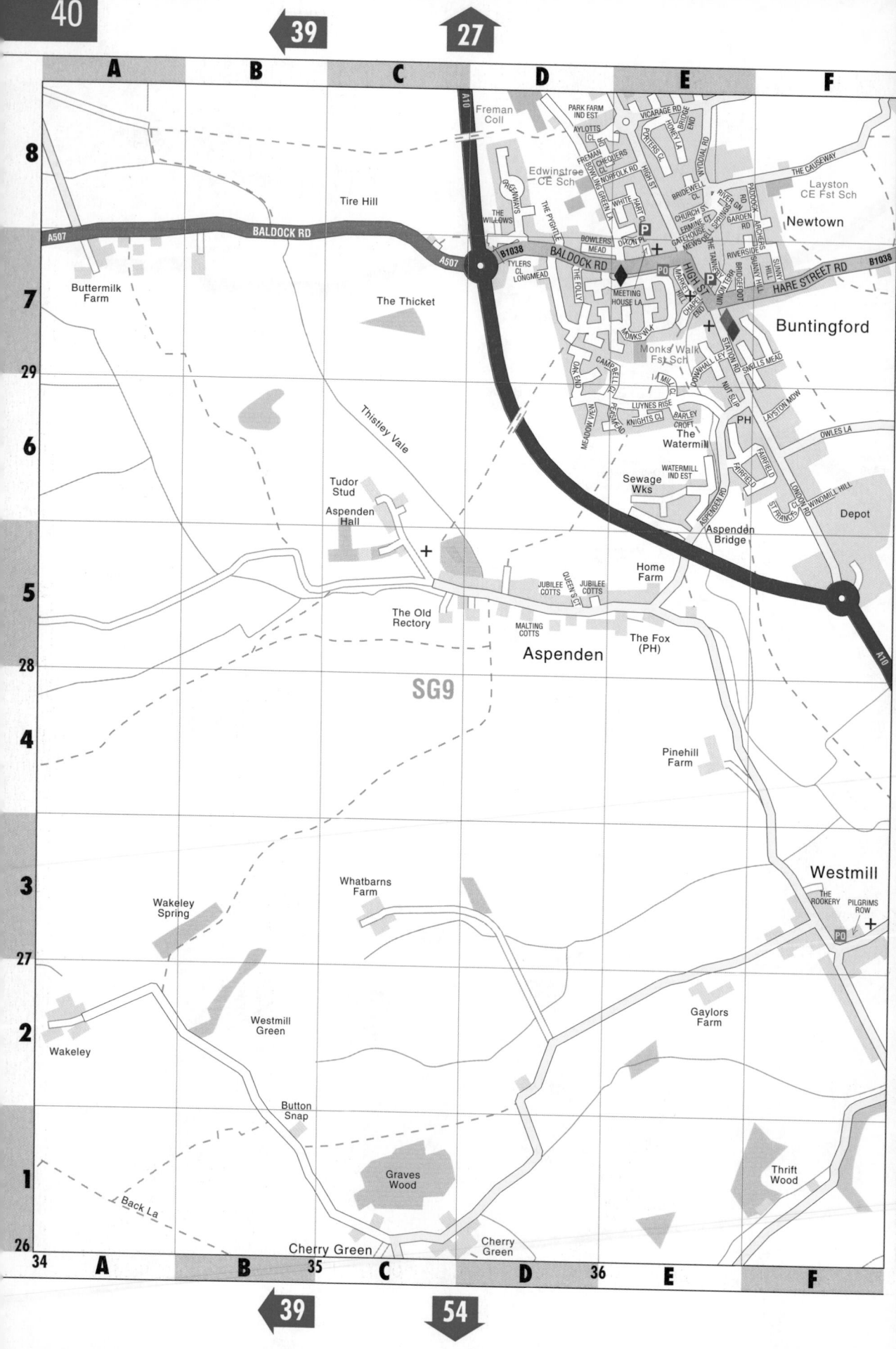

A507 BALDOCK RD

A507

Buttermilk Farm

Tire Hill

The Thicket

Thistley Vale

Tudor Stud

Aspenden Hall

The Old Rectory

Jubilee Cotts

Queen's Ct

Jubilee Cotts

Malting Cotts

Aspenden

The Fox (PH)

Home Farm

Aspenden Bridge

Sewage Wks

Watermill Ind Est

Depot

SG9

Pinehill Farm

Wakeley Spring

Whatbarns Farm

Westmill

THE ROOKERY

PILGRIMS ROW

PO

Westmill Green

Gaylors Farm

Wakeley

Button Snap

Graves Wood

Thrift Wood

Back La

Cherry Green

Cherry Green

Freman Coll

PARK FARM IND EST

AYLOTTS

VICARAGE RD

HONEY LA

PORTERS CL

BRIDGE END

WYDDIAL RD

THE CAUSEWAY

Edwinstree CE Sch

CHEQUERS

NORFOLK RD

FREMAN

HIGH ST

BRIDEWELL

CL

Layston CE Fst Sch

Newtown

GREENWAYS

THE WILLOWS

THE PIGHTLE

WHITE HART CL

CHURCH ST

ERMINE CT

GATEHOUSE MEWS

RIVER GN

GARDEN RD

PADDOCK CL

ARCHERS

B1038

BALDOCK RD

TYLERS CL

LONGMEAD

BOWLERS MEAD

DIXON PL

THE TANNERS

RIVERSIDE

SUNNY HILL

BRIDGEFOOT

HARE STREET RD

B1038

THE FOLLY

MEETING HOUSE LA

PO

HIGH ST

MARKET HILL

Buntingford

MONKS WALK

CHAPEL END

Monks Walk Fst Sch

CAMPBELL'S

MILL CL

SNELLS MEAD

LAYSTON MDW

OAK END

LUYNES RISE

PESTS END

BARLEY CROFT

KNIGHTS CL

DOWNHALL LEY

STATION RD

NUT SLIP

PH

OWLES LA

MEADOW RD

The Watermill

FAIRFIELD

FERFIELD

LONGMORE CL

WINDMILL HILL

ASPENDEN RD

ST FRANCIS

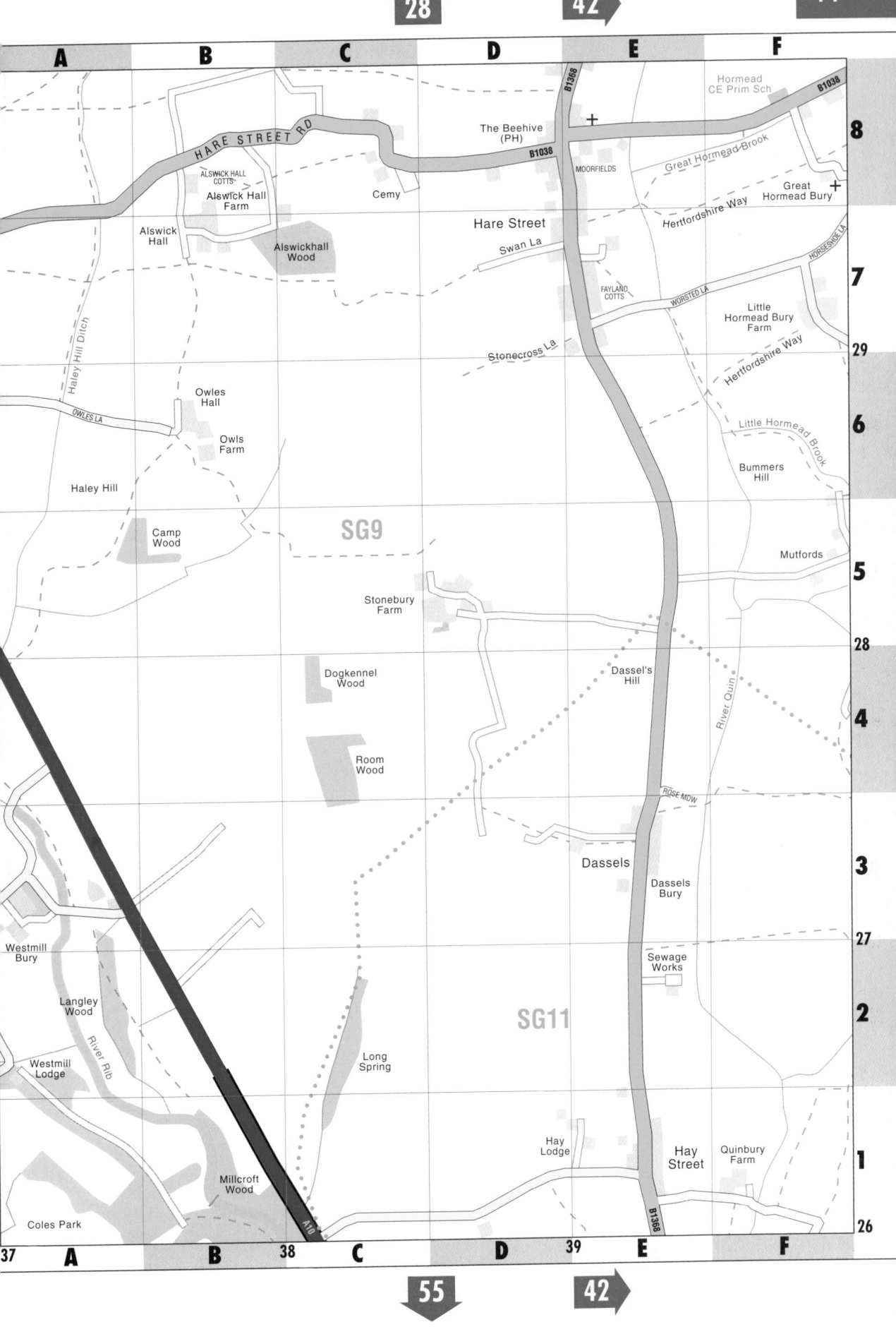

A B C D E F

8 7 29 6 5 28 4 3 27 2 1 26

HARE STREET RD

Alswick Hall Farm
ALSWICK HALL COTTS
Cemy
Alswick Hall
Alswickhall Wood

The Beehive (PH)
B1038
Moorfields
Hormead CE Prim Sch
B1038
Great Hormead Brook

Hare Street
Swan La
Hertfordshire Way
Great Hormead Bury

FAYLAND COTTS
WORSTED LA
HORSESHOE LA
Little Hormead Bury Farm

Stonecross La
Hertfordshire Way

Haley Hill Ditch
OWLES LA
Owles Hall
Owls Farm

Little Hormead Brook
Bummers Hill

Haley Hill

Camp Wood

SG9

Stonebury Farm

Mutfords

Dogkennel Wood

Dassel's Hill

River Quin

Room Wood

ROSE MDW

Dassels

Westmill Bury

Dassels Bury

Langley Wood

Sewage Works

SG11

River Rib

Westmill Lodge

Long Spring

Hay Lodge

Hay Street

Quinbury Farm

Millcroft Wood

A10

B1368

Coles Park

Three Tuns (PH)

B1038

HORSESHOE HILL

Great Hormead

8

JUBILEE COTTS

WILLOW CL

HORSESHOE LA

Church End Cottage

Sparksfield

7

The Thrift

Great Hormead Park

St Patrick's Wood

PARK VIEW

29

Glebe House

Balons Farm

Little Hormead

Little Hormead Brook

SG9

6

Bulls Farm

Fair Lady Wood

The Willows

Lady Wood

Mutfords

5

Mutton Hall

Duck Street Cottage

Hertfordshire Way

28

Furneux Pelham Hall

STRE

4

Shirley

Bradley Spring

High Wood

Patient End Farm

3

Hoare's La

Bozengreen Farm

Rotten Row

Hertfordshire Way

Patient End

27

Bozen Green

2

SG11

THE CAUSEWAY

Hole Farm Cott

1

Hole Farm

26

40 A B **41** C D **42** E F

CM23

8

Hall Wood

Stocking
Farm

Stocking Pelham
Hall

7

The Cock
(PH)

Violets
Spring

Stocking
Pelham

White Hart
Farm

Berden

29

Whitebarns

MEAD
VIEW

Crabb's
Green

6

Sports
Ground

CRABB'S LA

Crabb's Green
Farm

WHITEBARNS LA

Whitebarns
Cottages

Silla
Farm

GINNS RD

The Willows

El Tfmr Sta

SG9

Willows
Farm

5

28

River Ash

VIOLETS LA

GINNS RD   THE WASH

Furneux
Pelham

WHITEBARNS

Brewery

Lower
Farm

East End

Green's
Farm

4

+ PO

THE STREET

Furneux
Pelham
CE Prim Sch

LAKE
VILLAS

Old Mill
House

Eastend
Farm

The
Star
(PH)

+

The
Brewery
Tap
(PH)

THE OLD
COMMON

Barleycroft
End

The Brook

Recn
Gd

Clay
Chimneys

3

THE CAUSEWAY

Pheasant
Hall

27

Sewage
Works

Hixham
Cottages

Hixham Hall

2

Kings
Cottage

Kings

CM23

SG11

1

Oaken Spring

Heath
Farm

26

A   B   C   D   E   F

C5
1 CHAWORTH GN
2 ACWORTH CT
3 MOSSDALE CT
4 WOLFSBURG CT
5 THORNTONDALE
6 GREEN CT

7 WHARFDALE

A   B   C   D   E   F

LU3

Great Bramingham Wood

Sundon Park

Works

Lea Manor Recn Ctr

Lea Manor High Sch

Whitefield Jun & Inf Schs

Lealands High Sch

Liby

Five Springs Sch

Marsh Farm

North Luton Ind Est

Park Avenue Trad Est

Eagle Centre Way

Pirton Hill Jun & Inf Schs

TODDINGTON RD

1 Stoneways Cl
2 Green Bushes
3 Brocket Ct

Leagrave Common

Penhill Ct 1
Lea Bank Ct 2
Five Springs Ct 3

Playing Fields

Source of the River Lea or Lee

Well Head

Waulud's Bank

Waulud Prim Sch

Lea Bank

1 Woburn Ct
2 Playford Sq
3 Hanover Ct

1 Twigden Ct
2 The Heights
3 The Stepping Stones
4 Willow Ct
5 Nursery Par

Limbury

Leagrave

Mast

Allot Gdns

Recn Gd

St Martin de Porres RC Jun & Inf Schs

1 Clover Cl
2 Guernsey Cl
3 Clydesdale Cl
4 Pastures Ct
5 Leghorn Cres

HAVERDALE 1
STONESDALE 2

Leagrave Prim Sch

Downs View

Beechwood Jun & Inf Schs

Liby

LU4

Factory

Factory

Moorlands Prep Sch

Ickhield Way Path

1 Marbury Pl
2 Archway Rd
3 Marsh Ho
4 Caxton Cl

Leagrave High St

Ferrars Jun & Inf Schs

Luton & Dunstable (Faringdon Wing)

Luton Maternity

Challney Boys & Girls High Schs

WALLER AVE

Wingate Ct

Larkspur Gdns

Hathaway Cl 1
Swanston Grange 2
Downview 3
James Ct 4

Luton & Dunstable

DUNSTABLE RD

LU5

The Drummonds

Downside Jun & Inf Schs

DUNSTABLE

LU1

LU1

HATTERS WAY

04   A   B   05   C   D   06   E   F

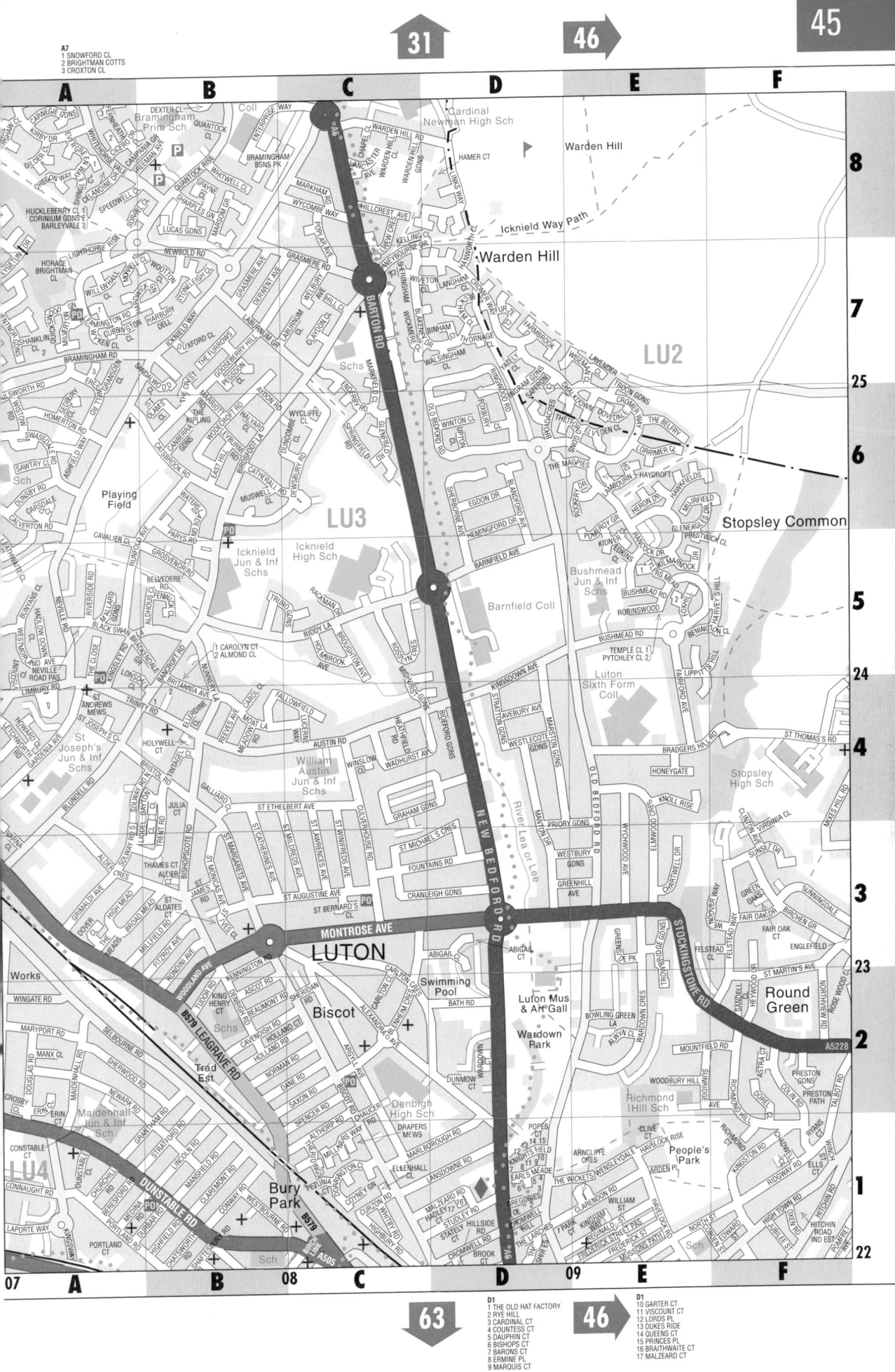

A   B   C   D   E   F

8

Whitehill Wood
Jamaica Plantation
Whitehill Farm
Beech Hill
Beechhill Plantation
Dog Kennel Farm
PH ST WEST A505
BEECH HILL

7

Whitehill Farm
Oaket Wood
North Lodge
Upshot Wood

25

Icehouse Plantation
East Lodge

6

Butterfield Green
Crem
Great Hayes Wood
Luton Univ Putteridge Bury
Dick's Gap
Manor Farm
Cemy
HITCHIN RD
Home Farm
Hawleydell Plantation

5

Recn Gd
Putteridge High Sch
Putteridge Recn Ctr
WEST LODGE COTTS
Mangrove Hall
Messina Plantation
WREN CL
NIGHTINGALE
JAYWOOD
CURLEW
MOUNT GRACE RD
CORNINGDALE
EDGEWOOD RD
ELMWOOD RD
GREEN RD
WOOD GREEN
SWIFTS GREEN
WILLIAM SUTTON CT
HAYES CL
CROWLAND RD
WOOD GREEN RD
ROGATE RD
ROXGROVE RD
SELSEY DR
BIRLING DR
RAVENBANK RD
PH

Luton Regional Sports Ctr
Putteridge Jun & Inf Schs
1 BALCOMBE CL
2 PEVENSEY CL
3 AMBERLEY CL
Mangrove Lodge

24

MULLION CL
JANSEL HO
PO
Putteridge Rd
Putteridge Par
ROCHESTER AVE
CHESFORD RD
MIDDLETON RD

LOTHAIR RD
VENETIA
DEL COTT
JELDERBERRY
GREENWAYS
CANNON LA
HAWTHORN AVE
COLLINGTREE
STAPLEFORD RD
APPLECROFT RD
WESTWAY
FIELD END
EASTFIELD RD
Mangrove Green
LU2

4

ST THOMAS'S RD
MIXES HILL CT
Liby
HAZELWOOD CL
RAVENSTHORPE
WANDON CL
BLACKTHORN DR
BRIAR CL
PEARTREE RD
Stopsley Jun & Inf Schs
Stopsley
WALNUT CL
DAHLIA CL
GREEN LA
Playing Field
Slipe Spring
1 WALTHAM CT
2 RINGMER CT
3 NINFIELD CT
4 MARY BRASH CT
Cockernhoe Endowed Jun Mix & Inf Sch
Cockernhoe Farm

TANCRED RD
RYECROFT WAY
BANBURY RISE
HITCHIN RD
FORREST
A505
Recn Gd
POP ARTS CL
AVON COTTS
SOWERBY AVE
ALFRISTON CL
LULLINGTON
KENVER
SEAFORD CL
PLUMPTON CL
HAYLING
SALTDEAN
TILGATE
1 BURFIELD CT
2 BROAD OAK CT
3 GARFIELD CT
4 SCOTFIELD CT
Cockernhoe
ELMTREE AVE
CHALK HILL

3

LYNWOOD AVE
SHELTON WAY
ARNOLD
STEPHENS CT
BRAYS RD
MOBLEY GN
LITTLE CHURCH RD
DITCHLING RD
1 CROFT RD
12 THE SEVERALLS
Allot Gdns
Slaughter's Wood
DELLFIELD CT
1 RENSHAW CL
2 BERROW CL
3 RESTON PATH
4 WARTON GN
5 BRANTON CL
Brickiln Wood

A505
A5228
HITCHIN RD
KINANCE CL
RICKYARDS
STRONNELL CL
ASHCROFT RD
BRAYS CT
SIBLEY CL
GIBBET'S MEAD
SLYPER GN
COPTHORNE
ROTHERFIELD

23

Sacred Heart Jun & Inf Schs
STEPHENS GDNS
Sch
NICHOLS
LITTLEFIELD RD
MANGROVE RD
CHALFONT WAY
Someries Jun & Inf Schs
HONSHAM CL
TRESCOTT CT
ROCHFORD DR
TAMPTON CT
RYLANDS HEATH

LUTON
Ramridge Jun & Inf Sch
MORETON
CLEVEDON RD
HANSWICK CT
YEOVIL CT
STYLES CT
KEEPERS
WIGMORE LA
HILL RD
BUCKINGHAM
KEMPSEY CL
ASTLEY
CLAVERLEY CT
ROSWELL CL
CRESSY
GREENRIGGS

2

MORETON PK
MORETON
UPWELL RD
WILLITON RD
MARSHALL RD
WHITECHURCH CL 1
WADDESDON CL 2
BRIMFIELD CL 3
WHITLEY GN 4
LINLEY DELL 5
BRILL CL
LINDSEY WAY
CORBRIDGE DR
WHITTINGHAM
HAWTREE
CUTLERS
WARMINSTER
ENNISMORE
A5228
FELIX AVE
PO
MORETON
RAMRIDGE'S
Ashcroft High Sch
BUCKINGHAM DR
SUSSEX CL
Wigmore
Wigmore Prim Sch
BRIERLEY
POLECAT
CHATTON
BIRTLEY
HAWSTEAD
PORTMEAD
BOWYALE
MALTHOUSE RD

VAUXHALL WAY
HARTSFIELD RD
BURNHAM RD
COPEHOUSE HILL
Crawley Green Rd
Superstore
Wigmore Park Ctr
COLWELL RISE
PELTON RD
WELDON
WIGMORE
LESBURY CL
CORBRIDGE DR
WHITTINGHAM
RADSTONE PL
THE DELL
BROOKVALE
FELBRIGG

1

Hart Hill
CHERRY TREE CL
KENNETH RD
ELMORE RD
STANFORD RD
EXTON AVE
RIDGE CL
CONGREVE RD
HIGHOVER RD
TAUNTON RD
WALCOT AVE
SAYWELL RD
BRENDON AVE
EATON VALLEY RD
PENFOLD CRES
SUMMERS RD
CARTERET RD
OVERFIELD RD
HIGH RIDGE
HOLLYBUSH RD
LYNEHAM RD
NETHERCOTT RD
EASTCOTT RD
HOLTSMERE
TIMWORTH
FRISTON GN
BARFORD
FALLOWFIELD
RAMFIELD
TAFFORD RD
RAINHAM WAY
NEWNHAM
HEMSTEAD
BARROWBY
BANASTON
EATON GREEN RD
Superstore
Wigmore Park Ctr
Hotel
Allot Gdns
1 PITSFORD TERR
2 ABBOTSWOOD PAR
3 ELMFIELD CT
4 POMFRET AVE

22

Wr Twr
HART LA
HARTS WOOD
TOWER
PLYMOUTH CL
PO
ROWELFIELD
FALCONERS RD
A505
PO
P
1 NAYLAND CL
2 ARDLEIGH GN
3 BAYLAM DELL
Playing Field

10   A   B   11   C   D   12   E   F

D1
1 CHELSWORTH CL
2 MUTFORD CROFT
3 MELFORD CL
4 PINFORD DELL
5 ALDERTON CL

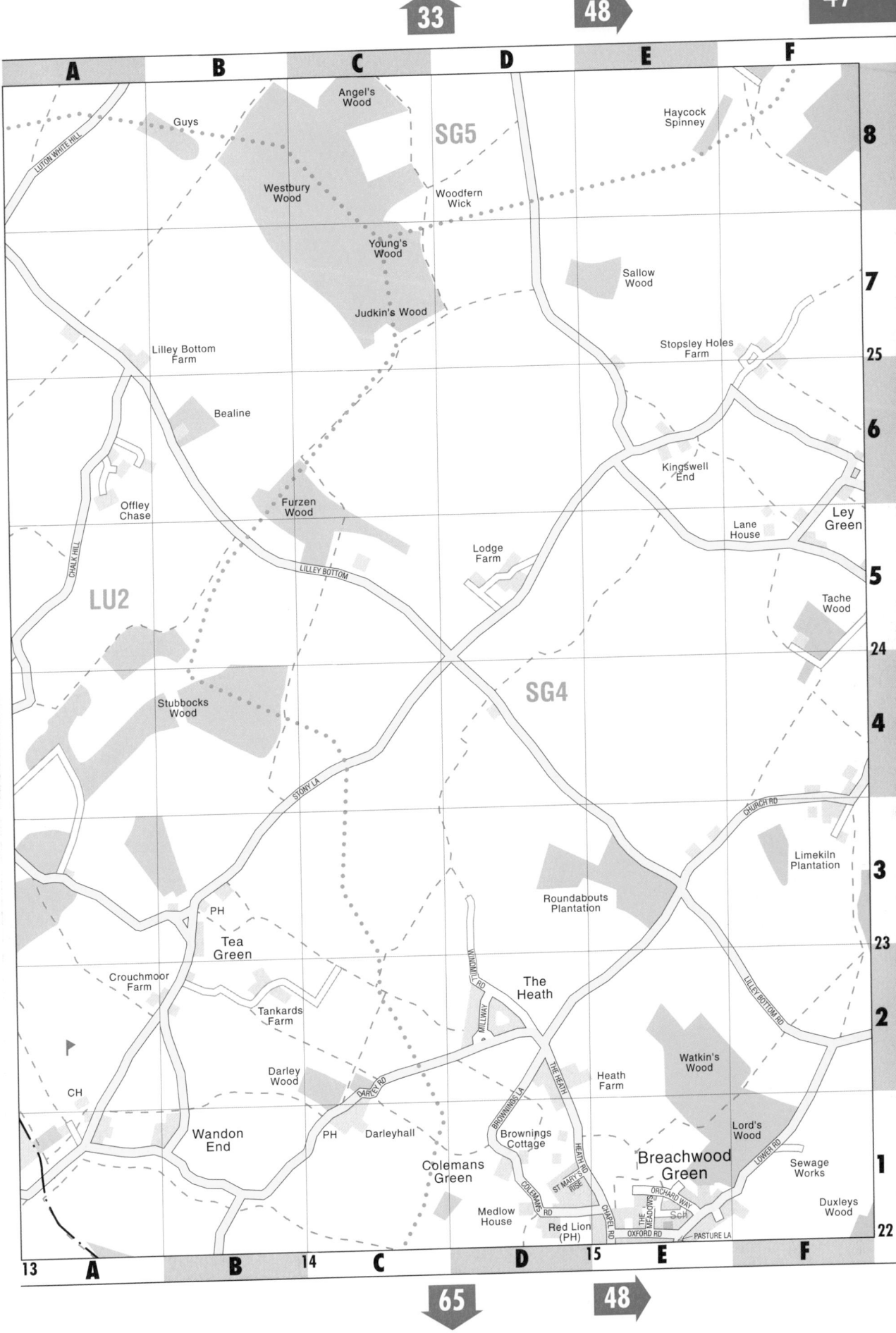

A **B** **C** **D** **E** **F**

Angel's Wood

Guys

SG5

Haycock Spinney

8

LUTON WHITE HILL

Westbury Wood

Woodfern Wick

Young's Wood

Sallow Wood

7

Judkin's Wood

Stopsley Holes Farm

25

Lilley Bottom Farm

6

Bealine

Kingswell End

Offley Chase

Furzen Wood

Lane House

Ley Green

CHALK HILL

LU2

LILLEY BOTTOM

Lodge Farm

Tache Wood

5

24

Stubbocks Wood

SG4

4

STONY LA

Limekiln Plantation

3

CHURCH RD

Roundabouts Plantation

23

PH

Tea Green

Crouchmoor Farm

The Heath

LILLEY BOTTOM RD

2

Tankards Farm

WINDMILL RD

Watkin's Wood

MILLWAY

CH

Darley Wood

Heath Farm

Lord's Wood

LOWER RD

Wandon End

PH

Darleyhall

DARLEY RD

BROWNINGS LA

Brownings Cottage

Breachwood Green

Sewage Works

Colemans Green

THE HEATH

ORCHARD WAY

Sch

Duxleys Wood

Medlow House

Red Lion (PH)

HEATH RD

ST MARY'S RISE

COLEMANS RD

THE MEADOWS

CHAPEL RD

OXFORD RD

PASTURE LA

1

22

13 **A** **B** **14** **C** **D** **15** **E** **F**

A B C D E F

8
West Wood
Sootfield Springs
The Warren
Gosmore Hill
Leggatts Plantation

7
Austage End
Castle Farm
Wain Wood
Bunyan's Cottage
Lincees Plantation
Tatmorehills La
Preston Rd

25
Chequers La
Templars La
Dower House
Princess Helena Coll

6
Wantsend Farm
Cox Green
Leggatts Farm
Pond Farm
Chequers Cotts
Church La
Red Lion (PH)
Temple Dinsley
Dead Woman's La
Back

Preston Hills
Preston
Preston Prim Sch
Crunnels Gn
School La
Ladygrove Cotts
Ladygrove Ct

5
PH
PO
Stony Wood
Preston Hills
Kiln Wood
Ladygrove Farm
Minsden Farm
Plough La

24
Parsonage Farm
Dean's Wood
Lady Grove

4
Church Rd
The Nursery
Whitehall Wood
Prestonhill Farm
Lady Grove
SG4
The Firs

Whitehall Farm
Hearnsfield Wood

3
Kingswalden Bury
King's Walden
Kingswalden Park (Deer Park)
Cedar Wood
Pinfold Wood

23
Frogmore
Frogmore Bottom
Foxholes Wood
Rookery Wood
Park Wood
Park Wood

2
Hanger Wood
Stagenhoe
Garden Wood
Lodge

1
Lilley Bottom Rd
Long Spinney
Chalkleys Wood

22
Law Hall Farm
Duxleys Wood
Stagenhoe Bottom Farm
Walk Wood

16 A 17 B C D 18 E F

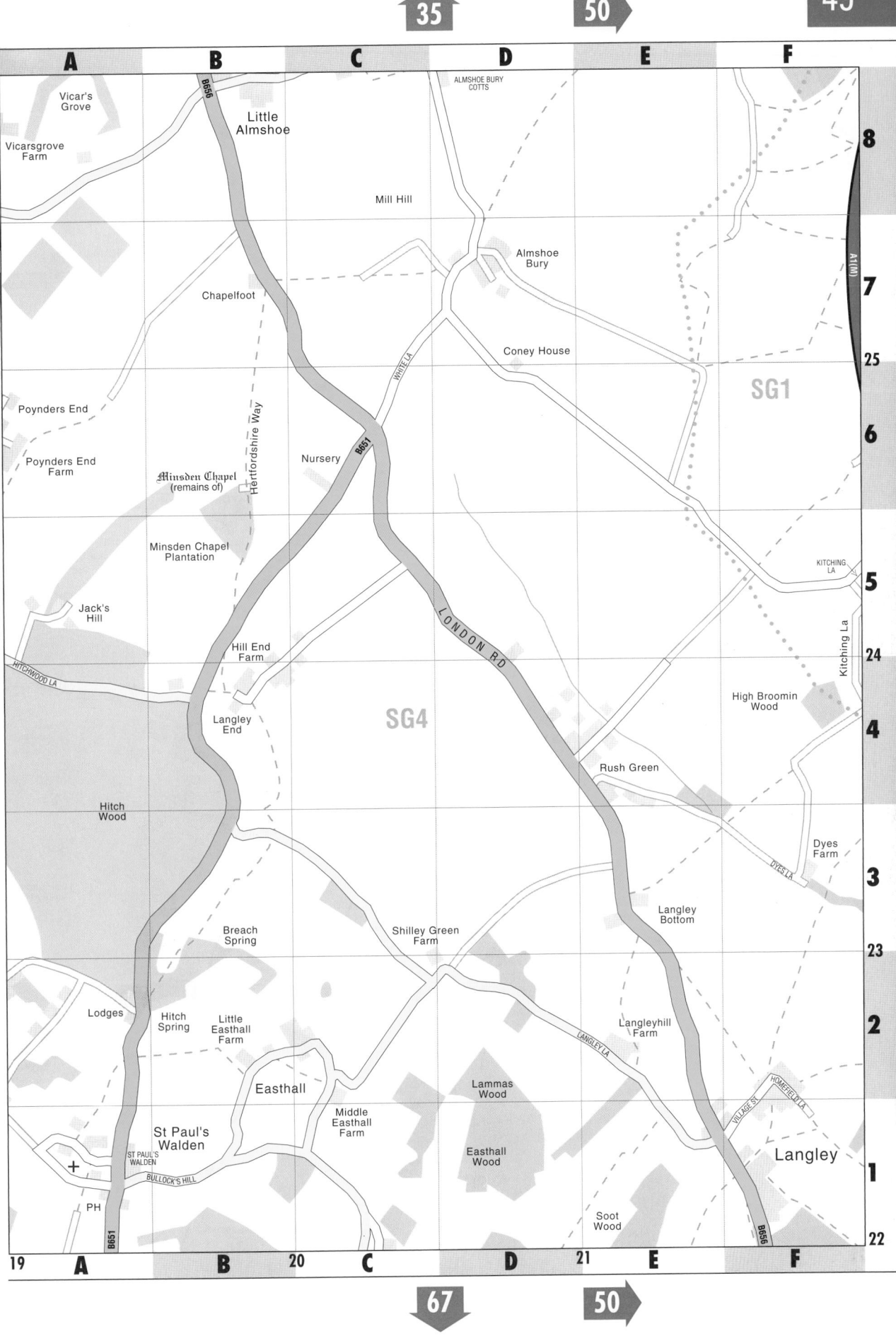

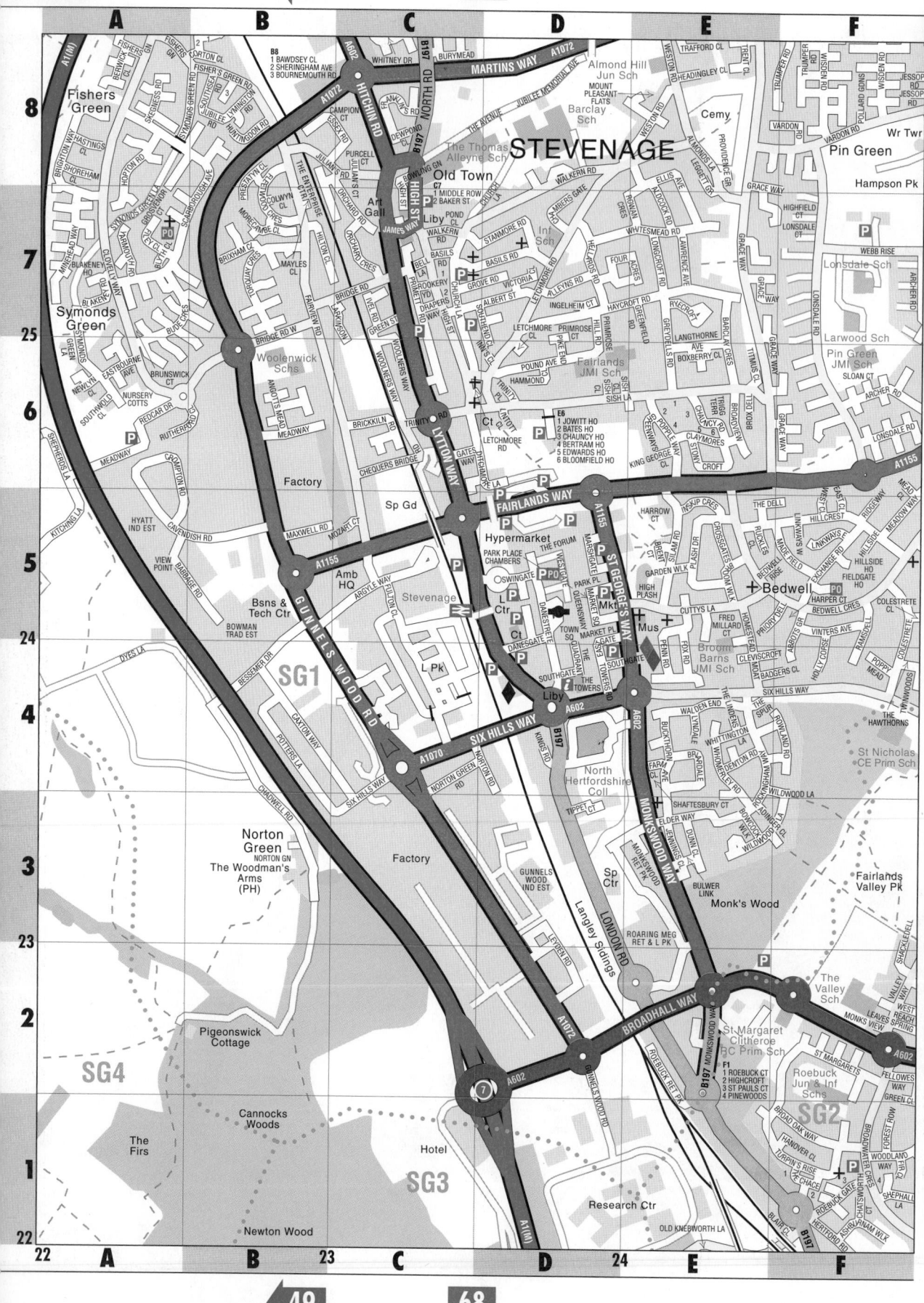

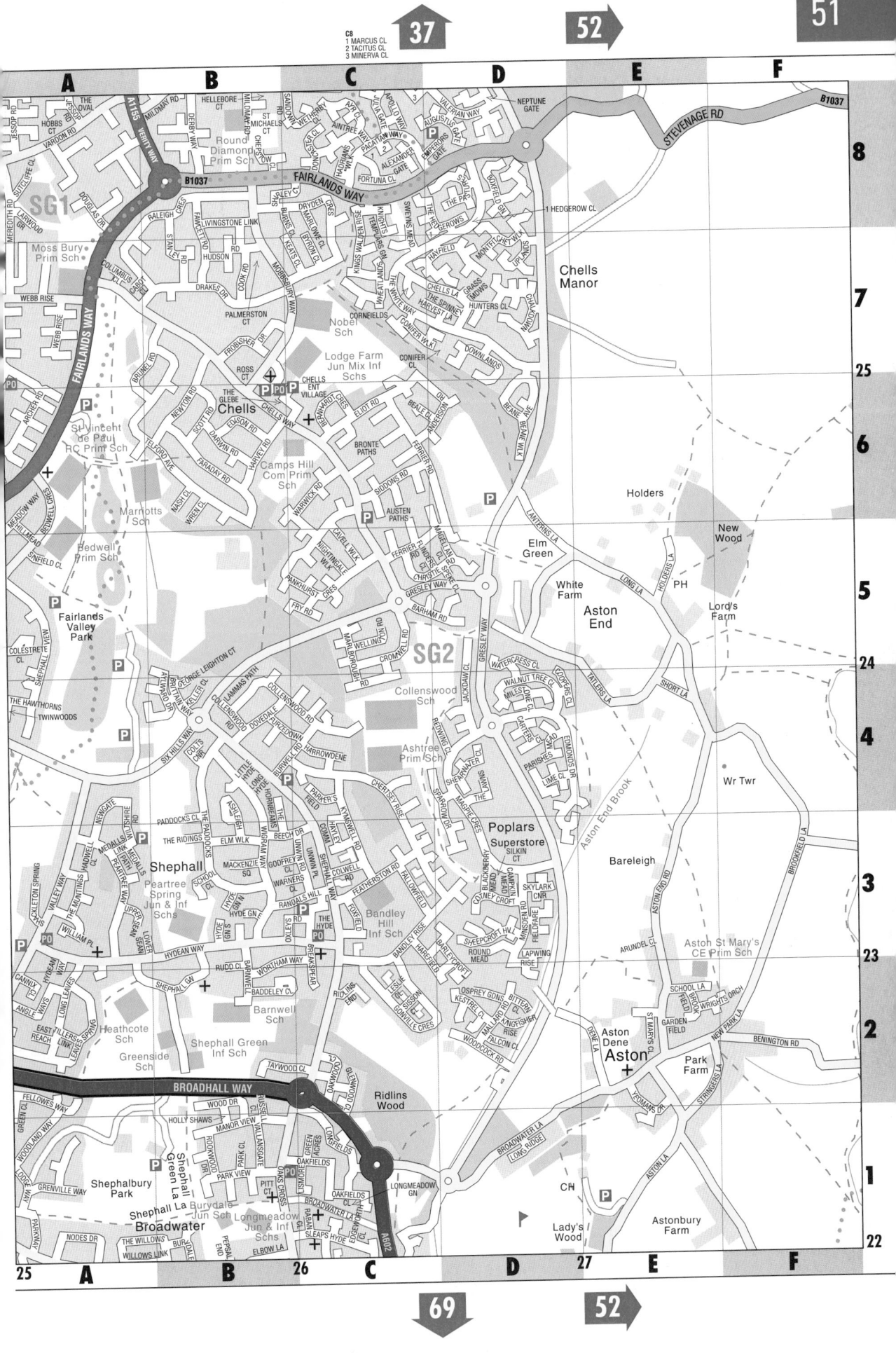

51
38

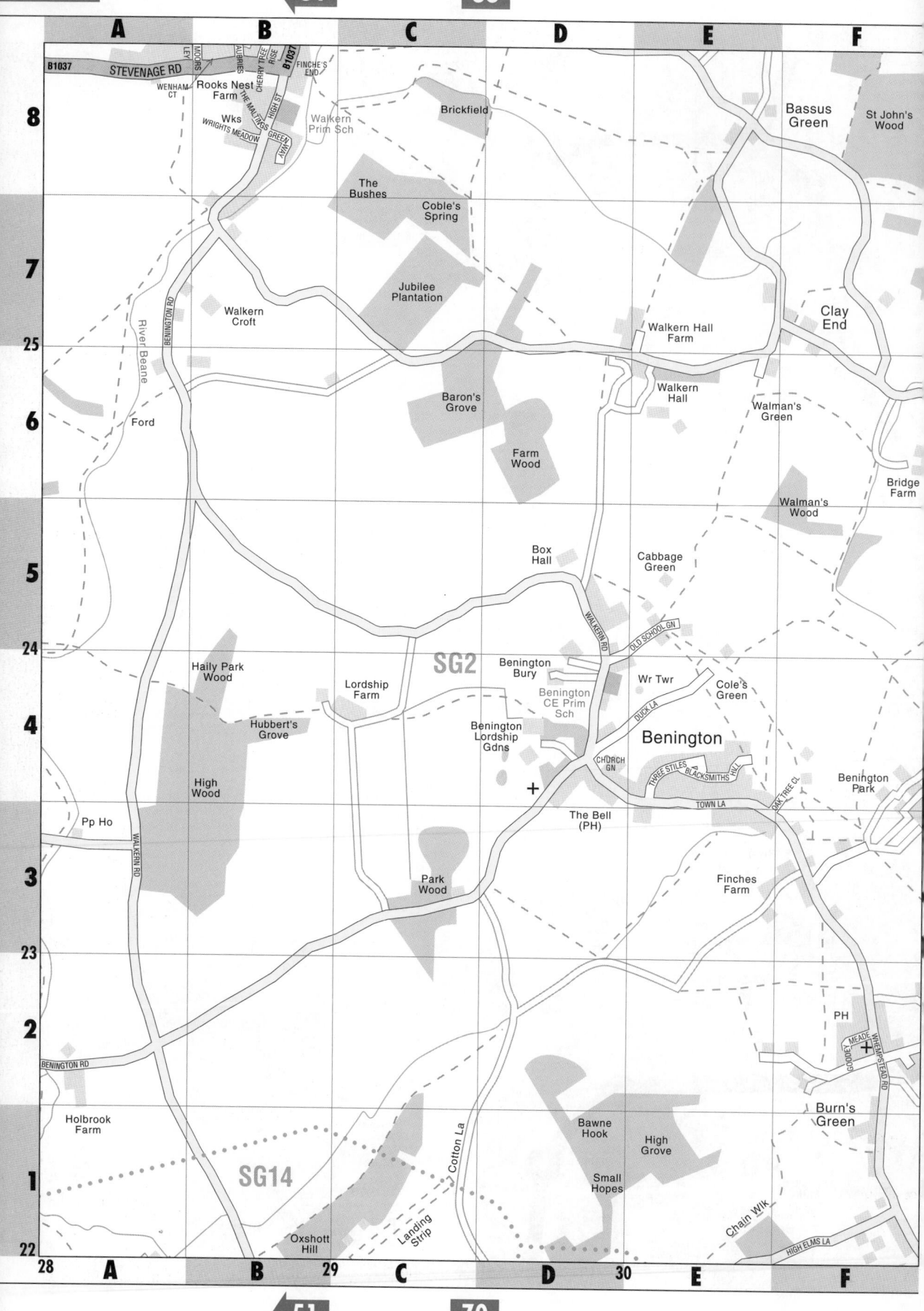

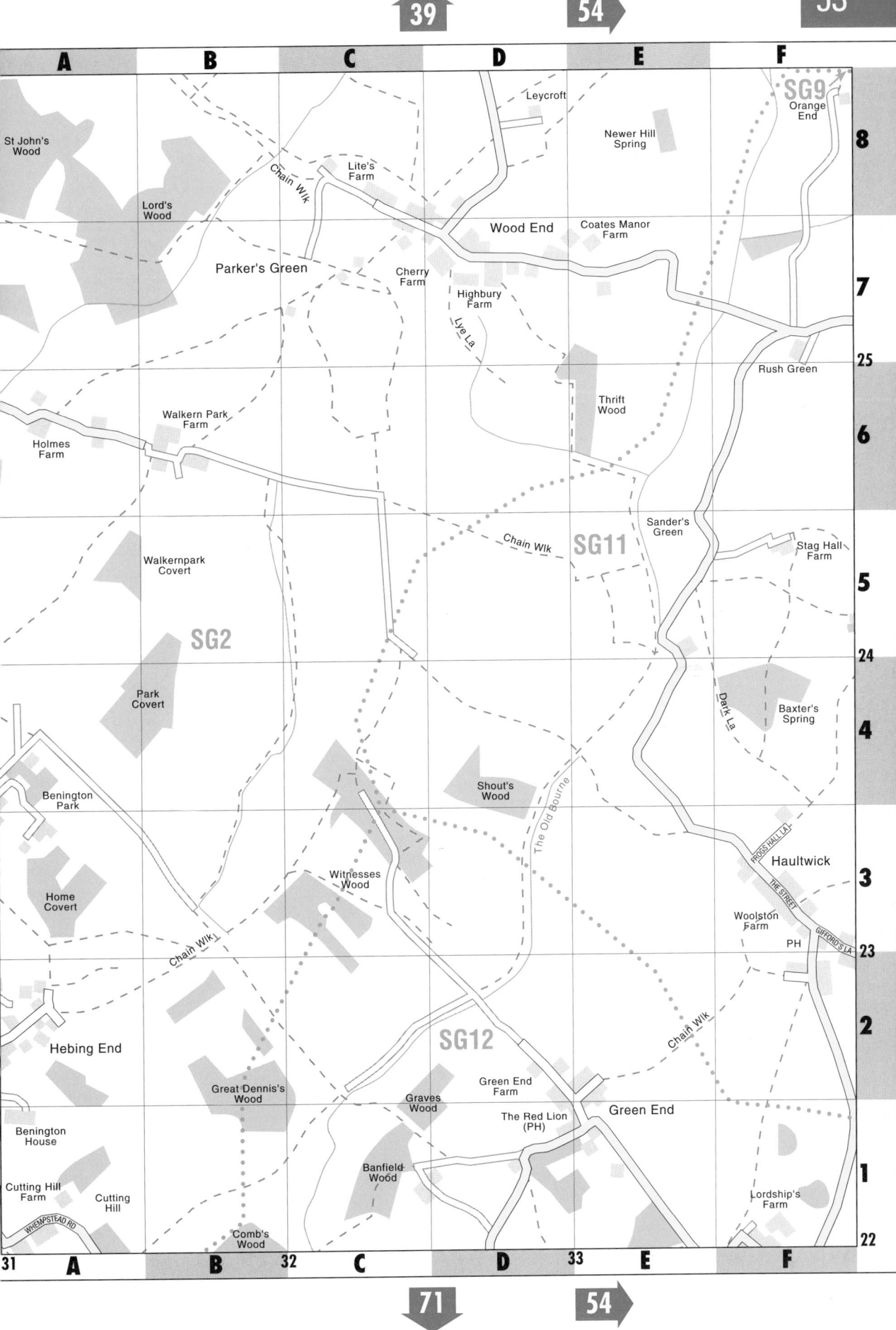

39
54

A   B   C   D   E   F

SG9
Orange
End

Leycroft

St John's
Wood

Newer Hill
Spring

8

Lord's
Wood

Chain Wlk

Lite's
Farm

Wood End

Coates Manor
Farm

Parker's Green

Cherry
Farm

Highbury
Farm

7

Lye La

Rush Green

25

Thrift
Wood

Holmes
Farm

Walkern Park
Farm

6

Chain Wlk

SG11

Sander's
Green

Stag Hall
Farm

5

Walkernpark
Covert

SG2

24

Dark La

Baxter's
Spring

4

Park
Covert

Shout's
Wood

The Old Bourne

Benington
Park

FROGS HALL LA

Haultwick

3

Home
Covert

Witnesses
Wood

THE STREET

Woolston
Farm

GIFFORD'S LA

Chain Wlk

PH

23

Chain Wlk

Hebing End

SG12

Chain Wlk

2

Great Dennis's
Wood

Graves
Wood

Green End
Farm

Green End

Benington
House

The Red Lion
(PH)

Lordship's
Farm

1

Cutting Hill
Farm

Cutting
Hill

Banfield
Wood

WHEMPSTEAD RD

Comb's
Wood

22

31   A   B   32   C   D   33   E   F

71
54

A **B** **C** **D** **E** **F**

Back La

Peasfield

Furtherfield
Spring

SG9

Tillers End
Farm

Coles
Park

The
Rectory

8

Cowley
Spring

Rush
Green
Cotts

7

Mill
Farm

25

6

The
Paddock

Nobles
Farm

Nasty

+

Munden
Bury

+

5

Great Munden

SG11

Chalk Wk

24

Bugby's
Farm

MENTLEY LA

4

The Plough
(PH)

Herringworth
Hall

Brockhold's
New Cover

Great Munden
Farm

Libury
Hall

Dane End Tributary

Stockalls

3

Great Munden
House

Brockhold's
New Clover

Brockhold's
Farm

23

GIFFORD'S LA

Hornbeam
Common

Goldsdell
Common

2

Overley
Common

Water
Twr

King's
Hill

Camps
Farm

Levens
Green

Levens Green
Farm

Old Hall
Green

Bandy
Common

Fellowsfield
Common

The Horse
and Groom
(PH)

PH

1

SG12

BEGGARMAN'S LA

22

A **B** **C** **D** **E** **F**

34 35 36

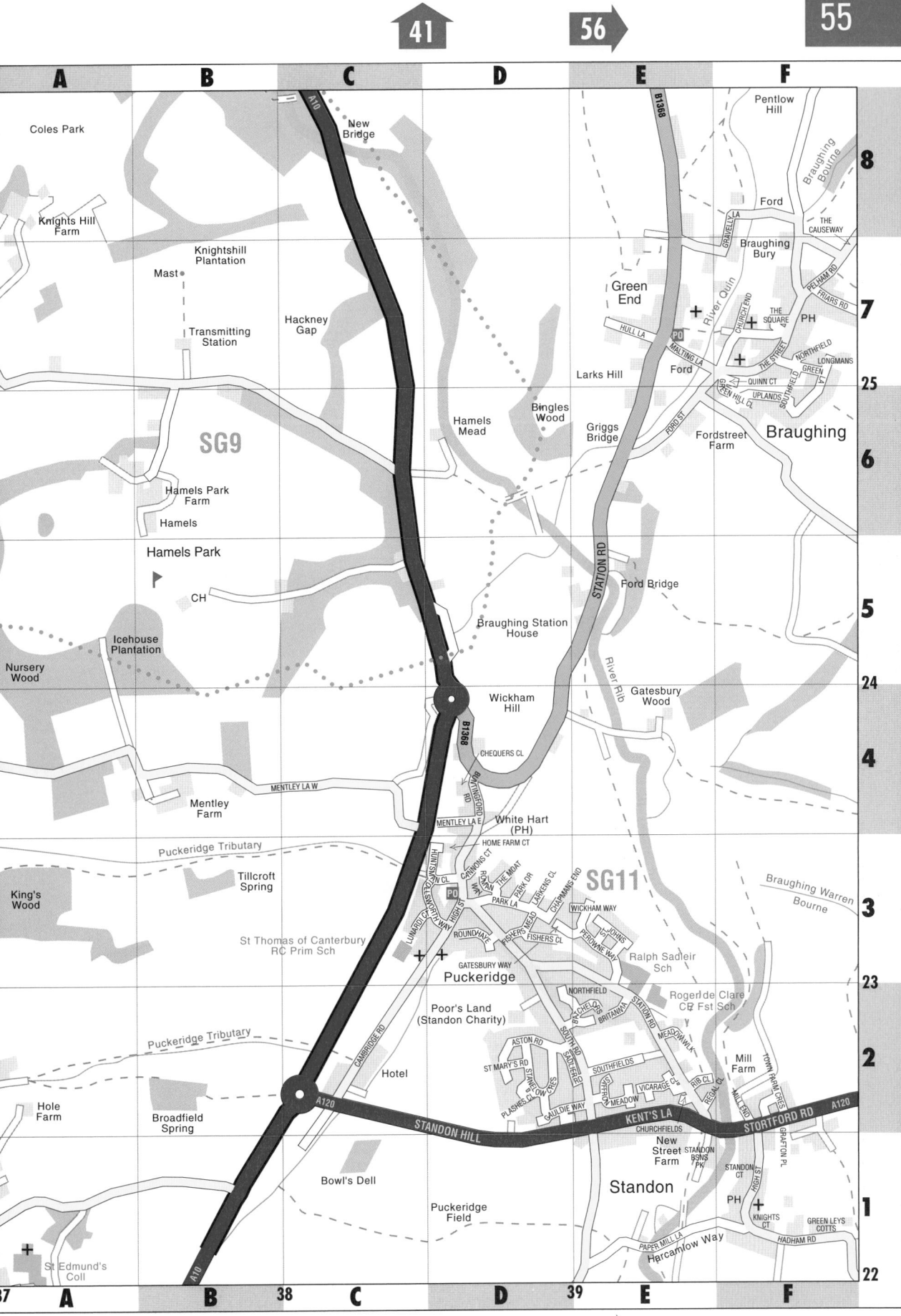

55
42

A   B   C   D   E   F

8

Braughing Bourne

THE CAUSEWAY

Hole Spring

Charleston House

Cockhamsted

Albury Hall Farm

7

FRIARS RD

Allot Gdns

Windcott

Harcamlow Way

Albury Hall Cottages

25

Flowerlands

Ferricks Wood

6

PARSONAGE

Fryers House   Nursery

Braughing Friars

Albury Water Tower

5

Sacombe Wood

Oldfield Cottages

Upp Hall

Ideal Farm

24

Braughing Warren Bourne

Piggotts Farm

The Warren

SG11

4

Harcamlow Way

Ash Plantation

New Wood

Albury End

Darney Wood

Warrenhill Cottage

3

HORSE CROSS

STANDON RD

Tilekiln Farm

Pockendon Field

23

A120

Ten Acre Wood

2

Poor's Land

Broken Green Cottages

Foxearth Wood

Jubilee

Broken Green

A120

Twiney Wood

Queer Wood

Wellpond Green

1

Standon Friars

PH

Lodge Farm

Highfield Farm

Westland Green

22

40   A   41   B   C   41   D   42   E   F

55
74

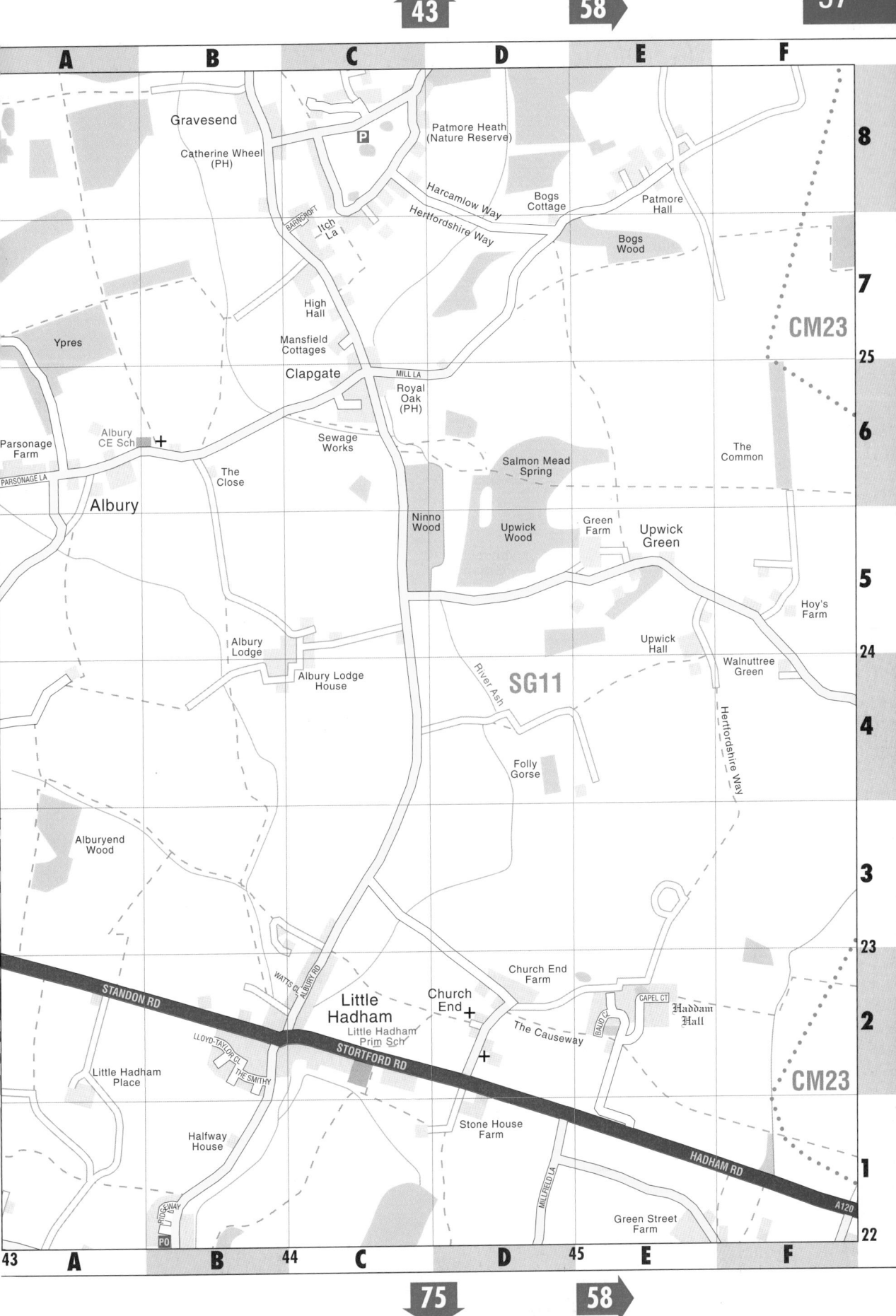

57

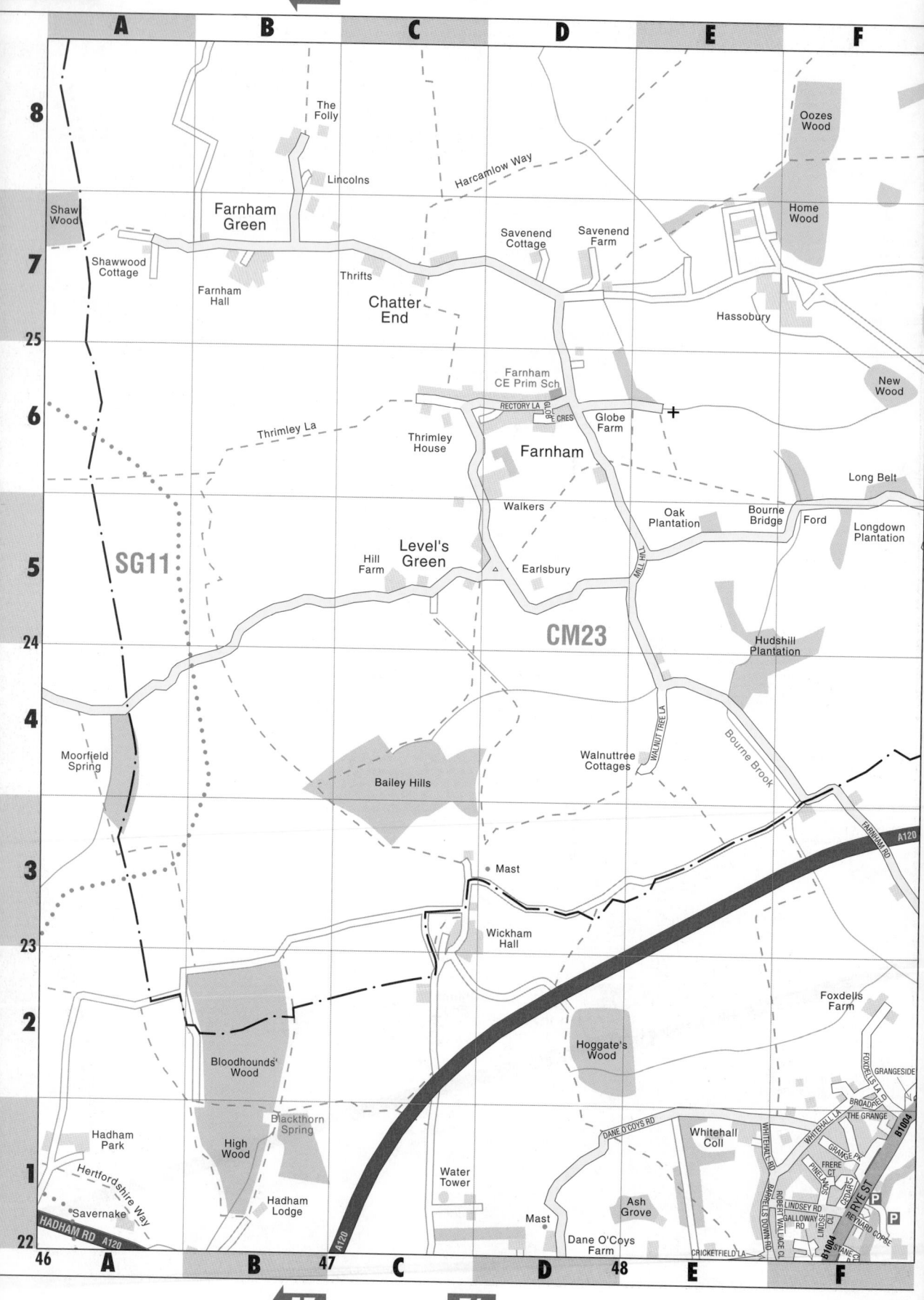

57
76

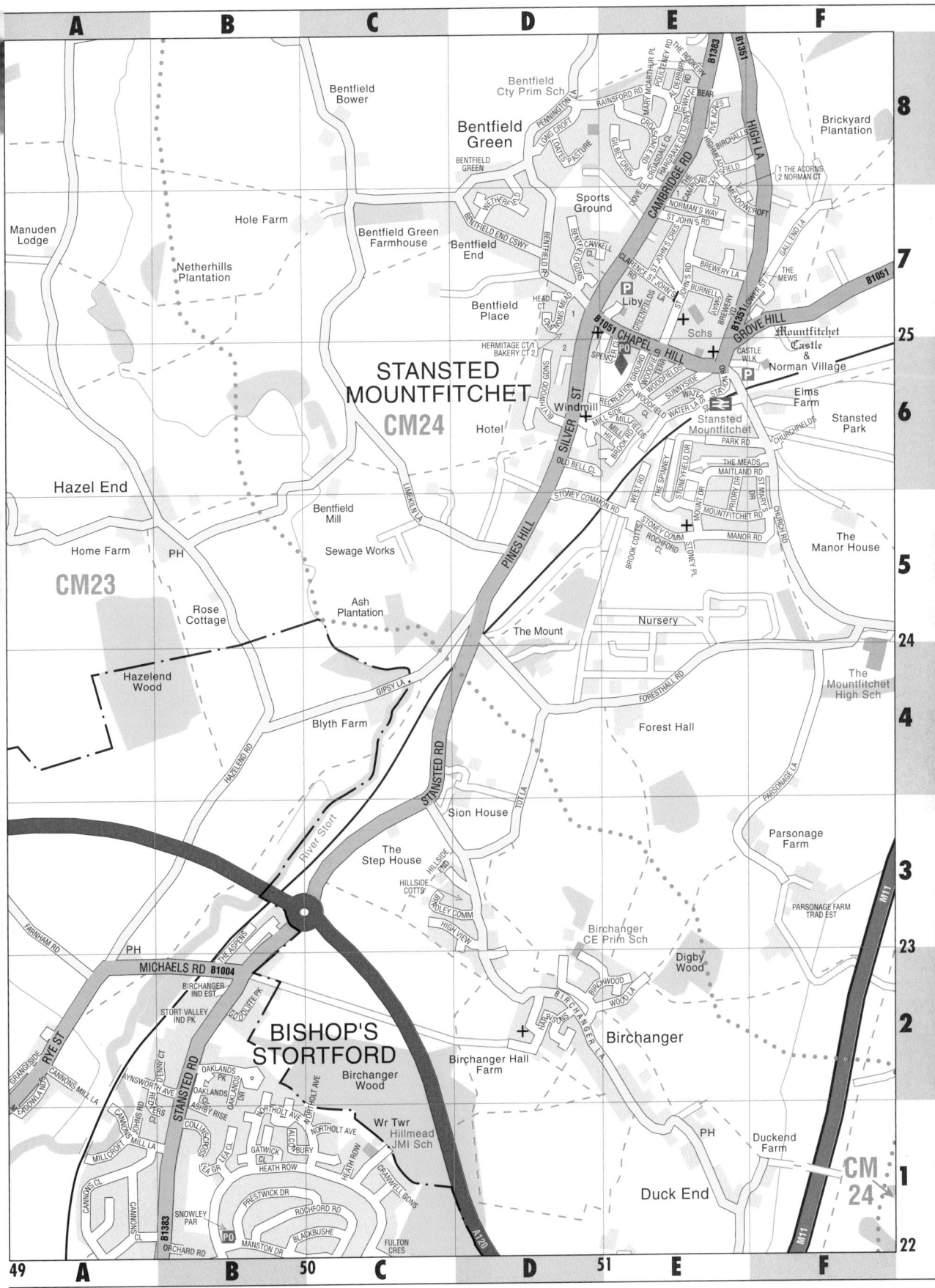

A B C D E F

8 7 25 6 5 24 4 3 23 2 1 22

Manuden Lodge

Bentfield Bower

Bentfield Green

Bentfield Cty Prim Sch

Brickyard Plantation

Hole Farm

Netherhills Plantation

Bentfield Green Farmhouse

Bentfield End

Sports Ground

1 THE ACORNS
2 NORMAN CT

CAMBRIDGE RD

HIGH LA

GALL END LA

THE MEWS

Liby

Schs

GROVE HILL

Mountfitchet Castle & Norman Village

Bentfield Place

STANSTED MOUNTFITCHET

CM24

Hermitage Ct1
Bakery Ct 2

CHAPEL HILL

Windmill

Hotel

SILVER ST

Recreation Ground

Woodfields

Sunnyside

Stansted Mountfitchet

Park Rd

Elms Farm

Stansted Park

The Manor House

Hazel End

CM23

Home Farm

PH

Rose Cottage

Bentfield Mill

Sewage Works

Ash Plantation

PINES HILL

Old Bell Cl

Stoney Common Rd

The Mount

Brook Cotts

Stoney Comm

Rochford Cl

Stoney Pl

Manor Rd

The Meads

Maitland Rd

Mountfitchet Rd

CHURCH RD

The Manor House

Nursery

The Mountfitchet High Sch

Hazelend Wood

GIPSY LA

Blyth Farm

STANSTED RD

Forest Hall

Foresthall Rd

Parsonage Farm

PARSONAGE LA

M11

River Stort

Sion House

TOTLA

The Step House

HILLSIDE RD

HILLSIDE COTTS

BIDLEY COMM

HIGH VIEW

Birchanger CE Prim Sch

Digby Wood

Parsonage Farm Trad Est

PH

FARNHAM RD

RYE ST

PH

THE ASPENS

MICHAELS RD B1004

Birchanger Ind Est

Stort Valley Ind Pk

GOLDCLIFFE PK

STANSTED RD

BISHOP'S STORTFORD

Birchanger Wood

BIRCHANGER LA

BIRCHANGER LA

WOOD LA

BIRCHWOOD

Birchanger

Duckend Farm

CM24

GRANGESIDE

CAVAN WAY

CANNONS CL

CANNONS MILL LA

B SIMONS

REEVES

AYNSWORTH AVE

OAKLANDS PK

COLLYERS CT

OAKLANDS AVE

OAKLANDS CL

ASHBY RISE

NORTHOLT AVE

ALCOCK

ASTBURY

NORTHOLT AVE

Birchanger Hall Farm

Wr Twr
Hillmead JMI Sch

Birchanger Wood

MILLCROFT

CANNONS MILL LA

CANNONS CL

B1383

ORCHARD RD

SNOWLEY PAR

PO

MANSTON DR

LEA CL

LEA GR

GATWICK CL

HEATH ROW

PRESTWICK DR

ROCHFORD RD

BLACKBUSHE

HEATH ROW

CRANWELL GDNS

FULTON CRES

A120

Duck End

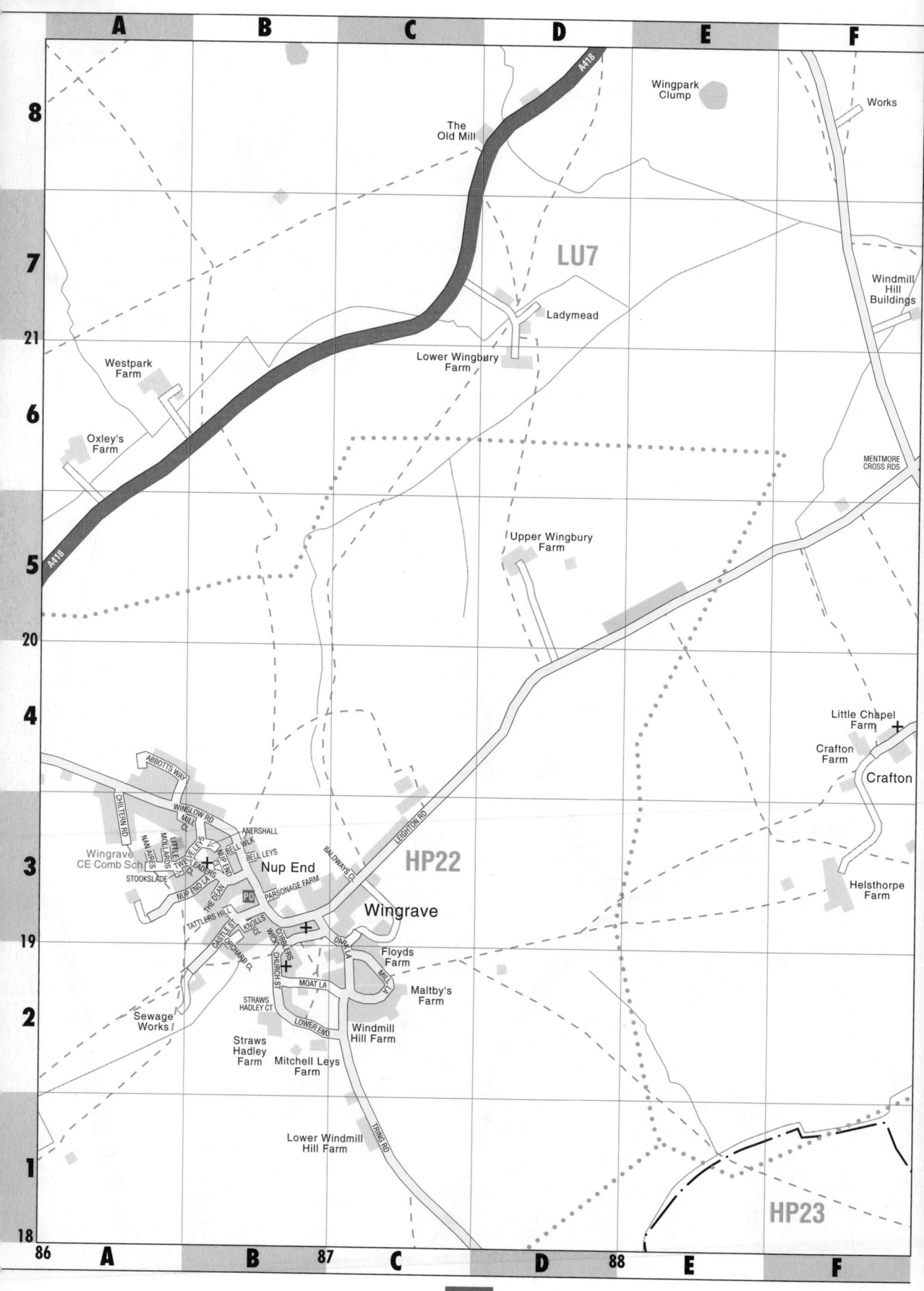

A B C D E F

8

LU7

7

21

6

Works

Wingpark Clump

The Old Mill

Ladymead

Lower Wingbury Farm

Windmill Hill Buildings

Westpark Farm

Oxley's Farm

MENTMORE CROSS RDS

5

20

Upper Wingbury Farm

A418

4

Little Chapel Farm

Crafton Farm

Crafton

ABBOTTS WAY

CHILTERN RD

WINSLOW RD

MILL CL

ANERSHALL

HP22

Helsthorpe Farm

3

Wingrave CE Comb Sch

NAN AIRES

MOLLARDS

LITTLE LEYS

TWELVE LEYS CL

BELL WLK

NUP END

BELL LEYS

Nup End

BALDWAYS CL

LEIGHTON RD

STOOKSLADE

NUP END LA

THE DEAN

PO

PARSONAGE FARM

Wingrave

19

TATTLERS HILL

CASTLE ST

ORCHARD CL

KNOLLS CL

COBBLERS WICK

CHURCH ST

DARK LA

MILL LA

Floyds Farm

Maltby's Farm

MOAT LA

2

Sewage Works

STRAWS HADLEY CT

LOWER END

Windmill Hill Farm

Straws Hadley Farm

Mitchell Leys Farm

1

Lower Windmill Hill Farm

TRING RD

HP23

18

86 A B 87 C D 88 E F

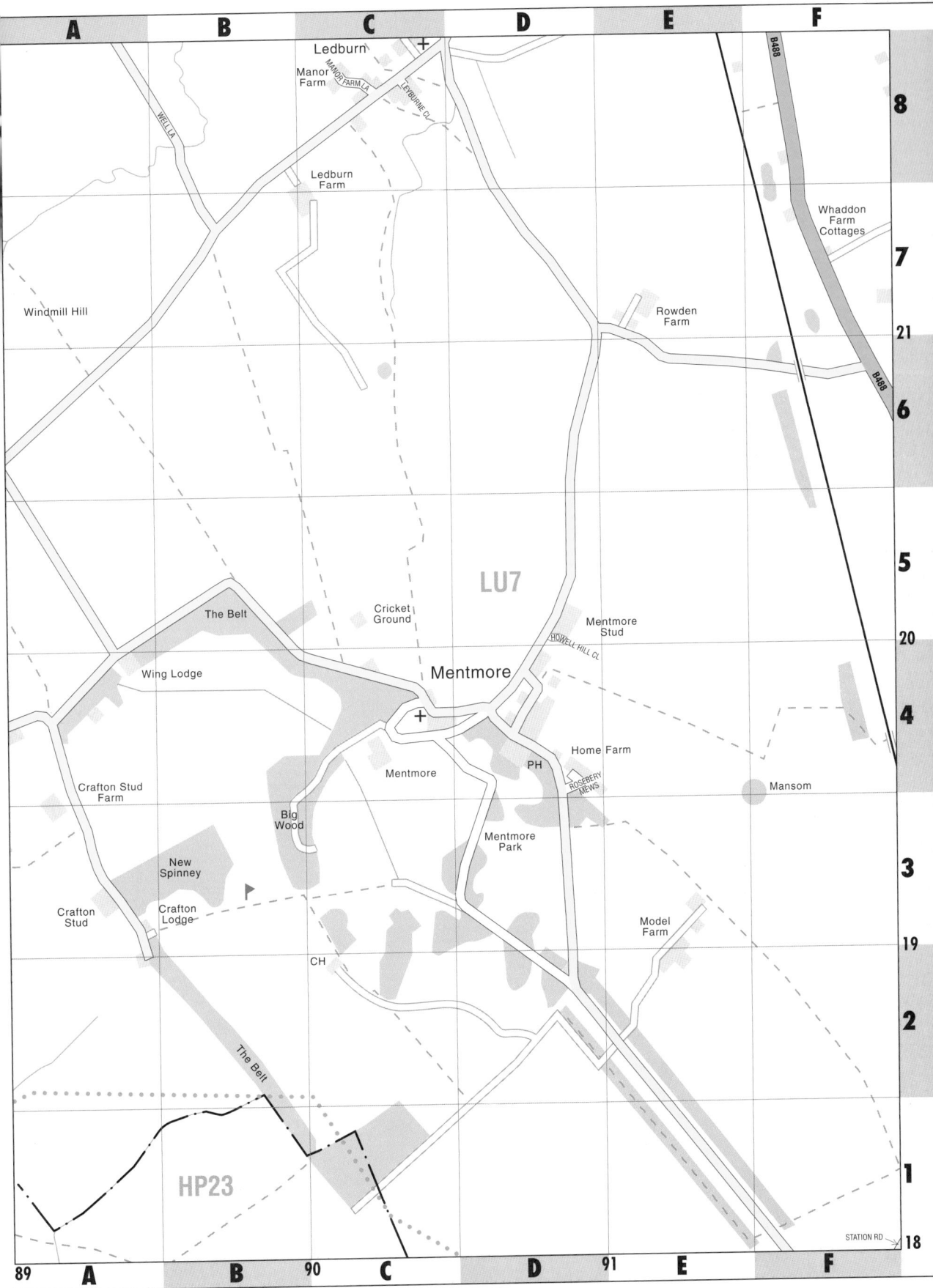

A B C D E F

Ledburn

Manor Farm
MANOR FARM LA
LEYBURNE CL

Ledburn Farm

B488

Whaddon Farm Cottages

8

7

21

Windmill Hill

B488

6

LU7

5

20

The Belt

Cricket Ground

Mentmore Stud

HOWELL HILL CL

Wing Lodge

Mentmore

4

Crafton Stud Farm

Mentmore

PH

Home Farm

ROSEBERY MEWS

Mansom

Big Wood

Mentmore Park

New Spinney

3

Crafton Stud

Crafton Lodge

Model Farm

19

CH

2

The Belt

1

HP23

STATION RD

18

89 A B 90 C D 91 E F

D7
1 MERSEY PL
2 CHARLOTTES CT
3 CRESTA HO
4 ALMA LINK
5 DUNSTABLE PL
6 PEEL ST

D8
7 PEEL PL

1 THE BARLEYCORN
2 DOWNTON CT
3 BEDFORD GDNS
4 THE MOUNT
5 VILLA CT

6 DEACONS CT
7 ST NINIAN'S CT
8 LANGHAM HO
9 COLLINGDON CT
10 CARDIGAN CT
11 CARDIGAN GDNS

E7
1 WILLIAMSON ST
2 BARBERS LA
3 WALLER STREET MALL
4 CHEAPSIDE SQ
5 SMITHS LANE MALL
6 SMITHS SQ

E7
7 THE GALLERY
8 MELSON SQ

E8
1 BUTTERWORTH PATH
2 BERKELEY PATH
3 WELBECK RD
4 ALBION ST

F8
1 ENTERPRISE CTR
2 SOUTHLYNN HO
3 HARTWOOD
4 LINDEN CT
5 HYDE HO
6 THE ABBEYGATE BSNS CTR

45

64

63

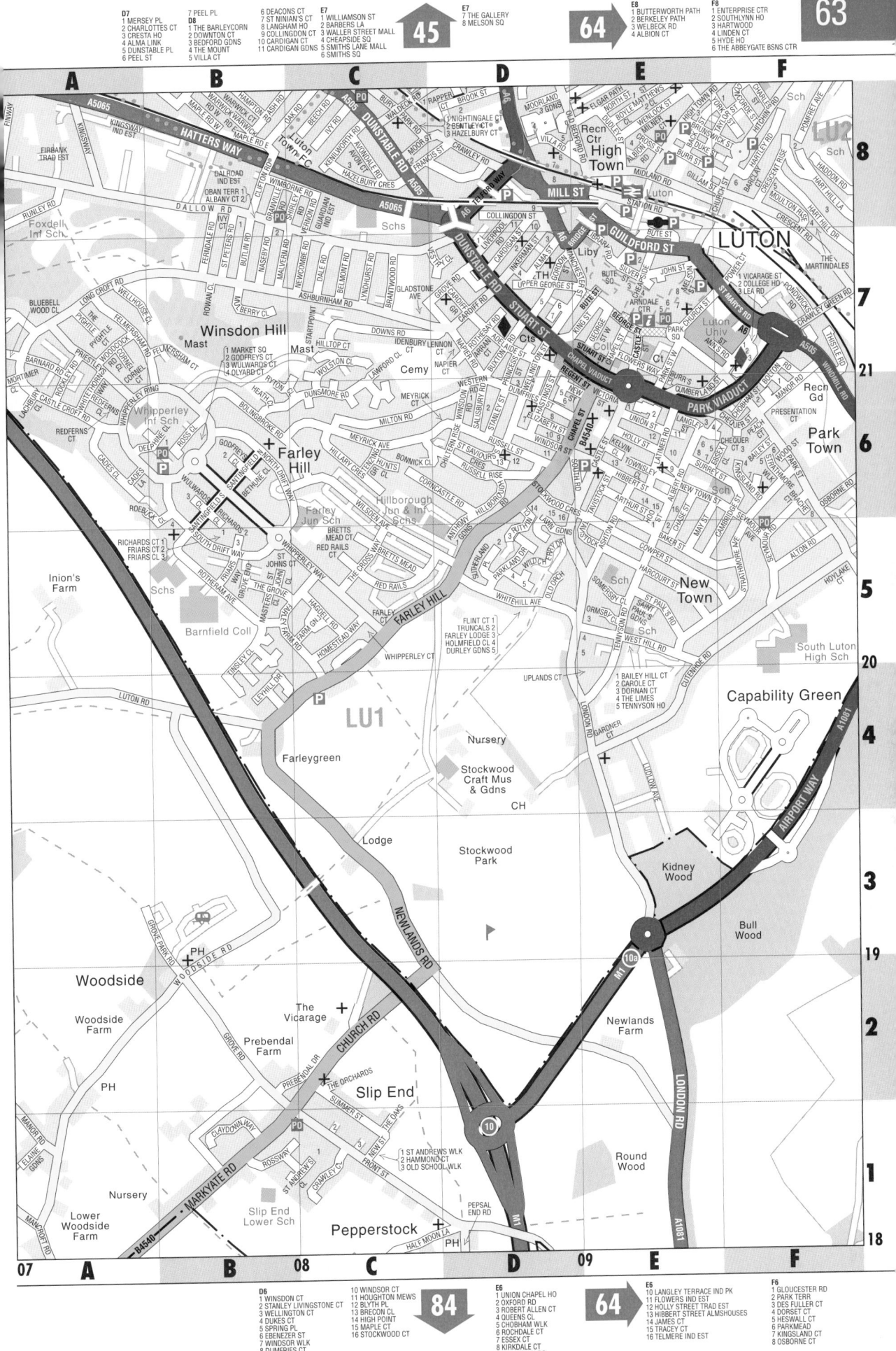

D6
1 WINSDON CT
2 STANLEY LIVINGSTONE CT
3 WELLINGTON CT
4 DUKES CT
5 SPRING PL
6 EBENEZER ST
7 WINDSOR WLK
8 DUMFRIES CT
9 ELIZABETH CT

10 WINDSOR CT
11 HOUGHTON MEWS
12 BLYTH PL
13 BRECON CL
14 HIGH POINT
15 MAPLE CT
16 STOCKWOOD CT

E6
1 UNION CHAPEL HO
2 OXFORD RD
3 ROBERT ALLEN CT
4 QUEENS CL
5 CHOBHAM WLK
6 ROCHDALE CT
7 ESSEX CT
8 KIRKDALE CT
9 NEW TOWN RD

E6
10 LANGLEY TERRACE IND PK
11 FLOWERS IND EST
12 HOLLY STREET TRAD EST
13 HIBBERT STREET ALMSHOUSES
14 JAMES CT
15 TRACEY CT
16 TELMERE IND EST

F6
1 GLOUCESTER RD
2 PARK TERR
3 DES FULLER CT
4 DORSET CT
5 HESWALL CT
6 PARKMEAD
7 KINGSLAND CT
8 OSBORNE CT

84

64

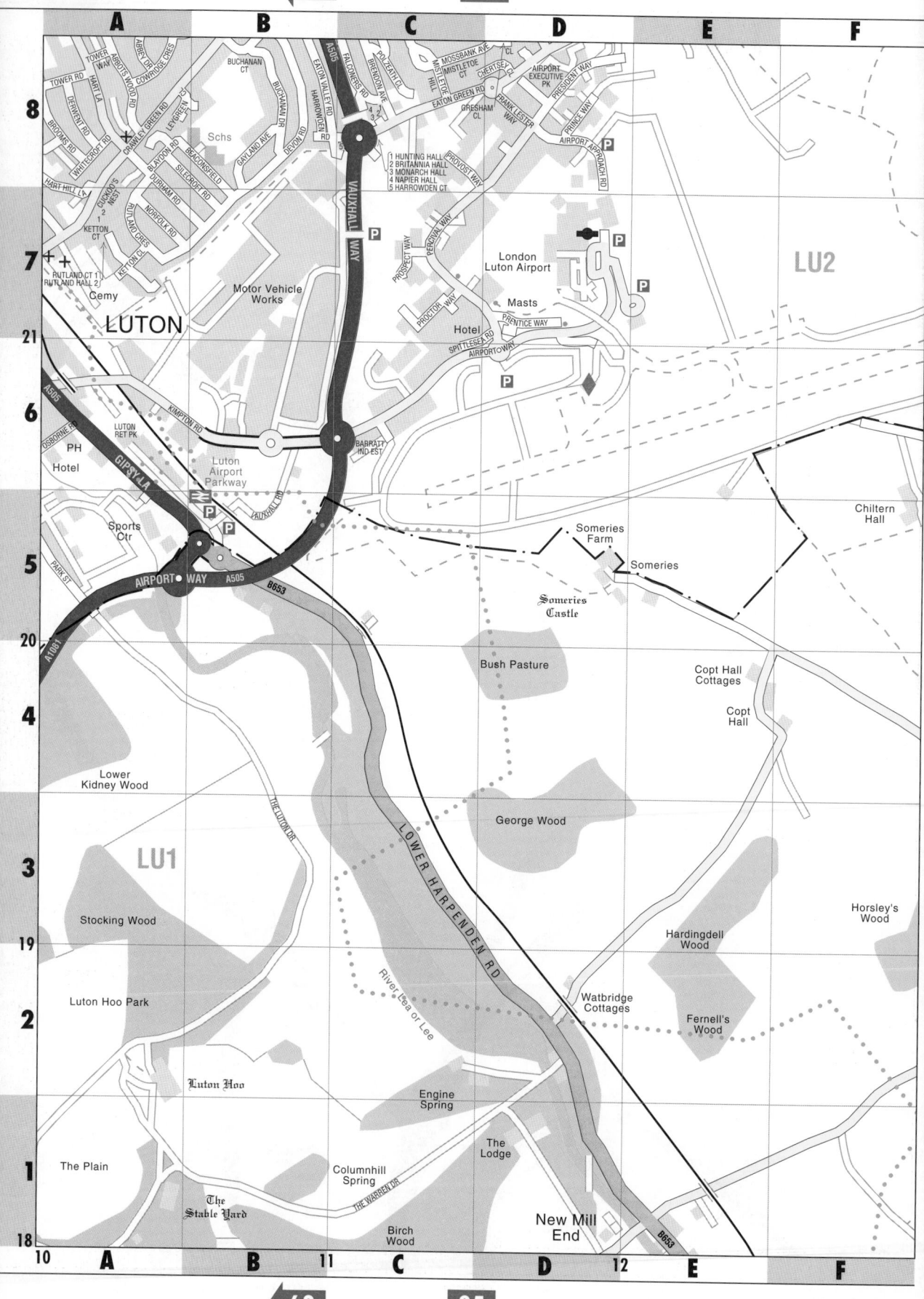

A **B** **C** **D** **E** **F**

8

7 LU2

21

6

Motor Vehicle Works

LUTON

Cemy

A505

Osborne Rd

Gipsy La

PH Hotel

Luton Ret Pk

Kimpton Rd

Luton Airport Parkway

BARRATT IND EST

London Luton Airport

Masts

Hotel

Prentice Way

Spittlesea Rd

Airport Way

Chiltern Hall

5 Sports Ctr

Airport Way A505 B653

Someries Farm

Someries

Park St

Someries Castle

Copt Hall Cottages

Copt Hall

20 A1081

Bush Pasture

4 Lower Kidney Wood

George Wood

Hardingdell Wood

Horsley's Wood

LU1

3 Stocking Wood

The Luton Dr

Lower Harpenden Rd

19

2 Luton Hoo Park

River Lea or Lee

Watbridge Cottages

Fernell's Wood

Luton Hoo

Engine Spring

1 The Plain

Columnhill Spring

The Warren Dr

The Lodge

The Stable Yard

New Mill End

18 Birch Wood

B653

A **B** **C** **D** **E** **F**

10 11 12

1 HUNTING HALL
2 BRITANNIA HALL
3 MONARCH HALL
4 NAPIER HALL
5 HARROWDEN CT.

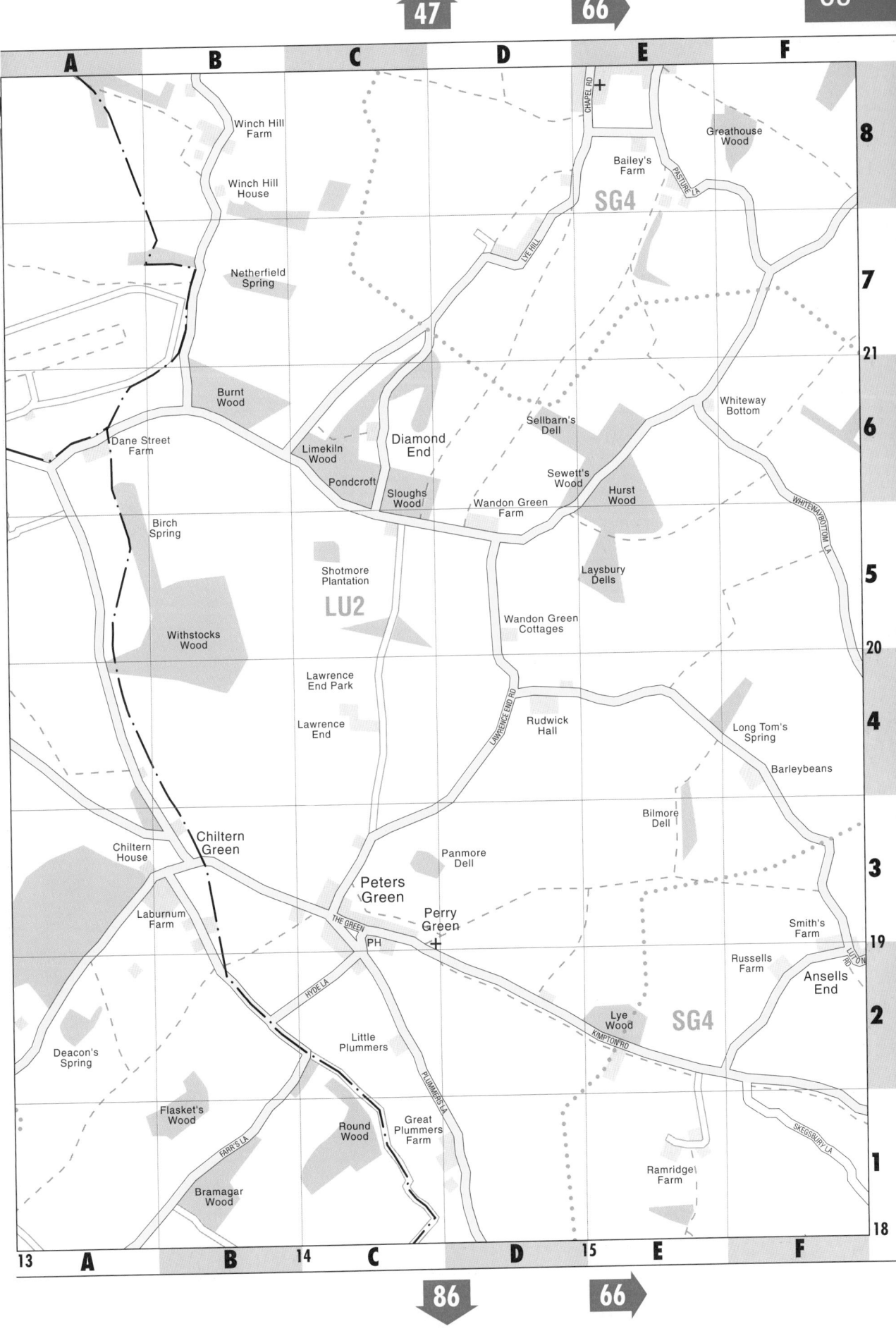

47
66

A B C D E F

8

Winch Hill
Farm

Greathouse
Wood

Winch Hill
House

Bailey's
Farm

CHAPEL RD

SG4

PASTURE LA

7

Netherfield
Spring

LYE HILL

21

Burnt
Wood

Sellbarn's
Dell

Whiteway
Bottom

6

Dane Street
Farm

Limekiln
Wood

Diamond
End

Pondcroft

Sewett's
Wood

Hurst
Wood

WHITEWAYBOTTOM LA

Sloughs
Wood

Wandon Green
Farm

Birch
Spring

Shotmore
Plantation

Laysbury
Dells

5

LU2

Withstocks
Wood

Wandon Green
Cottages

20

Lawrence
End Park

LAWRENCE END RD

Rudwick
Hall

Long Tom's
Spring

4

Lawrence
End

Barleybeans

Bilmore
Dell

Chiltern
Green

Chiltern
House

Panmore
Dell

3

Peters
Green

Smith's
Farm

THE GREEN

Perry
Green

Russells
Farm

LUTON RD

19

Laburnum
Farm

PH

Ansells
End

HYDE LA

Lye
Wood

SG4

2

Deacon's
Spring

Little
Plummers

KIMPTON RD

PLUMMERS LA

Flasket's
Wood

Round
Wood

Great
Plummers
Farm

Ramridge
Farm

1

FARR'S LA

SKEGSBURY LA

Bramagar
Wood

18

13 A B 14 C D 15 E F

86
66

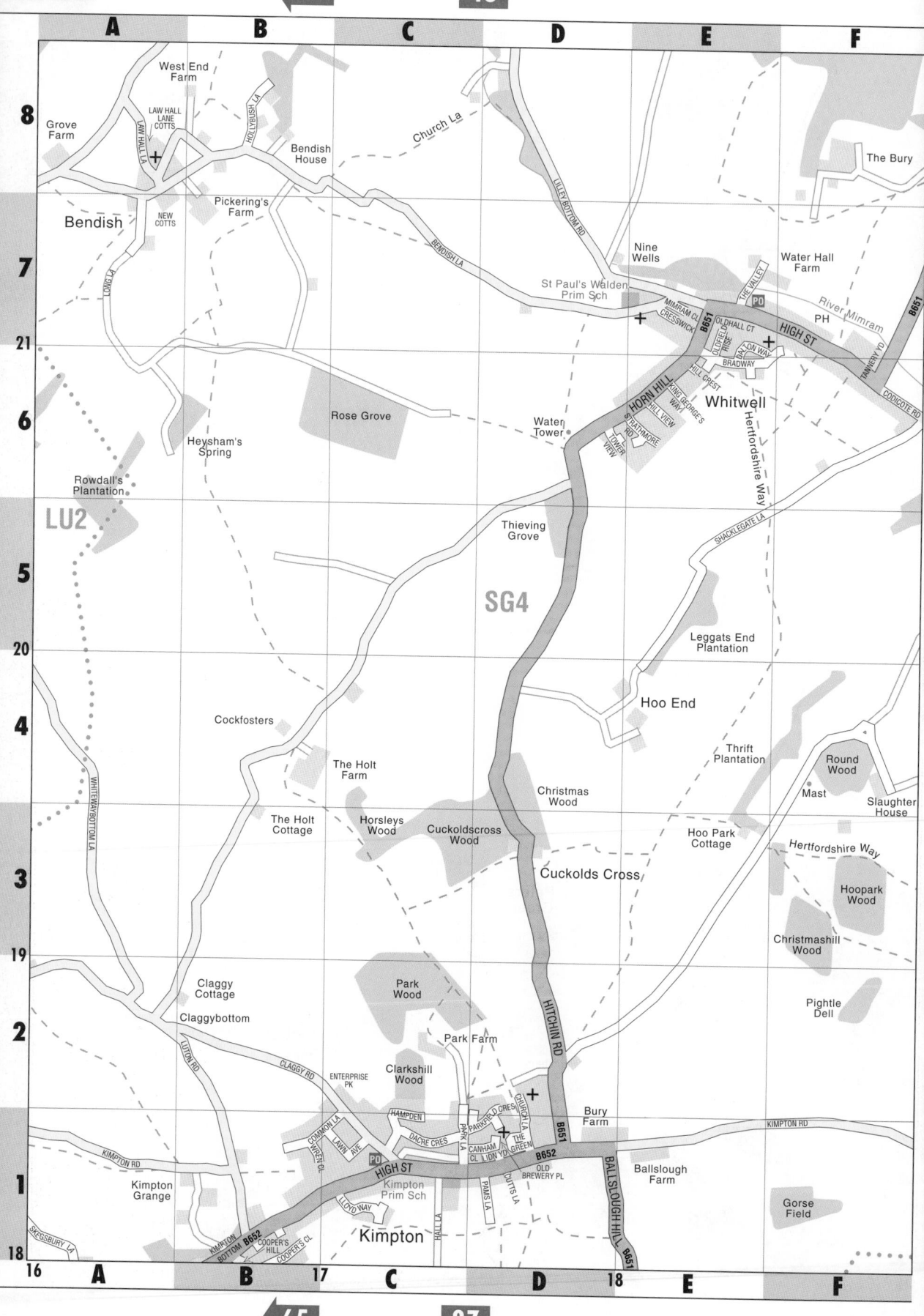

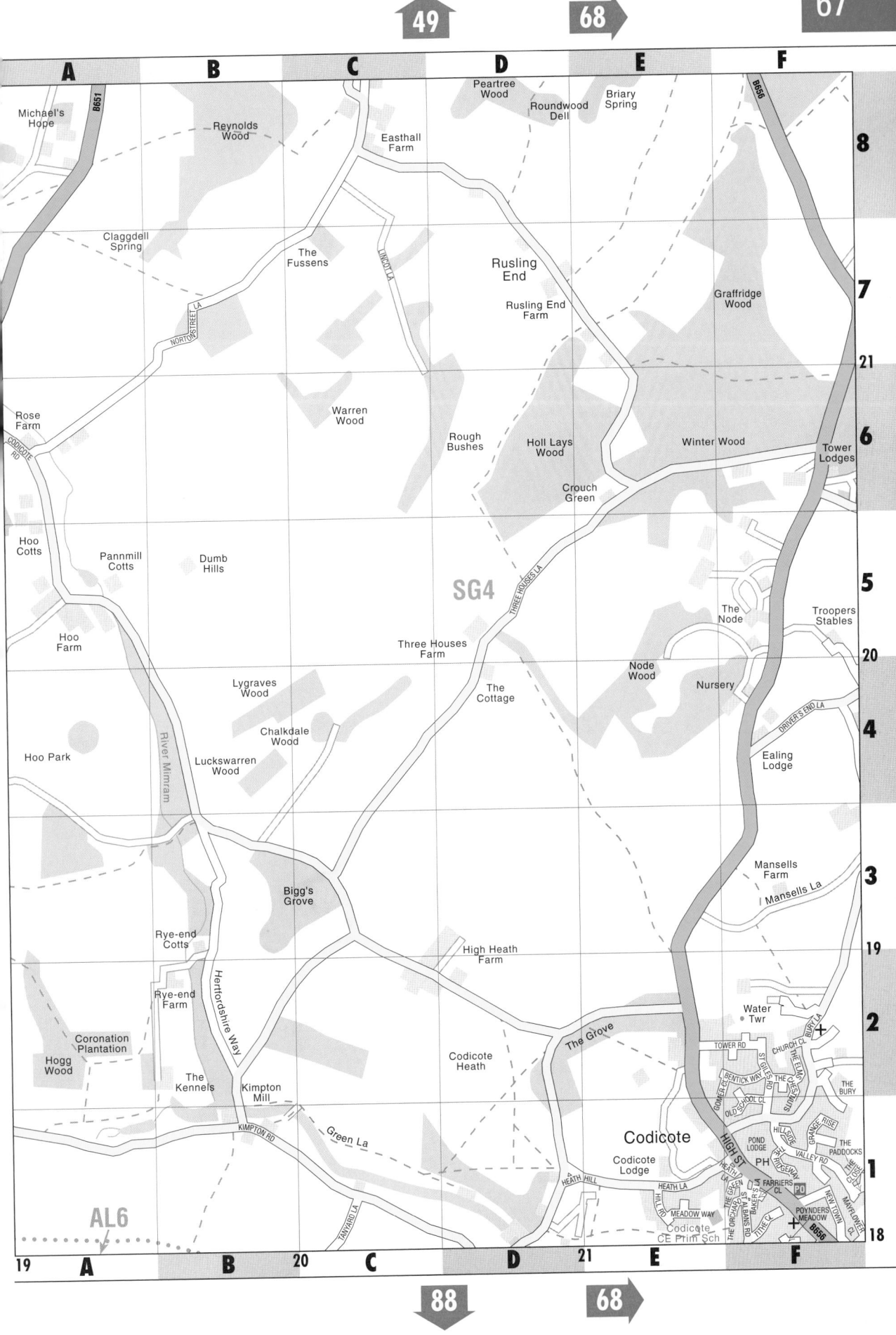

A B C D E F

8

7

21

6

5

20

4

3

19

2

1

18

19 A B 20 C D 21 E F

Michael's Hope
B651
Reynolds Wood
Easthall Farm
Peartree Wood
Roundwood Dell
Briary Spring
B656

Claggdell Spring
The Fussens
LINCOT LA
Rusling End
Graffridge Wood

NORTON STREET LA
Rusling End Farm

Rose Farm
CODICOTE RD
Warren Wood
Rough Bushes
Holl Lays Wood
Winter Wood
Tower Lodges

Crouch Green

Hoo Cotts
Pannmill Cotts
Dumb Hills
SG4
THREE HOUSES LA

Hoo Farm
Three Houses Farm
The Node
Troopers Stables

River Mimram
Lygraves Wood
The Cottage
Node Wood
Nursery
DRIVER'S END LA

Hoo Park
Chalkdale Wood
Ealing Lodge

Luckswarren Wood

Bigg's Grove
Mansells Farm
Mansells La

Rye-end Cotts
High Heath Farm

Hertfordshire Way
Rye-end Farm
Water Twr

Coronation Plantation
The Grove
TOWER RD
CHURCH CL
BURY LA

Hogg Wood
Codicote Heath
ST JOHN'S RD
THE ELMS
THE BURY

The Kennels
Kimpton Mill
Codicote
Codicote Lodge
Pond Lodge
HILL SIDE
GRANGE RISE
THE PADDOCKS

KIMPTON RD
Green La
TANYARD LA
Heath Hill
HEATH LA
HILL RD
MEADOW WAY
Codicote CE Prim Sch
POYNDERS MEADOW
B656

AL6

BENTICK WAY
GOMER CL
SCHOOL CL
OLD SCHOOL CL
HIGH ST
PH
PO
VALLEY RD
RIDGEWAY
NEW TOWN
MAYFLOWER CL

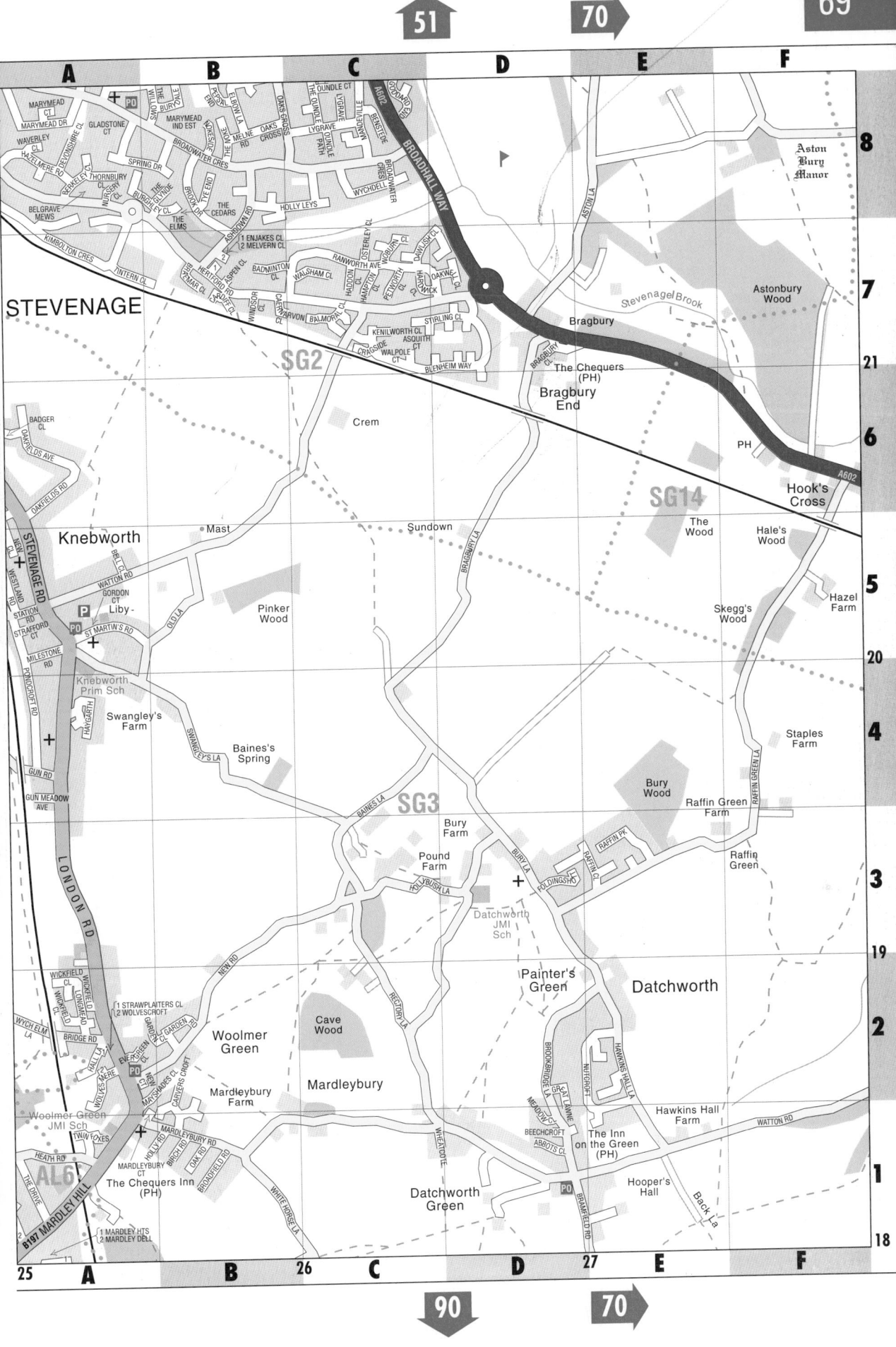

A B C D E F

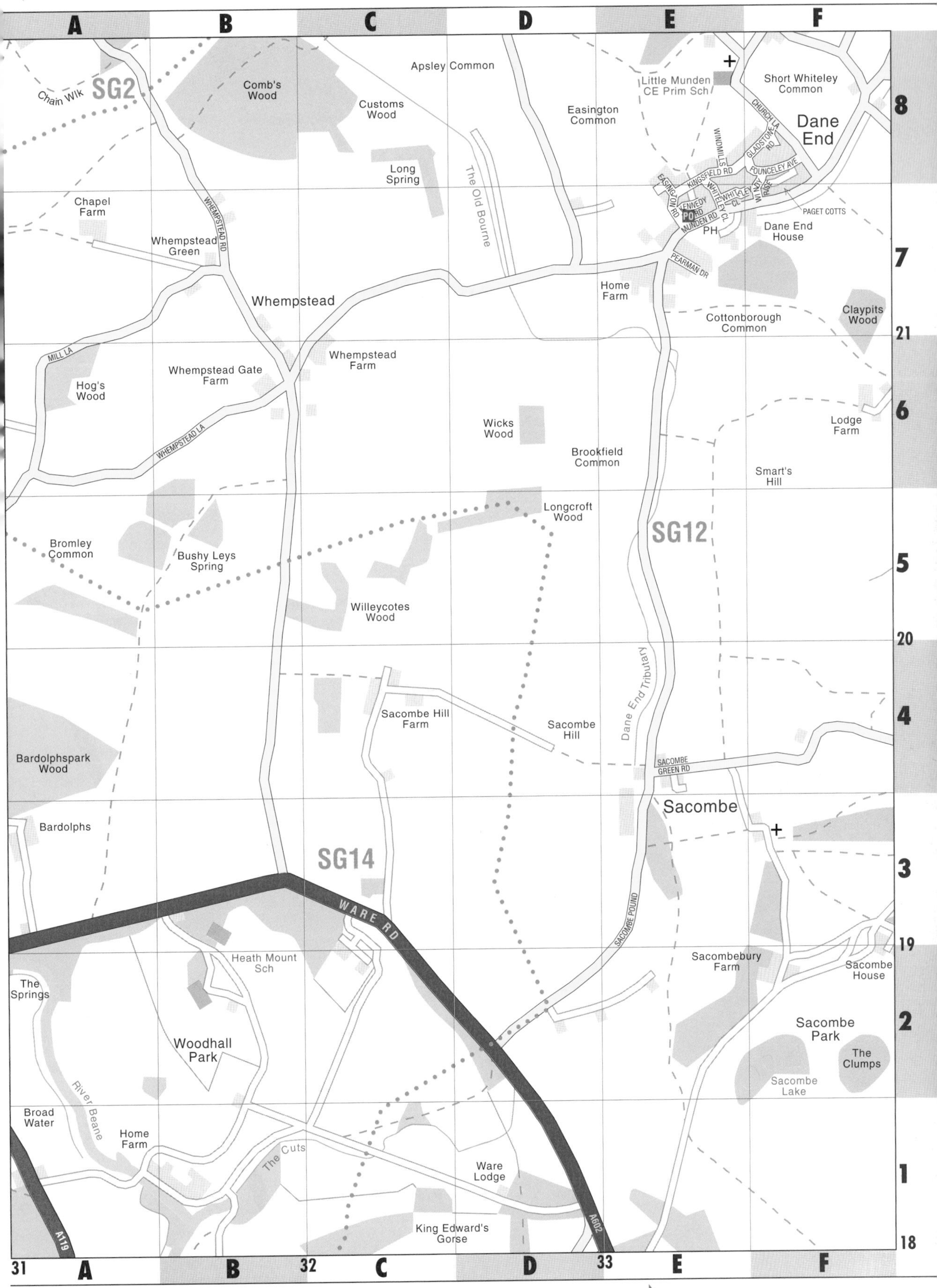

8

SG2

Chain Wlk

Comb's
Wood

Apsley Common

Customs
Wood

Easington
Common

+

Little Munden
CE Prim Sch

Short Whiteley
Common

Dane
End

Long
Spring

The Old Bourne

WINDMILLS

GLADSTONE RD

CHURCH LA

FOUNCELEY AVE

EASINGTON RD

KINGSFIELD RD

KENNEDY

WHITELEY CL

WHITELEY LA

MUNDEN RD

PO

RISBY

PAGET COTTS

7

Chapel
Farm

WHEMPSTEAD RD

Whempstead
Green

Home
Farm

PH

Dane End
House

PEARMAN DR

Dane End

Cottonborough
Common

Claypits
Wood

21

Whempstead

Whempstead
Farm

MILL LA

Hog's
Wood

Whempstead Gate
Farm

WHEMPSTEAD LA

Wicks
Wood

Brookfield
Common

Smart's
Hill

Lodge
Farm

6

Longcroft
Wood

SG12

5

Bromley
Common

Bushy Leys
Spring

Willeycotes
Wood

Dane End Tributary

20

Bardolphspark
Wood

Sacombe Hill
Farm

Sacombe
Hill

SACOMBE
GREEN RD

4

Bardolphs

SG14

Sacombe

+

3

WARE RD

Heath Mount
Sch

SACOMBE POUND

Sacombebury
Farm

Sacombe
House

19

The
Springs

Woodhall
Park

Sacombe
Park

The
Clumps

2

River Beane

Broad
Water

Home
Farm

The Cuts

Ware
Lodge

Sacombe
Lake

1

A119

A602

King Edward's
Gorse

18

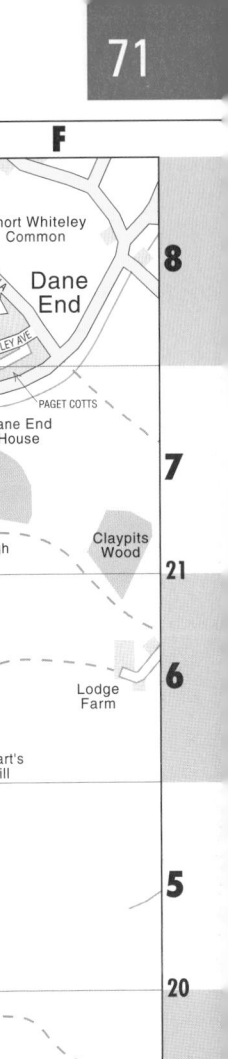

71
54

A B C D E F

8
Fullars Common
Moorfield Common
High Trees Farm
Hatchett Farm
Hatchett Poultry Farm
Beggarman's Wood
BEGGARMAN'S LA
Hill Farm

Trenchern Hills

7
Whitehill Farm
Langton's La
Shelly's Wood
Roughground Wood

21
CH
Cock's Wood
Potter's Green
Rigery Farm
RIGERY LA

6
Potter's Hall Farm
Labdens Farm

5
ROWNEY LA
Rowney Priory
Black Grove
A10
Willowtree Farm

20
Rowney Wood
LOWGATE LA
Standon Green End Farm

SG12
Knoll Farm

4
LOWGATE LA
Sacombe Green
Standon Green End
SG11
Mott's Wood
Barwick Tributary

3
Church Wood
Dilly Wood
The Bourne
Salmonsley Wood
DANE END RD

Low Wood

19
Home Wood
MARSHALL'S LA

Home Farm
Sutes
CAMBRIDGE COTTS

2
Gages Wood
Marshall's Farm
PH
Pullar Memorial Jun Mix Inf Sch

Furzeground Wood
Marshall's
High Cross
NORTH DR
POPLAR CL
PASSFIELD COTTS

1
Hazelwood Farm
Mark's Wood
SG12

Rennesley Garden Wood
Highcross Hill
Gravelpit Wood
A10

18
34 A B 35 C D 36 E F

71
93

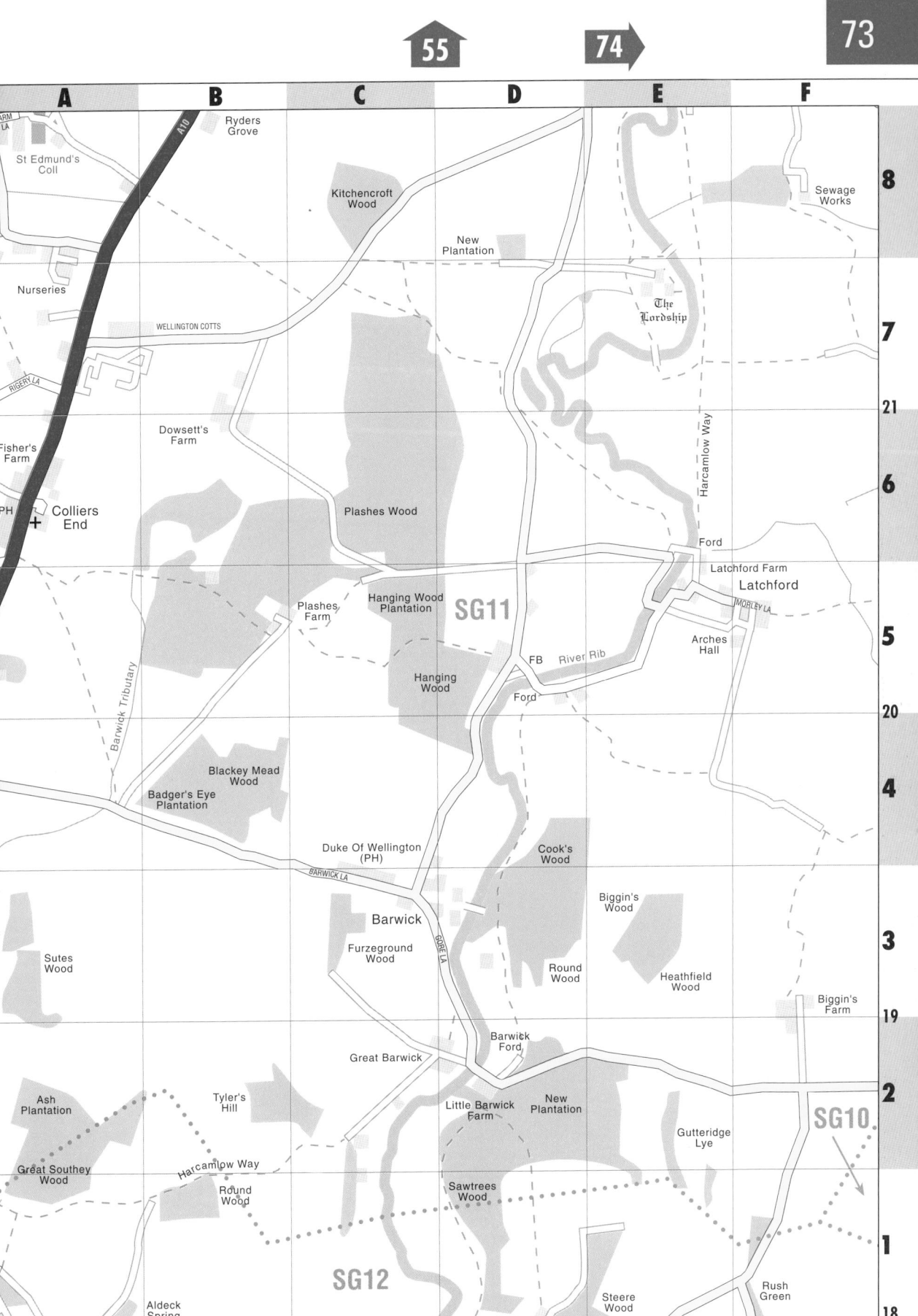

73
56

A B C D E F

8

Balsams

Bromley

Alder Wood

Westfield Farm

Little Balsams

Caley Wood

7

21

Bowles Wood

Bromleyhall Farm

SG11

Cambercroft Spring

Damsel's Spring

CH

6

The Wilderness

Standon Lodge Farm

BROMLEY LA

Chaldean Farm

5

Rector's Springs

Vineyard Spring

Spindle Bridge

20

WINDING HILL

4

Bartram's Wood

New Barns

NEW BARNS LA

B1004

SG10

Cox La

THE SQUARE

Much Hadham
The Bull (PH)

HIGH ST

CHURCH LA

3

PARK TERR

DIMPLE LA

19

Brand's Farm

Moor Place

St Andrews CE Prim Sch

Hertfordshire Way

The Barn Sch

2

Nimney Bourne

Blackcroft Farm

Hadham Cross

TOWER HILL

ASH MEADOW

WAL NUT CL

PO
PH

MATING LA

Nursery

Old Hall Farm

KETTLE GREEN RD

BROADFIELD CL

Broadfield Way

CULVER CT

WIDFORD RD

1

Kettle Green Farm

WINDMILL WAY LAURELDENE

Kettle Green

Moat Farm

MILLERS VIEW

STATION RD

B1004

18

SG12

40 A B 41 C D 42 E F

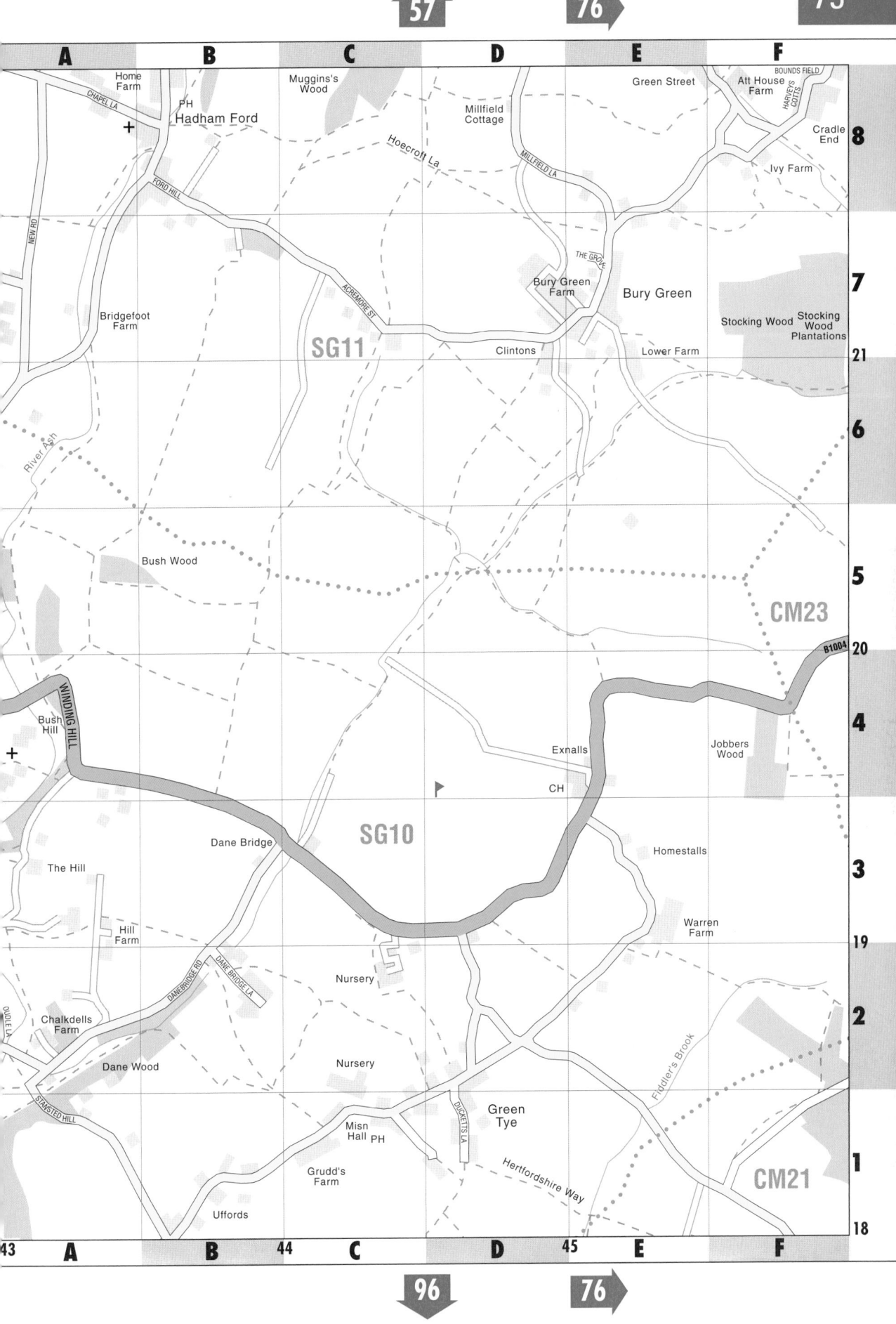

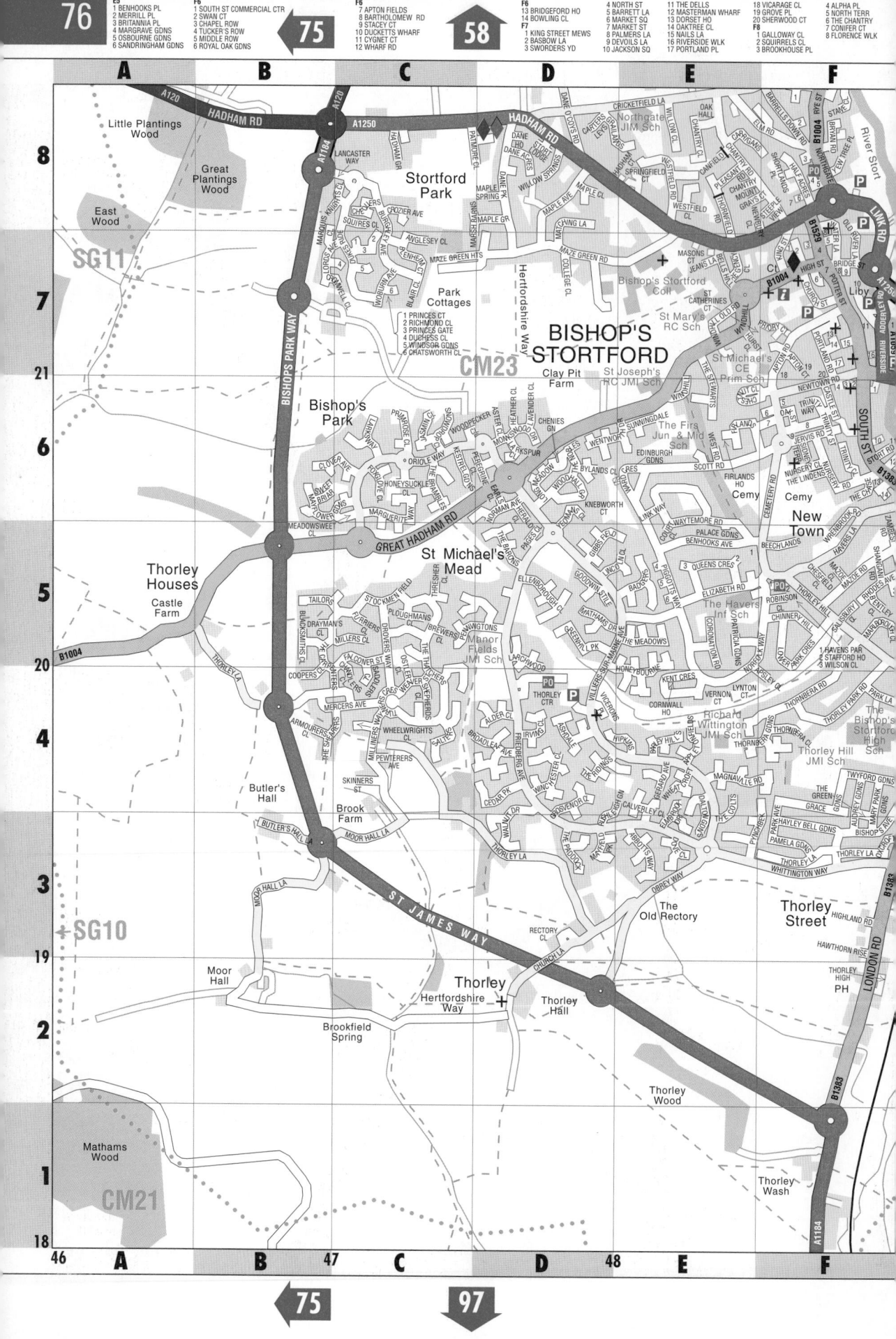

A7
1 THE CAUSEWAY
2 THE OLD MALTINGS
3 FULLER CT
4 LIMES CRES
5 RED LION CT
6 BAKERS CT

7 HOCKERILL CT
8 HARRINGTON CL
9 PRIORS
10 CLIFFORD CT
11 THOMAS HESKIN CT
12 MASTERMAN WHARF

B8
1 BOYD CL
2 HEATH ROW
3 STORTFORD HALL RD
4 GROSVENOR HO
5 EATON HO
6 BELGRAVE HO

59

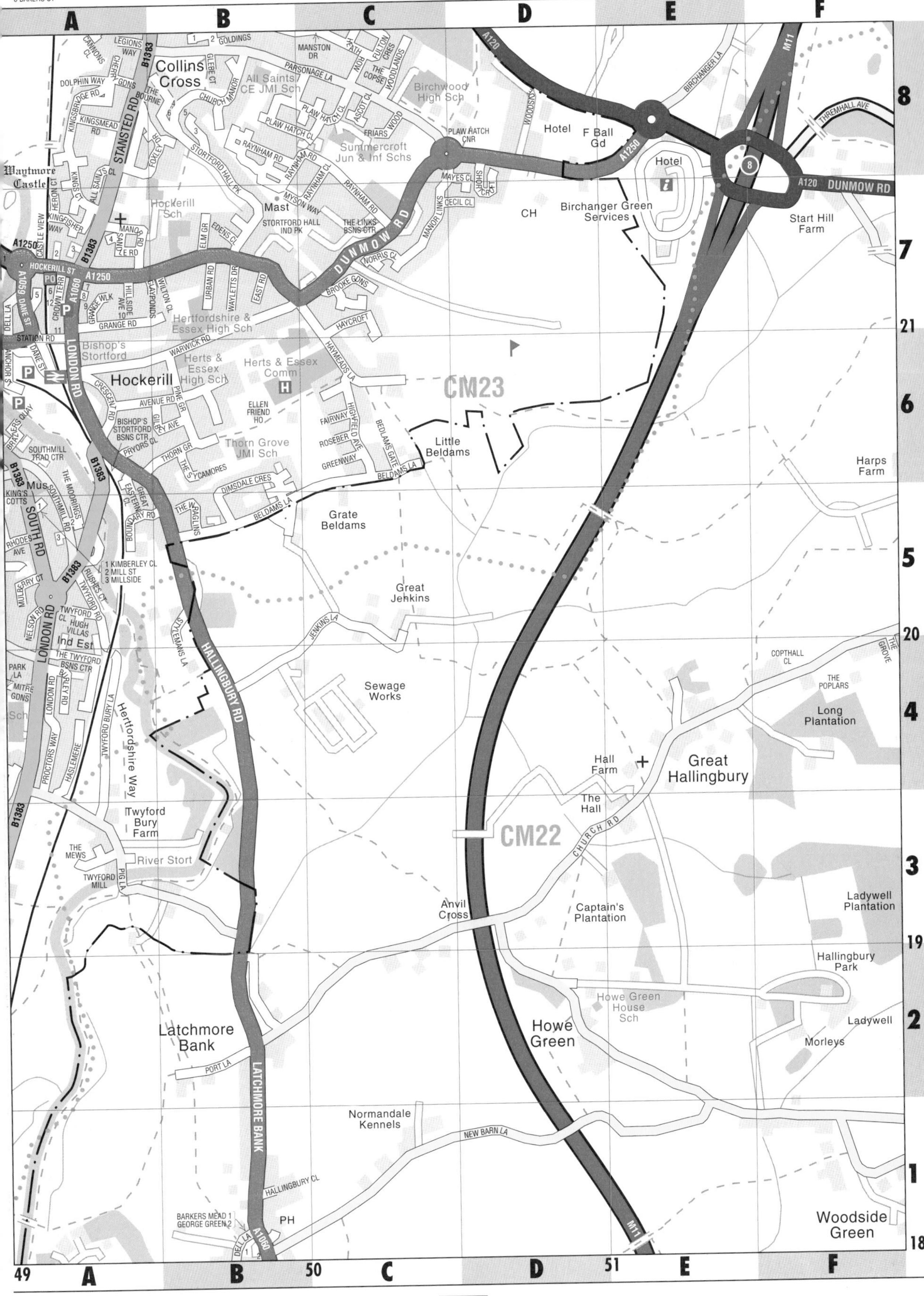

Collins Cross

Waytmore Castle

Bishop's Stortford

Hockerill

All Saints CE JMI Sch

Birchwood High Sch

Summercroft Jun & Inf Schs

Hotel
F Ball Gd

Hotel

Birchanger Green Services

Start Hill Farm

DUNMOW RD

Hertfordshire & Essex High Sch

Herts & Essex High Sch

Herts & Essex Comm

CM23

Little Beldams

Harps Farm

Thorn Grove JMI Sch

Grate Beldams

Great Jenkins

Copthall Cl

The Poplars

Long Plantation

Sewage Works

Hall Farm

Great Hallingbury

The Hall

CM22

Ladywell Plantation

Twyford Bury Farm

The Mews

Twyford Mill

River Stort

Anvil Cross

Captain's Plantation

Hallingbury Park

Howe Green House Sch

Howe Green

Ladywell

Morleys

Latchmore Bank

Normandale Kennels

NEW BARN LA

Woodside Green

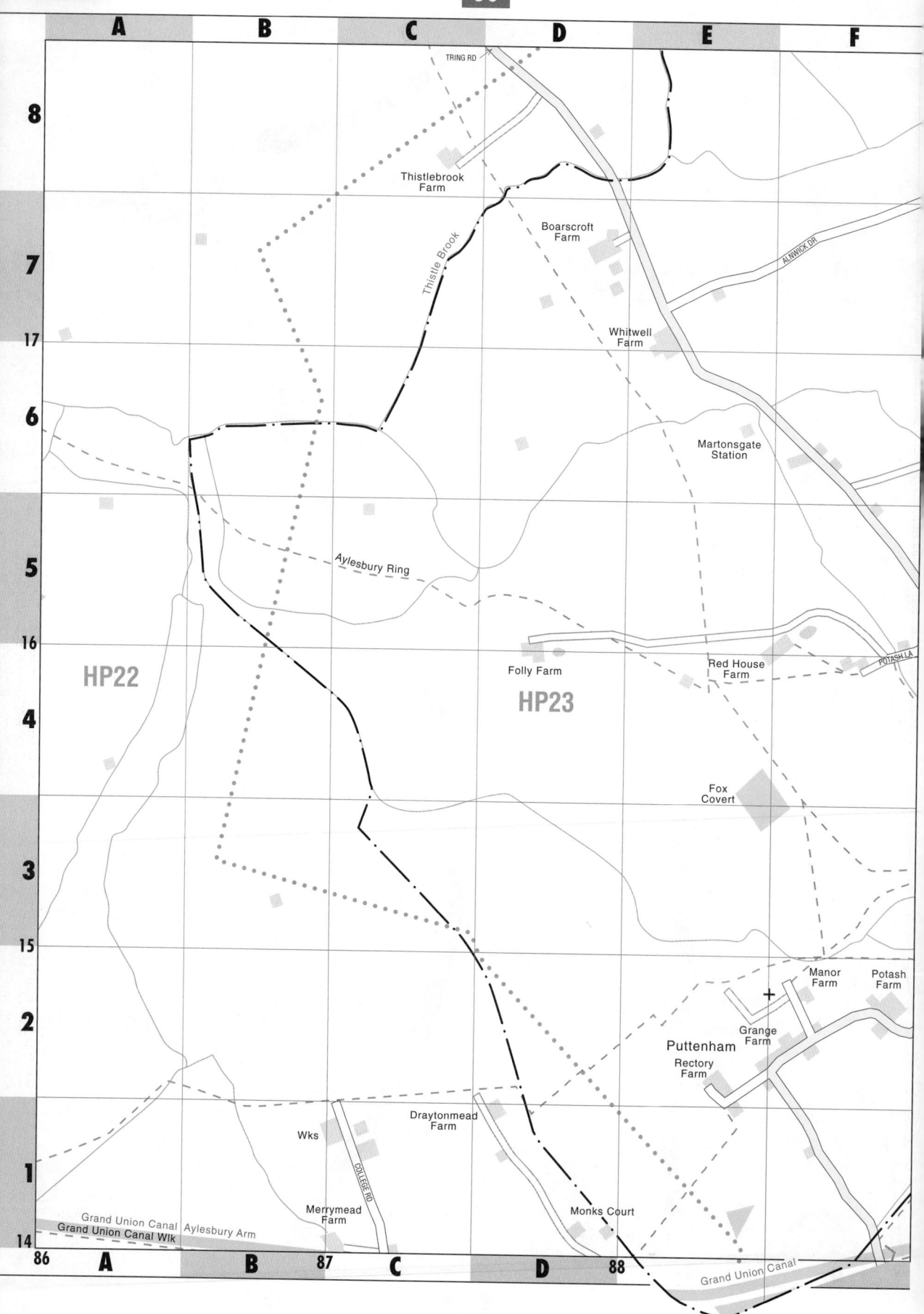

60

A   B   C   D   E   F

8

7

17

6

TRING RD

Thistlebrook
Farm

Thistle Brook

Boarscroft
Farm

ALNWICK DR

Whitwell
Farm

Martonsgate
Station

5

Aylesbury Ring

16

HP22

Folly Farm

HP23

Red House
Farm

POTASH LA

4

Fox
Covert

3

15

Manor
Farm

Potash
Farm

2

Grange
Farm

Puttenham

Rectory
Farm

Draytonmead
Farm

Wks

COLLEGE RD

1

Merrymead
Farm

Monks Court

14

Grand Union Canal Aylesbury Arm
Grand Union Canal Wlk

Grand Union Canal

86   A   B   87   C   D   88

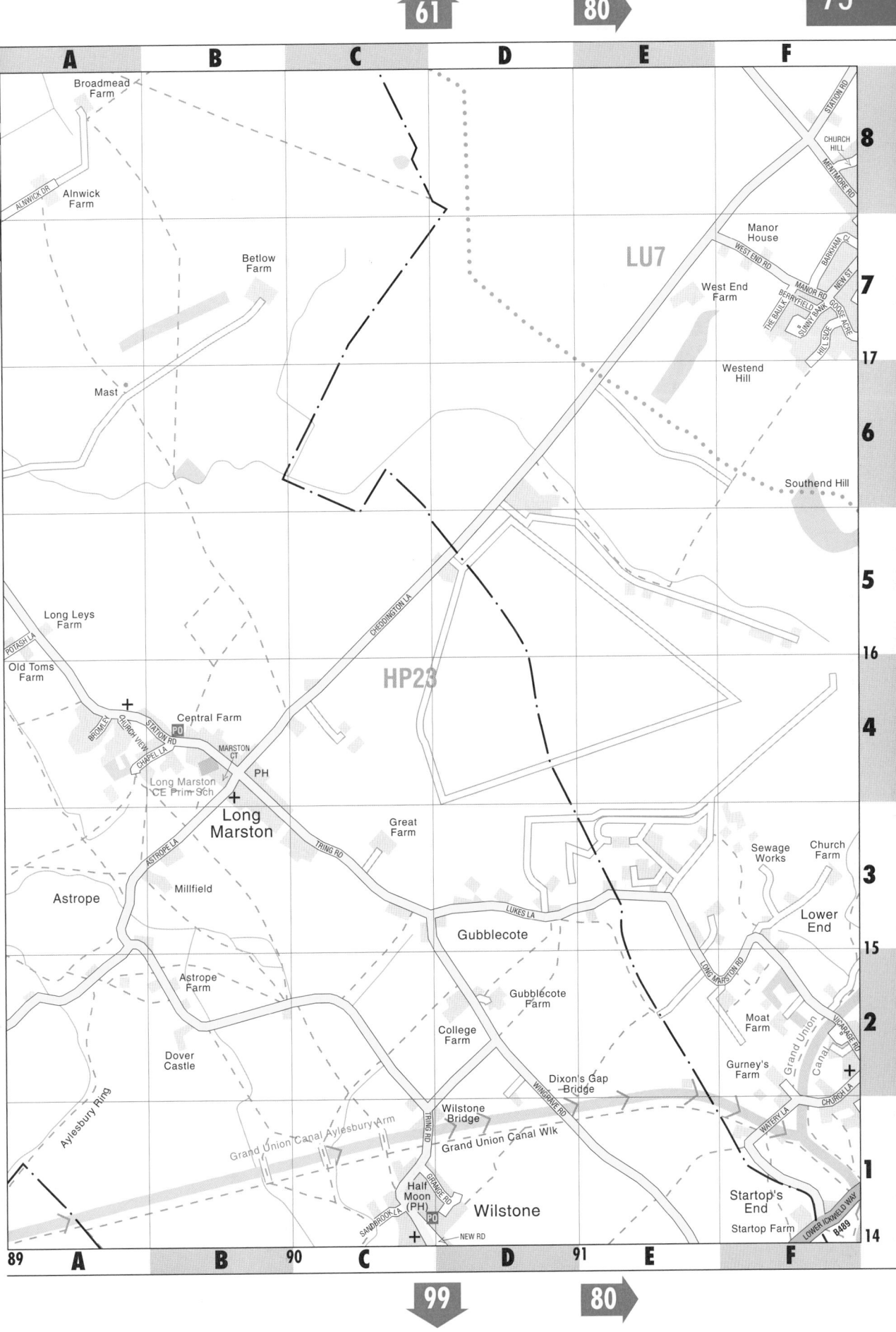

61 80

A B C D E F

8

LU7

CHURCH HILL

STATION RD

MENTMORE RD

Manor House

WEST END RD

Broadmead Farm

Alnwick Farm

ALNWICK DR

Betlow Farm

West End Farm

BARKHAM CL

NEW ST

MANOR RD

GOOSE ACRE

THE BAULK

BERRYFIELD

SUNNY BANK

HILL SIDE

7

17

Mast

Westend Hill

Southend Hill

6

Long Leys Farm

CHEDDINGTON LA

5

POTASH LA

Old Toms Farm

16

HP23

Central Farm

PO

STATION RD

+

CHURCH VIEW

BROMLEY

CHAPEL LA

MARSTON CT

PH

4

Long Marston CE Prim Sch

+

Long Marston

Great Farm

ASTROPE LA

TRING RD

Sewage Works

Church Farm

3

Astrope

Millfield

LUKES LA

Lower End

Gubblecote

15

Astrope Farm

Gubblecote Farm

LONG MARSTON RD

Moat Farm

VICARAGE RD

2

Dover Castle

College Farm

WINGRAVE RD

Gurney's Farm

Grand Union Canal

CHURCH LA

+

Dixon's Gap Bridge

Aylesbury Ring

Wilstone Bridge

Grand Union Canal Wlk

WATERY LA

1

Grand Union Canal Aylesbury Arm

TRING RD

GRANGE RD

Startop's End

LOWER ICKNIELD WAY

B489

Half Moon (PH)

PO

Wilstone

SANDBROOK LA

NEW RD

+

Startop Farm

14

89 A B 90 C D 91 E F

99 80

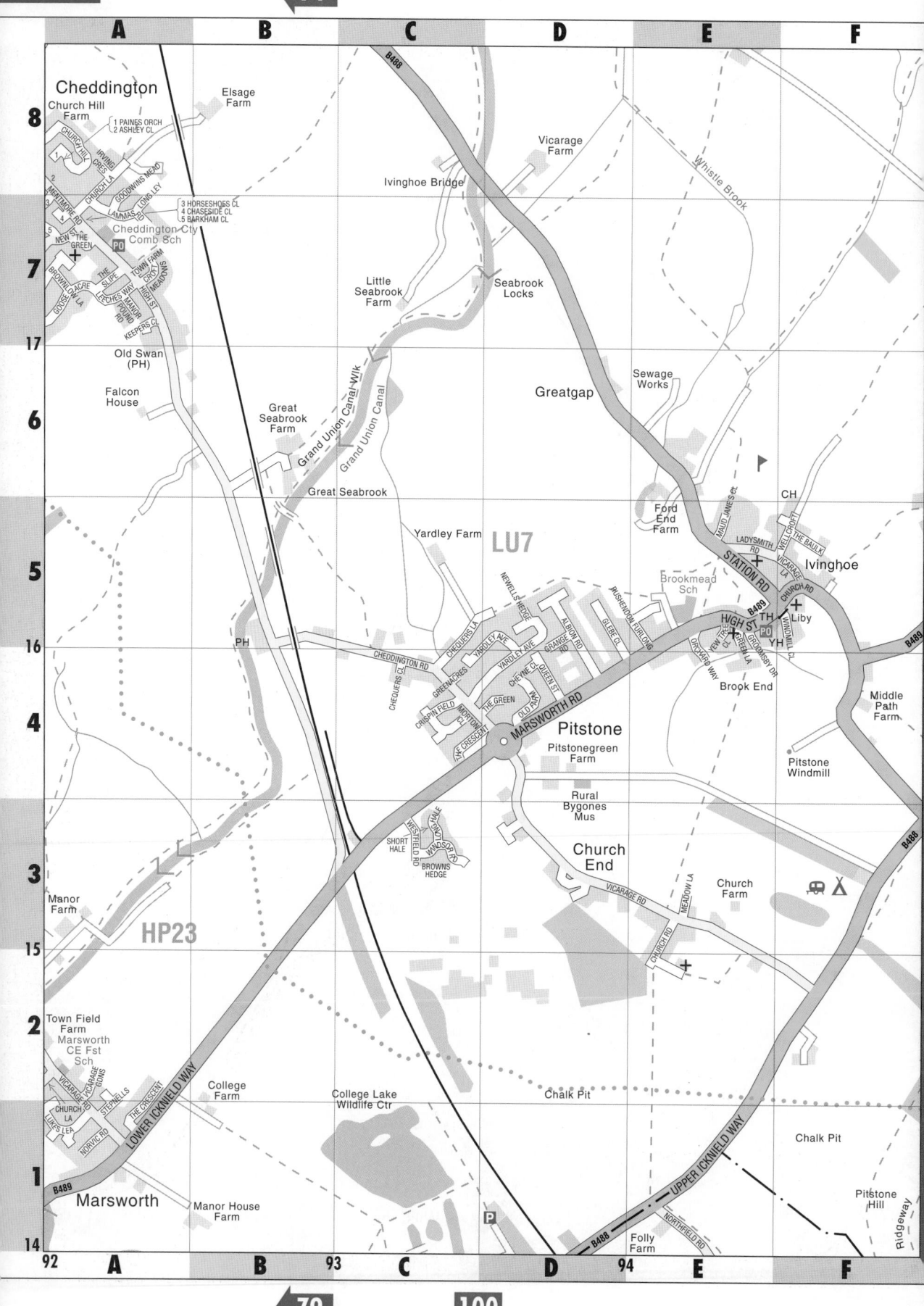

	A	B	C	D	E	F

Cheddington

Church Hill Farm

1 PAINES ORCH
2 ASHLEY CL

Elsage Farm

Ivinghoe Bridge

Vicarage Farm

Whistle Brook

3 HORSESHOES CL
4 CHASESIDE CL
5 BARKHAM CL

Cheddington Cty Comb Sch

PO

NEW ST
THE GREEN

Little Seabrook Farm

Seabrook Locks

Old Swan (PH)

Falcon House

Great Seabrook Farm

Grand Union Canal-Wik

Grand Union Canal

Greatgap

Sewage Works

Ford End Farm

CH

Ivinghoe

Great Seabrook

Yardley Farm

LU7

STATION RD

Liby

PH

CHEDDINGTON RD

NEWELLS HEDGE
CHEQUERS LA
YARDLEY AVE
ALBION RD
RUSHENDON FURLONG
GLEBE CL

B489 TH
HIGH ST PO
YH

Brookmead Sch

MAUD JANE'S ct
LADYSMITH RD
WELLCROFT
THE BAULK
VICARAGE LA
CHURCH RD
WINDMILL CL

B488

CHEQUERS CL
GREENACRES
GREENACRE
CHEYNE CL
QUEEN ST
OLD PARK
CRISPIN FIELD
MORTON CL

THE GREEN

GRANGE CL

ONSLOW WAY
NEW TREES
GREEN LA
GROOMS WAY

Brook End

Middle Path Farm

Pitstone

Pitstone Windmill

ELM CRESCENT
MARSWORTH RD

Pitstonegreen Farm

Rural Bygones Mus

SHORT HALE
WINDSOR RD
WESTFIELD RD
BROWNS HEDGE

VICARAGE RD

MEADOW LA

Church Farm

Church End

Manor Farm

HP23

CHURCH RD

Town Field Farm

Marsworth CE Fst Sch

College Farm

College Lake Wildlife Ctr

Chalk Pit

VICARAGE RD
VICARAGE GDNS
STEPNELLS
THE CRESCENT
CHURCH LA
LUKE'S LEA
NORVIC RD

LOWER ICKNIELD WAY

Chalk Pit

UPPER ICKNIELD WAY

Pitstone Hill

B489

Marsworth

Manor House Farm

P

B488

NORTHFIELD RD

Folly Farm

Ridgeway

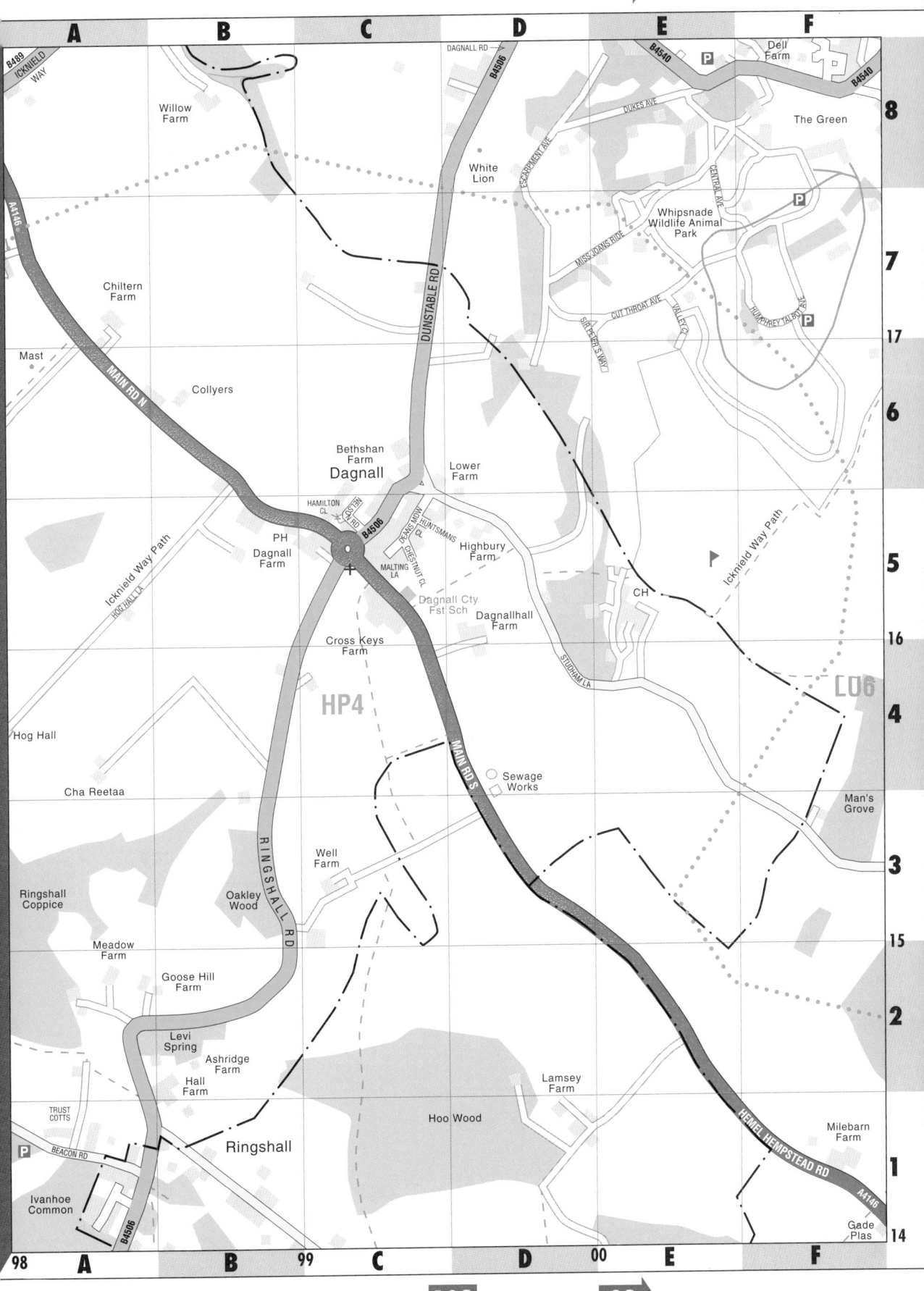

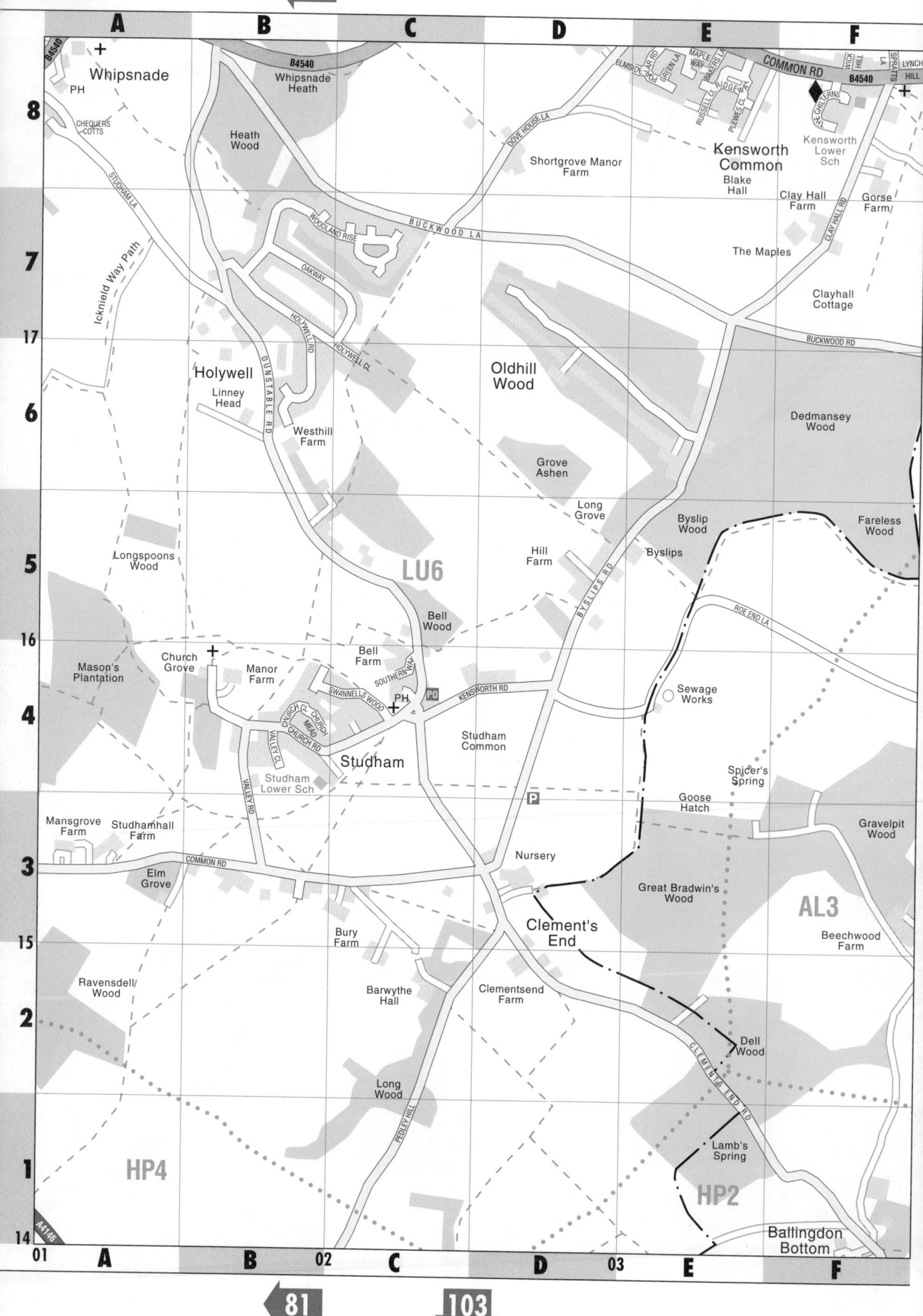

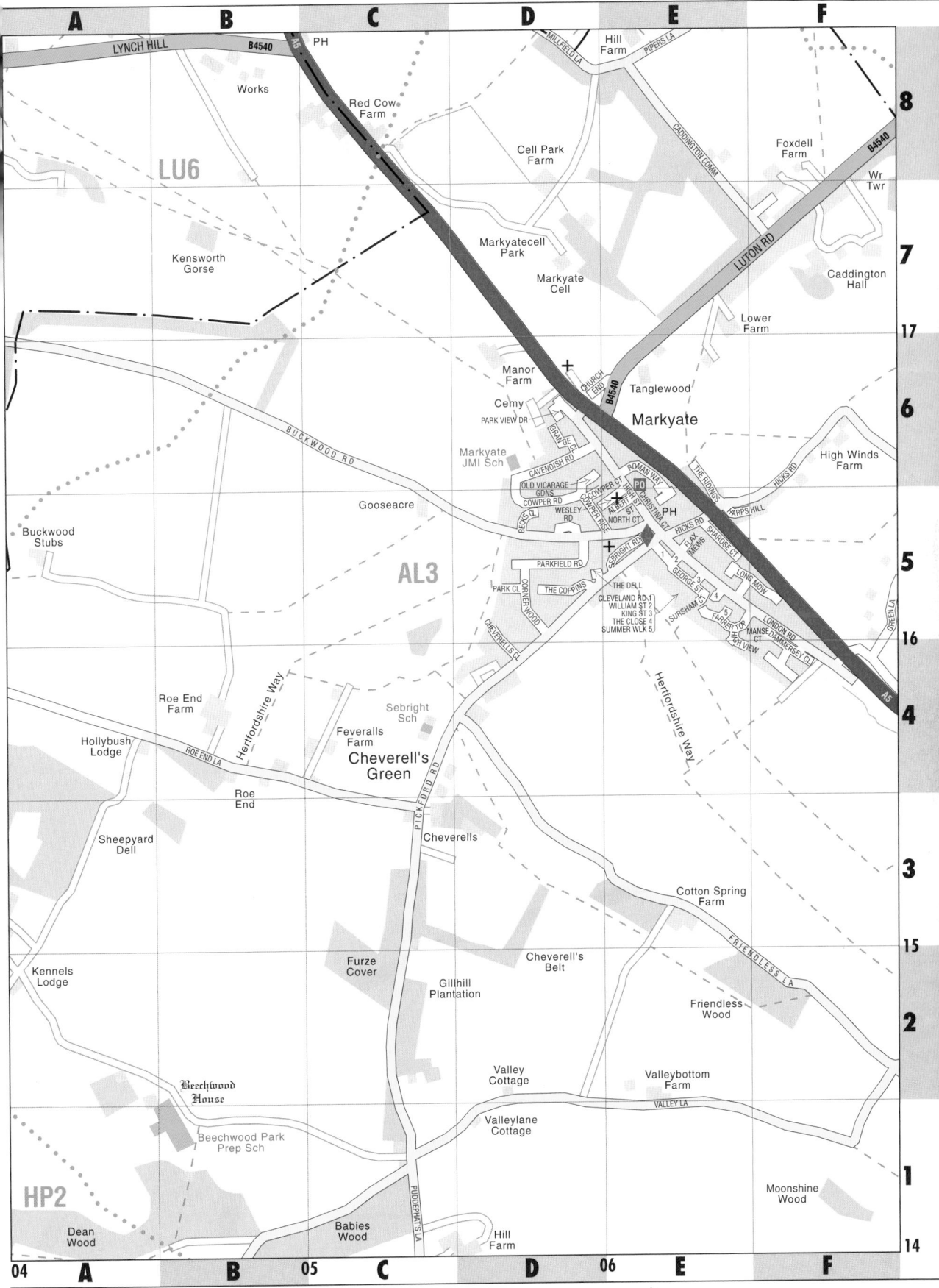

62
84
104
84

A B C D E F

8 7 17 6 5 16 4 3 15 2 1 14

LYNCH HILL B4540 PH

Works

Red Cow Farm

LU6

Hill Farm PIPERS LA

Cell Park Farm

CADDINGTON COMM

Foxdell Farm

B4540

Wr Twr

Kensworth Gorse

Markyatecell Park

Markyate Cell

LUTON RD

Caddington Hall

Lower Farm

BUCKWOOD RD

Manor Farm

Cemy

PARK VIEW DR

Tanglewood

CHURCH END

B4540

Markyate

Gooseacre

Markyate JMI Sch

CAVENDISH RD

OLD VICARAGE GDNS

COWPER RD

WESLEY RD

BEERS CL

COWPER CT

C C COWPER CT

CHRISTINA ST

COWPER RISE

NORTH CT

ALBERT ST

ROMAN WAY

THE RIDINGS

PO

HICKS RD

PH

High Winds Farm

HICKS RD

HARPS HILL

AL3

Buckwood Stubs

PARK CL

CORNER WOOD

THE COPPINS

PARKFIELD RD

SEBRIGHT RD

HICKS RD

LAX MEADS

SHAROSE CT

GEORGE ST

LONG MDW

THE DELL
CLEVELAND RD 1
WILLIAM ST 2
KING ST 3
THE CLOSE 4
SUMMER WLK 5

SURSHAM CT

FARRER CR

MANSE CT

HILL VIEW

LONDON RD

DAMMERSEY CL

GREEN LA

A5

CHEVERELL'S CL

Hertfordshire Way

Roe End Farm

Sebright Sch

Feveralls Farm

Cheverell's Green

Hollybush Lodge

ROE END LA

Roe End

PICKFORD RD

Cheverells

Hertfordshire Way

Sheepyard Dell

Cotton Spring Farm

FRIENDLESS LA

Kennels Lodge

Furze Cover

Gillhill Plantation

Cheverell's Belt

Friendless Wood

Beechwood House

Beechwood Park Prep Sch

Valley Cottage

Valleybottom Farm

VALLEY LA

Valleylane Cottage

Moonshine Wood

HP2

Dean Wood

PUDDEPHAT'S LA

Babies Wood

Hill Farm

A B C D E F
04 05 06

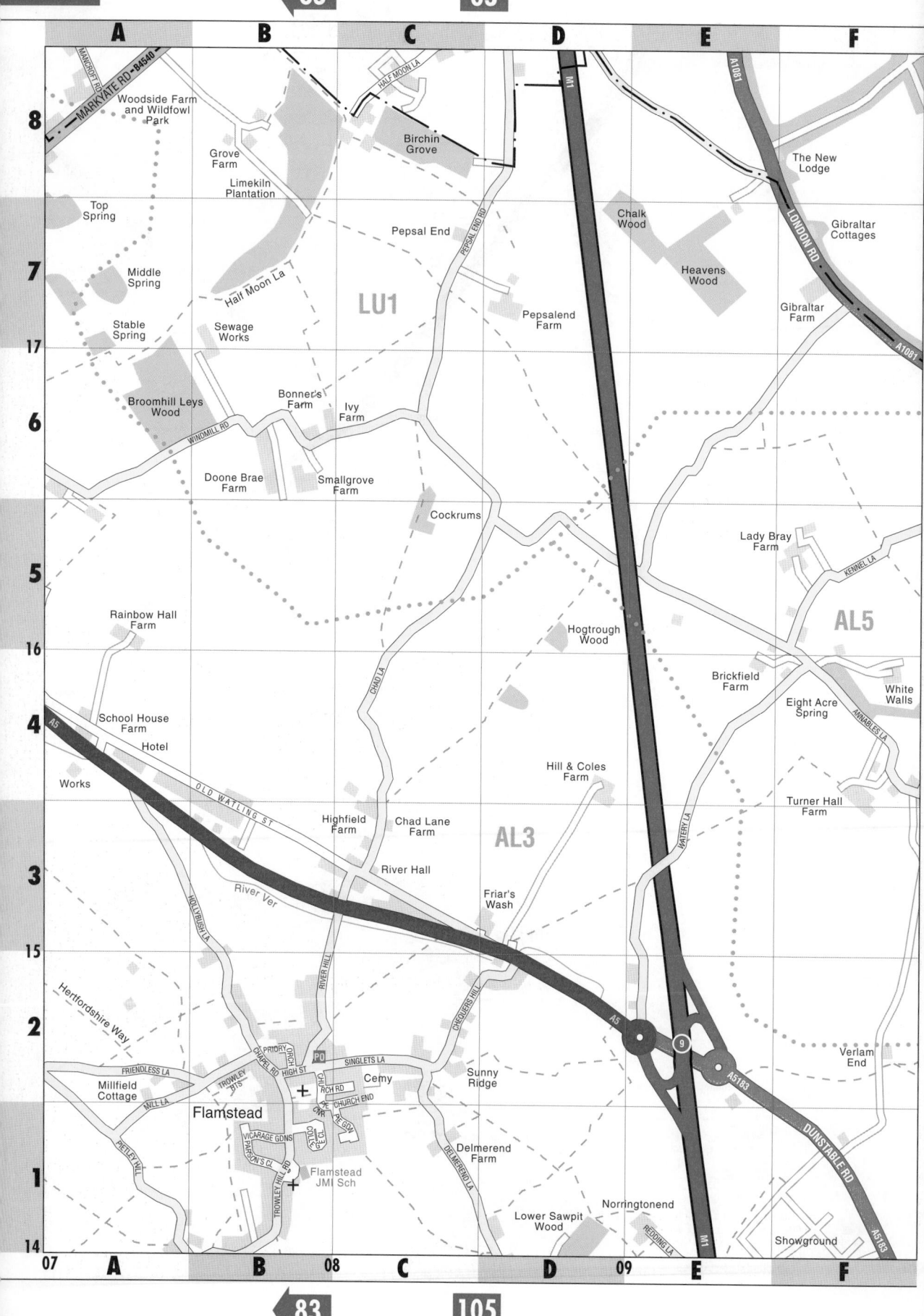

A · B · C · D · E · F

8

7

17

6

5

16

4

3

15

2

1

14

MARKYATE RD ~ B4540

Woodside Farm and Wildfowl Park

Grove Farm

Limekiln Plantation

Half Moon La

Birchin Grove

Top Spring

Middle Spring

Half Moon La

Pepsal End

LU1

Pepsalend Farm

PEPSAL END RD

M1

Chalk Wood

Heavens Wood

The New Lodge

A1081

LONDON RD

Gibraltar Cottages

Stable Spring

Sewage Works

Gibraltar Farm

A1081

Broomhill Leys Wood

WINDMILL RD

Bonner's Farm

Ivy Farm

Doone Brae Farm

Smallgrove Farm

Cockrums

Lady Bray Farm

KENNEL LA

AL5

Rainbow Hall Farm

CHAD LA

Hogtrough Wood

Brickfield Farm

Eight Acre Spring

White Walls

ANNABLES LA

A5

School House Farm

Hotel

OLD WATLING ST

Hill & Coles Farm

Turner Hall Farm

Works

Highfield Farm

Chad Lane Farm

AL3

River Ver

River Hall

Friar's Wash

WATERY LA

HOLLYBUSH LA

RIVER HILL

CHEQUERS HILL

A5

Hertfordshire Way

9

Verlam End

PRIORY

CHAPEL RD

CHURCH RD

HIGH ST

PO

SINGLETS LA

Cemy

Sunny Ridge

A5183

DUNSTABLE RD

Millfield Cottage

FRIENDLESS LA

TROWLEY BTS

MILL LA

RCH RD

CNR

CHURCH END

PL GDN

Flamstead

VICARAGE GDNS

PARSON'S CL

TROWLEY HILL RD

COLL CL

Delmerend Farm

DELMEREND LA

PIETLEY HILL

Flamstead JMI Sch

Norringtonend

Lower Sawpit Wood

REDDING LA

M1

Showground

A5183

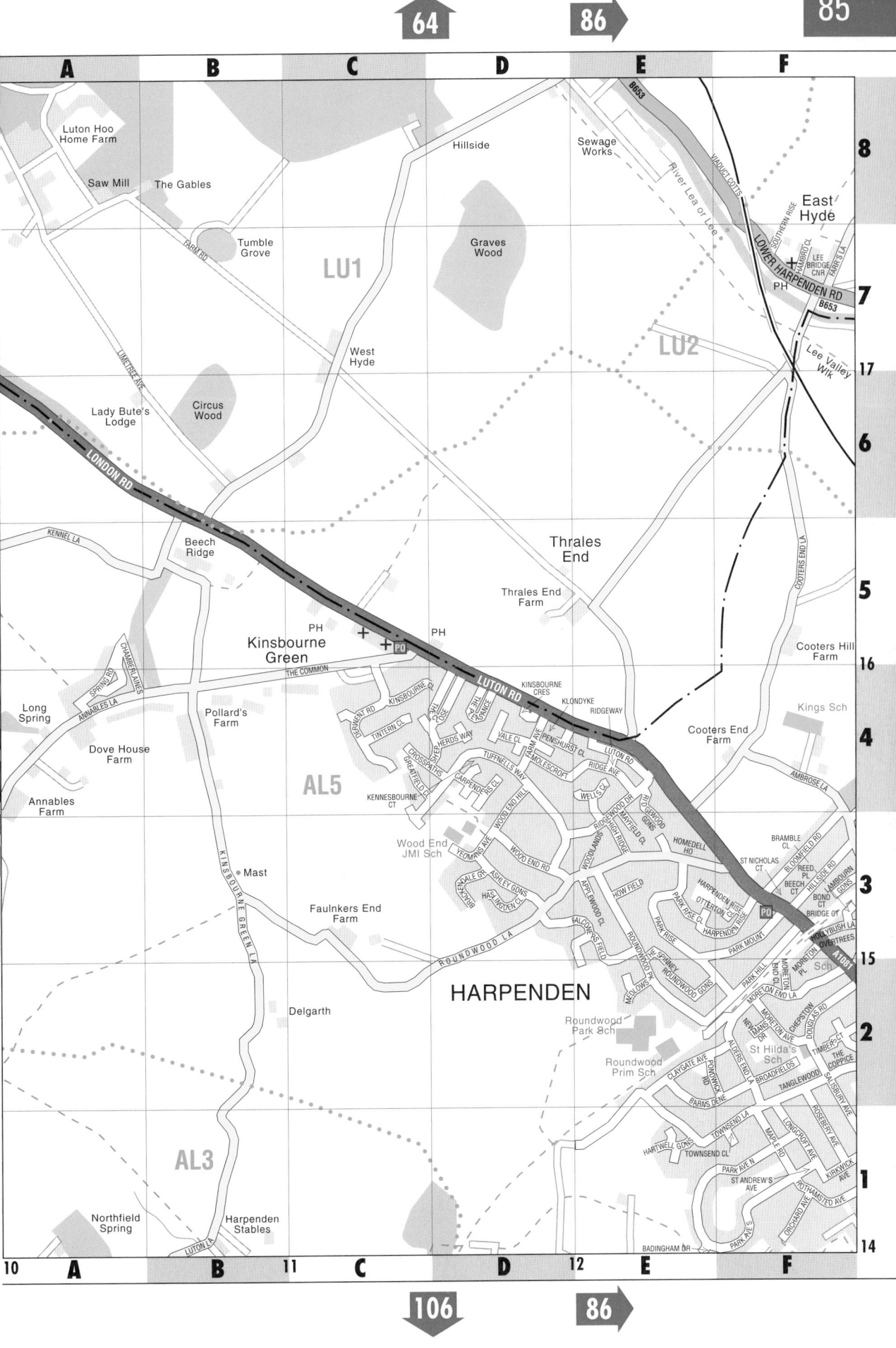

A B C D E F

8
7
17
6
5
16
4
3
15
2
1
14

Luton Hoo
Home Farm

Saw Mill

The Gables

FARM RD

Tumble
Grove

LU1

Hillside

Graves
Wood

Sewage
Works

B653

East
Hyde

LEE
HAMBRO CL
BRIDGE
CNR
FRM LA

LOWER HARPENDEN RD

PH

B653

LU2

Lee Valley
Wlk

VIADUCT COTTS

River Lea or Lee

SOUTHERN RISE

LIMETREE AVE

LONDON RD

Lady Bute's
Lodge

Circus
Wood

West
Hyde

KENNEL LA

Beech
Ridge

Thrales
End

Thrales End
Farm

COOTERS END LA

Cooters Hill
Farm

SPRING RD

CHAMBERLAINES

ANNABLES LA

PH

Kinsbourne
Green

PH

PO

THE COMMON

LUTON RD

Kinsbourne
Cres

Klondyke

Ridgeway

PH

Cooters End
Farm

Kings Sch

Long
Spring

Pollard's
Farm

DERWENT RD

KINSBOURNE

TINTERN CL

FARM AVE

VALE CL

PENSHURST CL

THE FONNE

Dove House
Farm

GREATFIELD CL

HERDS WAY

CROSSPATHS

TUFFNELLS WAY

RIDGE AVE

WELLS CL

Luton RD

MOLESCROFT

AMBROSE LA

AL5

KENNESBOURNE
CT

CARPENDERS CL

LUTON RD

Annables
Farm

Wood End
JMI Sch

YEOMANS AVE

BRACKENDALE GR

ASHLEY GDNS

HAS...INGTON CT

WOOD END RD

WOOD END HILL

APPLEWOOD CL

RIDGEWOOD DR

HIGH RIDGE

WOODLANDS

MAYFIELD CL

RIDGEWOOD

RIDGEWOOD GDNS

HOMEDELL
HO

St Nicholas
CT

BRAMBLE
CL

BLOOMFIELD RD

REED
PL

BEECH
CT

HILLSIDE RD

BOND
CT

BRIDGE CT

AMBOURN

KINSBOURNE GREEN LA

Mast

Faulnkers End
Farm

ROUNDWOOD LA

Delgarth

FALCONERS FIELD

HARPENDEN RISE

HOW FIELD

OTTERTON CL

PARK RISE CL

HARPENDEN RISE

PARK RISE

ROUNDWOOD DR

THE SPINNEY

ROUNDWOOD GDNS

PARK MOUNT

PARK HILL

MORETON
END LA

MORETON END CL

MOLYBUSH LA

Overtrees

PO

A1081

... Sch

HARPENDEN

Roundwood
Park Sch

MEADOWS PK

MORETON
DR

NEW MANS...
PL

MORETON AVE

DOUGLAS RD

CHEPSTOW RD

SALISBURY AVE

St Hilda's
Sch

TIMBERCRT

THE
COPPICE

AL3

Roundwood
Prim Sch

CLAYGATE AVE

PONSWICK
RD

ALDERS END LA

BROADFIELDS

BARNS DENE

TANGLEWOOD

Northfield
Spring

LUTON LA

Harpenden
Stables

HARTWELL GDNS

TOWNSEND LA

TOWNSEND CL

ST ANDREW'S
AVE

PARK AVE N

MAPLE RD

LONGCROFT AVE

ORCHARD RD

PARK AVE S

ROTHAMSTED AVE

ROSEBERY AVE

KIRKWICK
AVE

BADINGHAM DR

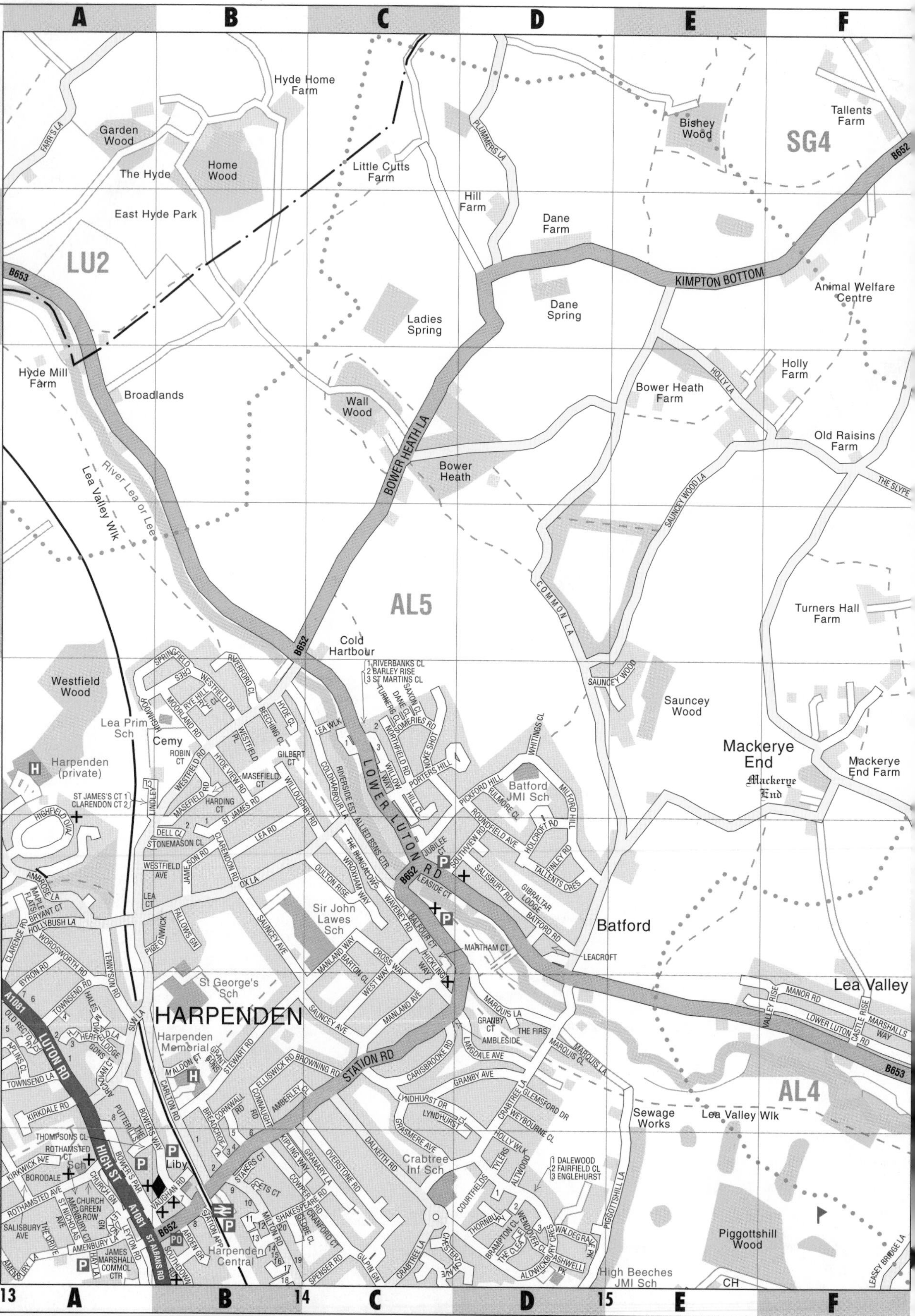

A2
1 LYDEKKER MEWS
2 GERARD CT
3 CORNELIA CT
4 HARDENWICK CT
5 SOUTHGATE CT
6 BERKELEY CT
7 FERNDALE
8 ANVIL HO

B1
1 CARLTON CT
2 CARLTON BANK
3 THE MEWS
4 CROFT CT
5 DEVONSHIRE RD
6 KINLOCH CT
7 VICTORIA RD
8 HARDING PAR
9 COLERIDGE CT

B1
10 BEAUMONT CT
11 COPPER BEECHES
12 MILTON CT
13 THE CEDARS
14 YARDLEY CT
15 KEATS HO
16 SHELLEY CT
17 AVON CT
18 FURZEDOWN CT

19 CHILTERN CT
20 HADDON CT

A B C D E F

Nursery

KIMPTON BOTTOM

B652

COOPER'S HILL

COOPER'S CL

HALL LA

B651

BALLSLOUGH HILL

8

Cottage Farm

SG4

Claggbottom Wood

Kimpton Hall Farm

Gunn's Lodge Cottages

7

The Dell

KIMPTON RD

Prior's Wood

Porter's End

LIME AVE

DRIVE

THE

17

WAY

BEECH

BLACKMORE MANOR

Blackmore End

Hall Wood

BIBBS HALL LA

6

BLACKMORE WAY

THE PADDOCKS

Bibbsworth Hall Farm

BROWNFIELD WAY

Hog's Plough

THE BROADWAY

FIRS DR

Cross Keys (PH)

Lamer Wood

AL6

Nursery

THE SLYPE

DALE AV

BURTON CL

Lamer House

5

P

Astridge Farm

Gustardwood Common

AL5

16

Gustard Wood

Lamer Park

4

MARSHALLS HEATH LA

Heron's Farm

AL4

Hertfordshire Way

CH

Home Farm

3

Cromwell Piggeries

Delaport House

CH

Lamer Farm

Marshalls Heath

15

Dairy Cottage

CODICOTE RD

P

2

PH

FOLLY FIELDS

The Folly

ROSE LA

CORY-WRIGHT WAY

PH

CHERRY TREE LA

LEASEY DELL DR

Cherry Trees

LOWER LUTON RD

GARDEN

Lea Valley Wlk

SHEEPCOTE LA

Leasey Bridge

LEASEY BRIDGE LA

KINGFISHER CL

STATION RD

CODICOTE RD

ABBOT JOHN MEWS

MOUNT RD

Sewage Works

1

Leasey Bridge Farm

Lea Valley Wlk

River Lea or Lee

PO

P

ASH GR

B651

HIGH ST

EAST LA

MEADS LA

1 OLD RECTORY GDNS
2 EAST MOUNT
3 BROCKET VIEW

B653

CANONS FIELD

14

16 A B 17 C D 18 E F

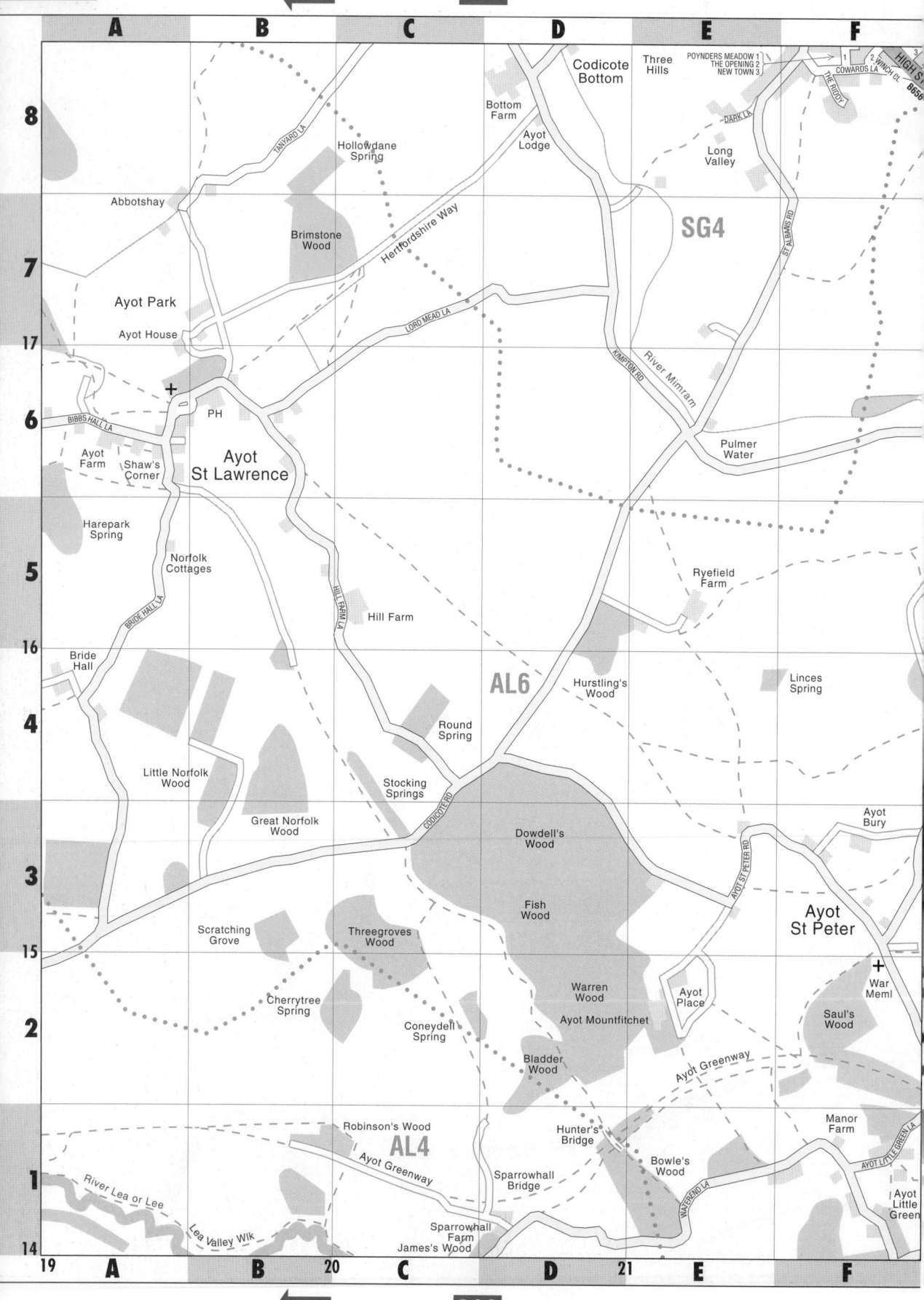

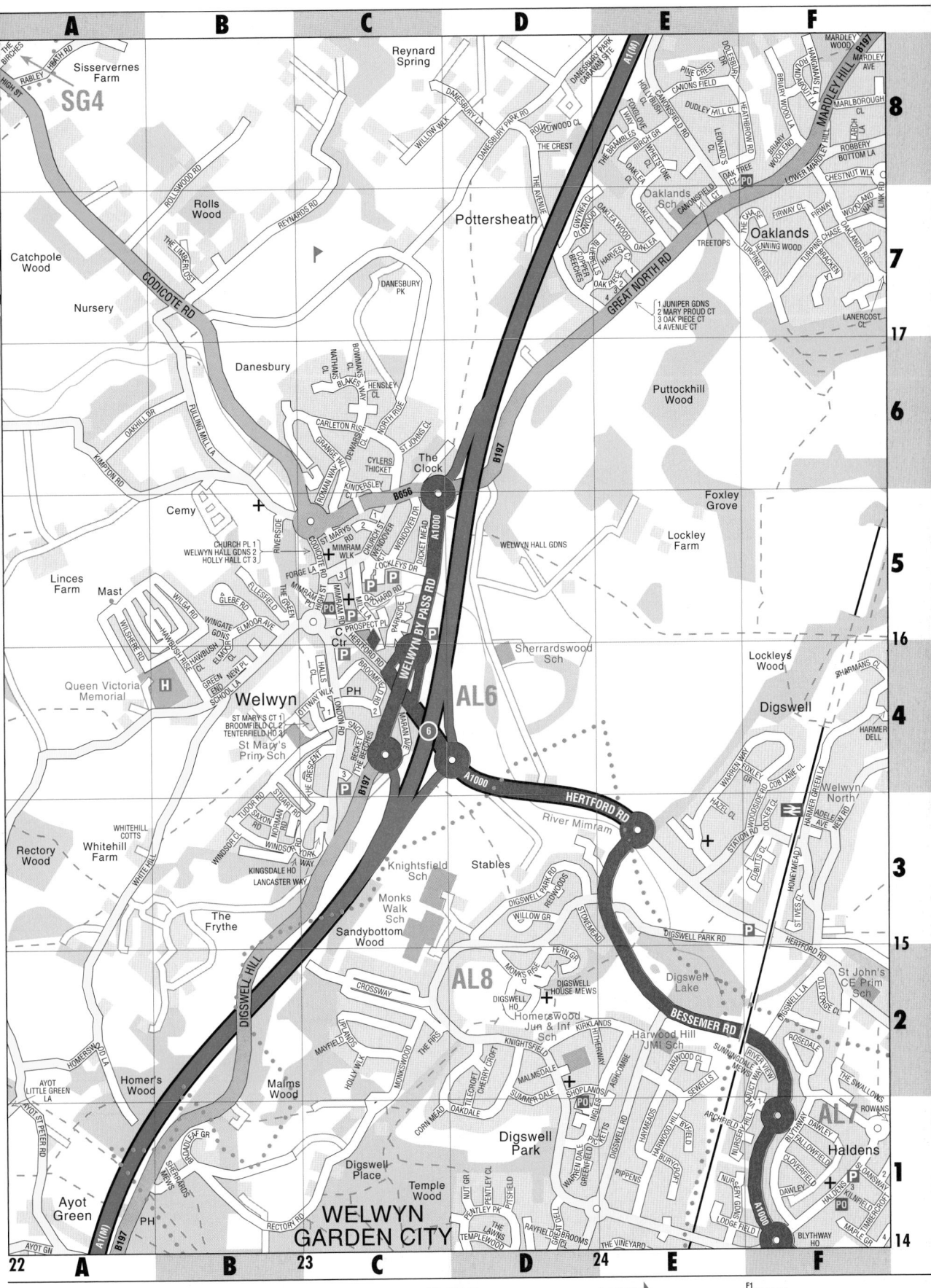

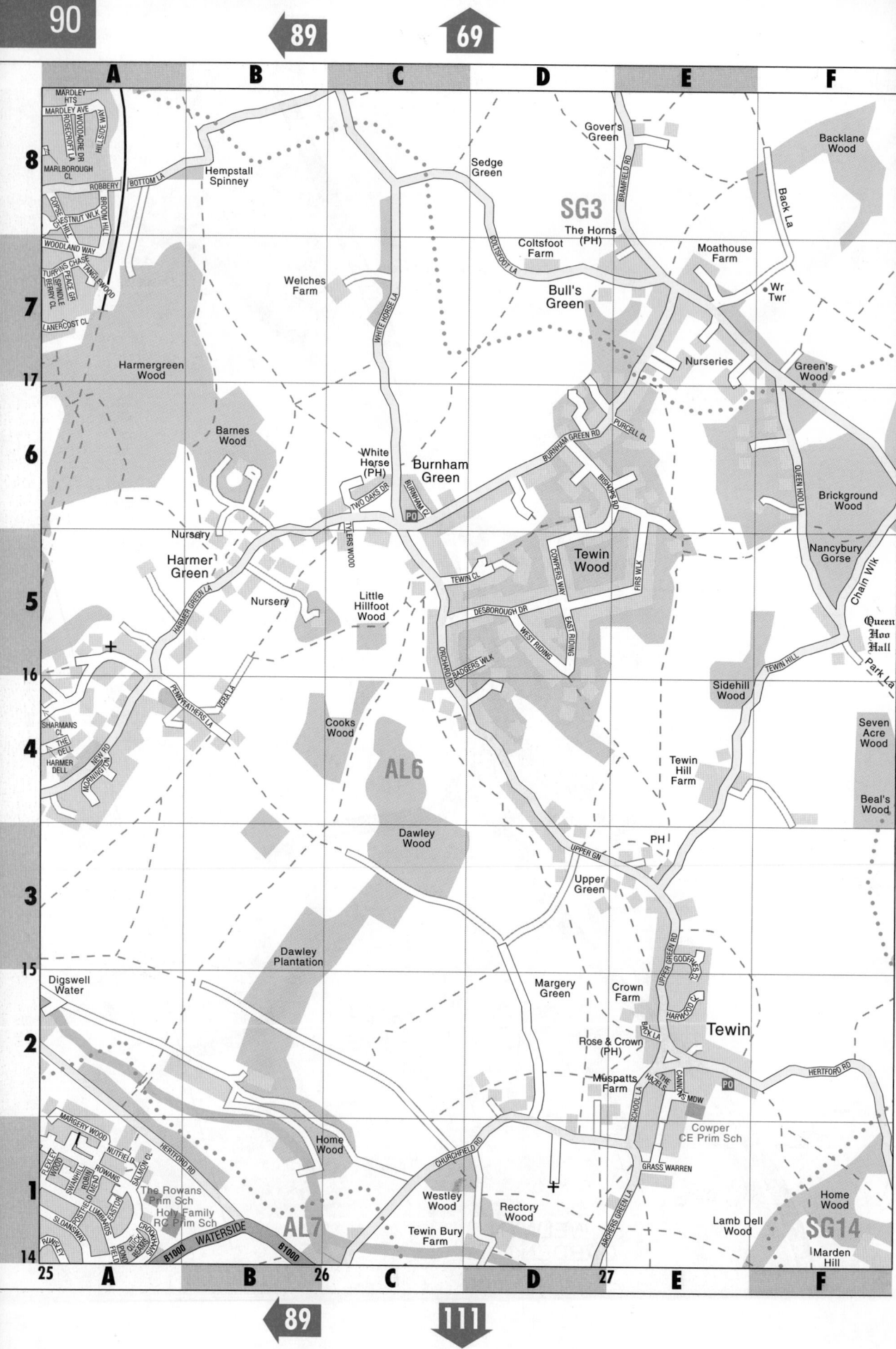

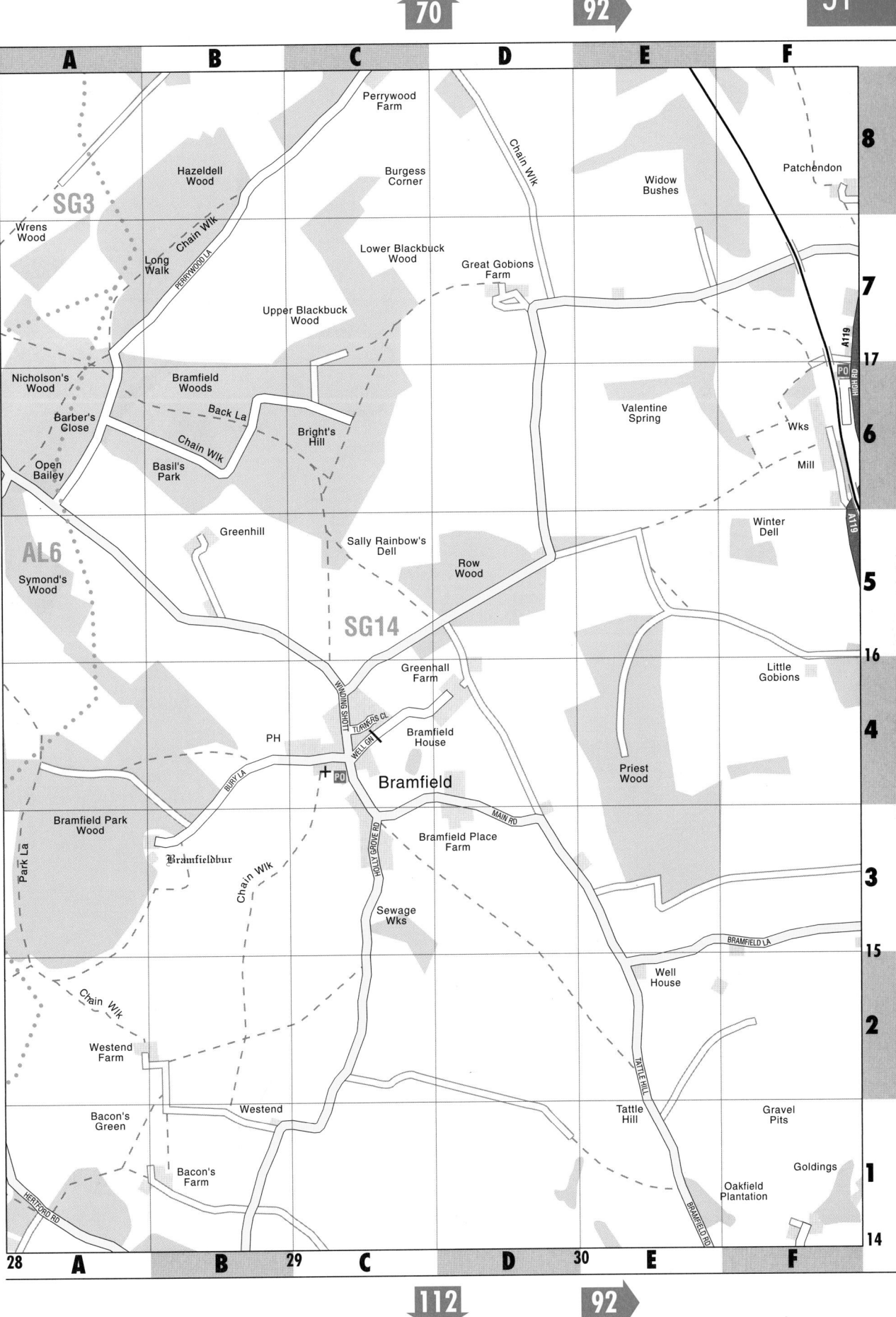

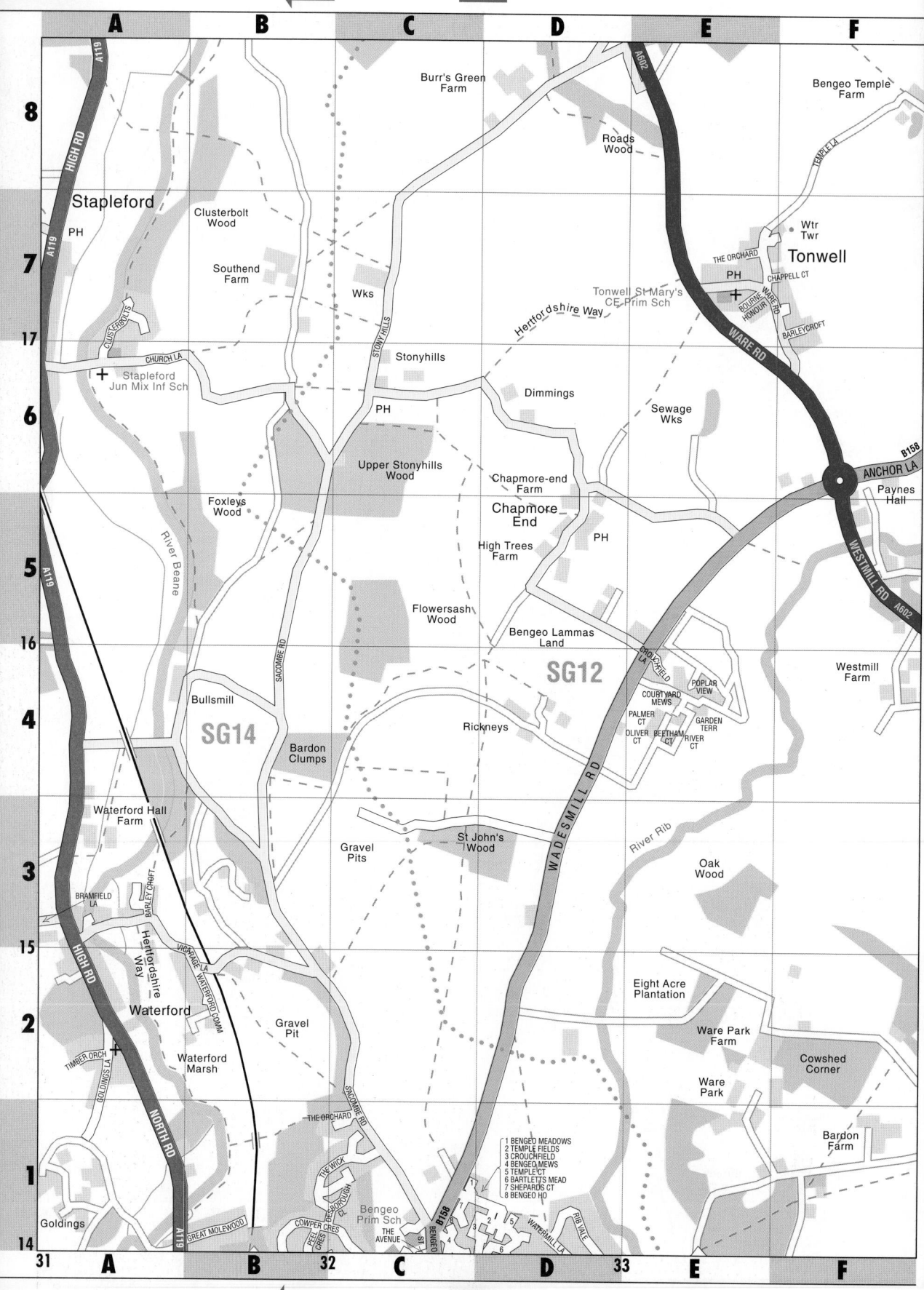

A B C D E F

8 7 17 6 5 16 4 3 15 2 1 14

SG11

Youngsbury

Lord's Wood
Chelsing Farm
Bourne Wood
Chelsing Cottages
Hertfordshire Way
Wadesmill
Upper Millfield Wood

Wade's Wood
Rennesley Farm
ANCHOR COTTS
B158 PH
PO
Thundridge
Old Church La
Thundridgehill

River Rib
ANCHOR LA
Chelsing Lodge
Sow & Pigs (PH)
WOODLANDS RD
DUCKETTS WOOD
COLD CHRISTMAS LA
Cowards

POLES LA
POLES PK
HANBURY DR
Hanbury Mews
Mole's Wood
Moles Farm
Little Fanhams

DOWNFIELD CT
Hanbury Manor
SG12
Wodson Park Sports & L Ctr
Round House
Great Cozens

Gravel Pit
Jubilee Plantation
South Lodge
Trinity Ctr
Dark La

WESTMILL RD
A602
C3
1 PEREGRINE HOUSE
2 FALCON CT
3 OSPREY HOUSE
4 KESTREL CT
ERMINE POINT BSNS PK
GENTLEMENS FIELD
THE LARCHES
St Mary's CE Jun Sch
Great Cozens

Gravel Pit
Cemy
Kingshill Inf Sch
Tower Prim Sch
Evergreen Rd

THE HYDE
WENGEO LA
Westmill Rd
CHURCH FIELD
Western House
Musley Inf Sch
H The Octagan

WARE

The Chauncy Sch
WATTON RD
B1004
St Catherine's CE Prim Sch
BALDOCK ST
A1170
PARK RD
Works
Works
HIGH ST
Ware Mus Liby
BURGAGE
Sacred Heart RC Prim Sch
STAR ST
B1004

Monastery
River Lea or Lee
Lea Valley Wlk
BROADMEADS
A119 HERTFORD RD
VIADUCT RD
A1170
WICKHAM WHARF
Widbury Musleigh
WIDBURY HILL
B1004

34 A 35 B C 36 D E F

D2
1 THUNDER HALL
2 THE BAKERY
3 ROKEWOOD MEWS
4 WAGGONERS YD
5 ST EVROUL CT
6 HARTFIELD CT
7 MONKS ROW
8 CAMERON CT
9 THE ALBION

D1
1 BLACK SWAN CT
2 CHURCH ROW MEWS
3 ST MARY'S CTYD
4 OMEGA CT
5 FRENCH HORN CT
6 LEASIDE WLK
7 DOLPHIN YD
8 WELLS YD
9 GEORGE WLK

10 RIVERSIDE MEWS
11 WATER ROW
12 BURGAGE CT
13 CHRISTOPHER CT
14 BECKETS WLK
15 STATION CT

E1
1 MILLACRES
2 OMEGA MALTINGS
3 ALBANY MEWS

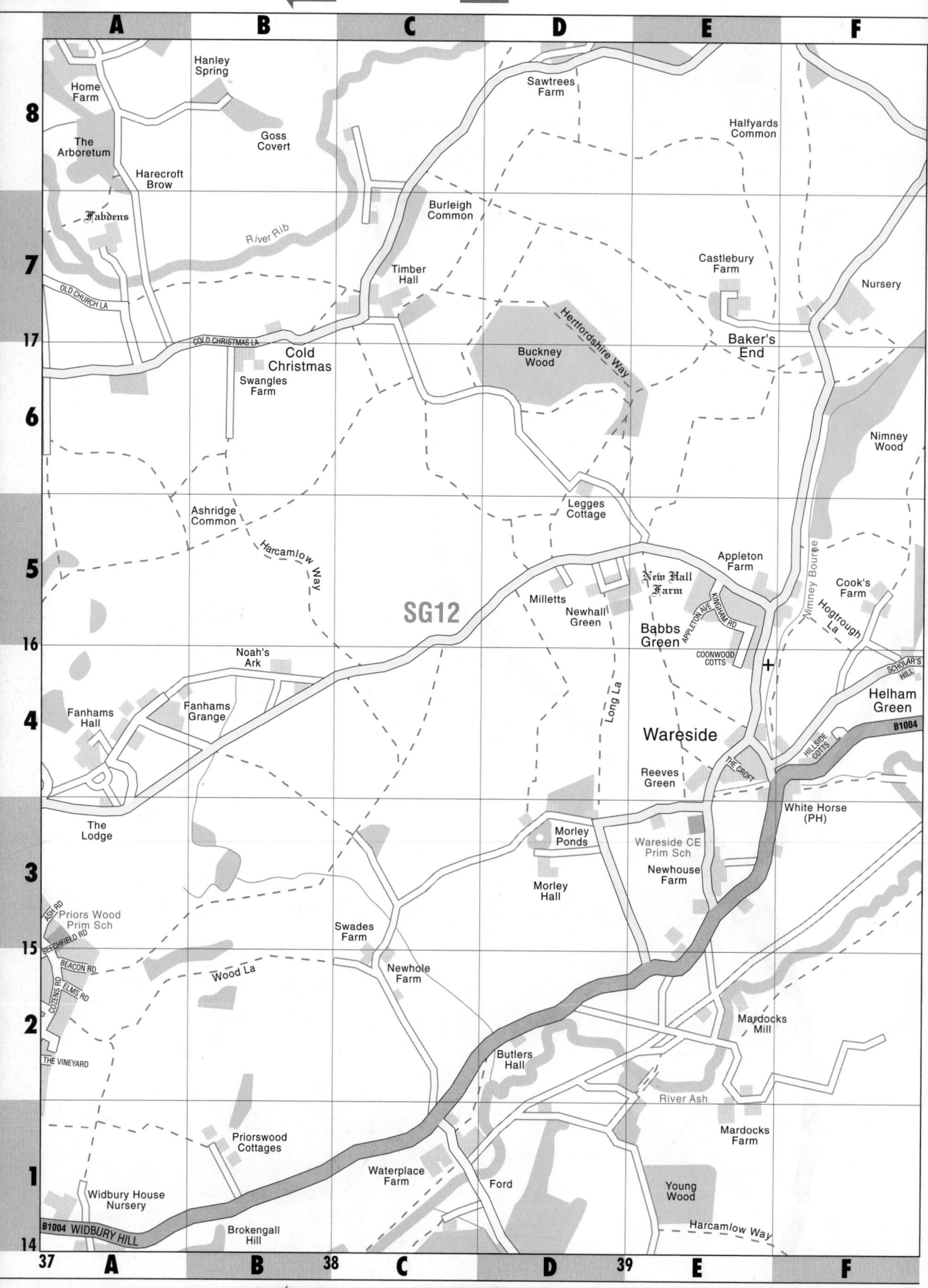

74
96

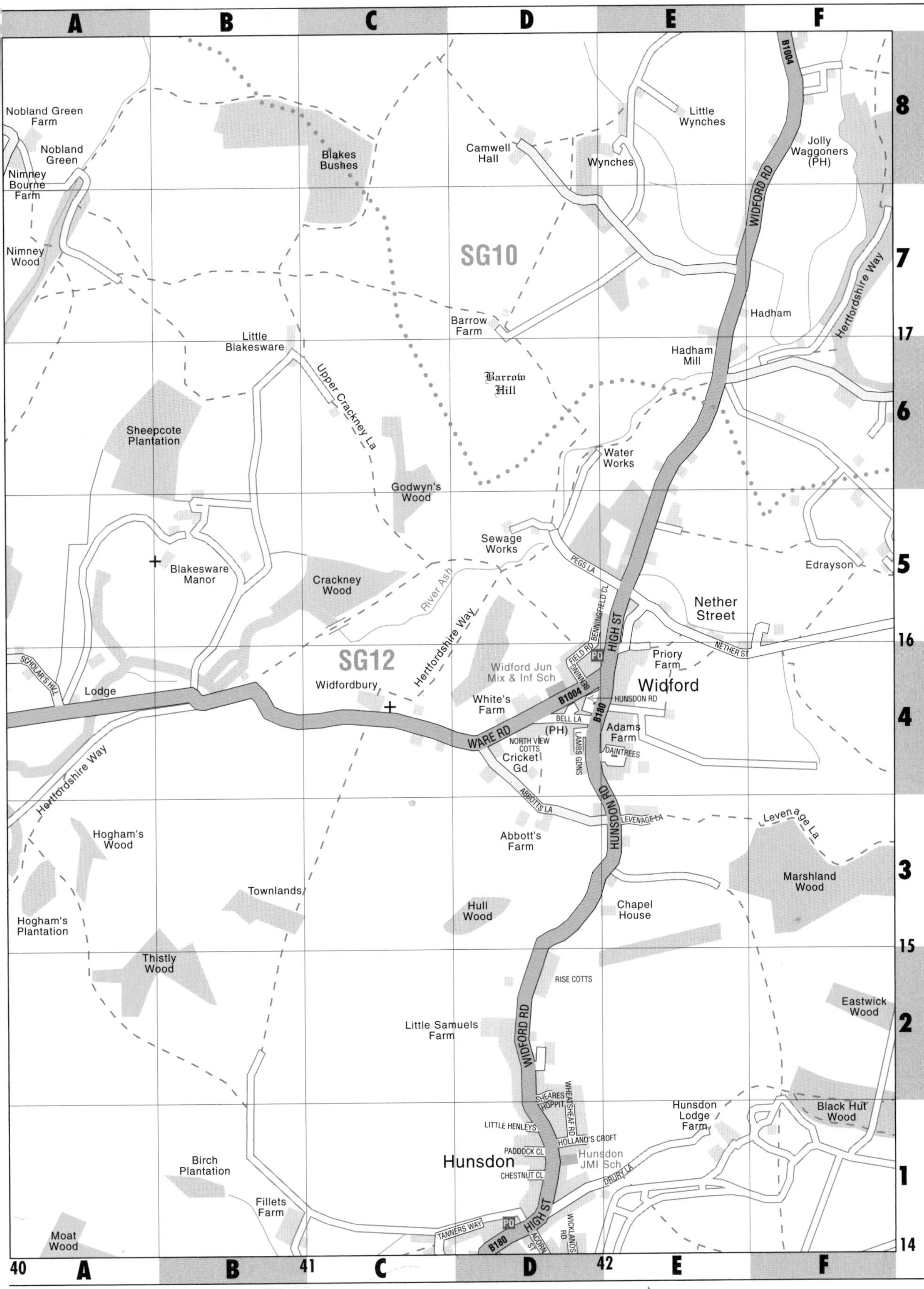

	A	B	C	D	E	F	

8

Nobland Green Farm

Nobland Green

Nimney Bourne Farm

Nimney Wood

Blakes Bushes

Camwell Hall

Little Wynches

Wynches

B1004

WIDFORD RD

Jolly Waggoners (PH)

Hertfordshire Way

SG10

7

17

Little Blakesware

Barrow Farm

Hadham

Hadham Mill

Upper Crackney La

Sheepcote Plantation

Barrow Hill

6

Water Works

Godwyn's Wood

Edrayson

5

Blakesware Manor

Crackney Wood

River Asp

Sewage Works

PEGS LA

Nether Street

16

Hertfordshire Way

SG12

Widfordbury

Widford Jun Mix & Inf Sch

HIGH ST

FIELD RD

PO

SKINNER'S

BENNINGFIELD CL

Priory Farm

NETHER ST

Widford

Lodge

White's Farm

WARE RD

B1004

B180

HUNSDON RD

Adams Farm

4

Hertfordshire Way

NORTH VIEW COTTS

(PH)

BELL LA

LAMBS GDNS

DAINTREES

Cricket Gd

ABBOTT'S LA

HUNSDON RD

LEVENAGE LA

Levenage La

Hogham's Wood

Abbott's Farm

Marshland Wood

3

Townlands

Hull Wood

Chapel House

15

Hogham's Plantation

Thistly Wood

WIDFORD RD

RISE COTTS

Eastwick Wood

2

Little Samuels Farm

Black Hut Wood

Hunsdon Lodge Farm

Birch Plantation

SHEARES HOPPIT

WHEATSHEAF RD

LITTLE HENLEYS

HOLLAND'S CROFT

PADDOCK CL

Hunsdon JMI Sch

OBURY LA

1

Fillets Farm

Hunsdon

CHESTNUT CL

Moat Wood

TANNERS WAY

PO

B180

HIGH ST

MORLEY

WICKLANDS RD

14

40	A		B	41	C		D	42	E		F	

116
96

A B C D E F

8

Blount's
Farm

Bucklers Hall
Farm

Brook La

Perry
Green

The Chase
Farm

Sacombs
Ash

SACOMBS ASH LA

Hertfordshire Way

7

The Hoops
Inn
(PH)

Hylands
Nursery

The Bourne

17

Warrens

The Queens Head
(PH)

6

South-end

Old
Park

Allen's
Green

Minges

St Elizabeth's
Sch & Home

Dukes
Farm

Covey's La

Allensgreen
Wood

SG10

5

Turtle
Farm

Chandlers

Fiddlers Brook

Chandlers La

NETHER ST

16

The
Rick

CM21

Hardings

4

Levenage
Spring

Gangies

3

Mole
Wood

Carters

Stonards

Hoskins
Farm

GANGIES HILL

Fryars

15

Lawns
Wood

Actons
Farm

The Manor
of Groves

CH

High
Trees

2

Queen's
Wood

Maplecroft
Wood

Jeffs

SG12

Battles
Wood

Great Pennys
Farm

Mabletts

1

Keeper's

Golden
Grove

Sayes
Coppice

CM20

14

43 A B 44 C D 45 E F

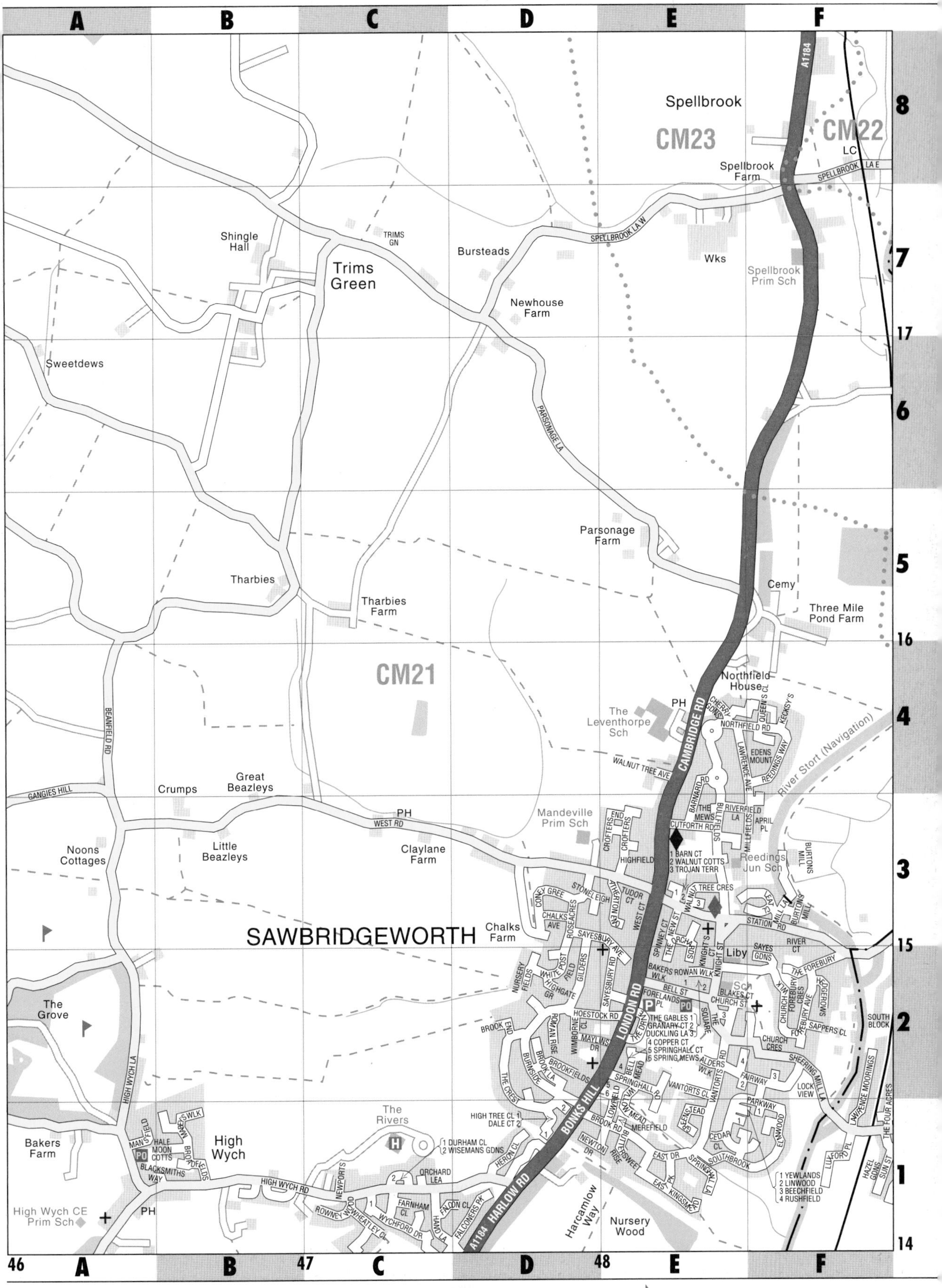

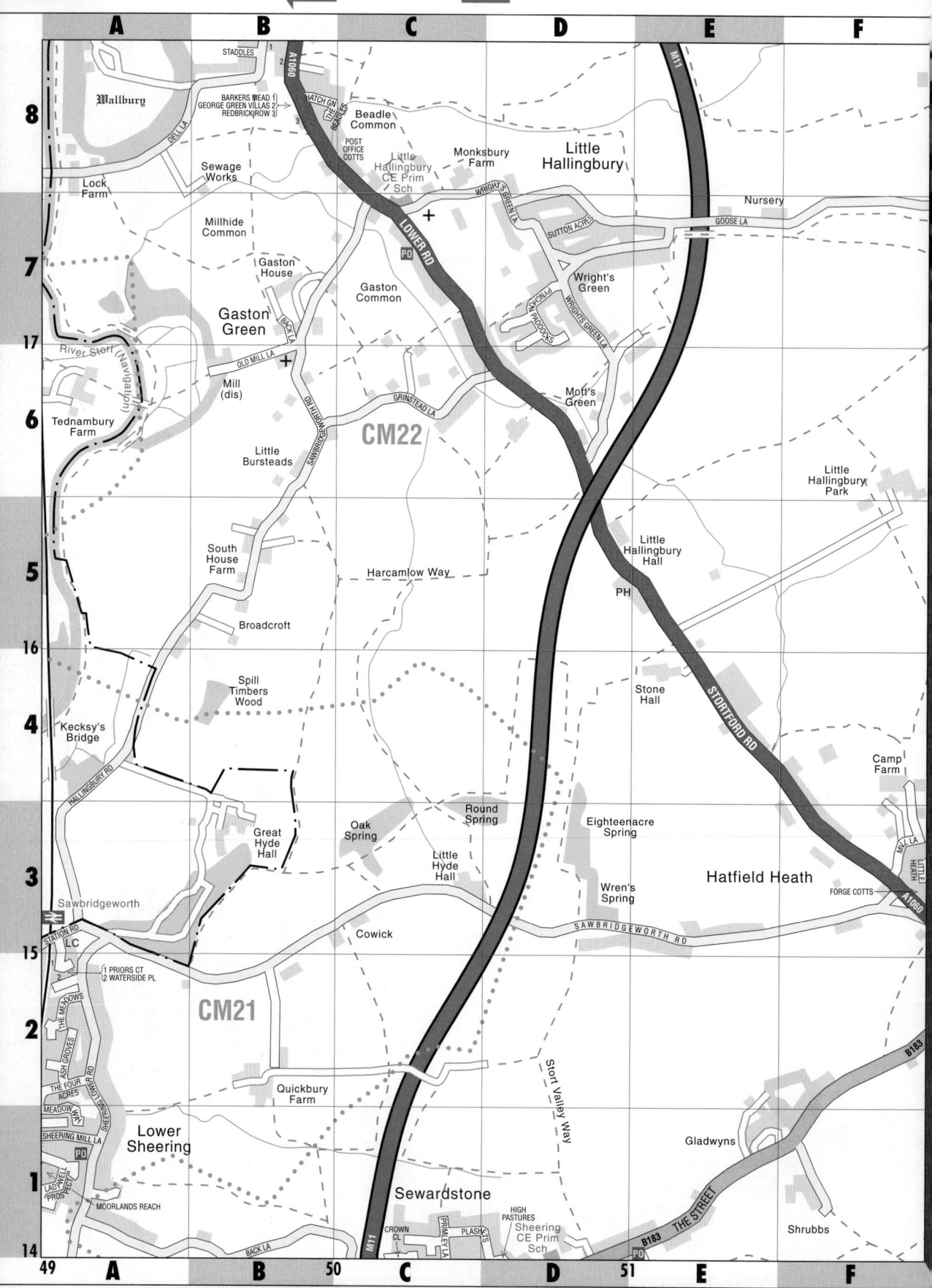

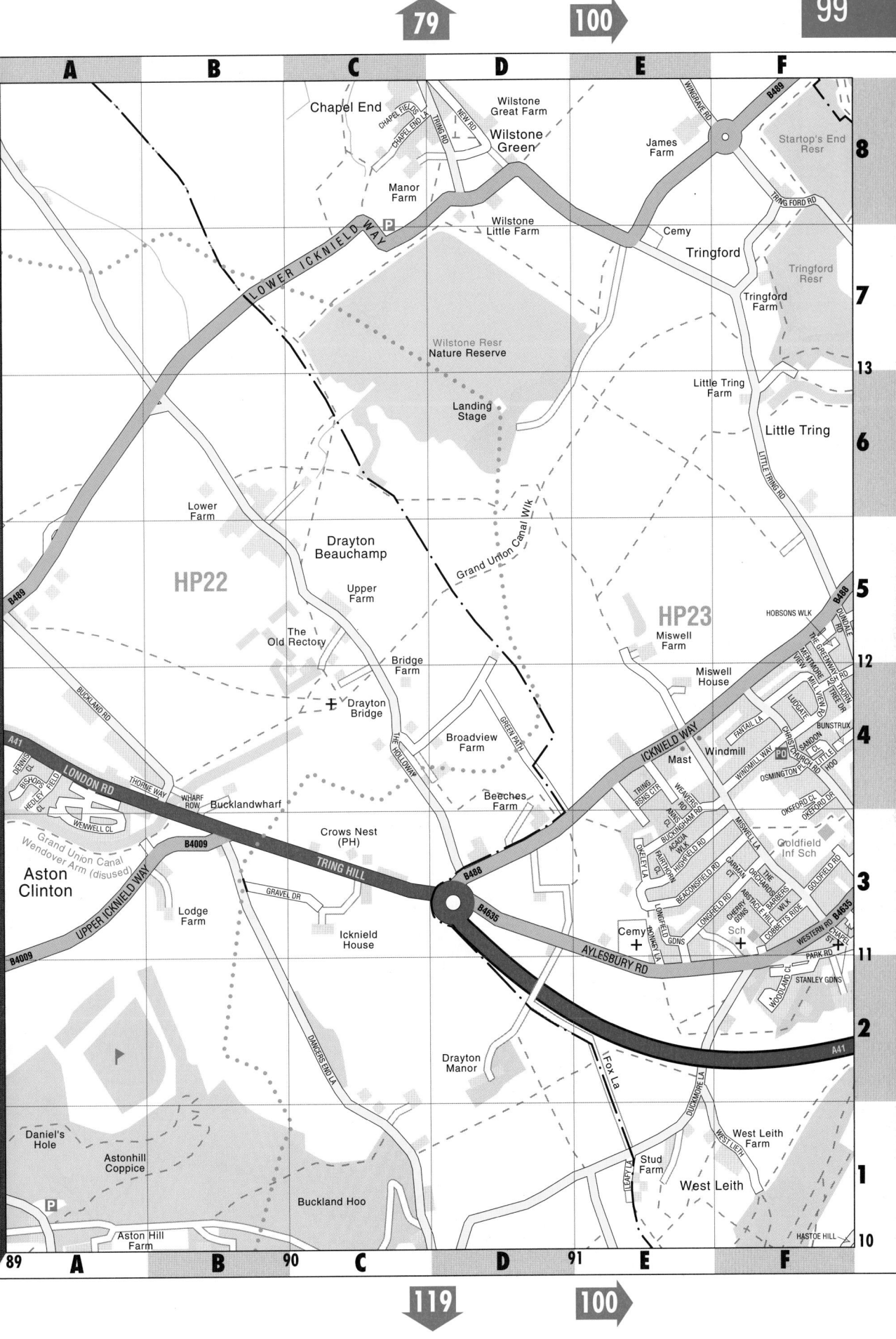

A   B   C   D   E   F

Chapel End
Wilstone
Great Farm
Wilstone
Green
James Farm
8
Manor
Farm
Wilstone
Little Farm
Cemy
Tringford
LOWER ICKNIELD WAY
P
Tringford
Resr
7
Tringford
Farm
13
Wilstone Resr
Nature Reserve
Little Tring
Farm
Landing
Stage
Little Tring
6
Grand Union Canal Wlk
Lower
Farm
Drayton
Beauchamp
HP22
Upper
Farm
HP23
Miswell
Farm
HOBSONS WLK
5
B489
12
B489
The Old Rectory
Miswell
House
4
Bridge
Farm
ICKNIELD WAY
Windmill
PO
Drayton
Bridge
THE HOLLOWAY
GREEN PATH
Broadview
Farm
Mast
Goldfield
Inf Sch
Beeches
Farm
3
A41
LONDON RD
THORNE WAY
WHARF
ROW
Bucklandwharf
Crows Nest
(PH)
B488
B4635
Sch
Aston
Clinton
Grand Union Canal
Wendover Arm (disused)
B4009
TRING HILL
Cemy
AYLESBURY RD
PARK RD
11
B4009
UPPER ICKNIELD WAY
GRAVEL DR
Lodge
Farm
Icknield
House
B4635
B488
STANLEY GDNS
2
A41
Drayton
Manor
Fox La
DUCKMORE LA
Daniel's
Hole
DANCERS END LA
WEST LIETH
West Leith
Farm
Astonhill
Coppice
Stud
Farm
West Leith
1
P
Buckland Hoo
LEAFY LA
HASTOE HILL
10

99
80

8

Marsworth Resr
Nature Reserve

College Lake Wildlife Ctr

UPPER ICKNIELD WAY

B488

Folly Bridge

Works

Grand Junction Arms (PH)

Bulbourne

Bulbourne Farm

Northfield Grange

7

TRING FORD RD

BULBOURNE RD

Gamnel Farm

Grand Union Canal

Grand Union Canal Wlk

Park Hill Farm

NORTHFIELD RD

Sewage Works

BULBOURNE CT

GAMNEL

13

Mill

LONGBRIDGE CL

BUSHEL WHARF

Tring Wharf

MARSHCROFT LA

6

New Mill

ICKNIELD WAY

ELIZABETH DR

CHAPEL MDW

SUTTON CL

PHEASANT CL

WINGRAVE RD

B486

ALBANY

ALDBURY GDNS

NEW MILL TERR

NETHERBY CL

HOLLYFIELD CL

RIDGE VIEW

Marshcroft Cottages

Clarke's Spring

5

B488

NEW RD

BLAINE

CYNLOG RD

FIELDS END

MULBERRY

NEW WAY

WOODBROOK CT

GROVE GDNS

PAINTERS

GRENADINE WAY

ELM TREE WLK

SILK MILL WAY

GWYNNE

ROSEBERY WAY

BUNYAN

DANVERS

CROUT

VERNEY

CHILTERN WAY

GROVE PK

HOLLYFIELD CL

GROVE RD

BEACON WAY

GRAVE ACRES

THE GROVE

Grove Road Prim Sch

PO

Clarke's Spring

HP23

12

MANOR RD

BETTY'S LA

EIGHT ACRES

KINGSLEY CL

EIGHT ACRES

BROOK ST

BROOKFIELD CL

SHAIGHS GN

Tring Sch

BEECH WLK

CARRINGTON PL

MORTIMER HILL

SYCAMORE DR

HARCOURT RD

HAWKWELL

THE BEECHES

GRANGE RD

WHITTINGHAM RD

STATION RD

Court Theatre

Pendley Farm

BEGGARS LA

4

BUNSTRUX

DUNDALE RD

DEANS FURLONG

DEANS CL

ST PETERS

FAVERSHAM CL

MEADOW

EVANS WAY

WEST RD

NURSERY

TREEHANGER CL

BEECH GR

DAMASK CL

Cow Lane Farm

COW LA

COW LA

Pendley Manor (Hotel)

Chestnut Wood

Lodge Bushes

3

DUNS CL

FRIARS WLK

P P

POND CL

P

CHURCH YD

SNUG

PLAITERS

MORTIMER RISE

B486

DUNSLEY PL

Upper Dunsley

Dunsley Farm

Sp Ctr

Pendley Beeches

WELLBROOK MEWS

PARSONAGES CL

Jun Sch

PARSONAGE CL

P

PO

Liby HIGH ST

i

OAKLAWN

MANSION DR

TRING

LONDON RD

1 GOLDFIELD RD
2 CHRISTCHURCH HO
3 DOLPHIN SQ
4 CLEMENT PL
5 GRACES MALTINGS
6 CROWN ROSE CT
7 THE TERRACE
8 MUSEUM CT
9 LOUISA COTTS
10 WEST PAS

CHRISTCHURCH RD

WESTERN RD

B4635

WOODS CL

HARROW YD

MANSARD CL

ARCHWAY CT

SURREY PL

Mus

QUEEN

KING

CHARLES

ALBERT ST

9

Park

CARPENTERS YD

ST

HENRY

THE FURLONG

PARK RD

The Arts Educational Schs

ODDY HILL

B4635

A4251

11

Woodlands Farm

HASTOE LA

Ridgeway

FOX RD

Langton Wood

THE TWIST

Park Farm

A4251

2

A41

Tring Park Nature Reserve

Bull's Wood

FOX CL

HIGHFIELD RD

MARY CROSSFIELD RD

THE BELMERS

THE HOSPICE

POLLYWICK RD

OSBORNE WAY

VICARAGE RD

THE HOLLIES

COMMON FIELD

Wigginton

Sch

THE FIRS

THE BIT

FIELDWAY

FIELD END CL

CRISHAM RD

VALPY CL

HEMP LA

Hill Green Farm

HASTOE HILL

MARLIN HILL

GRIMSDYKE RD

WICK RD

1

10

99
120

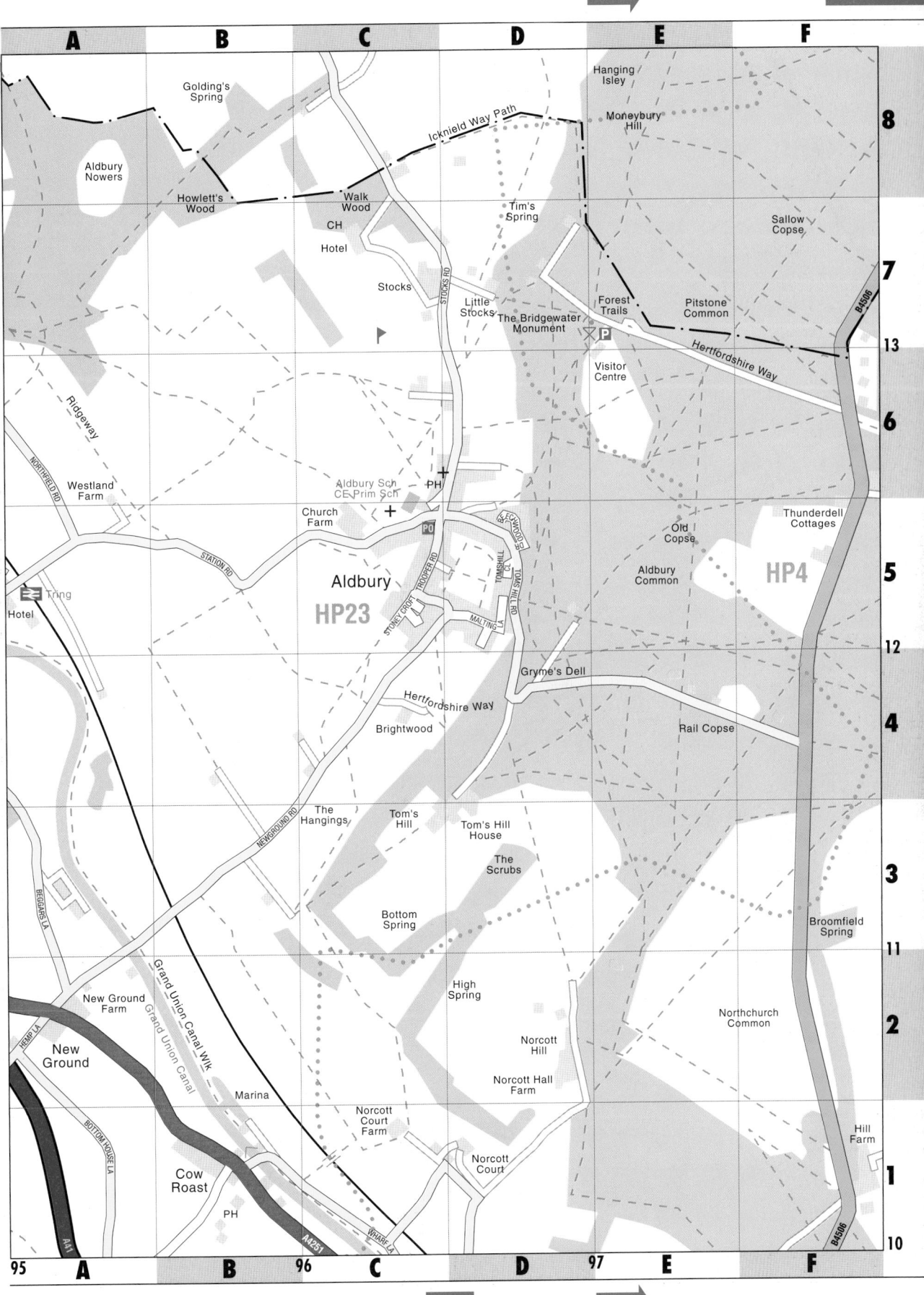

101
81

A   **B**   **C**   **D**   **E**   **F**

B4506

ALDERTON DR

8

GATESHEAD CL

KINGSHILL DR

PO

BRIDGEWATER CT

Bridgewater Arms (PH)

BEECH CL

CHURCH RD

Church Farm

Badger Wood

Little Gaddesden CE Sch

Hudnall Common Plantation

7

Pitstone Park Copse

Little Gaddesden

Hudnall Common

B4506

HUDNALL LA

POND LA

Hudnall

13

Ashridge

CH

THE LYE

CHAPEL CL

Hudnall Farm

6

Old Park Lodge

Ashridge Park

Golden Valley

Robin Hood Farm

Little Brownlow Farm

Little Gaddesden House

Prince's Riding

The Rookery

5

Thunderdell Wood

Hertfordshire Way

Home Farm

Lady Grove

Ashridge College (Gardens)

Ashridge Management Coll

Cromer Wood

CROMER CL

CROMER CL

NETTLEDEN RD

12

HP4

Harding's Rookery

4

Woodyard Cottage

Berkhamstead Common

Toll

Pulridge Wood

3

Little Coldharbour Farm

Coldharbour Spring

Coldharbour Farm

Golden Valley Farm

11

Furzefield Wood

Nettleden Lodge

Webb's Copse

2

Hertfordshire Way

Ashridge

HP1

Bluebell Spring

Brickkiln Cottage

Frithsden Beeches

1

Frithsden Gardens

10

98   **A**   **B**   99   **C**   **D**   00   **E**   **F**

101
122

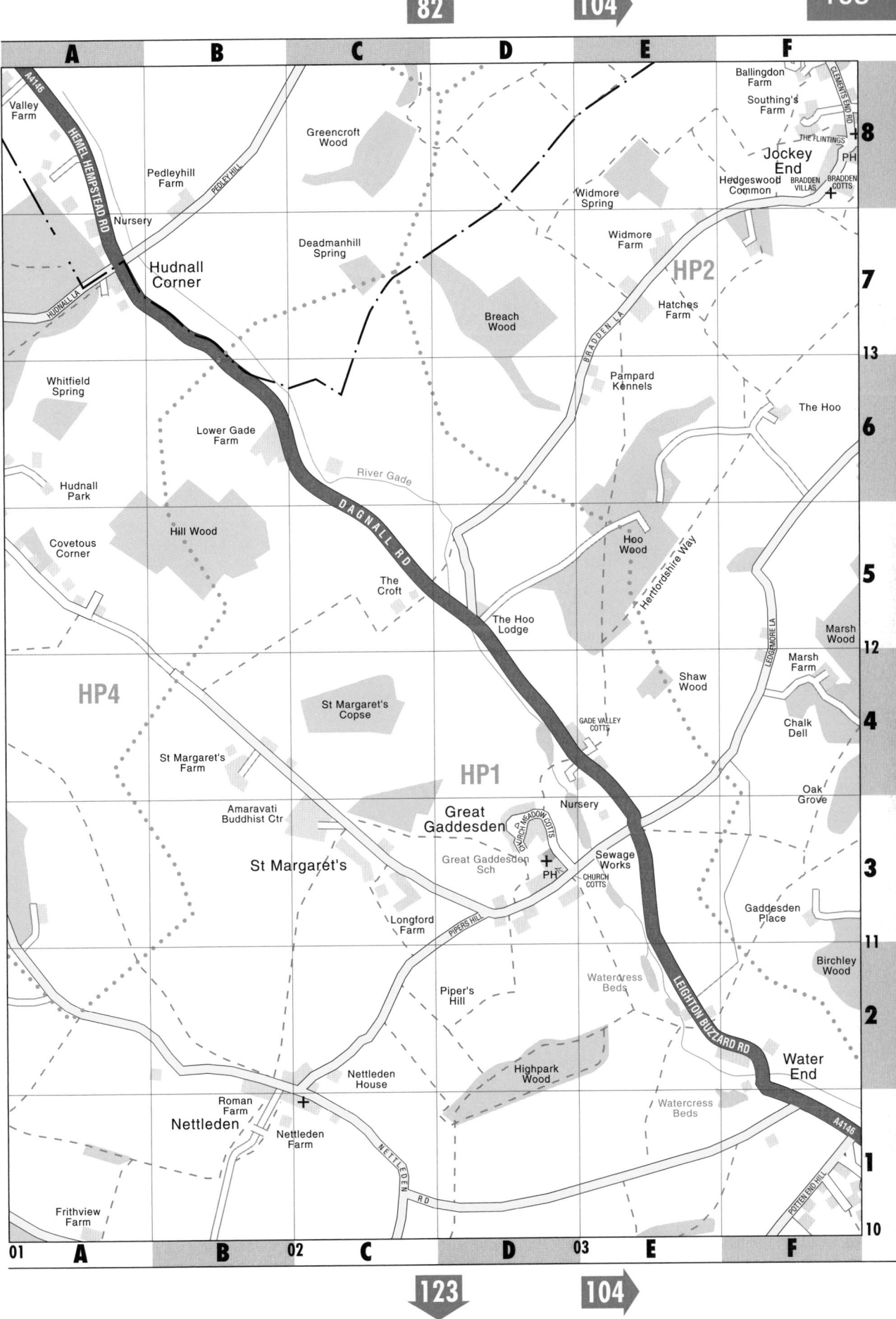

82
104

A B C D E F

8
7
13
6
5
12
4
3
11
2
1
10

Valley Farm

A414b

Ballingdon Farm

Southing's Farm

THE FLINTINGS

CLEMENTS END RD

Jockey End

PH

HEMEL HEMPSTEAD RD

Pedleyhill Farm

Greencroft Wood

Widmore Spring

Hedgeswood Common

BRADDEN VILLAS

BRADDEN COTTS

PEDLEY HILL

Nursery

Deadmanhill Spring

Widmore Farm

HP2

Hudnall Corner

Widmore

Hatches Farm

HUDNALL LA

Whitfield Spring

Breach Wood

BRADDEN LA

Pampard Kennels

The Hoo

Lower Gade Farm

River Gade

Hudnall Park

DAGNALL RD

Hoo Wood

Covetous Corner

Hill Wood

The Croft

Hertfordshire Way

Marsh Wood

The Hoo Lodge

Shaw Wood

LEDGEMORE LA

Marsh Farm

Chalk Dell

HP4

St Margaret's Copse

GADE VALLEY COTTS

Oak Grove

St Margaret's Farm

HP1

CHURCH MEADOW COTTS

Nursery

Amaravati Buddhist Ctr

Great Gaddesden

Great Gaddesden Sch

PH

Sewage Works

Gaddesden Place

St Margaret's

CHURCH COTTS

Longford Farm

PIPERS HILL

Birchley Wood

Piper's Hill

Watercress Beds

LEIGHTON BUZZARD RD

Nettleden House

Highpark Wood

Water End

Roman Farm

Watercress Beds

Nettleden

Nettleden Farm

A4146

NETTLEDEN RD

POTTEN END HILL

Frithview Farm

01 A B 02 C D 03 E F

123
104

103
83

A B C D E F

8 +
WEST DENE

Dean La

Babies Wood

Little Woodend Cottages

Yewtree Spring

AL3

Scratch Wood

Newland's Wood

Prior's Spring

WOOD END LA

Hertfordshire Way

Six Tunnels Farm

Whitehouse Farm

7

Abel's Grove

Wood End Farm

PUDDEPHAT'S LA

Water Twr

Puddephats Farm

13

LEDGEMORE LA

Gaddesden Row JMI Sch

Gaddesden Row

Green La

Upper Wood Farm

Gaddesden Hoo Cottages

The Lane House

Teakettle Wood

6

GADDESDEN ROW

Round Spring Wood

Ledgemore Farm

New Gorse

Golden Parsonage

Greenlane Wood

5

Long Wood

Ye Olde Chequers (PH)

Elmtree Farm

12

Marsh Wood

Stags End

Threecraft Wood

Corner Farm

GADDESDEN LA

Home Farm

London Wood

HP2

Hawbush Farm

4

Stable Wood

Big Wood

3

CUPID GREEN LA

Crown & Sceptre (PH)

Thomas's Wood

Birchley Wood

11

Briden's Camp

Eastbrookhay Farm

Millhill Farm

Millhill Gorse

Hogstrough Dell

2

Chalkpit Dell

Lovetts End Farm

Varney's Wood

DODDS LA

Red Lion (PH)

HP1

Wood Farm

Little Lovetts End Farm

ESSEX MEAD 1
ST AGNELLS LA 2
THE DEE 3
OLD MAPLE 4

SQUIRES RIDE

1

LEIGHTON BUZZARD RD
A4146

WOOTTON DR

10

04 A 05 B C 06 D E F

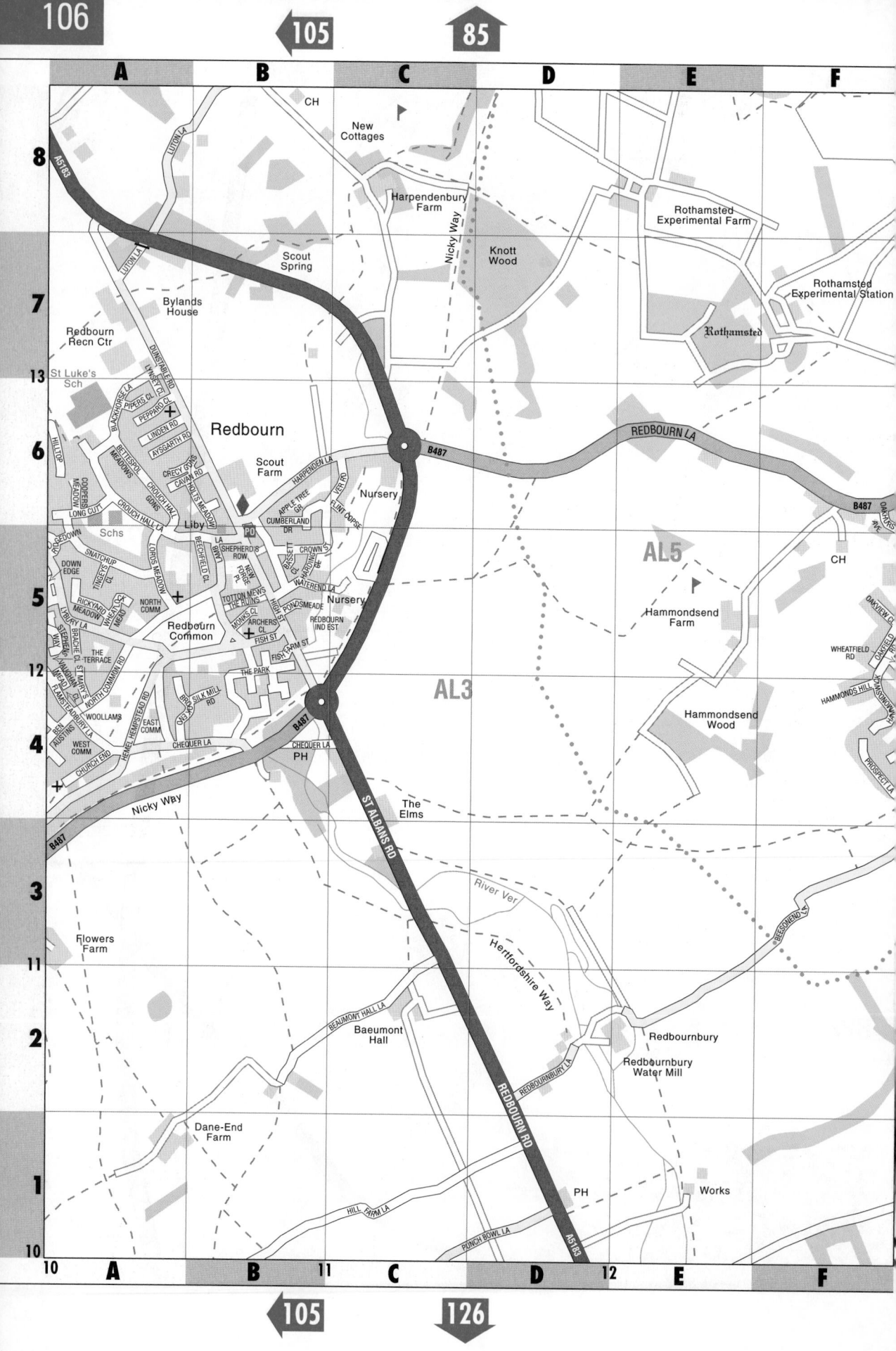

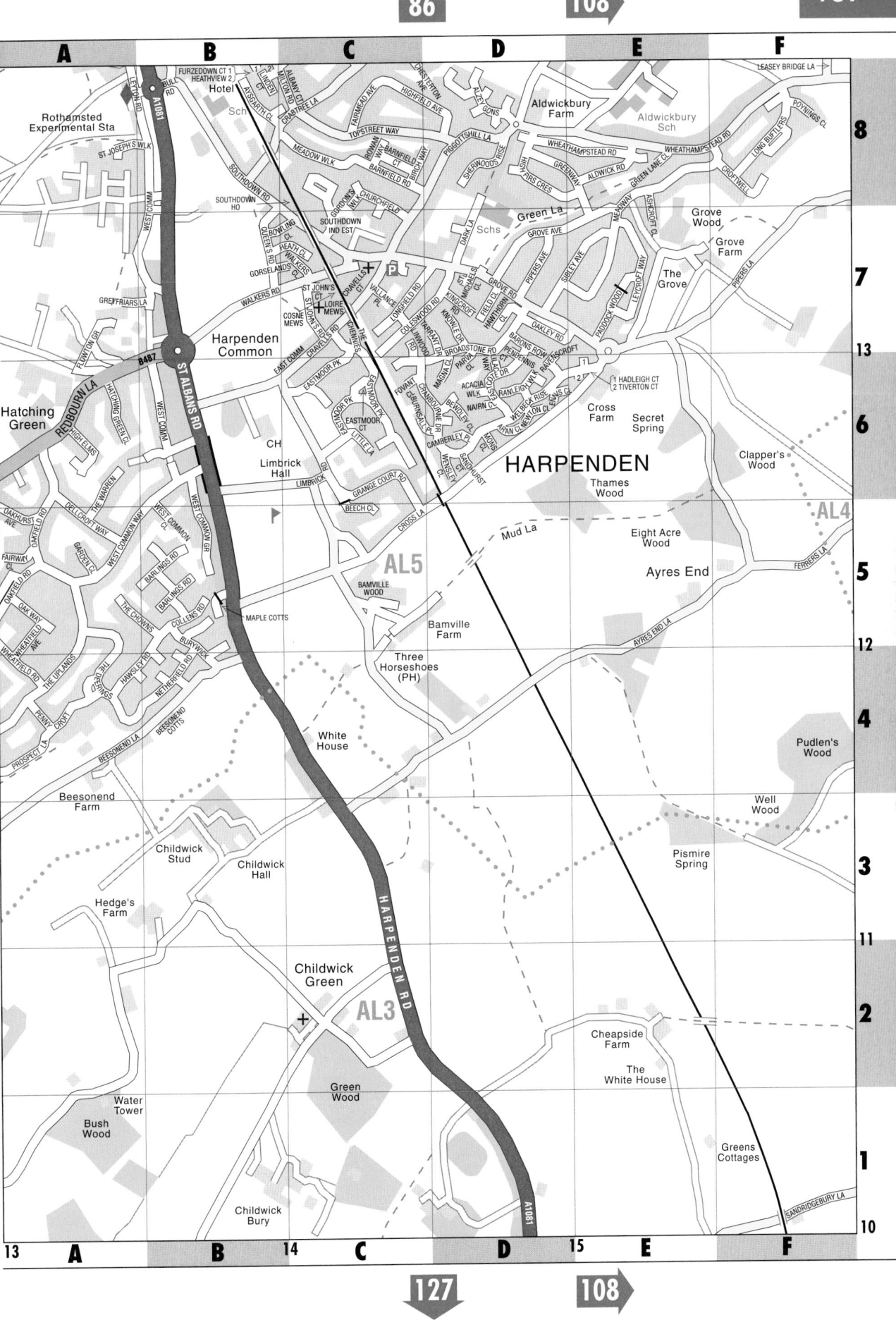

86
108

Rothamsted
Experimental Sta

FURZEDOWN CT 1
HEATHVIEW 2

Hotel

LEASEY BRIDGE LA

Aldwickbury
Farm

Aldwickbury
Sch

8

St JOSEPH'S WLK

CHESTERTON

ALEX
GDNS

WHEATHAMSTEAD RD

WHEATHAMSTEAD RD

GREENWAY

ALDWICK RD

GREENWAY

GREEN LANE CL

GREEN LANE CL

ASHCROFT CL

POYNINGS CL

LONG BUTLERS

CROFTWELL

GREYFRIARS LA

SOUTHDOWN
HO

HIGHFIELD AVE

FAIRMEAD AVE

TOPSTREET WAY

MEADOW WLK

BARNFIELD CL

BARNFIELD AVE

BIRCH WAY

PIGGOTTSHILL LA

SHERWOODS RISE

DARK LA

Schs

Green La

GROVE AVE

HIGH FIRS CRES

Grove
Wood

Grove
Farm

The
Grove

PIPERS LA

7

BOWLING
CL

QUEEN'S RD

HEATH CL

WALKERS
CL

GORSELANDS CL

WALKERS RD

SOUTHDOWN
IND EST

BOWMAN
WY

GORDONS
CL

CHURCHFIELD

CHURCHFIELD

GRAVELS
CL

VALLANCE
PL

LONGFIELD RD

COLESWOOD RD

ST JOHN'S
CT

LOIRE
MEWS

GROVE RD

KINGSCROFT

FIELD CL

HAWTHORN

GROVE RD

OAKLEY RD

BARONS ROW

PIPERS AVE

SIBLEY AVE

LEYCROFT WAY

PADDOCK WD

13

COSNE
MEWS

St JOHN'S RD

THE
DENZILS

ST JOHN'S RD

CRANBROOK

TARGARET RD

BROADSTONE RD

KNOWLE DR

WINDOOD

1 HADLEIGH CT
2 TIVERTON CT

Harpenden
Common

EAST COMM

EASTMOOR PK

EASTMOOR PK

EASTMOOR
CT

FOVANT

CRANBOURNE DR

CRANBOURNE DR

MACON
WAY

PAPDA

COTE DR

BARONS CROFT

6

Hatching
Green

High Elms

HATCHING GREEN CL

WEST COMM

WEST COMM

ST ALBANS RD

CH

Limbrick
Hall

LIMBRICK

GRANGE COURT RD

BEECH CL

LITTLE LA

CROSS LA

CAMBERLEY CL

BEVERLEY

NAIRN

RANLEIGH WLK

ACACIA
WLK

WEST BECK RISE

ARRAN CL

NEWTON CT

TEXAS CL

WENLEY RD

SANDHURST

Cross
Farm

Secret
Spring

HARPENDEN

Thames
Wood

Clapper's
Wood

AL4

13

FLOWTON GR

B487

REDBOURN LA

DELLCROFT WAY

THE WARREN

WEST COMMON GR

WEST COMMON

AL5

Eight Acre
Wood

Ayres End

FERRERS LA

5

OAKHURST
AVE

OAKFIELD RD

GARDEN CL

WEST COMMON WAY

BARLINGS RD

BARLINGS RD

COLLENS RD

THE CHOWNS

BURYWICK

MAPLE COTTS

BAMVILLE
WOOD

Bamville
Farm

Mud La

12

FAIRWAY
CL

OAK WAY

WHEATFIELD RD

THE UPLANDS

THE PEPPERS

HAWSLEY RD

NETHERFIELD RD

BEESONEND LA

BEESONEND
COTTS

Three
Horseshoes
(PH)

AYRES END LA

Pudlen's
Wood

4

PENNY CROFT

PROSPECT LA

White
House

Well
Wood

Beesonend
Farm

Childwick
Stud

Childwick
Hall

Pismire
Spring

3

HARPENDEN RD

Hedge's
Farm

11

Childwick
Green

AL3

Cheapside
Farm

The
White House

2

Water
Tower

Bush
Wood

Green
Wood

Greens
Cottages

A1081

SANDRIDGEBURY LA

1

Childwick
Bury

10

13 A
B
14
C
D
15
E
F

127
108

107
87

| | A | B | C | D | E | F |

8

WHEATHAMPSTEAD RD
Down Green House
PIPERS LA
Poultry Farm
HARPENDEN RD
AL5
Pipers

Lea Valley Wlk
BURY GN
ASH GR 1
OLD RECTORY GDNS 2
BREWHOUSE HILL
LATTIMORE RD
HIGH ASH RD
BUTTERFIELD RD
WICK AVE
BARTON RD
CHURCH ST
ST HELEN'S CL
HIGH MEADS
HIGH ST
B651
THE HILL
TOWN FARM
FOUR LIMES
WALNUT CT
OFFAS WAY
SAXON RD
CAESARS RD
HEWITT CL
VALE CT
BEECH CRES
WRIGHT CL
HILL
DYKE RD
DAVYS CL
HOUSDEN CL
SMALLWOOD CL
LAMB CT
GRANARY CL
ST THOMAS ST
BROCKET CL
PARKINSON CL
GARRARD WAY
NECTON RD
CONQUERORS HILL
MERCRIES RD
TUDOR RD
BATTLEVIEW
SHEEPCOTE LA
Marford Farm
MARFORD RD
The Nelson (PH)
CORY-WRIGHT WAY
B653
Belgic Oppidum
Liby
Sch

7
AMWELL LA
Amwell
Little Piggotts Wood
The Elephant & Castle (PH)
DOWN GREEN LA
Wheathampstead Sch
Wheathampstead

13
Stocking Wood
BULL LA
PH
Nomansland
Glen Nurseries
Wicked Lady (PH)
DYKE LA
BEECH HYDE LA
Beech Hyde Farm

6

West Farm
P
FERRERS LA
Pearman's Spring
PH

5
P
Nomansland Common
AL4
Darblay

12
Round Wood
Nomansland Farm
Coleman Green

4
Hillend Farm
COLEMAN GREEN LA
TOWER HILL LA
Hammond's Farm Cottages

3
HAMMONDS LA
Hammond's Farm

11
Langley Wood
Hertfordshire Way

2
AL3
SANDRIDGEBURY LA
POUND CL
SPENCER PL
HIGH ST
LANGLEY GR
SHOTFIELD
Sandridge Sch
FAIRSHOT CT
Harlowdell Spring

1
Sandridgebury
Sandridgebury Farm
The Green Man (PH)
HOPKINS CRES
CHURCH END
ST LEONARD'S CT
ANSON CL
LYNDON MEAD
GILES CL
Cemy
ST LEONARD'S CRES
HOUSE LA
JERSEY WAY
NORTHSIDE
HIGHFIELD RD
B651
ST ALBANS RD
REYNOLDS CRES
GIBBONS CL
Harefield
WOODCOCK HILL
Mast
Fairfolds
Fairfold's Farm

10
Sandridge

| 16 | A | B | 17 | C | D | 18 | E | F |

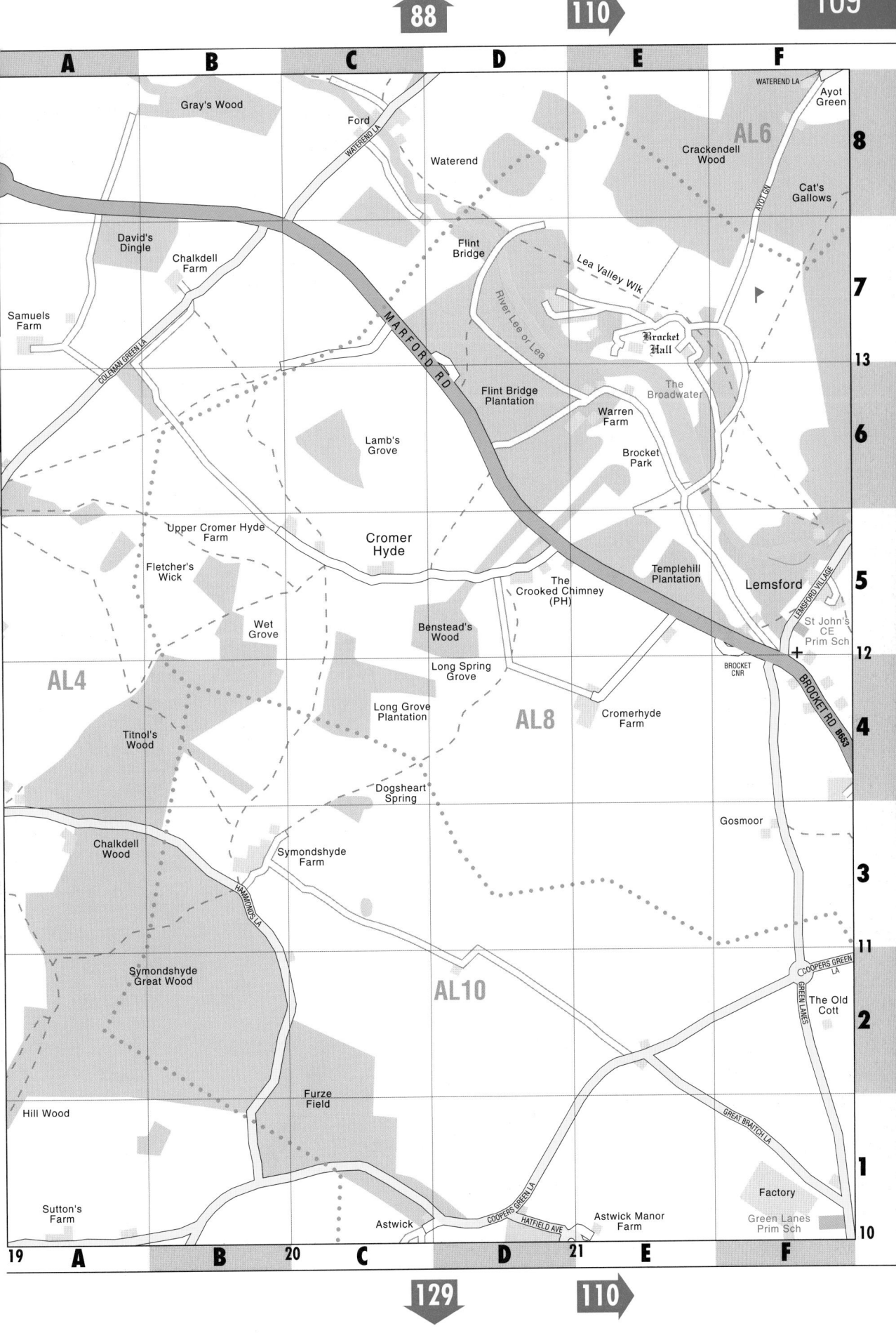

A B C D E F

WATEREND LA

Gray's Wood

Ford

Waterend

AL6

Crackendell
Wood

Ayot
Green

Cat's
Gallows

8

David's
Dingle

Chalkdell
Farm

Flint
Bridge

Lea Valley Wlk

AYOT LN

7

Samuels
Farm

MARFORD RD

River Lee or Lea

Brocket
Hall

13

COLEMAN GREEN LA

Flint Bridge
Plantation

The
Broadwater

Warren
Farm

6

Lamb's
Grove

Brocket
Park

Upper Cromer Hyde
Farm

Cromer
Hyde

Templehill
Plantation

Lemsford

5

Fletcher's
Wick

The Crooked Chimney
(PH)

LEMSFORD VILLAGE

St John's
CE
Prim Sch

12

AL4

Wet
Grove

Benstead's
Wood

BROCKET
CNR

+

Long Spring
Grove

Cromerhyde
Farm

Titnol's
Wood

Long Grove
Plantation

AL8

BROCKET RD B653

4

Dogsheart
Spring

Gosmoor

Chalkdell
Wood

Symondshyde
Farm

3

HAMMONDS LA

COOPERS GREEN
LA

11

Symondshyde
Great Wood

AL10

GREEN LANES

The Old
Cott

2

Furze
Field

Hill Wood

GREAT BRAITCH LA

1

Sutton's
Farm

Astwick

COOPERS GREEN LA

HATFIELD AVE

Astwick Manor
Farm

Factory

Green Lanes
Prim Sch

10

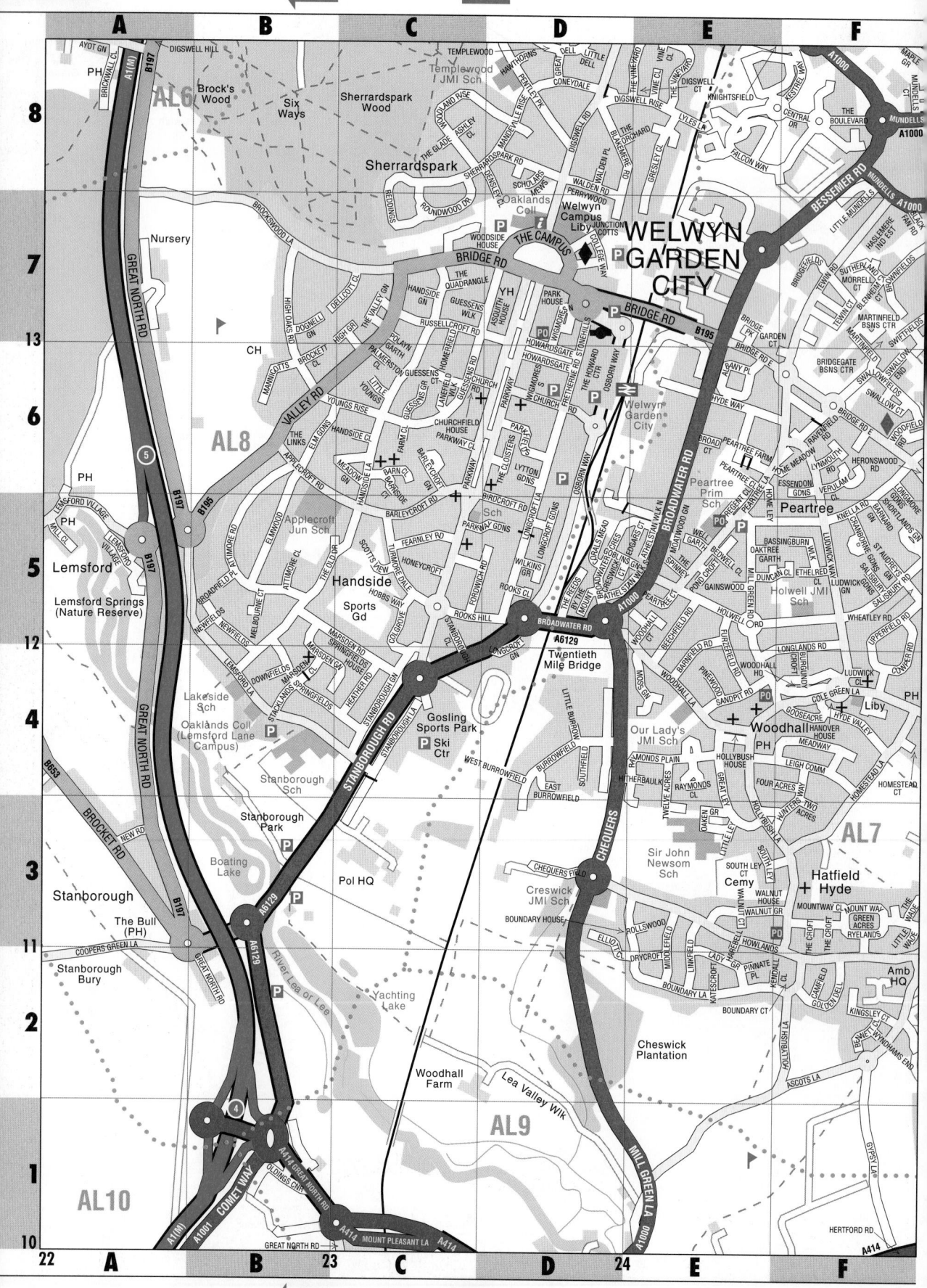

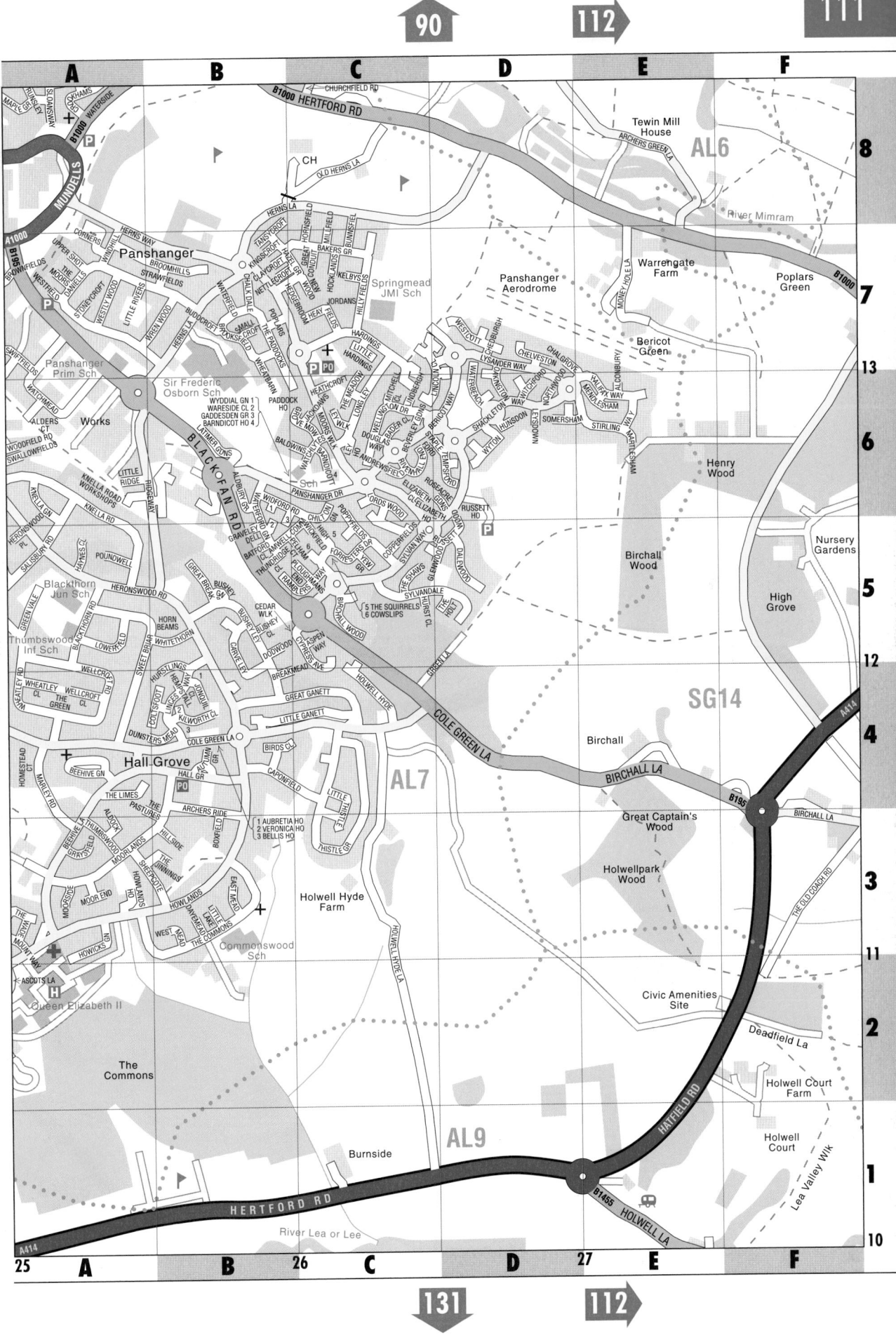

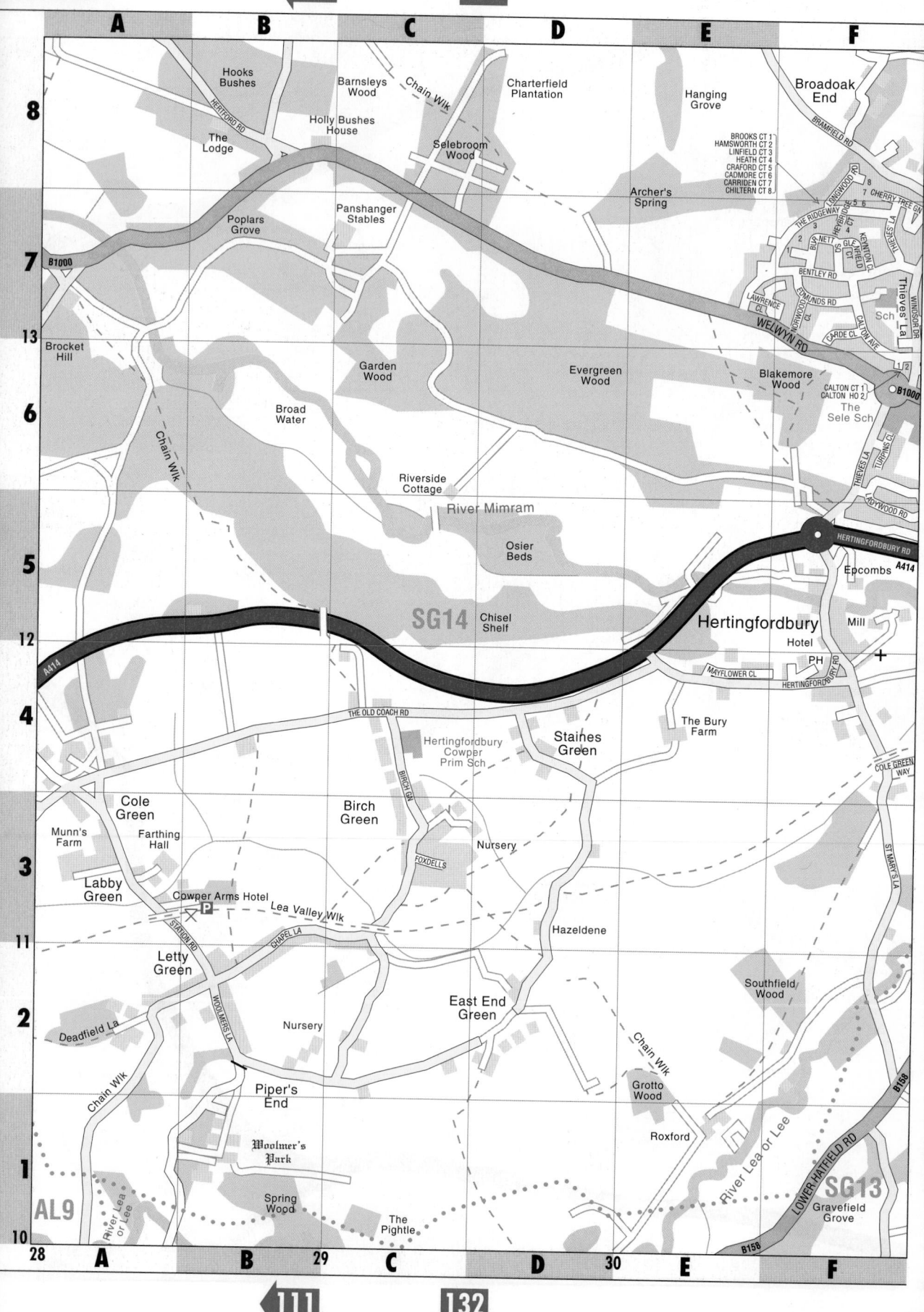

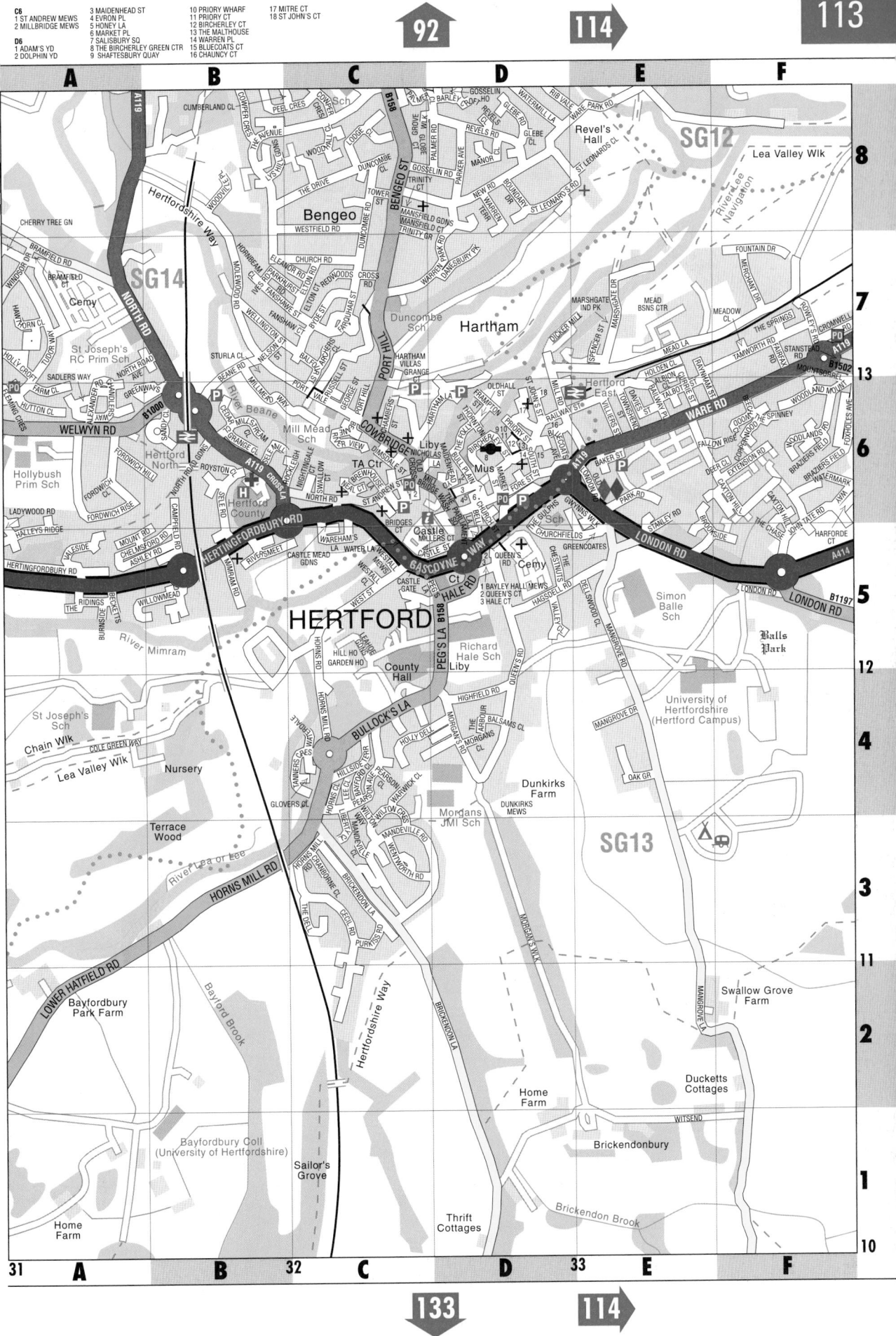

C6
1 ST ANDREW MEWS
2 MILLBRIDGE MEWS

D6
1 ADAM'S YD
2 DOLPHIN YD

3 MAIDENHEAD ST
4 EVRON PL
5 HONEY LA
6 MARKET PL
7 SALISBURY SQ
8 THE BIRCHERLEY GREEN CTR
9 SHAFTESBURY QUAY

10 PRIORY WHARF
11 PRIORY CT
12 BIRCHERLEY CT
13 THE MALTHOUSE
14 WARREN PL
15 BLUECOATS CT
16 CHAUNCY CT

17 MITRE CT
18 ST JOHN'S CT

A B C D E F

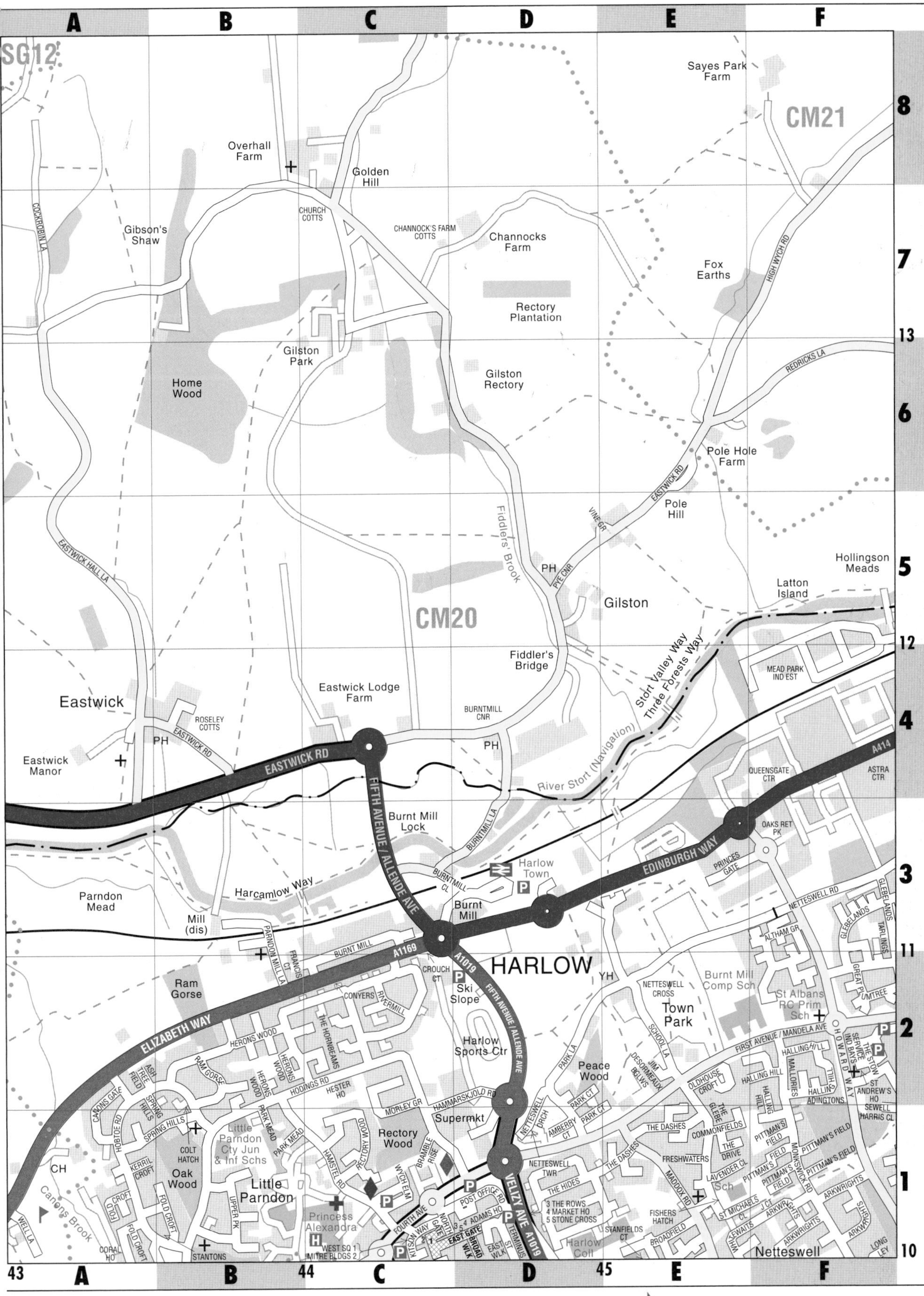

SG12

CM21
Sayes Park
Farm

Overhall
Farm

Golden
Hill

Gibson's
Shaw

CHURCH
COTTS

CHANNOCK'S FARM
COTTS

Channocks
Farm

Fox
Earths

HIGH WYCH RD

Gilston Park
Park

Home
Wood

Rectory
Plantation

Gilston
Rectory

REDRICKS LA

EASTWICK HALL LA

Pole Hole
Farm

Pole
Hill

EASTWICK RD

VINE GT

Hollingson
Meads

Fiddlers' Brook

PH
PYE CNR

CM20

Gilston

Latton
Island

Fiddler's
Bridge

Stort Valley Way
Three Forests Way

Mead Park
Ind Est

Eastwick

ROSELEY
COTTS

EASTWICK RD

Eastwick Lodge
Farm

BURNTMILL
CNR

PH

A414

PH

QUEENSGATE
CTR

ASTRA
CTR

Eastwick
Manor

EASTWICK RD

FIFTH AVENUE / ALLENDE AVE

Burnt Mill
Lock

River Stort (Navigation)

Edinburgh Way

PRINCES
GATE

OAKS RET
PK

Parndon
Mead

Harcamlow Way

BURNTMILL LA

BURNTMILL
CL

Harlow Town

NETTESWELL RD

Mill
(dis)

BURNT MILL

A1169

Burnt
Mill

A1019

HARLOW

YH

NETTESWELL
CROSS

Burnt Mill
Comp Sch

ALTHAM GR

Ram
Gorse

PARNDON MILL LA

FRANCIS

RIVERMILL

CONYERS

CROUCH
CT

Ski
Slope

FIFTH AVENUE / ALLENDE AVE

Town
Park

St Albans
RC Prim
Sch

Elizabeth Way

HERONS WOOD

THE HORNBEAMS

Harlow
Sports Ctr

Peace
Wood

PARK LA

SCHOOL LA

FIRST AVENUE

MANDELA AVE

HALLING HILL

HANDKERCHIEF

MALLORES

ST
ANDREW'S
HO

Little
Parndon
Cty Jun
& Inf Schs

Rectory
Wood

HAMMARSKJOLD RD

Supermkt

NETTESWELL TWR

THE DASHES

COMMONFIELDS

FRESHWATERS

THE
DRIVE

PITTMAN'S
FIELD

PITTMAN'S FIELD

Oak
Wood

Little
Parndon

Princess
Alexandra

POST OFFICE RD

VELIZY AVE

THE HIDES

3 THE ROWS
4 MARKET HO
5 STONE CROSS

FISHERS
HATCH

ARKWRIGHTS

CH

Canons Brook

WEST SQ 1
MITRE BLDGS 2

EAST GATE
BROAD
WLK

A1019

Harlow
Coll

STANFIELDS
CT

BROADFIELD

Netteswell

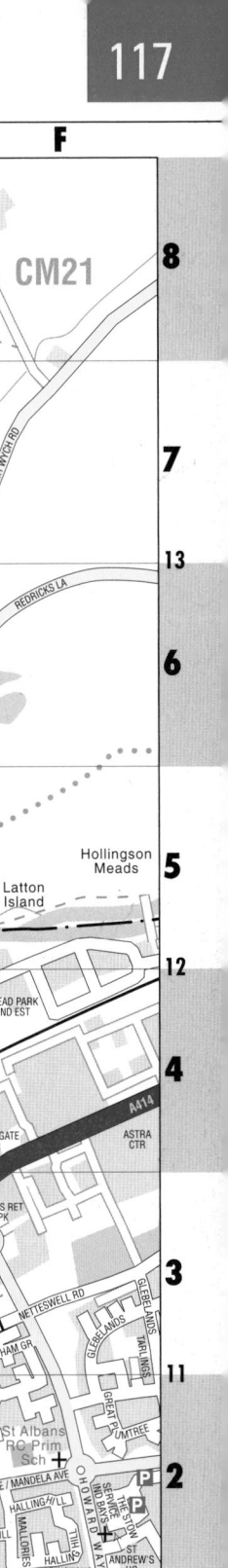

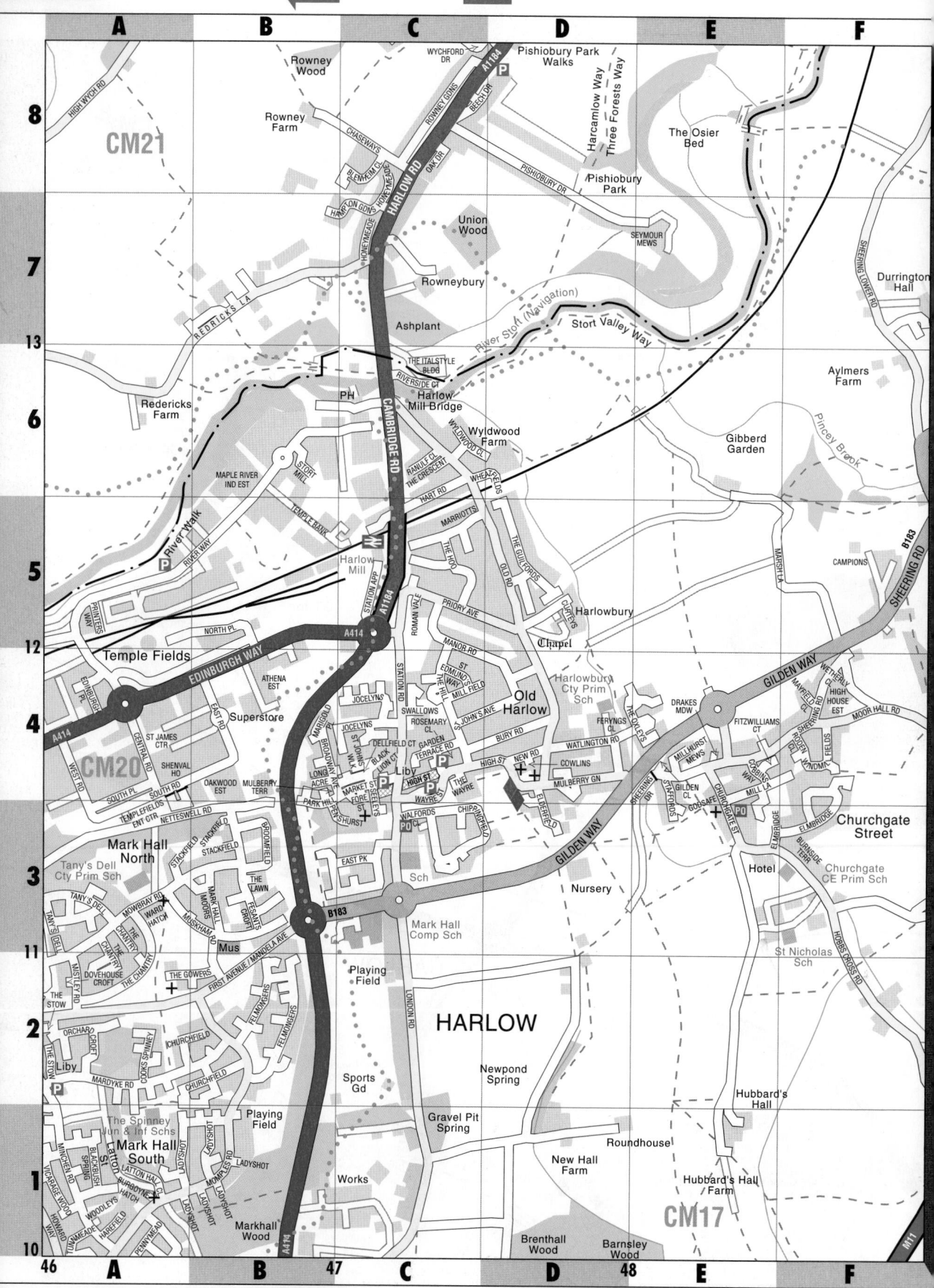

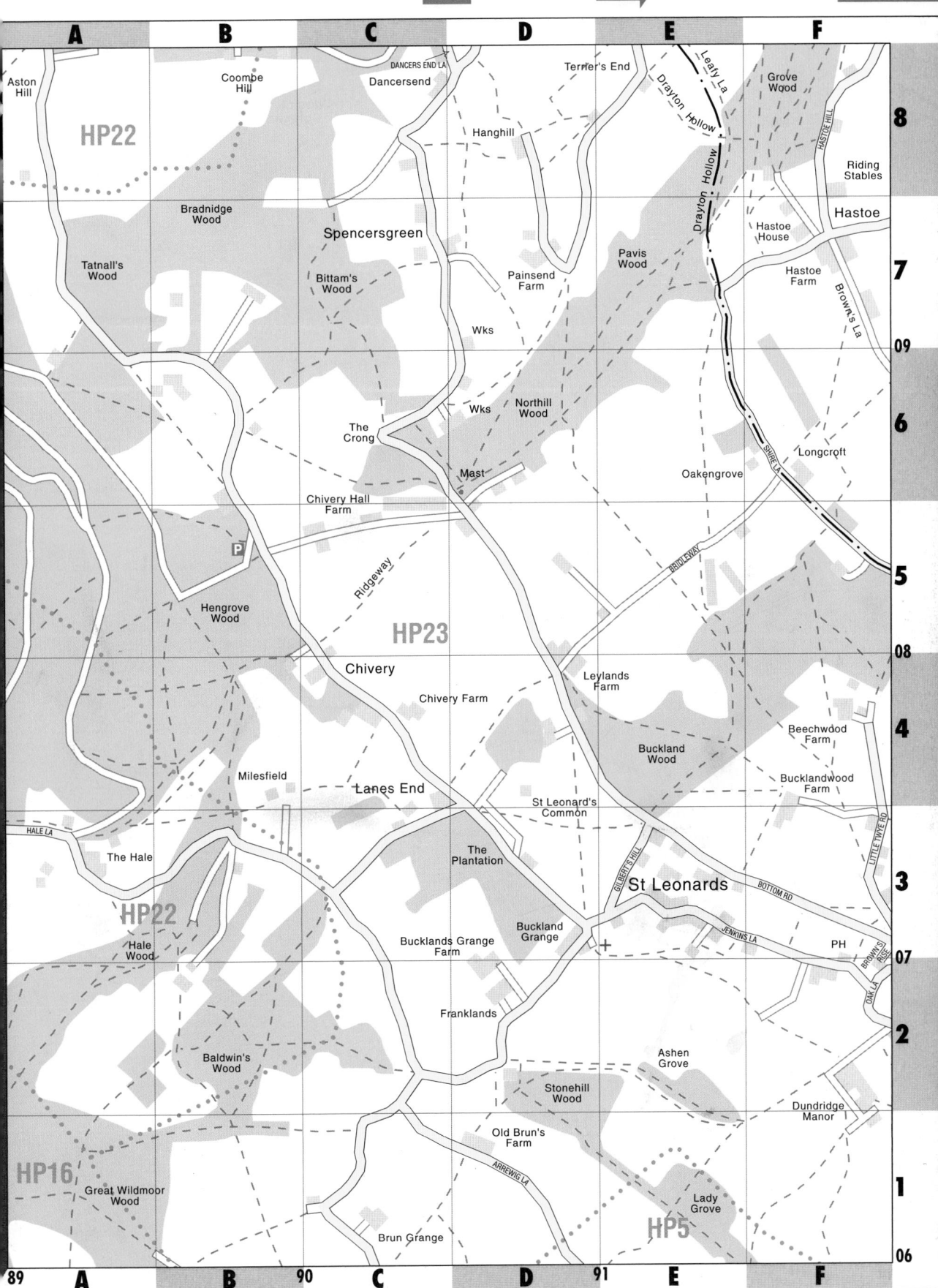

Aston Hill

HP22

Coombe Hill

DANCERS END LA
Dancersend

Hanghill

Terrier's End

Leafy La
Drayton Hollow

Grove Wood

8

Bradnidge Wood

Spencersgreen

Painsend Farm

Pavis Wood

Drayton Hollow

Riding Stables

HASTOE HILL

Hastoe

Tatnall's Wood

Bittam's Wood

Hastoe House

Hastoe Farm

7

Brown's La

Wks

09

The Crong

Wks

Northill Wood

SHIRE LA

Longcroft

6

Mast

Oakengrove

Chivery Hall Farm

Ridgeway

BRIDLEWAY

5

P

Hengrove Wood

HP23

08

Chivery

Chivery Farm

Leylands Farm

Beechwood Farm

4

Milesfield

Lanes End

St Leonard's Common

Buckland Wood

Bucklandwood Farm

LITTLE TWYE RD

HALE LA

The Hale

The Plantation

Buckland Grange

St Leonards

GILBERT'S HILL

BOTTOM RD

3

HP22

Hale Wood

Bucklands Grange Farm

JENKINS LA

PH

07

BROWN'S RISE

OAK LA

Franklands

Ashen Grove

2

Baldwin's Wood

Stonehill Wood

Dundridge Manor

HP16

Old Brun's Farm

ARREWIG LA

HP5

1

Great Wildmoor Wood

Lady Grove

06

Brun Grange

A   B   C   D   E   F

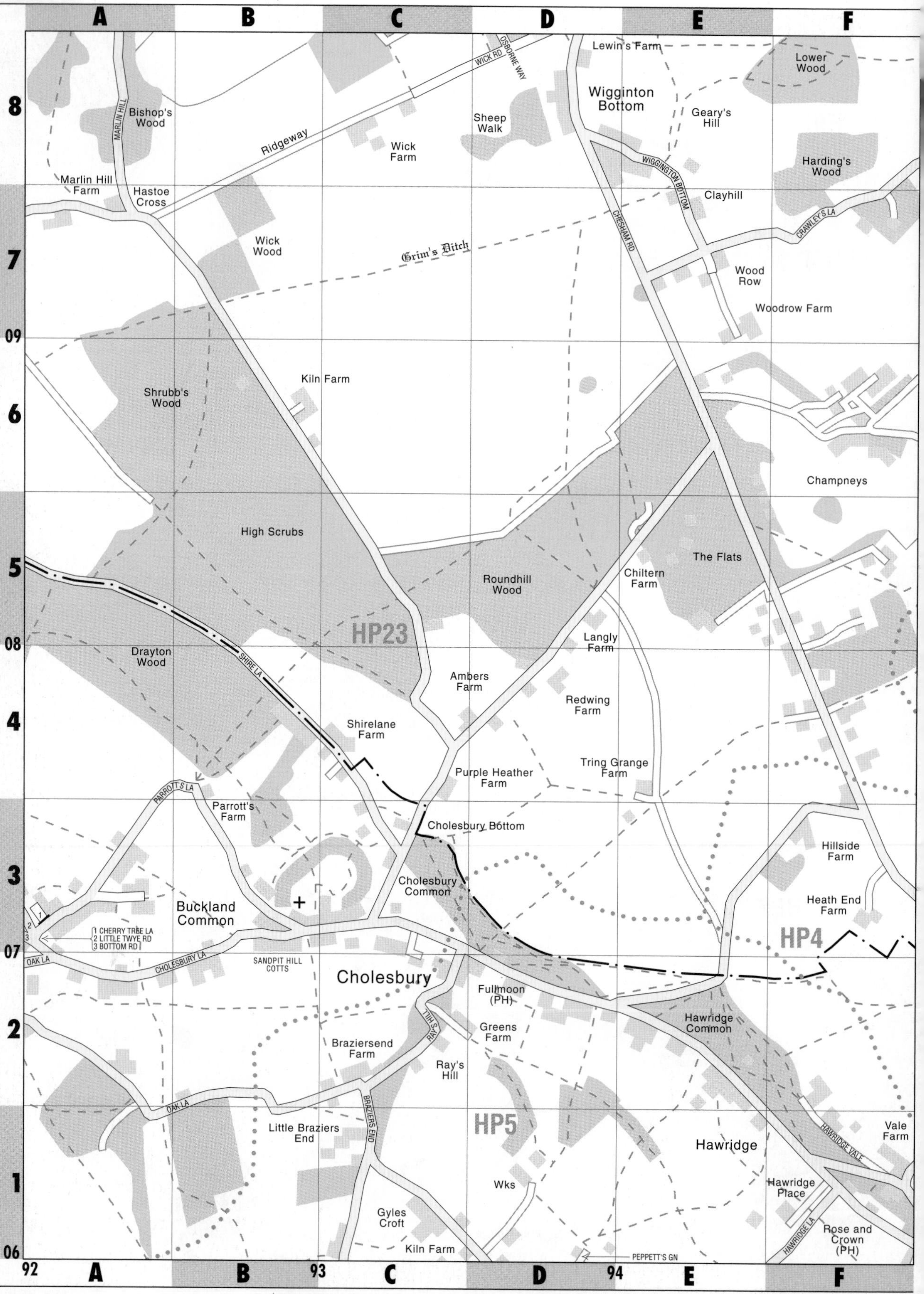

8
Bishop's Wood
Marlin Hill
Lewin's Farm
Wigginton Bottom
Geary's Hill
Lower Wood
WICK RD
OSBORNE WAY
Wick Farm
Sheep Walk
Harding's Wood

Marlin Hill Farm
Hastoe Cross
Ridgeway
Wick Wood
Grim's Ditch
WIGGINTON BOTTOM
CHESHAM RD
Clayhill
CRAWLEY'S LA
Wood Row

7

09
Shrubb's Wood
Kiln Farm
Woodrow Farm

6
Champneys

High Scrubs
The Flats

5
Roundhill Wood
Chiltern Farm
SHIRE LA

08
Drayton Wood
Langly Farm

4
Shirelane Farm
Ambers Farm
Redwing Farm
Tring Grange Farm

Parrott's Farm
PARROTT'S LA
Purple Heather Farm
Cholesbury Bottom
Hillside Farm

3
Buckland Common
Cholesbury Common
Heath End Farm
HP4

07
1 CHERRY TREE LA
2 LITTLE TWYE RD
3 BOTTOM RD
OAK LA
CHOLESBURY LA
SANDPIT HILL COTTS
Cholesbury
Fullmoon (PH)
Hawridge Common

2
Braziersend Farm
TILE KILN RD
Greens Farm
Ray's Hill

Little Braziers End
OAK LA
BRAZIERS END
HP5
Hawridge
HAWRIDGE VALE
Vale Farm

1
Wks
Hawridge Place
Gyles Croft
HAWRIDGE LA
Rose and Crown (PH)

06
Kiln Farm
PEPPETT'S GN

92   A   B   93   C   D   94   E   F

HP23

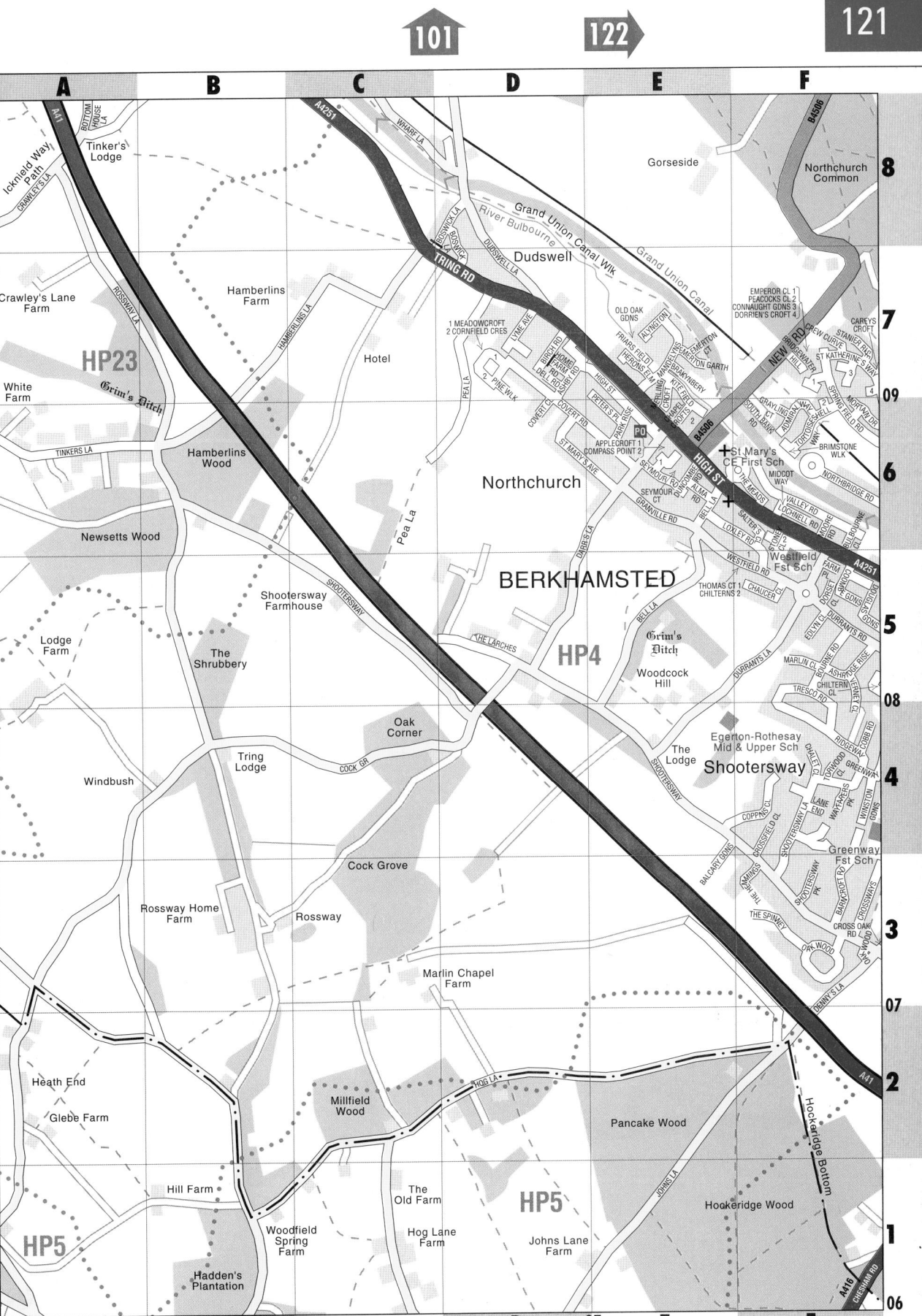

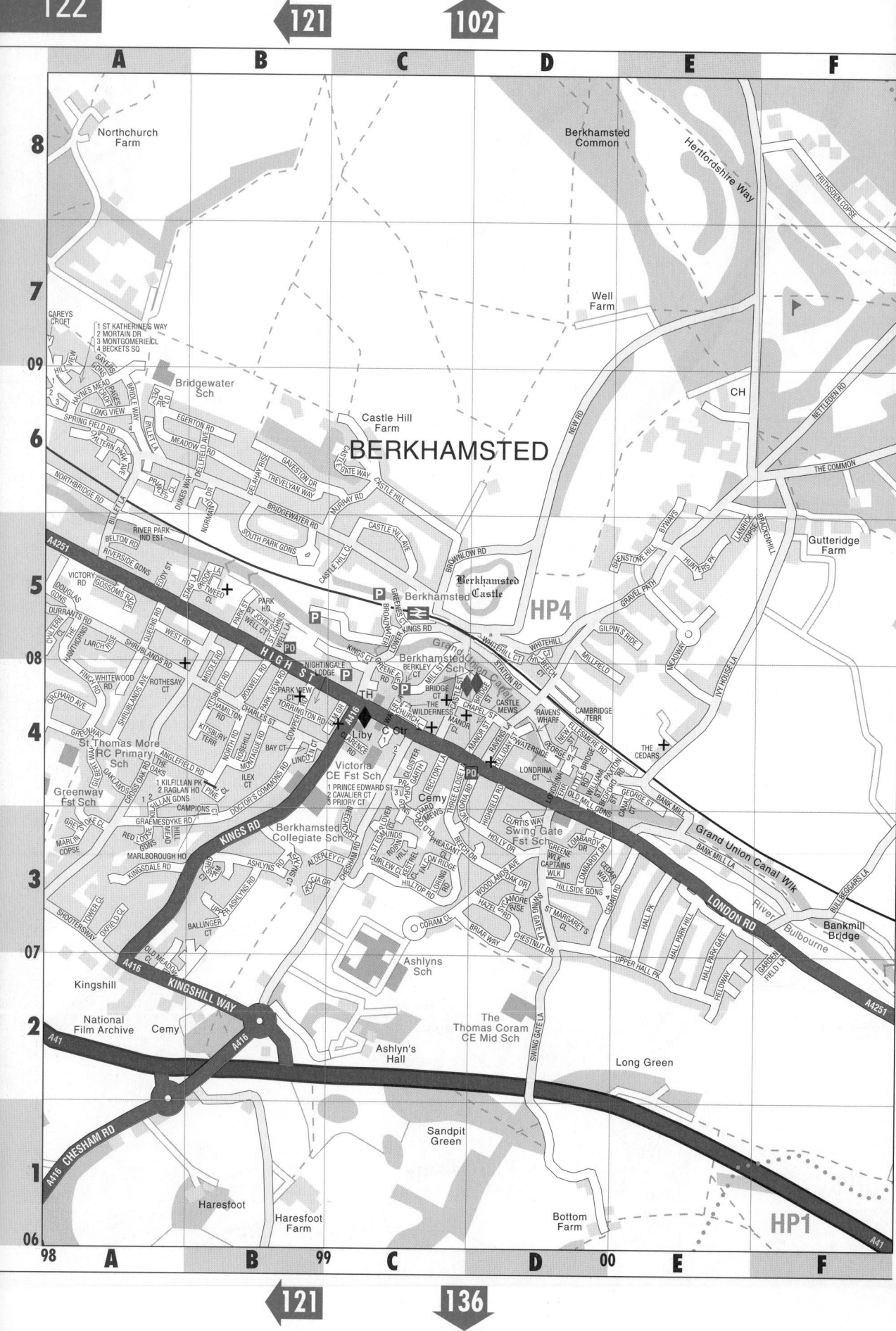

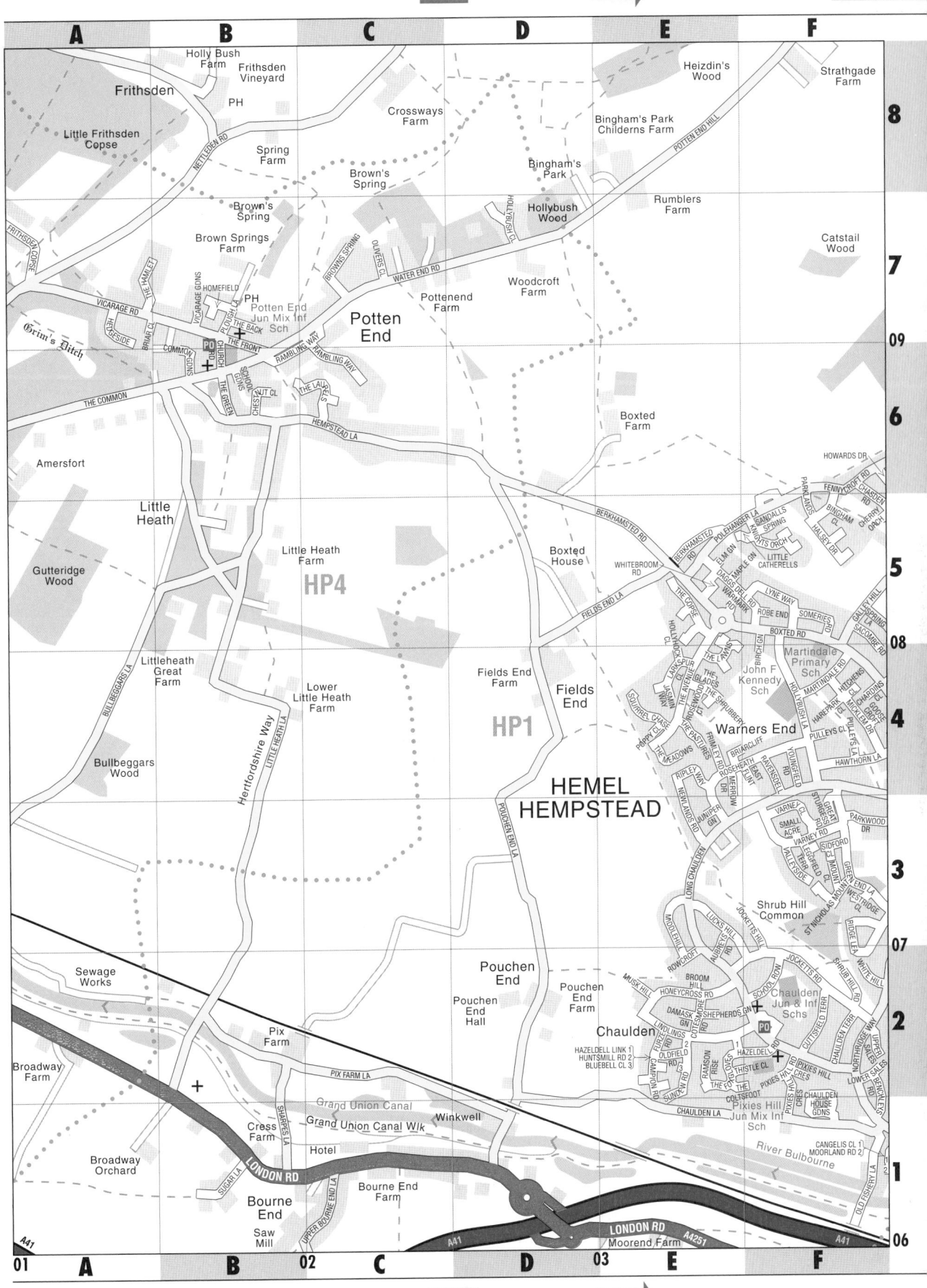

103
124
137
124

A B C D E F

8

Holly Bush Farm
Frithsden Vineyard
PH
Heizdin's Wood
Strathgade Farm
Little Frithsden Copse
Frithsden
Spring Farm
Crossways Farm
Bingham's Park Childerns Farm
POTTEN END HILL

NETTLEDEN RD

Brown's Spring
Bingham's Park
Rumblers Farm
7
Brown's Spring
Brown Springs Farm
Hollybush Wood
Catstail Wood

FRITHSDEN COPSE
BROWNS SPRING
OLIVERS CL
WATER END RD
HOLLYBUSH CL

Woodcroft Farm
THE HAMLET
Homefield
VICARAGE GDNS
PH
Potten End Jun Mix Inf Sch
Pottenend Farm

VICARAGE RD
HIGH ST
THE BACK
BRIAR CL
PLOUGH LA
09
Grim's Ditch
PO
Potten End
THE FRONT
RAMBLING WAY
RAMBLING WAY

HOWARDS DR

SCHOOL GDNS
CHESTNUT CL
THE LAWES

CHURCH RD
THE GREEN
6
THE COMMON
HEMPSTEAD LA
Boxted Farm

FENNYCROFT RD
CHASDEN RD
PARKLANDS

Amersfort

BERKHAMSTED RD

SANDALLS SPRING
ELM GN
POLCHANGER LA
ROOTS ORCH
DACRE MAPLE GN
CHERRY ORCH
BINGHAM CL
HALSEY DR
Little Heath
Boxted House
WHITEBROOM RD
LITTLE CATHERELLS
5

Gutteridge Wood
Little Heath Farm
HP4
BERKHAMSTED RD

THE COPSE
WARLAND
DAGS DELL RD
ROBE END
BOXTED RD
LYNE WAY
SOMERIES
GALLEY HILL
SACOMBE RD
08

FIELDS END RD

Martindale Primary Sch

Littleheath Great Farm
HOLLANDS CL
LARKSPUR CL
THE GLADE
THE SHRUBBERY
BIRCH GN
John F Kennedy Sch
MARTINDALE RD
HITCHENS
CHARDINS
4
Lower Little Heath Farm
Fields End Farm
Fields End
JASMIN CL
THE AVENUE
ROSEWOOD DR
FINLEY CT RD
HAREPARK
BICKERTON
PULLEYS LA
Warners End

HERTFORDSHIRE WAY
LITTLE HEATH LA
BULLBEGGARS LA
SQUIRREL CHASE
POPPY CL
THE MEADOWS
BRIARCLIFF
RAVENSTHILL
PULLEYS CL
HAWTHORN LA

HEMEL HEMPSTEAD
HP1
RIPLEY WAY
NEWLANDS RD
ROSEHEATH
MERROW
YOUNGFIELD
Bullbeggars Wood

JUNIPER GN
VARNEY RD
GREAT STURGESS RD
PARKWOOD DR
3
POUCHEN END LA
VARNEY CL
SMALL ACRE
VARNEY RD
SIDFORD
LEGFIELD
GREEN END LA
WESTRIDGE
07
Shrub Hill Common
LONG CHAULDEN
VALE SIDE
ST NICHOLAS MOUNT
RIDGE LEA
WHITE CROSS

Sewage Works

ROWCROFT
BROOM HILL
AUBREYS RD
JOCKETTS RD
SHRUB HILL RD
2
Pix Farm
MUSK HILL
HONEYCROSS RD
SCHOOL ROW
Chaulden Jun & Inf Schs
COTTSFIELD TERR
UPPER SALES

DAMASK GN
SHEPHERDS GN
LINDLINGS
PO
CHAULDEN TERR
NORTHRIDGE RD
Pouchen End
Pouchen End Hall
Pouchen End Farm
Chaulden
OLDFIELD
COTTSFIELD
HAZELDELL
PIXIES HILL CRES
LOWER SALES

PIX FARM LA
HAZELDELL LINK 1
HUNTSMILL RD 2
BLUEBELL CL 3
CAMPION RD
RAMSON RISE
THE CLOVES
THISTLE CL
PIXIES HILL RD
CHAULDEN HOUSE GDNS

Broadway Farm
Grand Union Canal
Winkwell
SUNDEW RD
COLTSFOOT
CHAULDEN LA
Pixies Hill Jun Mix Inf Sch
CANGELIS CL 1
MOORLAND RD 2
1
Grand Union Canal Wlk
River Bulbourne
Cress Farm
Hotel

SHARPES LA
SUGAR LA
LONDON RD
UPPER BOURNE END LA

Bourne End
Broadway Orchard
Saw Mill
Bourne End Farm
LONDON RD
A4251
Moorend Farm
OLD FISHERY LA

A41
01 A B 02 C D 03 E F
A41
A41
A4251
06

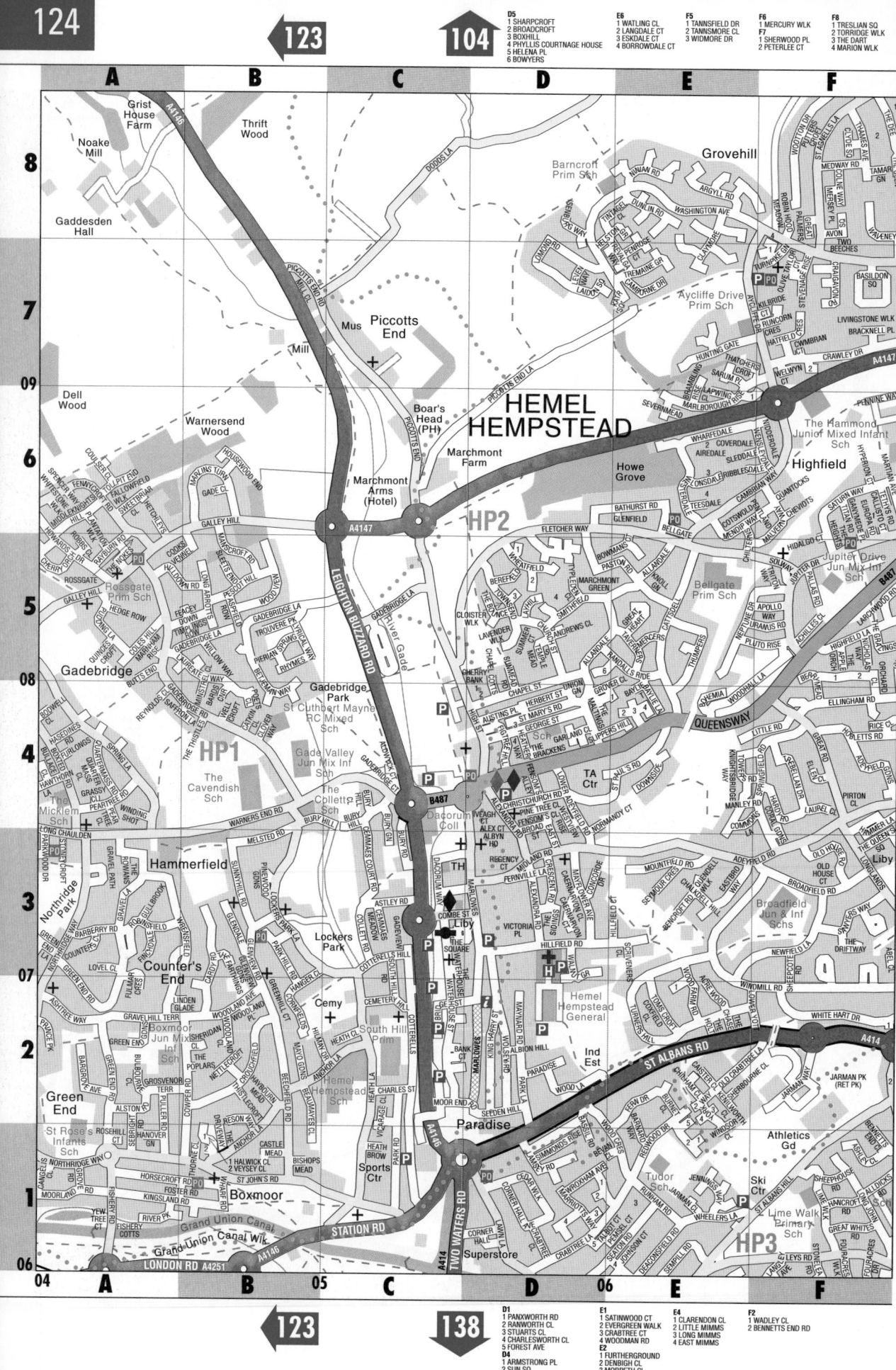

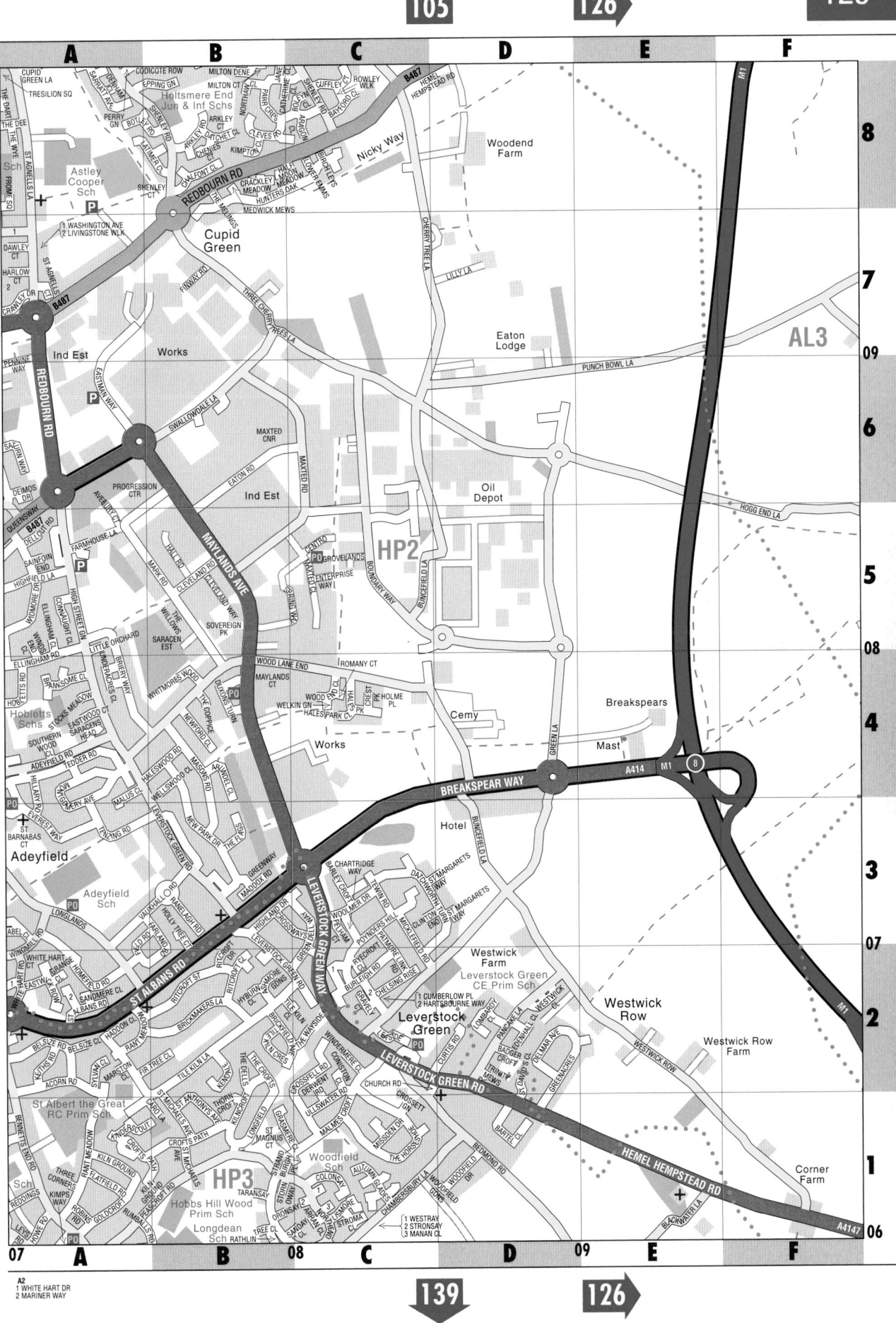

125
106

A   B   C   D   E   F

8

HILL FARM LA
Hill Farm

New Jerome
Cottage

A5183

Hertfordshire Way

7

PUNCH BOWL LA

Baker's
Farm

Shafford
Farm

09

Southend
Farm

Hogg
End

Whitehedge
Spring

REDBOURN RD

Bow
Bridge

6

Beech
Hyde

HOGG END LA

Old
Jeromes

River Ver

Butlers
Farm

Maynes
Farm

A5183

5

Kettlewell's
Farm

Kentish
Wood

Windmillhill
Wood

AL3

08

The
Vistas

Gorhambury

Shepherds
Cottages

4

Bruce's
Plantation

Gorhambury
(remains of)

HP2

Cypress
Wood

Brickkiln
Wood

Lord Bacon's
Mount

3

Temple
Cottage

Temple
Wood

Prae Wood
House

07

Stud
Cottages

Praewood
Farm

Prae Wood

2

M1

Westwick
Hall

Square
Wood

A4147

BEECHTREE LA

Hill End
Farm

7

1

M1

M10

HP3

HEMEL HEMPSTEAD RD

HP2

AL2

A4147

BEDMOND LA

MAYNE PL VE
SAMB
FLAVIAN CL
ARKETING
LIN VITA

POTTERSCROU LA

FLAVIAN CL
HADRIAN
CL

IGN
CL

AKEMAN CL 1
MEAUTYS 2

06

10   A   B   11   C   D   12   E   F

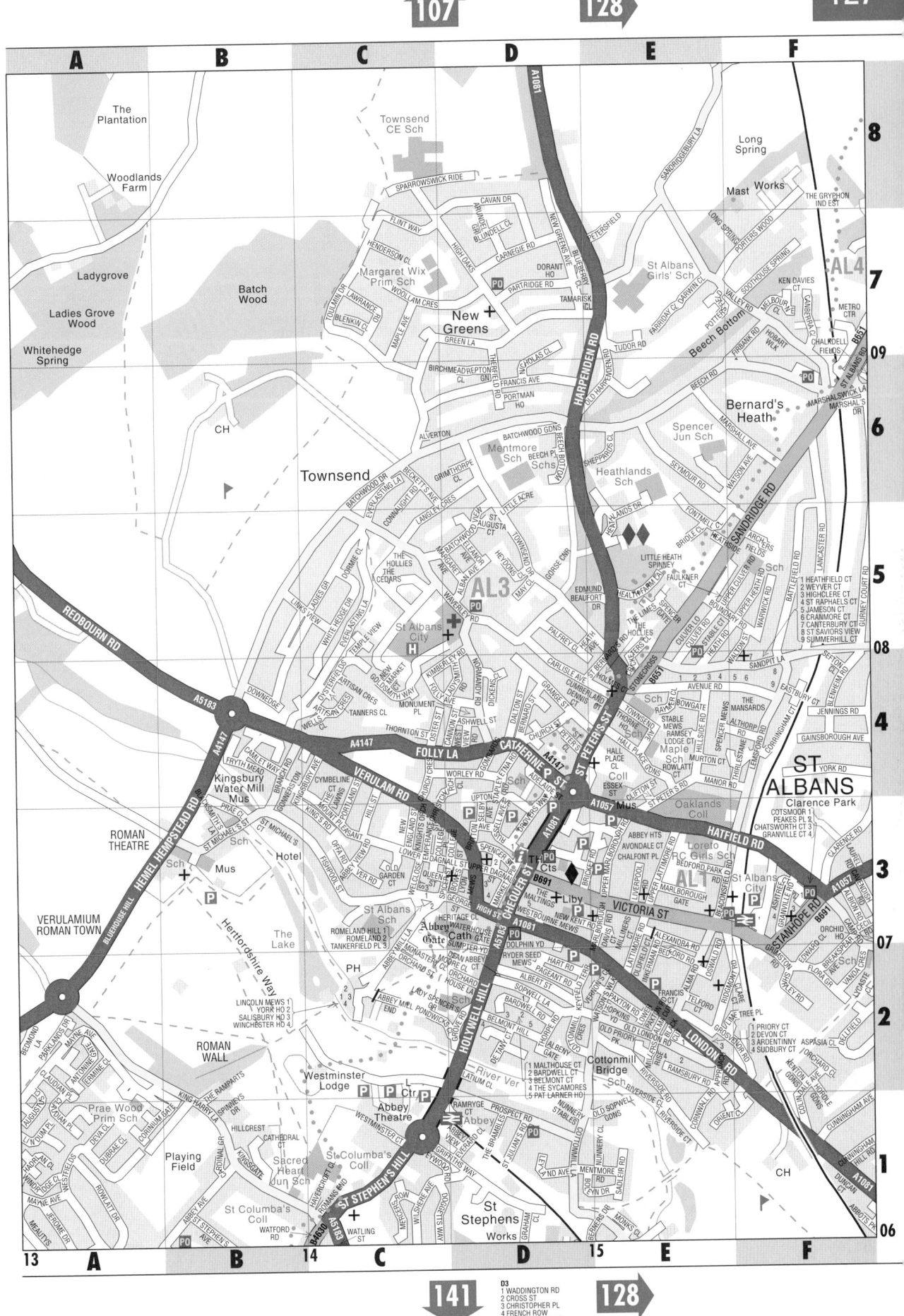

A B C D E F

8

7

09

6

5

08

4

3

07

2

1

06

13 A B 14 C D 15 E F

D3
1 WADDINGTON RD
2 CROSS ST
3 CHRISTOPHER PL
4 FRENCH ROW
5 HALF MOON MEWS

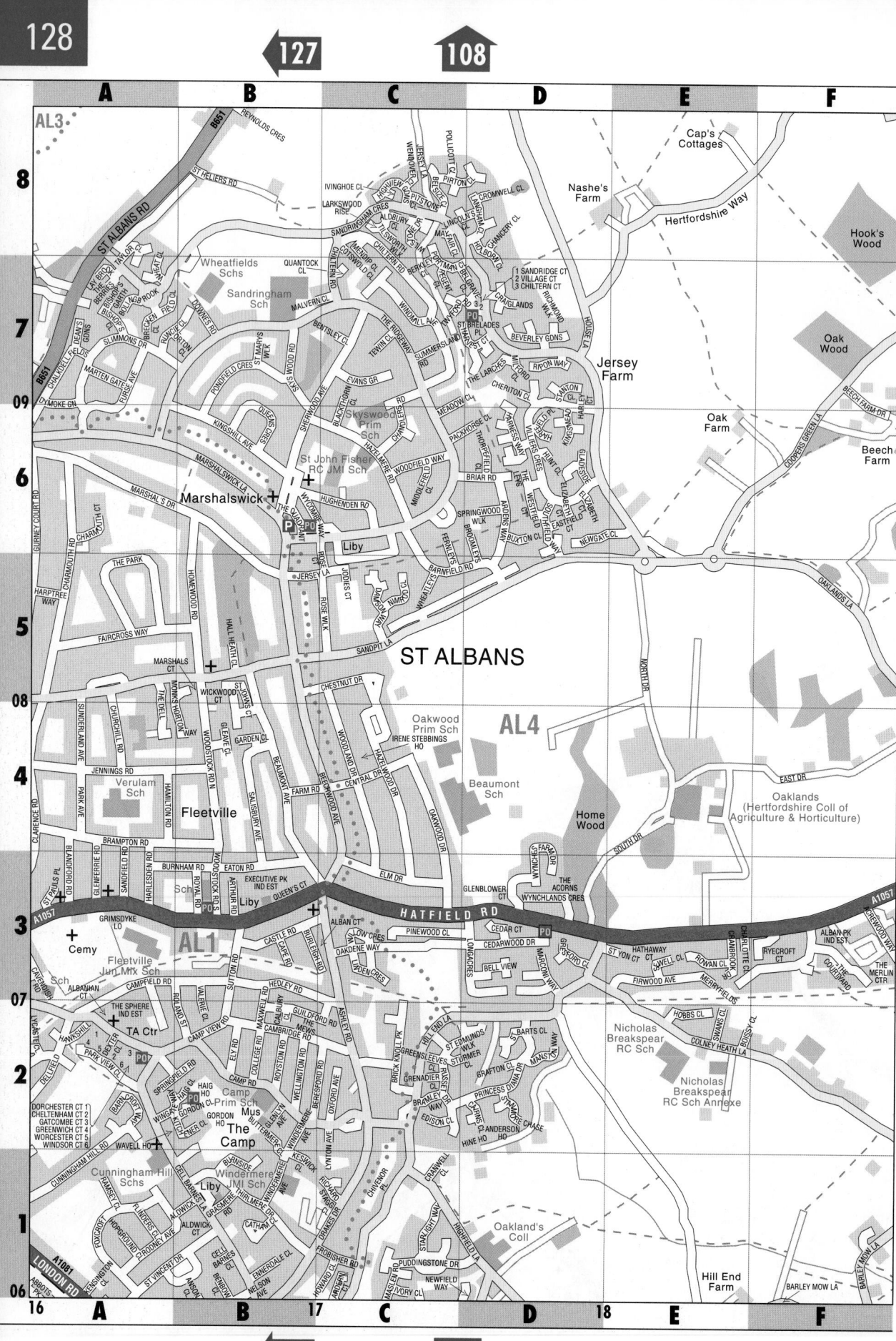

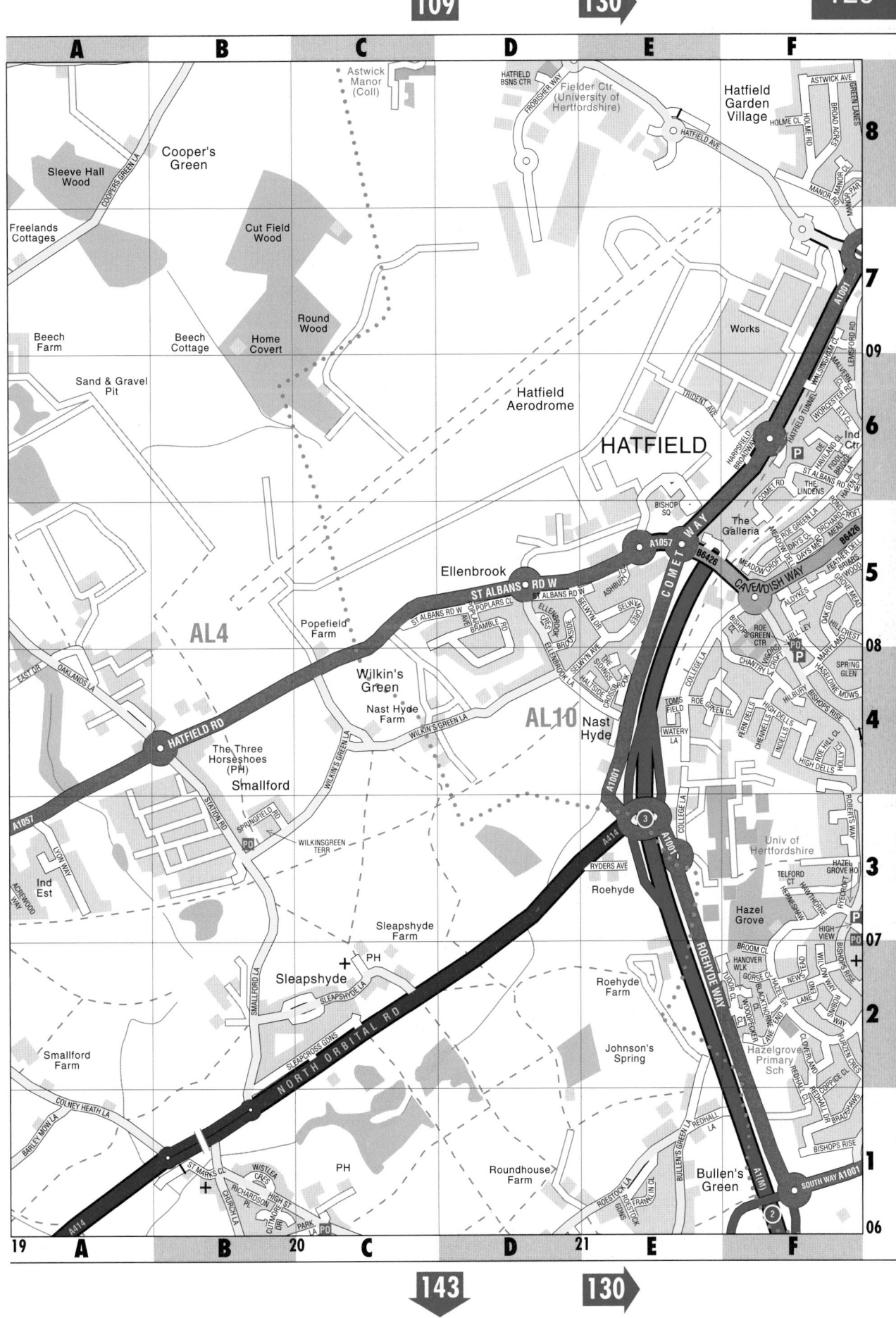

130

A6
1 QUEENSWAY HO
2 BROOMFIELD CT
3 LOTHAIR CT
4 GALLEYCROFT CT

◄ 129

110 ►

HATFIELD

A B C D E F

8

7

09

6

5

08

4

3

07

2

1

06

AL10

AL9

A2
1 ALMOND WLK
2 ROWAN WLK
3 GEAN WLK
4 SCHOLARS WLK
5 HAZEL GR
6 SHALLCROSS CRES
7 FURZEN CRES
8 STRAWBERRY FIELD

A3
1 LINNET WLK
2 MAGPIE WLK
B3
1 KINGSMILL CT
2 ALLEN CT
3 HAMILTON CT
4 RICHMOND CT

A B C D E F

B1455 HOLWELL LA B1455
Holwell Manor
Holwell Bridge
B158

Lea Valley Wlk

LOW RD 8

Essendonbury Farm

Lodge

SG13 7

Hillend Farm

Ox Wood

ESSENDON HILL

Larkinshill Grove

Parsonage 09

Hillend Cottages

THE TERRACE

Essendon 6

HANBURY COTTS

GLEBE CL
GLEBE CO
GLEBE HO
EAST VIEW

The Furze Field

Lower Westend Farm

Salisbury Crest (PH)

RECTORY CL

SCHOOL LA
SCHOOL CL

Essendon CE Prim Sch

FORGE COTTS

Pollard Wood

Rose & Crown (PH)

Brickkiln Wood

West End

ROSE LA

The Candlestick (PH)

HIGH RD

5

08

Edwards Wood

Wellington Wood

AL9

Essendon Place

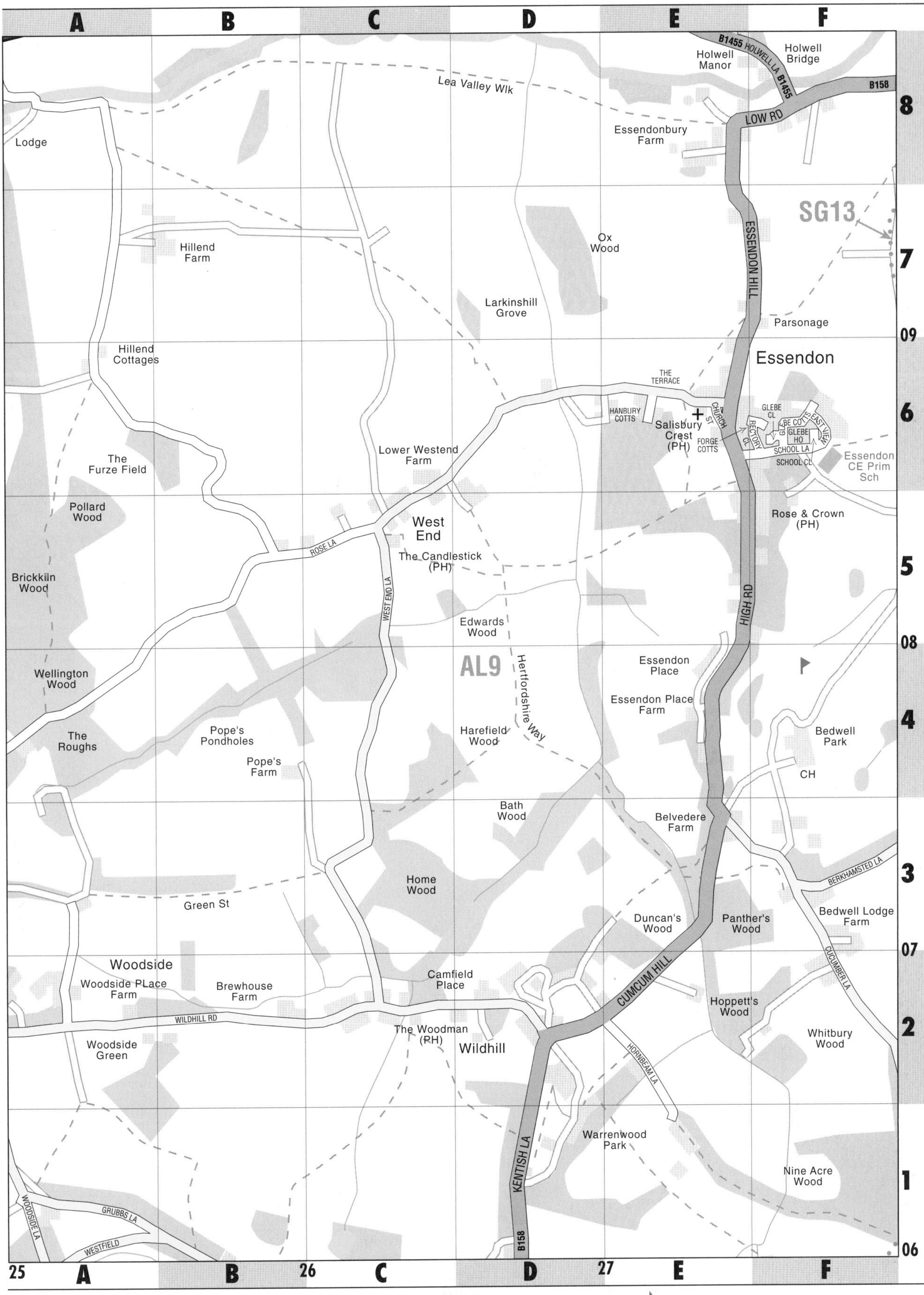

The Roughs

WEST END LA

Harefield Wood

Hertfordshire Way

Essendon Place Farm

Bedwell Park

4

Pope's Pondholes

CH

Pope's Farm

Bath Wood

Belvedere Farm

BERKHAMSTED LA

Home Wood

Green St

Duncan's Wood

Panther's Wood

Bedwell Lodge Farm

3

07

Woodside

CUMCUM HILL

Woodside PLace Farm

Brewhouse Farm

Camfield Place

Hoppett's Wood

Whitbury Wood

CUCUMBER LA

2

WILDHILL RD

The Woodman (PH)

Wildhill

HORNBEAM LA

Woodside Green

KENTISH LA

Warrenwood Park

Nine Acre Wood

1

WOODSIDE LA

GRUBBS LA

WESTFIELD

B158

06

25 A B 26 C D 27 E F

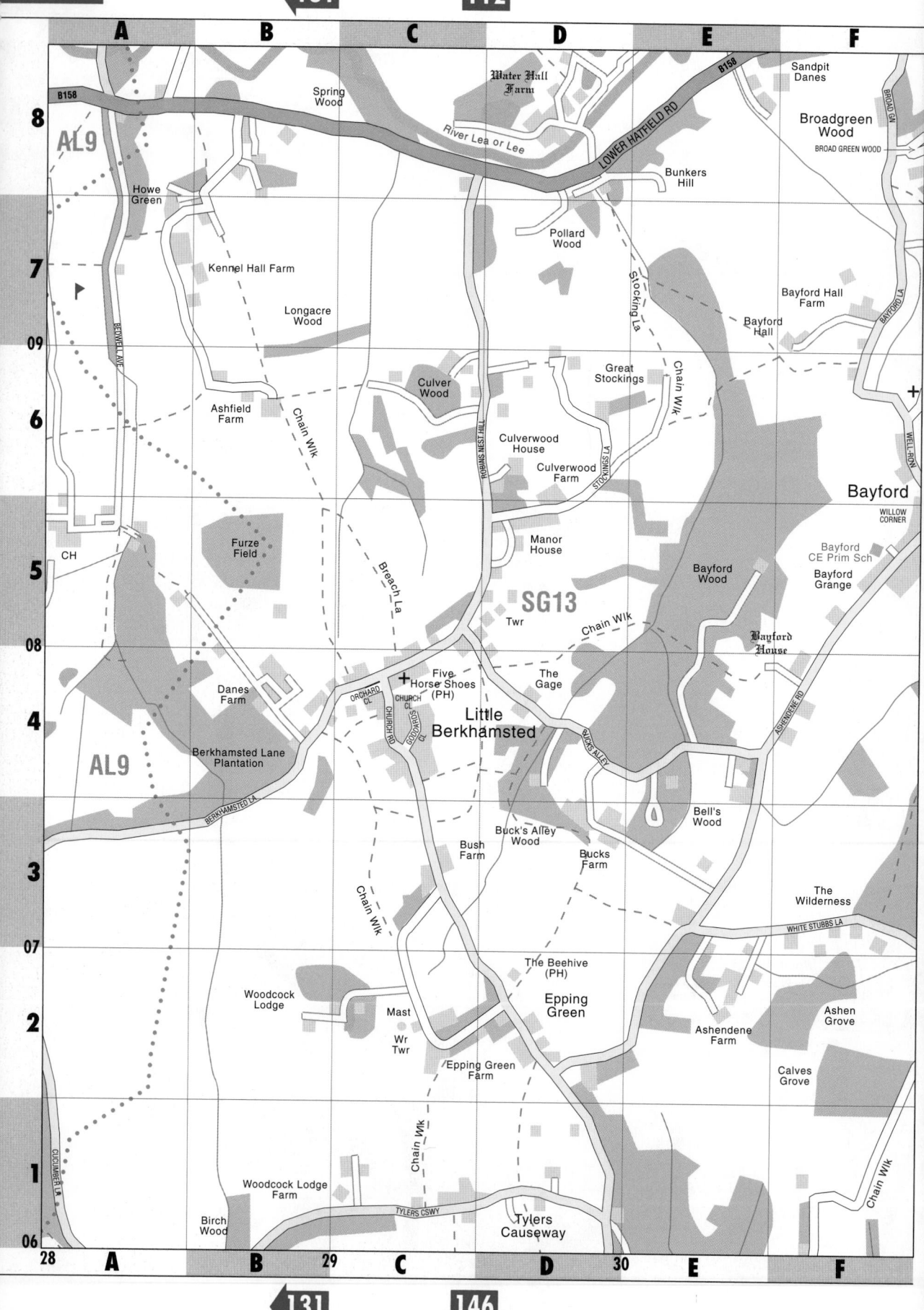

131
112
131
146

B158

AL9

Howe Green

Spring Wood

Water Hall Farm

River Lea or Lee

LOWER HATFIELD RD

B158

Sandpit Danes

Broadgreen Wood

BROAD GREEN WOOD

BROAD GN

Kennel Hall Farm

Longacre Wood

Pollard Wood

Bunkers Hill

Stocking La

Bayford Hall Farm

Bayford Hall

BAYFORD LA

09

Ashfield Farm

Chain Wlk

Culver Wood

Great Stockings

Chain Wlk

6

Culverwood House

Culverwood Farm

Bayford

WILLOW CORNER

WELL-RON

ROBINS NEST HILL

STOCKINGS LA

Manor House

Bayford Wood

Bayford CE Prim Sch

Bayford Grange

CH

Furze Field

Breach La

SG13

Twr

Chain Wlk

Bayford House

08

Danes Farm

AL9

Berkhamsted Lane Plantation

BERKHAMSTED LA

ORCHARD CL

CHURCH RD

CHURCH CL

STUBBS CL

Five Horse Shoes (PH)

Little Berkhamsted

The Gage

BUCKS ALLEY

ASHENGROVE RD

Bell's Wood

The Wilderness

WHITE STUBBS LA

07

Chain Wlk

Bush Farm

Buck's Alley Wood

Bucks Farm

3

The Beehive (PH)

Epping Green

Ashendene Farm

Ashen Grove

Woodcock Lodge

Mast

Wr Twr

Epping Green Farm

Calves Grove

Chain Wlk

Chain Wlk

Woodcock Lodge Farm

Birch Wood

TYLERS CSWY

Tylers Causeway

CUCUMBER LA

BESSWELL AVE

28

A

B

29

C

D

30

E

F

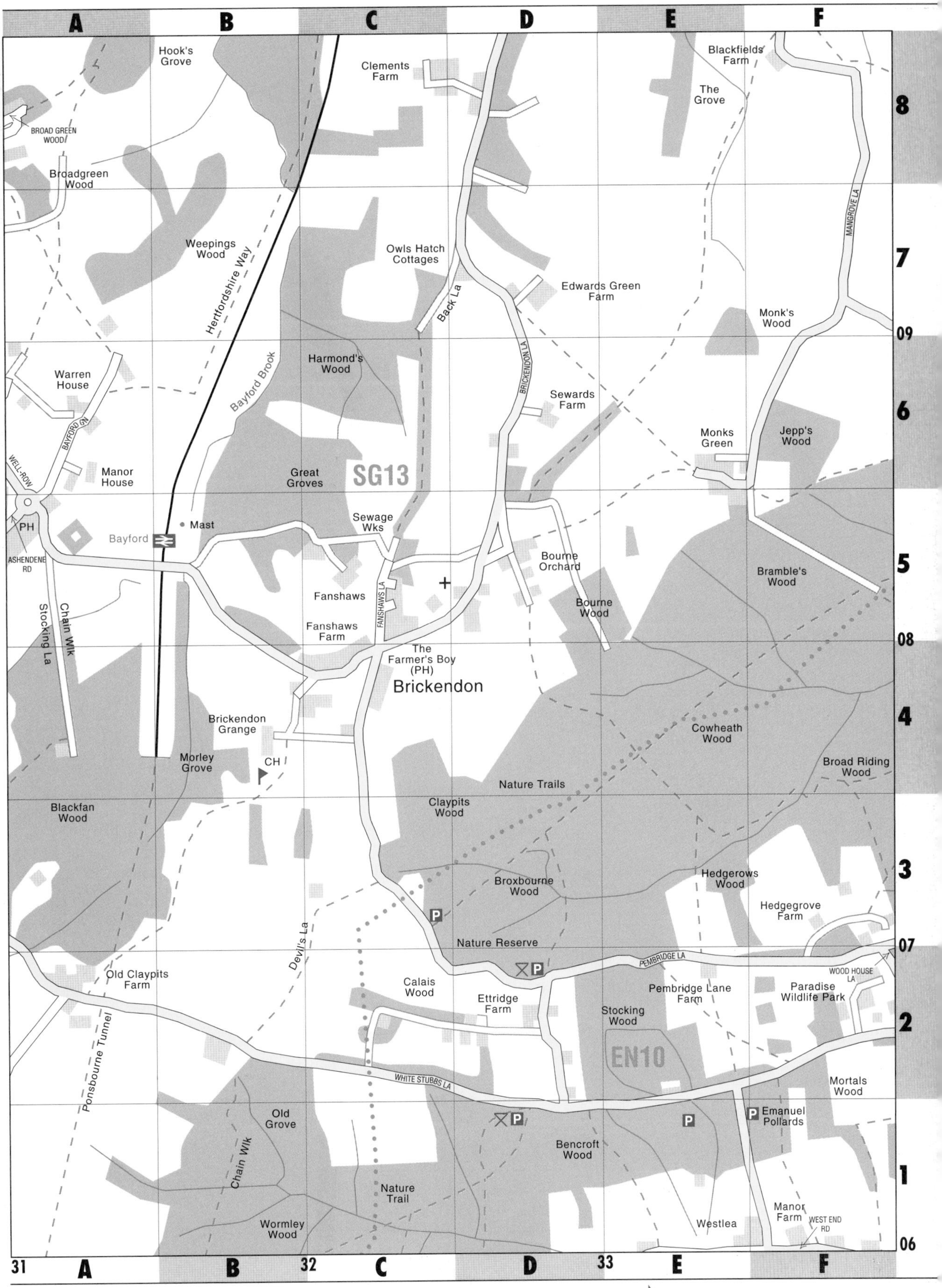

A   B   C   D   E   F

8

BROAD GREEN WOOD

Hook's Grove

Clements Farm

Blackfields' Farm

The Grove

Broadgreen Wood

7

Weepings Wood

Hertfordshire Way

Owls Hatch Cottages

Back La

Edwards Green Farm

Monk's Wood

MANGROVE LA

09

Warren House

Bayford Brook

Harmond's Wood

Brickendon La

Sewards Farm

Monks Green

Jepp's Wood

6

WELL-ROW

BAYFORD GN

Manor House

Great Groves

SG13

Sewage Wks

Bourne Orchard

Bramble's Wood

5

PH

ASHENDENE RD

Mast

Bayford

Fanshaws

Fanshaws La

Bourne Wood

08

Stocking La

Chain Wlk

Fanshaws Farm

The Farmer's Boy (PH)

Brickendon

Cowheath Wood

4

Brickendon Grange

Morley Grove

CH

Nature Trails

Claypits Wood

Broad Riding Wood

Blackfan Wood

Broxbourne Wood

Hedgerows Wood

3

Hedgegrove Farm

Devil's La

Nature Reserve

P

Pembridge La

WOOD HOUSE LA

07

Old Claypits Farm

Ponsbourne Tunnel

Calais Wood

P

Ettridge Farm

Pembridge Lane Farm

Paradise Wildlife Park

Stocking Wood

2

EN10

Mortals Wood

WHITE STUBBS LA

Old Grove

Chain Wlk

P

Bencroft Wood

P

P Emanuel Pollards

1

Nature Trail

Westlea

Manor Farm

WEST END RD

Wormley Wood

06

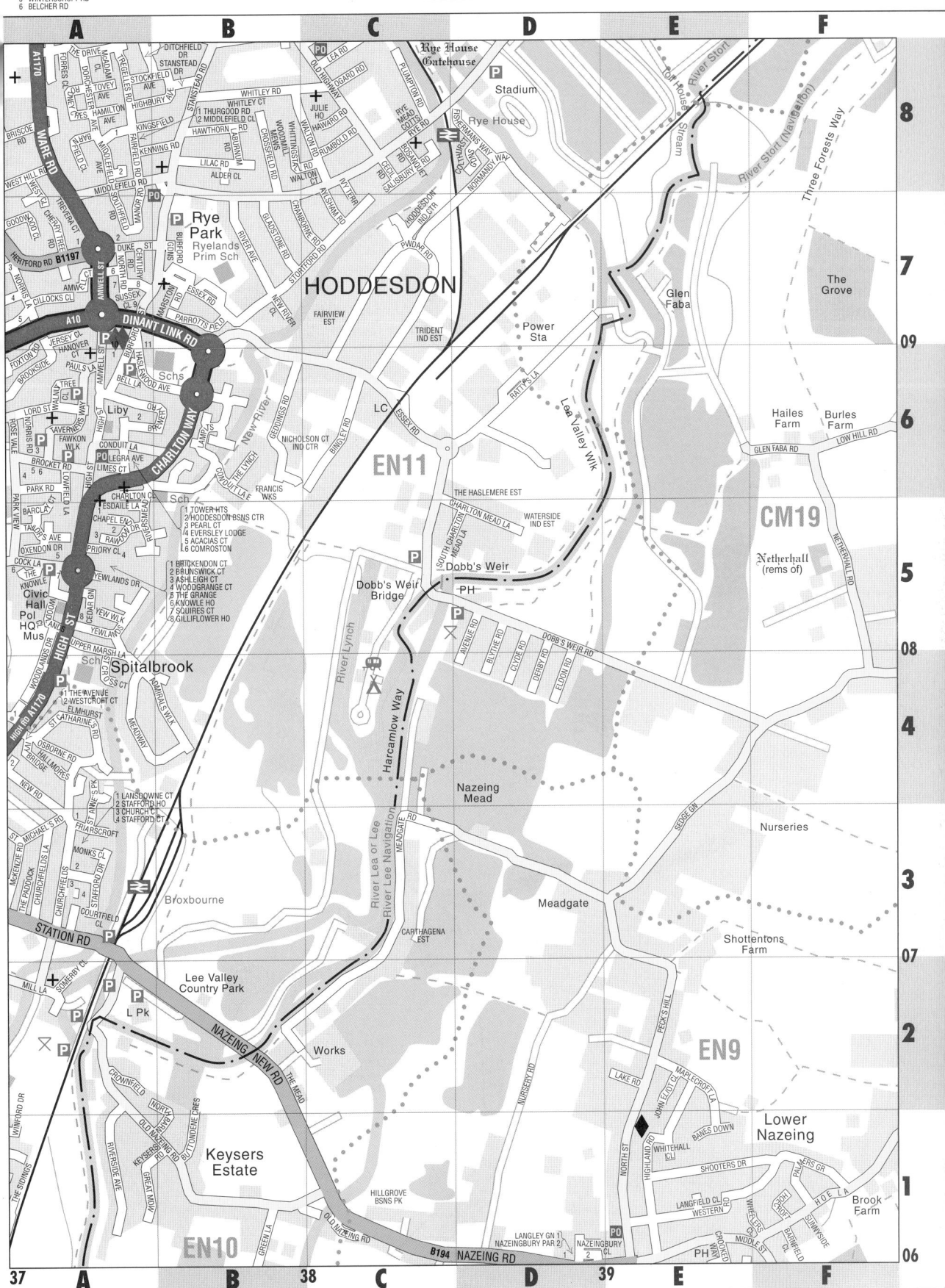

A7
1 FOURWAYS CT
2 CUMBERLAND CT
3 WESTFIELD RD
4 NORRIS RISE
5 WINTERSCROFT RD
6 BELCHER RD
7 ROMAN MEWS
8 ROMAN ST
9 BURFORD MEWS
10 TOWER CTR
11 BURFORD PL

HODDESDON

Rye Park
Ryelands Prim Sch

EN11

Rye House
Gatehouse

Stadium

Rye House

Glen Faba

The Grove

Power Sta

Hailes Farm

Burles Farm

CM19

Netherhall
(rems of)

Dobb's Weir
Dobb's Weir Bridge

Waterside Ind Est

Civic Hall
Pol HQ
Mus

Spitalbrook

Harcamlow Way

Nazeing Mead

Nurseries

Meadgate

Shottentons Farm

Broxbourne

EN9

Lee Valley Country Park

Works

Lower Nazeing

Keysers Estate

Hillgrove Bsns Pk

EN10

NAZEING RD

Brook Farm

122

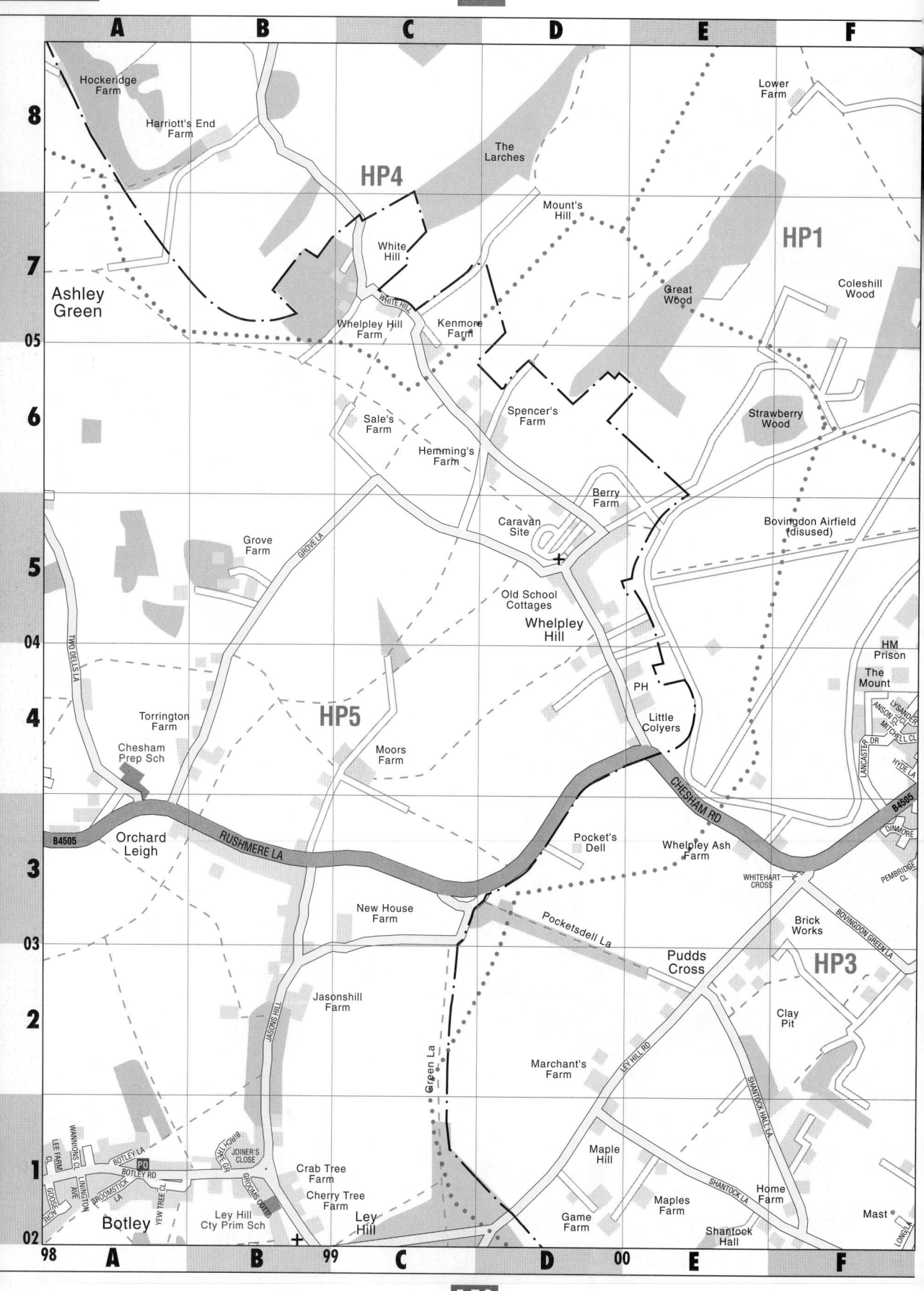

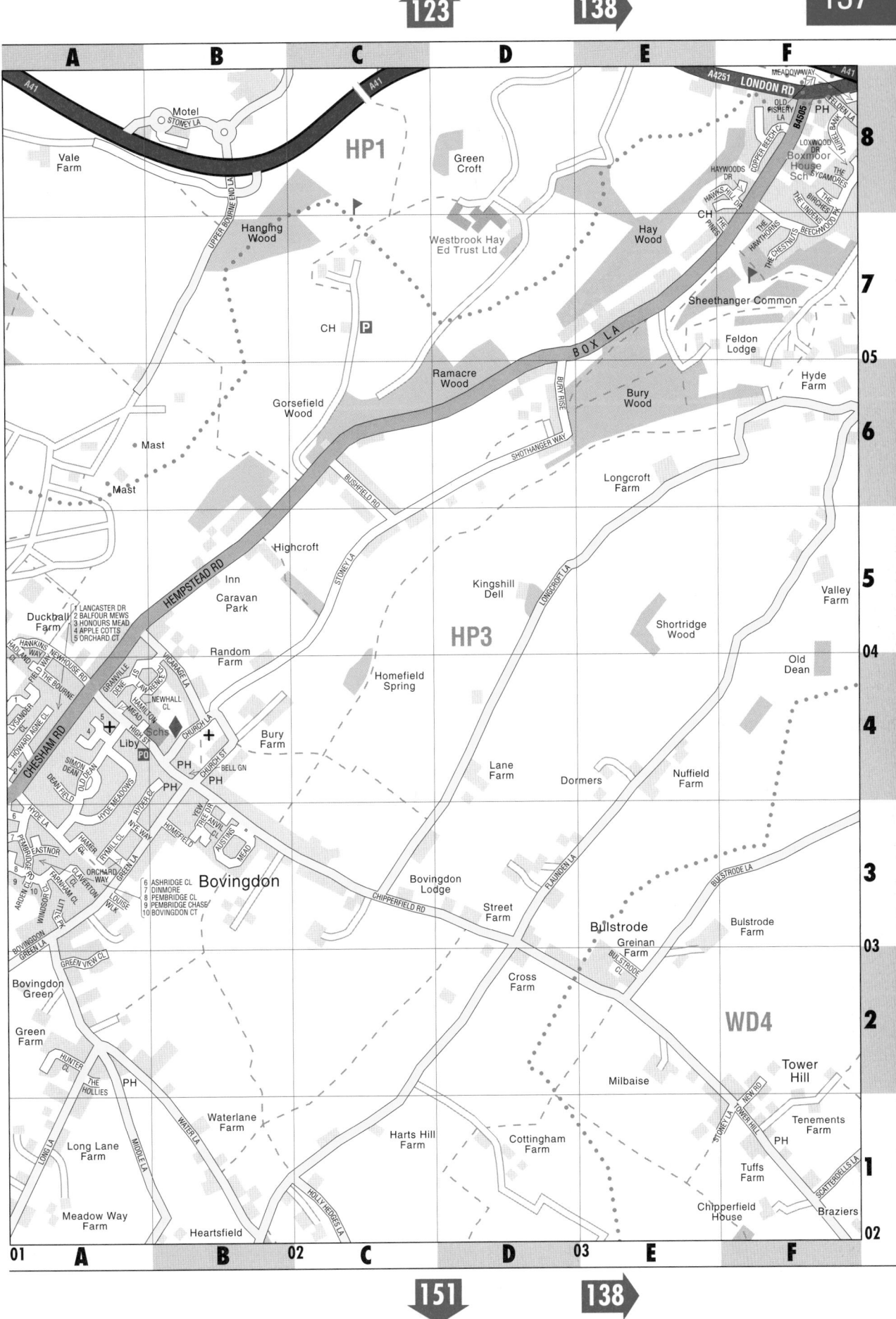

123
138
151
138

A B C D E F

8 7 05 6 5 04 4 3 03 2 02 1

01 A B 02 C D 03 E F

Vale Farm
Motel
STONEY LA
A41
HP1
Green Croft
A4251 LONDON RD
MEADOW WAY
A41
OLD FISHERY LA
B4505
PH
COPPER BEECH CT
LOXWOOD DR
Boxmoor House Sch
The SYCAMORES
HAYWOODS DR
HAWKS HILL
The PINES
CH
The BIRCHES
The LINDENS
The HAWTHORNS
The CHESTNUTS
BEECHWOOD
UPPER BOURNE END LA
Hanging Wood
Westbrook Hay Ed Trust Ltd
Hay Wood
CH
Sheethanger Common
Feldon Lodge
CH
P
BOX LA
Ramacre Wood
Bury Wood
Hyde Farm
Gorsefield Wood
BURY RISE
SHOTHANGER WAY
Longcroft Farm
Mast
BUSHFIELD RD
Mast
Highcroft
STONEY LA
Kingshill Dell
LONGCROFT LA
Valley Farm
Inn
Caravan Park
Shortridge Wood
Old Dean
Duckhall Farm
1 LANCASTER DR
2 BALFOUR MEWS
3 HONOURS MEAD
4 APPLE COTTS
5 ORCHARD CT
Random Farm
Homefield Spring
HP3
HEMPSTEAD RD
HANKINS
NEWHOUSE RD
FIELD
HAZEL WAY
THE BOURNE
GRANVILLE
DENE
LAWRENCE
HAMILTON
HEAD
NEWHALL CL
Schs
VICARAGE LA
CHURCH LA
Bury Farm
Lane Farm
Dormers
Nuffield Farm
LYSANDER
CL
HOWARD AGNE CL
High ST
Liby
PO
CHURCH ST
BELL GN
CHESHAM RD
SIMON DEAN
OLD DEAN
DEAN FIELD
PH
PH
PH
RYDE LA
HAMER CL
RYMILL CL
NYE LA
HYDE MEADOWS
GREEN LA
TREE TAPE
YEW LA
ANVIL CL
AUSTINS MEAD
Bovingdon Lodge
Street Farm
FLAUNDEN LA
Bulstrode
BULSTRODE LA
Bulstrode Farm
EASTNOR
PEMBRIDGE
GROVE
CLAVERTON
FARNHAM CL
ORCHARD WAY
WINDSOR CL
LITTLE
LOUISE WLK
GREEN WALK
6 ASHRIDGE CL
7 DINMORE
8 PEMBRIDGE CL
9 PEMBRIDGE CHASE
10 BOVINGDON CT
Bovingdon
CHIPPERFIELD RD
Cross Farm
Greinan Farm
BULSTRODE CL
WD4
BOVINGDON GREEN LA
GREEN VIEW CL
Bovingdon Green
Green Farm
Tower Hill
HUNTER CL
THE HOLLIES
PH
Milbaise
NEW RD
STONEY LA
TOWER HILL
PH
Tenements Farm
Long Lane Farm
WATER LA
MIDDLE LA
Waterlane Farm
HOLLY HEDGES LA
Harts Hill Farm
Cottingham Farm
Tuffs Farm
SCATTERDELLS LA
LONG LA
Meadow Way Farm
Heartsfield
Chipperfield House
Braziers

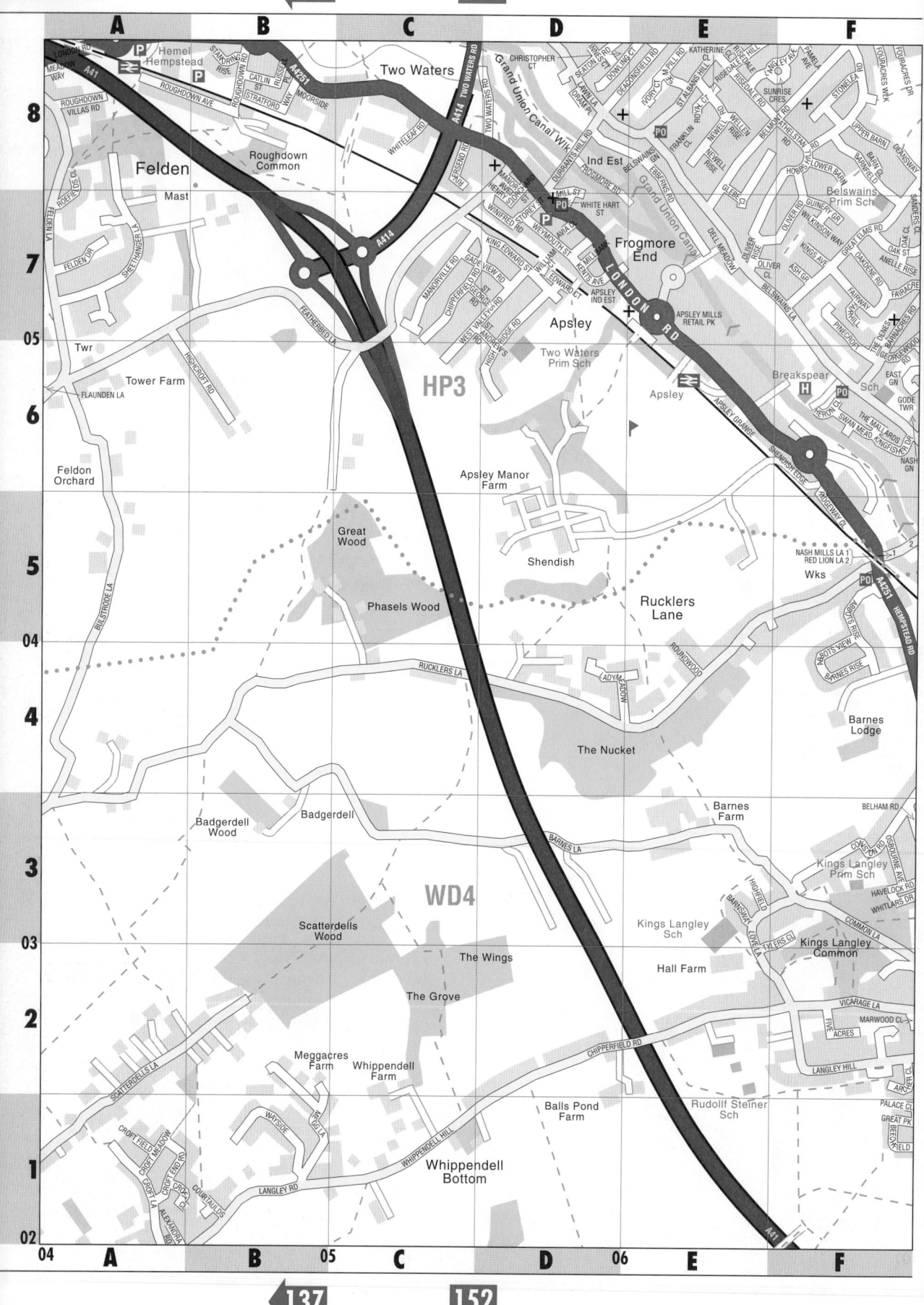

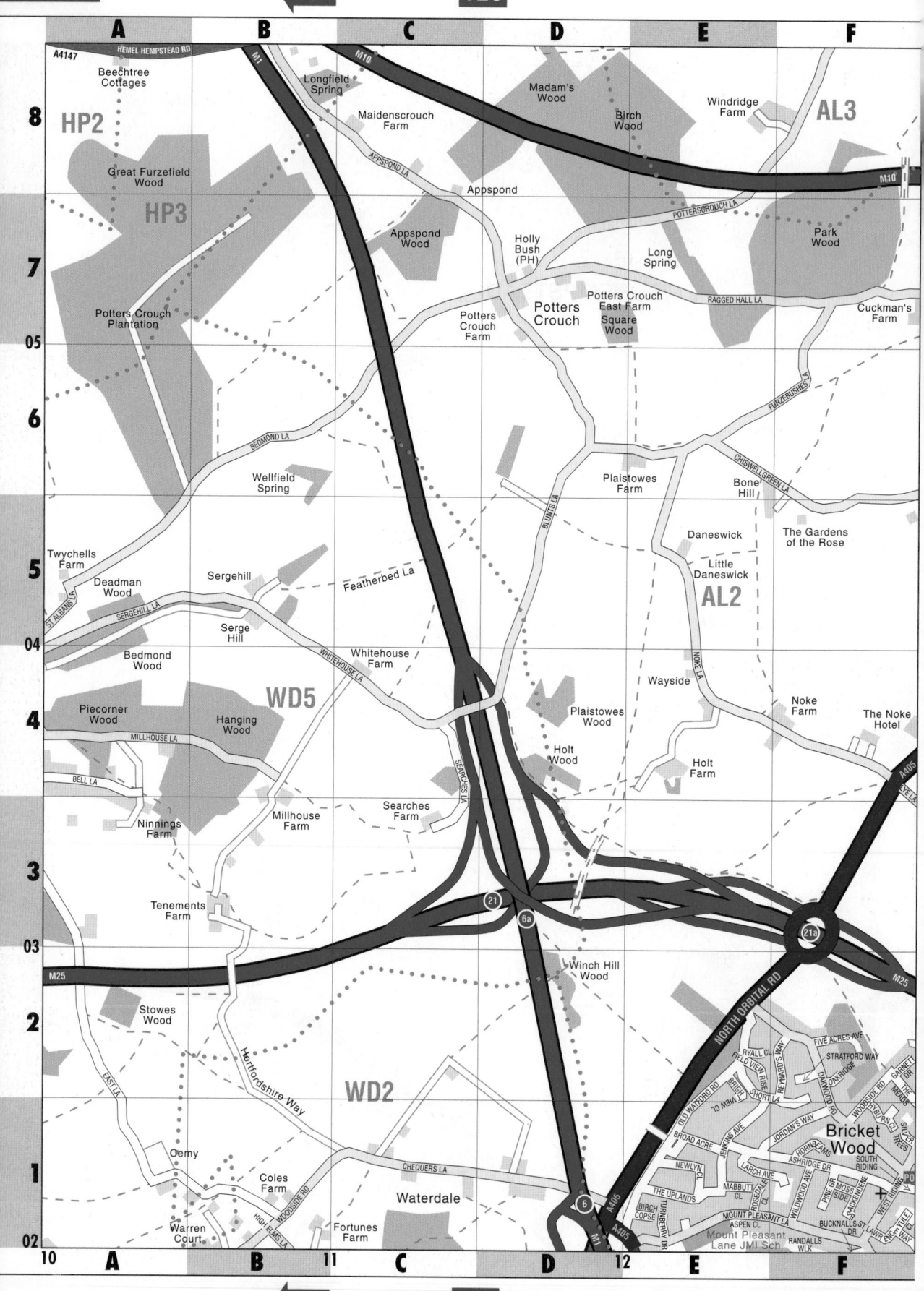

139
126

127
142

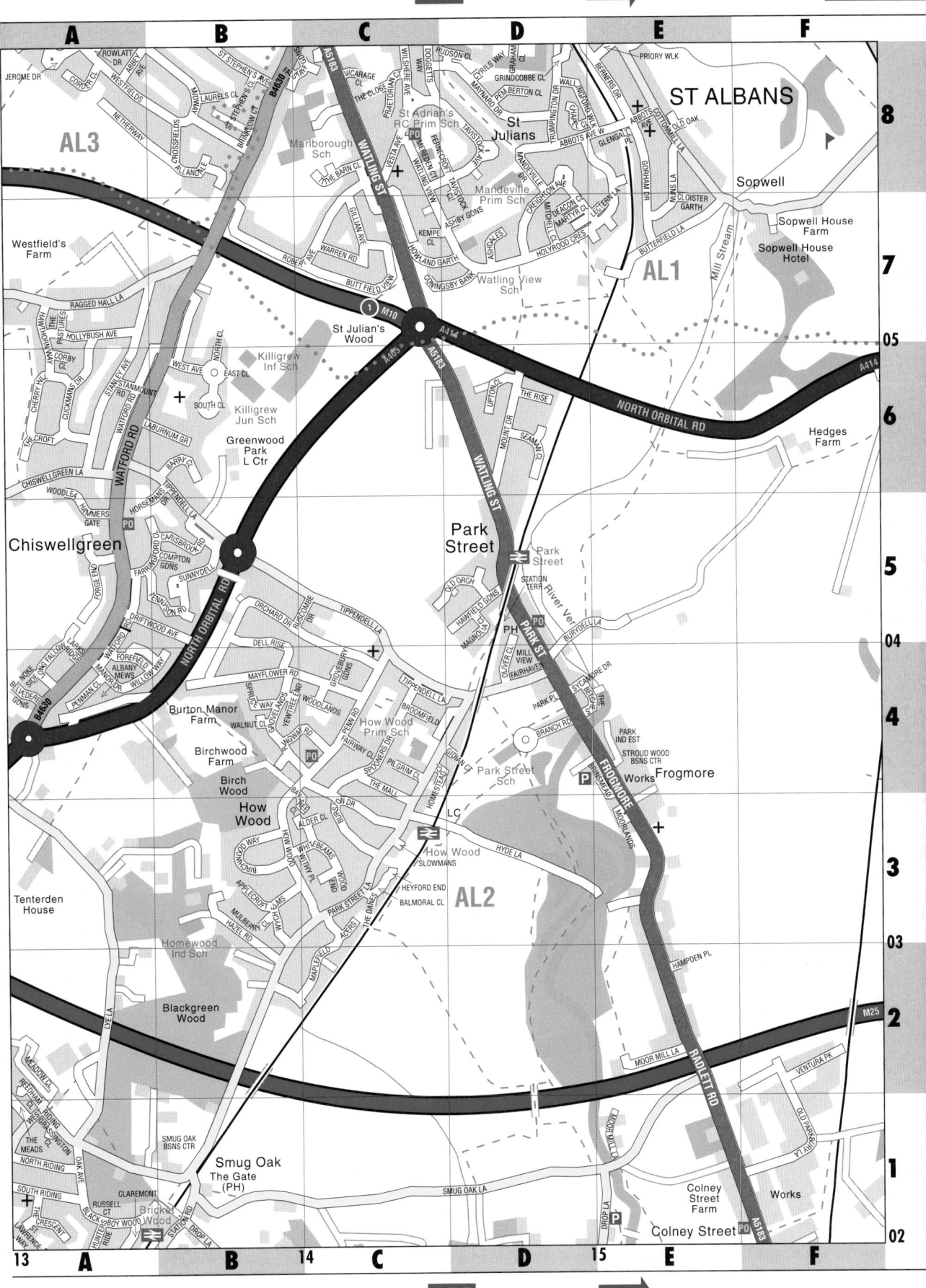

155
142

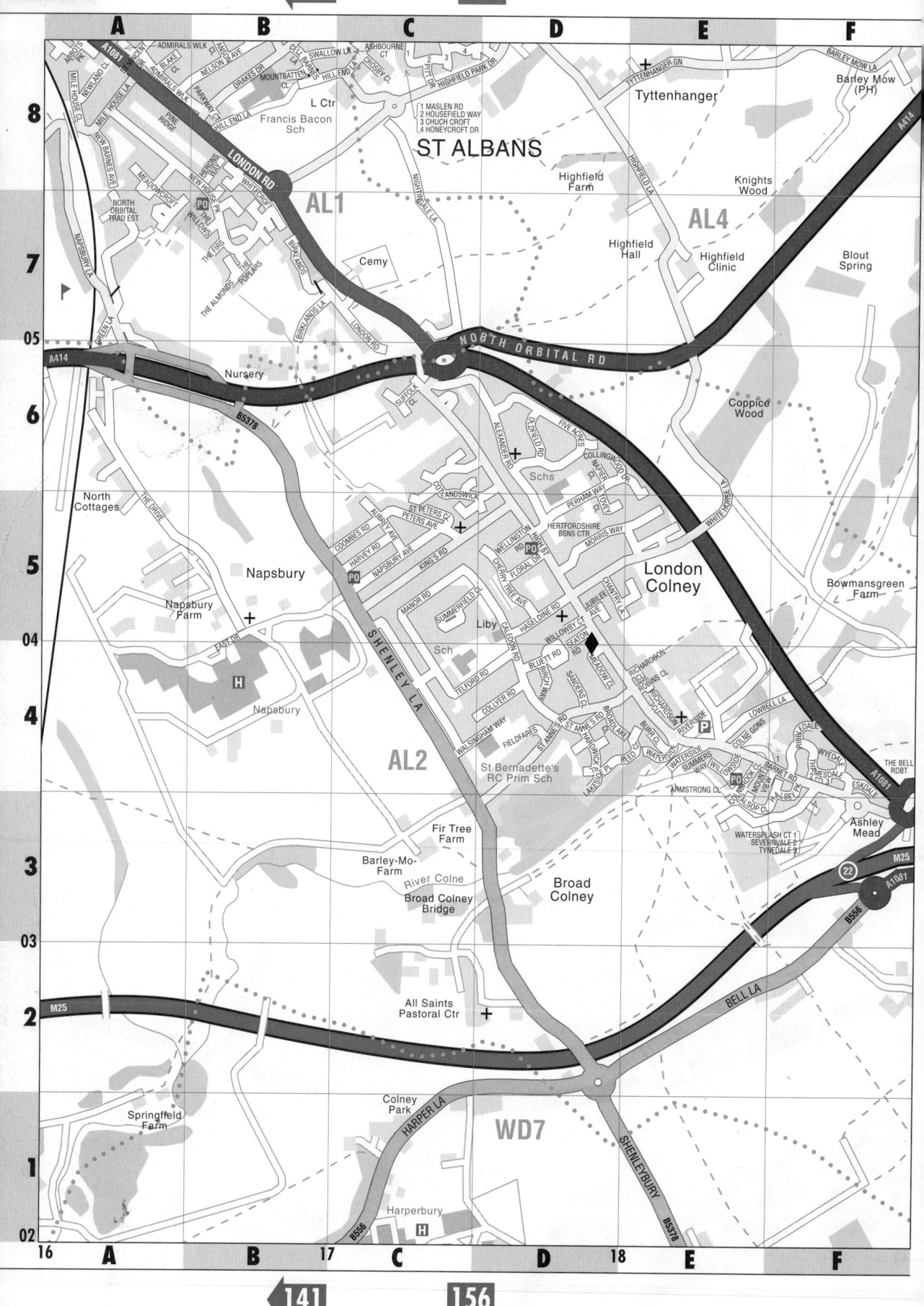

129

144

A B C D E F

8
7
05
6
5
04
4
3
03
2
1
02

NORTH ORBITAL RD
A414

Park Corner

HEATH PARK LA
CHURCH LA
PARK SIDE LA

SCHOLARS CT

HIGH ST

River Colne

Water Works

Windmill

Colney Heath
PH

Colney Heath Farm

ROESTOCK LA
MEADWAY
HALL GDNS
BENNETTS CL
FELLOWES LA

ADMIRALS CL

Roestock

BULLENS GREEN LA
DELLSOME LA

A1 (M)
2

DELLSOME LA

A1 (M)

Tollgate Wood

Warren Farm

Tollgate Farm

TOLLGATE RD

Frederick's Wood

Park Cottage

Tyttenhanger Farm

AL4

The Osierbeds

North Mymms Park

The New Plantation

Garden Wood

COURSERS RD

Coursers Farm

AL9

Tyttenhanger Park

Red Lodge

North Mymms Park

Walsingham Wood

Lodge Plantation

22
A1081
AL2

B556

Cangsley Grove

Cobs Ash

Potwells

Round Wood

03

EN6

Salisbury Hall Farm

Salisbury Hall

Mosquito Aircraft Mus

Redwell Wood Farm

Oak Lodge

Hawkshead Wood

Redwell Wood

Ridgehill Stud

Shenley Lodge Cottage

RECTORY LA

Ridgehill

Manor Lodge Sch

PACKHORSE LA

WD7

Shenley Lodge Farm

M25

B556
BLACKHORSE LA
ST ALBANS RD

Woodhill Farm

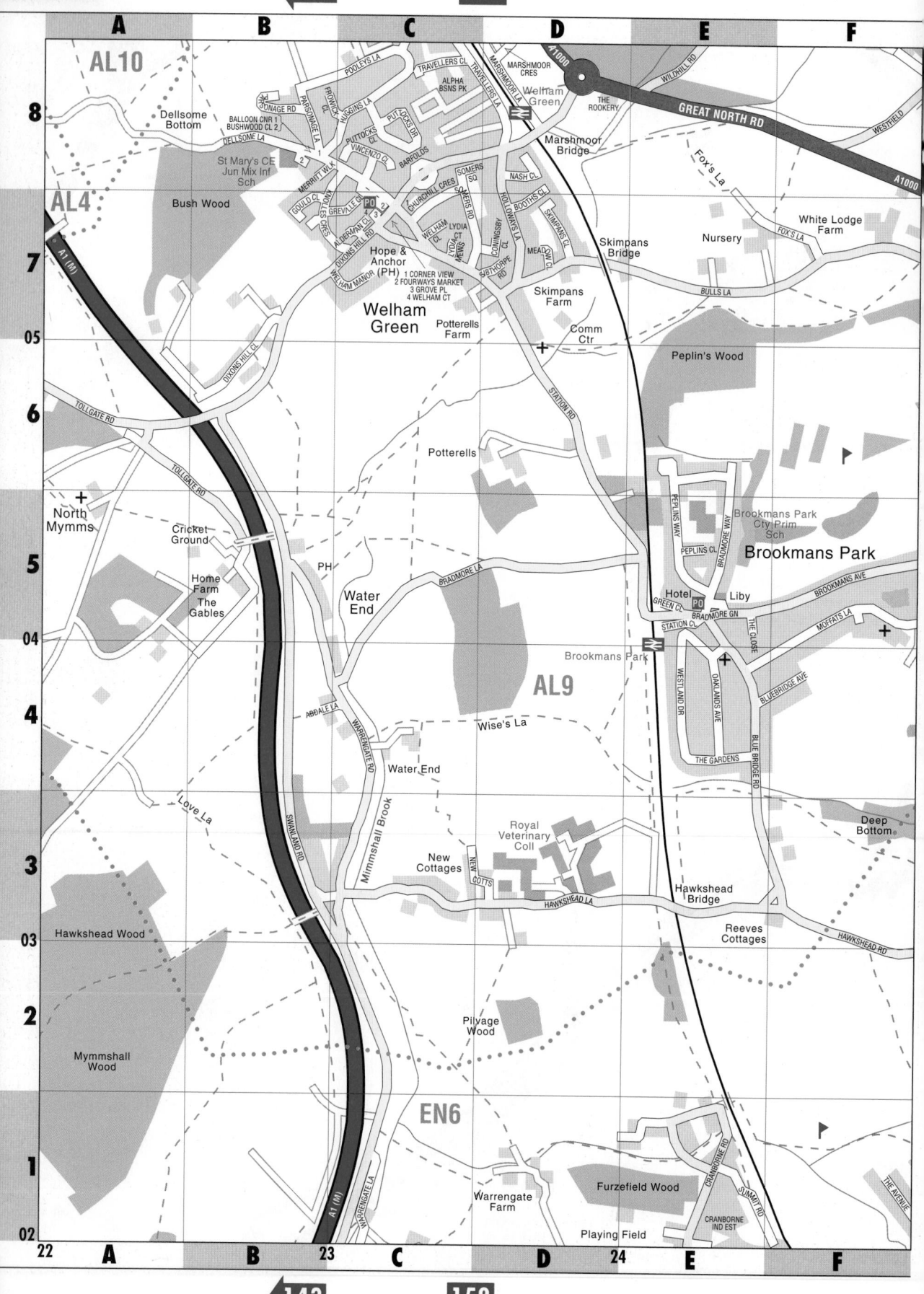

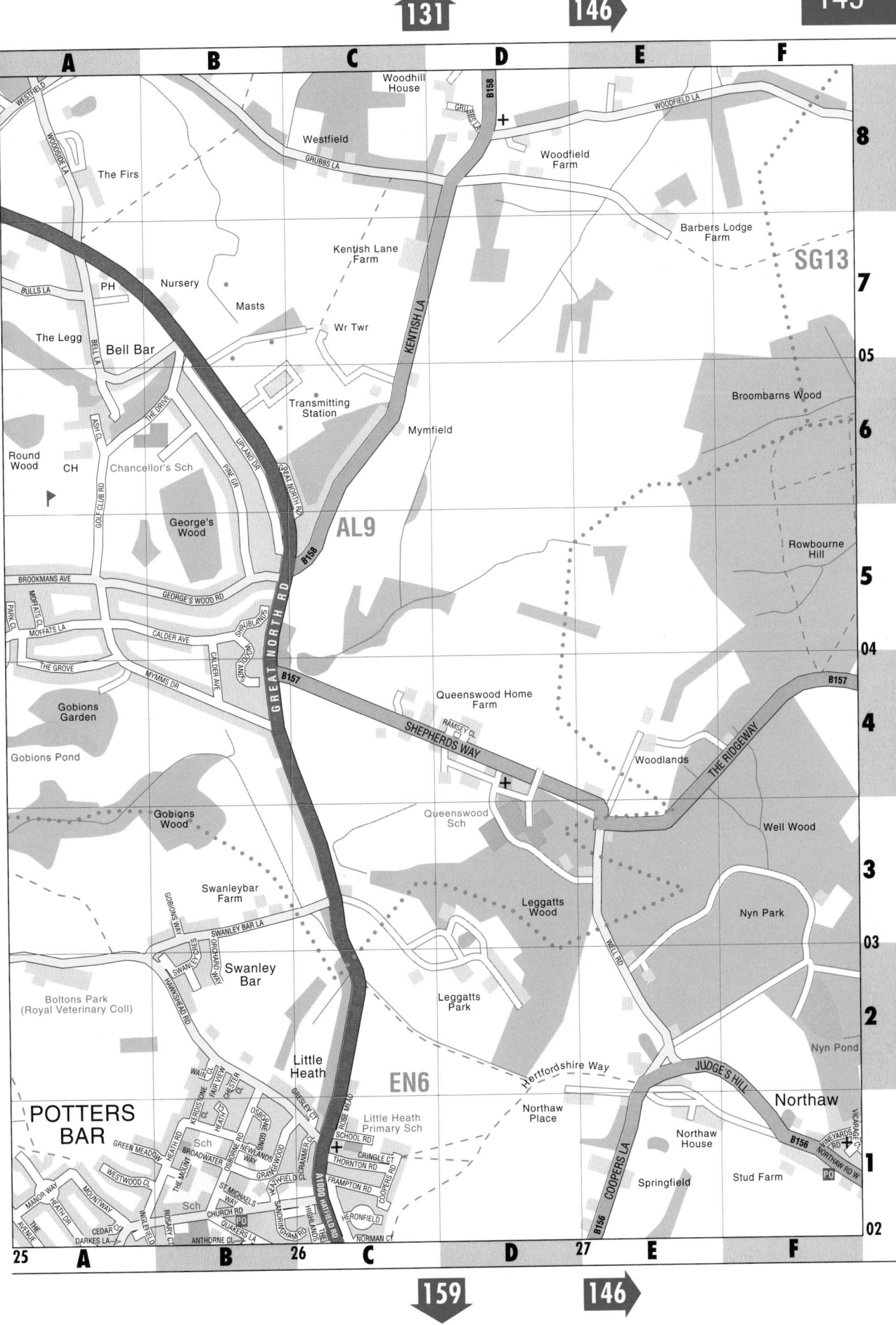

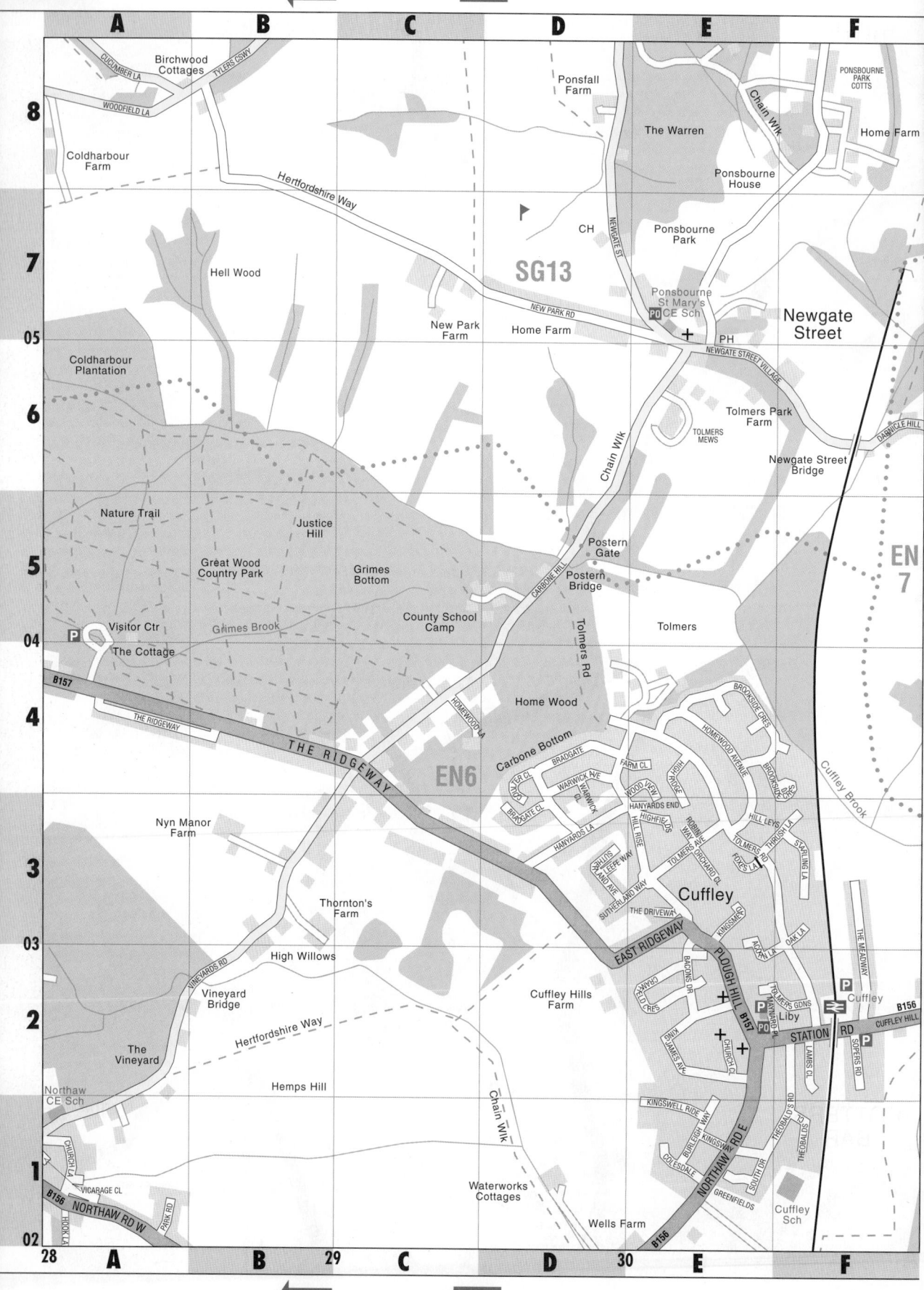

A B C D E F

8 The Roughs
Firs Wood
Wormleybury Brook
West End Rd
Wormley West End
SG13
Westfield Grove
Biggs Grove
EN10

7 Long Grove
Derry's Wood
Baisley's Wood
Beaumont Manor
Beaumont Rd
Thunderfield Grove Nature Reserve
Tunford Brook
Bread and Cheese Bridge

05
St Lawrence Farm
Chain Wlk
Tanfield Stud Farm
Bread and Cheese La
Gammon's La

6 Darnicle Hill
Bruce Cl
Walters Cl
Bitten Rd
Starkey Cl
Nightingale Rd
Dahl Cl
Shambrook Cl
Sexton Cl
Gladding Rd
Everett Rd
Lovering Rd
Bloomfield Rd
Wells Cl
Savill Cl
Sadler Cl
Sell Cl
Martin Rd
Burgess Cl
Wilkinson Cl
Hammond Street Rd
Smiths La
Beaumont View
Russet Rd
Pear Tree Wlk
Beechwood Cl
Appleby St
Gammon Farm
Nurseries
Richardson Cres

5 Burleigh Farm
Nurseries
EN7
Macintosh Cl 1
Hobby Horse Cl 2
Broadgreen Rd
Arrcress Rd
Great Stockwood Rd
Higgins Rd
Little Stock Rd
Argent Way
The Mount
Sheldon Cl
Maychroft Rd
Ruskin
Spencer Ave
Oaklands Rd
Milton Cl
Brangon Cl
Scaffield Cl
Hilton Cl
Hammond Cl
Holbeck La
Park La
Upper Shott
Lower Shott
Roundcroft
Adamsfield
Smart Cl
Jarvis Cleys 1
Tennand Cl 2
Cardinal Cl 3
Milton Ct 4
Headingley Cl 5

04
Nursery
Lucasend Farm
High View Farm
Crouch La
Lightswood Cl
Hammond Street
Southview Cl 1
The Poplars 2
Hazel Cl 3
Whitebeam Cl 4
Nurseries
Acacia Cl
The Acers
Foresters
The Firs
Sycamore Robinson Cl
Grenadine Cl
Glover Cl
Allwood
Coleridge Cl
Carvell Rd
Peakes Way
Dig Dag Hill
Byron Cl

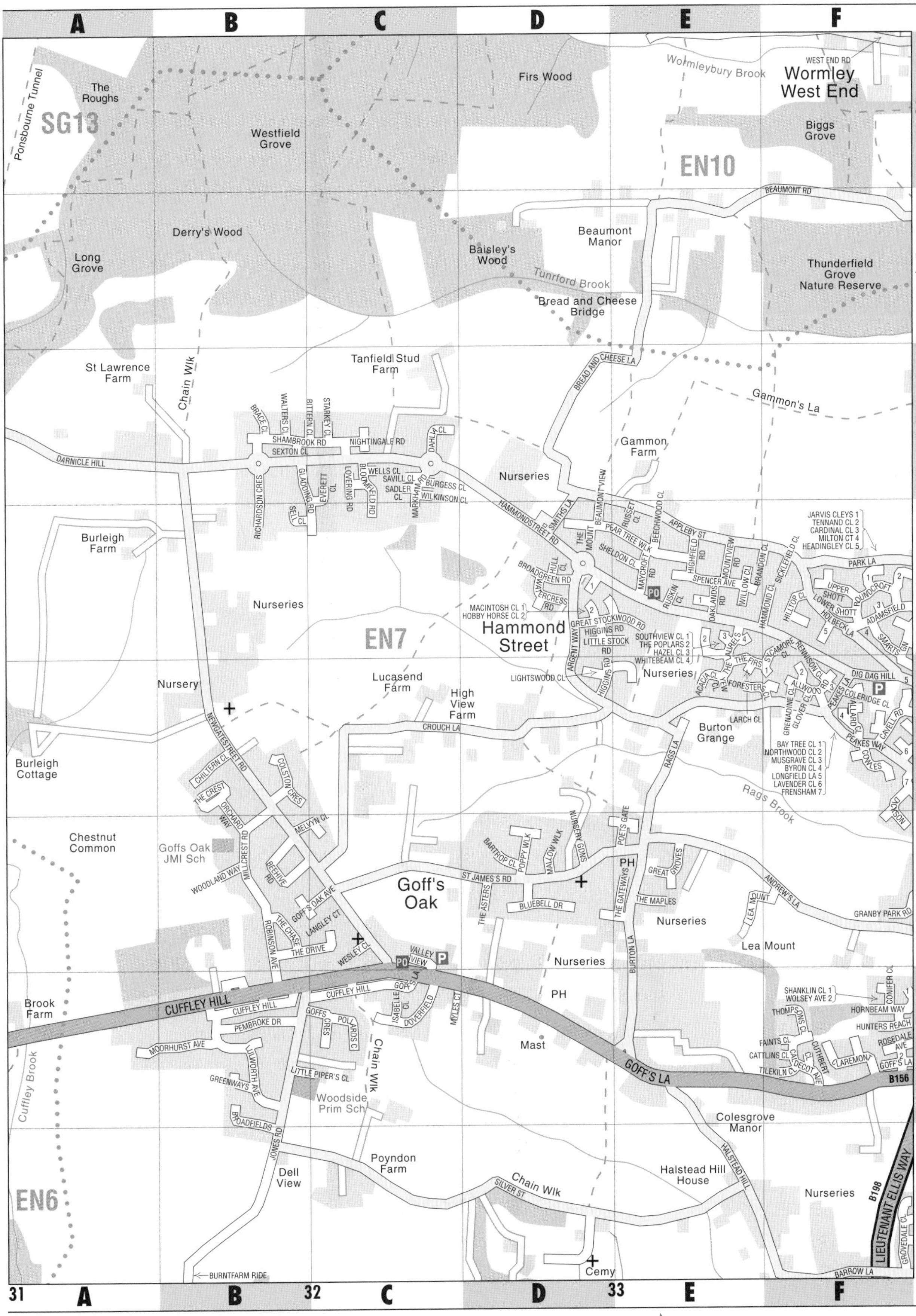

4 Burleigh Cottage
Newgatestreet Rd
Chiltern Cl
The Crest
Orchard Way
Colston Cres
Burton Grange
Larch Cl
Rags La
Rags Brook
Bay Tree Cl 1
Northwood Cl 2
Musgrave Cl 3
Byron Cl 4
Longfield La 5
Lavender Cl 6
Frensham 7

3 Chestnut Common
Goffs Oak JMI Sch
Woodland Way
Millcrest Rd
Beetle Rd
Goff's Oak Ave
Melvyn Cl
Langley Ct
Goff's Oak
Bartrop Cl
Poppy Wlk
Mallow Wlk
Ginns Rd
Runsome Wlk
Poets Gate
The Gateways
Great Groves
The Maples
Nurseries
Lea Quint
Andrew's La
Granby Park Rd
Lea Mount
St James's Rd
The Asters
Bluebell Dr
PH

03
The Chase
Robinson Ave
The Drive
Wesley Cl
Valley View
PO
Nurseries
Burton La
PH
Shanklin Cl 1
Wolsey Ave 2
Conifer Cl
Thompsons Cl
Hornbeam Way

2 Brook Farm
Cuffley Brook
Cuffley Hill
Moorhurst Ave
Pembroke Dr
Goffs Cres
Poll Ards Cl
Isabelle Cl
Doverfield
Myles Ct
Gort Cl
Mast
Goff's La
Faints Cl
Catlins Cl
Tilekiln La
Outhbert Cl
Decoy Ave
Claremon
Goff's La
Rosedale Ave
Hunters Reach
B156
Little Piper's Cl
Greenways
Ilworth Ave
Chain Wlk
Woodside Prim Sch
Broadfields
Jones Rd

1 EN6
Dell View
Poyndon Farm
Silver St
Chain Wlk
Halstead Hill House
Halstead Hill
Colesgrove Manor
Nurseries
Lieutenant Ellis Way
B198
Grovedale Cl

02 Burntfarm Ride
Cemy
Barrow La

31 A 32 B C 33 D E F

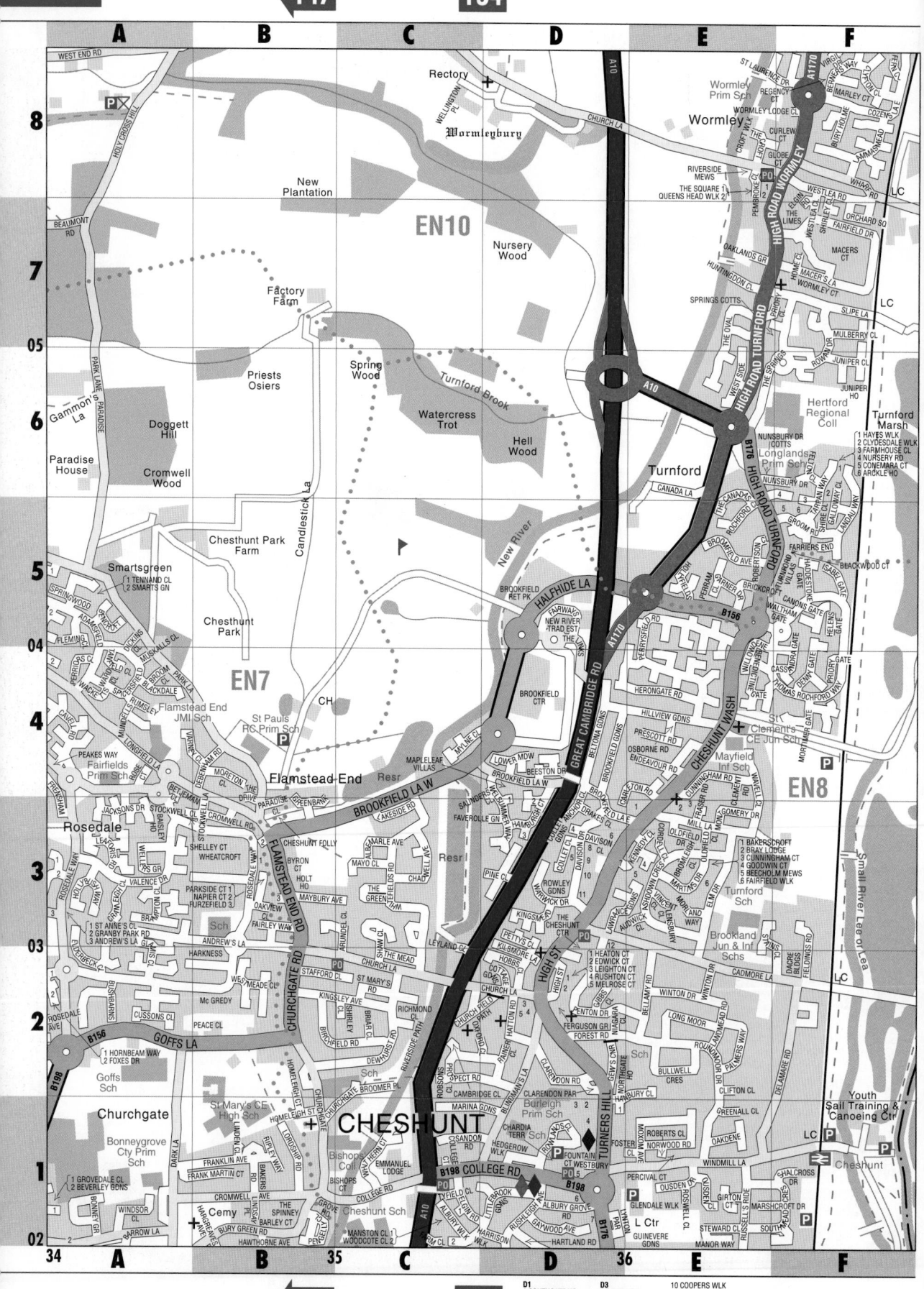

D1
1 SOUTHGATE HO
2 ALEXANDER CT
3 ROWLANDS CT
4 ANCIENT ALMSHOS
5 NEWNHAM PAR
6 MANORCROFT PAR
7 CLAYTON PAR

D3
1 CAMPINE CL
2 SOUTHBROOK DR
3 THE SPUR
4 CRAIGS WLK
5 BREEZE TERR
6 THE WHITE HO
7 THE COLONNADE
8 CEDAR LODGE
9 BLAXLAND TERR

10 COOPERS WLK
11 DOUGLAS HO
12 CADMORE CT

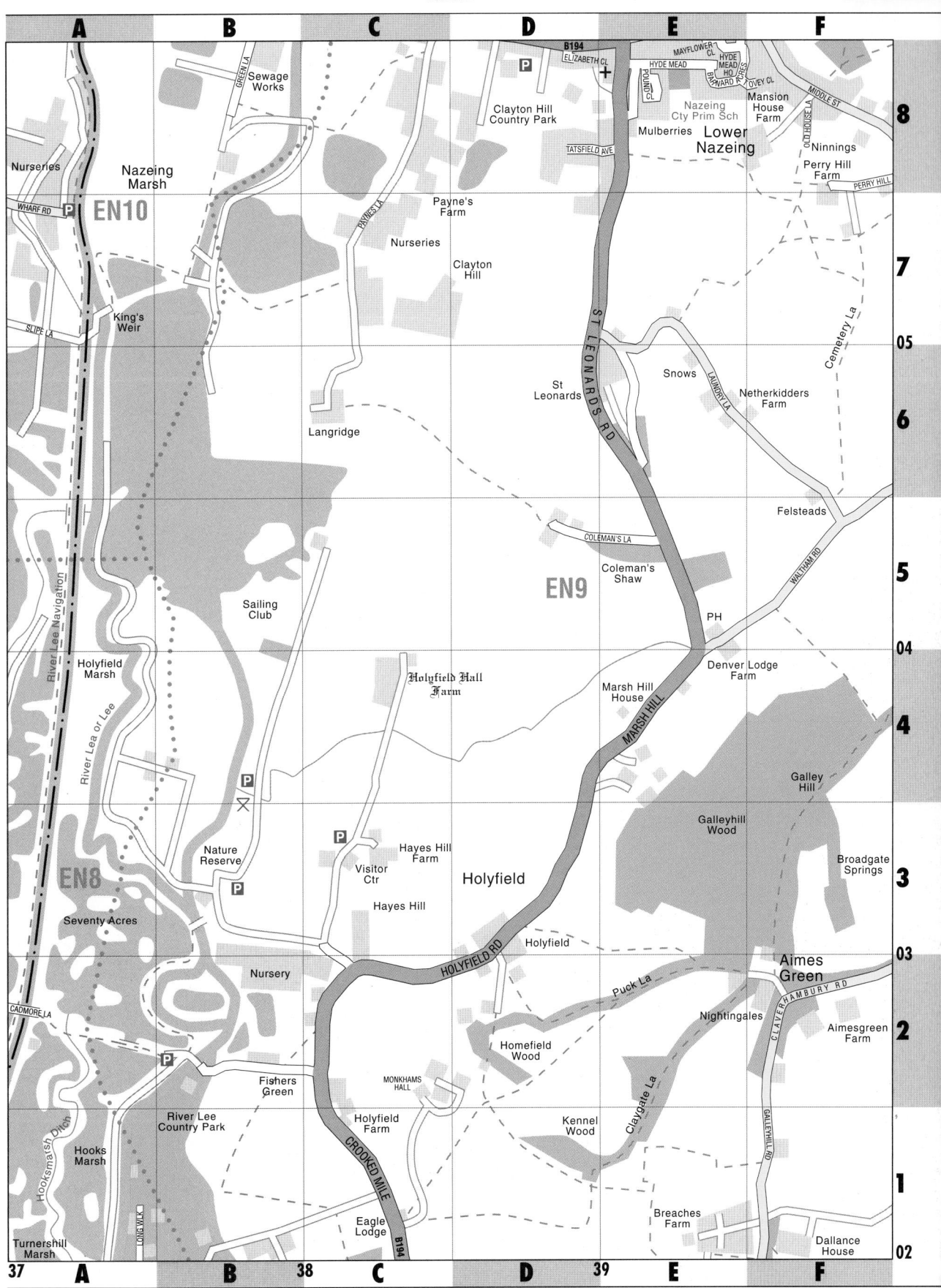

A **B** **C** **D** **E** **F**

Nurseries

Nazeing
Marsh

EN10

WHARF RD

SLIPE LA

King's
Weir

Sewage
Works

GREEN LA

PAYNES LA

Payne's
Farm

Nurseries

Clayton
Hill

Clayton Hill
Country Park

B194

ELIZABETH CL

TATSFIELD AVE

Mulberries

Lower
Nazeing

MAYFLOWER
CL

HYDE MEAD

HYDE
MEAD
HO

POUND CL

BARNARD

OVEY CL

CROSS

Nazeing
Cty Prim Sch

Mansion
House
Farm

MIDDLE ST

OLD HOUSE LA

Ninnings

Perry Hill
Farm

PERRY HILL

Cemetery La

8

7

05

6

Langridge

St
Leonards

ST LEONARDS RD

Snows

LAUNDRY LA

Netherkidders
Farm

Felsteads

WALTHAM RD

COLEMAN'S LA

Coleman's
Shaw

EN9

PH

5

04

Sailing
Club

Holyfield
Marsh

River Lea or Lee

River Lee Navigation

Holyfield Hall
Farm

Marsh Hill
House

MARSH HILL

Denver Lodge
Farm

4

Galley
Hill

Galleyhill
Wood

Broadgate
Springs

3

03

EN8

Seventy Acres

Nature
Reserve

Visitor
Ctr

Hayes Hill
Farm

Hayes Hill

Holyfield

HOLYFIELD RD

Holyfield

Aimes
Green

CLAVERHAMBURY RD

Puck La

Nightingales

Aimesgreen
Farm

2

CADMORE LA

Nursery

Fishers
Green

Hooksmarsh Ditch

LONG WLK

River Lee
Country Park

Holyfield
Farm

CROOKED MILE

MONKHAMS
HALL

Homefield
Wood

Kennel
Wood

Claygate La

GALLEYHILL RD

Breaches
Farm

Dallance
House

1

02

Turnershill
Marsh

Hooks
Marsh

Eagle
Lodge

B194

37 **A** **B** 38 **C** **D** 39 **E** **F**

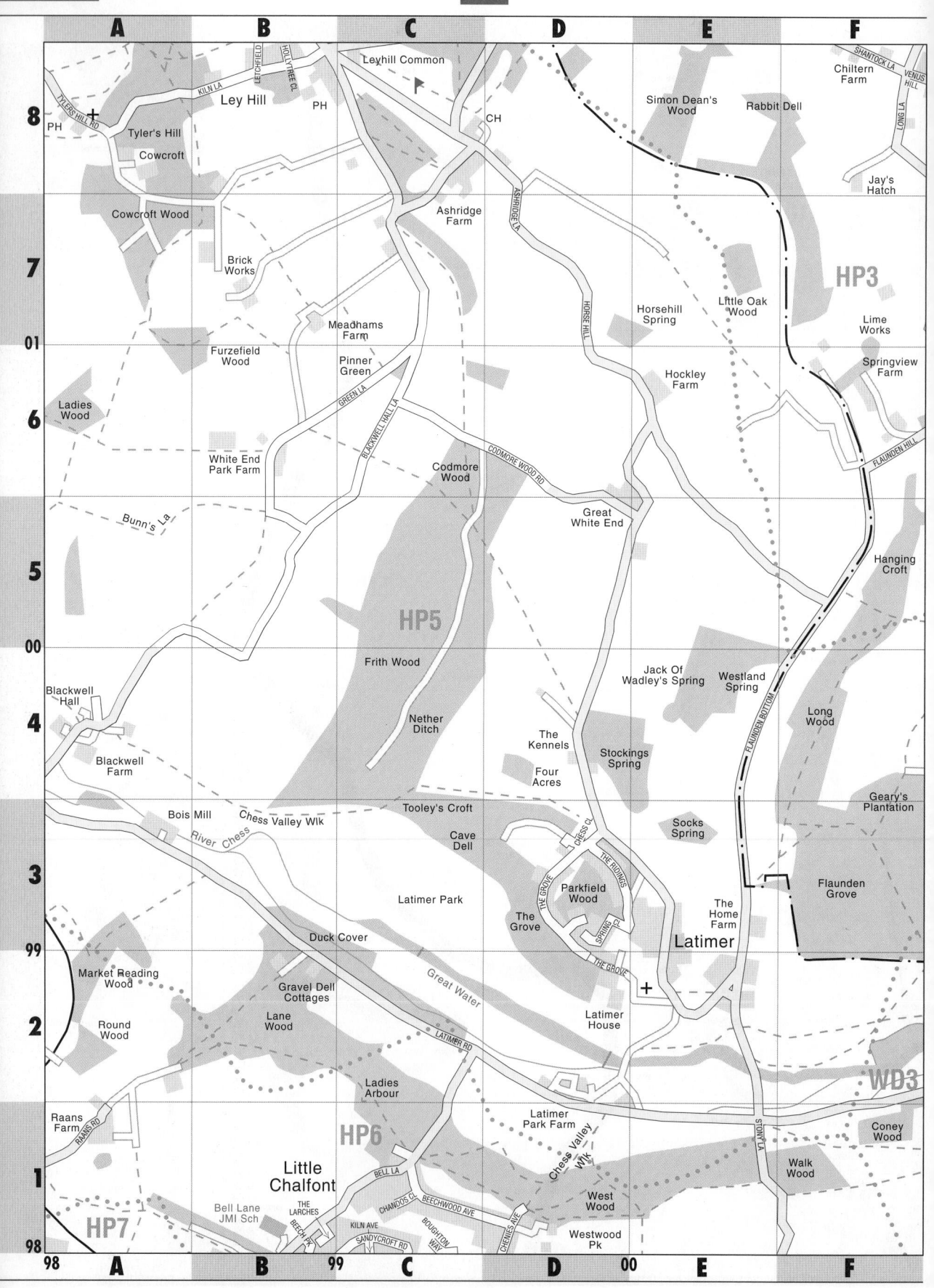

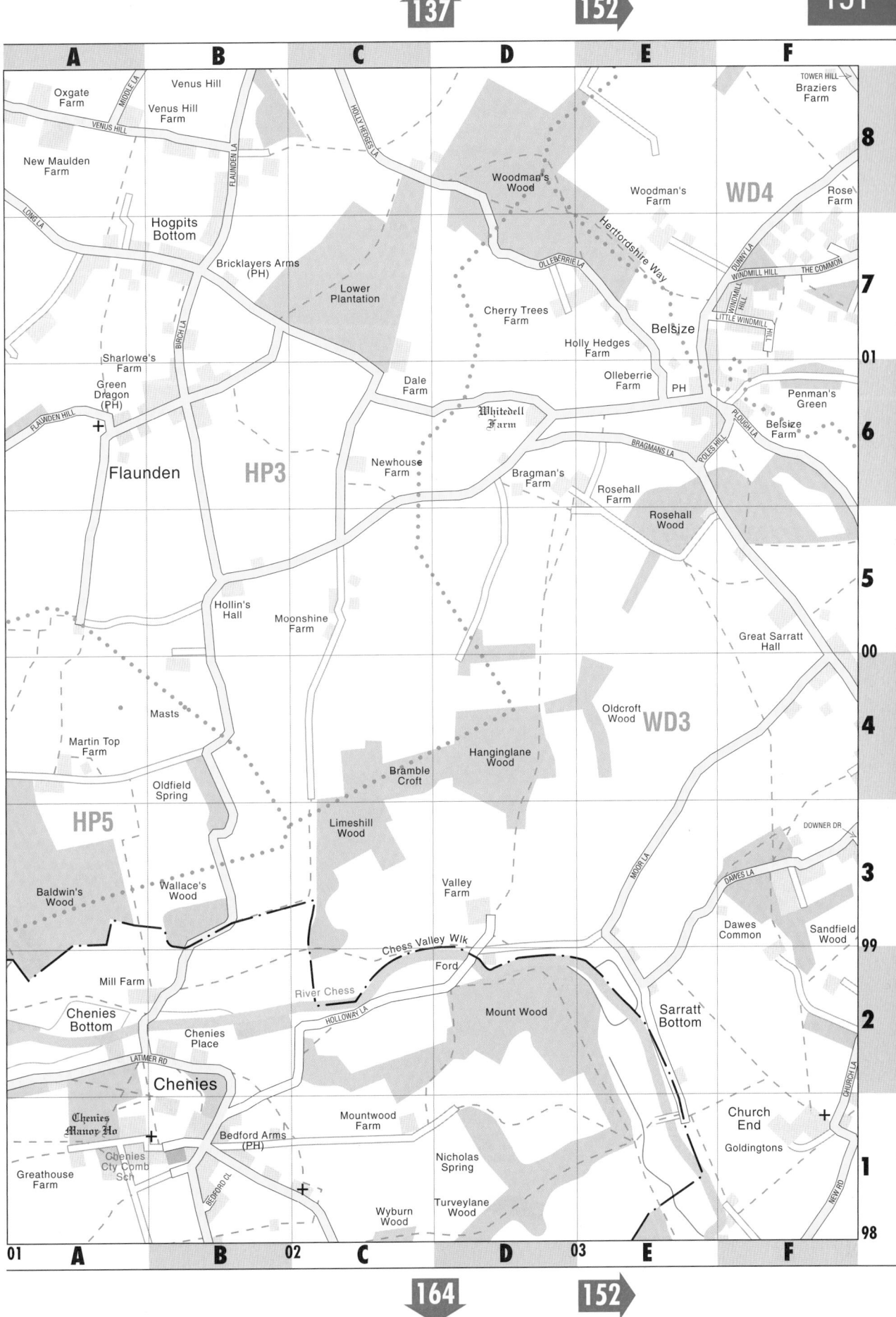

Oxgate Farm
Venus Hill
Venus Hill Farm
MIDDLE LA
VENUS HILL
New Maulden Farm
FLAUNDEN LA
LONG LA
Hogpits Bottom
Bricklayers Arms (PH)
HOLLY HEDGES LA
Lower Plantation
Woodman's Wood
Woodman's Farm
WD4
Rose Farm
TOWER HILL
Braziers Farm
THE COMMON
QUINNY LA
WINDMILL HILL
LITTLE WINDMILL HILL
WINDMILL HILL
Hertfordshire Way
OLLEBERRIE LA
Cherry Trees Farm
Belsize
Holly Hedges Farm
Olleberrie Farm
PH
BRAGMANS LA
POLES HILL
PLOUGH LA
Penman's Green
Belsize Farm
BIRCH LA
Sharlowe's Farm
Green Dragon (PH)
FLAUNDEN HILL
Flaunden
HP3
Dale Farm
Whitedell Farm
Newhouse Farm
Bragman's Farm
Rosehall Farm
Rosehall Wood
Hollin's Hall
Moonshine Farm
Great Sarratt Hall
Masts
Martin Top Farm
Oldfield Spring
HP5
Bramble Croft
Hanginglane Wood
Oldcroft Wood
WD3
DOWNER DR
Limeshill Wood
DAWES LA
MOOR LA
Baldwin's Wood
Wallace's Wood
Valley Farm
Dawes Common
Sandfield Wood
Chess Valley Wlk
Ford
Mount Wood
Sarratt Bottom
Mill Farm
River Chess
HOLLOWAY LA
Chenies Bottom
Chenies Place
LATIMER RD
Chenies
CHURCH LA
NEW RD
Chenies Manor Ho
Chenies Cty Comb Sch
BEDFORD CL
Bedford Arms (PH)
Mountwood Farm
Nicholas Spring
Church End
Goldingtons
Greathouse Farm
Wyburn Wood
Turveylane Wood

8
7
01
6
5
00
4
3
99
2
1
98

01
A
B
02
C
D
03
E
F

151 138

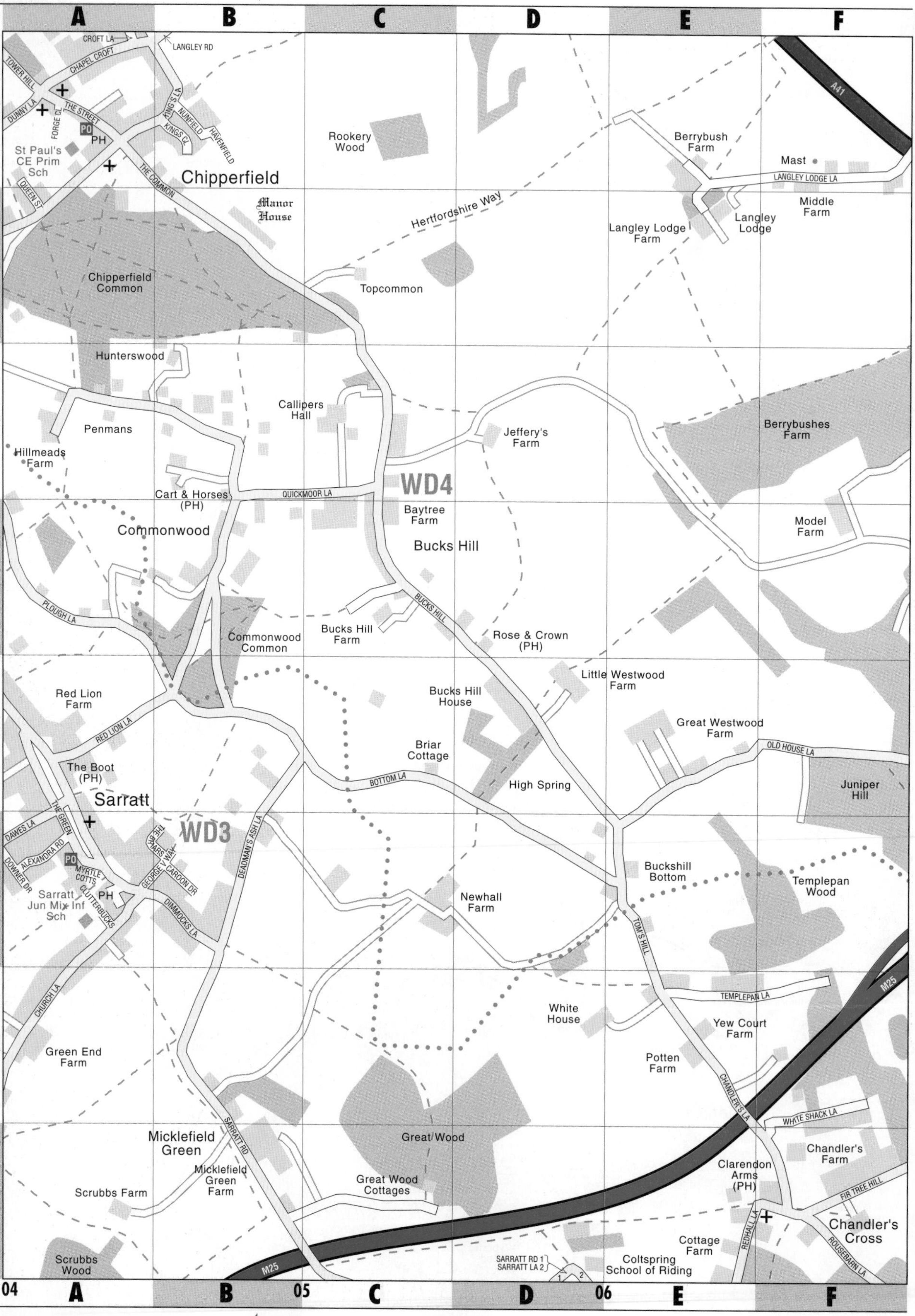

	A	B	C	D	E	F

8

CROFT LA
CHAPEL CROFT
LANGLEY RD
TOWER HILL
DUNNY LA
THE STREET
FORGE LA
KINGS CR
QUEEN ST
THE COMMON
NUNFIELD
HAVENFIELD
SNELL'S LA
PO
PH
St Paul's CE Prim Sch

Rookery Wood

Berrybush Farm

Mast ●

LANGLEY LODGE LA

Chipperfield

Manor House

Hertfordshire Way

Langley Lodge Farm

Langley Lodge

Middle Farm

7

Chipperfield Common

Topcommon

01

Hunterswood

Callipers Hall

Jeffery's Farm

Berrybushes Farm

6

Penmans

Hillmeads Farm

Cart & Horses (PH)

QUICKMOOR LA

WD4

Model Farm

Commonwood

Baytree Farm

Bucks Hill

5

PLOUGH LA

Commonwood Common

Bucks Hill Farm

Bucks Hill

Rose & Crown (PH)

00

Red Lion Farm

RED LION LA

Bucks Hill House

Little Westwood Farm

4

The Boot (PH)

Briar Cottage

High Spring

Great Westwood Farm

OLD HOUSE LA

Juniper Hill

THE GREEN
DAWES LA
ALEXANDRA RD
DOWNER DR
CHURCH LA
MYRTLE COTTS
PH
PO
GEORGE'S WAY
CARDON DR
CLUTTERBUCKS
DIMMOCKS LA
THE MEAD
BOTTOM LA
DEADMAN'S ASH LA

Sarratt

WD3

Sarratt Jun Mix Inf Sch

Newhall Farm

Buckshill Bottom

TOM'S HILL

Templepan Wood

3

99

TEMPLEPAN LA

M25

White House

Yew Court Farm

2

Green End Farm

Potten Farm

CHANDLER'S LA

WHITE SHACK LA

Micklefield Green

SARRATT RD

Great Wood

Chandler's Farm

FIR TREE HILL

1

Scrubbs Farm

Micklefield Green Farm

Great Wood Cottages

Clarendon Arms (PH)

REDHALL LA

Chandler's Cross

ROUSEBARN LA

98

Scrubbs Wood

M25

SARRATT RD 1
SARRATT LA 2
1 2

Coltspring School of Riding

Cottage Farm

04	A	B	05	C	D	06	E	F

151 165

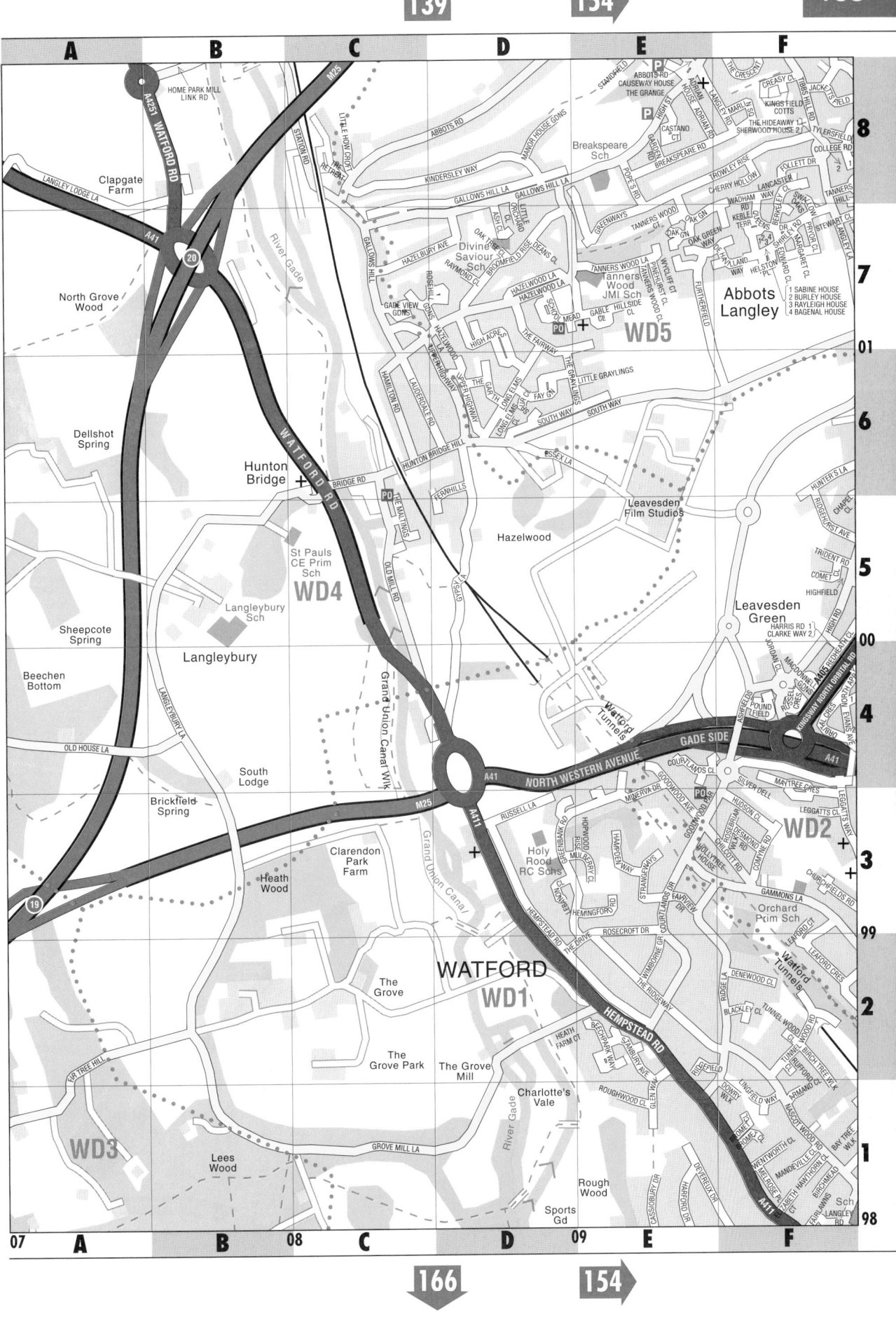

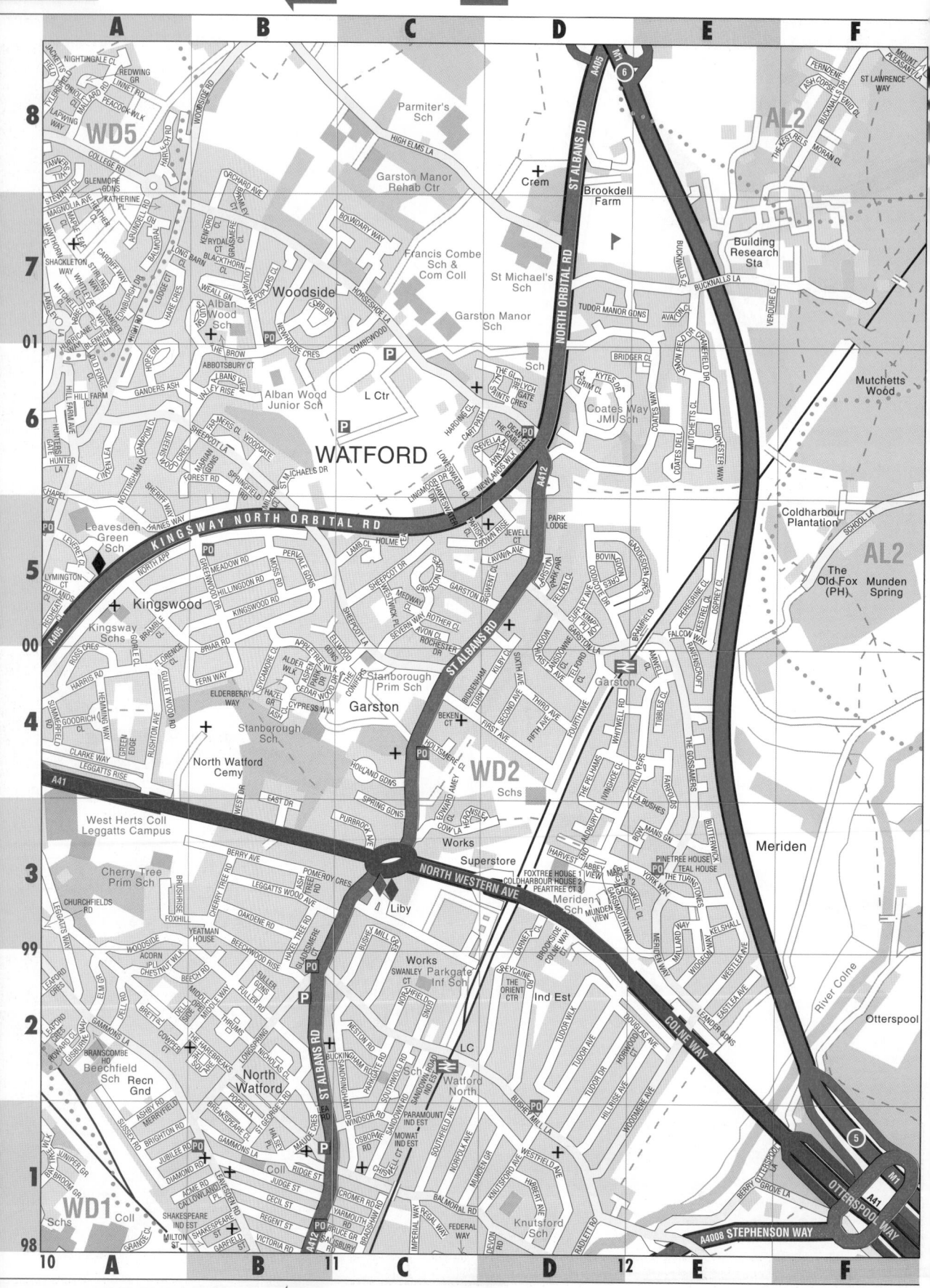

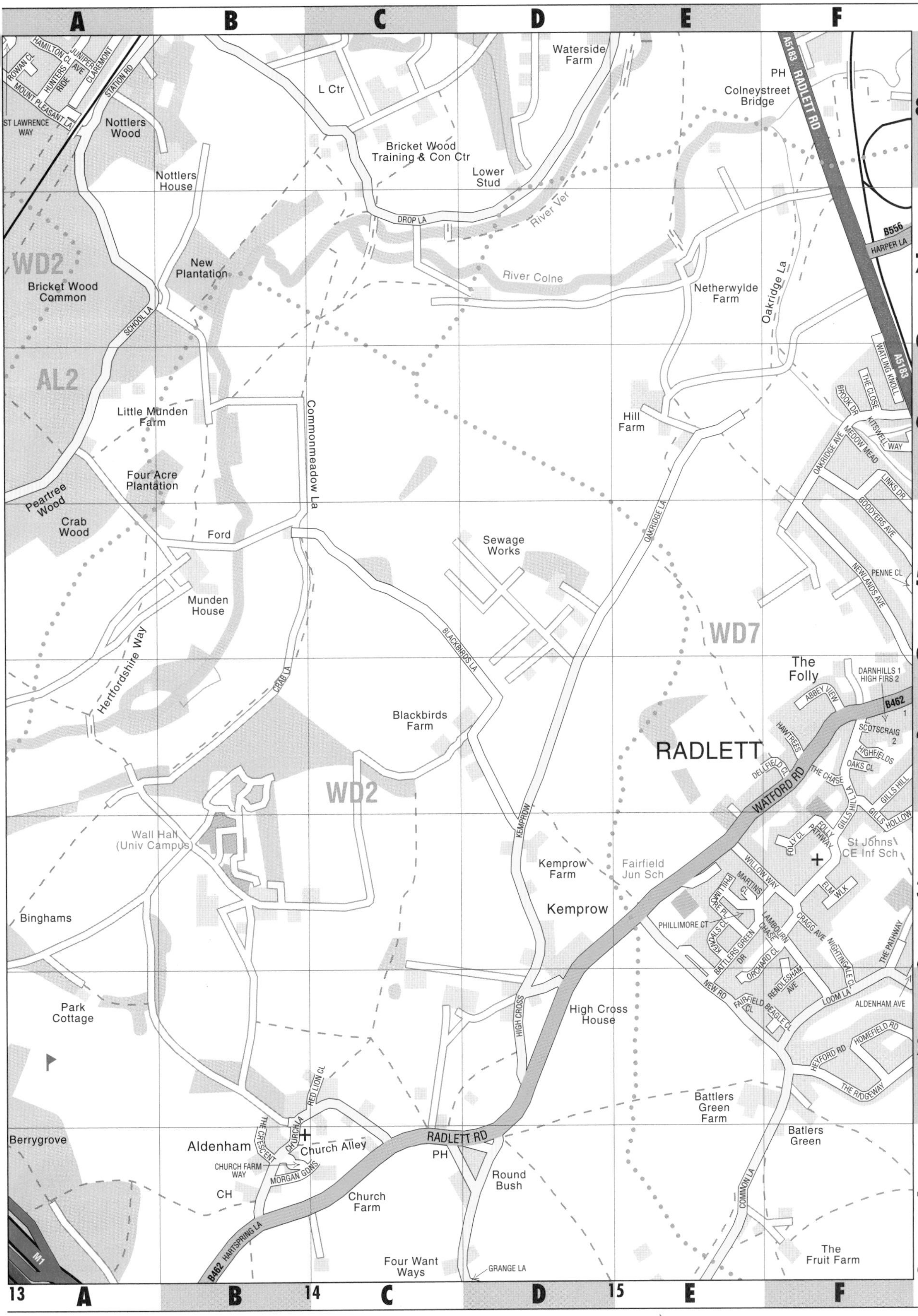

155 142

155 169

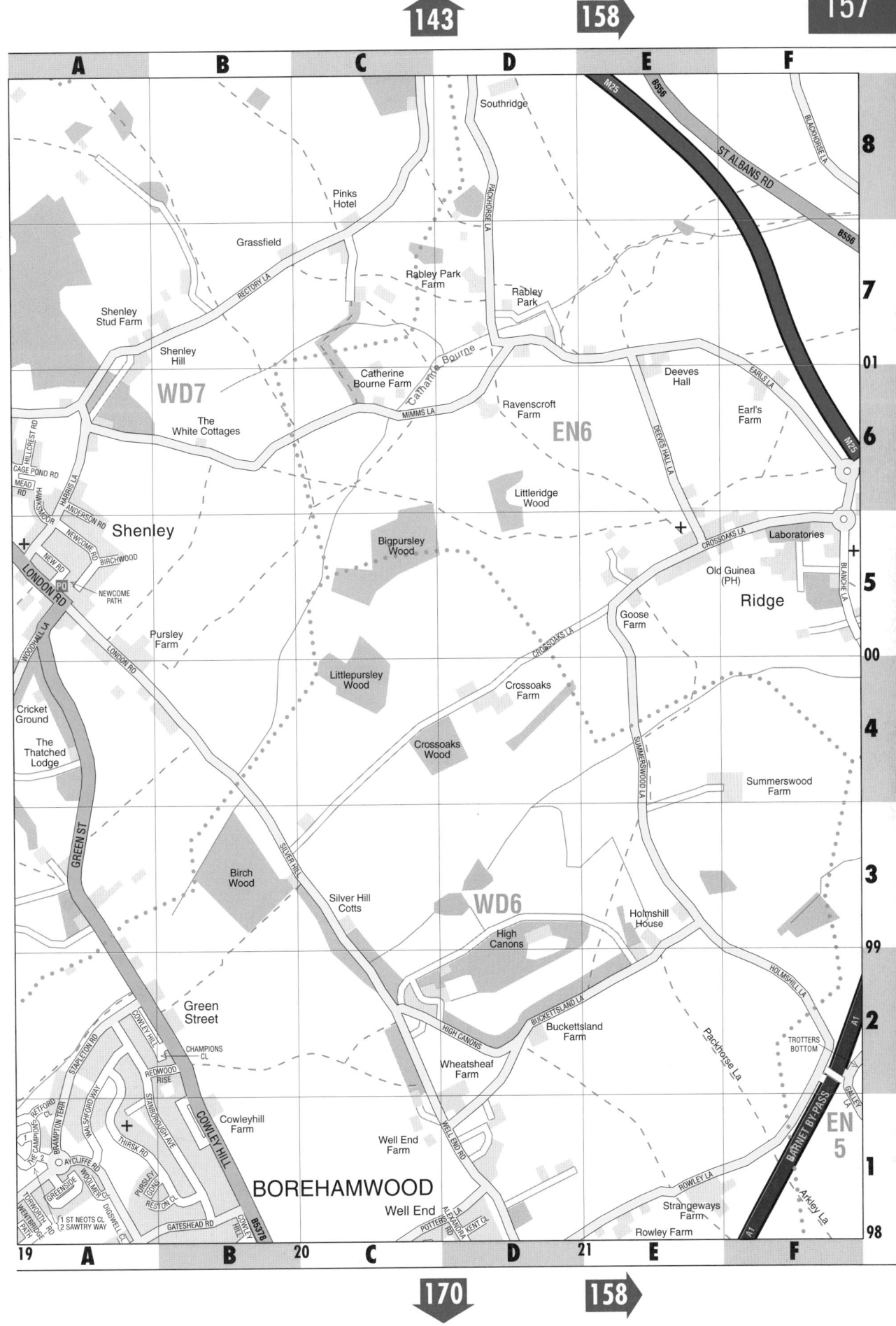

143
158

A B C D E F

8
7
01
6
5
00
4
3
99
2
1
98

Southridge

Pinks Hotel

Grassfield

Rabley Park Farm

Rabley Park

St ALBANS RD

B556

BLACKHORSE LA

B556

PACKHORSE LA

M25

Shenley Stud Farm

Shenley Hill

WD7

Catherine Bourne Farm

Catherine Bourne

MIMMS LA

Ravenscroft Farm

EN6

Deeves Hall

Earl's Farm

EARLS LA

M25

RECTORY LA

The White Cottages

Littleridge Wood

DEEVES HALL LA

CROSSOAKS LA

Laboratories

BLANCHE LA

HILLCREST RD

CAGE POND RD

MEAD RD

HAWKSHEAD

HARRIS LA

ANDERSON RD

NEWCOME RD

BIRCHWOOD

Shenley

NEWCOME PATH

Bigpursley Wood

Goose Farm

Old Guinea (PH)

Ridge

NEW RD

LONDON RD

PO

WOODHALL LA

Pursley Farm

Littlepursley Wood

CROSSOAKS LA

Crossoaks Farm

LONDON RD

Cricket Ground

The Thatched Lodge

Crossoaks Wood

SUMMERSWOOD LA

Summerswood Farm

GREEN ST

Birch Wood

SILVER HILL

Silver Hill Cotts

WD6

High Canons

Holmshill House

HOLMSHILL LA

A1

Green Street

CHAMPIONS CL

COWLEY HILL

STAPLETON RD

REDWOOD RISE

STANBROUGH AVE

THIRSK RD

COWLEY HILL

Cowleyhill Farm

High Canons

HIGH CANONS

BUCKETTSLAND LA

Buckettsland Farm

Packhorse La

TROTTERS BOTTOM

A1

BARNET BY-PASS

OAKLEY

EN 5

RETFORD CL

WALSHFORD WAY

BRAMPTON TERR

THE CAMPIONS

AYCLIFFE

GREENSIDE

WOLMER CL

PURSLEY GDNS

RESTON CL

DISSWELL CT

GATESHEAD RD

COWLEY HILL

BS276

Wheatsheaf Farm

WELL END RD

Well End Farm

ALEXANDRA LA

KENT CL

POTTERS LA

Rowley La

ROWLEY LA

Strangeways Farm

Rowley Farm

Arkley La

BARNET BY-PASS

A1

BOREHAMWOOD

Well End

DORROFIELD

1 ST NEOTS CL
2 SAWTRY WAY

WOODRIDGE
WEST PATH

19 A 20 B C 21 D E F

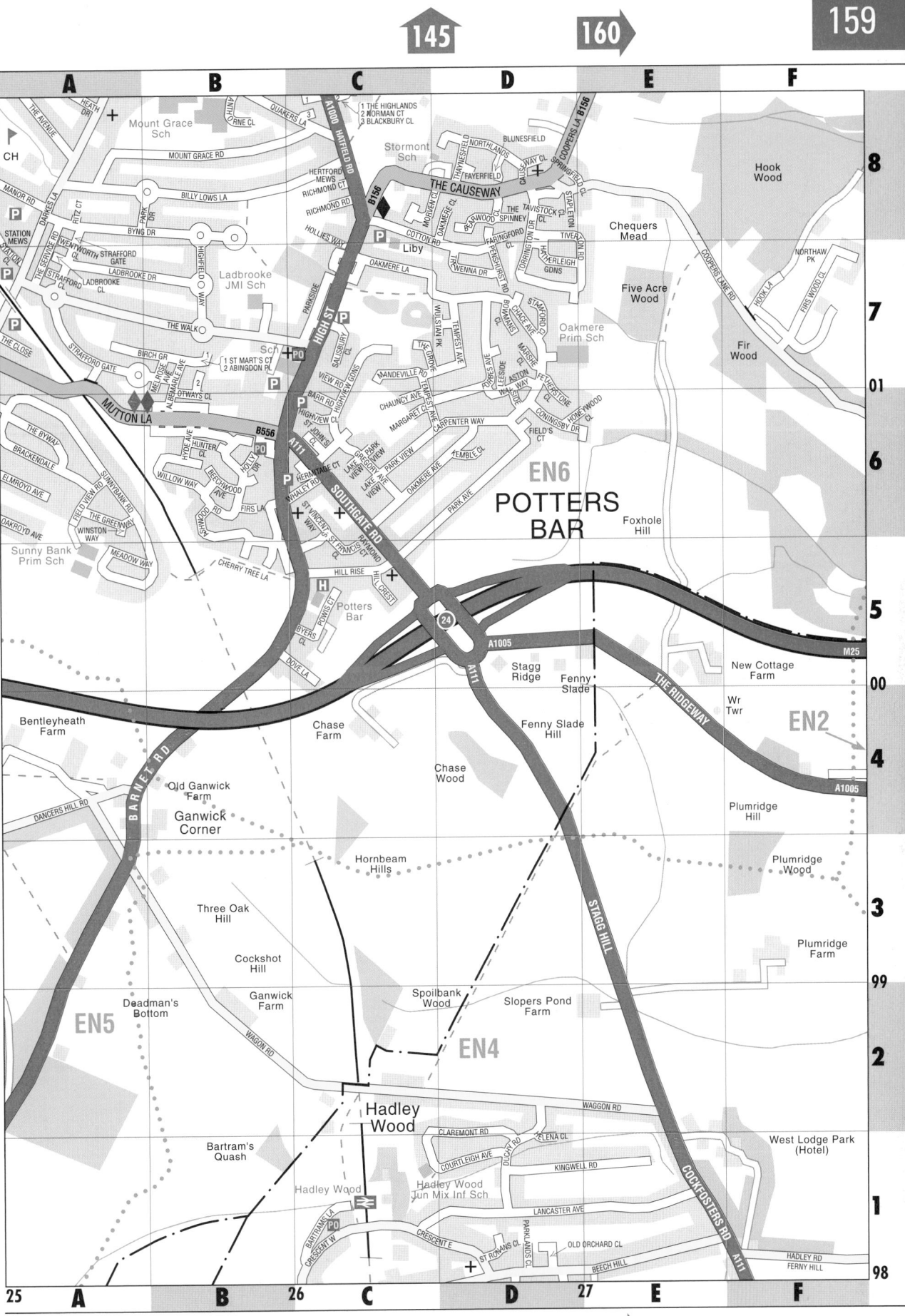

159
146

159

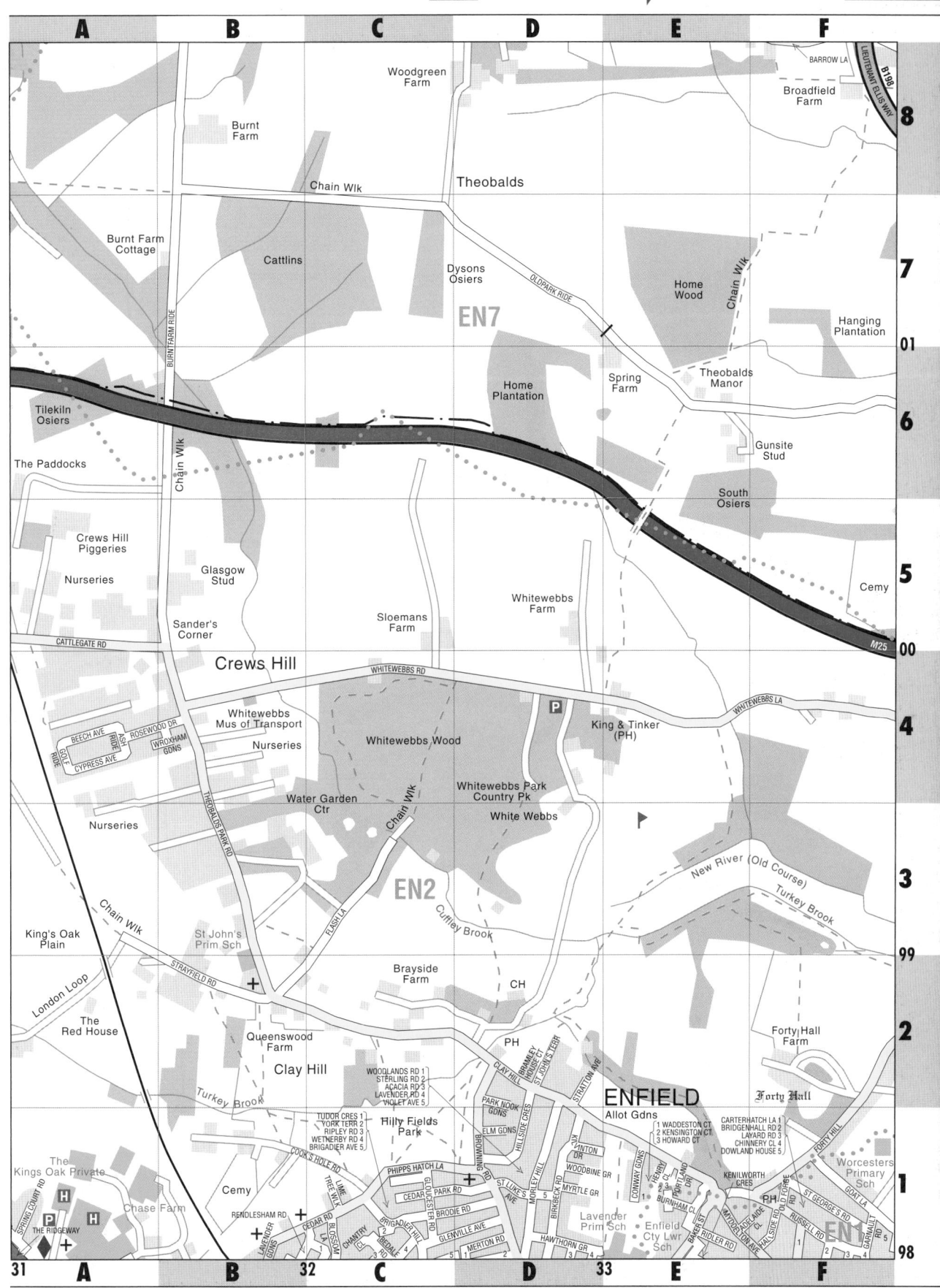

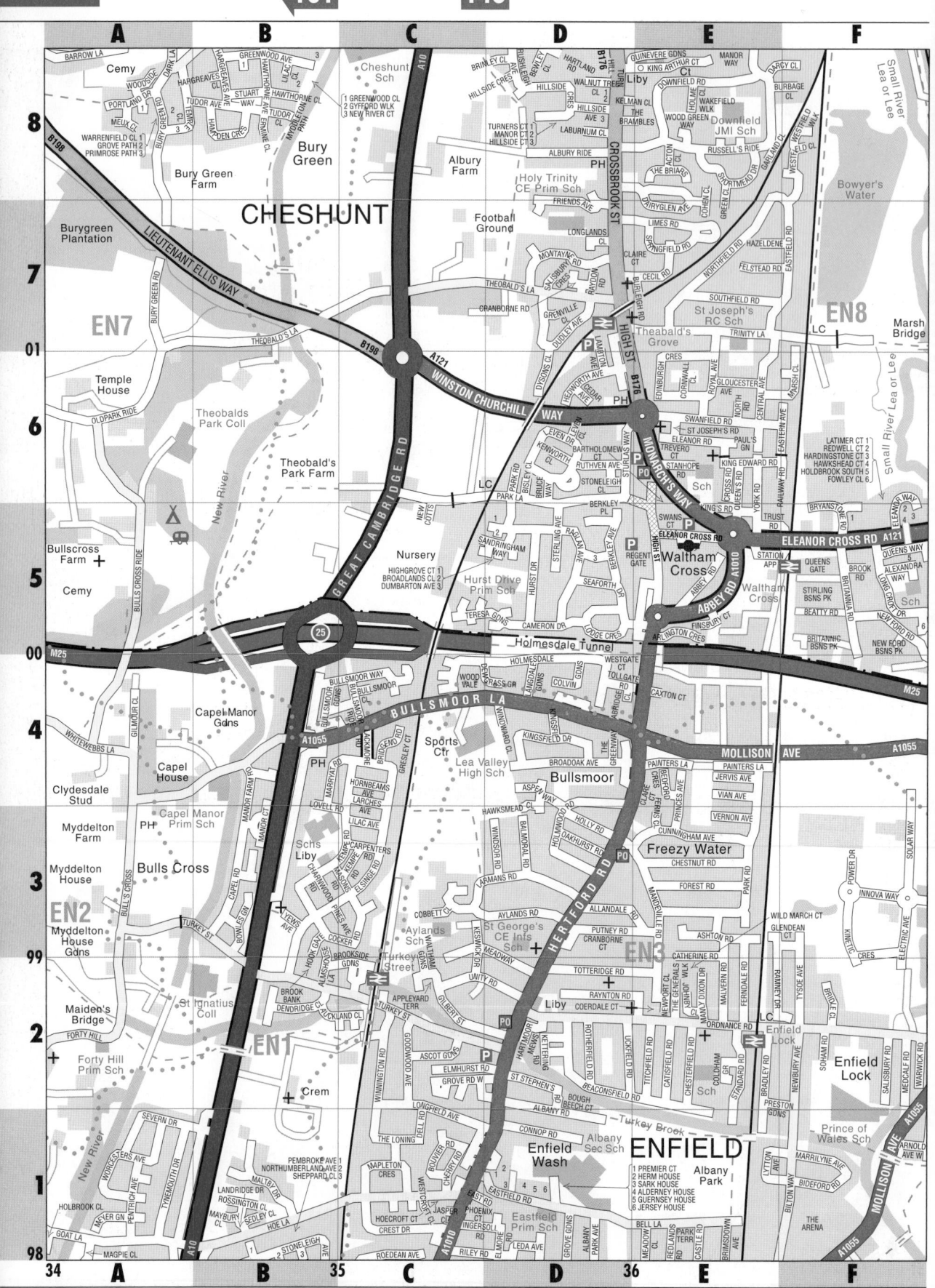

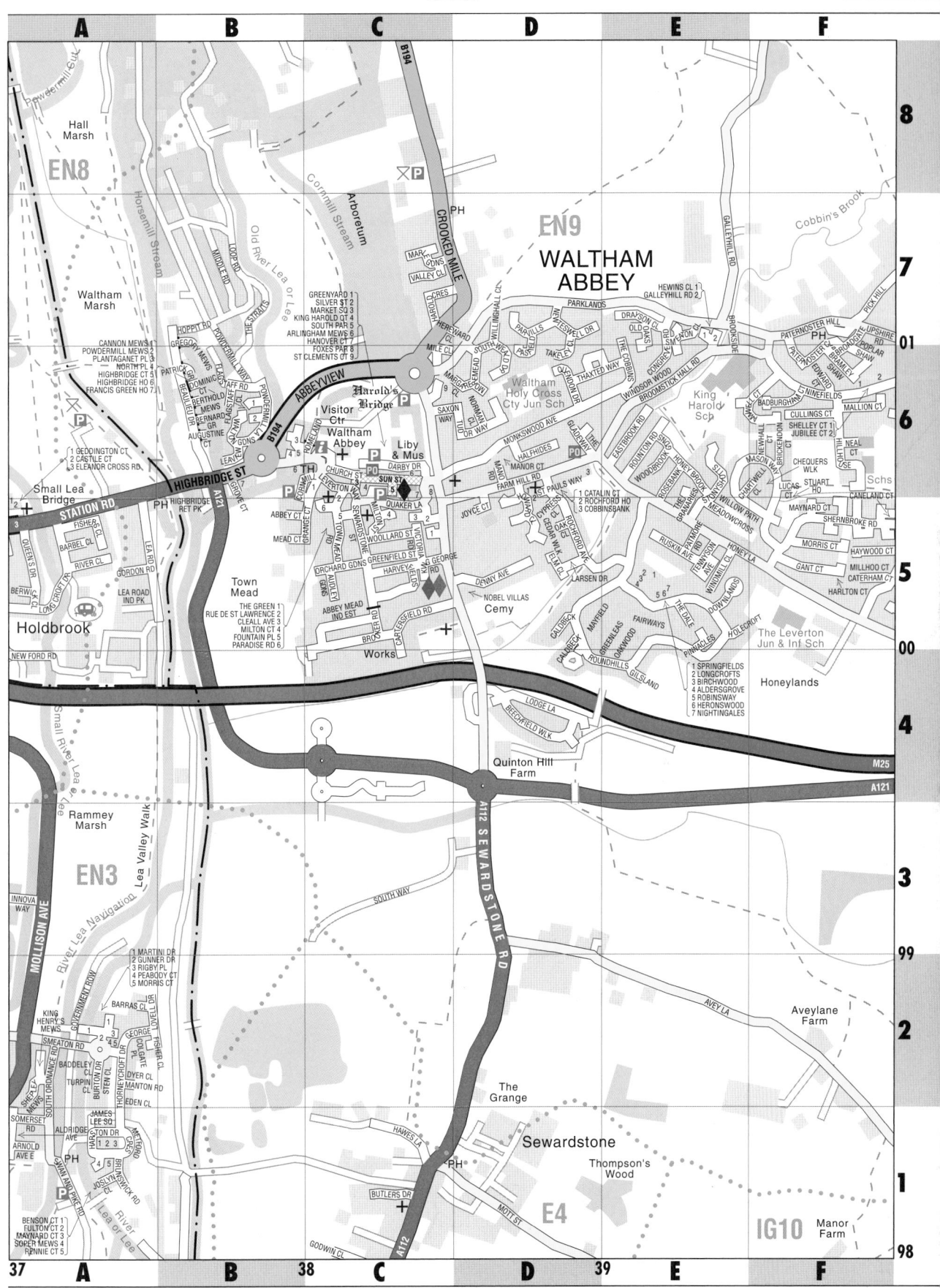

A   B   C   D   E   F

A404

AMERSHAM RD

8

← HP6

Old Hanging
Wood

Sarrattmill
House

Sarrattmill
Bridge

NEW RD

Little
Greenstreet
Farm

Chilton's
Wood

Bullscroft
Spring

Halsey's
Wood

HP8

Great
Greenstreet
Farm

CHENIES RD

St Clement Danes
Sch

NORTH HILL

7

Field Study
Centre

MARLINS CL

97

Whitelands
Wood

GREEN ST

Cemy

The Readings

SOLESBRIDGE LA

WARWICK LA

WATT'S CL

A404

6

Hillas
Wood

Carpenter's
Wood

RICKMANSWORTH RD

SOLESBRIDGE LA

P

+

WARWICK LA

Christ Church
CE Sch

BEECHWOOD PK

THE

FINCH GN

MARRIOTT

PADDOCKS

Chorleywood West

CARPENTERS WOOD DR

WHITELANDS AVE

BEECHWOOD AVE

BRUSHWOOD DR

GREENBURY
CL

ORCHARD CL

ORCHARD DR

HOMEFIELD RD

WOODSIDE

LAND LA

COMMON RD

Chorleywood
Common

DOG KENNEL LA

CEDAR
WLK

WILDWOOD

HOMEWOOD
CT

WOODLAND
PL

TERR

PARKFIELD

BADGERS CL

5

Newhouse
Farm

The Russell Sch

GRENVILLE CT 1
SWAN CT 2
STAG CT 3
SHERATON HOUSE 4

FARM RD

STREETS

GROVE
WAY

BLACKETTS WOOD DR

MAIN PAR

NEW PAR

1
2 3

Chorleywood

GATE
COTTS

COLLEY LAND

GILLIAT'S GN

CH

P

COMMON RD

WD3

►

CHORLEYWOOD

ARTICHOKE
DELL

HAYWOOD PK

SOUTH COTTAGE GDNS

SOUTH COTTAGE
DR

THE
BEECHES

SOUTH PARK AVE

96

BURTONS LA

CHALFONT LA

GROVEWOOD CL

SHIRE LA

HADDON RD

SOUTH RD

BERKS HILL

HILLSIDE RD

DOVER PK

P

P

Liby

NORTH RD

Chorleywood
Bottom

COMMON GATE RD

Chorleywood
Bottom

BERRY LA

M25

4

HP8

Philipshill
Farm

BURFIELD RD

QUICKLEY LA

QUICKLEY LA

FURZE VIEW

CASELL LA

WICK

CAPEL WAY

CAPELL RD

COMANS CL

HUBBARDS RD

TURNERS ORCH

KINGS FRM CL

CLEMENTS RD

Berry
Farm

Catlips Farm
Livery Stables

MANOR
COTTS

HERONSGATE RD

QUICKLEY RISE

PRENDERGAST
WAY

WINDERMERE LA

PENN WAY

KINGS
WAY

West
Clayton

3

BULLSLAND GDNS

QUICKLY BROW

LAWFORD AVE

LAWFORD CL

STAG LA

RYMAN
CT

Chorleywood
Prim Sch

PENN WAY

Penn
Farm

95

The
Swillett

LITTLE HILL

O'FIELD WATRS

Hill
Farm

SHEPHERD'S LA

2

Philipshill
Wood

Bullsland
Farm

BULLSLAND LA

BRADFORD RD

STOCKPORT RD

+

HALIFAX RD

LONG LA

Heronsgate

THE QUEENS DR

ASHLEYS

PYNEFIELD
HO

OATFIELD
ALDBURY
CHILTERN

NELD
WAY

HARRIER
WAY

WALKER
WAY

THELLUSSON
WAY

Mill End

1

Chiltern Open Air
Museum

Shire La

CHERRY TREE LA

NOTTINGHAM RD

Ladywalk

17

M25

DENHAM WAY NORTH
ORBITAL RD

A412

LONG LA

MILL
WAY

PENN
RD

WHITFIELD

HOME WAY

BRESFORD
BASING?

94

HP8

01   A   B   02   C   D   03   E   F

152
166

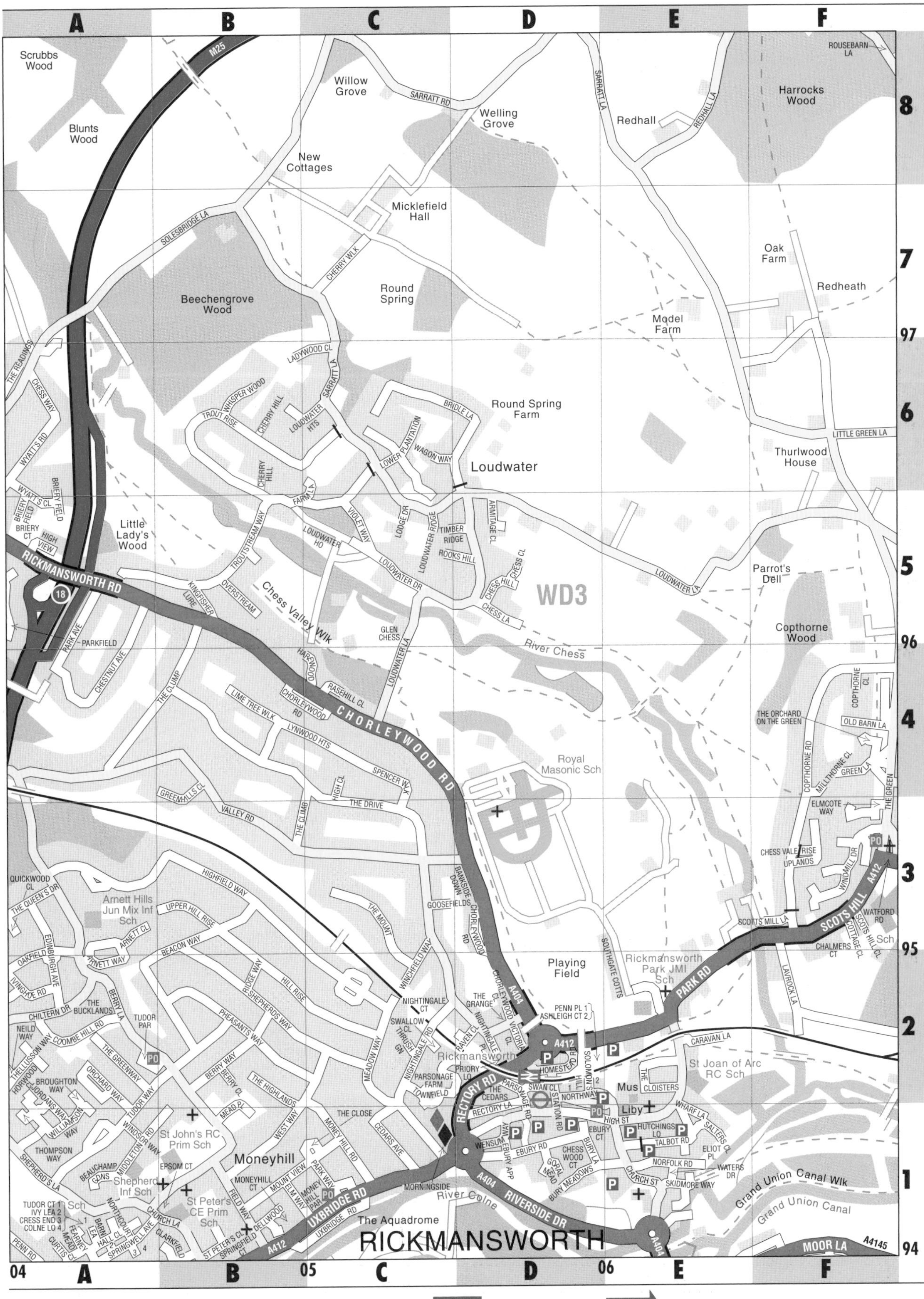

| | A | B | C | D | E | F |

8

Scrubbs Wood

M25

Willow Grove

SARRATT RD

Welling Grove

Redhall

REDHALL LA

SARRATT LA

Harrocks Wood

Blunts Wood

New Cottages

7

SOLESBRIDGE LA

CHERRY WLK

Micklefield Hall

Round Spring

Oak Farm

Redheath

THE READINGS

Beechengrove Wood

LADYWOOD CL

Model Farm

97

WYATTS RD

CHESS WAY

Round Spring Farm

LITTLE GREEN LA

6

TROUT RISE

WHISPER WOOD

CHERRY HILL

LOUDWATER HTS

SARRATT LA

BRIDLE LA

WAGON WAY

Thurlwood House

WYATTS RD

BRIERY FIELD

BRIERY CL

HIGH VIEW

CHERRY HILL

LOUDWATER HO

FARM LA

LOWER PLANTATION

Loudwater

ARMITAGE CL

Parrot's Dell

5

RICKMANSWORTH RD

(18)

KINGFISHER LURE

OVERSTREAM

TROUT STREAM WAY

Little Lady's Wood

VIOLET WAY

LODGE DR

LOUDWATER RIDGE

ROOKS HILL

CHESS HILL CL

CHESS HILL

CHESS LA

WD3

LOUDWATER LA

Copthorne Wood

PARK AVE

PARKFIELD

Chess Valley Wlk

LOUDWATER DR

GLEN CHESS

River Chess

THE ORCHARD ON THE GREEN

OLD BARN LA

96

CHESTNUT AVE

THE CLUMP

RASEHILL CL

HARWOOD

LOUDWATER LA

COPTHORNE CL

COPTHORNE RD

GREEN LA

MILLTHORNE CL

4

LIME TREE WLK

CHORLEYWOOD RD

LYNWOOD HTS

CHORLEYWOOD RD

Royal Masonic Sch

ELMCOTE WAY

THE GREEN

GREENHILLS CL

SPENCER WLK

HIGH CL

THE DRIVE

CHESS VALE RISE

UPLANDS

WINDMILL DR

PO

VALLEY RD

THE CLUMP

THE CLUMP

SCOTS MILL LA

A412

3

QUICKWOOD CL

Arnett Hills Jun Mix Inf Sch

UPPER HILL RISE

HIGHFIELD WAY

THE MOUNT

BANKSIDE DOWN

CHORLEYWOOD RD

GOOSEFIELDS

SCOTS MILL LA

WATFORD RD

Sch

THE QUEEN'S DR

ARNETT CL

BEACON WAY

A404

CHALMERS CT

95

OAKFIELD

EDINBURGH AVE

ARNETT WAY

RIDGE WAY

HILL RISE

Rickmansworth Park JMI Sch

PARK RD

LAVROCK LA

LONGDOE RD

BERRY LA

SHEPHERDS WAY

Playing Field

SOUTHGATE COTTS

CARAVAN LA

2

NEILD WAY

CHILTERN DR

THE BUCKLANDS

TUDOR PAR

PHEASANTS WAY

MEADOW WAY

NIGHTINGALE CT

SWALLOW CL

THRUSH GN

NIGHTINGALE RD

FAVELL CL

THE GRANGE

PENN PL 1

ASHLEIGH CT 2

VICTORIA

SOLOMONS HILL

St Joan of Arc RC Sch

THE CLOISTERS

HOLWELL WAY

HIDPWOOD

BROUGHTON WAY

ORCHARD WAY

BERRY WAY

BERRY LA

THE HIGHLANDS

Rickmansworth

PARSONAGE FARM

TOWNFIELD

PRIORY

HOMESTEAD

A412

Mus

WHARF LA

SALTERS

Liby

HUTCHINGS LO

TALBOT RD

1

JORDANS WAY

WILLIAMSON

COOMBE HILL RD

THE GREENWAY

PO

TUDOR WAY

THE HIGHLANDS

WEST WAY

THE CLOSE

CEDARS AVE

St John's RC Prim Sch

MONEYHILL RD

RECTORY RD

THE CEDARS

RECTORY LA

PASSAGE RD

SWAN CL

STATION RD

HIGH ST

CHESS WOOD

BURT LA

EBURY RD

NORFOLK RD

ELIOT CT PL

WATERS DR

SKIDMORE WAY

CHURCH ST

Grand Union Canal Wlk

THOMPSON WAY

BEAUCHAMP GDNS

WINDSOR WAY

MIDDLETON WAY

EPSOM CT

Moneyhill

MONEYHILL CT

PARK VIEW

MEADOW

PARK RD

WENSUM WAY

EBURY APP

GOVAL MEAD

BURY MEADOWS

Grand Union Canal

SHEPHERD'S LA

Shepherd Inf Sch

St Peter's CE Prim Sch

THE CLOSE

MORNINGSIDE

A404

RIVERSIDE DR

94

TUDOR CT 1

IVY LEA 2

CRESS END 3

COLNE LO 4

Sch

CHURCH LA

SPRINGWELL LA

A412

UXBRIDGE RD

The Aquadrome

River Colne

A404

MOOR LA

A4145

RICKMANSWORTH

| | A | B | C | D | E | F |

173
166

A B C D E F

8

Whippendell Wood

Merlin's Wood

Newland's Spring

Jacotts Hill

Cassiobury Inf Sch

Cassiobury Jun Mix Sch

HEMPSTEAD RD
A411
Heathdene Manor
Grandfield
LANGLEY RD
DEVEREUX DR
Kildonan Cl
WOODLAND DR

7

Waterdell Spring

Dell Wood

Grand Union Canal Wlk

HARFORD DR
BELLMOUNT WOOD AVE
CASSIOBURY DR
CARPENDER WALK
CONINGSBY DR
TREFUSIS WLK
LANGLEY WAY
DE VERE WLK
RICHMOND RD
BERCEAU WLK
The GARDENS
COTTAGE CL
TEMPL E
ORCHARD CL
ORCHARD C L
CASSIOBURY
GARDEN CL
BARKSIDE DR
STRATFORD RD

PD

97

Waterdell House

Long Newland's Spring

Cassiobury Park

6

Little Green Jun Sch
LITTLE GREEN LA
LINCOLN WAY
LINCOLN DR
NORWICH WAY
CANTERBURY WAY

CH

Watford

SWISS CL
SWISS AVE
CASSIOBURY PARK AVE
METROPOLITAN STATION APP
SHEPHERDS RD
Watford Gram Sch for Boys

A412

5

The GREEN
WHITEGATES CL
DUGDALES
LOVATTS
GROVE CRES
MANOR WAY
ROCHESTER WAY
LINCOLN WAY
LEWES WAY
DOVER WAY
LINKS WAY
LODGE END
LUDLOW WAY
RICHMOND WAY
WARWICK WAY
HASTINGS WAY
KENILWORTH DR
DURRANTS DR

WD3

GADE BANK
1 DORCHESTER CT
2 BERKELEY CT
3 GROSVENOR CT
4 CAVENDISH CT

GADE AVE
QUEEN MARY'S AVE
SHERATON MEWS
CASSIOBRIDGE RD
MAYTHORNE CL
RICKMANSWORTH RD
SAVANNA RD
The HOLLIES
CHERRY DALE
ARGYLE CT
KING GEORGES AVE
SOLAR CT
ASTRA CT
WHIPPENDELL RD
SYDNEY RD

WD1

The CHASE
ALWIN CT
CHESTNUT CT
BRAMBLE CL
OAKHURST
MILDRED AVE
KENSINGTON CL
QUEENS AVE
PRINCES AVE
EUSTON AVE
FINWAY CT

96

KINGS OAK
PARRYS CL
The GREEN
HANOVER CT
CHARTER HO
CHERWELL CL
OWENS WAY
REPTON WAY
DULWICH WAY
SHERBORNE WAY
WINCHESTER WAY
LANCING WAY
GIRTON WAY
SHAFTESBURY CT
CLAREMONT CRES
BALDWINS LA

DORROFIELD CL
CASSIOBRIDGE TERR
MAYFARE
SYCAMORE RD
REGENTS INT'CH
ASCOT RD
The BOULEVARD
Works
disused

TOLPITS CL
HAGDEN LA
A4145
HOLM OAK PK
WIGHT HO
MULL
ORKNEY
LUNDY HO
CRUSADER
WAY

4

York Mead Prim Sch
FULLER WAY
MALVERN WAY
BARTON WAY
RUGBY WAY
WINTON DR
WINTON CRES
WINTON APP
SYCAMORE RD
REGARS INT'CH
BLACKMOOR LA
VALLEY WLK
SYCAMORE RD

Croxley Green

Liby
Recn Gd
PO

Croxley CTR
MILLFIELD HO
HALTERS MEAD
GREENHILL CRES
Westfield Sch
CROXLEY VIEW

St Anthonys RC Prim Sch

COMBE HO 1
GOODWIN HO 2
GOSFORD HO 3
COUPER HO 4
CHAUNCEY HO 5
CUSSANS HO 6
COLBORNE HO 7

CRESHAM WAY
COMBE RD
HEALEY RD
HIGH VIEW
The ROUNDS
CHARLOCK
CROCKFORDS CH
CLYSTON RD
SCAMMEL WAY

3

A412
Sch
Croxley
WATFORD RD
THE GUILDHOUSE
DICKINSON AVE
DICKINSON SQ
THE GUILD HO
THE MAGISTERS
YORKE RD
NEW RD
GONVILLE AVE
EVANS CL
FRANKLAND RD
SPRINGFIELD CL
BEECHCROFT AVE
OAKLEIGH DR
HAZELWOOD
DUTTFIELD CR
BASILDON RD
BYEWATERS
GILL CL
HECKFORD CL
EVENSYDE
WOODSHOTS
CROXLEY CTR
FARADAY CL
GREENHILL CRES
MARSHFIELD
KELBLE CT
CHENIES
LATIMER CL
DEAKIN CL

Holywell

CHIRDLAND HO 8
FLETE HO 9
BENNECK HO 10
CHIDBROOK HO 11
REDDING HO 12
FLACKWELL HO 13
CHOLESBURY HO 14
WATFORD ENT CTR

Holywell JMI Sch
PO
TOLPITS LA

F3
1 THANET HO
2 KINTYRE HO
3 LEWIS HO
4 ISLAY HO
5 FARNE HO
6 BARRA HO
7 ALDERNEY HO
8 PURBECK HO
9 JERSEY HO
10 SARK HO
11 SKYE HO
12 BROWNSEA HO
13 SHETLAND HO
14 HARRIS HO

95

Harvey Road Prim Sch
ALL SAINTS LA
BATEMAN RD
HARVEY RD
FRANKLAND CL
MOOR LANE CROSSING
River Gade
Grand Union Canal

Works

Common Moor

THE COURTYARDS
CAXTON WAY

FLAUNDEN HO 1
CHALFONT HO 2
ASHLEY HO 3
WENDOVER HO 4
ASHRIDGE HO 5
AMERSHAM HO 6
TRING HO 7
MISSENDEN HO 8

Brightwells Spring

2

Croxleyhall Farm

DWIGHT RD
SUTHERLAND CT
CENTURY CT
METRO CTR
MOOR PK IND CTR
WOLSEY BSNS PK

Tolpits House

CHAFFINCH LA

Hampermill Lake

1

PEERGLOW IND EST
OLD'S BL
OLD'S APP
BYFLEET IND EST
VALE IND PK
Tolpits House
River Colne

MOOR LA
A4145

HA6

Merchant Taylors' Sch

94

07   A   B   08   C   D   09   E   F

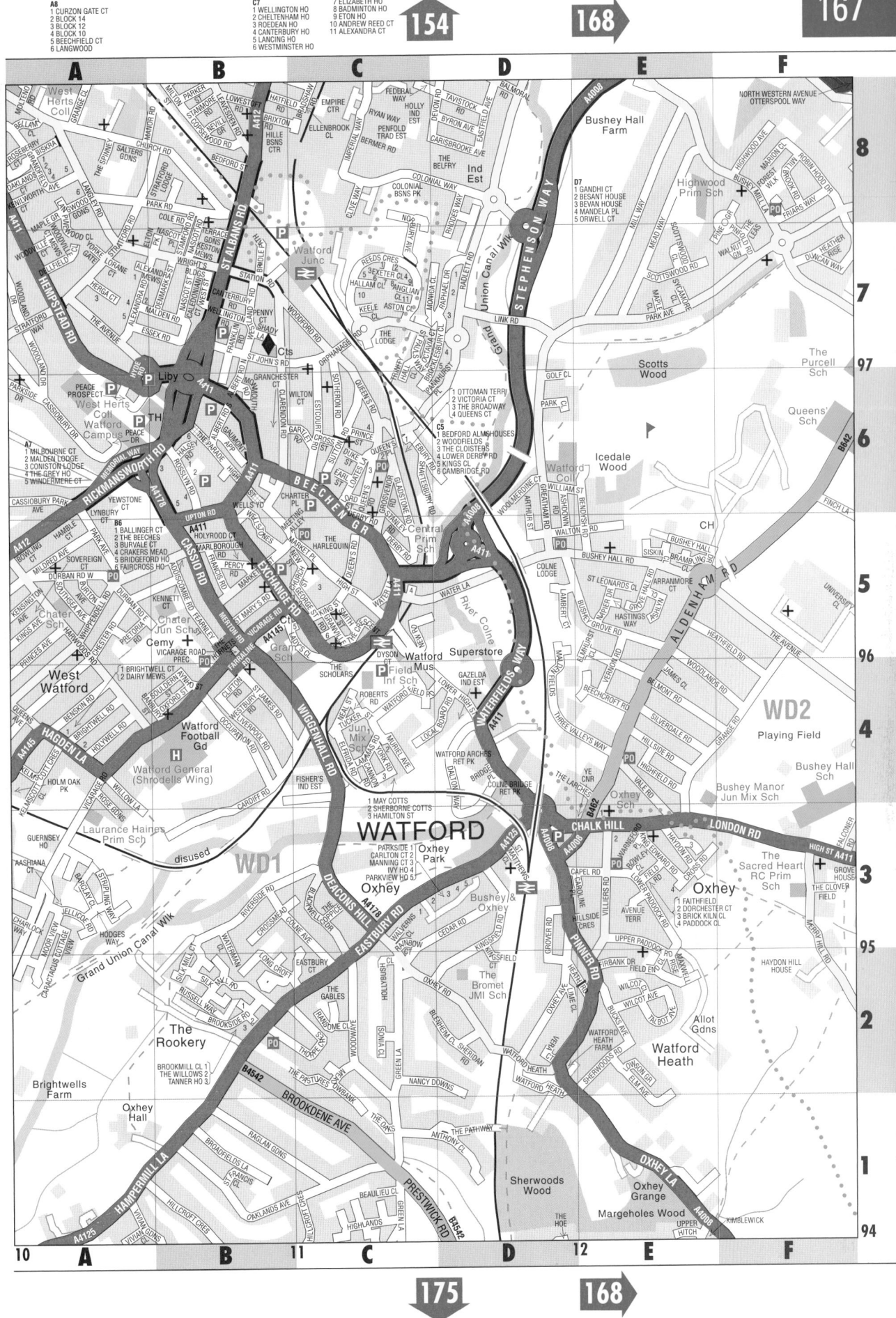

A8
1 CURZON GATE CT
2 BLOCK 14
3 BLOCK 12
4 BLOCK 10
5 BEECHFIELD CT
6 LANGWOOD

C7
1 WELLINGTON HO
2 CHELTENHAM HO
3 ROEDEAN HO
4 CANTERBURY HO
5 LANCING HO
6 WESTMINSTER HO

7 ELIZABETH HO
8 BADMINTON HO
9 ETON HO
10 ANDREW REED CT
11 ALEXANDRA CT

| A | B | C | D | E | F |

West Herts Coll

NORTH WESTERN AVENUE
OTTERSPOOL WAY

Bushey Hall Farm

D7
1 GANDHI CT
2 BESANT HOUSE
3 BEVAN HOUSE
4 MANDELA PL
5 ORWELL CT

Highwood Prim Sch

Highwood Prim Sch

Watford Junc

The Purcell Sch

Scotts Wood

Queens' Sch

1 OTTAWAN TERR
2 VICTORIA CT
3 THE BROADWAY
4 QUEENS CT

Icedale Wood

C5
1 BEDFORD ALMSHOUSES
2 WOODFIELDS
3 THE CLOISTERS
4 LOWER DERBY RD
5 KINGS CL
6 CAMBRIDGE RD

Watford Coll

CH

Bushey Hall

A7
1 MILBOURNE CT
2 MALDEN LODGE
3 CONISTON LODGE
4 THE GREY HO
5 WINDERMERE CT

Central Prim Sch

B6
1 BALLINGER CT
2 THE BEECHES
3 BURVALE CT
4 CRAKERS MEAD
5 BRIDGEFORD HO
6 FAIRCROSS HO

The Harlequin

UNIVERSITY CT

West Watford

Superstore

WD2

Playing Field

1 BRIGHTWELLY CT
2 DAIRY MEWS

Watford Field Inf Sch

GAZELDA IND EST

Bushey Hall Sch

Watford Football Gd

Jun Mix Sch

Bushey Manor Jun Mix Sch

Watford General (Shrodells Wing)

Watford Arches Ret Pk

COLNE BRIDGE RET PK

1 MAY COTTS
2 SHERBORNE COTTS
3 HAMILTON ST

Laurance Haines Prim Sch

WATFORD

Oxhey Park

Oxhey Sch

London Rd

Oxhey

The Sacred Heart RC Prim Sch

GROVE HOUSE

disused

WD1

PARKSIDE 1
CARLTON CT 2
MANNING CT 3
IVY HO 4
PARKVIEW HO 5

Oxhey

The Bromet JMI Sch

1 FAITHFIELD
2 DORCHESTER CT
3 BRICK KILN CL
4 PADDOCK CL

Bushey & Oxhey

Guernsey Ct

Aashiana

Hodges Way

Grand Union Canal Wlk

The Gables

Watford Heath Farm

Watford Heath

The Rookery

BROOKMILL CL 1
THE WILLOWS 2
TANNER HO 3

Brightwells Farm

Oxhey Hall

Allot Gdns

Sherwoods Wood

Oxhey Grange

Margeholes Wood

KIMBLEWICK

THE HOE

UPPER HITCH

| 8 |
| 7 |
| 97 |
| 6 |
| 5 |
| 96 |
| 4 |
| 3 |
| 95 |
| 2 |
| 1 |
| 94 |

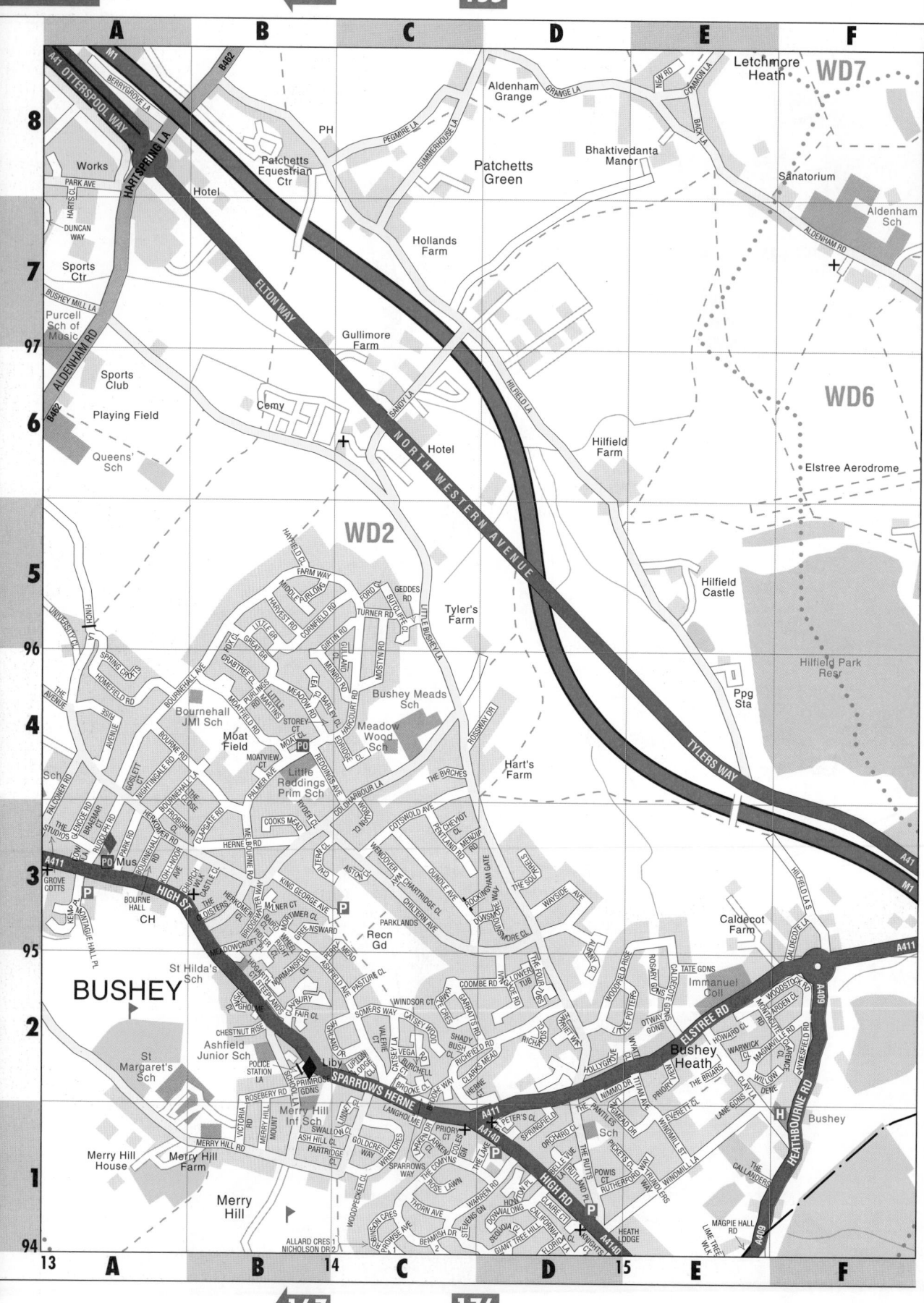

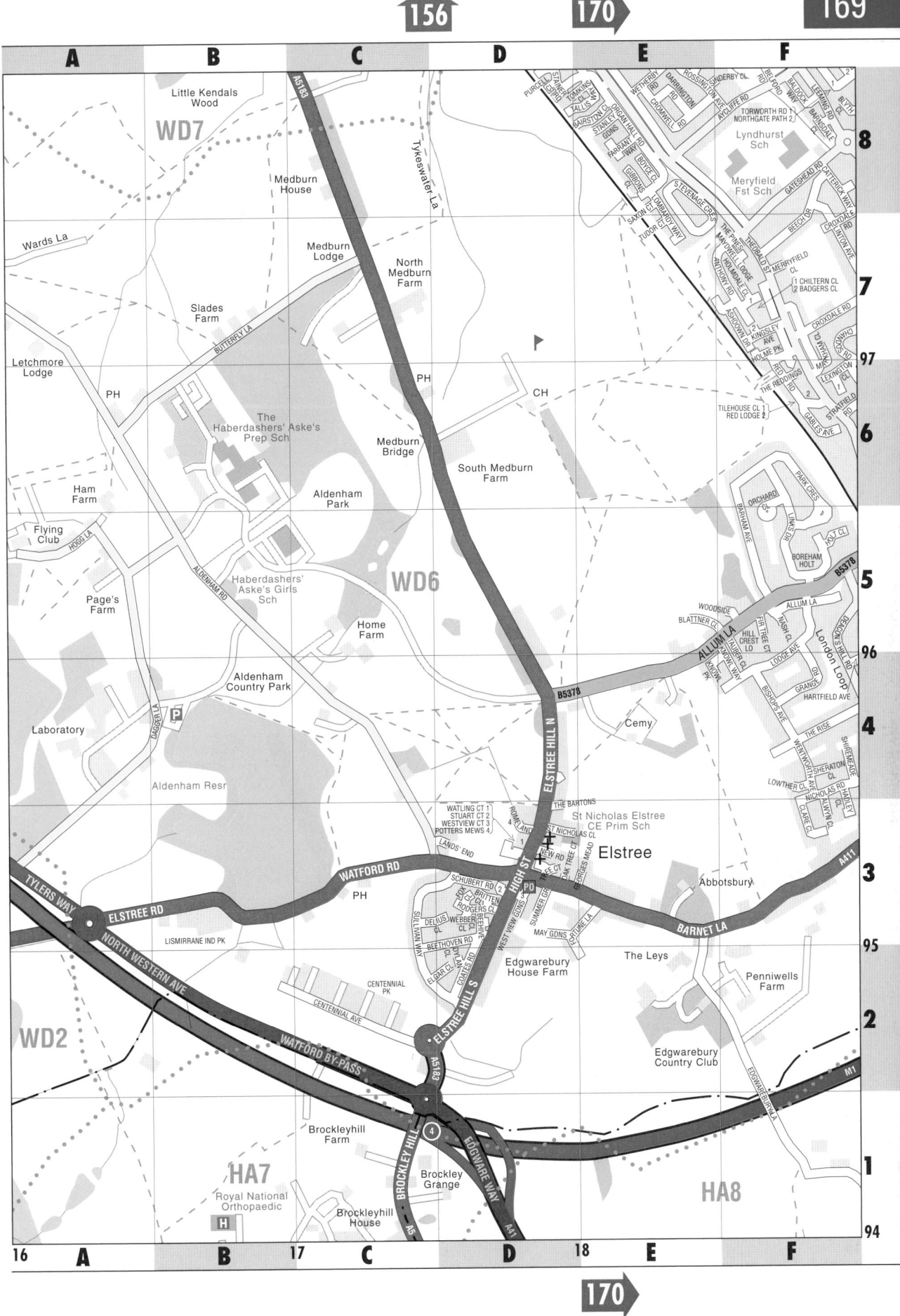

156
170
170

169
157

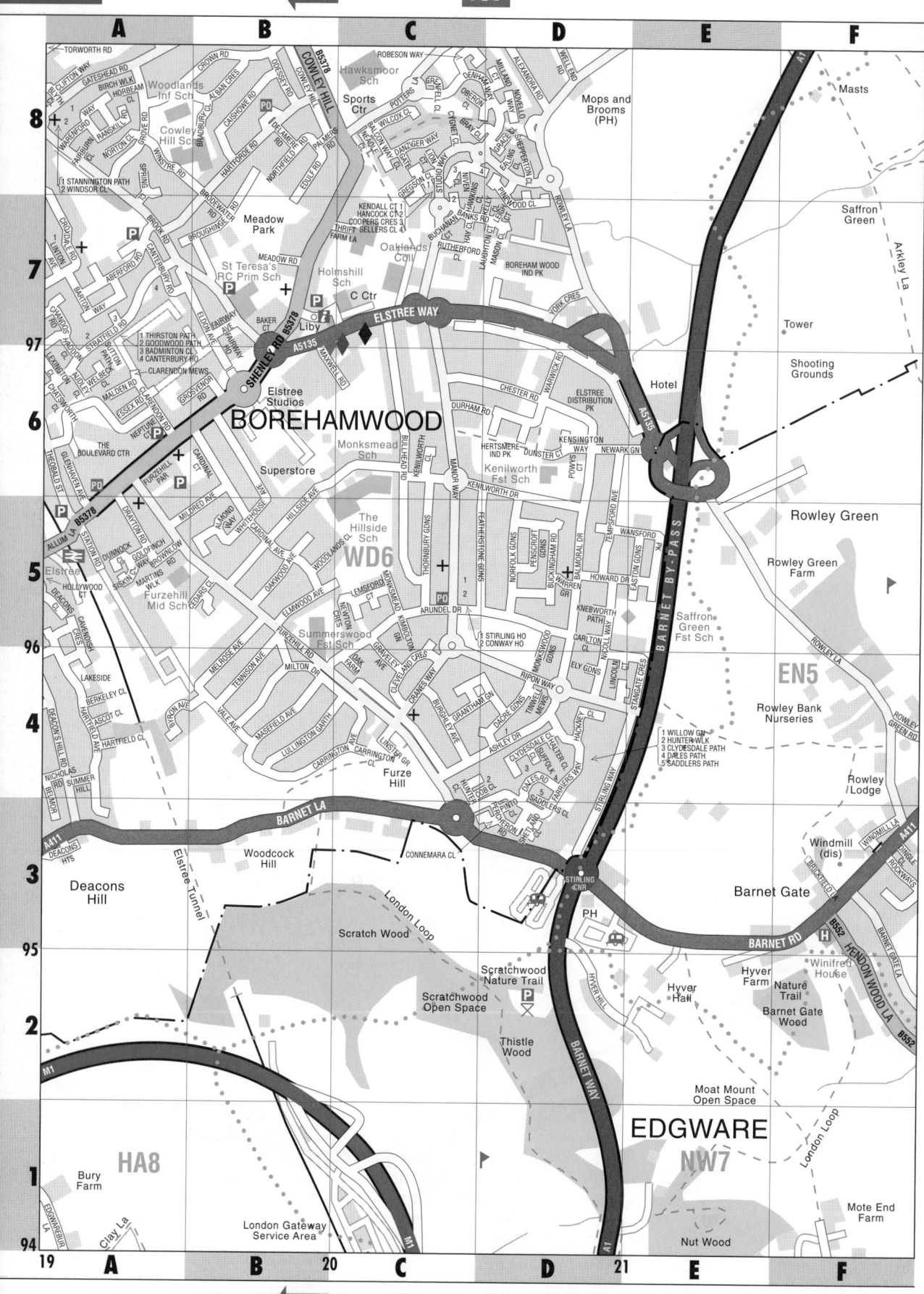

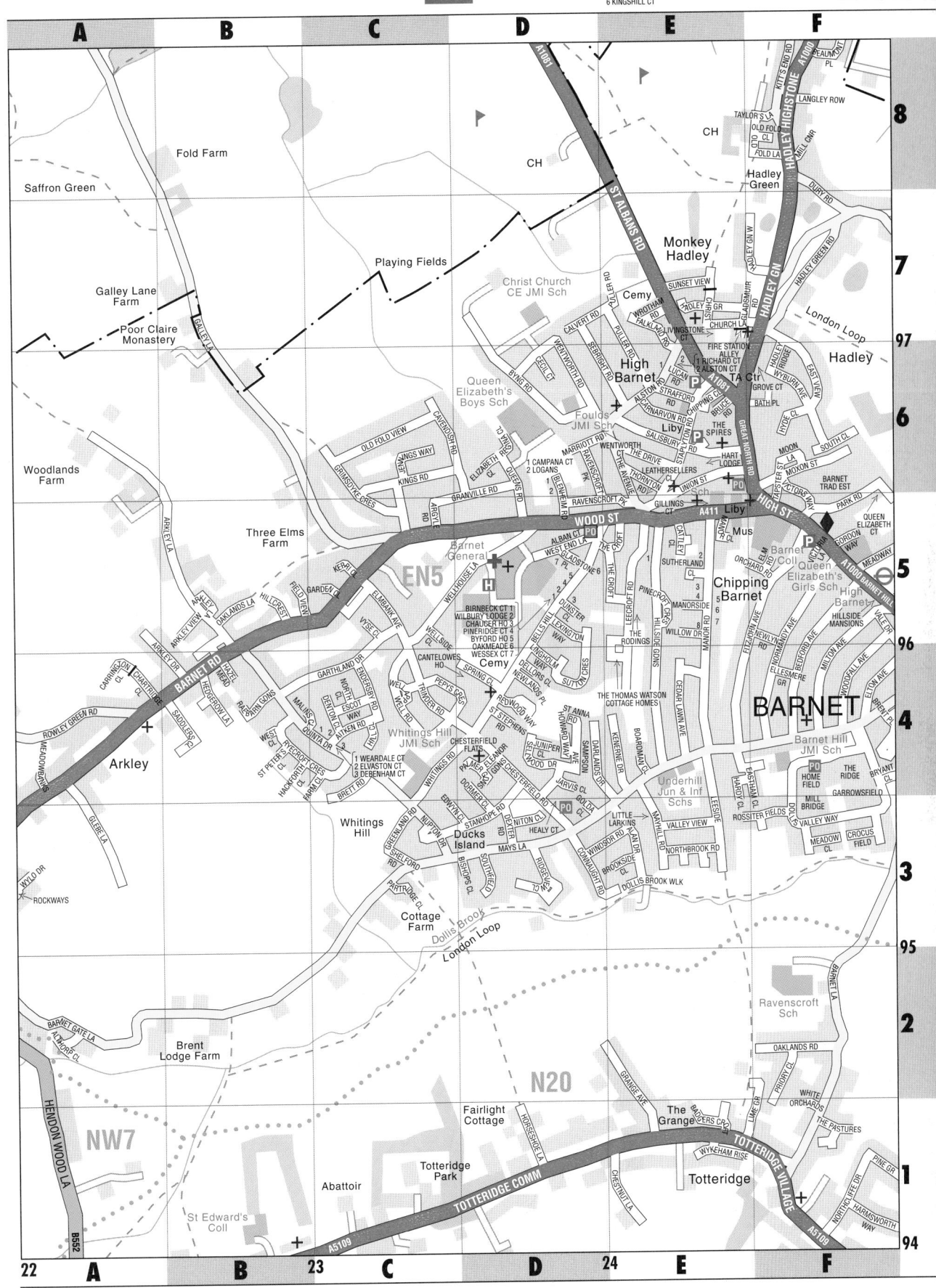

A B C D E F

8
7
97
6
5
96
4
3
95
2
1
94

22 A B 23 C D 24 E F

Saffron Green
Fold Farm
Galley Lane Farm
Poor Claire Monastery
Woodlands Farm
Playing Fields
Christ Church CE JMI Sch
Monkey Hadley
CH
CH
Hadley Green
Hadley
London Loop
Cemy
High Barnet
Queen Elizabeth's Boys Sch
Foulds JMI Sch
The Spires
Hart Lodge
Barnet General
Three Elms Farm
EN5
Arkley
Barnet Coll
Chipping Barnet
Queen Elizabeth's Girls Sch
High Barnet
Hillside Mansions
BARNET
Barnet Hill JMI Sch
Whitings Hill JMI Sch
Cemy
The Thomas Watson Cottage Homes
Underhill Jun & Inf Schs
Mill Bridge
Garrowsfield
Whitings Hill
Ducks Island
Little Larkins
Cottage Farm
Dollis Brook
London Loop
Ravenscroft Sch
Brent Lodge Farm
N20
Fairlight Cottage
The Grange
White Orchards
The Pastures
NW7
Abattoir
St Edward's Coll
Totteridge Park
TOTTERIDGE COMM
Totteridge
TOTTERIDGE VILLAGE
HENDON WOOD LA
ROCKWAYS

164

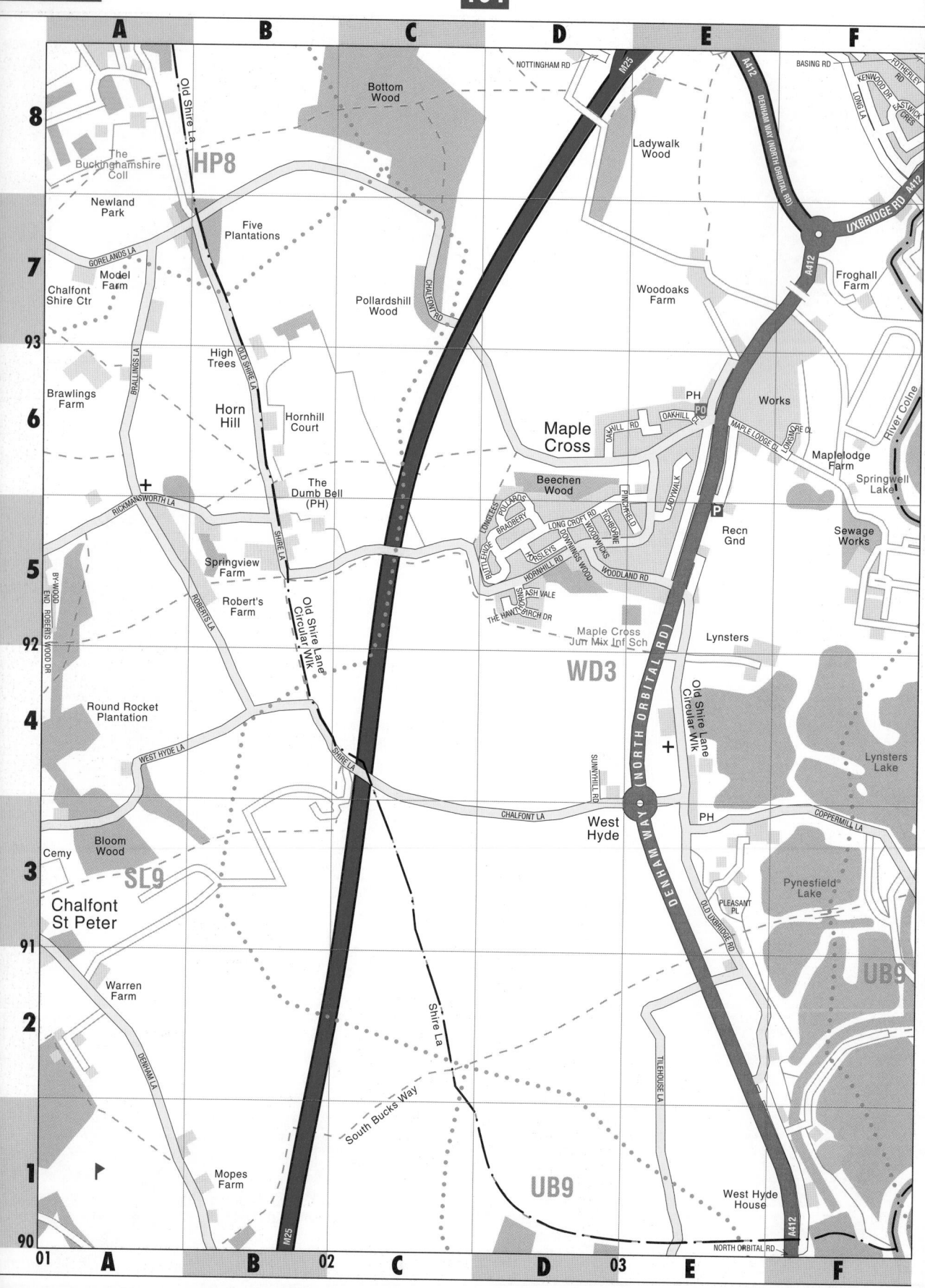

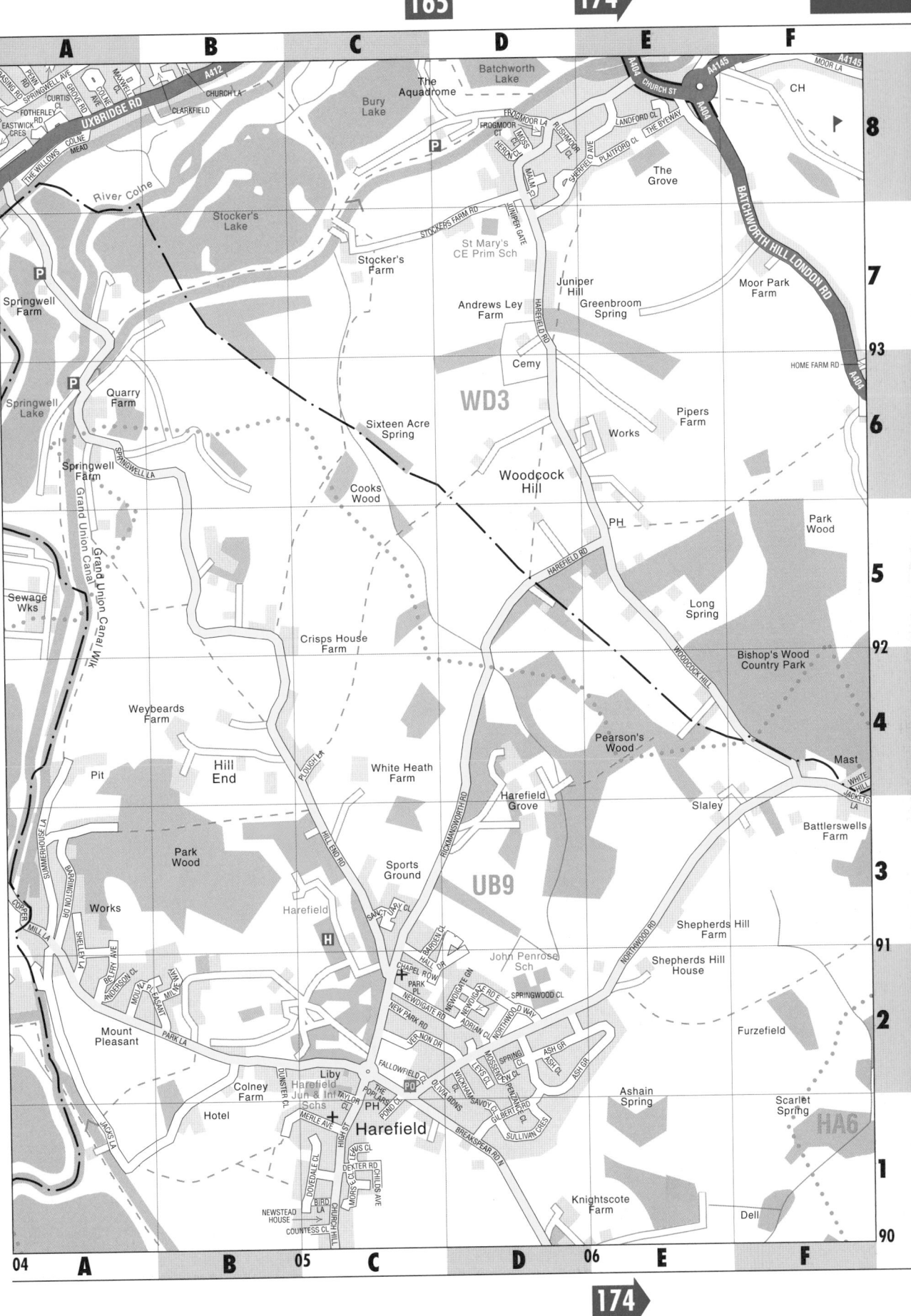

A B C D E F

8

A4145 MOOR LA A4145

Northwood Prep Boys Sch

Playing Fields

Merchant Taylors' Sch

HAMPERMILL LA A4125

WD1

SANDY LA

SANDY LODGE RD

ASKEW RD

EAST DR

SANDY LODGE LA

HAYLING RD

DUMFRIES CL

7

CH

PEMBROKE RD

MAIN AVE

WOLSEY MANS

NORTH APP

PARK MANS

PENN RD

Moor Park

CH

SANDY LODGE LA

CH

WESTBURY RD

THE ROVERS

BISHOPS AVE

ROSS AVE

FARRINGTON PL

PORT LAND RD

VALE CT

PHOENIX CL

CAPELLA RD

VEGA CRES

A4125

93

WD3

HOME FARM RD

Home Farm

THORNHILL RD

RUSSELL RD

ASTONS RD

BEDFORD RD

ORMONDE RD

WOLSEY RD

SOUTH APP

Moor Park

CROFTERS RD

WOODFIELD AVE

THE FAIRWAY

HERON WLK

ACROSS AVE

ALT AIR WAY

ADHARA

MARKAB RD

6

A404 LONDON RD

BATCHWORTH HEATH HILL

Batchworth Heath

PARK CL

ANSON WLK

OXFORD RD

OLD GANNON CL

HEATHSIDE RD

RUSSELL CL

NEVIL CL

HSIDE RD

BOURNE END RD

EASTBURY

EASTBURY RD

GROSVENOR RD

PARKSIDE CT

SHELLEY CL

HOLBEIN GATE

WESLEY AVE

Eastbury

DAVENHAM AVE

Batchworth Heath Farm

FARM RD

WHITE HILL

HA6

KEWFERRY DR

EBURY CL

TREE TOPS CL

St Martin's Sch

MEZEN

GROVE FARM PARK

BATCHWORTH LA

ST MARY'S AVE

SANDY LODGE CT

CLARE CT

EASTBURY AVE

EASTBURY PL

PINE CL

KILM WAY

FRITHWOOD AVE

5

White Hill

REEDESIDE RD

THIRLMERE GDNS

TANWORTH CEDAR PL

LANG TOFT CL

LANG

HILL RD

MOOR PARK RD

GROVE RD

WOODRIDGE WAY

ROFANT RD

EASTBURY RD

92

Lockwell

WHITE HILL

RISING HILL CL

Park Farm

Holy Trinity Sch

ELMS CL

SHERBORNE PL

WILDWOOD

HALLAND WAY

DENE RD

London Bible Coll

St Helen's Sch

Frithwood Prim Sch

WATFORD RD

CHERTSEY

4

Lockwell Wood

Mount Vernon & Watford

A4180

GLENSHEE CL

EATON GATE

BIRCH CT

HARRISON CL

COLLEGE WAY

WOODLEA GR

FIRS WLK

FOXE

WELCOTE DR

OAK CT

THE LARCHES

OAKLANDS GATE

TRINITY

OSBOURNE RD

CAREW RD

SENTIS CT

Liby

CHESTER PL

A4125

French Grove

RICKMANSWORTH RD

ROSECROFT CT

CLOSEMEAD CL

EATON GATE WAY

MALLARD

THE AVENUE

CHELWOOD CL

WEDGEWOOD CL

COPELAND

B469

GREEN LA

B469

WOODSIDE WAY

UB9

JACKET LA

The Riverside Club (Tennis Ctr)

Denville Hall

BITTSMEAD

SEVENOAKS CL

NORTHGATE

CH

THE GLEN

WILFORD

CLIVE RD

Northwood Coll

Northwood

MANSWORTH CL

FORGE LA

ASHURST

CHESTER RD

ROY RD

WYCHWOOD WAY

WOODSIDE WAY

3

MANOR HOUSE DR

HURST PL

DUCK'S HILL RD

TEAL DR

COVERT RD

COPSE WOOD WAY

SILVERWOOD CL

LINKSWAY

MAXWELL RD

CLINON CL

NAWSWORTH CL

DORMANS CL

LEAF CL

MURRAY RD

ELGIN DR

DRYSDALE CL

HIGHFIELD CL

REGINALD RD

CHURCH CT

EMMANUEL RD

TOWNSEND

CHURCH RD

HIGH ST

CHURCH RD

91

Deadman's Grove

NEAGH DR

DRAKES DR

FRINGEWOOD CL

KINGFISHER CL

NICHOLAS WAY

ROGERS RUFF

OAK GLADE

LONGWOOD CL

GRANGEDALE CL

ST THILA LA

NEW FARM LA

HIGHFIELD CRES

GREENHILLS

HIGHFIELD CL

PINNER RD

A4125

PO

VINCENT CT

HILLARD RD

ADDISON RD

2

Towers

A4180

DUCK'S HILL FARM

COPSE WOOD CL

THE BROAD WLK

NORTHWOOD

ATHENA PL

LYNWOOD DR

KNOLL CRES

LEEDS AVE

CHESTNUT WAY

THE DRIVE

ACRE WAY

ROBINA CL

YASMIN CL

PINNER RD A404

Northwood Hills

1

DUCKS HILL RD

Duck's Hill

Copse Wood

CH

KNOLL CRES

Cemy

90

Ashby Farm

WINCHESTER RD

CRANBOURNE RD

HIGHLAND RD

07 A B 08 C D 09 E F

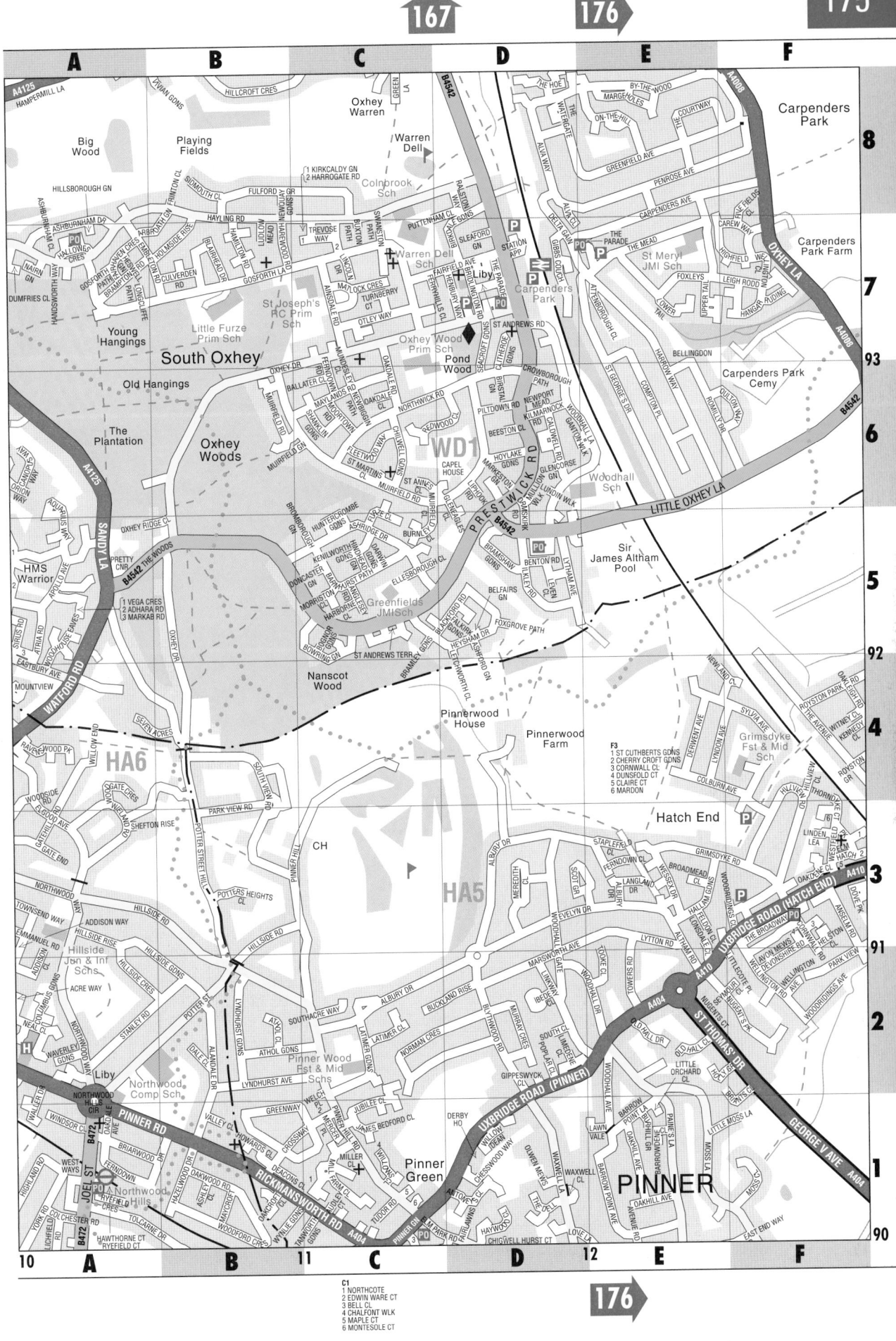

A B C D E F

8

WD1

WD2

BUSHEY

Stanmore Common

THE COMMON

7

Mutton Wood

Harrow Weald Common

Bentley Priory

HA7

93

Levels Wood

COMMON RD

Deer Park

6

Valley View Farm

Grimsdyke Hotel

The Kiln

Heriot's Wood

Burnt Oak Farm

Weald Wood

OLD REDDING

PH

Priory House

CH

Stony Wood

PH

Copse Farm

Lower Priory Farm

STANMORE

5

Oxheylane Farm

OXHEY LA

BROOKSHILL DR

Hillside

BROOKSHILL AVE

CLAMP HILL

Bentley Wood High Sch

92

HA5

HA3

Harrow Weald PK

BROOKSHILL

Harrow Coll, Harrow Weald Campus

Harrow Weald Cemy

4

The Bannister Sports Ctr

PARK DR

Lavender Gdns

UXBRIDGE RD (STANMORE) A410

A4008

OXHEY LA

UXBRIDGE RD (HARROW WEALD)

A410

3

Hatch End

UXBRIDGE RD (HATCH END)

A410

Superstore

Harrow Coll, Adult Learners Ctr

Whittlesea Sch

Recn Gd

Weald Fst & Mid Schs

91

Playing Field

Hatch End High Sch

Cedars Fst & Mid Sch

Harrow Weald

HIGH RD

College Ave

2

Shaftesbury Sch

St Teresa's Fst & Mid RC Sch

St Barnabas Sch

HIGH ST

Park Cres

Headstone Lane

HA2

Carmelite Cl

1

Pinner Park Farm

Sports Gd

Coll

HARROW

Belmont Fst & Mid Sch

90

GEORGE V AVE

A404

A409

HIGH ST

13 A B 14 C D 15 E F

Street names are listed alphabetically and show the locality, the Postcode District, the page number and a reference to the square in which the name falls on the map page

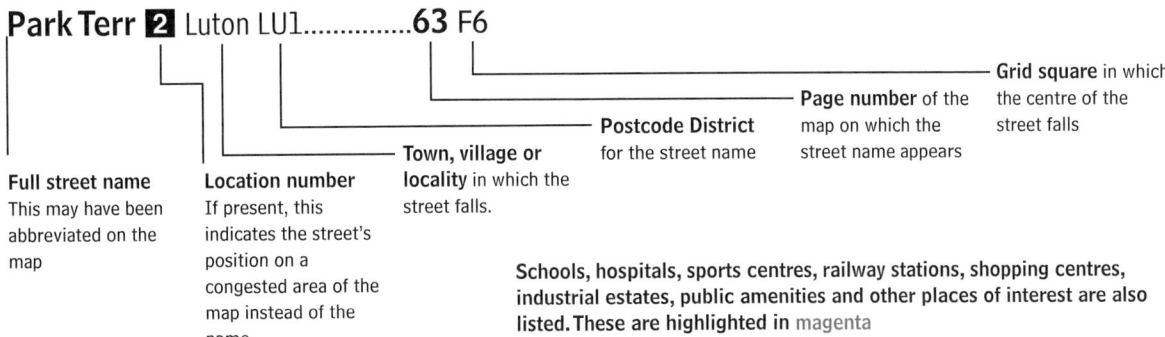

Park Terr 🔲 **Luton LU1..............63 F6**

Full street name
This may have been abbreviated on the map

Location number
If present, this indicates the street's position on a congested area of the map instead of the name

Town, village or locality in which the street falls.

Postcode District
for the street name

Page number of the map on which the street name appears

Grid square in which the centre of the street falls

Schools, hospitals, sports centres, railway stations, shopping centres, industrial estates, public amenities and other places of interest are also listed. These are highlighted in magenta

Abbreviations used in the index

App	Approach	Cl	Close	Espl	Esplanade	N	North	S	South
Arc	Arcade	Comm	Common	Est	Estate	Orch	Orchard	Sq	Square
Ave	Avenue	Cnr	Corner	Gdns	Gardens	Par	Parade	Strs	Stairs
Bvd	Boulevard	Cotts	Cottages	Gn	Green	Pk	Park	Stps	Steps
Bldgs	Buildings	Ct	Court	Gr	Grove	Pas	Passage	St	Street, Saint
Bsns Pk	Business Park	Ctyd	Courtyard	Hts	Heights	Pl	Place	Terr	Terrace
Bsns Ctr	Business Centre	Cres	Crescent	Ind Est	Industrial	Prec	Precinct	Trad	Trading Est
Bglws	Bungalows	Dr	Drive		Estate	Prom	Promenade	Wlk	Walk
Cswy	Causeway	Dro	Drove	Intc	Interchange	Ret Pk	Retail Park	W	West
Ctr	Centre	E	East	Junc	Junction	Rd	Road	Yd	Yard
Cir	Circus	Emb	Embankment	La	Lane	Rdbt	Roundabout		

Town and village index

Abbots Langley 153 F7	Chorleywood 164 E5	Hemel Hempstead 124 D6	Mentmore 61 D4	Spellbrook 97 E8
Albury 57 A6	Clothall 24 E4	Henlow 10 D8	Moor Park 174 D6	Standon 55 E1
Aldbury 101 C5	Cockernhoe 46 F3	Hertford 113 C5	Much Hadham 74 F3	Stanmore 176 F5
Anstey 29 B6	Codicote 67 E1	Hertford Heath 114 B3	Nettleden 103 B1	Stanstead Abbotts ...115 E4
Ardeley 38 F3	Colney Heath 143 D8	Hertingfordbury 112 E5	Newgate Street 146 F7	Stansted Mountfitchet ..59 C6
Arlesey 11 A4	Cottered 39 C7	Hexton 19 B2	Newnham 12 E8	Stapleford 92 A7
Ashley Green 136 A7	Crews Hill 161 B4	High Wych 97 B1	Northaw 145 F1	Steeple Morden 5 B8
Ashwell 4 D3	Croxley Green 166 A4	Hinxworth 3 C5	Northwood 174 E2	Stevenage 50 D8
Aspenden 40 D5	Cuffley 146 E3	Hitchin 34 E8	Nuthampstead 18 A2	Stocking Pelham 43 E7
Aston 51 E2	Dagnall 81 C6	Hoddesdon 135 C7	Oaklands 89 F7	Stotfold 11 E7
Aston Clinton 99 A3	Dane End 71 F8	Holdbrook 163 A5	Odsey 5 C1	Streatley 31 A5
Ayot St Lawrence 88 B6	Datchworth 69 E2	Holwell 21 B7	Park Street 141 D5	Studham 82 C4
Ayot St Peter 88 F3	Dunstable 44 A1	Hunsdon 95 D1	Pepperstock 63 C1	Tewin 90 E2
Baldock 23 E8	East Hyde 85 F8	Ickleford 21 E4	Peters Green 65 C3	Therfield 15 F7
Barkway 17 D4	Eastwick 117 A4	Jockey End 103 F8	Pinner 175 E1	Thundridge 93 E7
Barley 8 F1	Edgware 170 E1	Kelshall 15 D5	Pirton 20 E4	Tonwell 92 F7
Barnet 171 F4	Elstree 169 E3	Kensworth Common ...82 E8	Pitstone 80 D4	Tring 100 B3
Bayford 132 F6	Enfield 162 E1	Kimpton 66 C1	Potten End 123 C7	Walkern 38 A1
Benington 52 E4	Essendon 131 F6	King's Walden 48 A3	Potters Bar 159 D6	Wallington 25 D8
Berkhamsted 122 C6	Eyeworth 1 A8	Kings Langley 139 A1	Preston 48 D6	Waltham Abbey 163 D7
Birchanger 59 E2	Farnham 58 D6	Knebworth 69 A5	Radlett 156 C5	Ware 93 F2
Bishop's Stortford 76 D7	Flamstead 84 B1	Kneesworth 2 A5	Radwell 12 C4	Wareside 94 E4
Borehamwood 170 B6	Flaunden 151 A6	Langley 49 F1	Redbourn 106 B6	Watford 167 C3
Botley 136 A1	Furneux Pelham 43 A5	Latimer 150 F2	Reed 16 F5	Watton at Stone 70 D4
Bovingdon 137 B3	Gilston 117 E5	Lea Valley 86 F2	Rickmansworth 165 C1	Welham Green 144 C7
Bramfield 91 C4	Goff's Oak 147 C3	Letchworth 11 E2	Ridge 157 F5	Welwyn 89 B4
Braughing 55 F6	Graveley 36 C4	Letchworth 22 C5	Ringshall 81 B1	Welwyn Garden City ..110 E7
Breachwood Green 47 E1	Great Amwell 114 F5	Lilley 32 D2	Roydon 116 C1	Westmill 40 F3
Brent Pelham 30 B2	Great Chishill 9 F2	Little Berkhamsted ...132 C4	Royston 7 C5	Weston 24 C1
Brickendon 133 C4	Great Gaddesden 103 D3	Little Chalfont 150 B1	Rushden 25 F3	Wheathampstead 108 C7
Bricket Wood 140 F1	Great Hallingbury 77 E4	Little Gaddesden 102 D7	Sacombe 71 E3	Whipsnade 82 A8
Brookmans Park 144 F5	Great Hormead 42 B8	Little Hadham 57 C2	St Albans 127 F4	Whitwell 66 E6
Buckland 27 D8	Great Munden 54 C5	Little Hallingbury 98 D8	St Ippolyts 35 B3	Widford 95 E4
Buntingford 40 F7	Great Offley 33 D2	Little Wymondley 35 E3	St Leonards 119 E3	Wigginton 100 D1
Bushey 168 A2	Great Wymondley 35 F6	London Colney 142 E5	Sandon 15 B1	Wilstone 79 D1
Bygrave 13 C5	Guilden Morden 1 F4	Long Marston 79 B3	Sandridge 108 C1	Wingrave 60 C3
Caddington 62 D3	Hadley Wood 159 C2	Lower Nazeing 149 E8	Sarratt 152 A4	Woodside 63 A2
Chalfont St Peter 172 A3	Hammond Street 147 D5	Lower Stondon 10 A3	Sawbridgeworth 97 C3	Woolmer Green 69 B2
Cheddington 80 A8	Harefield 173 C1	Luton 45 C3	Sewardstone 163 D1	Wyddial 28 B3
Chenies 151 B2	Harlow 117 D2	Maple Cross 172 D6	Sheering 98 C1	
Cheshunt 148 C1	Harpenden 86 B2	Markyate 83 E6	Shenley 157 A5	
Chipperfield 152 B8	Harrow 176 E1	Marsworth 80 A1	Shillington 19 F8	
Chiswellgreen 141 A5	Hatfield 130 B8	Meesden 29 F6	Slip End 63 C2	
Cholesbury 120 C2	Hatfield Heath 98 E3	Meldreth 2 F8	South Oxhey 175 B7	

A

Aashiana Ct WD1 ...167 A3
Abbey Ave AL3 ...127 B1
Abbey Ct St Albans AL1 ...127 D2
Waltham Abbey EN9 ...163 B5
Abbey Dr
Abbots Langley WD5 ...154 A7
Luton LU2 ...46 A1
Abbey Hts AL1 ...127 E3
Abbey Jun Mix Inf Sch AL1 ...127 D2
Abbey Mead Ind Est EN9 163 C5
Abbey Mill End AL3 ...127 C2
Abbey Mill La AL3 ...127 C2
Abbey Rd EN8 ...162 E5
Abbey Sta AL1 ...127 D1
Abbey Theatre AL1 ...127 C1
Abbey View Radlett WD7 ..155 F4
St Albans AL1 ...127 D1
Watford WD2 ...154 D3
Abbey View Rd AL3 ...127 C3
Abbeygate Bsns Ctr The LU2 ...63 F8
Abbeyview EN9 ...163 C6
Abbis Orch SG5 ...21 E5
Abbot John Mews AL4 ...87 D1
Abbots Ave AL1 ...141 E8
Abbots Ave W AL1 ...141 D8
Abbots Cl SG3 ...69 D1
Abbots Ct LU2 ...46 A1
Abbots Gr SG1 ...50 F5
Abbots Langley Sch WD5 ...139 F1
Abbots Pk AL1 ...128 A1
Abbots Rd WD5 ...139 E1
Abbots Rise WD4 ...138 F5
Abbots View WD4 ...138 F4
Abbots Wood Rd LU2 ...64 A8
Abbotsbury Ct WD2 ...154 B7
Abbotswood Par LU2 ...46 A1
Abbotts Ct SG12 ...115 C4
Abbotts La SG12 ...95 D3
Abbotts Rd SG6 ...22 D6
Abbotts Rise SG12 ...115 D4
Abbotts Way
Bishop's Stortford CM23 ...76 E3
Stanstead Abbotts SG12 ...115 D4
Wingrave HP22 ...60 A4
Abbotts Yd SG8 ...7 D6
Abdale La AL9 ...144 C4
Abel Cl HP2 ...125 A3
Abel Smith Sch SG13 ...113 D6
Aberdale Gdns EN6 ...158 F7
Aberdeen Rd HA3 ...176 F1
Aberford Rd WD6 ...170 A7
Abigail Cl LU3 ...45 D3
Abigail Ct LU3 ...45 D3
Abingdon Pl EN6 ...159 B7
Abingdon Rd LU4 ...44 C3
Aboyne Lodge Sch AL3 ..127 D4
Abridge Cl EN8 ...162 D4
Abstacle Hill HP23 ...99 F3
Acacia Cl
Hammond Street EN7 ...147 E4
Stanmore HA7 ...176 E4
Acacia Gr HP4 ...122 B3
Acacia Rd EN2 ...161 D1
Acacia St AL10 ...130 A2
Acacia Wlk
Harpenden AL5 ...107 D6
Tring HP23 ...99 E3
Acacias Ct EN11 ...135 A6
Acers AL2 ...141 C3
Achilles Cl HP2 ...124 F5
Ackroyd Rd SG8 ...7 E8
Acme Rd WD2 ...154 B1
Acorn La EN6 ...146 E2
Acorn Pl WD2 ...154 A2
Acorn Rd HP3 ...125 A2
Acorns The St Albans AL4 .128 D3
Stansted Mountfitchet CM24 .59 E7
Acre Piece SG4 ...35 A6
Acre Way HA6 ...174 F2
Acre Wood HP2 ...124 E2
Acremore St SG11 ...75 C7
Acrewood Way AL4 ...128 F3
Acton Cl EN8 ...162 E8
Acworth Cres LU4 ...44 C5
Acworth Ct 2 LU4 ...44 C5
Adam's Yd 1 SG14 ...113 D6
Adams Ho CM20 ...117 D1
Adams Way HP23 ...100 B6
Adamsfield EN7 ...148 A5
Adderley Rd
Bishop's Stortford CM23 ...76 F7
Harrow HA3 ...176 F2
Addington Way LU4 ...44 D3
Addiscombe Rd WD1 ...167 B5
Addison Cl HA6 ...175 A2
Addison Way HA6 ...174 F2
Adelaide Cl EN1 ...161 F1
Adelaide St Luton LU1 ...63 D7
St Albans AL3 ...127 D4
Adele Ave AL6 ...89 F3
Adeyfield Gdns HP2 ...124 F4
Adeyfield Rd HP2 ...124 F3
Adeyfield Sch HP2 ...125 A3
Adhara Rd HA6 ...175 A5
Adinger Cl SG1 ...50 E3
Adingtons CM20 ...117 F2
Adlington Ct LU4 ...44 C4
Admiral St SG13 ...114 A6
Admiral Way HP4 ...121 F6
Admirals Cl AL4 ...143 E8
Admirals Ct HA6 ...174 F5
Admirals Wlk
Hoddesdon EN11 ...135 B4
St Albans AL1 ...142 A8
Adrian Cl UB9 ...173 D2
Adrian Ho WD5 ...153 E8
Adrian Rd WD5 ...153 E8
Adstone Rd LU1 ...62 F3
Ailsworth Rd LU3 ...45 A7
Ainsdale Rd WD1 ...175 C7
Ainsland Ct LU4 ...44 B2
Aintree Rd SG8 ...7 F6
Aintree Way SG1 ...51 C8
Airedale HP2 ...124 E6
Airport Approach Rd LU2 .64 D8
Airport Executive Pk LU2 .64 D8
Airport Way LU1,LU2 ...64 A5
Aitken Rd EN5 ...171 C4
Akeman Cl AL3 ...126 F1
Akeman St HP23 ...100 A3
Alamein Cl EN10 ...134 E3
Alan Dr EN5 ...171 E3
Alandale Dr HA5 ...175 B2
Alban Ave AL3 ...127 D5
Alban Cres WD6 ...170 B8
Alban Ct Barnet EN5 ...171 D5
St Albans AL1 ...128 C3
Alban Pk Ind Est AL4 ...128 F3
Alban Rd SG6 ...23 C3
Alban Wood Inf Sch WD2 ...154 B7
Alban Wood Jun Sch WD2 ...154 B6
Albanian Ct AL1 ...128 A2
Albans View WD2 ...154 B6
Albany Cl WD2 ...168 D3
Albany Ct Harpenden AL5 .107 C8
Luton LU1 ...63 B8
Albany Mews
Chiswellgreen AL2 ...141 A4
3 Ware SG12 ...93 E1
Albany Park Ave EN3 ...162 D1
Albany Pl AL7 ...110 E6
Albany Rd EN3 ...162 D1
Albany Sec Sch EN3 ...162 D1
Albany Terr HP23 ...100 B6
Albemarle Ave
Cheshunt EN8 ...148 C3
Potters Bar EN6 ...159 B7
Albeny Gate AL1 ...127 D2
Albert Rd Arlesey SG15 ...11 A4
Luton LU1 ...63 E6
Albert Rd N WD1 ...167 B6
Albert Rd S WD1 ...167 B6
Albert St Markyate AL3 ...83 E5
St Albans AL1 ...127 D2
Stevenage SG1 ...50 D7
Tring HP23 ...100 A3
Albion Cl SG13 ...113 E7
Albion Ct 4 LU2 ...63 E8
Albion Hill HP2 ...124 D2
Albion Rd Luton LU2 ...63 E8
Pitstone LU7 ...80 D5
St Albans AL1 ...127 F3
Albion The 9 SG12 ...93 D2
Albury CE Sch SG11 ...57 A6
Albury Cl LU3 ...31 A1
Albury Dr Pinner HA5 ...175 D3
Pinner HA5 ...175 E3
Albury Grove Rd EN8 ...148 D1
Albury Rd SG11 ...57 C2
Albury Ride EN8 ...162 D8
Albury Wlk EN8 ...148 C1
Albyn Ho HP2 ...124 D3
Alconbury
Bishop's Stortford CM23 ...59 B1
Welwyn Garden City AL7 ...111 E6
Aldbury CE Prim Sch HP23 ...101 C6
Aldbury Cl St Albans AL4 .128 C8
Watford WD2 ...154 D3
Aldbury Gdns HP23 ...100 B6
Aldbury Gr AL7 ...111 B6
Aldbury Rd WD3 ...164 F2
Aldcock Rd SG1 ...50 E7
Aldeburgh Cl SG1 ...36 A1
Aldenham Ave WD7 ...156 A3
Aldenham Ctry Pk WD6 ..169 B4
Aldenham Gr WD7 ...156 B5
Aldenham Rd
Bushey WD2 ...168 A6
Elstree WD6,WD2 ...169 B5
Radlett WD7 ...156 A4
Watford WD2 ...167 E5
Aldenham Sch WD6 ...168 F7
Alder Cl Baldock SG7 ...23 F7
Bishop's Stortford CM23 ...76 D4
Chiswellgreen AL2 ...141 C3
Hoddesdon EN11 ...135 B8
Alder Cres LU3 ...45 A3
Alder Ct LU3 ...45 B3
Alder Wlk WD2 ...154 B4
Alderbury Rd CM24 ...59 E8
Alderley Ct HP4 ...122 C3
Alderman Cl AL9 ...144 C7
Alderney Ho Enfield EN3 .162 D1
7 Watford WD1 ...166 F3
Alders Ct AL7 ...111 A6
Alders End La AL5 ...85 F2
Alders Wlk CM21 ...97 E2
Aldersgrove EN9 ...163 E5
Alderton Cl 5 LU2 ...46 D1
Alderton Dr HP4 ...102 B8
Alderwood Ho WD1 ...175 C7
Aldhous Cl LU3 ...45 B5
Aldock AL7 ...111 A3
Aldridge Ave EN3 ...163 A1
Aldridge Ct SG7 ...12 E1
Aldwick AL1 ...128 B1
Aldwick Ct AL1 ...128 B1
Aldwick Rd AL5 ...107 E8
Aldwickbury Cres AL5 ...86 D1
Aldwickbury Sch AL5 ...107 E8
Aldwyck Ct HP1 ...124 C4
Aldwyke Rise SG12 ...93 C3
Aldykes AL10 ...129 F5
Alesia Rd LU3 ...44 F6
Alex Ct HP2 ...124 D4
Alexander Ct 2 EN8 ...148 D1
Alexander Gate SG1 ...51 C8
Alexander Rd
Hertford SG14 ...113 A6
London Colney AL2 ...142 D6
Stotfold SG5 ...11 F6
Alexandra Ave LU3 ...45 C2
Alexandra Ct 11 WD1 ...167 C7
Alexandra Mews WD1 ...167 A7
Alexandra Rd
Borehamwood WD6 ...170 D8
Chipperfield WD4 ...138 A1
Hemel Hempstead HP2 ...124 D4
Hitchin SG5 ...21 F1
Kings Langley WD4 ...139 B1
Sarratt WD3 ...152 A3
St Albans AL1 ...127 E3
Watford WD1 ...167 A7
Alexandra Way EN8 ...162 F5
Aleyn Way SG7 ...13 B1
Alfriston Cl LU2 ...46 C3
Algar Cl HA7 ...176 F5
Alington La SG6 ...22 F3
All Saints CE Sch CM23 ...77 B8
All Saints Cl CM23 ...77 A8
All Saints Cres WD2 ...154 D6
All Saints La WD3 ...166 A3
All Saints Mews HA3 ...176 E4
Allandale
Hemel Hempstead HP2 ...124 D5
St Albans AL3 ...141 B8
Allandale Cres EN6 ...158 E7
Allandale Rd EN3 ...162 D3
Allard Cl EN7 ...147 F4
Allard Cres WD2 ...168 C1
Allard Way EN10 ...134 E2
Alldicks Rd HP3 ...124 F1
Allen Cl Shenley WD7 ...156 E7
Wheathampstead AL4 ...108 D7
Allen Ct 2 AL10 ...130 B3
Allenby Ave LU5 ...44 A1
Allendale LU3 ...31 A1
Allerton Cl WD6 ...156 F1
Allerton Rd WD6 ...156 F1
Alleyns Rd SG1 ...50 D7
Allied Bsns Ctr AL5 ...86 C3
Allison SG6 ...23 C5
Allton Rd SG16 ...10 A4
Allum La WD6 ...169 E5
Allwood Rd EN7 ...147 F4
Alma Ct WD6 ...156 F1
Alma Cut AL1 ...127 E2
Alma Link 4 LU1 ...63 D7
Alma Rd Berkhamsted HP4 .121 E6
St Albans AL1 ...127 E2
Alma Row HA3 ...176 D2
Alma St LU1 ...63 D7
Almond Cl LU3 ...45 B4
Almond Hill Jun Sch SG1 .50 E8
Almond Way
Borehamwood WD6 ...170 B5
Harrow HA2 ...176 C1
Almond Wlk 1 AL10 ...130 A2
Almonds La SG1 ...50 E8
Almonds The AL1 ...142 B7
Alms La SG7 ...4 D4
Almshoe Bury Cotts SG4 ..49 D8
Almshouse La EN1 ...162 B2
Alnwick Dr HP23 ...78 F7
Alpha Bsns Pk AL9 ...144 C8
Alpha Pl 4 CM23 ...76 F8
Alpine Cl SG4 ...35 A5
Alpine Way LU3 ...44 D8
Alpine Wlk HA7 ...176 E8
Alsop Cl AL2 ...142 E3
Alston Ct EN5 ...171 E6
Alston Rd Barnet EN5 ...171 E6
Hemel Hempstead HP1 ...124 A2
Alswick Hall Cotts SG9 ...41 B8
Altair Way HA6 ...174 F5
Altham Gr CM20 ...117 F3
Altham Rd HA5 ...175 E3
Althorp Cl NW1 ...171 A2
Althorp Rd Luton LU3 ...45 C1
St Albans AL1 ...127 F4
Alton Ave HA7 ...176 F3
Alton Rd LU1 ...63 F5
Altwood AL5 ...86 D1
Alva Cl WD1 ...175 D8
Alva Way WD1 ...175 D8
Alverton AL3 ...127 C6
Alwin Pl WD1 ...166 E5
Alwyn Cl
Borehamwood WD6 ...169 F3
Luton LU2 ...45 E2
Alyngton HP4 ...121 E7
Alzey Gdns AL5 ...107 D8
Amaravati Buddhist Ctr HP1 ...103 C3
Amberley Cl
Harpenden AL5 ...86 B2
Luton LU2 ...46 D4
Amberley Gn SG12 ...93 C4
Amberry Ct CM20 ...117 D1
Ambleside Harpenden AL5 .86 D2
Luton LU3 ...44 F5
Ambrose La AL5 ...85 F4
Amenbury Ct AL5 ...86 A1
Amenbury La AL5 ...86 A1
Amersham Ho WD1 ...166 E2
Amersham Rd HP6,WD3 ..164 B8
Ames Cl LU3 ...31 A1
Amor Way SG6 ...23 B6
Amwell Cl WD2 ...154 E4
Amwell Comm AL7 ...111 C5
Amwell Ct
Hoddesdon EN11 ...135 A7
Waltham Abbey EN9 ...163 E6
Amwell End SG12 ...93 D1
Amwell Hill SG12 ...114 F6
Amwell La
Stanstead Abbotts SG12 ...115 B5
Wheathampstead AL4 ...108 B7
Amwell Pl SG13 ...114 C4
Amwell St EN11 ...135 A7
Amwell View Sch SG12 ..115 B4
Anchor Cl EN8 ...148 D3
Anchor Cotts SG12 ...93 D7
Anchor La
Hemel Hempstead HP1 ...124 B1
Hemel Hempstead HP1 ...124 C2
Tonwell SG12 ...93 B6
Anchor Rd SG7 ...23 F7
Anchor St CM23 ...77 A6
Ancient Almshos 4 EN8 .148 D1
Anderson Cl UB9 ...173 A2
Anderson Ho AL4 ...128 D2
Anderson Rd
Shenley WD7 ...157 A6
Stevenage SG2 ...51 D6
Anderson's Ho 3 SG5 ...34 F8
Anderson's La SG9 ...29 A1
Andover Cl LU4 ...44 C6
Andrew Cl WD7 ...156 F6
Andrew Reed Ct 10 WD1 .167 C7
Andrew's La
Cheshunt EN7 ...148 B3
Goff's Oak EN7 ...147 F3
Andrews Cl HP2 ...124 D5
Andrews Lane Prim Sch EN7 ...148 B3
Andrewsfield AL7 ...111 C6
Anelle Rise HP3 ...138 F7
Anershall HP22 ...60 B3
Angel Cl LU4 ...44 D3
Angel Cotts SG5 ...33 D2
Angel Pavement SG8 ...7 D6
Angell's Mdw SG7 ...4 D4
Angle Ways SG2 ...51 B2
Anglefield Rd HP4 ...122 A4
Anglesey Cl CM23 ...76 C7
Anglesey Rd WD1 ...175 C5
Anglian Bsns Pk SG8 ...7 C7
Anglian Cl WD1 ...167 C7
Angotts Mead SG1 ...50 B6
Angus Cl LU4 ...44 A3
Anmer Gdns LU4 ...44 B4
Annables La AL5 ...85 A4
Annette Cl HA3 ...176 E1
Anns Cl HP23 ...99 E3
Ansell Ct SG1 ...36 B1
Anselm Rd HA5 ...175 F3
Anson Cl Bovingdon HP3 ...136 F4
Sandridge AL4 ...108 C1
St Albans AL1 ...128 B1
Anson Wlk HA6 ...174 C6
Anstee Rd LU4 ...44 B6
Anstey Fst Sch SG9 ...29 A6
Anthony Cl WD1 ...167 D1
Anthony Gdns LU1 ...63 D6
Anthony Rd WD6 ...169 F7
Anthorne Cl EN6 ...159 B8
Anthus Mews HA6 ...174 E3
Antoinette Ct WD5 ...139 F2
Antoneys Cl HA5 ...175 D1
Antonine Gate AL3 ...127 A2
Anvil Cl HP3 ...137 B3
Anvil Ct LU3 ...45 E5
Anvil Ho 8 AL5 ...86 A2
Apex Point AL9 ...130 C1
Aplins Cl AL5 ...86 A2
Apollo Ave HA6 ...175 A5
Apollo Way
Hemel Hempstead HP2 ...124 F5
Stevenage SG2 ...51 C8
Apple Cotts HP3 ...137 A4
Apple Orch The HP2 ...124 F5
Apple Tree Gr AL3 ...106 B6
Appleby St EN7 ...147 E5
Applecroft
Berkhamsted HP4 ...121 E6
Chiswellgreen AL2 ...141 B3
Lower Stondon SG16 ...10 B3
Applecroft Jun Sch AL8 ..110 B5
Applecroft Rd Luton LU2 ...46 C4
Welwyn Garden City AL8 ...110 B6
Appleford's Cl EN11 ...134 F8
Appleton Ave SG12 ...94 E5
Appleton Fields CM23 ...76 E4
Appletree Wlk WD2 ...154 B4
Appletrees SG5 ...34 D6
Applewood Cl AL5 ...85 E3
Appleyard Terr EN3 ...162 C2
Approach Rd AL1 ...127 E2
Approach The EN6 ...158 F7
Appspond La AL2 ...140 C8
April Pl CM21 ...97 F3
Apsley Cl CM23 ...76 F4
Apsley End Rd SG5 ...19 E6
Apsley Grange HP3 ...138 E6
Apsley Ind Est HP3 ...138 D7
Apsley Mills Ret Pk HP3 .138 E7
Apsley Sta HP3 ...138 E6
Apton Ct CM23 ...76 F7
Apton Fields 7 CM23 ...76 F6
Apton Rd CM23 ...76 F7
Aquadrome The WD3 ...173 C8
Aquarius Way HA6 ...175 A6
Aragon Cl HP2 ...125 C8
Aran Cl AL5 ...107 D6
Arbour Cl LU3 ...31 A1
Arbour The SG13 ...113 D4
Arbroath Gn WD1 ...175 B7
Arcade 5 SG5 ...34 E7
Arcade The Hatfield AL10 ..130 B6
Letchworth SG6 ...22 F6
Arcade Wlk 4 SG5 ...34 E7
Arcadian Ct AL5 ...86 A2
Arch Rd SG4 ...35 E4
Archer Cl WD4 ...138 F2
Archer Rd SG1 ...51 A6
Archers SG9 ...40 F8
Archers Cl Hertford SG14 .113 C7
Redbourn AL3 ...106 B5
Archers Fields AL1 ...127 F5
Archers Green La AL6 ...111 E8
Archers Ride AL7 ...111 B4
Archers Way SG6 ...22 D6
Arches The SG6 ...23 A7
Archfield AL7 ...89 E1
Archway Ho AL9 ...130 C6
Archway Par LU3 ...44 F4
Archway Rd LU3 ...44 E4
Arckle Ho EN10 ...148 F5
Ardeley St Lawrence CE Prim Sch SG2 ...38 F3
Arden Cl Bovingdon HP3 ...137 A3
Bushey WD2 ...168 F2
Arden Gr AL5 ...86 B1
Arden Pl LU2 ...45 E1
Arden Press Way SG6 ...23 B6
Ardens Way AL4 ...128 D6
Ardentinny AL1 ...127 E2
Ardern Ct AL1,AL4 ...128 C1
Ardleigh Gn LU2 ...46 E1
Ardross Ave HA6 ...174 E5
Arena Par SG6 ...22 F6
Arena The EN3 ...162 F1
Argent Way EN7 ...147 D5
Argyle Ct WD1 ...166 F5
Argyle Rd EN5 ...171 C5
Argyle Way SG1 ...50 C5
Argyll Ave LU3 ...45 C2
Argyll Rd HP2 ...124 E8
Arkley Ct HP2 ...125 B8
Arkley Dr EN5 ...171 B4
Arkley La EN5 ...171 B5
Arkley Rd HP2 ...125 B8
Arkley View EN5 ...171 B5
Arkwrights CM20 ...117 F1
Arlesey Ho SG15 ...11 A8
Arlesey New Rd SG5 ...22 B7
Arlesey Rd Henlow SG16 ...10 D8
Henlow SG16 ...10 E8
Ickleford SG5 ...21 F5
Arlesey Sta SG15 ...11 A8
Arlingham Mews EN9 ...163 C6
Arlington Cres EN8 ...162 E5
Armand Cl WD1 ...153 F1
Armitage Cl WD3 ...165 D5
Armitage Gdns LU4 ...44 D1
Armour Rise SG4 ...22 B2
Armourers Cl CM23 ...76 B4
Armstrong Cl AL2 ...142 E4
Armstrong Gdns WD7 ...156 E7
Armstrong Pl 1 HP1 ...124 D4
Arncliffe Cres LU2 ...45 E1
Arndale Ctr LU1 ...63 E7
Arnett Cl WD3 ...165 A3
Arnett Hills Jun Mix Inf Sch WD3 ...165 A3
Arnett Way WD3 ...165 A2
Arnold Ave E EN3 ...163 A1
Arnold Ave W EN3 ...162 F1
Arnold Cl Hitchin SG4 ...35 B8
Luton LU2 ...46 A3
Stevenage SG1 ...36 D2
Arnolds La SG7 ...3 D6
Arran Cl HP3 ...125 C1
Arran Ct LU1 ...63 D7
Arranmore Ct WD2 ...167 E5
Arretine Cl AL3 ...126 F1
Arrewig La HP5 ...119 D1
Arrow Cl LU3 ...44 E6
Arthur Gibbens Ct SG1 ...37 A1
Arthur Rd AL1 ...128 B3
Arthur St Luton LU1 ...63 E6
Watford WD2 ...167 D5
Artichoke Dell WD3 ...164 E4
Artillery Pl HA3 ...176 C3
Artisan Cres AL3 ...127 C4
Arts Educational Schs The HP23 ...100 B3
Arundel Cl Aston SG2 ...51 E3
Cheshunt EN8 ...148 C3
Hemel Hempstead HP2 ...125 B4
Arundel Dr WD6 ...170 C5
Arundel Gr AL3 ...127 D7
Arundel Rd LU4 ...44 F2
Arundell Rd WD5 ...154 A7
Ascot Cl
Bishop's Stortford CM23 ...77 C8
Borehamwood WD6 ...170 A4
Ascot Cres SG1 ...37 B1
Ascot Gdns EN3 ...162 C2
Ascot Ind Est SG6 ...23 B7
Ascot Rd Luton LU3 ...45 B2
Royston SG8 ...7 F6
Watford WD1 ...166 E4
Ascot Terr SG12 ...114 F7
Ascots La AL7 ...110 F2
Ash Cl
Abbots Langley WD5 ...153 D7

Ash Cl continued
Brookmans Park AL9 . . . . . .145 A6
Harefield UB9 . . . . .173 D2
Watford WD2 . . . . .154 B4
Ash Dr Hatfield AL10 . . . . . . .130 A2
Hitchin SG4 . . . . .35 A4
Ash Gr Harefield UB9 . . . . . . .173 D2
Hemel Hempstead HP3 . . . . .138 F7
Wheathampstead AL4 . . . . . . .87 C1
Ash Groves CM21 . . . . .98 A2
Ash Hill Cl WD2 . . . . .168 B1
Ash Mdw SG10 . . . . .74 F2
Ash Mill SG8 . . . . .17 C3
Ash Rd Luton LU4 . . . . .63 B6
Tring HP23 . . . . .99 F4
Ware SG12 . . . . .94 A3
Ash Ride EN2 . . . . .161 A4
Ash Tree Field CM20 . . . . . .117 A2
Ash Tree Rd WD2 . . . . .154 B3
Ash Vale WD3 . . . . .172 D5
Ash Way SG8 . . . . .7 F6
Ashanger La SG7 . . . . .24 D4
Ashborurne Sq HA6 . . . . . . .174 E4
Ashbourne Cl SG6 . . . . .23 B3
Ashbourne Ct AL4 . . . . .142 C8
Ashbourne Rd EN10 . . . . . . .134 F2
Ashbrook La SG4 . . . . .35 C3
Ashburnam Wlk SG2 . . . . . . .50 F1
Ashburnham Cl WD1 . . . . . .175 A7
Ashburnham Dr WD1 . . . . . .175 A7
Ashburnham Rd LU1 . . . . . . .63 C7
Ashbury Cl AL10 . . . . .129 E5
Ashby Ct HP2 . . . . .105 B1
Ashby Gdns AL1 . . . . .141 D7
Ashby Rd
Berkhamsted HP4 . . . . .121 D7
Watford WD1 . . . . .154 A1
Ashby Rise CM23 . . . . .59 B1
Ashcombe AL8 . . . . .89 E2
Ashcroft HA5 . . . . .176 A4
Ashcroft Cl AL5 . . . . .107 E8
Ashcroft Ct EN10 . . . . .134 F1
Ashcroft Rd LU2 . . . . .46 B3
Ashdale CM23 . . . . .76 D4
Ashdale Gdns LU3 . . . . .31 A1
Ashdale Gr HA7 . . . . .176 F4
Ashdales AL1 . . . . .141 D7
Ashdown SG6 . . . . .11 F1
Ashdown Cres EN8 . . . . .148 E3
Ashdown Dr WD6 . . . . .169 F7
Ashdown Rd
Stevenage SG2 . . . . .69 B8
Watford WD2 . . . . .167 D6
Ashendene Rd SG13 . . . . . . .132 F4
Ashfield Ave WD2 . . . . .168 C2
Ashfield Jun Sch WD2 . . . . .168 B2
Ashfield Way LU3 . . . . .45 A6
Ashfields WD2 . . . . .153 F4
Ashford Gn WD1 . . . . .175 D5
Ashleigh SG2 . . . . .51 B4
Ashleigh Ct
Hoddesdon EN11 . . . . .135 A5
Rickmansworth WD3 . . . . . .165 D2
Ashley Cl Cheddington LU7 . .80 A8
Hemel Hempstead HP3 . . . . .124 F1
Pinner HA5 . . . . .175 B1
Welwyn Garden City AL8 . . .110 C8
Ashley Ct AL10 . . . . .130 B6
Ashley Dr WD6 . . . . .170 D4
Ashley Gdns AL5 . . . . .85 D3
Ashley Ho WD1 . . . . .166 E2
Ashley Rd Hertford SG14 . . .113 E5
St Albans AL1 . . . . .128 C2
Ashleys WD3 . . . . .164 F2
Ashlyn Cl WD2 . . . . .167 E5
Ashlyns Ct HP4 . . . . .122 B3
Ashlyns Rd HP4 . . . . .122 B3
Ashlyns Sch HP4 . . . . .122 C2
Ashmore Gdns HP3 . . . . . . .125 B2
Ashridge Cl HP3 . . . . .137 A3
Ashridge College (Gdns)
HP4 . . . . .102 D5
Ashridge Dr
Bricket Wood AL2 . . . . .140 F1
South Oxhey WD1 . . . . .175 C5
Ashridge Ho WD1 . . . . .166 E2
Ashridge La HP5 . . . . .150 D7
Ashridge Management
Coll HP4 . . . . .102 C5
Ashridge Rise HP4 . . . . .121 F5
Ashton Rd Enfield EN3 . . . . .162 E3
Luton LU1 . . . . .63 E5
Ashton's La SG7 . . . . .23 F6
Ashtree Ct AL1 . . . . .127 F3
Ashtree Prim Sch SG2 . . . . .51 C4
Ashtree Way HP1 . . . . .124 A2
Ashurst Cl HA6 . . . . .174 E3
Ashville Way SG7 . . . . .13 A1
Ashwell SG1 . . . . .36 C2
Ashwell Ave LU3 . . . . .44 C8
Ashwell Cl SG4 . . . . .36 B4
Ashwell Comm SG4 . . . . .36 B4
Ashwell & Morden Sta SG7 .5 D2
Ashwell Par LU3 . . . . .44 C8
Ashwell Pk AL5 . . . . .86 D1
Ashwell Prim Sch SG7 . . . . . .4 D4
Ashwell Rd Bygrave SG7 . . . .13 C4
Guilden Morden SG8 . . . . .1 F1
Hinxworth SG7 . . . . .3 E5
Newnham SG7 . . . . .12 F8
Ashwell Village Mus SG7 . . . .4 D4
Ashwood Rd EN6 . . . . .159 B6
Askew Rd HA6 . . . . .174 D8

Aspasia Cl AL1 . . . . .127 F2
Aspen Cl
Bricket Wood AL2 . . . . .140 E1
Stevenage SG2 . . . . .69 B7
Aspen Park Dr WD2 . . . . . . .154 B4
Aspen Way Enfield EN3 . . . .162 D4
Welwyn Garden City AL7 . . .111 C5
Aspenden Rd SG9 . . . . .40 E6
Aspens The
Bishop's Stortford CM23 . . . .59 B3
Hitchin SG4 . . . . .35 A6
Aspfield Row HP1 . . . . .124 B5
Asquith Cl SG2 . . . . .69 C7
Asquith Ho AL8 . . . . .110 D7
Ass House La HA3 . . . . .176 B6
Astall Cl HA3 . . . . .176 E2
Aster Cl AL3 . . . . .76 D6
Asters The CM7 . . . . .76 D6
Astley Cooper Sch HP2 . . . .125 A8
Astley Gn LU2 . . . . .46 D2
Astley Rd HP1 . . . . .124 C3
Aston Cl Bushey WD2 . . . . . .168 C3
Stevenage SG1 . . . . .36 C2
Watford WD1 . . . . .167 C7
Aston End Rd SG2 . . . . .51 E3
Aston La SG2 . . . . .69 E8
Aston Rd SG11 . . . . .55 D2
Aston Rise SG4 . . . . .35 B6
Aston St Mary's
CE Prim Sch SG2 . . . . .51 E4
Aston View HP2 . . . . .105 A1
Aston Way EN6 . . . . .159 D7
Astonia Ho SG7 . . . . .23 F7
Astons Rd HA6 . . . . .174 C6
Astra Ct Luton LU2 . . . . .45 F2
Watford WD1 . . . . .166 F4
Astra Ctr CM20 . . . . .117 F4
Astral Cl SG16 . . . . .10 B3
Astrope La HP23 . . . . .79 B3
Astwick Ave AL10 . . . . .129 F8
Astwick Rd Stotfold SG5 . . . .3 A2
Stotfold SG5 . . . . .11 F8
Athelstan Rd HP3 . . . . .138 F8
Athelstan Wlk N AL7 . . . . . .110 E5
Athelstan Wlk S AL7 . . . . . .110 D5
Athelstone Rd HA3 . . . . .176 D1
Athena Est CM20 . . . . .118 B4
Athena Pl HA6 . . . . .174 F2
Atherstone Rd LU4 . . . . .44 D1
Atherton End CM21 . . . . .97 E3
Athlone Cl WD7 . . . . .156 B3
Athol Cl HA5 . . . . .175 B2
Athol Gdns HA5 . . . . .175 B2
Atholl Cl LU3 . . . . .44 D8
Atria Rd HA6 . . . . .175 A5
Attenborough Cl WD1 . . . . .175 E7
Attimore Cl AL8 . . . . .110 B5
Attimore Rd AL8 . . . . .110 B5
Aubretia Ho AL7 . . . . .111 B4
Aubrey Ave AL2 . . . . .142 C5
Aubrey Gdns LU4 . . . . .44 B6
Aubrey La AL3 . . . . .105 E2
Aubreys SG6 . . . . .23 A2
Aubreys Rd HP1 . . . . .123 E3
Aubries SG2 . . . . .38 B1
Auckland Cl EN1 . . . . .162 B2
Auckland Rd EN6 . . . . .158 E7
Audley Cl WD6 . . . . .170 A6
Audley Ct HA5 . . . . .175 C1
Audley Gdns EN9 . . . . .163 C5
Audrey Gdns CM23 . . . . .76 F4
Audwick Cl EN8 . . . . .148 E3
Augustine Ct EN9 . . . . .163 B6
Augustine Rd HA3 . . . . .176 C1
Augustus Cl AL3 . . . . .127 A1
Augustus Gate SG2 . . . . .51 D8
Austen Paths SG2 . . . . .51 C6
Austin Rd LU3 . . . . .45 C4
Austins Mead HP3 . . . . .137 B3
Austins Pl HP2 . . . . .124 D4
Autumn Glades HP3 . . . . . . .125 C1
Autumn Gr AL7 . . . . .111 B4
Avalon Cl WD2 . . . . .154 E7
Avebury Ave LU2 . . . . .45 D4
Avebury Ct AL6 . . . . .89 E7
Avenue App WD4 . . . . .139 A1
Avenue Ct AL6 . . . . .89 E7
Avenue One SG6 . . . . .23 C6
Avenue Rd
Bishop's Stortford CM23 . . . .77 B6
Hoddesdon EN11 . . . . .135 D5
Pinner HA5 . . . . .175 E1
St Albans AL1 . . . . .127 E4
Avenue Rise WD2 . . . . .168 A4
Avenue Terr WD1 . . . . .167 E3
Bushey WD2 . . . . .167 F5
Hemel Hempstead HP1 . . . . .123 E4
Hertford SG14 . . . . .113 B8
Hitchin SG4 . . . . .35 A7
Luton LU4 . . . . .44 D5
Northwood HA6 . . . . .174 C4
Oaklands AL6 . . . . .89 D7
Potters Bar EN6 . . . . .145 A1
Radlett WD7 . . . . .156 B5
Stevenage SG1 . . . . .50 D8
Stotfold SG5 . . . . .11 F6
Watford WD1 . . . . .167 A7
Avey La EN9 . . . . .163 E2
Avia Cl HP3 . . . . .138 D7
Avior Dr HA6 . . . . .174 F6
Avocet SG6 . . . . .11 E1
Avon Chase SG16 . . . . .10 B4
Avon Cl WD2 . . . . .154 C5
Avon Cotts LU2 . . . . .45 B1
Avon Ct Harpenden AL5 . . . .86 B1
Luton LU1 . . . . .63 C8
Avon Mews HA5 . . . . .175 F2

Avon Rd SG16 . . . . .10 B4
Avon Sq HP2 . . . . .124 F8
Avondale Cl AL1 . . . . .127 E3
Avondale Rd LU1 . . . . .63 C6
Axe Cl LU3 . . . . .44 E6
Aycliffe Dr HP2 . . . . .124 E7
Aycliffe Drive Prim Sch
HP2 . . . . .124 E7
Aycliffe Rd WD6 . . . . .156 F1
Aylands Cl HA3 . . . . .45 B6
Aylands Rd EN3 . . . . .162 D3
Aylands Sch EN3 . . . . .162 C3
Aylesbury Rd HP23 . . . . .99 E3
Ayllot Ct SG14 . . . . .70 D4
Aylotts Cl SG9 . . . . .40 D8
Aylsham Rd EN11 . . . . .135 C8
Aylward Dr SG2 . . . . .51 B4
Aynho St WD1 . . . . .167 B4
Aynsworth Ave CM23 . . . . . .59 B2
Ayot Gn Ayot St Peter AL6 . .89 A1
Hatfield AL6 . . . . .109 F8
Ayot Little Green La AL6 . . .88 F1
Ayot St Peter Rd AL6 . . . . . .88 E3
Ayr Cl SG8 . . . . .51 C8
Ayres End La AL3,AL5 . . . . .107 C5
Aysgarth Cl AL5 . . . . .107 B8
Aysgarth Rd AL3 . . . . .106 A6

B

Baas Hill EN10 . . . . .134 D2
Baas Hill Cl EN10 . . . . .134 E2
Baas La EN10 . . . . .134 D3
Babbage Rd SG1 . . . . .50 B5
Back La Buckland SG9 . . . . . .27 D8
Little Hallingbury CM22 . . . . .98 A3
Preston SG4 . . . . .48 D6
Radlett WD2 . . . . .168 E8
Sheering CM22 . . . . .98 B1
Tewin AL6 . . . . .90 E2
Back St Ashwell SG7 . . . . .4 C3
Luton LU2 . . . . .63 E8
Back The HP4 . . . . .123 B7
Bacon's Yd SG7 . . . . .4 D4
Bacons Dr EN6 . . . . .146 E2
Badburgham Ct EN9 . . . . . . .163 F6
Baddeley Cl
Holdbrook EN3 . . . . .163 A2
Stevenage SG2 . . . . .51 B2
Bader Cl Stevenage SG1 . . . . .36 F1
Welwyn Garden City AL7 . . .111 C6
Badger Cl SG3 . . . . .69 A6
Badger Croft HP2 . . . . .125 D2
Badger Way AL10 . . . . .130 B3
Badgers Cl
Borehamwood WD6 . . . . . . .169 F7
Hertford SG13 . . . . .114 B6
Stevenage SG1 . . . . .50 E4
Badgers Croft
Barnet HP2 . . . . .171 E1
Hoddesdon EN10 . . . . .134 E2
Badgers Wlk
Chorleywood WD3 . . . . .164 F5
Tewin AL6 . . . . .90 C5
Badingham Dr AL5 . . . . .85 E1
Badminton Cl
Borehamwood WD6 . . . . . . .170 A7
Stevenage SG2 . . . . .69 B7
Badminton Ho WD1 . . . . . . .167 C7
Badminton Pl EN10 . . . . . . .134 E3
Bagenal Ho WD5 . . . . .153 F7
Bagwicks Cl LU3 . . . . .44 E7
Bailey Hill Ct LU1 . . . . .63 E5
Bailey St LU1 . . . . .63 F6
Baines La SG3 . . . . .69 C4
Baird Cl WD2 . . . . .168 B3
Bairstow Cl WD6 . . . . .169 E8
Baisley Ho EN7 . . . . .148 A3
Baker Cl WD6 . . . . .170 B7
Baker St Enfield EN1 . . . . . .161 E1
Hertford SG13 . . . . .113 E6
Luton LU1 . . . . .63 E5
Potters Bar EN6 . . . . .158 E5
Stevenage SG1 . . . . .50 C7
Baker's La SG4 . . . . .67 F1
Bakers Ct CM23 . . . . .77 A7
Bakers Gr AL7 . . . . .111 C7
Bakers La Barley SG8 . . . . .8 F2
Kensworth Common LU6 . . . .82 E8
Bakers Rd EN7 . . . . .148 B1
Bakers Wlk CM21 . . . . .97 E2
Bakerscroft EN8 . . . . .148 E3
Bakery Ct CM24 . . . . .59 D6
Bakery The SG12 . . . . .93 D2
Bakewell Cl LU4 . . . . .44 C1
Balcary Gdns HP4 . . . . .121 C4
Balcombe Cl LU2 . . . . .46 D4
Balcon Way WD6 . . . . .170 C8
Baldock Ind Est SG7 . . . . . . .23 F7
Baldock La SG6 . . . . .23 D4
Baldock Rd Aspenden SG9 . .40 B8
Letchworth SG6 . . . . .23 B5
Stotfold SG5 . . . . .12 A5
Therfield SG8 . . . . .6 C4
Baldock St Royston SG8 . . . . .7 C6
Ware SG12 . . . . .93 D2
Baldock Sta SG7 . . . . .12 F1
Baldock Way WD6 . . . . .169 F8
Baldways Cl HP22 . . . . .60 D3
Baldwins AL7 . . . . .111 C6
Baldwins La WD3 . . . . .166 B5
Balfour AL5 . . . . .86 C3
Balfour Mews HP3 . . . . .137 A4
Balfour St SG14 . . . . .113 C7
Baliol Rd SG5 . . . . .34 F8
Ballater Cl WD1 . . . . .175 C6

Ballinger Ct
Berkhamsted HP4 . . . . .122 B3
Watford WD1 . . . . .167 B6
Balloon Cnr AL9 . . . . .144 B8
Ballslough Hill SG4 . . . . .66 D1
Balmoral Cl
Chiswellgreen AL2 . . . . .141 C3
Stevenage SG2 . . . . .69 C7
Balmoral Dr WD6 . . . . .170 D5
Balmoral Rd
Abbots Langley WD5 . . . . . .154 A7
Enfield EN3 . . . . .162 D3
Hitchin SG5 . . . . .21 E1
Watford WD2 . . . . .154 C1
Balmore Wood LU3 . . . . .31 B1
Balsams Cl SG13 . . . . .113 D4
Bampton Rd LU4 . . . . .44 B2
Bamville Wood AL5 . . . . . . .107 C5
Banbury Cl LU4 . . . . .44 F4
Banbury St WD1 . . . . .167 B4
Bancroft SG5 . . . . .34 F7
Bancroft Rd Harrow HA3 . . .176 C1
Luton LU3 . . . . .45 B5
Bandley Hill Inf Sch SG2 . . .51 C3
Bandley Rise SG2 . . . . .51 C3
Banes Down EN9 . . . . .135 E1
Bank Cl LU4 . . . . .44 C4
Bank Ct HP1 . . . . .124 C2
Bank Mill HP4 . . . . .122 E4
Bank Mill La HP4 . . . . .122 E3
Banks Rd WD6 . . . . .170 C7
Bankside Down WD3 . . . . . .165 D3
Bannister Gdns SG8 . . . . .7 E8
Bannister Sports Ctr The
HA3 . . . . .176 C4
Barbel Cl EN8 . . . . .163 A5
Barberry Rd HP1 . . . . .124 A3
Barbers La LU1 . . . . .63 E7
Barbers Wlk HP23 . . . . .99 F3
Barchester Rd HA3 . . . . .176 D1
Barclay Cl
Hertford Heath SG13 . . . . . .114 B4
Watford WD1 . . . . .167 A3
Barclay Cres SG1 . . . . .50 E7
Barclay Ct
Hoddesdon EN11 . . . . .135 A5
Luton LU2 . . . . .63 F8
Barclay Sch SG1 . . . . .50 D8
Barden Cl UB9 . . . . .173 C3
Bards Cnr HP1 . . . . .124 B4
Bardwell Cl AL1 . . . . .127 D2
Bardwell Rd AL1 . . . . .127 D2
Barfolds AL9 . . . . .144 C8
Barford Rise LU2 . . . . .46 D1
Bargrove Ave HP1 . . . . .124 A2
Barham Ave WD6 . . . . .169 F5
Barham Rd SG2 . . . . .51 C5
Barkers Mead
Bishop's Stortford CM22 . . . .77 B1
Little Hallingbury CM22 . . . . .98 B8
Barkham Cl LU7 . . . . .79 F7
Barking Cl LU4 . . . . .44 B6
Barkway Fst Sch SG8 . . . . . . .17 E6
Barkway Hill SG8 . . . . .17 E6
Barkway Rd SG8 . . . . .7 E5
Barkway St SG8 . . . . .7 D5
Barley CE Fst Sch SG8 . . . . . .9 A1
Barley Cl WD2 . . . . .168 B3
Barley Croft
Hemel Hempstead HP2 . . . . .125 C3
Hertford SG14 . . . . .113 D8
Stapleford SG14 . . . . .92 A3
Barley Ct EN7 . . . . .148 B1
Barley Hills CM23 . . . . .76 E4
Barley La LU4 . . . . .44 C5
Barley Mow La AL4 . . . . . . .142 F8
Barley Ponds Cl SG12 . . . . . .93 F1
Barley Ponds Rd SG12 . . . . .93 F1
Barley Rd Great Chishill SG8 . .9 A7
Great Chishill SG8 . . . . .9 C2
Barley Rise Baldock SG7 . . . .24 B8
Harpenden AL5 . . . . .86 C4
Barleycorn The LU3 . . . . . . .63 D8
Barleycroft Buntingford SG9 .40 E6
Stevenage SG2 . . . . .51 D3
Tonwell SG12 . . . . .92 F7
Barleycroft Gn AL8 . . . . . . .110 C6
Barleycroft Rd AL8 . . . . .110 C5
Barleyvale LU3 . . . . .45 A8
Barlings Rd AL5 . . . . .107 B5
Barmor Cl HA2 . . . . .176 B1
Barn Cl
Hemel Hempstead HP3 . . . . .138 F8
Radlett WD7 . . . . .156 A4
Welwyn Garden City AL8 . . .110 C8
Barn Ct CM21 . . . . .97 E3
Barn Lea WD3 . . . . .165 A1
Barn Sch The SG10 . . . . .74 F2
Barnacres Rd HP3 . . . . .139 A8
Barnard Acres EN9 . . . . .149 E8
Barnard Gn AL7 . . . . .110 F5
Barnard Rd Luton LU1 . . . . . .63 A7
Sawbridgeworth CM21 . . . . .97 E4
Barnard Way HP3 . . . . .124 E1
Barncroft SG11 . . . . .57 C7
Barncroft Prim HP2 . . . . .124 D8
Barncroft Rd HP4 . . . . .121 F3
Barncroft Way AL1 . . . . .128 A2
Barndell Cl SG5 . . . . .11 F6
Barndicot Ho AL7 . . . . .111 C6
Barnes La WD4 . . . . .138 D3
Barnes Rise WD4 . . . . .138 F4
Barnet By-Pass
Borehamwood EN5 . . . . . . .170 E5
Potters Bar EN5 . . . . .158 A3
Barnet Coll of F Ed EN5 . . .171 F5

Barnet Gate La EN5 . . . . . .170 F3
Barnet General Hospl
EN5 . . . . .171 D5
Barnet Hill EN5 . . . . .171 F5
Barnet Hill
Jun Mix Inf Sch EN5 . . . . .171 F4
Barnet La Barnet EN5,N20 . .171 F1
Borehamwood WD6 . . . . . . .170 B3
Barnet Mus EN5 . . . . .171 E5
Barnet Rd Barnet EN5 . . . . .170 E3
London Colney AL2 . . . . . . .142 F4
Potters Bar EN6,EN5 . . . . . .159 A4
Barnet Trad Est EN5 . . . . . .171 F6
Barnet Way NW7 . . . . .170 D2
Barnfield HP3 . . . . .138 F8
Barnfield Ave LU2 . . . . .45 D5
Barnfield Coll
Luton, Farley Hill LU1 . . . . . .63 B5
Luton, Stopsley Common LU2 45 D5
Luton, Warden Hill LU3 . . . . .45 B8
Barnfield Ct AL5 . . . . .107 C8
Barnfield Rd
Harpenden AL5 . . . . .107 C8
St Albans AL4 . . . . .128 C5
Welwyn Garden City AL7 . . .110 E4
Barnhurst Path WD1 . . . . . .175 C5
Barns Dene AL5 . . . . .85 E2
Barnsdale Cl WD6 . . . . .169 F8
Barnside Ct AL8 . . . . .110 C6
Barnston Cl LU2 . . . . .46 D1
Barnsway WD4 . . . . .138 E3
Barnview Lo HA3 . . . . .176 E2
Barnwell SG2 . . . . .51 B2
Barnwell Sch SG2 . . . . .51 B2
Baron Ct SG1 . . . . .36 B1
Barons Ct LU2 . . . . .45 D1
Barons Row AL5 . . . . .107 D7
Barons The CM23 . . . . .76 D5
Baronsmere Ct EN5 . . . . . . .171 E5
Barr Rd EN6 . . . . .159 C6
Barra Cl HP3 . . . . .139 C8
Barra Ho WD1 . . . . .166 F3
Barras Cl EN3 . . . . .163 A4
Barratt Ind Est LU2 . . . . .64 C6
Barratt Way HA3 . . . . .176 D1
Barrells Down Rd CM23 . . . .58 E1
Barrett La CM23 . . . . .76 F7
Barrington Dr UB9 . . . . .173 A3
Barrington Rd SG6 . . . . .22 F4
Barrow La EN7 . . . . .147 F1
Barrow Point Ave HA5 . . . . .175 E1
Barrow Point La HA5 . . . . . .175 E1
Barrowby Cl LU2 . . . . .46 D1
Barrowdene Cl HA5 . . . . . . .175 E1
Barry Cl AL2 . . . . .141 B6
Bartel Cl HP3 . . . . .125 D1
Bartholomew Court
Sh Pavilion HP2 . . . . .162 E6
Bartholomew Rd CM23 . . . .76 F6
Bartletts Mead SG14 . . . . . . .92 D1
Barton Cl AL5 . . . . .86 C3
Barton Rd Hexton SG5 . . . . . .19 A1
Luton LU3 . . . . .45 C7
Wheathampstead AL4 . . . . . .108 C8
Barton Way
Borehamwood WD6 . . . . . . .170 A7
Croxley Green WD3 . . . . . . .166 B4
Bartons The WD6 . . . . .169 D3
Bartrams La EN4 . . . . .159 C1
Bartrop Cl EN7 . . . . .147 D3
Barwick La SG11 . . . . .73 C3
Basbow La CM23 . . . . .76 F7
Basildon Cl WD1 . . . . .166 C3
Basildon Sq HP2 . . . . .124 F7
Basils Rd SG1 . . . . .50 D7
Baslow Cl HA3 . . . . .176 D2
Bassett Cl AL3 . . . . .106 B5
Bassil Rd HP2 . . . . .124 D2
Bassingbourne Rd EN10 . . .134 F3
Bassingburn Wlk AL7 . . . . . .110 F5
Batchelors SG12 . . . . .55 E2
Batchwood Dr AL3 . . . . .127 C3
Batchwood Gdns AL3 . . . . . .127 C6
Batchwood View AL3 . . . . . .127 D5
Batchworth Heath Hill
WD3 . . . . .174 A6
Batchworth Hill
London WD3 . . . . .173 F7
Batchworth La HA6 . . . . .174 D5
Bateman Rd WD3 . . . . .166 A3
Bates Ho SG1 . . . . .50 E6
Batford Cl AL7 . . . . .111 B5
Batford Jun Mix Inf Sch
AL5 . . . . .86 D4
Batford Rd AL5 . . . . .86 D3
Bath Pl EN5 . . . . .171 F6
Bath Rd LU3 . . . . .45 D2
Bathurst Rd HP2 . . . . .124 C4
Batterdale AL9 . . . . .130 C6
Battlefield Rd AL1 . . . . .127 F5
Battleview AL4 . . . . .108 E8
Baud Cl SG11 . . . . .57 E2
Baulk The Cheddington LU7 .79 F7
Lilley LU2 . . . . .32 D2
Pitstone LU7 . . . . .80 F5
Bay Cl LU4 . . . . .44 B6
Bay Ct HP4 . . . . .122 B4
Bay Tree Cl
Chiswellgreen AL2 . . . . .141 C3
Hammond Street EN7 . . . . . .147 F4
Bay Tree Wlk WD1 . . . . .154 A1

Bayford CE Prim Sch SG13 132 F5
Bayford Cl
Hemel Hempstead HP2 125 C8
Hertford SG13 113 C4
Bayford Gn SG13 133 A6
Bayford La SG13 132 F7
Bayford Sta SG13 133 B5
Bayfordbury Coll (Univ of Hertfordshire) SG13 113 B1
Bayhurst Dr HA6 174 F4
Baylam Dell LU2 46 E1
Bayley Hall Mews SG14 113 D5
Baylie Ct HP2 124 E4
Baylie La HP2 124 E4
Bayworth SG6 23 B5
Beacon Ct SG13 114 C3
Beacon Rd Ringshall HP4 81 A1
Ware SG12 94 A2
Beacon Way
Rickmansworth WD3 165 B3
Tring HP23 100 C5
Beaconsfield LU2 64 B8
Beaconsfield Rd
Enfield EN3 162 D2
Hatfield AL10 130 C6
St Albans AL1 127 E3
Tring HP23 99 E3
Beadles The CM22 98 B8
Beadlow Rd LU4 44 A4
Beagle Cl WD7 155 F2
Beale Cl SG2 51 C6
Beamish Dr WD2 168 C1
Beane Ave SG2 51 D6
Beane Rd Hertford SG14 113 B7
Watton at Stone SG14 70 D4
Beane River View SG14 113 C6
Beane Wlk SG2 51 D6
Beaneside The SG14 70 D4
Beanfield Rd CM21 97 A4
Beanley Cl LU2 46 E2
Bear La SG7 4 D4
Bearton Ave SG5 34 E8
Bearton Ct SG5 21 E1
Bearton Gn SG5 21 D1
Bearton Rd SG5 21 E1
Bearwood Cl EN6 159 D8
Beatty Rd EN8 162 F5
Beauchamp Gdns WD3 165 A1
Beaulieu Cl WD1 167 C1
Beaulieu Dr EN9 163 B6
Beaumayes Cl HP1 124 B2
Beaumont Ave AL1 128 B4
Beaumont Cl 3 SG5 34 D8
Beaumont Ct 10 AL5 86 B1
Beaumont Gate WD7 156 A4
Beaumont Hall La AL3 106 C2
Beaumont Pl EN5 171 F8
Beaumont Rd
Hammond Street EN7 147 F7
Luton LU3 45 B2
Beaumont Sch AL4 128 C4
Beaumont View EN7 147 D5
Beazley Cl SG12 93 E2
Becket Gdns AL6 89 C4
Beckets Sq HP4 122 A6
Beckets Wlk 14 SG12 93 D1
Beckett's Ave AL3 127 C6
Becketts SG14 113 A5
Beckfield La SG9 26 D7
Beckham Cl LU2 45 D7
Becks Cl AL3 83 D5
Bedale Rd EN2 161 C1
Bede Cl HA5 175 D2
Bede Ct HP4 102 C8
Bedford Almshouses 1 WD1 167 C5
Bedford Ave EN5 171 F4
Bedford Cl WD3 151 B1
Bedford Cres EN3 162 E4
Bedford Gdns 3 LU2 63 D8
Bedford Park Rd AL1 127 E3
Bedford Rd Hitchin SG5 34 E7
Ickleford SG5 21 D5
Letchworth SG6 22 D7
Lower Stondon SG16 10 B3
Moor Park HA6 174 D6
St Albans AL1 127 E2
Bedford St
Berkhamsted HP4 122 D4
Hitchin SG5 34 D7
Watford WD2 167 B8
Bedmond La
Bricket Wood AL3,WD5 140 B6
St Albans AL3 126 F1
Bedmond Rd
Abbots Langley WD5 139 E7
Hemel Hempstead HP3 125 D1
Hemel Hempstead WD5 139 F2
Bedmond Village Prim Sch WD5 139 F3
Bedwell Ave AL9 132 A7
Bedwell Cl AL7 110 E5
Bedwell Cres SG1 50 F5
Bedwell Prim Sch SG1 51 A5
Bedwell Rise SG1 50 E5
Beech Ave Crews Hill EN2 161 A4
Radlett WD7 156 A5
Beech Bottom AL3 127 D6
Beech Cl Harpenden AL5 107 C5
Hatfield AL10 130 A4
Beech Cres AL4 108 D7
Beech Ct
Berkhamsted HP4 122 D4
Harpenden AL5 85 F3
Beech Dr
Berkhamsted HP4 122 C3
Borehamwood WD6 169 F7
Sawbridgeworth CM21 118 C8
Stevenage SG2 51 B3
Beech Farm Dr AL4 128 F7
Beech Gr HP23 100 C4
Beech Hill
Hadley Wood EN4 159 E1
Letchworth SG6 22 D7
Luton LU2 46 D8
Beech Hill Prim Sch LU4 45 B1
Beech Ho EN11 134 F6
Beech Hyde La AL4 108 F6
Beech Hyde Prim Sch AL4 108 D7
Beech Mews SG12 114 D7
Beech Pk HP6 150 B1
Beech Pl AL3 127 D6
Beech Rd Luton LU1 63 C8
St Albans AL3 127 E6
Watford WD2 154 B2
Beech Ridge SG7 23 F6
Beech Way AL4 87 B6
Beech Wlk HP23 100 C4
Beechcroft
Berkhamsted HP4 122 C3
Datchworth SG3 69 D1
Beechcroft Ave WD3 166 C4
Beechcroft Rd WD2 167 E4
Beechen Gr WD1 167 C6
Beeches The
Chorleywood WD3 164 F4
Hitchin SG4 35 A6
Park Street AL2 141 D4
Royston SG8 7 D6
Tring HP23 100 C4
2 Watford WD1 167 B6
Welwyn AL6 89 C4
Beechfield
Hoddesdon EN11 115 A2
Kings Langley WD4 138 F1
Sawbridgeworth CM21 97 F2
Beechfield Cl AL3 106 B5
Beechfield Ct 5 WD1 167 A8
Beechfield Rd
Hemel Hempstead HP1 124 B2
Ware SG12 93 F2
Welwyn Garden City AL7 110 E5
Beechfield Sch WD2 154 A2
Beechfield Wlk EN9 163 D4
Beeching Cl AL5 86 B4
Beechlands CM23 76 F5
Beecholm Mews EN8 148 E3
Beechpark Way WD1 153 E2
Beechtree La AL3 126 B2
Beechwood Ave
Chorleywood WD3 164 B5
Little Chalfont HP6 150 C1
Potters Bar EN6 159 B6
St Albans AL1 128 C4
Beechwood Cl Baldock SG7 23 F5
Hammond Street EN7 147 E5
Hertford SG13 113 F6
Hitchin SG5 21 D2
Beechwood Dr HP23 101 D5
Beechwood Inf Sch LU4 44 E4
Beechwood Jun Sch LU4 44 E4
Beechwood Park Prep Sch AL3 83 B1
Beechwood Pk
Chorleywood WD3 164 F5
Hemel Hempstead HP3 137 F7
Beechwood Rd LU4 44 E3
Beechwood Rise WD2 154 B2
Beecroft La SG2 38 C2
Beehive Cl WD6 169 D3
Beehive Gn AL7 111 A4
Beehive La AL7 111 A3
Beehive Rd EN7 147 B3
Beesonend Cotts AL5 107 B4
Beesonend La AL3,AL5 106 E3
Beeston Cl WD1 175 D6
Beeston Dr EN8 148 D4
Beetham Ct SG14 92 E4
Beethoven Rd WD6 169 D3
Beeton Cl HA5 176 A3
Beggarman's La SG11 72 D8
Beggars Bush La WD1,WD3 166 D4
Beggars La HP23 101 A3
Beken Ct WD2 154 C4
Belcher Rd 6 EN11 135 A7
Beldam Ave SG8 7 E5
Beldams La CM23 77 B5
Belfairs WD1 175 D5
Belford Rd WD6 156 F1
Belfry Ave UB9 173 A2
Belfry The Luton LU2 45 E6
Watford WD2 167 D8
Belgrave Ave WD1 166 F4
Belgrave Cl AL4 128 C7
Belgrave Dr WD4 139 C3
Belgrave Ho 6 CM23 77 B8
Belgrave Mews SG2 69 A8
Belgrave Rd LU4 44 D5
Belham Rd WD4 139 A3
Bell Acre SG6 23 B4
Bell Acre Gdns SG6 23 B4
Bell Cl
Abbots Langley WD5 139 F4
Hitchin SG4 35 B6
Knebworth SG3 69 A5
3 Pinner HA5 175 C1
Bell Farm Ind Est SG8 18 B2
Bell Gn HP3 137 B4
Bell La
Abbots Langley WD5 140 A4
Bell La *continued*
Berkhamsted HP4 121 E5
Brookmans Park AL9 145 A7
Enfield EN3 162 E1
Hertford SG14 113 D6
Hoddesdon, Broxbourne EN11 134 E2
Hoddesdon, Spitalbrook EN11 135 A6
Little Chalfont HP6 150 C1
Nuthampstead SG8 18 B2
Shenley AL2 142 E2
Stevenage SG1 50 C7
Widford SG12 95 D4
Bell Lane Jun Mix Inf Sch HP6 150 B1
Bell Leys HP22 60 B3
Bell Mead CM21 97 E2
Bell Rdbt The AL2 142 F4
Bell Row SG7 23 E7
Bell St CM21 97 E2
Bell View AL4 128 D3
Bell Wlk HP22 60 B3
Bellamy Cl Knebworth SG3 68 F5
Watford WD1 167 A8
Bellamy Rd EN8 148 E2
Belle Vue La WD2 168 D1
Belle Vue Rd SG12 93 F1
Bellerby Rise LU4 44 B6
Bellfield Ave HA3 176 D4
Bellgate HP2 124 E6
Bellgate Prim HP2 124 E5
Bellingdon WD1 175 E7
Bellis Ho AL7 111 B4
Bellmount Wood Ave WD1 166 E8
Bells Hill Barnet EN5 171 D5
Bishop's Stortford CM23 76 E7
Belmers Rd HP23 100 D1
Belmont Ct AL1 127 D2
Belmont Fst & Mid Sch HA3 176 F1
Belmont Hill AL1 127 D2
Belmont Lodge HA3 176 D3
Belmont Rd
Hemel Hempstead HP3 138 E8
Luton LU1 63 C7
Watford WD2 167 E4
Belmor WD6 170 A3
Belper Rd LU4 44 D2
Belsize Cl
Hemel Hempstead HP3 125 A2
St Albans AL4 128 C8
Belsize Rd Harrow HA3 176 D3
Hemel Hempstead HP3 125 A2
Belswains Gn HP3 138 E8
Belswains La HP3 138 F7
Belswains Prim Sch HP3 138 F7
Belton Rd HP4 122 A5
Beltona Gdns EN8 148 D4
Belvedere Gdns AL2 141 A4
Belvedere Rd LU3 45 B5
Bembridge Gdns LU3 44 F7
Ben Austins AL3 106 A4
Benbow Cl AL1 128 B1
Benchley Hill SG4 35 C8
Benchleys Rd HP1 123 F2
Bencroft EN7 148 A5
Bencroft Rd HP2 124 E3
Bencroft Wood EN10 133 D1
Bendish La SG4 66 C7
Bendysh Rd WD2 167 E5
Benedictine Gate EN8 148 E4
Benford Rd EN11 134 F4
Bengarth Dr HA3 176 D1
Bengeo Ho SG14 92 C1
Bengeo Mdws SG14 92 C1
Bengeo Mews SG14 92 C1
Bengeo Prim Sch SG14 92 C1
Bengeo St SG14 113 C8
Benhooks Ave CM23 76 E5
Benhooks Pl 1 CM23 76 E5
Benington CE Prim Sch SG2 52 D4
Benington Cl LU2 45 F5
Benington Lordship Gdns SG2 52 D4
Benington Rd Aston SG2 51 F2
Benington SG2 52 A7
Bennett Cl
Northwood HA6 174 F3
Welwyn Garden City AL7 110 F2
Bennett Ct SG6 23 B3
Bennetts Cl AL4 143 D8
Bennetts End Cl HP3 124 F1
Bennetts End Rd HP3 125 A1
Bennetts La SG9 25 F4
Bennettsgate HP3 139 A8
Bennick Ho WD1 166 E3
Benningfield SG12 95 D5
Benningfield Rd SG12 95 D4
Benskin Rd WD1 167 A4
Benslow La SG4 35 A7
Benslow Rise SG4 35 A8
Benson Cl LU3 44 F7
Benson Ct EN3 163 A1
Benstede SG2 69 C8
Bentfield Cty Prim Sch CM24 59 D8
Bentfield End Cswy CM24 59 D7
Bentfield Gdns CM24 59 D8
Bentfield Green CM24 59 D8
Bentfield Rd CM24 59 D7
Bentick Way SG4 67 F2
Bentley Cl CM23 76 F5
Bentley Ct LU1 63 C8
Bentley Heath La EN5 158 F4
Bentley Lodge WD2 176 E8
Bentley Rd SG14 112 F7
Bentley Wood High Sch HA3 176 F5
Benton Rd WD1 175 D5
Bentsley Cl AL4 128 C7
Berceau Wlk WD1 166 E8
Berefield HP2 124 D5
Beresford Rd Luton LU4 45 A1
Rickmansworth WD3 164 F1
St Albans AL1 128 C2
Bericot Way AL7 111 D6
Berkeley SG6 23 A4
Berkeley Cl
Abbots Langley WD5 153 F8
Borehamwood WD6 170 A4
6 Hitchin SG5 34 D8
Potters Bar EN6 158 F7
Stevenage SG2 69 A8
Ware SG12 93 C2
Berkeley Ct
Croxley Green WD3 166 D4
6 Harpenden AL5 86 A2
Berkeley Path 2 LU2 63 E8
Berkeley Sq HP2 105 C1
Berkhamsted Castle HP4 122 D5
Berkhamsted Collegiate Sch Berkhamsted HP4 122 B4
Berkhamsted HP4 122 C4
Berkhamsted La AL9 132 B3
Berkhamsted Rd HP1 123 E5
Berkhamsted Sta HP4 122 C5
Berkley Ave EN8 162 D5
Berkley Cl AL4 128 C7
Berkley Ct HP4 122 C4
Berkley Pl EN8 162 D5
Berks Hill WD3 164 C4
Bermer Rd WD2 167 C8
Bernard Gr EN9 163 B6
Bernard St AL3 127 D4
Bernard's Heath Inf Sch AL1 127 F5
Berners Dr AL1 141 E8
Berners Way EN10 148 F8
Bernhardt Cres SG2 51 C6
Berries The AL4 128 A7
Berrow Cl LU2 46 E2
Berry Ave WD2 154 B3
Berry Cl WD3 165 B2
Berry Grove La WD2 154 E1
Berry La WD3 165 A2
Berry Leys LU3 44 E7
Berry Way WD3 165 B2
Berryfield LU7 79 F7
Berrygrove La WD2 168 A8
Berrymead HP2 124 F5
Berthold Mews EN9 163 B6
Bertram Ho 4 SG1 50 E6
Berwick Cl Harrow HA7 176 F4
Holdbrook EN8 163 A5
Stevenage SG1 50 A8
Berwick Rd WD6 156 F1
Besant Ho 2 WD2 167 D7
Besford Cl LU2 46 E2
Bessemer Cl SG5 21 E2
Bessemer Dr SG1 50 B4
Bessemer Rd AL7,AL8 89 E2
Bethune Cl LU1 63 B6
Betjeman Cl EN7 148 A3
Betjeman Rd SG8 2 D1
Betjeman Way HP1 124 B4
Betony Vale SG8 7 E5
Bettespol Mdws AL3 106 A6
Betty's La HP23 100 A4
Bevan Cl HP3 124 E1
Bevan Ho 3 WD2 167 D7
Beverley Cl SG8 7 B8
Beverley Gdns
Cheshunt EN7 148 A1
St Albans AL4 128 D7
Welwyn Garden City AL7 111 C6
Beverley Rd Luton LU4 44 F1
Stevenage SG1 37 B2
Beverly Cl EN10 134 E2
Bevil Ct EN11 115 A1
Bewdley Cl AL5 107 D6
Bewley Cl EN8 162 D8
Bexhill Rd LU2 46 D2
Beyers Gdns EN11 115 A1
Beyers Prospect EN11 115 A1
Beyers Ride EN11 115 A1
Bibbs Hall La SG4,AL6 87 E6
Biddenham Turn WD2 154 C4
Bideford Gdns LU3 45 D4
Bideford Rd EN3 162 F1
Bidwell Cl SG6 23 B5
Biggin Hill SG9 28 D7
Biggin La SG5 34 F7
Bignells Cnr EN6 158 B5
Billet La HP4 122 A6
Billy Lows La EN6 159 B8
Bilton Rd SG4 21 F2
Bilton Way Enfield EN3 162 F1
Luton LU1 44 F1
Bingen Rd SG5 21 C1
Bingham Cl HP1 123 F5
Binghams Park Childrens Farm HP1 123 E8
Bingley Rd EN11 135 C6
Binham Cl LU2 45 D7
Binyon Cres HA7 176 F5
Birch Copse AL2 140 E1
Birch Ct HA6 174 C4
Birch Dr Hatfield AL10 130 A4
Maple Cross WD3 172 D5
Birch Gn
Hemel Hempstead HP1 123 F5
Hertingfordbury SG14 112 C4
Birch Gr Oaklands AL6 89 E8
Potters Bar EN6 159 B7
Birch La HP3 151 B7
Birch Leys HP2 125 C8
Birch Link LU4 45 C1
Birch Pk HA3 176 C3
Birch Rd
Berkhamsted HP4 121 D7
Woolmer Green SG3 69 B1
Birch Tree Gr HP5 136 B1
Birch Tree Wlk WD1 153 F2
Birch Way Harpenden AL5 107 C8
London Colney AL2 142 D4
Birch Wlk WD6 170 A8
Birchall La SG14 111 E4
Birchall Wood AL7 111 C5
Birchalls CM24 59 E8
Birchanger CE Prim Sch CM23 59 D2
Birchanger Ind Est CM23 59 B2
Birchanger La CM23 59 D2
Birchen Gr LU2 45 F3
Bircherley Ct 12 SG14 113 D6
Bircherley Green Ctr The 8 SG14 113 D6
Bircherley St SG14 113 D6
Birches The Bushey WD2 168 C4
Codicote SG4 89 A8
Hemel Hempstead HP3 137 F8
Letchworth SG6 22 E8
Birchfield Rd EN8 148 C2
Birchmead WD1 153 F1
Birchmead Cl AL3 127 D6
Birchway AL10 130 B7
Birchwood
Birchanger CM23 59 D2
Shenley WD7 157 A5
Waltham Abbey EN9 163 E5
Birchwood Ave AL10 130 A7
Birchwood Cl AL10 130 A7
Birchwood High Sch CM23 77 C8
Birchwood Way AL2 141 B3
Bird La UB9 173 C1
Birdcroft Rd AL8 110 D5
Birdie Way SG13 114 B7
Birds Cl AL7 111 B4
Birds Hill SG6 23 A6
Birdsfoot La LU3 45 B6
Birkbeck Rd EN2 161 D1
Birkdale Gdns WD1 175 D7
Birklands AL1 142 B7
Birklands La AL1 142 B7
Birling Dr LU2 46 C4
Birnbeck Ct EN5 171 D5
Birstal Gn WD1 175 D6
Birtley Croft LU2 46 E1
Biscot Rd LU3 45 C2
Bishop Ken Rd HA3 176 F2
Bishop Sq AL10 129 E5
Bishop Wood CE Jun Sch HP23 100 A3
Bishop's Ave CM23 76 F3
Bishop's Cl AL4 128 A7
Bishop's Garth AL4 128 A7
Bishop's Hatfield Girls' Sch AL10 130 A5
Bishop's Palace (rem of) AL9 130 D6
Bishop's Stortford Bsns Ctr CM23 77 A6
Bishop's Stortford Coll CM23 76 E7
Bishop's Stortford High Sch The CM23 76 F4
Bishop's Stortford Sta CM23 77 A6
Bishop's Wood Ctry Pk WD3 173 F4
Bishops Ave
Borehamwood WD6 169 F4
Moor Park HA6 174 F7
Bishops Cl Barnet EN5 171 D3
Hatfield AL10 129 F5
Bishops' Coll EN8 148 B1
Bishops Ct Cheshunt EN8 148 B1
6 Luton LU3 45 D1
Bishops Field HP22 99 A4
Bishops Mead HP1 124 B1
Bishops Park Way CM23 76 B7
Bishops Rd AL6 90 E6
Bishops Rise AL10 129 F2
Bishopscote Rd LU3 45 B3
Biskra WD1 167 A8
Bisley Cl EN8 162 D6
Bit The HP23 100 D1
Bittern Cl
Hammond Street EN7 147 C6
Stevenage SG2 51 D2
Bittern Way SG6 11 E1
Black Boy Wood AL2 141 A1
Black Cut AL1 127 E2
Black Fan Rd
Welwyn Garden City AL7 110 F7
Welwyn Garden City AL7 111 B6
Black Lion Ct CM17 118 C4
Black Lion Hill WD7 156 F7
Black Smiths Cl SG12 115 A7
Black Swan Ct 1 SG12 93 D1
Black Swan La LU3 45 A5
Blackberry Mead SG2 51 D3
Blackbirds La WD2 155 C5
Blackbury Cl EN6 159 C8
Blackbush Spring CM20 118 A1
Blackbushe CM23 59 C1
Blackdale EN7 148 A4
Blacketts Wood Dr WD3 164 B5
Blackford Rd WD1 175 D5

Blackhorse Cl SG4 .....35 A5
Blackhorse La Hitchin SG4 .35 A5
Redbourn AL3 ....106 A6
Ridge EN6 ....157 F8
Blackhorse Rd SG6 ....23 C8
Blackley LU1 WD1 .....153 F2
Blackmoor La WD1 ....166 D4
Blackmore SG6 ....23 B3
Blackmore Manor AL4 ..87 B6
Blackmore Way AL4 ....87 B6
Blacksmith Cl HP1 .....11 F7
Blacksmith's La Reed SG8 .16 D5
St Albans AL3 ....127 B3
Blacksmiths Cl CM23 ...76 B5
Blacksmiths Hill SG2 ...52 E4
Blacksmiths Way CM21 ..97 D1
Blackthorn Cl
St Albans AL4 ....128 C6
Watford WD2 ....154 B7
Blackthorn Dr LU2 ......46 C4
Blackthorn Jun Sch AL7 .111 A5
Blackthorn Rd AL7 .....111 A5
Blackthorne Cl AL10 ...129 F2
Blackwater La HP3 ....125 E1
Blackwell Cl HA3 ......176 D3
Blackwell Dr WD1 .....167 C3
Blackwell Hall La HP5 .150 C6
Blackwell Rd WD4 .....139 A2
Blackwood Ct EN7 .....148 F5
Bladon Cl SG4 ....35 F3
Blaine HP23 ....100 A6
Blair Cl
Bishop's Stortford CM23 ....76 C7
Hemel Hempstead HP2 ..105 B1
Stevenage SG2 ....50 F1
Blairhead Dr WD1 .....175 B7
Blake Rd Royston SG8 ...2 D1
St Albans AL1 ....142 A8
Blakemere Rd AL8 .....110 D8
Blakemore End Rd SG4 ..35 D3
Blakeney Dr LU2 ....45 C7
Blakeney Ho SG1 ......50 A7
Blakeney Rd SG1 ......50 A7
Blakes Ct CM21 ....97 E2
Blakes Way AL6 ....89 C6
Blanche La EN6 ....157 F5
Blandford Ave LU2 .....45 D6
Blandford Rd AL1 .....128 A3
Blanes The SG12 ....93 C3
Blattner Cl WD6 ......169 E5
Blaxland Terr 9 EN8 ..148 D3
Blaydon Rd LU2 ....64 A8
Blenheim Cl
Sawbridgeworth CM21 ..118 C8
Watford WD1 ....167 D2
Blenheim Cres LU3 .....45 C2
Blenheim Ct
Bishop's Stortford CM23 ...76 C4
Welwyn Garden City AL7 .110 F7
Blenheim Rd Barnet EN5 .171 D5
St Albans AL1 ....127 F4
Blenheim Way SG2 .....69 D7
Blenhiem Rd WD5 .....154 A7
Blenkin Cl AL3 ....127 C7
Blind La SG2 ....38 F5
Blindman's La EN8 ....148 D2
Block 10 4 WD1 ....167 A8
Block 12 3 WD1 ....167 A8
Block 14 2 WD1 ....167 A8
Bloomfield Ave LU2 .....46 A1
Bloomfield Ho 6 SG1 ..50 E6
Bloomfield Rd
Hammond Street EN7 ..147 C6
Harpenden AL5 ....85 F3
Blossom La EN2 ......161 C1
Blue Bridge Rd AL9 ...144 E4
Bluebell Cl
Hemel Hempstead HP1 ..123 E4
Hertford SG13 ....114 A6
Bluebell Dr
Abbots Langley WD5 ...139 F4
Goff's Oak EN7 ....147 D3
Bluebell Wood Cl LU1 ..63 A7
Bluebells AL6 ....89 D7
Blueberry Cl AL3 .....127 D7
Bluebridge Ave AL9 ...144 F4
Bluecoat Yd SG12 ......93 D1
Bluecoats Ave SG14 ...113 D6
Bluecoats Ct 15 SG14 ..113 D6
Bluehouse Hill AL3 ....127 A3
Bluett Rd AL2 ....142 D4
Blundell Cl AL3 ....127 D7
Blundell Rd LU3 ....45 A4
Blunesfield EN6 ....159 D8
Blunts La AL2 ....140 D5
Blyth Cl
Borehamwood WD6 ...170 A8
Stevenage SG1 ....50 A7
Blyth Pl 12 LU1 ....63 D6
Blythe Rd EN11 ....135 D5
Blythway AL7 ....89 F1
Blythway Ho AL7 ....89 F1
Blythwood Gdns CM24 ..59 D6
Blythwood Rd HA5 ....175 D2
Boardman Cl EN5 .....171 E4
Bockings SG5 ....38 C1
Bodmin Rd LU4 ....44 F3
Bodwell Cl HP1 ....124 A4
Bogmoor Rd SG8 ....18 A8
Bognor Gdns WD1 ....175 C5
Bohemia HP2 ....124 E4
Boissy Cl AL4 ....128 E2
Boleyn Cl HP2 ....125 C8
Boleyn Dr AL1 ....127 D1
Bolingbroke Rd LU1 ...63 B6
Bolingbrook AL4 ......128 A7
Bolney Gn LU2 ....46 D3
Bolton Rd LU1 ....63 F7

Boltons Park (Royal
Veterinary Coll) EN6 .145 A2
Bond Cl AL5 ....85 F3
Bondor Bsns Ctr SG7 ...23 F7
Boniface Gdns HA3 ...176 B3
Boniface Wlk HA3 ....176 B3
Bonks Hill CM21 ....97 D1
Bonney Dr EN7 ....148 A1
Bonnick Cl LU1 ....63 C6
Booths Cl AL9 ....144 D7
Boreham Holt WD6 ...169 F5
Borehamwood Ind Pk
WD6 ....170 D7
Bornedene EN6 ....158 E8
Borodale AL5 ....86 A1
Borough Way EN6 ....158 E7
Borrell Cl EN10 ......134 F3
Borrowdale Ct 4 HP2 ..124 E6
Borton Ave SG16 ....10 B4
Bosanquet Rd EN11 ...135 C8
Boscombe Ct SG6 ......23 B6
Bosmore Rd LU3 ....44 F5
Boswell Cl WD7 ......156 E7
Boswell Dr SG5 ....21 E4
Boswell Gdns SG1 .....36 D1
Boswick La HP4 ......121 D8
Botley La HP5 ....136 A1
Botley Rd Botley HP5 .136 A1
Hemel Hempstead HP2 .125 B8
Bottom House La HP23 .101 A1
Bottom La WD3,WD4 ..152 C4
Bottom Rd HP23 .....119 F3
Bough Beech Ct EN3 ..162 D2
Boughton Way HP6 ...150 C1
Boulevard Ctr The WD6 .170 A6
Boulevard The
Watford WD1 ....166 D4
Welwyn Garden City AL7 .110 F8
Boulton Rd SG1 ....37 C2
Bounce The HP2 ......124 D5
Boundary Cl EN5 .....171 F8
Boundary Ct AL7 .....110 F2
Boundary Dr SG14 ...113 D8
Boundary Ho AL7 ....110 D3
Boundary La AL7 .....110 E2
Boundary Rd
Bishop's Stortford CM23 .77 A5
St Albans AL1 ....127 E5
Boundary Way
Hemel Hempstead HP2 .125 C5
Watford WD2 ....154 C7
Bounds Field SG11 ....75 F8
Bourne End Rd HA6 ..174 E6
Bourne Hall HP2 .....168 A3
Bourne Honour SG12 ..92 E7
Bourne Rd
Berkhamsted HP4 .....121 F5
Bushey WD2 ....168 A4
Bourne The
Bishop's Stortford CM23 ..77 A8
Bovingdon HP3 ....137 A4
Ware SG12 ....93 D2
Bournehall Ave WD2 ..168 A4
Bournehall
Jun Mix Inf Sch WD2 .168 B4
Bournehall La WD2 ...168 A4
Bournehall Rd WD2 ...168 A3
Bournemouth Rd 3 SG1 .50 B8
Bouvier Rd EN3 ....154 D5
Bovingdon Cres WD2 .154 D5
Bovingdon Ct HP3 ....137 A3
Bovingdon Green La
HP3 ....136 D7
Bovingdon Prim Sch
HP3 ....137 B4
Bovingdon Sch HP3 ..137 B4
Bowbrook Vale LU2 ....46 F1
Bowcock Wlk SG1 .....50 E3
Bower Heath La AL5 ...86 C6
Bower's Par AL5 ....86 A1
Bowers Way AL5 ....86 A1
Bowershott SG6 ....23 A4
Bowes Lyon Mews AL3 .127 B3
Bowgate AL1 ....127 E4
Bowlers Mead SG9 ....40 D7
Bowles Gn EN1 ......162 B3
Bowling Cl
14 Bishop's Stortford CM23 .76 F6
Harpenden AL5 ......107 C2
Bowling Ct WD1 ......167 A5
Bowling Gn SG1 ....50 C8
Bowling Green La
Buntingford SG9 ......40 D8
Luton LU2 ....45 E2
Bowling Rd SG12 ......93 E1
Bowman Trad Est SG1 ..50 B5
Bowmans Ave SG4 .....35 B6
Bowmans Ct
Potters Bar EN6 .....159 D7
Welwyn AL6 ....89 C6
Bowmans Ct HP2 .....124 E5
Bowmans Gn WD2 ...154 A1
Bowmansgreen Prim Sch
AL2 ....142 C4
Bowring Gn WD1 ....175 C5
Bowyer's Cl SG5 ....21 D1
Bowyers 6 HP2 ......124 D5
Box La
Hemel Hempstead HP3 .137 E7
Hoddesdon EN11 .....134 E6
Boxberry Cl SG1 ....50 E5
Boxfield AL7 ....111 B3
Boxfield Gn SG2 ....51 D8

Boxgrove Cl LU2 ....46 C5
Boxhill 3 HP2 ....124 D5
Boxmoor House Sch
HP3 ....137 F8
Boxmoor Jun Mix Inf Sch
HP1 ....124 A2
Boxted Cl LU4 ....44 C5
Boxted Rd HP1 ....123 F5
Boxtree La HA3 ......176 D3
Boxtree Rd HA3 ......176 D3
Boxwell Rd HP4 ......122 B4
Boyce Cl WD6 ....169 E8
Boyd Cl 1 CM23 ....77 B8
Boyle Cl LU2 ....63 E8
Brace Cl EN7 ....147 B6
Braceby Cl LU3 ....44 F6
Brache Cl AL3 ....106 A5
Brache Ct LU1 ....63 F6
Bracken La AL6 ....89 F7
Brackendale EN6 .....159 A6
Brackendale Gr
Harpenden AL5 ....85 D3
Luton LU3 ....45 B5
Brackenden AL2 ......140 F1
Brackenhill HP4 ......122 F5
Brackens The HP2 ....124 D4
Bracklesham Gdns LU2 ..46 D3
Bracknell Pl HP2 .....124 F7
Bradbery WD3 ....172 D5
Bradbury Cl WD6 ....170 B8
Bradden Cotts HP2 ...103 F8
Bradden La HP1,HP2 ..103 E7
Bradden Villas HP2 ...103 F8
Bradford Rd WD3 ....164 C2
Bradgate EN6 ....146 D4
Bradgate Ct EN6 .....146 D3
Bradgers Hill Rd LU2 ..45 E4
Bradley Comm CM23 ..59 C3
Bradley Rd Enfield EN3 .162 E2
Luton LU4 ....44 D1
Bradleys Cnr SG1 .....35 C8
Bradman Way SG1 .....37 A1
Bradmore Gn AL9 ....144 E5
Bradmore La AL9 ....144 C5
Bradmore Way AL9 ...144 E5
Bradshaw Rd WD2 ...154 C1
Bradshaws AL10 .....129 F1
Bradway SG4 ....66 E6
Braemar Cl SG2 ....69 B7
Braemar Ct WD2 .....168 A3
Braeside Cl HA5 .....176 A3
Bragbury Cl SG2 ......69 D7
Bragbury La SG2,SG3 ..69 D5
Bragmans La WD3 ...151 E6
Braham Ct 2 SG5 .....34 E7
Brain Cl AL10 ....130 B6
Braithwaite Ct 16 LU3 .45 D1
Brakynbery HP4 .....121 E7
Brallings La SL9 ......172 A1
Bramble Cl Harpenden AL5 .85 F3
Luton LU4 ....44 C4
Watford WD2 ....154 A5
Bramble Rd Hatfield AL10 .129 D5
Luton LU4 ....44 C4
Bramble Rise CM20 ...117 C1
Brambles The
Bishop's Stortford CM23 .76 C6
Cheshunt EN8 ....162 D8
Oaklands AL6 ....89 E8
Royston SG8 ....7 E5
St Albans AL1 ....127 D1
Stevenage SG1 ....36 D2
Ware SG12 ....93 C3
Brambling Cl WD2 ...167 E5
Brambling Rise HP2 ..124 E6
Bramfield Hitchin SG4 ..35 B6
Watford WD2 ....154 E5
Bramfield Ct SG14 ...113 A7
Bramfield La SG14 ....91 F3
Bramfield Pl HP2 ....105 A1
Bramfield Rd
Datchworth SG3 ....90 E8
Hertford SG14 ....112 F8
Bramhanger Acre LU3 ..44 D7
Bramingham Bsns Pk LU3 .45 B8
Bramingham Prim Sch
LU3 ....45 B8
Bramingham Rd LU3 ..44 F6
Bramleas WD1 ....166 F5
Bramley Cl SG7 ....12 F1
Bramley Ct WD2 .....154 B8
Bramley Gdns WD1 ..175 D5
Bramley House Ct EN2 .161 D2
Bramley Shaw EN9 ...163 F6
Bramley Way AL4 ....128 C2
Brampton Cl
Cheshunt EN7 ....148 A3
Harpenden AL5 ....86 D1
Brampton Park Rd SG5 ..21 E1
Brampton Rd Royston SG8 ..7 F6
South Oxhey WD1 ....175 A7
St Albans AL1 ....128 A4
Brampton Terr WD6 ..157 A1
Bramshaw Gdns WD1 .175 D5
Bramshott Cl SG4 .....34 F5
Branch Cl AL10 ......130 C7
Branch Rd
Park Street AL2 ......141 D4
St Albans AL1 ....127 B4
Brand St SG5 ....34 E7
Brandles Rd SG6 ......23 A3
Brandles Sch SG7 .....23 E7
Brandon Cl EN7 .....147 E5
Branksome Cl HP2 ...125 A4
Branscombe Ho WD2 .175 D5
Branton Cl LU2 ....46 E2
Brantwood Rd LU1 ....63 C7
Bray Cl WD6 ....170 C8

Bray Lodge EN8 .....148 E3
Brayes Manor SG5 ....11 C3
Brays Ct LU2 ....46 B3
Brays Rd LU2 ....46 B3
Braziers End HP5 ....120 C1
Braziers Field SG13 ..113 F6
Braziers Quay CM23 ...77 A6
Breachwood Green
Jun Mix Inf Sch SG4 ..47 E1
Bread & Cheese La EN7 .147 D6
Breadcroft La AL5 .....86 B1
Breakmead AL7 ......111 B4
Breaks Rd AL10 .....130 B6
Breakspear SG2 ....51 C3
Breakspear Ave AL1 ..127 F2
Breakspear Coll WD5 .139 F1
Breakspear Hospl HP3 .138 E1
Breakspear Rd N UB9 .173 D1
Breakspear Way HP2 .125 D4
Breakspeare Cl WD2 ..154 B1
Breakspeare Rd WD5 .153 E8
Breakspeare Sch WD5 .153 E8
Brecken Cl AL4 ......128 A7
Brecon Cl 18 LU1 .....63 D6
Breeze Terr 5 EN8 ...148 D3
Brendon Ave LU2 ......46 C1
Brent Ct SG1 ....50 E5
Brent Pl EN5 ....171 F4
Brett Pl WD2 ....154 A2
Brett Rd EN5 ....171 C4
Bretts Mead LU1 ......63 C5
Bretts Mead Ct LU1 ..63 C5
Brewers Ct CM23 .....76 C5
Brewery La Baldock SG7 .23 E8
Stansted Mountfitchet CM24 .59 E7
Brewery Rd EN11 ....135 B6
Brewery Yd CM24 .....59 F7
Brewhouse Hill AL4 ..108 C8
Brewhouse La SG14 ..113 C6
Briants Cl HA5 ......175 F1
Briar Cl Cheshunt EN8 .148 C2
Luton LU2 ....46 C4
Potten End HP4 .....123 A7
Briar Patch La SG6 ....22 D3
Briar Rd St Albans AL4 .128 D6
Watford WD2 ....154 B4
Briar Way HP4 ....122 D3
Briarcliff HP1 ....123 E4
Briardale Stevenage SG1 .50 E4
Ware SG12 ....93 C3
Briarley Cl EN10 .....134 F1
Briars Cl AL10 ....130 A5
Briars La AL10 ....130 A5
Briars The Bushey WD2 .168 E2
Cheshunt EN8 ....162 E8
Hertford SG13 ......114 A6
Sarratt WD3 ....152 A3
Briars Wood AL10 ....130 A5
Briarwood Dr HA6 ...175 A1
Briary La SG6 ....7 C5
Briary Wood End AL6 ..89 F7
Briary Wood La AL6 ...89 F7
Brick Kiln Cl WD1 ....167 E3
Brick Kiln La SG4 .....34 C5
Brick Knoll Pk AL1 ...128 C2
Brickcroft EN10 .....148 E5
Brickendon Ct
Hoddesdon EN11 .....135 A5
Waltham Abbey EN9 .163 F6
Brickendon La SG13 ..133 D6
Bricket Rd AL1 ......127 D3
Bricket Wood Sta AL2 .141 A1
Brickfield AL10 .....130 A2
Brickfield Ho HP3 ...125 B2
Brickfield Ct AL10 ...130 B2
Brickfield La EN5 ....170 F5
Brickfields The SG12 ..93 B2
Brickkiln Rd SG1 .....50 C6
Brickly Rd LU4 ....44 C5
Brickmakers La HP3 ..125 B2
Brickwall Cl AL6 .....110 A8
Brickwall Cl AL6 ......88 A5
Bride Hall La AL6 .....88 A5
Bridewell Cl SG9 ......40 E8
Bridge Cl
Berkhamsted HP4 ....122 D4
Harpenden AL5 ....85 F3
Radlett WD7 ....156 B4
Bridge Gate SG9 ......40 E8
Bridge Foot SG12 .....93 D2
Bridge Pk AL7 ....110 F2
Bridge Pl WD1 ......167 D4
Bridge Rd
Abbots Langley WD4 .153 C6
Letchworth SG6 ......22 F6
Welwyn Garden City AL8 .110 C7
Woolmer Green SG3 ...69 A2
Bridge Rd E AL7 .....110 F6
Bridge Rd W AL7 .....50 C7
Bridge St
Berkhamsted HP4 ....122 D4
Bishop's Stortford CM23 .76 F7
Hemel Hempstead HP1 .124 C2
Hitchin SG5 ....34 E6
Kneesworth SG8 ....2 B8
Luton LU1 ....63 E8
Bridgefields AL7 .....110 F7
Bridgefoot SG9 ....40 E7
Bridgeford Ho
13 Bishop's Stortford CM23 .76 F6
5 Watford WD1 ....167 B6
Bridgend Rd EN1 ....162 C4
Bridgenhall Rd EN1 ..161 C1
Bridger Cl WD2 ......154 E6
Bridges Ct SG14 .....113 C6
Bridges Rd HA7 ......176 F5
Bridgewater Ct HP4 ..102 C4

Bridgewater Hill HP4 .121 F7
Bridgewater Monument
The HP4 ....101 E7
Bridgewater Rd HP4 .122 B5
Bridgewater Sch HP4 .122 B5
Bridgewater Way WD2 .168 B3
Bridle Cl Enfield EN3 ..162 F2
Hoddesdon EN11 .....115 A2
St Albans AL3 ....127 E5
Bridle La WD3 ....165 D6
Bridle Path WD2 .....167 B7
Bridle Way
Berkhamsted HP4 ....122 A6
Great Amwell SG12 ..115 A6
Bridle Way (N) EN11 .115 B2
Bridle Way (S) EN11 .115 A1
Bridleway HP23 ......119 E5
Bridlington Rd WD1 .175 D7
Brierley Cl LU2 ....46 D2
Briery Ct WD3 ....165 A5
Briery Field WD3 ....165 A5
Briery Way HP2 ......125 A4
Brigadier Ave EN2 ...161 C1
Brigadier Hill EN2 ...161 C1
Brightman Cotts 2 LU3 .45 A7
Brighton Rd WD2 ....154 A1
Brighton Way SG1 .....50 A8
Brightview Cl AL2 ....140 E2
Brightwell Ct WD1 ...167 A4
Brightwell Rd WD1 ...167 A4
Brill Cl LU2 ....46 D2
Brimfield Cl LU2 ......46 D2
Brimsdown Ave EN3 .162 E1
Brimstone Wlk HP4 ..121 F6
Brinklow Ct AL3 .....141 B8
Brinley Cl EN8 ....162 D8
Brinsley Rd HA3 .....176 D1
Brinsmead AL2 ......141 E4
Briscoe Cl EN11 .....134 F8
Briscoe Rd EN11 ....134 F8
Bristol Rd LU3 ....45 B4
Britannia SG11 ....55 E2
Britannia Ave LU3 ....45 B4
Britannia Hall LU2 ....64 C8
Britannia Pl 3 CM23 ..76 E5
Britannia Rd EN8 ...162 F5
Britannic Bsns Pk EN8 .162 F5
Brittain Way SG12 ....51 B4
Britten Cl WD6 ......169 D3
Britton Ave AL3 .....127 D3
Brixham Cl SG1 ....50 B7
Brixton Rd WD2 .....167 B8
Broad Acre AL2 .....140 E1
Broad Acres AL10 ...129 F8
Broad Ct AL7 ....110 E6
Broad Gn SG13 ......132 F8
Broad Green Wood
SG13 ....133 A8
Broad Mead LU3 ......45 A3
Broad Oak Ct LU2 ....46 D3
Broad Oak Way SG2 ..50 F1
Broad St HP2 ....124 D4
Broad Wlk CM20 ....117 D1
Broad Wlk The HA6 ..174 C1
Broadacres LU2 ....45 D6
Broadcroft
2 Hemel Hempstead HP2 .124 D5
Letchworth SG6 ......22 F2
Broadfield
Bishop's Stortford CM23 .58 F2
Harlow CM20 ....117 E1
Broadfield Cl SG10 ...74 E1
Broadfield Ct WD2 ...176 E8
Broadfield Inf Sch HP2 .124 F3
Broadfield Jun Sch HP2 .124 F3
Broadfield Pl AL8 ....110 B5
Broadfield Rd
Hemel Hempstead HP2 .124 F3
Woolmer Green SG3 ...69 B3
Broadfield Way SG10 ..74 F1
Broadfields
Goff's Oak EN7 ......147 B2
Harpenden AL5 ....85 F2
Harrow HA2 ....176 B1
High Wych CM21 ......97 B1
Broadfields Cty Prim Sch
CM20 ....117 E1
Broadfields Cl WD1 ..167 B1
Broadgate EN9 ......163 F7
Broadgreen Rd EN7 .147 D5
Broadhall Way SG2 ...51 B2
Broadlake Cl AL2 ....142 D4
Broadlands CI EN8 ..162 D5
Broadlawns Ct HA3 .176 B2
Broadleaf Ave CM23 ..76 D4
Broadleaf Gr AL8 .....89 B1
Broadley Gdns WD7 .156 E7
Broadmead SG4 ....35 B5
Broadmead Cl HA5 ..175 E3
Broadmead Ind Sch LU1 .63 E3
Broadmeadow Ride SG4 .35 A4
Broadmeads SG12 ....93 D1
Broadoak Ave EN3 ..162 D4
Broadstone Rd AL5 ..107 D7
Broadwater SG1 ......50 E6
Broadwater
Berkhamsted HP4 ....122 C5
Potters Bar EN6 .....145 A4
Broadwater Ave SG6 ..22 E5
Broadwater Cres
Stevenage SG2 ....69 C8
Welwyn Garden City AL7 .110 D5
Broadwater Dale SG6 .22 E5
Broadwater La SG2 ...51 D1
Broadwater Rd AL7 ..110 E6

Broadway SG6 . . . . .22 F5
Broadway Ave CM17 . . . . .118 B4
Broadway Ct SG6 . . . . .22 E3
Broadway The
  Harrow HA3 . . . . .176 F1
  Hatfield AL9 . . . . .130 C6
  Kimpton AL4 . . . . .87 B5
  Pinner HA5 . . . . .175 F3
  Watford WD1 . . . . .167 C6
Brocket Cnr AL8 . . . . .109 F4
Brocket Ct LU4 . . . . .44 D5
Brocket Rd Hatfield AL8 . . .110 A3
  Hoddesdon EN11 . . . . . . .135 A6
Brocket View AL4 . . . . . . .108 D8
Brockett Cl AL8 . . . . .110 B6
Brockhurst Cl HA7 . . . . . .176 F4
Brocklesbury Cl WD2 . . . .167 D7
Brockley Hill HA7 . . . . . . .169 C1
Brockswood La AL8 . . . . . .110 B7
Brockswood Prim Sch
  HP2 . . . . .105 C1
Brockwell Shott SG2 . . . . .38 B1
Brodewater Rd WD6 . . . . .170 B7
Brodie Rd EN2 . . . . .161 C1
Bromborough Gn WD1 . . .175 C5
Bromet Cl WD1 . . . . .153 F1
Bromet Jun Mix Inf Sch
  The WD1 . . . . .167 D2
Bromleigh Cl EN8 . . . . . . .148 E1
Bromley HP23 . . . . .79 A4
Bromley La SG10 . . . . .74 D6
Brompton Cl LU3 . . . . .44 F8
Bronte Cres HP1 . . . . .105 B1
Bronte Paths SG2 . . . . . . .51 C6
Brook Bank EN1 . . . . .162 B2
Brook Cotts CM24 . . . . . . .59 E5
Brook Ct LU3 . . . . .45 D1
Brook Dr Radlett WD7 . . . .155 F6
  Stevenage SG2 . . . . .69 B8
Brook End Borehamwood AL3 . .106 A4
  Sawbridgeworth CM21 . . . .97 D2
Brook Field SG1 . . . . .51 E2
Brook La
  Berkhamsted HP4 . . . . . .122 B5
  Sawbridgeworth CM21 . . . .97 D2
Brook Rd
  Borehamwood WD6 . . . . .170 A7
  Sawbridgeworth CM21 . . . .97 D2
  Stansted Mountfitchet CM24 .59 E6
Brook St Luton LU3 . . . . . .63 D8
  Stotfold SG5 . . . . .11 E6
  Tring HP23 . . . . .100 B4
Brook View SG4 . . . . .35 F6
Brookbridge La SG3 . . . . . .69 D2
Brookdene Ave WD1 . . . . .167 C1
Brookdene Dr HA6 . . . . . .174 F4
Brooke Cl WD2 . . . . .168 C2
Brooke Gdns CM23 . . . . . .77 C7
Brooke Rd SG8 . . . . .7 D8
Brooke Way WD2 . . . . . . .168 C2
Brooker Rd EN8 . . . . .163 C5
Brookfield Cl HP23 . . . . . .100 B4
Brookfield Ct EN8 . . . . . . .148 E4
Brookfield Gdns EN8 . . . . .148 E4
Brookfield La SG2 . . . . . . .51 F3
Brookfield La E EN8 . . . . .148 E3
Brookfield La W EN8 . . . . .148 C4
Brookfield Ret Pk EN8 . . . .148 D5
Brookfields CM21 . . . . . . .97 D2
Brookhill SG2 . . . . .68 F8
Brookhouse Pl 3 CM23 . . .76 F8
Brookland Jun & Inf Schs
  EN8 . . . . .148 E3
Brooklands Cl LU4 . . . . . . .44 C6
Brooklands Gdns EN6 . . . .158 E7
Brookmans Ave AL9 . . . . .144 F5
Brookmans Park
  Cty Prim Sch AL9 . . . . . .144 E5
Brookmans Park Sta
  AL9 . . . . .144 E5
Brookmead Sch LU7 . . . . .80 E5
Brookmill WD1 . . . . .167 B2
Brooks Ct SG14 . . . . .112 F7
Brooksfield AL7 . . . . .111 B7
Brookshill HA3 . . . . .176 B5
Brookshill Ave HA3 . . . . . .176 E5
Brookshill Dr HA3 . . . . . . .176 D5
Brookside Hatfield AL10 . . .129 D5
  Hertford SG13 . . . . .113 C5
  Hoddesdon EN11 . . . . . . .135 A6
  Letchworth SG6 . . . . .22 F5
  Potters Bar EN6 . . . . . . .158 A7
  Waltham Abbey EN9 . . . . .163 E7
  Watford WD2 . . . . .154 D3
Brookside Cl EN5 . . . . . . .171 E3
Brookside Cres EN6 . . . . .146 E4
Brookside Gdns EN1 . . . . .162 C2
Brookside Rd WD1 . . . . . .167 B2
Broom Barns
  Jun Inf Sch SG1 . . . . .50 E5
Broom Cl
  Hammond Street EN7 . . . .148 A4
  Hatfield AL10 . . . . .129 F2
Broom Gr Knebworth SG3 . .68 F5
  Watford WD1 . . . . .154 A1
Broom Hill
  Hemel Hempstead HP1 . . .123 C2
  Welwyn AL6 . . . . .90 A8
Broom Wlk SG1 . . . . .50 E5
Broomer Pl EN8 . . . . .148 C2
Broomfield
  Chiswellgreen AL2 . . . . . .141 C4
  Harlow CM20 . . . . .118 B3
Broomfield Ave EN10 . . . . .148 E5
Broomfield Cl AL6 . . . . . . .89 C4

Broomfield Ct 2 AL10 . . . .130 A6
Broomfield Rd AL6 . . . . . .89 C4
Broomfield Rise WD5 . . . .153 D7
Broomhills AL4 . . . . .128 D6
Brooms Cl AL8 . . . . .89 D1
Brooms Rd LU2 . . . . .64 A8
Broomstick Hall Rd EN9 . .163 E6
Broomstick La HP5 . . . . . .136 A1
Broughinge Rd WD6 . . . . .170 B7
Broughton Ave LU3 . . . . . .45 C5
Broughton Hill SG6 . . . . . .23 B6
Broughton Way WD3 . . . . .165 A2
Brow The WD2 . . . . .154 B6
Brown's Cl AL4 . . . . .44 D5
Brown's Cnr SG9 . . . . .27 F3
Brown's Rise HP23 . . . . . .119 F3
Brownfield Way AL4 . . . . . .87 B6
Brownfields AL7 . . . . .110 F7
Browning Dr SG4 . . . . .35 B8
Browning Rd Enfield EN2 . .161 D1
  Harpenden AL5 . . . . .86 C2
  Luton LU4 . . . . .44 A2
Brownings La SG2 . . . . . . .47 D1
Brownlow La LU7 . . . . .80 A7
Brownlow Rd
  Berkhamsted HP4 . . . . . .122 C5
  Borehamwood WD6 . . . . .170 A5
Browns Hedge LU7 . . . . . .80 C3
Browns Spring HP4 . . . . . .123 C7
Brownsea Ho 12 WD1 . . . .166 F3
Brox Dell SG1 . . . . .50 E6
Broxbourne CE Prim Sch
  EN10 . . . . .134 F2
Broxbourne Sch The
  EN10 . . . . .134 E1
Broxbourne Sta EN10 . . . .135 A3
Broxbournebury Mews
  EN10 . . . . .134 C3
Broxley Mead LU4 . . . . . . .44 D5
Bruce Gr WD2 . . . . .154 C1
Bruce Rd Barnet EN5 . . . . .171 E6
  Harrow HA3 . . . . .176 E1
Bruce Way EN8 . . . . .162 D6
Brunel Rd SG2 . . . . .51 B7
Brunswick Ct
  Hoddesdon EN11 . . . . . . .135 A5
  Stevenage SG1 . . . . .50 A7
Brunswick Rd EN3 . . . . . .163 A1
Brunswick St LU2 . . . . . . .63 F8
Brushrise WD2 . . . . .154 A3
Brushwood Dr WD3 . . . . .164 C5
Brussels Way LU3 . . . . . . .44 D8
Bryan Rd CM23 . . . . .76 F8
Bryanstone Rd EN8 . . . . .162 F5
Bryant Cl EN5 . . . . .171 F4
Bryant Ct AL5 . . . . .86 A3
Bryce Cl SG12 . . . . .93 D3
Bsns Ctr E SG6 . . . . .23 C6
Bsns Ctr W SG6 . . . . .23 C6
Buchanan Ct
  Borehamwood WD6 . . . . .170 C7
  Luton LU2 . . . . .64 B8
Buchanan Dr LU2 . . . . . . .64 B8
Buckettsland La WD6 . . . .157 D2
Buckingham Dr LU2 . . . . . .46 D2
Buckingham Rd
  Borehamwood WD6 . . . . .170 D5
  Tring HP23 . . . . .99 E3
  Watford WD2 . . . . .154 C2
Buckinghamshire Coll
  The HP8 . . . . .172 A8
Buckland Rd HP22 . . . . . . .99 A4
Buckland Rise HA5 . . . . . .175 D5
Bucklands The WD3 . . . . .165 A2
Buckle Cl LU3 . . . . .44 F7
Bucklers Cl EN10 . . . . . . .134 F1
Bucklersbury SG5 . . . . . . .34 E6
Bucknalls Cl WD2 . . . . . . .154 E4
Bucknalls Dr AL2 . . . . . . .154 F8
Bucknalls La WD2 . . . . . . .154 E4
Bucks Alley SG13 . . . . . . .132 D4
Bucks Ave WD1 . . . . .167 E2
Bucks Hill WD4 . . . . .152 C5
Buckthorn Ave SG1 . . . . . .50 E4
Buckton Rd WD6 . . . . . . .156 F1
Buckwood La LU6 . . . . . . .82 C7
Buckwood Rd AL3 . . . . . . .83 C6
Buddcroft AL7 . . . . .111 B7
Bude Cres SG1 . . . . .50 A7
Bulbourne Cl
  Berkhamsted HP4 . . . . . .121 F6
  Hemel Hempstead HP1 . . .124 A4
Bulbourne Ct HP23 . . . . . .100 A7
Bulbourne Rd HP23 . . . . .100 B7
Bull La Buckland SG9 . . . . .27 C8
  Cottered SG9 . . . . .39 C8
  Wheathampstead AL4 . . . .108 A6
Bull Plain SG14 . . . . .113 D6
Bull Rd AL5 . . . . .107 B8
Bull Stag Gn AL9 . . . . . . .130 C7
Bull's Cross EN2 . . . . .162 A3
Bullace Cl HP1 . . . . .124 A4
Bullbeggars La CM24 . . . .123 A4
Bullen's Green La AL4 . . . .143 E8
Bullfields CM21 . . . . .97 E3
Bullhead Rd WD6 . . . . . . .170 C6
Bullock's Hill SG4 . . . . . . .49 B1
Bullock's La SG13 . . . . . . .113 C4
Bullrush Cl AL10 . . . . .130 B4
Bulls Cross Ride EN7 . . . .162 A5
Bulls La AL9 . . . . .144 E7
Bullsland Gdns WD3 . . . . .164 B3
Bullsland La WD3 . . . . . . .164 B3
Bullsmoor Cl EN8 . . . . . . .162 C4
Bullsmoor Gdns EN8 . . . .162 B4
Bullsmoor La EN1,EN3 . . .162 C4
Bullsmoor Ride EN8 . . . . .162 C4

Bullsmoor Way EN8 . . . . .162 C4
Bullwell Cres EN8 . . . . . . .148 E2
Bulstrode Cl HP3 . . . . . . .137 E3
Bulstrode La
  Chipperfield HP3 . . . . . . .137 F3
  Hemel Hempstead HP3 . . .138 A5
Bulwer Link SG1 . . . . .50 E3
Buncefield La HP2 . . . . . .125 C5
Bungalows The AL5 . . . . . .86 C3
Bunkers La HP3 . . . . .139 B7
Bunnsfield AL7 . . . . .111 C7
Bunstrux HP23 . . . . .100 A4
Bunting Rd LU4 . . . . .44 A4
Buntingford Rd SG11 . . . . .55 D4
Bunyan Cl Pirton SG5 . . . .20 D4
  Tring HP23 . . . . .100 B5
Bunyan Rd SG5 . . . . .34 F8
Bunyans Cl LU3 . . . . .45 A5
BUPA Bushey Hospl
  WD2 . . . . .168 F1
Burbage Cl EN8 . . . . .162 E8
Burchell Ct WD2 . . . . .168 C2
Burfield Cl AL10 . . . . .130 A7
Burfield Ct LU2 . . . . .46 D3
Burfield Rd WD3 . . . . .164 C4
Burford Cl LU3 . . . . .31 A1
Burford Gdns EN11 . . . . . .135 B7
Burford Mews 9 EN11 . . . .135 A7
Burford Pl 11 EN11 . . . . . .135 A7
Burford Way SG5 . . . . . . .21 D2
Burgage Ct 12 SG12 . . . . .93 D1
Burgage La SG12 . . . . . . .93 D1
Burge End La SG5 . . . . . . .20 C5
Burgess Ct EN7 . . . . .147 C6
Burgess Ct WD6 . . . . .156 F1
Burghley Ave
  Bishop's Stortford CM23 . .76 C7
  Borehamwood WD6 . . . . .170 C4
Burghley Cl SG2 . . . . .69 A8
Burgoyne Hatch CM20 . . . .118 A1
Burgundy Croft AL7 . . . . .110 F4
Burhill Gr HA5 . . . . .175 E1
Burleigh Mead AL9 . . . . . .130 C7
Burleigh Prim Sch EN8 . . .148 D1
Burleigh Rd
  Cheshunt EN8 . . . . .162 E7
  Hemel Hempstead HP2 . . .125 C2
  Hertford SG13 . . . . .114 A7
  St Albans AL1 . . . . .128 B3
Burleigh Way EN6 . . . . . . .146 E1
Burley SG6 . . . . .11 F2
Burley Ho WD5 . . . . .153 F7
Burley Rd CM23 . . . . .77 A4
Burnell Rise SG6 . . . . .22 D5
Burnell Wlk SG6 . . . . .22 E5
Burnells Way CM24 . . . . . .59 E7
Burnet Cl HP3 . . . . .124 E2
Burnett Ave SG16 . . . . . . .10 B4
Burnett Sq SG14 . . . . . . .112 F7
Burnham Cl
  Datchworth AL6 . . . . .90 C6
  Enfield EN1 . . . . .161 E1
Burnham Green Rd
  AL6,SG3 . . . . .90 D6
Burnham Rd Luton LU2 . . . .46 B2
  St Albans AL1 . . . . .128 B3
Burnley Cl WD1 . . . . .175 C5
Burns Cl Hitchin SG4 . . . . .35 B8
  Stevenage SG2 . . . . .51 C8
Burns Dr HP2 . . . . .105 B1
Burns Rd SG8 . . . . .7 D8
Burnsall Pl AL5 . . . . .107 C6
Burnside Hertford SG14 . . .113 A5
  Hoddesdon EN11 . . . . . . .134 F6
  Sawbridgeworth CM21 . . . .97 D2
  St Albans AL1 . . . . .128 B1
Burnside Cl AL10 . . . . . . .130 A8
Burnside Terr CM17 . . . . .118 F3
Burnt Cl LU3 . . . . .44 F7
Burnt Mill CM20 . . . . .117 C3
Burnt Mill Cty Comp Sch
  CM20 . . . . .117 F2
Burntfarm Ride EN2,EN7 . .161 B7
Burntmill Cl CM20 . . . . . .117 C3
Burntmill Cnr CM20 . . . . .117 D4
Burntmill La CM20 . . . . . .117 D3
Burr Cl AL2 . . . . .142 E4
Burr St LU2 . . . . .63 E8
Burr's Pl LU1 . . . . .63 E6
Burrowfield AL7 . . . . .110 D4
Burrs La SG8 . . . . .17 C3
Bursland SG2 . . . . .22 D6
Burston Dr AL2 . . . . .141 C3
Burton Ave WD1 . . . . . . .167 A5
Burton Cl AL4 . . . . .87 C5
Burton Dr EN3 . . . . .163 A2
Burton La EN7 . . . . .147 E3
Burtons La WD3 . . . . .164 A4
Burtons Mill CM21 . . . . . .97 F3
Burvale Ct 3 WD1 . . . . . .167 B6
Burwell Rd SG2 . . . . .51 C4
Bury Cotts AL3 . . . . .105 C5
Bury End SG5 . . . . .20 D4
Bury Gn
  Hemel Hempstead HP1 . . .124 C4
  Wheathampstead AL4 . . . .108 C8
Bury Green Rd
  Cheshunt EN7 . . . . .162 A7
  Cheshunt EN7 . . . . .162 B8
Bury Hill HP1 . . . . .124 C4
Bury Hill Cl HP1 . . . . .124 C4
Bury Holme EN10 . . . . . . .148 F8
Bury La Bramfield SG14 . . .91 B4
  Codicote SG4 . . . . .67 F2
  Datchworth SG3 . . . . .69 D3
  Rickmansworth WD3 . . . .165 D1
  Streatley LU3 . . . . .31 A5
Bury Mdws WD3 . . . . .165 D1

Bury Mead SG15 . . . . .11 A7
Bury Mead Rd SG5 . . . . . .21 F1
Bury Park Rd LU1 . . . . . . .63 C8
Bury Rd Harlow CM17 . . . .118 D4
  Hatfield AL10 . . . . .130 C6
  Hemel Hempstead HP1 . . .124 C3
Bury Rise HP3 . . . . .137 D6
Bury The SG4 . . . . .67 F2
Bury Wlk AL8 . . . . .89 E1
Burydale Jun Sch SG2 . . . .51 B1
Burydell La AL2 . . . . .141 D5
Buryfield Terr SG12 . . . . . .93 C1
Buryfield Way SG12 . . . . . .93 C1
Burymead AL7 . . . . .36 C1
Burywick AL5 . . . . .107 B5
Bush Hall La AL9 . . . . . . .130 D8
Bush Spring SG7 . . . . .13 A1
Bushbarns EN7 . . . . .148 A2
Bushby Ave EN10 . . . . . . .134 F1
Bushel Wharf HP23 . . . . . .100 A6
Bushell Gn WD2 . . . . .176 D8
Bushey Cl AL7 . . . . .111 B5
Bushey Gn AL7 . . . . .111 B5
Bushey Grove Rd WD2 . . .167 E5
Bushey Hall Dr WD2 . . . . .167 E5
Bushey Hall Rd WD2 . . . . .167 E5
Bushey Hall Sch WD2 . . . .167 F4
Bushey Heath Prim Sch
  WD2 . . . . .168 D1
Bushey Ley AL7 . . . . .111 B5
Bushey Manor
  Jun Mix Sch WD2 . . . . . .167 A4
Bushey Meads Sch WD2 . .168 C4
Bushey Mill Cres WD2 . . . .154 C3
Bushey Mill La
  Bushey WD2 . . . . .167 E6
  Watford WD2 . . . . .154 D1
Bushey Mus WD2 . . . . . . .168 A3
Bushey & Oxhey Sta
  WD1 . . . . .167 D3
Bushfield Rd HP3 . . . . . . .137 C6
Bushmead Inf Sch LU2 . . . .45 E5
Bushmead Jun Sch LU2 . . .45 E5
Bushmead Rd LU2 . . . . . . .45 E5
Bushwood Cl AL9 . . . . . . .144 B8
Bute Sq LU1 . . . . .63 E7
Bute St LU1 . . . . .63 E7
Butely Rd LU4 . . . . .44 B5
Butler's Hall La CM23 . . . .76 B3
Butlers Dr E4 . . . . .163 C1
Butlin Rd LU1 . . . . .63 B7
Butt Field View AL1 . . . . . .141 C7
Butterfield Green Rd LU2 . .46 A6
Butterfield La AL1 . . . . . . .141 E7
Butterfield Rd AL4 . . . . . .108 C7
Butterfly La WD6 . . . . . . .169 B7
Buttermere Cl AL1 . . . . . .128 B2
Butterwick WD2 . . . . .154 E3
Butterworth Path 1 LU2 . .63 E8
Buttlehide WD3 . . . . .172 D5
Butts End HP1 . . . . .124 A5
Butts The EN10 . . . . .148 E5
Buttsmead HA6 . . . . .174 C3
Buxton Cl AL4 . . . . .128 D6
Buxton Path WD1 . . . . . . .175 C7
Buxton Rd LU1 . . . . .63 D7
Buxtons La SG8 . . . . .1 F3
Buzzard Rd LU4 . . . . .44 A4
By The Mount AL7 . . . . . .110 D5
By-The-Wood WD1 . . . . . .175 E8
By-Wood End SL9 . . . . . . .172 A5
Byde St SG14 . . . . .113 C7
Bye Way The HA3 . . . . . . .176 F2
Byers Cl EN6 . . . . .159 C5
Byewaters WD1 . . . . .166 C3
Byeway The WD3 . . . . . . .173 E8
Byfield AL8 . . . . .89 E1
Byfield Cl LU4 . . . . .44 B1
Byfleet Ind Est WD1 . . . . .166 B1
Byford Ho EN5 . . . . .171 D5
Bygrave SG1 . . . . .36 C2
Bygrave Rd SG7 . . . . .12 F1
Bylands Cl CM23 . . . . .76 D6
Byng Dr EN6 . . . . .159 A8
Byng Rd EN5 . . . . .171 D6
Byrd Wlk SG7 . . . . .23 F7
Byron Ave
  Borehamwood WD6 . . . . .170 A4
  Watford WD2 . . . . .154 D1
Byron Cl
  Hammond Street EN7 . . . .147 F4
  Hitchin SG4 . . . . .35 B8
  Stevenage SG2 . . . . .51 C7
Byron Ct EN3 . . . . .148 B3
Byron Pl HP2 . . . . .105 B1
Byron Rd Harpenden AL5 . .86 A2
  Harrow HA3 . . . . .176 F1
  Luton LU4 . . . . .44 B2
  Royston SG8 . . . . .7 E8
Byslips Rd LU6 . . . . .82 D5
Byway The EN6 . . . . .159 A6
Byways HP4 . . . . .122 C4

C

Cabot Cl SG2 . . . . .51 A7
Caddington Comm AL3 . . .83 E8
Caddis Cl HA7 . . . . .176 F3
Cade Cl SG6 . . . . .12 C1
Cades La LU1 . . . . .63 A6
Cades La LU1 . . . . .63 A6
Cadia Cl LU1 . . . . .62 E4
Cadmore Ct
  12 Cheshunt EN8 . . . . . .148 D3
  Hertford SG14 . . . . .112 F7
Cadmore La EN8 . . . . . . .148 E2

Cadwell Ct SG4 . . . . .22 A2
Cadwell La SG4 . . . . .22 A2
Caernarvon Cl
  Hemel Hempstead HP2 . . .124 D3
  Stevenage SG2 . . . . .69 B7
Caernarvon Ct HP2 . . . . . .124 D3
Caesars Rd AL4 . . . . .108 E8
Cage Pond Rd WD7 . . . . .156 F6
Cairn Way HA7 . . . . .176 F4
Cairns Cl AL4 . . . . .128 C3
Caishowe Rd WD6 . . . . . .170 B8
Caister Cl
  Hemel Hempstead HP2 . . .124 E2
  Stevenage SG2 . . . . .36 A1
Calbury Cl AL1 . . . . .128 B2
Caldbeck EN9 . . . . .163 D5
Caldecot Ave EN7 . . . . . . .147 C6
Caldecot Way EN10 . . . . .134 F1
Caldecote Gdns WD2 . . . .168 E2
Caldecote La WD2 . . . . . .168 F3
Caldecote Rd SG7 . . . . . . .12 E8
Calder Ave AL9 . . . . .145 B5
Caldwell Rd WD1 . . . . . . .175 C6
Caleb Cl LU4 . . . . .44 F2
Caledon Rd AL2 . . . . .142 D5
Caledonian Ct WD1 . . . . . .167 B7
California SG7 . . . . .12 F1
California La WD2 . . . . . . .168 D1
Callanders The WD2 . . . . .168 E1
Callisto Ct HP2 . . . . .124 F6
Callowland Pl WD2 . . . . . .154 B1
Calnwood Rd LU4 . . . . . . .44 C3
Calton Ave SG14 . . . . . . .112 F7
Calton Ct SG14 . . . . .112 F6
Calton Rd LU3 . . . . .45 A6
Calton Ho SG14 . . . . .112 F6
Calverley Cl CM23 . . . . . . .76 E4
Calvert Rd EN5 . . . . .171 D7
Calverton Rd LU3 . . . . . . .45 A6
Cam Ctr SG4 . . . . .22 A3
Cam Sq SG4 . . . . .22 A3
Camberley Pl AL5 . . . . . . .107 D6
Camborne Dr HP2 . . . . . .124 E7
Cambrian Way HP2 . . . . . .124 F6
Cambridge Cl EN8 . . . . . .148 C2
Cambridge Cotts SG11 . . .72 E2
Cambridge Cres SG8 . . . . .2 A8
Cambridge Dr EN6 . . . . . .158 E8
Cambridge Rd
  Barkway SG8 . . . . .17 D5
  Barley SG8 . . . . .9 A3
  Harlow CM20 . . . . .118 C6
  Hitchin SG4 . . . . .22 C2
  Sawbridgeworth CM21 . . . .97 E4
  St Albans AL1 . . . . .128 B2
  Standon SG11 . . . . .55 D8
  Stansted Mountfitchet CM24 .59 E8
  6 Watford WD1 . . . . . . .167 C5
Cambridge St LU1 . . . . . . .63 F6
Cambridge Terr HP4 . . . . .122 D4
Cameron Cl 8 SG12 . . . . .93 D2
Cameron Dr EN8 . . . . . . .162 D5
Camfield AL7 . . . . .110 F2
Camford Way LU3 . . . . . . .44 A8
Camlet Way AL3 . . . . .127 B4
Camp Prim Sch AL1 . . . . .128 B2
Camp Rd AL1 . . . . .128 B2
Camp View Rd AL1 . . . . . .128 B2
Campana Ct EN5 . . . . . . .171 D6
Campania Gr LU3 . . . . . . .45 A8
Campbell Cl
  Buntingford SG9 . . . . .40 E7
  Hitchin SG4 . . . . .35 B8
Campers Ave SG6 . . . . . . .22 E5
Campers Rd SG6 . . . . .22 E5
Campers Wlk SG6 . . . . . . .22 E5
Campfield Rd
  Hertford SG14 . . . . .113 B5
  St Albans AL1 . . . . .128 A3
Campfield Way SG6 . . . . . .22 D5
Campine Cl 1 EN8 . . . . . .148 D3
Campion Cl WD2 . . . . . . .154 A6
Campion Ct SG1 . . . . .50 C8
Campion Rd HP1 . . . . . . .123 E2
Campion Way SG8 . . . . . . .7 E5
Campions CM17 . . . . .118 F5
Campions Ct HP4 . . . . . . .122 B3
Campions The
  Borehamwood WD6 . . . . .157 A1
  Stansted Mountfitchet CM24 .59 E8
Campkin Mead SG2 . . . . . .51 D3
Camps Hill
  Com Prim Sch SG2 . . . . . .51 B6
Campus Five SG6 . . . . . . .23 C7
Campus The AL8 . . . . . . .110 D7
Canada La EN10 . . . . .148 E6
Canadas The EN10 . . . . . .148 E6
Canal Ct HP4 . . . . .122 D4
Canberra Cl Kneesworth SG8 . .2 B5
  St Albans AL3 . . . . .127 F7
Canberra Gdns LU3 . . . . . .45 B6
Candlefield Cl HP3 . . . . . .139 A8
Candlefield Rd HP3 . . . . . .139 A8
Candlefield Wlk HP3 . . . . .139 A8
Caneland Ct EN9 . . . . . . .163 F5
Canfield CM23 . . . . .76 D5
Cangelis Cl HP1 . . . . .124 A1
Canham Cl SG4 . . . . .66 D1
Cannix Cl SG2 . . . . .51 A2
Cannon Ho 1 SG4 . . . . . .34 F6
Cannon La LU2 . . . . .46 B5
Cannon Mews EN9 . . . . . .163 B6
Cannon Rd WD1 . . . . .167 C4
Cannon St AL3 . . . . .127 D4
Cannon's Cl SG8 . . . . .1 F5
Cannons Cl CM23 . . . . . . .59 A5
Cannons Ct SG11 . . . . . . .55 D3
Cannons Mdw AL6 . . . . . .90 C3
Cannons Mead CM24 . . . .59 D7

Cannons Mill La CM23 59 A1
Canons Cl WD7 156 B4
Canons Field Oaklands AL6 89 E8
Wheathampstead AL6 87 D1
Canons Gate
Cheshunt EN8 148 F5
Harlow CM20 117 A2
Canons Rd SG12 93 C2
Canonsfield Ct AL6 89 E7
Canonsfield Rd AL6 89 E8
Canopus Way HA6 175 A6
Cantelowes Ho EN5 171 D4
Canterbury Cl Luton LU3 44 F4
Northwood HA6 174 F4
Canterbury Ct AL1 127 F4
Canterbury Ho
Borehamwood WD6 170 A7
4 Watford WD1 167 C7
Canterbury Rd
Borehamwood WD6 170 A7
Watford WD1 167 B7
Canterbury Way
Croxley Green WD3 166 C6
Stevenage SG1 36 F2
Cape Rd AL1 128 B3
Capel Ct SG11 57 E2
Capel Ho WD1 175 D6
Capel Manor Gdns EN7 162 D4
Capel Manor Prim Sch EN1 162 B4
Capel Rd Enfield EN1 162 B3
Watford WD1 167 E3
Capell Ave WD3 164 C4
Capell Rd WD3 164 D4
Capell Way WD3 164 D4
Capella Rd HA6 174 F6
Capelvere Wlk WD1 166 E8
Caponfield AL7 111 B4
Capron Rd LU4 44 E4
Captains Wlk HP4 122 D3
Caractacus Cottage View WD1 167 A3
Caractacus Gn WD1 166 F3
Caravan La WD3 165 E2
Carbone Hill EN6,SG13 146 D5
Carde Cl SG14 112 F7
Cardiff Cl SG2 69 B7
Cardiff Gr LU1 63 D7
Cardiff Pl SG8 2 A8
Cardiff Rd Luton LU1 63 D7
Watford WD1 167 B4
Cardiff Way WD5 154 A7
Cardigan Ct 10 LU1 63 D8
Cardigan Gdns 11 LU1 63 D8
Cardigan St LU1 63 D7
Cardinal Ave WD6 170 B5
Cardinal Cl EN7 147 F5
Cardinal Ct
Borehamwood WD6 170 B6
3 Luton LU2 45 D1
Cardinal Gr AL3 127 B1
Cardinal Newman High Sch LU2 31 C1
Cardinals Gate SG8 7 C6
Cardy Rd HP1 124 B3
Carew Rd HA6 174 F4
Carew Way WD1 175 F7
Careys Croft HP4 122 A7
Carisbrook Rd AL2 141 B5
Carisbrooke Ave WD2 167 D8
Carisbrooke Rd
Harpenden AL5 86 C2
Luton LU4 44 E1
Carleton Rd EN8 148 E4
Carleton Rise AL6 89 C6
Carlisle Ave AL3 127 D4
Carlton Bank 2 AL5 86 B1
Carlton Cl
Borehamwood WD6 170 D5
Luton LU3 45 C2
Carlton Cres LU3 45 C2
Carlton Ct
1 Harpenden AL5 86 B1
Watford WD1 167 C3
Carlton Rd AL5 86 B2
Carman Ct HP23 99 F3
Carmelite Cl HA3 176 C2
Carmelite Rd
Harrow HA3 176 C1
Luton LU4 44 A3
Carmelite Way HA3 176 C1
Carmelite Wlk HA3 176 C2
Carmen Ct WD6 156 F1
Carnaby Rd EN10 134 E3
Carnarvon Rd EN5 171 E6
Carnegie Gdns LU3 45 A8
Carnegie Rd AL3 127 D7
Caro La HP3 125 B1
Carol Cl LU3 45 B4
Carole Ct LU1 63 E5
Caroline Pl WD1 167 E3
Carolyn Ct LU3 45 B4
Caroon Dr WD3 152 B3
Carpenders Ave WD1 175 E8
Carpenders Cl AL5 85 D4
Carpenders Park Sta WD1 175 D7
Carpenter Way EN6 159 D6
Carpenters Rd EN1 162 C3
Carpenters The CM23 76 B5
Carpenters Wood Dr WD3 164 B5
Carpenters Yd HP23 100 A3
Carriden Ct SG14 112 F8
Carrigans CM23 76 E8
Carrington Ave WD6 170 C4
Carrington Cl Barnet EN5 171 A4
Borehamwood WD6 170 C4
Carrington Pl HP23 100 C5
Carrington Sq HA3 176 C3
Carsdale Cl LU3 45 A6
Cart Path WD2 154 C6
Carteret Rd LU2 46 C1
Carterhatch La EN1 161 F1
Carters Cl Arlesey SG15 11 A7
Aston SG2 51 D4
Carters La SG5 34 A6
Carters Leys CM23 76 D8
Carters Way SG15 11 A7
Carters Wlk SG15 11 A7
Cartersfield Rd EN9 163 C5
Carthagena Est EN9 135 C3
Cartwright Rd Royston SG8 7 D5
Stevenage SG1 37 C2
Carve Ley AL7 111 B5
Carvers Croft SG3 69 B2
Cary Wlk WD7 156 B5
Cashio La SG6 23 A8
Caslon Way SG6 11 F1
Cassandra Gate EN8 148 F4
Cassio Rd WD1 167 B5
Cassiobridge Rd WD1 166 E5
Cassiobridge Terr WD3 166 D4
Cassiobury Dr WD1 166 F7
Cassiobury Inf Sch WD1 166 E8
Cassiobury Jun Mix Sch WD1 166 E8
Cassiobury Park Ave WD1 166 F6
Castano Ct WD5 153 E8
Castellane Cl 1 HA7 176 F3
Castile Ct EN8 163 A5
Castings Ho SG6 23 A7
Castle Cl Bushey WD2 168 B3
Hoddesdon EN11 115 C1
Castle Croft Rd LU1 63 A6
Castle Gate SG14 113 C5
Castle Gate Way HP4 122 C6
Castle Hill HP4 122 C6
Castle Hill Ave HP4 122 C5
Castle Hill Cl HP4 122 C5
Castle Mead HP1 124 B1
Castle Mead Gdns SG14 113 C6
Castle Mews HP4 122 D4
Castle Rd Enfield EN3 162 E1
Hoddesdon EN11 115 C1
St Albans AL1 128 B3
Castle Rise AL4 86 F2
Castle St
Berkhamsted HP4 122 C4
Bishop's Stortford CM23 76 F6
Hertford SG14 113 D5
Luton, High Town LU1 63 E7
Luton, New Town LU1 63 E6
Wingrave HP22 60 B3
Castle View CM23 77 A7
Castle Wlk CM24 59 E6
Castles Cl SG5 11 F8
Catalin Ct EN9 163 D6
Caterham Ct EN9 163 F5
Catesby Gn LU3 31 A1
Catham Cl AL1 128 B1
Cathedral Ct AL3 127 B1
Catherall Rd LU3 45 B6
Catherine Cl HP2 125 B8
Catherine Rd EN3 162 E3
Catherine St AL3 127 D4
Catisfield Rd EN3 162 E2
Catkin Cl HP1 124 B4
Catlin St HP3 138 B8
Catsbrook Rd LU3 45 B6
Catsdell Bottom HP3 139 B8
Catsey La WD2 168 C2
Catsey Wood WD2 168 C2
Catterick Way WD6 169 F8
Cattlegate Hill EN6 160 D7
Cattlegate Rd
Crews Hill EN2 161 A5
Northaw EN6 160 D6
Cattley Cl EN5 171 E5
Cattlins Cl EN7 147 F2
Cattsdell HP2 124 E5
Causeway Cl EN6 159 D8
Causeway Ho WD5 153 E8
Causeway The
1 Bishop's Stortford CM23 77 A7
Braughing SG9,SG11 42 D1
Brent Pelham SG9 30 B1
Buntingford SG9 40 F8
Furneux Pelham SG9 43 A4
Kneesworth SG8 2 A5
Potters Bar EN6 159 D8
Therfield SG8 15 F7
Cautherly La SG12 115 A5
Cavalier SG1 36 B1
Cavalier Cl LU3 45 A5
Cavalier Ct HP4 122 C4
Cavan Ct AL10 130 A4
Cavan Dr AL3 127 D8
Cavan Rd AL3 106 A6
Cavell Rd EN7 148 A4
Cavell Wlk SG2 51 C5
Cavendish Cres WD6 170 A5
Cavendish Ct WD3 166 D4
Cavendish Rd Barnet EN5 171 C6
Luton LU3 45 B2
Markyate AL3 83 D6
St Albans AL1 127 F3
Stevenage SG1 50 B5
Cavendish Sch The HP1 124 B4
Cavendish Way AL10 129 F5
Cawkell Cl CM24 59 D7
Caxton Ct Enfield EN3 162 E4
Luton LU3 44 F4
Caxton Hill SG13 113 F6
Caxton Rd EN11 115 B2
Caxton Way
Moor Park WD1 166 D2
Stevenage SG1 50 B4
Cecil Cl CM23 77 D7
Cecil Cres AL10 130 B7
Cecil Ct EN5 171 D6
Cecil Rd Brickendon SG13 113 C3
Cheshunt EN8 162 E7
Hoddesdon EN11 135 C8
Potters Bar EN6 158 B7
St Albans AL1 127 F3
Cecil St WD2 154 B1
Cedar Ave Cheshunt EN8 162 D6
Ickleford SG5 21 E4
Cedar Cl Hertford SG14 113 B6
Potters Bar EN6 145 A1
Sawbridgeworth CM21 97 E1
Ware SG12 114 D8
Cedar Cres SG8 7 B6
Cedar Ct
Bishop's Stortford CM23 58 F1
St Albans AL4 128 D3
Cedar Dr HA5 176 A4
Cedar Gn EN11 135 A5
Cedar Lawn Ave EN5 171 E4
Cedar Lodge 8 EN8 148 D3
Cedar Park Rd EN2 161 C1
Cedar Pk CM23 76 D4
Cedar Pl HA6 174 C4
Cedar Rd
Berkhamsted HP4 122 E3
Enfield EN2 161 C1
Hatfield AL10 130 A4
Watford WD1 167 D3
Cedar Way HP4 122 D3
Cedar Wlk
Chorleywood WD3 164 F5
Hemel Hempstead HP3 124 D1
Waltham Abbey EN9 163 D5
Welwyn Garden City AL7 111 B5
Cedar Wood Dr WD2 154 B4
Cedars Ave WD3 165 C1
Cedars Cl WD6 170 B5
Cedars Fst & Mid Sch HA3 176 C2
Cedars The
Berkhamsted HP4 122 E4
13 Harpenden AL5 86 B1
Rickmansworth WD3 165 D2
St Albans AL3 127 C5
Stevenage SG2 69 B8
Cedarwood Dr AL4 128 D3
Celandine Dr LU3 45 A8
Cell Barnes Cl AL1 128 B1
Cell Barnes La AL1 128 B1
Cemetery Hill HP1 124 C2
Cemetery Rd CM23 76 F6
Cemmaes Court Rd HP1 124 C3
Cemmaes Mdw HP1 124 C3
Centennial Ave WD6 169 C2
Centennial Pk WD6 169 C2
Central App SG6 22 F6
Central Ave Cheshunt EN8 162 E6
Henlow SG16 10 B3
Whipsnade LU6 81 E8
Central Dr St Albans AL4 128 C4
Welwyn Garden City AL7 110 F8
Central Prim Sch WD1 167 C5
Central Rd CM20 118 A4
Central Way HA6 174 E3
Centro HP2 125 C5
Century Ct WD1 166 C2
Century Rd
Hoddesdon EN11 135 A7
Ware SG12 93 D2
Cervantes Ct HA6 174 F3
Chace Ave EN6 159 D7
Chace The SG2 50 F1
Chad La AL3 84 C4
Chadwell SG12 114 C8
Chadwell Ave EN8 148 C3
Chadwell Cl LU2 45 F1
Chadwell Rd SG1 50 B3
Chadwell Rise SG12 114 C8
Chaffinch La WD1 166 F2
Chaffinches Gn HP3 139 A7
Chagney Cl SG6 22 E6
Chalet Cl HP4 121 F4
Chalfont Cl HP2 125 B8
Chalfont Ho WD1 166 E2
Chalfont La
Chorleywood WD3 164 B4
Maple Cross WD3 172 D3
Chalfont Pl AL1 127 E3
Chalfont Rd WD3,SL9 172 C7
Chalfont Shire Ctr HP8 172 A7
Chalfont Way LU2 46 D2
Chalfont Wlk 4 HA5 175 C1
Chalgrove AL7 111 D7
Chalk Dale AL7 111 B7
Chalk Field SG6 23 C3
Chalk Hill Great Offley LU2 47 A5
Watford WD1 167 E3
Chalk Hills SG7 23 F5
Chalkdell Fields AL4 128 A7
Chalkdell Hill HP2 124 E3
Chalkdell Path 8 SG5 34 D8
Chalkdown Luton LU2 45 E6
Stevenage SG2 51 D7
Chalks Ave CM21 97 D3
Challney Boys High Sch LU4 44 D2
Challney Cl LU4 44 D2
Challney Girls High Sch LU4 44 D2
Chalmers Ct WD3 165 F3
Chalton Rd LU4 44 C5
Chamberlaines AL5 85 A5
Chambers Gate SG1 50 D7
Chambers La SG5 21 E4
Chambers' St SG14 113 C6
Chambersbury La HP3 139 A7
Chambersbury Prim Sch HP3 139 B8
Champions Cl WD6 157 B2
Champions Gn EN11 115 A1
Champions Way EN11 115 A1
Chancellor's Sch AL9 145 A6
Chancellors Rd SG1 36 D1
Chancery Cl AL4 128 D8
Chandler's La WD3 152 E2
Chandlers Cl CM23 76 C4
Chandlers Rd AL4 128 C6
Chandlers Way SG14 113 A6
Chandos Cl HP6 150 C1
Chandos Rd
Borehamwood WD6 170 A7
Luton LU4 44 F1
Channock's Farm Cotts CM20 117 C7
Chantry Cl
Bishop's Stortford CM23 76 E8
Enfield EN2 161 C1
Kings Langley WD4 139 A2
Chantry Ct AL10 130 A4
Chantry La Hatfield AL10 129 F4
Hatfield AL10 130 A4
Little Wymondley SG4 35 F2
London Colney AL2 142 D5
Chantry Mount CM23 76 E8
Chantry Pl HA3 176 B2
Chantry Rd
Bishop's Stortford CM23 76 E8
Harrow HA3 176 B2
Chantry The
6 Bishop's Stortford CM23 76 F8
Harlow CM20 118 A2
Chaomans SG6 22 F3
Chapel Cl
Little Gaddesden HP4 102 D6
Luton LU2 45 C8
St Albans AL1 141 D8
Chapel Cotts HP2 124 D4
Chapel Croft WD4 152 A8
Chapel Crofts HP4 121 E6
Chapel End
Buntingford SG9 40 E7
Hoddesdon EN11 135 A5
Chapel End La HP23 99 C8
Chapel Fields HP23 99 C8
Chapel Hill CM24 59 E6
Chapel La
Hertingfordbury SG14 112 B3
Little Hadham SG11 75 A8
Long Marston HP23 79 B4
Chapel Mdw HP23 100 B6
Chapel Pl SG5 11 F6
Chapel Rd
Breachwood Green SG4 65 E8
Flamstead AL3 84 B2
Chapel Row
3 Bishop's Stortford CM23 76 F6
Harefield UB9 173 C2
6 Hitchin SG5 34 F8
Chapel St
Berkhamsted HP4 122 D4
Hemel Hempstead HP2 124 D4
Hinxworth SG7 3 D6
Luton, High Town LU1 63 E7
Luton, New Town LU1 63 E6
Tring HP23 99 F3
Chapel Viaduct LU1 63 E7
Chapel Way WD5 139 F4
Chapelfields SG12 115 D4
Chapman Rd SG1 36 B1
Chapmans End SG11 55 D3
Chappell Ct SG12 92 E7
Chapter House Rd LU4 44 A3
Chard Dr LU3 31 B1
Chardia Terr EN8 148 D1
Chardins Cl HP1 123 F4
Charles St
Berkhamsted HP4 122 B4
Hemel Hempstead HP1 124 C2
Luton LU2 63 F8
Tring HP23 100 A3
Charlesworth Cl 4 HP3 124 D1
Charlock Way WD1 166 F3
Charlotte Cl AL4 128 E3
Charlottes Ct 2 LU1 63 D7
Charlton Cl EN11 135 A6
Charlton Mead La EN11 135 D5
Charlton Rd SG5 34 D5
Charlton Way EN11 135 B6
Charlwood Cl HA3 176 E4
Charlwood Rd LU4 44 B1
Charmbury Rise LU2 46 A4
Charmouth Ct AL1 128 A6
Charmouth Rd AL1 128 A5
Charndon Cl LU3 31 B1
Charnwood Rd EN1 162 B3
Charter Ho WD3 166 A4
Charter Pl WD1 167 C6
Chartley Ave HA7 176 F4
Chartridge Cl Barnet EN5 171 A4
Bushey WD2 168 C3
Chartridge Way HP2 125 C3
Chartwell Cl EN9 163 E6
Chartwell Ct 8 EN5 171 E5
Chartwell Dr LU2 45 E3
Chartwell Rd HA6 174 F4
Charwood Cl WD7 156 E6
Chasden Rd HP1 123 F5
Chase Cl SG15 11 A8
Chase Farm Hospl EN2 161 A1
Chase Hill Rd SG15 11 A7
Chase St LU1 63 E6
Chase The
Bishop's Stortford CM23 76 F6
Goff's Oak EN7 147 B3
Great Amwell SG12 115 A6
Hemel Hempstead HP2 124 E2
Hertford SG13 113 F6
Oaklands AL6 89 F7
Radlett WD7 155 F4
Watford WD1 166 E5
Chaseside Cl LU7 80 A7
Chaseways CM21 118 C8
Chasten Hill SG6 22 D7
Chater Inf Sch WD1 167 A5
Chater Jun Sch WD1 167 B5
Chatsworth Cl
Bishop's Stortford CM23 76 C7
Borehamwood WD6 170 A6
Chatsworth Ct
St Albans AL1 127 F3
Stevenage SG2 50 F1
Chatsworth Rd LU4 45 B1
Chatteris Cl LU4 44 D4
Chatterton SG6 23 C5
Chatton Cl LU2 46 E2
Chaucer Cl HP4 121 F5
Chaucer Ct EN11 115 A1
Chaucer Ho EN5 171 D5
Chaucer Rd Luton LU3 45 C2
Royston SG8 7 C8
Chaucer Way Hitchin SG4 35 C7
Hoddesdon EN11 115 A2
Chaucer Wlk HP2 105 B1
Chaul End La LU4 44 E1
Chaul End Rd
Caddington LU1 62 D6
Luton LU4 44 B1
Chaulden House Gdns HP1 123 F1
Chaulden Jun & Inf Schs HP1 123 F2
Chaulden La HP1 123 E1
Chaulden Terr HP1 123 F2
Chauncey Ho WD1 166 E3
Chauncy Ave EN6 159 C6
Chauncy Cl SG12 93 D3
Chauncy Ct 16 SG14 113 D6
Chauncy Gdns SG7 13 B1
Chauncy Ho 3 SG1 50 E6
Chauncy Rd SG1 50 E6
Chauncy Sch The SG12 93 B2
Chaworth Gn 1 LU4 44 C5
Cheapside LU1 63 E7
Cheapside Sq 4 LU1 63 E7
Chedburgh AL7 111 D7
Cheddington Cty Comb Sch LU7 80 A7
Cheddington La HP23 79 C5
Cheddington Rd LU7 80 C4
Cheffins Rd EN11 114 F1
Chells Ent Village SG2 51 C6
Chells La SG2 51 D7
Chells Way SG2 51 B6
Chelmsford Rd SG14 113 B5
Chelsea Fields EN11 115 B2
Chelsing Rise HP2 125 C2
Chelsworth Cl 1 LU2 46 D1
Cheltenham Ct AL1 128 A2
Cheltenham Ho 2 WD1 167 C7
Chelveston AL7 111 D7
Chelwood Ave AL10 130 A8
Chelwood Cl HA6 174 C3
Chenduit Way HA7 176 F5
Cheney Rd LU4 44 C5
Chenies Ave HP6 150 D1
Chenies Cty Comb Sch WD3 151 B1
Chenies Ct HP2 125 B8
Chenies Gn CM23 76 D6
Chenies Manor Ho WD3 151 A1
Chenies Rd WD3 164 D7
Chenies Way WD1 166 E2
Chennells AL10 129 F4
Chennells Cl SG4 22 B2
Chennies The AL5 107 C7
Chepstow AL5 85 F2
Chepstow Cl SG1 51 B8
Chequer Ct LU1 63 F6
Chequer La AL3 106 B4
Chequer St Luton LU1 63 F6
St Albans AL1 127 D3
Chequers
Bishop's Stortford CM23 76 C8
Hatfield AL9 130 D8
Welwyn Garden City AL7 110 D3
Chequers Bridge Rd SG1 50 C6
Chequers Cl
Buntingford SG9 40 D8
Pitstone LU7 80 C4
Standon SG11 55 D4
Stotfold SG5 12 A6
Chequers Cotts
Preston SG4 48 D6
Whipsnade LU6 82 A8
Chequers Field AL7 110 D3
Chequers Hill AL3 84 C2
Chequers La
Abbots Langley WD2 140 C1
Pitstone LU7 80 C5
Preston SG4 48 D7
Chequers Wlk EN9 163 F6
Cheriton Cl AL4 128 D7
Cherry Bank HP2 124 D5
Cherry Cl SG3 68 F4
Cherry Croft AL8 89 D2

Cherry Croft Gdns 2
  HA5 . . . .**175** F3
Cherry Ct HA5 . . . .**175** D2
Cherry Dr SG8 . . . .**7** E7
Cherry Gdns
  Bishop's Stortford CM23 . . . .**77** A8
  Sawbridgeworth CM21 . . .**97** E4
  Tring HP23 . . . .**99** F3
Cherry Hill
  Chiswellgreen AL2 . . . .**141** A6
  Harrow HA3 . . . .**176** E4
  Rickmansworth WD3 . . . . .**165** B6
Cherry Hills WD1 . . . . . .**175** D5
Cherry Hollow WD5 . . . .**153** F8
Cherry Orch HP1 . . . . . .**124** A5
Cherry Rd EN3 . . . .**162** C1
Cherry Tree Ave AL2 . . .**142** D5
Cherry Tree Cl
  Arlesey SG15 . . . .**11** A4
  Luton LU2 . . . .**46** A1
Cherry Tree Gn SG14 . . . .**112** F7
Cherry Tree La
  Cholesbury HP23 . . . .**120** A3
  Chorleywood WD3 . . . . . .**164** C1
  Hemel Hempstead HP2 . . .**125** C7
  Potters Bar EN6 . . . .**159** B5
  Wheathampstead AL4 . . . . .**87** A3
Cherry Tree Prim Sch
  WD2 . . . .**154** A3
Cherry Tree Rd
  Hoddesdon EN11 . . . .**135** A7
  Watford WD2 . . . .**154** A3
Cherry Tree Rise SG2 . . . .**38** B1
Cherry Trees SG16 . . . . . .**10** B3
Cherry Way AL10 . . . . . .**130** A2
Cherry Wlk WD3 . . . . . .**165** C7
Cherrydale WD1 . . . .**166** F5
Chertsey Cl LU2 . . . .**64** D8
Chertsey Rise SG2 . . . . . .**51** C4
Cherwell Rd WD3 . . . . . .**166** A4
Chesfield Cl CM23 . . . . . .**76** E5
Chesford Rd LU2 . . . .**46** C4
Chesham Ct HA6 . . . .**174** F4
Chesham Prep Sch HP5 . .**136** A4
Chesham Rd
  Berkhamsted HP4 . . . . . .**122** C3
  Bovingdon HP3 . . . .**136** E3
  Wigginton HP23 . . . .**120** E7
Chesham Way WD1 . . . . .**166** F5
Cheshunt Centre The
  EN8 . . . .**148** D3
Cheshunt Rd EN8 . . . . . .**148** B3
Cheshunt Sch EN8 . . . . . .**148** C1
Cheshunt Sta EN8 . . . . . .**148** F1
Cheshunt Wash EN8 . . . .**148** E4
Cheslyn Cl LU2 . . . .**46** E2
Chess Cl Latimer HP5 . . . .**150** D3
  Rickmansworth WD3 . . . . .**165** D5
Chess Hill WD3 . . . .**165** D5
Chess La WD3 . . . .**165** D5
Chess Vale Rise WD3 . . . .**165** F3
Chess Way WD3 . . . .**165** A6
Chesswood Ct WD3 . . . . .**165** D1
Chesswood Way HA5 . . . .**175** D1
Chester Ave LU4 . . . .**44** E3
Chester Cl Luton LU4 . . . . .**44** F2
  Potters Bar EN6 . . . .**145** B2
Chester Ho HA6 . . . .**174** F3
Chester Pl HA6 . . . .**174** E3
Chester Rd
  Borehamwood WD6 . . . . .**170** D6
  Northwood HA6 . . . .**174** F3
  Stevenage SG1 . . . .**37** A1
  Watford WD1 . . . .**167** A5
Chesterfield Flats EN5 . .**171** D4
Chesterfield
  Inf & Jun Sch EN3 . . . . . .**162** E2
Chesterfield Rd
  Barnet EN5 . . . .**171** D4
  Enfield EN3 . . . .**162** E2
Chesterton Ave AL5 . . . . .**86** D1
Chestnut Ave Henlow SG16 .**10** C3
  Luton LU3 . . . .**44** C8
  Northwood HA6 . . . .**174** F2
  Rickmansworth WD3 . . . . .**165** A4
  Ware SG12 . . . .**93** F3
Chestnut Cl
  Bishop's Stortford CM23 . . .**76** E6
  Dagnall HP4 . . . .**81** C5
  Hunsdon SG12 . . . .**95** D1
  Potten End HP4 . . . .**123** E3
Chestnut Ct 4 Hitchin SG5 .**34** D8
  Watford WD1 . . . .**166** E5
Chestnut Dr
  Berkhamsted HP4 . . . . . .**122** D4
  Harrow HA3 . . . .**176** F2
  St Albans AL4 . . . .**128** C5
Chestnut La Barnet N20 . .**171** E1
  Kneesworth SG8 . . . .**2** B6
Chestnut Rd EN3 . . . .**162** E2
Chestnut Rise WD2 . . . . .**168** B2
Chestnut Wlk Hitchin SG4 . .**35** A4
  Royston SG8 . . . .**7** E6
  Stevenage SG1 . . . .**36** D1
  Watford WD2 . . . .**154** A2
Chestnuts The
  Codicote SG4 . . . .**67** F2
  Hemel Hempstead HP3 . . .**137** F7
  Hertford SG13 . . . .**113** D5
Cheverells Cl AL3 . . . .**83** D4
Cheviot Cl Bushey WD2 . . .**168** C3
  Luton LU3 . . . .**44** D7
Cheviot Rd LU3 . . . .**44** D7
Cheviots Hatfield AL10 . . .**130** A3
  Hemel Hempstead HP2 . . .**124** F6

Cheyne Cl Pitstone LU7 . . .**80** D4
  Ware SG12 . . . .**93** D3
Cheynes Inf Sch LU3 . . . . .**44** D8
Chicheley Gdns HA3 . . . .**176** C3
Chicheley Rd HA3 . . . . . .**176** C3
Chichester Way WD2 . . . .**154** E6
Chigwell Hurst Ct HA5 . . .**175** D1
Chilcott Rd WD2 . . . .**153** F3
Chilcourt SG8 . . . .**7** C6
Childbrook Ho WD1 . . . .**166** E3
Childs Ave UB9 . . . .**173** C1
Childwick Ct HP3 . . . .**139** B8
Chilham CI HP2 . . . .**124** E2
Chiltern Ave WD2 . . . . . .**168** C3
Chiltern Cl
  Borehamwood WD6 . . . . .**169** F7
  Bushey WD2 . . . .**168** B3
  Goff's Oak EN7 . . . .**147** B4
  Ware SG12 . . . .**93** D3
Chiltern Ct
  19 Harpenden AL5 . . . . . .**86** B1
  Hertford SG14 . . . .**112** F8
  St Albans AL4 . . . .**128** D7
Chiltern Dr WD3 . . . .**165** A2
Chiltern Gdns LU4 . . . . . .**44** F3
Chiltern Open Air Mus
  HP8 . . . .**164** A1
Chiltern Park Ave HP4 . . .**122** A4
Chiltern Rd Baldock SG7 . . .**23** F6
  Hitchin SG4 . . . .**35** A7
  St Albans AL4 . . . .**128** C7
  Wingrave HP22 . . . .**60** A3
Chiltern Rise LU1 . . . .**63** D6
Chiltern View SG6 . . . . . .**22** D5
Chiltern Way HP23 . . . . .**100** C5
Chilterns
  Berkhamsted HP4 . . . . . .**121** F6
  Hatfield AL10 . . . .**130** A2
  Hemel Hempstead HP2 . . .**124** E5
Chilterns The Hitchin SG4 . .**35** A6
  Kensworth Common LU6 . . .**82** F8
Chilton Gn AL7 . . . .**111** C6
Chilvers Bank SG7 . . . . . .**23** E7
Chilwell Gdns WD1 . . . . .**175** C6
Chilworth Gate EN10 . . . .**134** F1
Chindit Cl EN10 . . . .**134** E3
Chinnery Cl EN1 . . . .**161** F1
Chinnery Hill CM23 . . . . . .**76** F5
Chipperfield Rd
  Bovingdon HP3 . . . .**137** C3
  Hemel Hempstead HP3 . . .**138** C7
  Kings Langley WD4 . . . . .**138** D2
Chipping Cl EN5 . . . .**171** E6
Chippingfield CM17 . . . . .**118** C3
Chirdland Ho WD1 . . . . .**166** E3
Chishill Rd Barley SG8 . . . . .**9** A2
  Great Chishill SG8 . . . .**9** F3
Chishill Windmill SG8 . . . . .**9** C2
Chiswell Ct WD2 . . . .**154** C1
Chiswellgreen La AL2 . . . .**140** E6
Chittenden Cl EN9 . . . . . .**115** B1
Chivenor Pl AL4 . . . .**128** C1
Chobham St LU1 . . . .**63** F6
Chobham Wlk 5 LU1 . . . .**63** E6
Cholesbury La HP23 . . . . .**120** B2
Chorleywood
  Bottom WD3 . . . .**164** D4
Chorleywood Cl WD3 . . . .**165** D2
Chorleywood Prim Sch
  WD3 . . . .**164** C3
Chorleywood Rd WD3 . . .**164** C4
Chorleywood Sta WD3 . . .**164** D5
Chouler Gdns SG1 . . . .**36** C2
Chowns The AL5 . . . .**107** A5
Christ Church
  CE Jun Mix Inf Sch EN5 **171** D7
Christ Church
  CE Prim Sch SG12 . . . . . .**93** E1
Christ Church CE Sch
  WD3 . . . .**164** F5
Christ Church La EN5 . . . .**171** E7
Christchurch Cl AL3 . . . . .**127** D4
Christchurch Cres WD7 . .**156** A3
Christchurch Ho HP23 . . .**100** A3
Christchurch Rd
  Hemel Hempstead HP2 . . .**124** D4
  Tring HP23 . . . .**99** F4
Christie Cl EN10 . . . .**134** F3
Christie Rd SG2 . . . .**51** D5
Christina Ct AL3 . . . .**83** E5
Christopher Ct
  Hemel Hempstead HP3 . . .**138** D8
  16 Ware SG12 . . . .**93** D1
Christopher Pl 3 AL3 . . . .**127** D3
Christy's Yd SG7 . . . .**3** D6
Church Cl Codicote SG4 . . . .**67** F2
  Cuffley EN6 . . . .**146** E2
  Little Berkhamsted SG13 . .**132** C4
  Northwood HA6 . . . .**174** F3
  Radlett WD7 . . . .**156** A3
  Studham LU6 . . . .**82** B4
Church Cotts
  Gilston CM20 . . . .**117** C7
  Great Gaddesden HP1 . . .**103** D3
Church Cres
  Sawbridgeworth CM21 . . . .**97** F2
  St Albans AL3 . . . .**127** C4
Church Ct SG11 . . . .**55** E2
Church End Arlesey SG15 . .**11** A8
  Barley SG8 . . . .**9** A1
  Braughing SG11 . . . .**55** F7
  Flamstead AL3 . . . .**84** C2
  Markyate AL3 . . . .**83** D6
  Redbourn AL3 . . . .**106** A4
  Sandridge AL4 . . . .**108** C2
  Walkern SG2 . . . .**38** C2
Church Farm Way WD2 . .**155** B1
Church Field SG12 . . . .**93** B3

Church Field Path EN8 . .**148** C2
Church Gn Benington SG2 . .**52** D4
  Great Wymondley SG4 . . . .**35** E6
  Harpenden AL5 . . . .**86** A1
Church Green Row AL5 . . .**86** A1
Church Hill
  Abbots Langley WD5 . . . .**139** F4
  Cheddington LU7 . . . .**80** A8
  Harefield UB9 . . . .**173** C1
  Hertford Heath SG13 . . . .**114** C4
Church La Arlesey SG15 . . .**11** A7
  Ashwell SG7 . . . .**4** D4
  Barkway SG8 . . . .**17** C4
  Berkhamsted HP4 . . . . . .**122** C4
  Bishop's Stortford CM23 . . .**76** D3
  Bovingdon HP3 . . . .**137** B4
  Cheddington LU7 . . . .**80** A8
  Cheshunt EN8 . . . .**148** C2
  Colney Heath AL4 . . . . . .**143** B8
  Dane End SG12 . . . .**71** F8
  Graveley SG4 . . . .**36** C4
  Guilden Morden SG8 . . . . . .**1** F5
  Harrow HA3 . . . .**176** F2
  Hatfield AL9 . . . .**130** C5
  Hoddesdon EN10 . . . .**134** C1
  Kimpton SG4 . . . .**66** D1
  Kings Langley WD4 . . . . .**139** A2
  Letchworth SG6 . . . .**12** C1
  Marsworth HP23 . . . .**79** F1
  Much Hadham SG10 . . . . .**74** F3
  Northaw EN6 . . . .**146** A1
  Preston SG4 . . . .**48** D6
  Radlett WD2 . . . .**155** B1
  Reed SG8 . . . .**16** E5
  Rickmansworth WD3 . . . . .**165** B5
  Royston SG8 . . . .**7** D6
  Sarratt WD3 . . . .**152** A2
  Stapleford SG14 . . . .**92** A6
  Stevenage SG1 . . . .**50** C7
  Therfield SG8 . . . .**15** F7
  Weston SG4 . . . .**24** D1
Church Manor CM23 . . . . .**77** B8
Church Mead
  Roydon CM19 . . . .**116** B1
  Studham LU6 . . . .**82** B4
Church Meadow Cotts
  HP1 . . . .**103** D3
Church Path SG4 . . . .**35** F3
Church Pl AL6 . . . .**89** C5
Church Rd Flamstead AL3 . . .**84** B2
  Great Hallingbury CM22 . . .**77** D3
  Hemel Hempstead HP3 . . .**125** C2
  Hertford SG13 . . . .**113** C7
  King's Walden SG4 . . . . . .**47** F3
  Little Berkhamsted SG13 . .**132** C4
  Little Gaddesden HP4 . . . .**102** D8
  Northwood HA6 . . . .**174** F3
  Pitstone, Church End LU7 . .**80** E3
  Pitstone, Ivinghoe LU7 . . . .**80** F5
  Potten End HP4 . . . .**123** B6
  Potters Bar EN6 . . . .**145** B1
  Slip End LU1 . . . .**63** B1
  Stansted Mountfitchet CM24 .**59** F5
  Stotfold SG5 . . . .**11** F6
  Streatley LU3 . . . .**31** A6
  Studham LU6 . . . .**82** B4
  Watford WD1 . . . .**167** B8
  Welwyn Garden City AL8 . .**110** D6
Church Row Mews 2
  SG12 . . . .**93** D1
Church St Baldock SG7 . . . .**12** E1
  Bishop's Stortford CM23 . . .**76** F7
  Bovingdon HP3 . . . .**137** B4
  Buntingford SG9 . . . .**40** E8
  Essendon AL9 . . . .**131** E6
  Guilden Morden SG8 . . . . . .**1** F5
  Hatfield AL9 . . . .**130** C5
  Hemel Hempstead HP2 . . .**124** D5
  Hertford SG14 . . . .**113** D6
  Luton LU2 . . . .**63** E7
  Luton, High Town LU2 . . . .**63** F8
  Rickmansworth WD3 . . . . .**165** E1
  Sawbridgeworth CM21 . . . .**97** E2
  Shillington SG5 . . . .**19** F8
  St Albans AL3 . . . .**127** D4
  Waltham Abbey EN9 . . . . .**163** C6
  Ware SG12 . . . .**93** D1
  Watford WD1 . . . .**167** C5
  Welwyn AL6 . . . .**89** C5
  Wheathampstead AL4 . . . .**108** D8
  Wingrave HP22 . . . .**60** B2
Church Street Ind Est
  SG12 . . . .**93** D1
Church View
  Hoddesdon EN10 . . . .**134** F3
  Long Marston HP23 . . . . . .**79** A4
Church Wlk Bushey WD2 . .**168** A3
  Sawbridgeworth CM21 . . . .**97** F3
Church Yd Hitchin SG5 . . . .**34** E7
  Tring HP23 . . . .**100** A3
Churchfield Barley SG8 . . . .**9** A1
  Harlow CM20 . . . .**118** B2
  Harpenden AL5 . . . .**107** C8
Churchfield Ho AL8 . . . . .**110** C6
Churchfield Rd AL6 . . . . . .**90** C1
Churchfields
  Hertford SG13 . . . .**113** D5
  Hoddesdon EN10 . . . .**135** A3
  Standon SG11 . . . .**55** E2
  Stansted Mountfitchet CM24 .**59** F6
Churchfields La EN10 . . . .**135** A3
Churchfields Rd WD2 . . . .**153** F3
Churchgate Cheshunt EN8 **148** B3
  7 Hitchin SG5 . . . .**34** E7
Churchgate CE Prim Sch
  CM17 . . . .**118** F3
Churchgate Rd EN8 . . . . .**148** B2
Churchgate St CM17 . . . .**118** E4

Churchill Cres AL9 . . . . . .**144** C8
Churchill Rd Luton LU4 . . .**45** A1
  St Albans AL1 . . . .**128** A4
Churchyard Wlk 6 SG5 . . .**34** E7
Cicero Dr LU3 . . . .**45** A8
Cillocks Cl EN11 . . . .**135** A7
Claggy Rd SG4 . . . .**66** B2
Claire Ct Bushey WD2 . . . .**168** D1
  Cheshunt EN8 . . . .**162** D7
  5 Pinner HA5 . . . .**175** F3
Clamp Hill HA7 . . . .**176** E5
Clapgate Rd WD2 . . . .**168** B3
Clare Cl WD6 . . . .**169** F3
Clare Cres SG7 . . . .**23** E6
Clare Ct Enfield EN3 . . . . .**162** E4
  Northwood HA6 . . . .**174** F5
  St Albans AL1 . . . .**127** F2
Claremont
  Bricket Wood AL2 . . . . . .**155** A8
  Goff's Oak EN7 . . . .**147** F2
Claremont Cres WD3 . . . .**166** C4
Claremont Rd
  Hadley Wood EN4 . . . . . .**159** D2
  Harrow HA3 . . . .**176** E1
  Luton LU4 . . . .**45** B1
Clarence Cl WD2 . . . .**168** F2
Clarence Rd
  Berkhamsted HP4 . . . . . .**122** C4
  Harpenden AL5 . . . .**86** A3
  St Albans AL1 . . . .**128** A4
  Stansted Mountfitchet CM24 .**59** E7
Clarendon Cl 1 HP2 . . . .**124** E4
Clarendon Ct
  Harpenden AL5 . . . .**86** A3
  Moor Park HA6 . . . .**174** F5
Clarendon Mews WD6 . . .**170** A6
Clarendon Par EN8 . . . . . .**148** C2
Clarendon Rd
  Borehamwood WD6 . . . . .**170** A6
  Cheshunt EN8 . . . .**148** D2
  Harpenden AL5 . . . .**86** B3
  Luton LU2 . . . .**45** E1
  Watford WD1 . . . .**167** B6
Clarion Cl SG5 . . . .**33** C2
Clarion Ho SG5 . . . .**33** C2
Clark Rd SG8 . . . .**7** D7
Clarke Way WD2 . . . .**154** A4
Clarke's Rd AL10 . . . .**130** B7
Clarke's Spring HP23 . . . .**100** F5
Clarkfield WD3 . . . .**165** B1
Clarks Cl SG12 . . . .**93** D3
Clarks Mead WD2 . . . . . .**168** D2
Claudian Pl AL3 . . . .**127** A1
Claverhambury Rd EN9 . .**149** F2
Claverley Gn LU2 . . . .**46** E2
Claverton Cl HP3 . . . .**137** A3
Clay Hall Rd LU6 . . . .**82** F7
Clay La WD2 . . . .**168** E2
Claybury WD2 . . . .**168** B2
Claybush Rd SG7 . . . .**4** D3
Claydown Way LU1 . . . . . .**63** B1
Claydon Cl LU3 . . . .**45** C7
Claygate Ave AL5 . . . .**85** E2
Claymore HP2 . . . .**124** E7
Claymore Dr SG5 . . . .**21** F5
Claymores SG1 . . . .**50** E6
Clayponds CM23 . . . .**77** B7
Clayton Hill Ctry Pk EN9 **149** D8
Clayton Par 7 EN8 . . . . . .**148** D1
Cleall Ave EN9 . . . .**163** C5
Cleave The AL5 . . . .**86** D1
Clement Pl HP23 . . . .**100** A3
Clement Rd EN8 . . . .**148** C2
Clements End Rd LU6 . . . .**82** E2
Clements Rd WD3 . . . . . .**164** D4
Clements St SG12 . . . .**93** E1
Clevedon Rd LU2 . . . .**46** B2
Cleveland Cres WD6 . . . . .**170** C4
Cleveland Rd
  Hemel Hempstead HP2 . . .**125** B5
  Markyate AL3 . . . .**83** E5
Cleveland Way HP2 . . . . .**125** B5
Cleves Rd HP2 . . . .**125** B8
Cleviscroft SG1 . . . .**50** E4
Clewer Cres HA3 . . . .**176** D2
Clifford Ct LU4 . . . .**44** D5
Clifford Ct 10 CM23 . . . . .**77** A7
Clifton Cl EN8 . . . .**148** E2
Clifton Rd Luton LU1 . . . . .**63** E8
  Watford WD1 . . . .**167** B4
Clifton St AL1 . . . .**127** E4
Clifton Way
  Borehamwood WD6 . . . . .**170** A8
  Ware SG12 . . . .**93** D2
Climb The WD3 . . . .**165** B3
Clinton Ave LU2 . . . .**45** F3
Clinton End HP2 . . . .**125** C3
Clitheroe Gdns WD1 . . . .**175** D7
Clive Cl EN6 . . . .**158** F8
Clive Ct LU2 . . . .**45** E1
Clive Par HA6 . . . .**174** E3
Clive Way WD1 . . . .**167** C8
Cloister Garth
  Berkhamsted HP4 . . . . . .**122** C4
  St Albans AL1 . . . .**141** E7
Cloister Lawns SG6 . . . . . .**22** F4
Cloister Wlk HP2 . . . .**124** D5
Cloisters Rd
  Letchworth SG6 . . . .**23** A4
  Luton LU4 . . . .**44** B3
Cloisters The
  Bushey WD2 . . . .**168** B3
  Kings Langley WD4 . . . . .**139** A2
  Rickmansworth WD3 . . . . .**165** E2
  3 Watford WD1 . . . .**167** C5
  Welwyn Garden City AL8 . .**110** D6

Clonard Way HA5 . . . . . .**176** A5
Close The Baldock SG7 . . . .**23** E7
  Brookmans Park AL9 . . . .**144** E5
  Bushey WD2 . . . .**168** A4
  Codicote SG4 . . . .**67** F1
  Harpenden AL5 . . . .**85** D4
  Hinxworth SG7 . . . .**3** D6
  Luton LU3 . . . .**45** A5
  Markyate AL3 . . . .**83** E5
  Potters Bar EN6 . . . .**159** A7
  Radlett WD7 . . . .**155** F6
  Rickmansworth WD3 . . . . .**165** B1
  Royston SG8 . . . .**7** F7
  St Albans AL1 . . . .**141** C8
  Wallington SG9 . . . .**25** E5
  Ware SG12 . . . .**93** E1
Closemead Cl HA6 . . . . . .**174** C4
Clothall Rd Baldock SG7 . . .**23** F8
  Clothall SG7 . . . .**24** C6
Clovelly Way SG1 . . . .**50** A7
Clover Ave CM23 . . . .**76** B6
Clover Cl LU4 . . . .**44** A3
Clover Field The WD2 . . .**167** F3
Clover Way HP1 . . . .**124** B4
Cloverfield AL7 . . . .**89** F1
Cloverland AL10 . . . .**129** F2
Clump The WD3 . . . .**165** B4
Clusterbolts SG14 . . . .**92** A7
Clutterbucks WD3 . . . . . .**152** A3
Clyde Rd EN11 . . . .**135** D5
Clyde Sq HP2 . . . .**124** F8
Clyde St SG13 . . . .**114** A6
Clydesdale Cl WD6 . . . . . .**170** C4
Clydesdale Ct LU4 . . . .**44** A3
Clydesdale Path WD6 . . . .**170** C4
Clydesdale Rd Luton LU4 . .**44** A3
  Royston SG8 . . . .**7** C7
Clydesdale Wlk EN10 . . . .**148** F5
Clyfton Cl EN10 . . . .**148** F8
Clyston Rd WD1 . . . .**166** F3
Coach Dr SG4 . . . .**34** F5
Coach House
  Cloisters 1 SG7 . . . .**23** E7
Coachman's La SG7 . . . . . .**23** D8
Coates Dell WD2 . . . .**154** E6
Coates Rd WD6 . . . .**169** D2
Coates Way WD2 . . . .**154** E6
Coates Way
  Jun Mix Inf Sch WD2 . . . .**154** E6
Cob Cl WD6 . . . .**170** C4
Cob Lane Cl AL6 . . . .**89** F4
Cobb Gn WD2 . . . .**154** B7
Cobb Rd HP4 . . . .**121** F4
Cobbett Cl EN3 . . . .**162** C1
Cobbetts Ride HP23 . . . . .**99** F3
Cobbins The EN9 . . . .**163** E6
Cobbins Way CM17 . . . . .**118** E4
Cobbinsbank EN9 . . . .**163** D6
Cobblers Wick HP22 . . . . .**60** B3
Cobden Hill WD7 . . . .**156** B2
Cobden St LU2 . . . .**45** F1
Cobham Rd SG12 . . . .**93** F2
Cobmead AL10 . . . .**130** B7
Cock Gr HP23 . . . .**121** C4
Cock La Brent Pelham CB11 .**30** D7
  Hoddesdon EN11 . . . .**134** D4
Cockbush Ave SG13 . . . . .**114** B7
Cocker Rd EN1 . . . .**162** C5
Cockernhoe Endowed
  Jun Mix Inf Sch LU2 . . . . .**46** E3
Cockfosters Rd EN4 . . . . .**159** E1
Cockle Way WD7 . . . .**156** C6
Cockrobin La CM20 . . . . .**117** A7
Codicote
  CE Prim Sch SG4 . . . .**67** E1
Codicote Dr WD2 . . . .**154** D5
Codicote Heights SG4 . . . .**68** B1
Codicote Ho SG1 . . . .**36** C1
Codicote Rd Ayot St Lawrence
  AL4, AL6, SG4 . . . .**88** C3
  Welwyn AL6 . . . .**89** B7
  Wheathampstead AL4 . . . .**87** D1
  Whitwell SG4 . . . .**66** F6
Codicote Row HP2 . . . . . .**105** B1
Codmore Wood Rd HP5 . .**150** D6
Coerdale Ct EN3 . . . .**162** E2
Cohen Cl EN8 . . . .**162** E8
Colborne Ho WD1 . . . . . .**166** E3
Colbron Cl SG7 . . . .**4** C4
Colburn Ave HA5 . . . .**175** E4
Colchester Rd HA6 . . . . . .**175** A1
Cold Christmas La SG12 . .**93** E6
Coldham Gr EN3 . . . .**162** E2
Coldharbour La
  Bushey WD2 . . . .**168** A2
  Harpenden AL5 . . . .**86** C4
Cole Green La
  Hertingfordbury AL7 . . . .**111** D4
  Welwyn Garden City AL7 . .**111** B4
Cole Green Way SG14 . . .**113** A4
Cole Rd WD1 . . . .**167** B8
Colebrook Ave LU3 . . . . . .**44** C7
Coleman Green La
  Sandridge AL4 . . . .**108** L4
  Wheathampstead AL4 . . . .**109** A7
Coleman's La EN9 . . . . . .**149** E5
Colemans Cl SG5 . . . .**20** D4
Colemans Rd SG4 . . . .**47** D1
Coleridge Cl
  Hammond Street EN7 . . . .**147** F4
  Hitchin SG4 . . . .**35** B8
Coleridge Cres HP2 . . . . .**105** B1
Coleridge Ct 9 AL5 . . . . . .**86** B1
Coles Gn WD2 . . . .**168** C1
Coles Hill HP1 . . . .**124** A5
Coledale EN6 . . . .**146** E1
Colestrete SG1 . . . .**50** F5
Colestrete Cl SG1 . . . .**51** A5

Coleswood Rd AL5 ......107 C7
Colgate Ct EN5 ....171 E4
Colgate Pl EN3 ....163 A2
Colgrove AL8 ....110 C5
Colin Rd LU2 ....45 F2
Colindale Ave AL1 ......127 F1
Colindale Ct HA3 ....176 E2
College Ave HA3 ....176 E2
College Cl
  Bishop's Stortford CM23 ...76 D7
  Flamstead AL3 ....84 B1
  Harrow HA3 ....176 E3
  Ware SG12 ....114 D8
College Ct Cheshunt EN8 ..148 C7
College Hill Rd HA3 .....176 E3
College Ho LU1 ....63 F7
College La AL10 ....129 E4
College Lake Wildlife Ctr
  HP23 ....100 C8
College Pl AL3 ....127 C3
College Rd
  Abbots Langley WD5 ...154 A8
  Aston Clinton HP22 ....78 C1
  Cheshunt EN8 ....148 D1
  Harrow HA3 ....176 E2
  Hertford Heath SG13 ..114 D2
  Hitchin SG5 ....34 F8
  Hoddesdon EN11 .....134 F8
  St Albans AL1 ....128 B2
College St AL3 ....127 D3
College Way
  Northwood HA6 ....174 D4
  Welwyn Garden City AL8 ..110 D7
Collens Rd AL5 ....107 B5
Collenswood Rd SG2 ....51 B4
Collenswood Sch SG2 ...51 C4
Collet Cl EN8 ....148 D3
Collet Gdns EN8 ....148 D3
Collett Rd
  Hemel Hempstead HP1 ..124 C3
  Ware SG12 ....93 D2
Collett Sch The HP1 ....124 B4
Colley Land WD3 ....164 D5
Collingdon Ct 9 LU1 ...63 D8
Collingdon St LU1 ......63 D8
Collings Wells Cl LU1 ...62 E4
Collingtree LU2 ....46 B4
Collingwood Ct SG8 ....7 D7
Collingwood Dr AL2 ....142 D6
Collins Cross CM23 ....59 B1
Collison Cl SG4 ....22 C2
Collyer Rd AL2 ....142 D4
Colmer Pl HA3 ....176 D3
Colnbrook Cl AL2 ......142 E4
Colnbrook Sch WD1 ....175 C7
Colne Ave
  Rickmansworth WD3 ...173 A8
  Watford WD1 ....167 D4
Colne Bridge Ret Pk
  WD1 ....167 D4
Colne Gdns AL2 ....142 E4
Colne Lo WD3 ....165 A1
Colne Lodge WD2 ......167 D5
Colne Mead WD3 ......173 A8
Colne Way
  Hemel Hempstead HP2 ..124 F8
  Watford WD2 ....154 D3
Colne Way Ct WD2 .....154 D3
Colney Heath La AL4 ...128 C2
Colonial Bsns Pk WD2 ..167 C8
Colonial Way WD2 .....167 D8
Colonnade The 7 EN8 ..148 C8
Colonsay HP3 ....125 C1
Colston Cres EN7 ......147 B4
Colt Hatch CM20 ......117 B1
Colthurst Gdns EN11 ...135 D8
Colts Cnr SG2 ....51 B4
Colts Croft SG8 ....9 E2
Colts The CM23 ....76 E4
Coltsfield CM24 ....59 E8
Coltsfoot AL7 ....111 B4
Coltsfoot Dr SG8 ......7 E6
Coltsfoot Gn LU4 ......44 A5
Coltsfoot La SG3 ......90 D7
Coltsfoot Rd SG12 .....93 E3
Coltsfoot The HP1 .....123 E4
Columbus Cl SG2 ......51 A7
Columbus Gdns HA6 ...175 A2
Colvin Gdns EN8 ......162 D4
Colwell Rd SG2 ....51 C3
Colwell Rise LU2 ......46 E2
Colwyn Cl SG1 ....50 B7
Colyer Cl AL6 ....89 C3
Combe Ho WD1 ....166 E3
Combe Rd WD1 ....166 F3
Combe St HP1 ....124 C3
Combewood WD2 .....154 C7
Comet Cl WD2 ....153 F5
Comet Rd AL10 ....129 F6
Comet Way AL10,AL9 ..129 C5
Commerce Way SG6 ...22 F6
Common Field HP23 ...100 D1
Common Gate Rd WD3 .164 E4
Common Gdns HP4 ....123 B6
Common La Ashwell SG7 ....4 B6
  Harpenden AL5 ....86 D5
  Kimpton SG4 ....66 B1
  Kings Langley WD4 ...138 F3
  Radlett WD7,WD2 .....155 B1
Common Rd
  Chorleywood WD3 ....164 D5
  Kensworth Common LU6 ...82 F8
  Stanmore HA7 ....176 D7
  Stotfold SG5 ....11 F7
  Studham LU6 ....82 B3
Common Rise SG4 .....22 A1
Common The
  Chipperfield WD4 .....152 B8

Common The continued
  Harpenden AL5 ....85 C4
  Hatfield AL10 ....130 A6
  Potten End HP4 ....123 A6
  Stanmore HA7 ....176 F8
Common View SG6 ....23 B8
Common View Sq SG6 ..23 A8
Common Wharf SG12 ...93 E1
Commonfields CM20 ...117 E1
Commons La HP2 .....124 E4
Commons The AL7 ....111 B3
Commonswood Sch AL7 ..111 B3
Compass Point HP4 ...121 E6
Compton Ave LU4 .....44 D4
Compton Gdns AL2 ...141 B5
Compton Pl WD1 .....175 E6
Comroston EN11 ......135 A6
Comyne Rd WD2 .....153 F3
Comyns The WD2 ....168 C1
Concorde Dr HP2 .....124 D3
Concorde St LU2 .....63 F8
Conduit La
  Great Hormead SG9 ......29 B1
  Hoddesdon EN11 ....135 A6
Conduit La E EN11 ....135 B6
Conemara Ct EN10 ...148 F5
Coney Cl AL10 ....130 B3
Coney Gree CM21 ....97 D3
Coneydale AL8 ....110 D8
Congreve Rd WD3 ....164 D5
Conifer Cl Goff's Oak EN7 ..147 E2
  Stevenage SG2 ....51 D7
Conifer Ct 7 CM23 ...76 F8
Conifer Wlk SG2 .....51 C7
Conifers The WD2 ....154 C4
Coningesby Dr WD1 ..166 E7
Coningsby Bank AL1 ..141 D7
Coningsby Cl WD7 ....144 D7
Coningsby Ct WD7 ...156 A3
Coningsby Dr EN6 ....159 D6
Coniston Cl HP3 .....125 C2
Coniston Lodge 3 WD1 ..167 A7
Coniston Rd
  Abbots Langley WD4 ..139 A4
  Kings Langley WD4 ...138 F3
  Luton LU3 ....44 F5
Connaught Cl HP2 ....125 A5
Connaught Gdns HP4 ..121 F7
Connaught Rd
  Barnet EN5 ....171 D3
  Harpenden AL5 ......86 B2
  Harrow HA3 ....176 F2
  Luton LU4 ....44 F1
  St Albans AL1 ....127 C6
Connemara Cl WD6 ...170 D3
Conner's Cl SG8 .....1 F4
Connop Rd EN3 ......162 D1
Conquerors Hill AL4 ..108 E8
Conquest Cl SG4 .....34 F5
Constable Ct LU4 ....45 A1
Constantine Cl SG1 ..36 F1
Constantine Pl SG7 ...13 B1
Convent Cl SG5 ......34 F8
Conway Cl Stevenage SG2 ..51 D4
  Bishop's Stortford CM23 ..76 B4
Conway Cres WD6 ...170 C8
Conway Gdns HA3 ...176 E4
Conway Ho WD6 .....170 C5
Conway Rd LU4 ......45 B1
Conyers CM20 ....117 C2
Cook Rd SG2 ....51 B7
Cook's Hole Rd EN2 ..161 C1
Cooks Mead WD2 ...168 B3
Cooks Spinney CM20 ..118 A4
Cooks Vennel HP1 ...124 B5
Cooks Way Hatfield AL10 ..130 B3
  Hitchin SG4 ....22 A1
Coombe Gdns HA4 ..121 F5
Coombe Hill Rd WD3 ..165 A2
Coombe Rd Bushey WD2 ..168 D2
  Kelshall SG8 ....6 A1
Coombelands Rd SG8 ..2 E1
Coombes Rd AL2 .....142 C5
Coonwood Cotts SG12 ..94 E4
Cooper's Cl SG4 .....66 B1
Cooper's Hill SG4 ....87 B8
Coopers Cl Aston SG2 ..51 D4
  Bishop's Stortford CM23 ..76 B4
Coopers Cres WD6 ...170 C8
Coopers Gn SG6 .....22 D7
Coopers Green La
  AL4,AL8,AL10 ....109 D1
Coopers La EN6 ......145 E1
Coopers Lane Rd EN6 ..160 B6
Coopers Rd EN6 .....145 E1
Coopers Mdw AL3 ...106 A6
Coopers Wlk 10 EN8 ..148 D3
Cooters End La AL5 ...85 F5
Copenhagen Cl LU3 ...44 D8
Copmans Wick WD3 ..164 D4
Coppens The SG5 ...12 A5
Copper Beech Cl HP3 ..137 F8
Copper Beeches
  11 Harpenden AL5 ...86 B1
  Oaklands AL6 ....89 D7
Copperfields Luton LU4 ..44 C3
  Royston SG8 ....7 C6
Coppermill La WD3,UB9 ..172 F3
Copperwood SG13 ...113 F6
Coppice Cl Harrow HA7 ..176 F4
  Hatfield AL10 ....129 F1
Coppice Mead SG5 ...11 E5
Coppice The
  Harpenden AL5 ......85 F2
  Hemel Hempstead HP2 ..125 B4
  Watford WD1 ....167 C3
  Wigginton HP23 .....100 C1
Coppings The EN11 ...115 A1
Coppins Cl HP4 ......121 F4

Coppins The Harrow HA3 ..176 E4
  Markyate AL3 ....83 D5
Copse Cl LU4 ....174 C1
Copse Hill AL6 ....90 A8
Copse The
  Bishop's Stortford CM23 ..77 C8
  Hemel Hempstead HP1 ..123 E5
  Hertford SG13 ....114 A6
Copse Way LU3 ......44 D8
Copse Wood Way HA6 ..174 C2
Copsewood Rd WD2 ..167 B8
Copthall CM22 ....77 F4
Copthorne LU2 ......46 D3
Copthorne Ave EN10 ..134 F3
Copthorne Cl WD3 ...165 F4
Copthorne Rd WD3 ...165 F4
Coral Gdns HP4 .....124 F3
Coral Ho CM20 ......117 A1
Corals Mead AL7 ....110 D5
Coram Cl HP4 ....122 C3
Corbridge Dr LU2 ....46 E1
Corby Cl AL3 ....141 A6
Cordell Cl EN8 ......148 E3
Corder Cl AL3 ....141 A8
Coreys Mill La SG1 ...36 C3
Corfe Cl 4 HP2 .....124 E2
Corinium Gate AL3 ...127 A1
Corinium Gdns LU3 ..45 A8
Corn Mead AL8 .....89 C1
Corncastle Rd LU1 ...63 D6
Corncrake Cl LU2 ....46 C5
Corncroft AL10 ......130 B7
Cornel Cl LU1 ....63 A7
Cornel Ct LU1 ....63 A7
Cornelia Ct 8 AL5 ...86 A2
Corner Cl SG6 ......22 E6
Corner Hall HP3 ....124 D1
Corner Hall Ave HP3 ..124 D1
Corner View AL9 ....144 C7
Corner Wood AL3 ...83 D5
Cornerfield AL10 ....130 B8
Corners AL7 ....111 A7
Cornfield Cres HP4 ..121 D7
Cornfield Rd WD2 ...168 B5
Cornfields
  Hemel Hempstead HP1 ..124 B2
  Stevenage SG2 ....51 C7
Cornwall Cl Cheshunt EN8 ..162 E6
  3 Pinner EN8 ....175 F3
Cornwall Ho CM23 ...76 E4
Cornwall Rd
  Harpenden AL5 ......86 B2
  Pinner HA5 ....175 F3
  St Albans AL1 ....127 E1
Coronation Ave SG8 ..7 C5
Coronation Rd
  Bishop's Stortford CM23 ..76 E5
  Ware SG12 ....93 D2
Corringham Ct AL1 ...127 F4
Corton Cl SG1 ....50 B8
Cory-Wright Way AL4 ..87 E1
Cosgrove Way LU1 ...44 D1
Cosne Mews AL5 ....107 C7
Cotefield LU4 ....44 C3
Cotesmore Rd HP1 ..123 E2
Cotlandswick AL2 ...142 C5
Cotney Croft SG2 ...51 D3
Cotsmoor AL1 ......127 F3
Cotswold HP2 ......124 E6
Cotswold Ave WD2 ..168 C3
Cotswold Bsns Pk LU1 ..62 D2
Cotswold Cl AL4 ....128 C8
Cotswold Gdns LU3 ..44 C7
Cotswolds AL10 .....130 A3
Cottage Cl
  Croxley Green WD3 ..165 F3
  Watford WD1 ....166 F7
Cottage Gdns EN8 ...148 C2
Cottered Rd SG9 ....26 F1
Cotterells HP1 ......124 C2
Cotterells Hill HP1 ..124 C3
Cotton Dr SG13 .....114 B7
Cotton Field AL10 ...130 B7
Cotton Rd EN6 .....159 C8
Cottonmill Cres AL1 ..127 D2
Coucil Cotts SG6 ...23 B2
Coulser Cl HP1 .....124 A6
Coulson Ct LU1 .....62 F8
Coulter Cl EN6 .....146 D4
Council Cotts SG7 ...12 C4
Counters Cl HP1 ....124 A3
Countess Anne
  CE Prim Sch AL9 ...130 C6
Countess Cl UB9 ...173 C1
Countess Ct 4 LU2 ..45 D1
Couper Ho WD1 ....166 E3
Coursers Rd AL2,AL4 ..143 C6
Court Cl CM23 ......76 E5
Courtaulds WD4 ....138 B1
Courtenay Ave HA3 ..176 C2
Courtenay Gdns HA3 ..176 C1
Courtfield Cl EN10 ..135 A3
Courtfields AL5 .....86 D1
Courtlands Cl WD2 ..153 E4
Courtlands Dr WD1 ..153 E3
Courtleigh Ave EN4 ..159 D1
Courtway The WD1 ..175 E8
Courtyard Mews SG12 ..92 E4
Courtyard The AL4 ...128 F3
Courtyards The WD1 ..166 D2
Covent Garden Cl LU4 ..44 F3
Coventry Cl SG1 ....37 B1
Coverdale
  Hemel Hempstead HP2 ..124 E6
  Luton LU4 ....44 B6
Covert Cl HP4 ......121 D6
Covert Rd HP4 ......121 D6
Covert The HA6 ....174 C2

Cow La Bushey WD2 ..168 A3
  Tring HP23 ....100 D4
Coward Rd WD2 .....154 C3
Cowards La SG4 ....88 F8
Cowbridge SG14 ....113 C6
Cowdray Cl LU2 .....46 C3
Cowley Hill Sch WD6 ..170 A8
Cowlins CM17 ......118 D4
Cowley Rd
  Berkhamsted HP4 ...122 B4
  Harpenden AL5 .....83 D5
  Hemel Hempstead HP1 ..124 B2
  Markyate AL3 ....83 D5
  Welwyn Garden City AL7 ..110 A4
Cowper CE Prim Sch AL6 ..90 E2
Cowper Cres SG14 ..92 B1
Cowper Ct Markyate AL3 ..83 D5
  Watford WD2 ....154 A2
Cowper Rd
  Berkhamsted HP4 ...122 B4
  Harpenden AL5 .....83 D5
  Hemel Hempstead HP1 ..124 B2
  Markyate AL3 ....83 D5
  Welwyn Garden City AL7 ..110 A4
Cowper Rise AL3 ...83 D5
Cowper St LU1 .....63 E5
Cowpers Way AL6 ..90 D5
Cowridge Cres LU2 ..64 A8
Cowslip Cl SG8 ....7 F5
Cowslip Hill SG6 ...22 E7
Cowslips AL7 ......111 C5
Cox Cl WD7 ....156 F7
Cox's Way SG15 ...11 A6
Coxfield Cl HP2 ....124 E2
Coyney Gn LU2 ....45 C1
Cozens La E EN10 ..134 F1
Cozens La W EN10 ..134 F1
Cozens Rd SG12 ...94 A2
Crab La WD2 ....155 B4
Crab Tree La SG5 ...20 D4
Crab Tree Rd SG3 ...68 F4
Crabb's La SG9 .....43 F6
Crabbes Cl SG5 ....34 E7
Crabtree Cl Bushey WD2 ..168 B4
  Hemel Hempstead HP3 ..124 D1
Crabtree Ct 8 HP3 ..124 E1
Crabtree Dell SG6 ..23 B3
Crabtree Inf Sch AL5 ..86 C1
Crabtree La Harpenden AL5 ..86 C1
  Hemel Hempstead HP3 ..124 D1
Crackley Mdw HP2 ..125 B8
Cradock Rd LU4 ....44 B1
Craford Ct SG14 ...112 F7
Cragg Ave WD7 ....155 F3
Cragside SG2 ......69 C7
Craig Mount WD7 ..156 B4
Craigavon Rd HP2 ..124 F7
Craiglands AL4 .....128 D7
Craigs Wlk 4 EN8 ..148 D3
Craigweil Ave WD7 ..156 B4
Crakers Mead 4 WD1 ..167 B6
Cranberry Ave SG5 ..34 D6
Cranborne Cl
  Brickendon SG13 ...113 C3
  Potters Bar EN6 ....158 E8
Cranborne Cres EN6 ..158 E8
Cranborne Ct EN3 ..162 D3
Cranborne Gdns AL7 ..110 E5
Cranborne Ind Est EN6 ..144 E1
Cranborne Par EN6 ..158 D8
Cranborne Prim Sch
  EN6 ....158 F8
Cranborne Rd
  Cheshunt EN8 ......162 D7
  Hatfield AL10 ......130 B6
  Hoddesdon EN11 ...135 C7
  Potters Bar EN6 ....144 E1
Cranbourne SG1 ...36 B1
Cranbourne Dr
  Harpenden AL5 .....107 D6
  Hoddesdon EN11 ...115 C2
Cranbourne Prim Sch
  EN11 ....115 B2
Cranbourne Rd HA6 ..174 F1
Cranbrook Cl SG12 ..93 D3
Cranbrook Dr Luton LU3 ..44 D8
  St Albans AL4 ......128 C3
Crane Mead SG12 ..114 E8
Cranefield Dr WD2 ..154 E6
Cranes Way WD6 ..170 C4
Cranfield Cres EN6 ..146 E2
Cranford Ct AL5 ...86 C1
Cranleigh Cl EN7 ...148 A3
Cranleigh Gdns LU3 ..45 D3
Cranmer Cl EN6 ....145 C1
Cranmore Ct AL1 ...127 E4
Cranwell Cl AL4 ....128 C1
Cranwell Gdns CM23 ..59 C1
Cravells Ct AL5 ....107 C2
Cravells Rd AL5 ....107 C2
Crawford Rd AL10 ..130 A2
Crawley Cl LU1 ....63 C1
Crawley Dr HP2 ....124 F7
Crawley Green Inf Sch
  LU2 ....64 B8
Crawley Green Rd
  Luton, Hart Hill LU2 ..64 A8
  Luton, Wigmore LU2 ..46 D1
Crawley Rd LU1 ....63 D8
Crawley's La HP23 ..120 F7
Creamery Ct SG6 ...23 C3
Creasy Cl WD5 ....153 F8
Crecy Gdns AL3 ...106 A4
Creighton Ave AL1 ..141 D8
Crescent E EN4 ....159 C1
Crescent Rd
  Bishop's Stortford CM23 ..77 A3
  Hemel Hempstead HP2 ..124 D3
  Luton LU2 ....63 F8
Crescent Rise LU2 ..63 F8
Crescent The
  Abbots Langley WD5 ..139 F1

Crescent The continued
  Ardeley SG2 ....38 F2
  Bricket Wood AL2 ...141 A1
  Caddington LU1 .....62 E3
  Cottered SG9 ....39 D7
  Croxley Green WD3 ..166 B3
  Harlow CM17 ....118 C6
  Henlow SG16 ....10 C4
  Hitchin SG5 ....21 D1
  Letchworth SG6 ....23 A5
  Marsworth HP23 ...80 A1
  Pitstone LU7 ....80 C4
  Radlett WD2 ....155 B1
  St Ippolyts SG4 .....35 A3
  Watford WD1 ....167 C5
  Welwyn AL6 ....89 C4
Crescent W EN4 ...159 C1
Cress End WD3 ....165 A1
Cresset Cl SG12 ...115 C3
Cresswick SG4 ....66 E7
Crest Dr EN3 ......162 C1
Crest Pk HP2 ......125 C4
Crest The Goff's Oak EN7 ..147 B4
  Luton LU3 ....45 B7
  Oaklands AL6 ....89 D8
  Sawbridgeworth CM21 ..97 D2
  Ware SG12 ....93 D3
Cresta Cl LU5 .....44 A2
Cresta Ho 3 LU1 ...63 D7
Creswick Ct AL7 ...110 D5
Creswick Jun Mix Inf Sch
  AL7 ....110 D3
Crew Curve HP4 ...121 F7
Crews Hill EN2 ....160 F5
Crews Hill Sta EN2 ..160 F5
Crib St SG12 ......93 D2
Cricketer's Rd SG15 ..11 A4
Cricketers Cl AL3 ..127 E4
Cricketfield La CM23 ..76 E8
Cringle Ct EN6 ....145 C1
Crispin Field LU7 ..80 C4
Croasdaile Rd CM24 ..59 E8
Croasdale Cl CM24 ..59 E8
Crocus Field EN5 ..171 E3
Croft Cl WD4 ......138 A1
Croft Ct 4 Harpenden AL5 ..86 B1
  Hitchin SG5 ....34 E7
Croft End Rd WD4 ..138 A1
Croft Field
  Chipperfield WD4 ..138 A1
  Hatfield AL10 ......130 A5
Croft La Chipperfield WD4 ..138 A1
  Letchworth SG6 ....12 B1
Croft Mdw AL10 ...138 A1
Croft Mdws LU7 ...80 A7
Croft Rd Luton LU2 ..46 B3
  Ware SG12 ....93 C2
Croft The Barnet EN5 ..171 E5
  Chiswellgreen AL2 ..141 A6
  Hoddesdon EN10 ...148 B8
  Luton LU3 ....44 D8
  Wareside SG12 ....94 E4
  Welwyn Garden City AL7 ..110 F3
Croft Wlk EN10 ....148 E8
Crofters CM21 .....97 E3
Crofters End CM21 ..97 E3
Crofters Rd HA6 ...174 E6
Crofts Path HP3 ...125 B1
Crofts The
  Hemel Hempstead HP3 ..125 B2
  Stotfold SG5 ....11 F6
Croftwell AL5 .....107 E8
Cromer Cl HP4 ....102 E5
Cromer Rd WD2 ...154 C4
Cromer Way
  Luton, Stopsley Common LU2 ..45 E6
  Luton, Warden Hill LU2 ..45 D7
Cromer Windmill SG2 ..38 E6
Crompton Rd SG1 ..50 A6
Cromwell Ave EN7 ..148 B1
Cromwell Cl
  Bishop's Stortford CM23 ..76 B7
  St Albans AL4 ......128 D8
Cromwell Gn SG6 ..23 B8
Cromwell Hill LU2 ..45 D1
Cromwell Rd
  Borehamwood WD6 ..169 E8
  Cheshunt EN8 ......148 B3
  Hertford SG13 .....114 A7
  Letchworth SG6 ....23 B8
  Luton LU3 ....45 D1
  Stevenage SG2 ....51 C5
  Ware SG12 ....93 F2
Cromwell Way SG5 ..20 D4
Crooked Mile EN9 ..163 C2
Crooked Way EN9 ..135 E1
Crookhams AL7 ...90 A1
Crop Comm AL10 ..130 B7
Crosby Cl Luton LU4 ..45 A2
  St Albans AL4 .....142 C4
Cross La Harpenden AL5 ..107 C5
  Hertford SG14 .....113 B6
Cross Oak Rd HP4 ..122 A4
Cross Rd Cheshunt EN8 ..162 E6
  Hertford SG14 .....113 C2
  Watford WD1 ......167 E3
Cross St Letchworth SG6 ..22 F7
  2 St Albans AL3 ...127 C3
  Ware SG12 ....93 E1
  Watford WD1 ......167 C6
Cross Way AL5 ....86 C3
Cross Way The
  Harrow HA3 ......176 E1
  Luton LU1 ....63 C5

Crossbrook AL10 . . . . .129 E4
Crossbrook St EN8 . . . . . . .162 D8
Crossett Gn HP3 . . . . .125 C1
Crossfell Rd HP3 . . . . .125 C2
Crossfield Cl HP4 . . . . .121 F4
Crossfield Rd EN11 . . . . . . .135 B8
Crossfields AL3 . . . . .141 B8
Crossgates SG1 . . . . .50 E5
Crosslands LU1 . . . . .62 E3
Crossleys SG6 . . . . .11 F2
Crossmead WD1 . . . . .167 B3
Crossoaks La Ridge EN6 . . .157 F5
  Shenley EN6 . . . . .157 D5
Crosspath The WD7 . . . . . .156 A4
Crosspaths AL5 . . . . .85 C4
Crossway Pinner HA5 . . . . .175 B1
  Welwyn Garden City AL8 . .89 C2
Crossways Barley SG8 . . . . . .8 F1
  Berkhamsted HP4 . . . . . . .121 F3
  Hemel Hempstead HP3 . . .125 B3
Crouch Ct CM20 . . . . .117 C3
Crouch Hall Gdns AL3 . . . .106 A6
Crouch Hall La AL3 . . . . . . .106 A6
Crouch La EN7 . . . . .147 C4
Crouchfield
  Hemel Hempstead HP1 . . .124 B2
  Hertford SG14 . . . . .92 C1
Crouchfield La SG14 . . . . . .92 E4
Crow Furlong SG5 . . . . .34 D7
Crowborough Path WD1 . .175 D6
Crowland Rd LU2 . . . . .46 C5
Crown Cl CM22 . . . . .98 C1
Crown La SG8 . . . . .16 F5
Crown Lodge SG15 . . . . . . .11 A4
Crown Rd WD6 . . . . .170 B8
Crown Rise WD2 . . . . .154 D5
Crown Rose Ct HP23 . . . . .100 A3
Crown St AL3 . . . . .106 B5
Crown Terr CM23 . . . . .77 A7
Crownfield EN10 . . . . .135 A2
Croxdale Rd WD6 . . . . .170 A7
Croxley Cl WD1 . . . . .166 D4
Croxley Sta WD3 . . . . .166 B3
Croxley View WD1 . . . . . . .166 E3
Croxton Cl [3] LU3 . . . . .45 A7
Crozier Ave CM23 . . . . .76 C8
Crunnel's Gn SG4 . . . . .48 E5
Crusader Way WD1 . . . . . .166 F1
Cubbington Cl LU3 . . . . . . .45 A7
Cubitt Cl SG4 . . . . .35 C7
Cubitts Cl AL6 . . . . .89 F3
Cublands SG13 . . . . .114 B6
Cuckmans Dr AL2 . . . . .141 A6
Cuckoo's Nest LU2 . . . . . . .64 A7
Cucumber La AL9 . . . . .132 A1
Cuffley Ave WD2 . . . . .154 D5
Cuffley Cl LU3 . . . . .44 F4
Cuffley Ct HP2 . . . . .125 C8
Cuffley Hill EN7 . . . . .147 B2
Cuffley Sta EN6 . . . . .146 F1
Cuffley Sta EN6 . . . . .146 F2
Cullera Cl HA6 . . . . .174 F4
Cullings Ct EN9 . . . . .163 F6
Culver Cl SG10 . . . . .74 F1
Culver Lo AL1 . . . . .127 E5
Culver Rd AL1 . . . . .127 E5
Culverden Rd WD1 . . . . . . .175 B7
Culverhouse Rd LU3 . . . . . .45 C3
Culworth Cl LU1 . . . . .62 E3
Cumberland Cl
  Hemel Hempstead WD5 . .139 E7
  Hertford SG14 . . . . .113 C8
Cumberland Ct
  [2] Hoddesdon EN11 . . . . .135 A7
  St Albans AL3 . . . . .127 E4
Cumberland Dr AL3 . . . . . .106 B6
Cumberland St LU1 . . . . . . .63 E6
Cumberlow Pl HP2 . . . . . . .125 C2
Cumcum Hill AL9 . . . . .131 E2
Cundalls Rd SG12 . . . . .93 E2
Cunningham Ave
  Enfield EN3 . . . . .162 A4
  St Albans AL1 . . . . .127 F1
Cunningham Ct EN8 . . . . . .148 E3
Cunningham Hill Inf Sch
  AL1 . . . . .128 A1
Cunningham Hill
  Jun Mix Sch AL1 . . . . . . .128 A1
Cunningham Hill Rd AL1 . .128 A1
Cunningham Rd EN8 . . . . . .148 E4
Cupid Green La
  Great Gaddesden HP2 . . . .104 E3
  Hemel Hempstead HP2 . . .105 A1
Curlew Cl
  Berkhamsted HP4 . . . . . . .122 C3
  Letchworth SG6 . . . . .11 E1
Curlew Ct EN10 . . . . .148 F8
Curlew Rd LU2 . . . . .46 C5
Currie St SG13 . . . . .113 E6
Curteys CM17 . . . . .118 C6
Curtis Cl WD3 . . . . .165 A1
Curtis Rd HP3 . . . . .125 D2
Curtis Way HP4 . . . . .122 D3
Curzon Gate Ct [1] WD1 . .167 A8
Curzon Rd LU3 . . . . .45 C1
Cussans Ho WD1 . . . . .166 E3
Cussons Cl EN7 . . . . .148 A2
Cut Throat Ave HP4,LU6 . .81 E7
Cutenhoe Rd LU1 . . . . .63 E4
Cutforth Rd CM21 . . . . .97 E3
Cuthbert Cl EN7 . . . . .147 F2
Cutlers Gn LU2 . . . . .64 F6
Cutmore Dr AL4 . . . . .129 B1
Cutts La SG4 . . . . .66 D1
Cuttsfield Terr HP1 . . . . . .123 F2

Cuttys La SG1 . . . . .50 E5
Cwmbran Ct HP2 . . . . .124 F7
Cygnet Cl
  Borehamwood WD6 . . . . .170 C8
  Northwood HA6 . . . . .174 C4
Cygnet Ct [11] CM23 . . . . . . .76 F6
Cylers Thicket AL6 . . . . . . .89 C6
Cymbeline Ct AL3 . . . . . . .127 C4
Cypress Ave
  Crews Hill EN2 . . . . .161 A4
  Welwyn Garden City AL7 . .111 C5
Cypress Cl EN9 . . . . .163 D5
Cypress Rd HA3 . . . . .176 D1
Cypress Wlk WD2 . . . . . . .154 B4
Cyrils Way AL1 . . . . .141 D8

D

Dacorum Coll of F Ed
  HP1 . . . . .124 C4
Dacorum Way HP1 . . . . . . .124 C3
Dacre Bldgs EN8 . . . . .148 F2
Dacre Cres SG4 . . . . .66 C1
Dacre Gdns WD6 . . . . .170 D4
Dacre Gn SG8 . . . . .7 F6
Dacre Rd SG5 . . . . .35 A8
Dagger La WD6 . . . . .169 B4
Daggs Dell Rd HP1 . . . . . . .123 E5
Dagnall Cty Fst Sch HP4 . .81 C5
Dagnall Rd
  Great Gaddesden HP1 . . . .103 C5
  Whipsnade HP4,LU6 . . . . .81 D8
Dagnalls SG6 . . . . .22 F2
Dahlia Cl
  Hammond Street EN7 . . . .147 C6
  Luton LU2 . . . . .46 B4
Daintrees SG12 . . . . .95 E4
Daintry Lodge HA6 . . . . . .174 F3
Dairy Cotts SG5 . . . . .19 B2
Dairy Mews WD1 . . . . .167 A4
Daisy Ct SG6 . . . . .23 A8
Dalby Cl LU4 . . . . .44 B3
Dale Ave AL4 . . . . .87 B5
Dale Cl Hitchin SG4 . . . . . .34 F4
  Pinner HA5 . . . . .175 B2
Dale Ct CM21 . . . . .97 D1
Dale La LU1 . . . . .63 C7
Dale The Letchworth SG6 . .22 E5
  Waltham Abbey EN9 . . . . .163 E5
Dales Path WD6 . . . . .170 D4
Dales Rd WD6 . . . . .170 D4
Daleside Dr EN6 . . . . .158 F6
Dalewood
  Welwyn Garden City AL7 . .111 D5
Dalkeith Rd AL5 . . . . .86 C1
Dallow Inf Sch LU1 . . . . . . .63 C8
Dallow Jun Sch LU1 . . . . . .63 C8
Dallow Rd LU1 . . . . .63 B8
Dallow Road Jun & Inf Sch
  LU1 . . . . .63 C8
Dalroad Ind Est LU1 . . . . . .63 B8
Dalton Cl LU3 . . . . .31 B1
Dalton Gdns CM23 . . . . . . .76 E4
Dalton St AL3 . . . . .127 D4
Dalton Way Watford WD1 .167 D4
  Whitwell SG4 . . . . .66 E7
Daltry Cl SG1 . . . . .36 C2
Daltry Rd SG1 . . . . .36 C2
Damask Cl Tring HP23 . . . .100 C4
  Weston SG4 . . . . .37 B8
Damask Gn HP1 . . . . .123 E2
Damask Green Rd SG4 . . . .37 B8
Dame Alice Owen's Sch
  EN6 . . . . .158 E6
Dammersey Cl AL3 . . . . . . .83 F4
Damson Way AL4 . . . . .128 C5
Dancers End La HP23 . . . . .99 C2
Dancers Hill Rd EN5 . . . . .158 E3
Dancote SG3 . . . . .68 F5
Dane Acres CM23 . . . . .76 D8
Dane Bridge La SG10 . . . . .75 B2
Dane Cl Harpenden AL5 . . .86 C4
  Stotfold SG5 . . . . .11 F8
Dane End Ho SG1 . . . . .36 C1
Dane End La SG4 . . . . .37 E5
Dane End Rd SG11 . . . . . . .72 E3
Dane Ho CM23 . . . . .76 D8
Dane O'Coys Rd CM23 . . . .58 C1
Dane Pk CM23 . . . . .76 D8
Dane Rd LU3 . . . . .45 C2
Dane St CM23 . . . . .77 A7
Danebridge Rd SG10 . . . . . .75 B2
Danefield Rd SG5 . . . . .20 C4
Danemead EN11 . . . . .115 A1
Danes The AL2 . . . . .141 C3
Danesbury La AL6 . . . . .89 D8
Danesbury Park Caravan
  Site AL6 . . . . .89 D8
Danesbury Park Rd AL6 . . .89 D8
Danesbury Pk
  Hertford SG14 . . . . .113 D7
  Welwyn AL6 . . . . .89 C7
Danescroft SG6 . . . . .12 A1
Danesgate SG1 . . . . .50 D4
Danestrete SG1 . . . . .50 D5
Daniells AL7 . . . . .111 A7
Danvers Croft HP23 . . . . . .100 C5
Danvers Dr LU3 . . . . .31 C1
Danziger Way WD6 . . . . . .170 C8
Darby Dr
  Waltham Abbey EN9 . . . . .163 C6
  Welwyn AL6 . . . . .68 D3
Darcy Cl EN7 . . . . .162 E8
Dark La Cheshunt EN7 . . . .148 A1
  Codicote SG4 . . . . .88 E8
  Harpenden AL5 . . . . .107 D7

Dark La continued
  Sandon SG9 . . . . .15 B1
  Wingrave HP22 . . . . .60 C3
Darkes La EN6 . . . . .159 A8
Darlands Dr EN5 . . . . .171 D4
Darley Rd LU2,SG4 . . . . . . .47 C2
Darnhills WD7 . . . . .155 F4
Darnicle Hill EN7 . . . . .147 A6
Darr's La HP4 . . . . .121 D6
Darrington Rd WD6 . . . . . .169 E8
Darwin Cl
  Hemel Hempstead HP2 . . .105 B1
  St Albans AL3 . . . . .127 E7
Darwin Gdns WD1 . . . . . . .175 C6
Darwin Rd SG2 . . . . .51 B6
Dashes The CM20 . . . . . . .117 C1
Datchet Cl HP2 . . . . .125 B8
Datchworth
  Jun Inf Sch SG3 . . . . .69 D3
Datchworth Turn HP2 . . . .125 C3
Dauphin Ct [5] LU2 . . . . . . .45 D1
Davenham Ave HA6 . . . . . .174 F5
Daventer Dr HA7 . . . . .176 F3
David Evans Ct SG6 . . . . . .22 D7
Davies St SG13 . . . . .113 E6
Davis Cres SG5 . . . . .20 D4
Davis Ct AL1 . . . . .127 E3
Davis' Row SG15 . . . . .11 A4
Davison Cl AL10 . . . . .148 D3
Davison Dr EN8 . . . . .148 D3
Davys Cl AL4 . . . . .108 E7
Dawes La WD3 . . . . .151 F3
Dawley AL7 . . . . .89 F1
Dawley Ct HP2 . . . . .125 A7
Dawlish Cl SG2 . . . . .69 C7
Dawlish Rd LU4 . . . . .44 F3
Dawson Cl SG16 . . . . .10 C5
Day's Cl SG8 . . . . .7 C5
Dayemead AL7 . . . . .111 B3
Days Cl AL10 . . . . .129 F5
Days Mead AL10 . . . . .129 F5
De Haviland Cl AL10 . . . . .129 F6
De Haviland Ct WD7 . . . . .156 E7
De Haviland Way WD5 . . .153 F7
De Tany Ct AL1 . . . . .127 D2
De Vere Wlk WD1 . . . . . . .166 E7
Deacon Cl AL1 . . . . .141 D7
Deacon's Hill Rd WD6 . . . .170 A4
Deacons Cl
  Borehamwood WD6 . . . . .170 A5
  Pinner HA5 . . . . .175 B1
Deacons Ct [6] LU2 . . . . . . .63 D8
Deacons Hill WD1 . . . . . . .167 C3
Deacons Hts WD6 . . . . . . .170 A3
Deacons Way SG5 . . . . .21 C5
Deaconsfield Rd HP3 . . . . .138 E8
Dead Woman's La SG4 . . . .48 C7
Deadman's Ash La WD3 . . .152 B3
Deakin Cl WD1 . . . . .166 E2
Dean Cl WD2 . . . . .154 D1
Dean Field HP3 . . . . .137 A4
Dean Moore Cl AL1 . . . . . .127 D5
Dean The HP22 . . . . .60 B3
Dean's Gdns AL4 . . . . .128 A7
Deans Cl
  Abbots Langley WD5 . . . . .153 D7
  Tring HP23 . . . . .100 A4
Deans Furlong HP23 . . . . .100 A4
Deans Mdw HP4 . . . . .81 C5
Deanscroft SG3 . . . . .68 F5
Deard's End La SG3 . . . . . .68 F6
Deards Wood SG3 . . . . .68 F5
Debenham Ct EN5 . . . . . . .171 C4
Debenham Rd EN7 . . . . . . .148 B4
Dee The HP2 . . . . .124 F8
Deep Denes LU2 . . . . .46 A2
Deepdene EN6 . . . . .158 D8
Deeping Cl SG3 . . . . .68 F4
Deer Cl SG13 . . . . .113 F6
Deerfield Cl SG12 . . . . .93 D2
Deerings The AL5 . . . . .107 A4
Deerswood Ave AL10 . . . . .130 B3
Deeves Hall La EN6 . . . . . .157 E6
Deimos Dr HP2 . . . . .125 A6
Delahay Rise HP4 . . . . .122 B6
Delamare Rd EN8 . . . . .148 F2
Delamere Rd WD6 . . . . . . .170 B8
Delcroft SG12 . . . . .93 C2
Delfield Gdns LU1 . . . . .62 E4
Delius Cl WD6 . . . . .169 C3
Dell Cl AL5 . . . . .86 B3
Dell La Bishop's Stortford,
  Hockerill CM23 . . . . .77 A7
  Bishop's Stortford,
  Latchmore Bank CM22 . . . .77 E1
  Spellbrook CM22 . . . . .98 A8
Dell Mdw HP3 . . . . .138 E7
Dell Rd Berkhamsted HP4 . .121 D7
  Enfield EN3 . . . . .162 C1
  Watford WD2 . . . . .154 A2
Dell Rise AL2 . . . . .141 B5
Dell Side WD2 . . . . .154 A2
Dell Springs SG9 . . . . .40 E8
Dell The Baldock SG7 . . . . .23 E6
  Brickendon SG13 . . . . . . .113 C3
  Caddington LU1 . . . . .62 E3
  Luton LU2 . . . . .46 A3
  Markyate AL3 . . . . .83 D5
  Moor Park HA6 . . . . .174 E8
  Pinner HA5 . . . . .175 D1
  Radlett WD7 . . . . .156 A4
  Royston SG8 . . . . .7 C5
Dellcot Cl LU2 . . . . .46 B4
Dellcott Cl AL8 . . . . .110 C7

Dellcroft Way AL5 . . . . . . .107 A5
Dellcut Rd HP2 . . . . .125 A5
Dellfield
  Berkhamsted HP4 . . . . . . .122 A6
  St Albans AL1 . . . . .127 F2
  Thundridge SG12 . . . . .93 D8
Dellfield Ave HP4 . . . . .122 B6
Dellfield Cl Radlett WD7 . .155 F4
  Watford WD1 . . . . .167 A7
Dellfield Ct Harlow CM17 .118 C4
  Luton LU2 . . . . .46 D2
Dellfield Rd AL10 . . . . .130 A5
Dellmeadow WD5 . . . . . . .139 E1
Dellors Cl EN5 . . . . .171 D4
Dells The
  [11] Bishop's Stortford CM23 . .76 F7
  Hemel Hempstead HP3 . . .125 B1
Dells Wood Cl EN11 . . . . . .114 F1
Dellsome La
  Colney Heath AL4,AL9,AL10 .143 F8
  Welham Green AL9 . . . . . .144 B8
Dellswood Cl SG13 . . . . . .113 E5
Dellwood WD3 . . . . .165 B1
Delmar Ave HP2 . . . . .125 D2
Delmer Ct WD6 . . . . .156 F1
Delmerend La AL3 . . . . .84 C1
Delphine Cl LU1 . . . . .63 B6
Delta Gain WD1 . . . . .175 D7
Demontfort Rise SG12 . . . .93 C3
Denbigh Cl [2] HP2 . . . . . . .124 C2
Denbigh High Sch LU3 . . . .45 B2
Denbigh Inf Sch LU3 . . . . . .45 B2
Denbigh Jun Sch LU3 . . . . .45 B2
Denbigh Rd LU3 . . . . .45 B2
Denby SG6 . . . . .23 B4
Dencora Way LU3 . . . . .44 B8
Dendridge Cl EN1 . . . . . . .162 B2
Dene La SG2 . . . . .51 E2
Dene Rd HA6 . . . . .174 D4
Denes The HP3 . . . . .138 F7
Denewood Cl WD1 . . . . . . .153 F2
Denham Cl
  Hemel Hempstead HP2 . . .125 A8
  Luton LU3 . . . . .44 E8
Denham La SL9 . . . . .172 A2
Denham Way WD6 . . . . . . .170 C8
Denham Way
  (North Orbital Rd) WD3 .172 E4
Denmark Cl LU3 . . . . .44 E8
Denmark St WD1 . . . . .167 B7
Dennis Cl AL3 . . . . .127 D4
Dennis St SG14 . . . . .59 B2
Denny Ave EN9 . . . . .163 D5
Denny Ct CM23 . . . . .59 B2
Denny Gate EN8 . . . . .148 F4
Denny's La HP4 . . . . .121 F3
Densley Cl AL8 . . . . .110 D8
Denton Cl Barnet EN5 . . . .171 C4
  Luton LU4 . . . . .44 B3
Denton Ho WD1 . . . . .175 C7
Denton Rd SG1 . . . . .50 E4
Dents Cl SG6 . . . . .23 C3
Derby Ave HA3 . . . . .176 D2
Derby Ho HA5 . . . . .175 D1
Derby Rd
  Hoddesdon EN11 . . . . . . .135 D4
  Luton LU4 . . . . .44 D4
  Watford WD1 . . . . .167 C5
Derby Way SG1 . . . . .51 B8
Derwent Ave Luton LU3 . . .45 B7
  Pinner HA5 . . . . .175 A4
Derwent Lower Sch SG16 .10 B5
Derwent Rd
  Harpenden AL5 . . . . .85 C4
  Hemel Hempstead HP3 . . .125 C2
  Henlow SG16 . . . . .10 B4
  Luton LU2 . . . . .64 A8
Des Fuller Ct [3] LU1 . . . . .63 F6
Desborough Cl SG14 . . . . . .92 F1
Desborough Dr AL6 . . . . . .90 D5
Desborough Rd SG4 . . . . . .35 C8
Desmond Rd WD2 . . . . . . .153 F3
Deva Cl AL3 . . . . .127 A1
Devereux Dr WD1 . . . . . . .153 E1
Devoils La [9] CM23 . . . . . .76 F7
Devon Ct AL1 . . . . .127 E2
Devon Rd Luton LU2 . . . . . .64 B8
  Watford WD2 . . . . .167 D8
Devonshire Cl SG2 . . . . . . .69 A8
Devonshire Rd
  [5] Harpenden AL5 . . . . . .86 B1
  Pinner HA5 . . . . .175 F2
Dewars Cl AL6 . . . . .89 C6
Dewes Green Rd CM23 . . . .30 F1
Dewgrass Gr EN8 . . . . .162 B4
Dewhurst Rd EN8 . . . . . . .148 C2
Dewhurst St Mary
  CE Prim Sch EN8 . . . . . . .148 C2
Dewpond Cl SG1 . . . . .50 C8
Dewsbury Rd LU3 . . . . .45 C6
Dexter Cl Luton LU3 . . . . . .31 B1
  St Albans AL1 . . . . .128 A2
Dexter Rd Barnet EN5 . . . .171 C3
  Harefield UB9 . . . . .173 C1
Diamond Ind Ctr SG6 . . . . .23 C7
Diamond Rd WD2 . . . . .154 A1
Dickens Cl AL3 . . . . .127 D4
Dickens Ct HP2 . . . . .105 B1
Dicker Mill SG13 . . . . .113 D7
Dicket Mead AL6 . . . . .89 C5
Dickins Cl EN7 . . . . .148 A5
Dickinson Ave WD3 . . . . . .166 A3
Dickinson Sq WD3 . . . . . . .166 A3
Dickson EN7 . . . . .147 F4
Dig Dag Hill EN7 . . . . .147 F4
Digswell Rd WD6 . . . . .157 A1

Digswell House Mews
  AL8 . . . . .89 D2
Digswell La AL7 . . . . .89 F2
Digswell Park Rd
  Welwyn Garden City AL8 . . .89 D3
  Welwyn Garden City AL8 . . .89 E3
Digswell Rd AL8 . . . . .89 E1
Digswell Rise AL8 . . . . .110 E8
Dimmocks La WD3 . . . . . . .152 B3
Dimsdale Cres CM23 . . . . . .77 B6
Dimsdale St SG14 . . . . .113 C6
Dinant Link Rd EN11 . . . . .135 B7
Dingle Cl EN5 . . . . .170 F3
Dinmore HP3 . . . . .136 F3
Ditchfield Rd EN11 . . . . . . .115 A1
Ditchling Cl LU2 . . . . .46 C3
Ditchmore La SG1 . . . . .50 D6
Ditton Gn LU2 . . . . .46 E3
Divine Saviour
  RC Prim Sch WD1 . . . . . .153 D7
Divot Pl SG13 . . . . .114 B7
Dixies Cl SG7 . . . . .4 D3
Dixon Pl SG9 . . . . .40 E7
Dixons Hill Cl AL9 . . . . . . .144 B6
Dixons Hill Rd AL9 . . . . . .144 C4
Dobb's Weir Rd EN11 . . . .135 D5
Docklands SG5 . . . . .20 D4
Doctor's Commons Rd
  HP4 . . . . .122 B4
Dodds La HP2 . . . . .104 E1
Dodwood AL7 . . . . .111 B5
Dog Kennel La
  Chorleywood WD3 . . . . . .164 F5
  Hatfield AL10 . . . . .130 A6
  Royston SG8 . . . . .7 D6
Doggetts Way AL1 . . . . . . .127 C1
Dognell Gn AL8 . . . . .110 B7
Dolesbury Dr AL6 . . . . .89 E8
Dollis Brook Wlk EN5 . . . .171 E3
Dollis Valley Way EN5 . . . .171 F3
Dolphin Ct HA3 . . . . .176 E1
Dolphin Sq HP23 . . . . .100 A3
Dolphin Way CM23 . . . . . . .77 A6
Dolphin Yd
  [2] Hertford SG14 . . . . . .113 C6
  St Albans AL1 . . . . .127 D3
  [7] Ware SG12 . . . . .93 D1
Dominic Ct EN9 . . . . .163 B6
Doncaster Cl SG1 . . . . .51 E4
Doncaster Gn WD1 . . . . . . .175 C5
Donkey La HP23 . . . . .99 E2
Donne Cl SG8 . . . . .7 C8
Dorant Ho AL3 . . . . .127 D7
Dorchester Ave EN11 . . . . .135 A8
Dorchester Ct
  Croxley Green WD3 . . . . . .166 D4
  St Albans AL3 . . . . .128 A2
  Watford WD1 . . . . .167 E3
Dordans Rd LU4 . . . . .44 F4
Dorel Cl LU2 . . . . .45 C2
Dormans Cl HA6 . . . . .174 F4
Dormer Cl EN5 . . . . .171 D4
Dormie Cl AL3 . . . . .127 C5
Dornan Cl LU1 . . . . .63 E5
Dorrien's Croft HP4 . . . . . .121 F7
Dorrington Cl LU3 . . . . .45 C1
Dorrofield Cl WD3 . . . . . . .166 C4
Dorset Cl HP4 . . . . .121 F5
Dorset Ct [4] LU1 . . . . .63 F6
Dorset Ho [13] CM23 . . . . . .76 F7
Douglas Ave WD2 . . . . . . .154 E2
Douglas Dr SG1 . . . . .51 A8
Douglas Ho [11] EN5 . . . . . .148 D3
Douglas Rd Harpenden AL5 .85 F2
  Luton LU4 . . . . .45 A4
Douglas Way AL7 . . . . .111 C6
Dove Cl
  Bishop's Stortford CM23 . . .76 E3
  Stansted Mountfitchet CM24 .59 E4
Dove Ct AL10 . . . . .130 A3
Dove House La LU6 . . . . . . .82 D8
Dove La EN6 . . . . .159 C5
Dove Pk
  Chorleywood WD3 . . . . . .164 C4
  Pinner HA5 . . . . .176 A3
Dovedale Luton LU2 . . . . . .45 E6
  Stevenage SG2 . . . . .51 B4
  Ware SG12 . . . . .93 C3
Dovedale Cl UB9 . . . . .173 C1
Dovehouse Croft CM20 . . .118 A2
Dovehouse Hill LU2 . . . . . .46 B1
Dover Cl LU3 . . . . .45 A3
Dover Way WD3 . . . . .166 C5
Doverfield EN7 . . . . .147 C2
Dower Ct [1] SG4 . . . . .34 F4
Dowland Ho EN1 . . . . .161 F1
Dowling Ct HP3 . . . . .138 D8
Down Edge AL3 . . . . .105 F5
Down Green La AL4 . . . . . .108 B7
Downalong WD2 . . . . .168 D1
Downedge AL3 . . . . .127 B4
Downer Dr WD3 . . . . .152 A3
Downes Rd AL4 . . . . .128 B7
Downfield Cl SG13 . . . . . . .114 C4
Downfield Ct SG12 . . . . . . .93 E8
Downfield
  Jun Mix Inf Sch EN8 . . . .162 E8
Downfield Rd
  Cheshunt EN8 . . . . .162 E8
  Hertford Heath SG13 . . . .114 C5
Downfields AL8 . . . . .110 B4
Downhall Ley SG9 . . . . .40 E7
Downings Wood WD3 . . . . .172 D5
Downlands Baldock SG7 . . .13 A4
  Luton LU1 . . . . .44 C2
  Royston SG8 . . . . .7 C6
  Stevenage SG2 . . . . .51 D7
  Waltham Abbey EN9 . . . . .163 E5

Downs La AL10 130 A3
Downs Rd LU1 63 C7
Downs The AL10 130 A3
Downs View LU4 44 D4
Downsfield AL10 130 B2
Downside HP2 124 E4
Downside Inf Sch LU4 44 E1
Downside Jun Sch LU4 44 E1
Downsway Ct SG8 7 C6
Downton Ct 2 LU3 63 D8
Downview LU4 44 B2
Dowry Wlk WD1 153 F1
Drakes Cl EN8 148 D3
Drakes Dr Northwood HA6 174 B2
St Albans AL1 128 C1
Stevenage SG2 51 B7
Drakes Mdw CM17 118 E4
Drakes Way AL10 130 B3
Drapers Mews LU3 45 C1
Drapers Way SG1 50 C7
Drayman's Cl CM23 76 B5
Drayson Cl EN9 163 E7
Drayton Ave EN6 158 E7
Drayton Rd
Borehamwood WD6 170 A5
Luton LU4 44 A3
Driftway SG8 16 E4
Driftway The HP2 124 F3
Driftwood Ave AL2 141 B5
Drive The Barnet EN5 171 E6
Brookmans Park AL9 145 B6
Cheshunt EN7 148 B3
Goff's Oak EN7 147 B3
Harlow CM20 117 E1
Harpenden AL5 86 A1
Hertford SG14 113 C8
Hoddesdon EN11 135 A8
Kimpton AL4 87 B7
London Colney AL2 142 A5
Northwood HA6 174 E2
Oaklands AL6 69 A1
Potters Bar EN6 158 F7
Radlett WD7 156 A5
Rickmansworth WD3 165 C3
Sawbridgeworth CM21 97 E2
Watford WD1 153 E2
Driver's End La SG4,SG3 68 A4
Driveway The Cuffley EN6 146 E3
Hemel Hempstead HP1 124 B1
Dromey Gdns HA3 176 F3
Drop La AL2 155 C7
Drovers Way
Bishop's Stortford CM23 76 C5
Hatfield AL10 130 B8
St Albans AL1 127 D3
Drummond Dr HA7 176 F3
Drummond Ride HP23 100 A5
Drummonds The LU4 44 C2
Drury La SG12 95 E1
Drycroft AL7 110 E2
Dryden Cres SG2 51 C8
Dryden Rd HA3 176 F2
Drysdale Cl HA6 174 E3
Dubbs Knoll Rd SG8 1 F5
Dubrae Cl AL3 127 A1
Duchess Cl CM23 76 C7
Duchy Rd EN4 159 D1
Duck La SG2 52 E4
Duck's Hill Rd HA6 174 B1
Ducketts La SG10 75 D1
Ducketts Mead CM19 116 B1
Ducketts Wharf 10 CM23 76 F6
Ducketts Wood SG12 93 E6
Duckling La CM21 97 E2
Duckmore La HP23 99 E2
Dudley Ave EN8 162 D7
Dudley Hill Cl AL6 89 E8
Dudley St LU2 63 E8
Dudswell La HP4 121 D7
Dugdale Ct SG5 21 C1
Dugdale Hill La EN6 158 E7
Dugdales WD3 166 A5
Duke St Hoddesdon EN11 135 A7
Luton LU2 63 E8
Watford WD1 167 C6
Duke's La SG5 34 F8
Dukes Ave LU6 81 E8
Dukes Ct 4 LU1 63 D6
Dukes Ride
Bishop's Stortford CM23 76 C7
13 Luton LU2 45 D1
Dukes Way HP4 122 A6
Dulwich Way WD3 166 A4
Dumbarton Ave EN8 162 D5
Dumfries Cl WD1 175 A7
Dumfries Ct 8 LU1 63 D6
Dumfries St LU1 63 D6
Duncan Cl AL7 110 E5
Duncan Ct AL1 127 F1
Duncan Way WD2 167 F7
Duncombe Cl
Hertford SG14 113 C8
Luton LU3 45 C6
Duncombe Rd
Berkhamsted HP4 121 E6
Hertford SG14 113 C8
Duncombe Sch SG14 113 C7
Duncots Cl SG5 21 E3
Dundale Prim Sch HP23 100 A5
Dundale Rd HP23 100 A4
Dunfermline Ho WD1 175 C7
Dunhams La SG6 23 C6
Dunkirks Mews SG13 113 D4
Dunlin SG6 11 E1
Dunlin Rd HP2 124 E8
Dunmow Ct LU3 45 D2
Dunmow Rd CM23 77 C7
Dunn Cl SG1 50 E3
Dunnock Cl WD6 170 A5
Dunny La WD4 151 F7
Dunsby Rd LU3 45 A6
Dunsford Ct 4 HA5 175 F3
Dunsley Pl HP23 100 B3
Dunsmore Cl WD2 168 D3
Dunsmore Rd LU1 63 C6
Dunsmore Way WD2 168 D3
Dunstable Cl LU4 45 A1
Dunstable Ct LU4 44 F2
Dunstable Pl 5 LU1 63 D7
Dunstable Rd
Caddington LU1 62 C3
Dagnall AL3 81 C7
Luton LU1,LU4 45 F2
Redbourn AL3 106 A7
Studham LU6 82 B6
Dunster Cl Barnet EN5 171 D5
Harefield UB9 173 B2
Dunster Ct WD6 170 D6
Dunster Rd HP2 105 B1
Dunsters Mead AL7 111 B4
Dunston Hill HP23 100 A4
Durban Rd E WD1 167 A5
Durban Rd W WD1 167 A5
Durbar Rd LU4 45 B1
Durham Cl
Sawbridgeworth CM21 97 C1
Stanstead Abbotts SG12 115 B5
Durham Rd
Borehamwood WD6 170 C6
Luton LU2 64 A7
Stevenage SG1 37 A1
Durley Gdns LU1 63 D5
Durrant Ct HA3 176 E2
Durrants Dr WD3 166 C5
Durrants Hill Rd HP3 138 D8
Durrants La HP4 121 F5
Durrants Rd HP4 121 F5
Dury Rd EN5 171 F7
Duxford Cl LU3 45 B7
Duxons Turn HP2 125 B4
Dwight Rd WD1 166 D2
Dyer Ct EN3 163 A2
Dyes La SG4 49 F3
Dyke La AL4 108 E7
Dylan Cl WD6 169 D2
Dymoke Gn AL4 128 A7
Dymokes Way EN11 115 A1
Dyrham La EN5 158 A3
Dyson Ct WD1 167 C5
Dysons Cl EN8 162 D6

E

Eagle Centre Way LU4 44 B7
Eagle Cl LU4 44 A4
Eagle Ct Baldock SG7 12 E1
Hertford SG13 114 B7
Eagle Way AL10 130 A3
Ealing Cl WD6 170 D8
Earl St WD1 167 C6
Earls Cl CM23 76 D6
Earls Hill Gdns SG8 7 C6
Earls La EN6 157 F6
Earls Meade LU2 45 D1
Earlsmead SG6 22 F3
Easington Rd SG12 71 E7
Easingwold Gdns LU1 62 F8
East Burrowfield AL7 110 D4
East Cl Chiswellgreen AL2 141 B6
Hitchin SG4 22 B1
Stevenage SG1 50 F5
East Comm
Harpenden AL5 107 C7
Redbourn AL3 106 A4
East Dr London Colney AL2 142 B5
Moor Park WD1 174 E8
Sawbridgeworth CM21 97 E1
St Albans AL4 128 F4
Watford WD2 154 B3
East End Way HA5 175 F1
East Flint HP1 123 F4
East Gate CM20 117 D1
East Gn HP3 139 A6
East Herts Hospl SG13 114 A7
East Hill LU3 45 B6
East La
Abbots Langley WD5 140 A2
Wheathampstead AL4 87 D1
East Lodge La EN2 160 E4
East Mead AL7 111 B3
East Mimms 4 HP2 124 E4
East Mount AL4 87 D1
East Pk Harlow CM17 118 C3
Sawbridgeworth CM21 97 E1
East Rd
Bishop's Stortford CM23 77 B7
Enfield EN3 162 C1
Harlow CM20 118 B4
East Reach SG2 51 A2
East Ridgeway EN6 146 E3
East Riding AL6 90 D5
East St
Hemel Hempstead HP2 124 D3
Lilley LU2 32 D2
Ware SG12 93 D1
East View Barnet EN5 171 F6
Essendon AL9 131 F6
St Ippolyts SG4 35 C2
East Wlk CM20 117 D1
Eastbourne Ave SG1 50 A6
Eastbrook Prim Sch
HP2 125 A8
Eastbrook Rd EN9 163 E6
Eastbrook Way HP2 124 E3
Eastbury Ave HA6 174 F5
Eastbury Cl HA6 174 E5
Eastbury Ct St Albans AL1 127 F4
Watford WD1 167 C2
Eastbury Farm
Jun Mix Inf Sch HA6 174 F6
Eastbury Pl HA6 174 F5
Eastbury Rd
Northwood HA6 174 E4
Watford WD1 167 C3
Eastcheap SG6 22 F6
Eastcote Dr AL5 107 D6
Eastcott Cl LU2 46 D1
Eastern Ave Cheshunt EN8 162 F6
Henlow SG16 10 C3
Eastern Way SG6 12 A1
Eastfield Ave WD2 167 D8
Eastfield Cl LU2 46 C4
Eastfield Ct AL4 128 D6
Eastfield Prim Sch EN3 162 D1
Eastfield Rd
Cheshunt EN8 162 F7
Enfield EN3 162 D1
Royston SG8 7 E6
Eastgate SG1 50 D5
Eastglade HA6 174 F5
Easthall Ho SG1 36 C1
Eastham Cl EN5 171 F4
Eastholm SG6 23 A8
Eastholm Gn SG6 23 A8
Eastlea Ave WD2 154 E2
Eastman Way HP2 125 A6
Eastmoor Ct AL5 107 C6
Eastmoor Pk AL5 107 C6
Eastnor HP3 137 A3
Easton Gdns WD6 170 E5
Eastor AL7 90 A1
Eastwick Cres WD3 172 F8
Eastwick Hall La CM20 117 A5
Eastwick Rd
Eastwick CM20 117 B4
Gilston CM20 117 E6
Eastwick Row HP2 125 A2
Eastwood Ct HP2 125 A4
Eaton Gate HA6 174 C4
Eaton Green Rd LU2 64 D8
Eaton Ho 5 CM23 77 B8
Eaton Pl LU2 46 D1
Eaton Rd
Hemel Hempstead HP2 125 B6
St Albans AL1 128 B3
Eaton Valley Rd LU2 64 B8
Ebberns Rd HP3 138 E8
Ebenezer St 6 LU1 63 D6
Ebury App WD3 165 D1
Ebury Cl HA6 174 C5
Ebury Ct WD3 165 D1
Ebury Rd
Rickmansworth WD3 165 D1
Watford WD1 167 C6
Echo Hill SG8 7 C5
Eddy St HP4 122 A5
Eden Cl EN3 163 A2
Edenhall Cl HP2 125 D2
Edens Cl CM23 77 B7
Edens Mount CM21 97 F4
Edgars Ct AL7 110 E5
Edgbaston Dr WD7 156 E7
Edgbaston Rd WD1 175 B7
Edgcott Cl LU3 31 B1
Edgecote Cl LU1 62 E3
Edgehill Gdns LU3 44 C8
Edgewood Dr LU2 46 C6
Edgeworth Cl SG2 51 C1
Edgware Way HA8 169 D1
Edgwarebury La
WD6,HA8 169 F1
Edinburgh Ave WD3 165 A2
Edinburgh Cres EN8 162 E6
Edinburgh Dr WD5 154 A7
Edinburgh Gdns CM23 76 E6
Edinburgh Pl CM20 118 A4
Edinburgh Way CM20 117 E3
Edison Cl AL4 128 C2
Edison Rd SG2 51 B6
Edkins Cl LU2 45 E5
Edlyn Cl HP4 121 F5
Edmonds Dr SG2 51 D4
Edmund Beaufort Dr
AL3 127 E5
Edmunds Rd SG14 112 F7
Edridge Cl WD2 168 C4
Edulf Rd WD6 170 B8
Edward Amey Cl WD2 154 C3
Edward Cl
Abbots Langley WD5 153 F7
St Albans AL1 127 F2
Edward Ct
Hemel Hempstead HP3 138 D7
Waltham Abbey EN9 163 F6
Edward St LU2 45 F1
Edwards Ho 5 SG1 50 E6
Edwick Ct EN8 148 D2
Edwin Ware Ct 2 HA5 175 C1
Edwinstree CE Sch SG9 40 D8
Edwyn Cl EN5 171 D3
Egdon Dr LU2 45 D6
Egerton Rd HP4 122 B6
Egerton-Rothesay
Mid & Upper Sch HP4 121 E4
Eight Acres HP23 100 A4
Eighth Ave LU3 44 D7
Eisenberg Cl SG7 13 B1
Elaine Gdns LU1 63 A1
Elbow La
Hertford Heath SG13 134 B7
Stevenage SG2 51 B1
Eldefield SG6 22 D7
Elder Ct WD2 176 E8
Elder Rd SG12 93 F3
Elder Way SG1 50 E3
Elderbeck Cl EN7 148 A2
Elderberry Cl LU2 46 B4
Elderberry Dr SG4 35 A4
Elderberry Way WD2 154 B4
Elderfield CM17 118 D4
Eldon Ave WD6 170 B7
Eldon Rd Hoddesdon EN11 135 D4
Luton LU4 44 C1
Eleanor Ave AL3 127 D5
Eleanor Cross Rd EN8 162 F5
Eleanor Gdns EN5 171 D4
Eleanor Rd Cheshunt EN8 162 E6
Hertford SG14 113 C7
Eleanor Way EN8 162 F5
Electric Ave EN3 162 F3
Elfrida Rd WD1 167 C4
Elgar Cl WD6 169 D2
Elgar Path LU2 63 E8
Elgin Dr HA6 174 E3
Elgin Ho SG4 35 A6
Elgin Rd Cheshunt EN8 148 C1
Hoddesdon EN10 148 F8
Elgood Ave HA6 175 A3
Eliot Pl WD3 165 E1
Eliot Rd Royston SG8 7 D8
Stevenage SG2 51 C6
Elizabeth Cl Barnet EN5 171 D6
Lower Nazeing EN9 149 D8
Welwyn Garden City AL7 111 C6
Elizabeth Ct 9 Luton LU1 63 D6
St Albans AL4 128 D6
Watford WD1 153 F1
Elizabeth Dr HP23 100 B6
Elizabeth Ho
7 Watford WD1 167 C7
Welwyn Garden City AL7 111 C6
Elizabeth Rd CM23 76 E5
Elizabeth St LU1 63 D6
Elizabeth Way CM20 117 B2
Ellen Cl HP2 124 F4
Ellen Friend Ho CM23 77 B6
Ellenborough Cl CM23 76 D5
Ellenbrook Cl WD2 167 C8
Ellenbrook Cres AL10 129 D5
Ellenbrook La AL10 129 D4
Ellenhall Cl LU3 45 C1
Ellerdine Cl LU3 45 B4
Ellesborough Cl WD1 175 C5
Ellesfield AL6 89 B5
Ellesmere Gr EN5 171 F4
Ellesmere Rd HP4 122 D4
Ellice SG6 23 B4
Ellingham Cl HP2 125 A5
Ellingham Rd HP2 124 F4
Elliott Cl AL7 110 D3
Ellis Ave SG1 50 E8
Elliswick Rd AL5 86 B2
Ells Ct LU2 45 F1
Ellwood Gdns WD2 154 C5
Elm Ave Caddington LU1 62 E3
Watford WD1 167 E2
Elm Cl EN9 163 D5
Elm Dr Cheshunt EN8 148 E3
Hatfield AL10 130 A4
St Albans AL4 128 C3
Elm Gdns Enfield EN2 161 D1
Welwyn Garden City AL8 110 B6
Elm Gn HP1 123 E5
Elm Gr Berkhamsted HP4 122 C4
Bishop's Stortford CM23 77 B7
Watford WD2 154 A2
Elm Hatch HA5 175 F3
Elm Park Rd HA5 175 D1
Elm Pk SG7 23 F8
Elm Rd Barnet EN5 171 F5
Bishop's Stortford CM23 76 F8
Elm Terr HA3 176 D2
Elm Tree Wlk
Chorleywood WD3 164 F5
Tring HP23 100 A5
Elm Way WD3 165 B1
Elm Wlk Radlett WD7 155 F3
Royston SG8 7 F7
Stevenage SG2 51 B3
Elmbank Ave EN5 171 C5
Elmbridge CM17 118 F3
Elmbrook Dr CM23 76 E3
Elmcote HA5 175 D1
Elmcote Way WD3 165 F3
Elmfield Cl EN6 158 E6
Elmfield Ct LU2 46 A1
Elmfield Rd EN6 158 E6
Elmhurst EN10 135 A4
Elmhurst Cl WD2 167 E5
Elmhurst Rd EN3 162 C2
Elmoor Ave AL6 89 B5
Elmoor Cl AL6 89 B4
Elmore Rd Enfield EN3 162 D1
Luton LU2 46 A1
Elmroyd Ave EN6 158 F6
Elmroyd Cl EN6 158 F6
Elms Cl SG4 35 E3
Elms Rd Harrow HA3 176 E3
Ware SG12 94 A2
Elms The Codicote SG4 67 F2
Hertford SG13 114 A6
Stevenage SG2 69 B8
Elmscroft Gdns EN6 158 F7
Elmside LU6 82 E8
Elmside Wlk SG5 34 E7
Elmtree Ave LU2 46 E3
Elmwood
Sawbridgeworth CM21 97 F1
Welwyn Garden City AL8 110 B5
Elmwood Ave Baldock SG7 23 F7
Borehamwood WD6 170 B5
Elmwood Cres LU2 45 E3
Elmwood Ct SG7 23 F8
Elsinge Rd EN1 162 C3
Elstree Distribution Pk
WD6 170 D6
Elstree Hill N WD6 169 D4
Elstree Hill S WD6 169 D2
Elstree Rd Bushey WD2 168 E2
Elstree WD6 169 A3
Hemel Hempstead HP2 105 A1
Elstree Sta WD6 170 A5
Elstree Studios WD6 170 B6
Elstree Way WD6 170 C7
Elton Ave EN5 171 F4
Elton Ct SG14 113 C7
Elton Pk WD1 167 B7
Elton Rd SG14 113 C7
Elton Way WD2 168 B7
Elvaston Ct EN5 171 C4
Elveden Cl LU2 45 E6
Elvington Gdns LU3 31 B1
Ely Cl Hatfield AL10 129 F6
Stevenage SG1 37 B1
Ely Gdns WD6 170 D4
Ely Rd AL1 128 B2
Ely Way LU4 44 D4
Embleton Rd WD1 175 A7
Emerald Ct WD6 156 F1
Emerald Rd LU4 44 A3
Emerton Ct HP4 121 E7
Emerton Garth HP4 121 E7
Emma Rothschild Ct
HP23 100 A5
Emma's Cres SG12 115 B4
Emmanuel Lodge EN8 148 C1
Emmanuel Rd HA6 174 F3
Emmer Gn LU2 46 F2
Emmitt Cl WD7 156 E6
Emperor Cl HP4 121 F7
Emperors Gate SG2 51 D8
Empire Ctr WD2 167 C8
Empress Rd LU3 44 E4
Endeavour Rd EN8 148 E4
Enderby Rd LU3 45 C6
Enderley Cl HA3 176 E2
Enderley Rd HA3 176 E2
Endersby Rd EN5 171 C4
Endymion Ct AL10 130 C6
Endymion Mews AL10 130 C6
Endymion Rd AL10 130 C6
Enfield Cty Lower Sch
EN2 161 E1
Enfield Lock Sta EN3 162 E2
Englefield LU2 45 F3
Englehurst AL5 86 D1
Enid Cl AL2 154 F8
Enjakes Cl SG2 69 B7
Ennerdale Cl AL1 128 B1
Ennis Cl AL5 107 D6
Ennismore Cl SG6 23 C3
Ennismore Gn LU2 46 F1
Enslow Cl LU1 62 E3
Enterprise Ctr 1 LU2 63 F8
Enterprise Ctr The SG1 50 B8
Enterprise Pk SG4 66 C2
Enterprise Way
Hemel Hempstead HP2 125 C5
Luton LU3 45 B8
Enville Ho WD1 175 C7
Epping Forest District
Mus EN9 163 C6
Epping Gn HP2 125 B8
Epping Way LU3 44 C8
Epsom Ct WD3 165 B1
Ereswell Rd LU3 45 A7
Erin Cl LU4 45 A2
Erin Ct LU4 45 A2
Ermine Cl Cheshunt EN7 162 B8
Royston SG8 7 D8
St Albans AL3 127 A2
Ermine Ct SG9 40 E8
Ermine Pl 8 LU2 45 D1
Ermine Point Bsns Pk
SG12 93 B3
Ermine St SG12 93 D7
Erskine Ho WD1 175 D7
Escarpment Ave HP4,LU6 81 D8
Escot Way EN5 171 C4
Esdaile La EN11 135 A5
Eskdale London Colney AL2 142 F4
Luton LU4 44 C5
Eskdale Ct 3 HP2 124 E6
Essendon CE Prim Sch
AL9 131 F6
Essendon Gdns AL7 110 F6
Essendon Hill AL9 131 E6
Essex Cl LU1 63 F6
Essex Ct 7 LU1 63 E6
Essex La WD4 153 D6
Essex Mead HP2 105 A1
Essex Rd
Borehamwood WD6 170 A6
Hoddesdon EN11 135 C6
Stevenage SG1 50 B8
Watford WD1 167 B7
Essex St AL1 127 E4
Estcourt Rd WD1 167 C6
Estfeld Cl EN11 115 B1
Ethelred Cl AL7 110 F5
Etna Rd AL3 127 D4
Eton Ho 9 WD1 167 C7
Etonbury Mid Sch SG15 11 C7
Europa Rd HP2 124 F6
Euston Ave WD1 166 F4
Evan's Cl WD3 166 A4

Evans Ave WD2 153 F4
Evans Gr AL4 128 C7
Evans Way HP23 100 B4
Evedon Cl LU3 44 F6
Evelyn Dr HA5 175 D3
Evelyn Rd LU5 44 A1
Evensyde WD1 166 D3
Everard Cl AL1 127 D1
Everest Cl SG15 11 B5
Everest Way HP2 125 A3
Everett Cl Bushey WD2 168 E1
Hammond Street EN7 147 C6
Everett Ct WD7 156 A5
Evergreen Cl SG3 69 A2
Evergreen Rd SG12 93 F3
Evergreen Way LU3 45 A8
Evergreen Wlk 2 HP3 124 E1
Everlasting La AL3 127 C5
Eversden Ct HP2 105 B1
Eversley Lodge EN11 135 A6
Evron Pl 4 SG14 113 D6
Exchange Rd
Stevenage SG1 50 F5
Watford WD1 167 B5
Executive Pk Ind Est AL1 128 B3
Exeter Cl Stevenage SG1 37 B2
Watford WD1 167 C7
Explorer Dr WD1 166 F3
Extension Rd SG13 113 F6
Exton Ave LU2 46 A1
Eynsford Ct SG4 34 F6
Eynsford Rd LU4 44 D3
Eywood Rd AL1 127 C1

F

Faggots Cl WD7 156 C4
Faints Cl EN7 147 F2
Fair Cl WD2 168 B2
Fair Oak Ct LU2 45 F3
Fair Oak Dr LU2 45 F3
Fair View EN6 145 B2
Fairacre HP3 138 F7
Fairacre Ct HA6 174 E3
Fairacres Cl EN6 158 F6
Fairburn Cl WD6 170 A8
Faircross Ho 6 WD1 167 B6
Faircross Way AL1 128 A5
Fairfax Ave LU3 44 D7
Fairfax Rd SG13 113 F7
Fairfield Buntingford SG9 40 F6
Northwood HA6 175 A1
Fairfield Ave WD1 175 D7
Fairfield Cl Harpenden AL5 86 D1
Hatfield AL10 130 C8
Radlett WD7 155 E2
Fairfield Dr EN10 148 F7
Fairfield Hospl SG5 11 C2
Fairfield Jun Sch WD7 155 E3
Fairfield Rd EN11 135 A8
Fairfield Way SG4 35 D8
Fairfield Wlk EN8 148 E3
Fairfields Prim Sch EN7 148 A4
Fairfolds WD2 154 E4
Fairford Ave LU2 45 E4
Fairgreen Rd LU1 62 F3
Fairhaven AL2 141 D4
Fairhaven Cres WD1 175 A7
Fairhill HP3 138 F7
Fairlands Jun Mix Inf Sch
SG1 50 D6
Fairlands Lo WD6 170 A5
Fairlands Way SG1 51 A7
Fairlawns Pinner WD1 175 D1
Watford WD1 153 F1
Fairley Way EN7 148 B3
Fairmead Ave AL5 107 C8
Fairseat Cl WD2 176 E8
Fairshot Ct AL4 108 D2
Fairthorn Cl HP23 99 E3
Fairview Dr WD1 153 E3
Fairview Est EN11 135 C7
Fairview Rd SG1 50 B7
Fairway
Bishop's Stortford CM23 77 C6
Hemel Hempstead HP3 138 F7
Sawbridgeworth CM21 97 F2
Ware SG12 114 C8
Fairway Ave WD6 170 B7
Fairway Cl
Chiswellgreen AL2 141 C4
Harpenden AL5 107 A5
Fairway Ho WD6 170 B6
Fairway The
Abbots Langley WD5 153 D7
Moor Park HA6 174 E6
Fairways Cheshunt EN8 148 D5
Waltham Abbey EN9 163 E5
Faithfield WD1 167 E3
Falcon Cl Hatfield AL10 130 A3
Northwood HA6 174 E3
Sawbridgeworth CM21 97 C1
Stevenage SG2 51 D2
Falcon Ct 2 SG12 93 C3
Falcon Ridge HP4 122 C3
Falcon Way Watford WD2 154 E5
Welwyn Garden City AL7 110 E8
Falconer Rd WD2 168 A3
Falconer Sch WD2 168 A4
Falconer St CM23 76 C5
Falconers Field AL5 85 E3
Falconers Pk CM21 97 D1
Falconers Rd LU2 46 B1
Falkirk Gdns WD1 175 D5
Falkland Rd EN5 171 E7
Fallow Rise SG13 113 F6
Fallowfield Luton LU3 45 C4
Stevenage SG2 51 C3
Welwyn Garden City AL7 89 F1
Fallowfield Cl UB9 173 C2
Fallowfield Wlk HP1 124 A6
Fallows Gn AL5 86 B3
Falstaff Gdns AL1 141 C8
Falstone Gn LU2 46 E1
Fanhams Hall Rd SG12 93 F3
Fanhams Rd SG12 93 E2
Fanshaw Ct SG14 113 C7
Fanshawe Cres SG12 93 C2
Fanshawe St SG14 113 B7
Fanshaws La SG13 133 C5
Fantail La HP23 99 F4
Far End AL10 130 B2
Faraday Cl Luton LU4 44 C1
Watford WD1 166 D3
Faraday Rd SG2 51 B6
Faringdon Rd LU4 44 C3
Faringford Cl EN6 159 D8
Farland Rd HP2 125 B3
Farley Ct LU1 63 C5
Farley Farm Rd LU1 63 B5
Farley Hill LU1 63 C5
Farley Jun Sch LU1 63 C6
Farley Lodge LU1 63 D5
Farm Ave AL5 85 D4
Farm Cl Barnet EN5 171 C4
Borehamwood WD6 156 E1
Cheshunt EN8 148 C1
Cuffley EN6 146 E4
Hertford SG14 113 A6
Letchworth SG6 12 A1
Roydon CM19 116 B1
Stevenage SG1 50 E4
Welwyn Garden City AL8 110 C6
Farm Gn LU1 63 C5
Farm Hill Rd EN9 163 D6
Farm La
Rickmansworth WD3 165 C6
Standon SG11 73 A8
Farm Pl HP4 121 F5
Farm Rd Harpenden LU1 85 B7
Little Chalfont WD3 164 A5
Northwood HA6 174 C5
St Albans AL1 128 B4
Farm Way Bushey WD2 168 B5
Moor Park HA6 174 F6
Farmbrook LU2 45 D7
Farmers Cl WD2 154 B6
Farmhouse Cl EN10 148 F6
Farmhouse La HP2 125 A5
Farmstead Rd HA3 176 D1
Farne Ho 5 WD1 166 F3
Farnham CE Prim Sch
CM23 58 D6
Farnham Cl
Bovingdon HP3 137 A3
Sawbridgeworth CM21 97 C1
Farnham Rd CM23 58 F3
Farquhar St SG14 113 C7
Farr's La LU2 65 B1
Farraline Rd WD1 167 B5
Farrant Way WD6 169 E8
Farrer Top AL3 83 E5
Farriday Cl AL3 127 E7
Farriers SG12 115 A6
Farriers Cl Baldock SG7 12 E1
Codicote SG4 67 F1
Farriers End EN10 148 F5
Farriers Way WD6 170 D4
Farringford Cl AL2 141 B5
Farrington Pl HA6 174 F6
Farrow Cl LU3 31 C1
Farthing Dr SG6 23 C3
Farthings The HP1 124 B3
Faulkner Ct AL1 127 E5
Faverolle Gn EN8 148 D3
Faversham Cl HP23 100 A4
Fawbert & Barnard Inf Sch
CM21 97 E2
Fawbert & Barnard Sch
CM17 118 C3
Fawcett Rd SG2 51 B7
Fawkon Wlk EN11 135 A6
Fawn Ct AL9 130 C7
Fay Gn WD5 153 D6
Fayerfield EN6 159 D8
Fayland Cotts SG9 41 E7
Feacey Down HP1 124 B5
Fearney Mead WD3 165 A1
Fearnhill Sch SG6 22 C5
Fearnley Rd AL8 110 C5
Fearnley St WD1 167 B5
Feather Dell AL10 130 A5
Featherbed La HP3 138 B7
Featherston Rd SG2 51 C3
Featherstone Gdns
WD6 170 C5
Federal Way WD2 167 C8
Felbrigg Cl LU2 46 F2
Felden Cl Pinner HA5 175 E3
Watford WD2 154 D5
Felden Dr HP3 138 A7
Felden La HP3 138 A7
Felix Ave LU2 46 A2
Fellowes La AL4 143 E8
Fellowes Way SG2 51 A2
Fells Cl SG5 34 F8
Felmersham Ct LU1 63 B7
Felmersham Rd LU1 63 A7
Felmongers CM20 118 B2
Felstead Cl LU2 45 F3
Felstead Rd EN8 162 E7
Felstead Way LU2 45 F3
Felton Cl
Borehamwood WD6 156 E1
Cheshunt EN10 148 F6
Luton LU2 46 D1
Fen End SG5 11 F8
Fennycroft Rd HP1 124 A6
Fensom's Alley HP2 124 D4
Fensom's Cl HP2 124 D4
Fenwick Cl LU3 45 B5
Ferguson Gr EN8 148 D2
Fermor Cres LU2 46 C1
Fern Cl EN10 148 F8
Fern Dells AL10 129 F4
Fern Dr HP3 124 E2
Fern Gr AL8 89 D2
Fern Way WD2 154 B4
Ferndale 7 Harpenden AL5 86 A2
Much Hadham SG10 74 F2
Ferndale Rd Enfield EN3 162 E2
Luton LU1 63 B7
Ferndene AL2 154 F8
Ferndown HA6 175 A1
Ferndown Cl HA5 175 E3
Ferndown Rd WD1 175 C6
Fernecroft AL1 141 D8
Fernheath LU3 31 A1
Fernhills WD4 153 D6
Fernleigh Ct HA2 176 B1
Fernleys AL4 128 C5
Ferns Cl EN3 162 E3
Fernville La HP2 124 D3
Ferny Hill EN4 159 F1
Ferrars Cl LU4 44 B1
Ferrars Inf Sch LU4 44 B3
Ferrars Jun Sch LU4 44 B3
Ferrers La AL4 108 B5
Ferrier Rd SG2 51 C6
Ferryhills Cl WD1 175 C7
Feryngs Cl CM17 118 D4
Fesants Croft CM20 118 B3
Fetherstone Cl EN6 159 D7
Fiddle Bridge La AL10 129 F6
Fiddlebridge Ind Ctr
AL10 129 F6
Fidler Pl WD2 168 B3
Field Cl Harpenden AL5 107 D7
St Albans AL4 128 A7
Field Cres SG8 7 F7
Field End Cl Luton LU2 46 C4
Watford WD1 167 E2
Wigginton HP23 100 D1
Field Fare Gn LU4 44 A5
Field Inf Sch WD1 167 C4
Field La SG6 22 F4
Field Rd
Hemel Hempstead HP2 125 A3
Watford WD1 167 E3
Field View EN5 171 B5
Field View Rd EN6 159 A6
Field View Rise AL2 140 E2
Field Way Bovingdon HP3 137 A4
Hoddesdon EN11 115 C2
Rickmansworth WD3 165 B1
Field's Ct EN6 159 D6
Fielder Ctr
(Univ of Herts) AL10 129 D8
Fielders Way WD7 156 E6
Fieldfare Letchworth SG6 11 E1
Stevenage SG2 51 D3
Fieldfares AL2 142 D4
Fieldgate Ho SG1 50 F5
Fieldgate Rd LU4 44 D2
Fieldings Rd EN8 148 F2
Fields End HP23 100 A6
Fields End La HP1 123 E5
Fieldway
Berkhamsted HP4 122 E2
Stanstead Abbotts SG12 115 B4
Wigginton HP23 100 D1
Fifth Ave Letchworth SG6 23 C6
Watford WD2 154 D4
Fifth Avenue / Allende
Ave CM20 117 C3
Figtree Hill HP2 124 D4
Filey Cl SG1 50 A7
Filmer Rd LU4 44 E4
Filton Ho WD1 175 D7
Finch Cl Hatfield AL10 130 A3
Luton LU4 44 A4
Finch Gn WD3 164 F5
Finch La WD2 168 A5
Finch Rd HP4 122 A4
Finchdale HP1 124 A3
Finche's End SG2 52 B8
Finches The
Hertford SG13 114 B6
Hitchin SG4 35 A7
Finley Rd AL5 86 D3
Finsbury Ct EN8 162 E5
Finsbury Rd LU4 44 D5
Finucane Rise WD2 176 C8
Finway LU1 63 A8
Finway Ct WD1 166 F4
Finway Rd HP2 125 B7
Fir Cl SG2 50 F1
Fir Tree Cl HP3 125 B2
Fir Tree Ct WD6 169 F5
Fir Tree Hill WD3 153 A2
Firbank Dr WD1 167 E2
Firbank Rd AL3 127 F7
Firbank Trad Est LU1 63 A8
Fire Station Alley EN5 171 E7
Firecrest SG6 11 E1
Firlands CM23 76 E6
Firlands Ho CM23 76 E6
Firs Cl Hatfield AL10 130 B4
Hitchin SG5 34 D8
Firs Dr AL4 87 C5
Firs Jun & Mid Sch The
CM23 76 E6
Firs La EN6 159 B6
Firs The
Hammond Street EN7 147 E4
Harpenden AL5 86 D2
St Albans AL1 142 B7
Welwyn Garden City AL8 89 C2
Wigginton HP23 100 D1
Firs Wlk Northwood HA6 174 D4
Tewin AL6 90 E5
Firs Wood Cl EN6 159 F7
First Ave WD2 154 D4
First Avenue / Mandela
Ave CM20 117 F2
First Garden City
Heritage Mus SG6 23 A5
Firthesden Vinyard HP4 123 B8
Firway AL6 89 F7
Firway Cl AL6 89 F7
Firwood Ave AL4 128 E3
Fish Farm St AL3 106 B5
Fish Hill SG8 7 D6
Fish St AL3 106 B5
Fisher Cl Holdbrook EN3 163 A2
Kings Langley WD4 139 A2
Fisher Rd HA3 176 F1
Fisher's Green Rd SG1 50 B8
Fisher's Ind Est WD1 167 C4
Fishermans Way EN11 135 D8
Fishers Cl Holdbrook EN8 163 A5
Standon SG11 55 D3
Fishers Gn SG1 36 A1
Fishers Hatch CM20 117 E1
Fishers Mead SG11 55 D3
Fishery Cotts HP1 124 A1
Fishery Rd HP1 124 A1
Fishponds Rd SG5 34 E8
Fishpool St AL3 127 C3
Fitzjohn Ave EN5 171 F5
Fitzroy Ave LU3 45 B3
Fitzwarin Cl LU3 44 E8
Fitzwilliams Ct CM17 118 E4
Five Acres
Kings Langley WD4 138 F2
London Colney AL2 142 D6
Stansted Mountfitchet CM24 59 E8
Five Acres Ave AL2 140 F2
Five Fields Cl WD1 175 F7
Five Oaks Caddington LU1 62 F4
Hatfield AL10 130 B2
Five Oaks Mid Sch LU1 62 F3
Five Oaks Prim Sch
AL10 130 A3
Five Springs LU3 44 E6
Five Springs Ct LU3 44 E6
Five Springs Sch LU3 44 F7
Flags The HP2 125 B3
Flagstaff Cl EN9 163 B6
Flagstaff Rd EN9 163 B6
Flamstead End
Jun Mix Inf Sch EN7 148 A4
Flamstead End Rd EN8 148 B3
Flamstead
Jun Mix Inf Sch AL3 84 B1
Flamsteadbury La AL3 106 A4
Flash La EN2 161 C3
Flatfield Rd HP3 125 A1
Flaunden Bottom HP5 150 E4
Flaunden Hill HP3 151 A6
Flaunden Ho WD1 166 E2
Flaunden La HP3 137 D3
Flavian Cl AL3 126 F1
Flax Mews AL3 83 E5
Flecker Cl HA7 176 F5
Fleet The SG8 7 C6
Fleetville Inf Sch AL1 128 B3
Fleetville Jun Mix Sch
AL1 128 A3
Fleetwood SG6 23 B4
Fleetwood Cres SG1 50 B7
Fleetwood Way WD1 175 C6
Fleming Cl EN7 148 A5
Fleming Cres SG14 113 A6
Fletcher Way HP2 124 D6
Flete Ho WD1 166 E3
Flexley Wood AL7 90 A1
Flinders Cl St Albans AL1 128 A1
Stevenage SG2 51 D5
Flint Cl LU3 44 E7
Flint Copse AL3 106 C6
Flint Ct LU1 63 D5
Flint Rd SG6 23 C8
Flint Way AL3 127 C7
Flintings The HP2 103 F8
Flora Gr AL1 127 F2
Floral Dr AL2 142 D5
Florence Ave LU3 44 D6
Florence Cl WD2 154 A4
Florence St SG5 34 F8
Florence Wlk 8 CM23 76 F8
Flowers Ind Est 11 LU1 63 E6
Flowers Way LU1 63 E7
Flowton Gr AL5 107 A7
Fold Croft CM20 117 A1
Foldingshott SG3 69 D3
Follett Dr WD5 153 F8
Folly Ave AL3 127 C4
Folly Cl Hitchin SG4 35 A5
Radlett WD7 155 F3
Folly Fields AL4 87 B2
Folly La Caddington LU1 62 E4
St Albans AL3 127 C4
Folly Pathway WD7 155 F3
Folly The Buntingford SG9 40 D7
Hertford SG14 113 D6
Folly View SG12 115 B4
Fontmell Cl AL3 127 E5
Fontwell Cl HA3 176 E3
Football Cl SG7 12 E1
Forbes Ave EN6 159 D7
Ford Cl WD2 168 C5
Ford Hill SG11 75 B8
Ford St SG11 55 E6
Fordham Cl SG7 4 D4
Fordham Rd SG8 7 E5
Fordhams Wood
(Nature Reserve) SG8 6 F4
Fordwich Cl SG14 113 A6
Fordwich Hill SG14 113 A6
Fordwich Rd AL8 110 C5
Fordwich Rise SG14 113 A6
Fore St Harlow CM17 118 C4
Hatfield AL9 130 C6
Hertford SG14 113 D6
Weston SG4 24 B1
Forebury Ave CM21 97 F2
Forebury Cres CM21 97 F2
Forebury The CM21 97 F2
Forefield AL2 141 A4
Forelands Pl CM21 97 E2
Forest Ave 5 HP3 124 D1
Forest Rd Cheshunt EN8 148 D2
Enfield EN3 162 E3
Watford WD2 154 B6
Forest Row SG2 50 F1
Forest Wlk WD2 167 F8
Foresters Cl EN7 147 E4
Foresthall Rd CM24 59 E4
Forfar Ho WD1 175 C7
Forge Cl Chipperfield WD4 152 A8
5 Hitchin SG5 34 F8
Forge Cotts Essendon AL9 131 E6
Hatfield Heath CM22 98 F3
Forge End AL2 141 A5
Forge La Northwood HA6 174 E3
Welwyn AL6 89 C5
Forres Cl EN11 135 A8
Forres Prim Sch EN11 115 B1
Forrest Cres LU2 46 A3
Forresters Dr AL7 111 C5
Fortnums Acre HA7 176 F4
Fortuna Cl SG1 51 C8
Fortune La WD6 169 D3
Forty Hall EN2 161 F2
Forty Hill EN2 161 F1
Forty Hill Prim Sch EN2 162 A2
Fosman Cl 7 SG5 34 D8
Foster Cl Cheshunt EN8 148 E1
Stevenage SG1 36 D1
Foster Dr SG4 35 A5
Foster Rd HP1 124 B1
Foston Cl LU3 44 F6
Fotherley Rd WD3 172 F8
Foulds Jun Mix Inf Sch
EN5 171 D6
Founceley Ave SG12 71 F8
Founders Rd EN11 115 B1
Fountain Ct EN8 148 D1
Fountain Dr SG13 113 F7
Fountain Pl EN9 163 C5
Fountains Rd LU3 45 D3
Four Acres Stevenage SG1 50 D7
Welwyn Garden City AL7 110 F4
Four Acres The CM21 98 A2
Four Limes AL4 108 D8
Four Swannes Prim Sch
EN8 162 E6
Four Tubs The WD2 168 D2
Fouracres SG6 23 A3
Fouracres Dr HP3 124 F1
Fouracres Wlk HP3 124 F1
Fourth Ave Harlow CM20 117 C1
Letchworth SG6 23 C7
Luton LU3 44 D7
Watford WD2 154 D4
Fourways Ct 1 EN11 135 A7
Fourways Market AL9 144 C7
Fovant SG1 36 B1
Fovant Cl AL5 107 C6
Fowley Cl EN8 162 F5
Fowlmere Rd SG8 9 F8
Fox Cl Bushey WD2 168 B5
Elstree WD6 169 D3
Wigginton HP23 100 D1
Fox Cnr SG8 1 F5
Fox Hill SG8 1 F5
Fox Hill Rd SG8 1 F5
Fox La SG8 15 F7
Fox Rd Stevenage SG1 50 E4
Wigginton HP23 100 C2
Fox's La AL9 144 F7
Foxbury Cl LU2 45 D6
Foxcroft AL1 128 A1
Foxdell HA6 174 D4
Foxdell Inf Sch LU1 63 A8
Foxdell Jun Sch LU1 62 E8
Foxdells SG14 112 C3
Foxdells La CM23 58 F2
Foxes Cl SG13 114 B6
Foxes Dr EN7 148 A2
Foxes La EN6 146 E3
Foxes Par EN9 163 C6
Foxfield SG2 51 C3
Foxfield Cl HA6 174 F4
Foxglove Bank SG8 7 F5
Foxglove Cl
Bishop's Stortford CM23 76 C6
Hatfield AL10 130 B4
Foxglove Way AL6 89 E8
Foxgloves The HP1 123 E2
Foxgrove Path WD1 175 D5
Foxhill Luton LU2 45 E5
Watford WD2 154 A3
Foxholes Ave SG13 113 F6
Foxhollows AL10 130 B7

Foxlands Cl WD2 . . . . .154 A5
Foxley Dr CM23 . . . . .77 B8
Foxley Gr AL6 . . . . .89 F4
Foxleys WD1 . . . . .175 E7
Foxton Rd EN11 . . . . .135 A6
Foxtree Ho WD2 . . . . .154 E3
Frampton Rd EN6 . . . . . . .145 C1
Frampton St SG14 . . . . . . .113 D6
Francis Ave AL3 . . . . .127 D6
Francis Bacon Sch AL1 . . . .142 B8
Francis Cl Hitchin SG4 . . . .35 A5
Stotfold SG5 . . . . .11 E6
Francis Combe Sch &
Com Coll 154 C7
Francis Ct Harlow CM20 . . .117 B2
St Albans AL1 . . . . .127 E2
Francis Green Ho EN9 . . . .163 B6
Francis Rd Hinxworth SG7 . .3 C6
Ware SG12 . . . . .93 D2
Watford WD1 . . . . .167 B5
Francis St LU1 . . . . .63 D8
Francis Wks EN11 . . . . . . .135 B6
Frank Martin Ct EN7 . . . . .148 B1
Frankland Cl WD3 . . . . . . .166 A2
Frankland Rd WD3 . . . . . .166 B3
Franklin Ave EN7 . . . . . . .148 B1
Franklin Cl
Colney Heath AL4 . . . . . . .129 E6
Hemel Hempstead HP3 . . . .138 E8
Pirton SG5 . . . . .20 D4
Franklin Gdns SG4 . . . . . .22 B1
Franklin Rd WD1 . . . . . . .167 B7
Franklin's Rd SG1 . . . . . . .50 C8
Franks Cl SG16 . . . . .10 B5
Franshams WD2 . . . . .176 D8
Fraser Rd EN6 . . . . .148 E3
Fred Millard Ct SG1 . . . . . .50 E1
Frederick St LU2 . . . . .45 E1
Frederick Street Pas LU2 . . .45 E1
Freeman Ave LU3 . . . . . . .45 B8
Freemans Cl SG5 . . . . . . .21 D1
Freewaters Cl SG5 . . . . . .21 E4
Freman Coll SG9 . . . . .40 D8
Freman Dr SG9 . . . . .40 D8
French Horn Ct SG12 . . .93 D1
French Horn La AL10 . . . . .130 B6
French Row AL3 . . . . . . .127 D3
French's Cl SG12 . . . . .115 B4
Frensham EN7 . . . . .148 A4
Frensham Dr SG4 . . . . . . .22 C2
Frere Ct CM23 . . . . .58 F1
Freshwater Cl LU3 . . . . . . .44 F7
Freshwaters Cl CM17 . . . . .117 E1
Fretherne Rd AL8 . . . . . . .110 D6
Friars Cl LU1 . . . . .63 B5
Friars Ct LU1 . . . . .63 B5
Friars Field HP4 . . . . .121 E7
Friars Rd Braughing SG11 . .56 A7
Weston SG4 . . . . .24 B1
Friars Way Bushey WD2 . . .167 F8
Kings Langley WD4 . . . . . .139 A1
Luton LU1 . . . . .63 B5
Friars Wlk HP23 . . . . .100 A4
Friars Wood CM23 . . . . . . .77 C8
Friarscroft EN10 . . . . .135 A4
Friday Furlong SG5 . . . . . .34 C8
Friedberg Ave CM23 . . . . . .76 D4
Friendless La AL3 . . . . . . .83 F2
Friends Ave EN8 . . . . .162 D7
Friesian Cl LU4 . . . . .44 A3
Frimley Rd HP1 . . . . .123 E4
Fringewood Cl HA6 . . . . . .174 B2
Frinton Cl WD1 . . . . .175 B8
Friston Gn LU2 . . . . .46 D1
Frithsden Copse HP4 . . . . .122 F8
Frithwood Ave HA6 . . . . . .174 F4
Frithwood Prim Sch
HA6 . . . . .174 F4
Frobisher Cl WD2 . . . . . . .168 A3
Frobisher Dr SG2 . . . . . . .51 B7
Frobisher Rd AL1 . . . . . . .128 C1
Frobisher Way AL10 . . . . . .129 D8
Froghall La SG2 . . . . .38 B1
Frogmoor Ct WD3 . . . . . . .173 D6
Frogmoor La WD3 . . . . . . .173 D8
Frogmore AL2 . . . . .141 C4
Frogmore Hill SG14 . . . . . .70 B7
Frogmore Ho SG1 . . . . . . .36 C1
Frogmore Rd HP3 . . . . . . .138 D8
Frogmore St HP23 . . . . . . .100 A3
Frogs Hall La SG11 . . . . . .53 F3
Frome Cl LU4 . . . . .44 E4
Frome Sq HP2 . . . . .125 A8
Front St LU1 . . . . .63 C1
Front The HP4 . . . . .123 B7
Frowick Cl AL9 . . . . .144 B4
Frowyke Cres EN6 . . . . . . .158 A4
Fry Rd SG2 . . . . .51 C5
Fryth Mead AL3 . . . . .127 B4
Fulbeck Way HA2 . . . . . . .176 C1
Fulbourne Cl LU4 . . . . . . .44 E2
Fulford Gr WD1 . . . . .175 B8
Fuller Ct CM23 . . . . . . .77 C7
Fuller Gdns WD2 . . . . . . .154 B2
Fuller Rd WD2 . . . . .154 B2
Fuller Way WD3 . . . . .166 A4
Fullers Ct SG6 . . . . .22 E7
Fulling Mill La AL6 . . . . . . .89 B6
Fulmar Cres HP1 . . . . . . .124 A3
Fulmore Cl AL5 . . . . .86 D4
Fulton Cl SG1 . . . . .50 C5
Fulton Cres CM23 . . . . . . .77 C8
Fulton Ct
Borehamwood WD6 . . . . . .156 F1
Holdbrook EN3 . . . . .163 A1
Furlay Cl SG6 . . . . .22 D7
Furlong The HP23 . . . . . . .100 A3

Furlong Way SG12 . . . . . . .115 A7
Furlongs HP1 . . . . .124 A4
Furneux Pelham
CE Prim Sch SG9 . . . . . . .43 A4
Furriers Cl CM23 . . . . .76 C5
Furrowfield AL10 . . . . .130 B7
Furrows The LU3 . . . . .45 B7
Furse Ave AL4 . . . . .128 A7
Furtherfield WD5 . . . . . . .153 E7
Furtherground HP2 . . . .124 E2
Furze Cl Luton LU2 . . . . . .45 D7
South Oxhey WD1 . . . . . . .175 C5
Furze Gr SG8 . . . . .7 E5
Furze Rd HP1 . . . . .123 D2
Furze View WD3 . . . . .164 C4
Furzebushes La AL2 . . . . . .140 F6
Furzedown SG2 . . . . .51 B4
Furzedown Ct AL5 . . . . .86 B1
Furzefield EN8 . . . . .148 B3
Furzefield Cl SG6 . . . . . . .158 A6
Furzefield Ctr The EN6 . . . .158 D8
Furzefield Rd AL7 . . . . . . .110 E4
Furzehill Mid Sch WD6 . . . .170 A5
Furzehill Par WD6 . . . . . . .170 A6
Furzehill Rd WD6 . . . . . . .170 B5
Furzen Cres AL10 . . . . . . .129 F2

G

Gable Cl
Abbots Langley WD5 . . . . .153 E7
Pinner HA5 . . . . .176 A3
Gables Ave WD6 . . . . .169 F6
Gables The
Sawbridgeworth CM21 . . . .97 E2
Watford, The Rookery WD1 . .167 E2
Watford, Woodside WD2 . . .154 D6
Gaddesden Cres WD2 . . . .154 E5
Gaddesden Gr AL7 . . . . . .111 B6
Gaddesden La AL3 . . . . . .105 C4
Gaddesden Row
Great Gaddesden HP2 . . . .104 C6
Jockey End HP2 . . . . .103 F8
Gaddesden Row
Jun Mix Inf Sch HP2 . . . . .104 B6
Gade Ave WD1 . . . . .166 E5
Gade Bank WD1 . . . . .166 D5
Gade Cl
Hemel Hempstead HP1 . . . .124 B6
Watford WD1 . . . . .166 E5
Gade Side WD1 . . . . .153 E4
Gade Valley WD4 . . . . . . .153 E4
Gade Valley Cotts HP1 . . . .103 E4
Gade Valley
Jun Mix Inf Sch HP1 . . . . .124 B4
Gade View Gdns WD4 . . . .153 C7
Gade View Rd HP3 . . . . . .138 D7
Gadebridge Ct HP1 . . . . . .124 C4
Gadebridge La
Hemel Hempstead HP1 . . . .124 B5
Hemel Hempstead HP1 . . . .124 C5
Gadebridge Rd HP1 . . . . . .124 B4
Gadeview HP1 . . . . .124 C3
Gadswell Cl WD2 . . . . . . .154 E3
Gage Cl SG8 . . . . .7 D7
Gainsborough Ave AL1 . . . .127 F4
Gainsford Cres SG4 . . . . . .22 C2
Gainswood AL7 . . . . .110 E5
Gaitskell Ho WD6 . . . . . . .170 D5
Gall End La CM24 . . . . . . .59 F7
Galleria The AL10 . . . . . . .129 F5
Gallery The LU1 . . . . . . .63 E7
Galley Gn SG13 . . . . .115 A2
Galley Hill HP1 . . . . .124 B6
Galley La EN5 . . . . .171 B7
Galleycroft Ct AL10 . . . .130 A6
Galleyhill Rd EN9 . . . . . . .163 E7
Galleywood SG5 . . . . .21 D4
Galliard Cl LU3 . . . . .45 B4
Gallows Cl
 Bishop's Stortford CM23 . .76 F8
Cheshunt EN10 . . . . .148 F5
Galloway Rd CM23 . . . . . .58 F1
Gallows Hill WD4 . . . . . . .153 C7
Gallows Hill La WD5 . . . . . .153 D8
Galston Rd LU3 . . . . .44 D8
Gammons La WD1,WD2 . . .154 A2
Ganders Ash WD2 . . . . . . .154 A6
Gandhi Ct WD2 . . . . . . .167 D7
Gangies Hill CM21 . . . . . . .97 A4
Gant Ct EN9 . . . . .163 F5
Ganton Wlk WD1 . . . . . . .175 E6
Ganymede Pl HP2 . . . . . . .124 F6
Gaping La SG5 . . . . .34 D7
Garden Ave AL10 . . . . . . .130 A3
Garden Cl Barnet EN5 . . . .171 C5
Harpenden AL5 . . . . .107 A5
Royston SG8 . . . . .7 E7
St Albans AL1 . . . . .128 B4
Watford WD1 . . . . .166 F7
Woolmer Green SG3 . . . . . .69 B2
Garden Ct
Hoddesdon EN10 . . . . . . .134 F4
Welwyn Garden City AL7 . . .110 E7
Wheathampstead AL4 . . . . .87 D1
Garden Field
Jun Mix Inf Sch AL3 . . . . .127 D6
Garden Ho SG13 . . . . . . .113 C5
Garden La SG8 . . . . .7 D7
Garden Rd
Abbots Langley WD5 . . . . .153 D8
Buntingford SG9 . . . . .40 E8
Woolmer Green SG3 . . . . . .69 B2
Garden Row SG5 . . . . . .34 F8

Garden Terr SG12 . . . . . . .92 E4
Garden Terrace Rd
CM17 . . . . .118 C4
Garden Wlk Royston SG8 . . .7 E7
Stevenage SG1 . . . . .50 E5
Gardenia Ave LU3 . . . . . . .45 A4
Gardens of the Rose The
AL2 . . . . .140 F5
Gardens The Baldock SG7 . .23 E8
Brookmans Park AL9 . . . . .144 E4
Henlow SG16 . . . . .10 D8
Stotfold SG5 . . . . .11 E6
Gardiners La SG7 . . . . .4 D7
Gardner Ct LU1 . . . . .63 E4
Gareth Ct WD6 . . . . .156 F1
Garfield Ct LU2 . . . . .46 D3
Garfield St WD2 . . . . .154 B1
Garland Cl
Cheshunt EN8 . . . . .162 E8
Hemel Hempstead HP2 . . . .124 D4
Garland Rd SG12 . . . . . . .93 E1
Garnault Rd EN1 . . . . . . .161 F1
Garner Dr EN10 . . . . .148 E5
Garnett Cl WD2 . . . . .154 D3
Garnett Dr AL2 . . . . .140 D4
Garrard Way AL4 . . . . . . .108 D8
Garratts Rd WD2 . . . . . . .168 C2
Garretts Mead LU2 . . . . . .46 B3
Garrison Ct SG4 . . . . . . .34 F7
Garrowsfield EN5 . . . . . . .171 F4
Garsmouth Way WD2 . . . . .154 D3
Garston Cres WD2 . . . . . .154 C5
Garston Dr WD2 . . . . .154 C5
Garston Inf Sch WD2 . . . . .154 D4
Garston La WD2 . . . . .154 D5
Garston Manor Medical
Rehabilitation Ctr
WD2 . . . . .154 C8
Garston Manor Sch
WD2 . . . . .154 C7
Garston Park Par WD2 . . . .154 D5
Garston Sta WD2 . . . . . . .154 D4
Garter Ct LU2 . . . . .45 D1
Garth Rd SG6 . . . . .22 E3
Garth The WD3 . . . . .153 D6
Garthland Dr EN5 . . . . . . .171 C4
Gartlet Rd WD1 . . . . .167 C6
Gas La SG8 . . . . .17 C3
Gascoigne Cecil Jun Sch
AL10 . . . . .130 B7
Gascoyne Cecil Prim Sch
AL10 . . . . .130 A7
Gascoyne Cl EN6 . . . . . . .158 A7
Gascoyne Way
SG13,SG14 . . . . .113 D5
Gatcombe Ct AL1 . . . . . . .128 A2
Gate Cl WD6 . . . . .170 C8
Gate Cotts WD3 . . . . .164 D5
Gate End HA6 . . . . .175 A3
Gatecroft HP3 . . . . .139 A8
Gatehall Gdns LU3 . . . . . . .31 B1
Gatehill Rd HA6 . . . . .175 A3
Gatehouse Mews SG9 . . . .40 E8
Gates Way SG1 . . . . .50 C6
Gatesbury Way SG11 . . . . .55 D3
Gatesden Cl HP4 . . . . . . .102 A3
Gateshead Rd WD6 . . . . . .170 A8
Gateway Cl HA6 . . . . .174 C4
Gateways The EN7 . . . . . .147 E3
Gatwick Cl CM23 . . . . .59 B1
Gauldie Way SG11 . . . . . . .55 D2
Gaumont App WD1 . . . . . .167 B6
Gaunts Way LU2 . . . . .46 D1
Gaveston Dr HP4 . . . . . . .122 B6
Gayland Ave LU2 . . . . .64 B8
Gayton Cl LU3 . . . . .45 B4
Gaywood Ave EN8 . . . . . . .148 D1
Gazelda Ind Est WD1 . . . . .167 D4
Geddes Rd WD2 . . . . .168 C5
Geddings Rd EN11 . . . . . .135 B6
Geddington Ct EN8 . . . . . .163 A5
Generals Wlk The EN3 . . . .162 E2
Gentle Ct SG7 . . . . .23 E8
Gentlemens Field SG12 . . . .93 B3
George Green CM22 . . . . . .77 B1
George Green Villas
CM22 . . . . .98 B8
George La SG8 . . . . .7 D6
George Leighton Ct SG2 . . .51 B4
George Lovell Dr EN3 . . . . .163 A2
George St
Berkhamsted HP4 . . . . . . .122 D4
Hemel Hempstead HP2 . . . .124 D4
Hertford SG14 . . . . .113 C6
Luton LU1 . . . . .63 E7
Markyate AL3 . . . . .83 E5
St Albans AL3 . . . . .127 D3
Watford WD1 . . . . .167 C5
George St W LU1 . . . . . . .63 E7
George Street Prim Sch
HP2 . . . . .124 D4
George V Ave HA5 . . . . . . .175 F1
George V Way WD3 . . . . . .152 B3
George Wlk SG12 . . . . . .93 D1
George's Wood Rd AL9 . . . .145 B5
Georges Mead WD6 . . . . . .169 E8
Georgewood Rd HP3 . . . . .139 A7
Georgina Ct SG15 . . . . . . .11 A3
Gerard Ave CM23 . . . . . . .76 E4
Gerard Ct AL5 . . . . .86 A2
Gernon Rd SG6 . . . . .22 F5
Gernon Wlk SG6 . . . . .22 F5
Gew's Cnr EN8 . . . . .148 D2
Giant Tree Hill WD2 . . . . . .168 C4
Gibbons Cl
Borehamwood WD6 . . . . . .169 E8
Sandridge AL4 . . . . .108 C1

Gibbons Way SG3 . . . . . . .68 F5
Gibbs Cl EN8 . . . . .148 D2
Gibbs Couch WD1 . . . . . . .175 D7
Gibbs Field CM23 . . . . . . .76 D5
Gibraltar Lodge AL5 . . . . . .86 D3
Gibson Cl SG4 . . . . .35 B7
Gidian Ct AL2 . . . . .141 D4
Gifford's La SG11 . . . . .54 A2
Gilbert Cl AL5 . . . . .86 B4
Gilbert St EN3 . . . . .162 C2
Gilbert Way HP4 . . . . .122 A4
Gilbert's Hill HP23 . . . . . . .119 E3
Gilbey Ave CM23 . . . . .77 B6
Gilbey Cres CM24 . . . . . . .59 E8
Gildea Cl HA5 . . . . .176 A3
Gilden Cl CM17 . . . . .118 E4
Gilden Ct CM17 . . . . .118 D3
Gilder Cl LU3 . . . . .45 A8
Gilderdale LU4 . . . . .44 B6
Gilders CM21 . . . . .97 D2
Giles Cl AL4 . . . . .108 C1
Giles Inf Sch SG1 . . . . . . .37 A1
Giles Jun Sch SG1 . . . . . . .37 A1
Gill Cl WD1 . . . . .166 C3
Gillam St LU2 . . . . .63 E8
Gillan Gn WD2 . . . . .176 C8
Gillian Ave AL1 . . . . .141 C4
Gillian Ho HA3 . . . . .176 E4
Gilliat's Gn WD3 . . . . .164 D5
Gilliflower Ho EN11 . . . . . .135 A5
Gillings Ct EN5 . . . . .171 E5
Gillison Cl SG6 . . . . .23 B5
Gills Hill WD7 . . . . .155 F4
Gills Hill La WD7 . . . . .155 F3
Gills Hollow WD7 . . . . .155 F3
Gilmour Cl EN2 . . . . .162 A4
Gilpin Cl AL5 . . . . .86 C1
Gilpin Rd SG12 . . . . .114 E8
Gilpin's Gallop SG12 . . . . .115 B4
Gilpin's Ride HP4 . . . . . . .122 E5
Gilsland EN9 . . . . .163 E4
Ginns Rd SG9 . . . . .43 D6
Gippeswyck Cl HA5 . . . . . .175 D2
Gipsy La
Bishop's Stortford CM23 . . .59 C4
Knebworth AL6,SG3 . . . . . .68 E4
Luton LU1 . . . . .64 A6
Girdle Rd SG4 . . . . .22 A2
Girons Ct SG4 . . . . .35 B7
Girtin Rd WD2 . . . . .168 C5
Girton Ct EN8 . . . . .148 E1
Girton Way WD3 . . . . .166 C4
Gisburne Way WD2 . . . . . .154 A2
Gladding Rd EN7 . . . . . . .147 B6
Glade The Baldock SG7 . . . .23 E8
Letchworth SG6 . . . . .22 F3
Welwyn Garden City AL8 . . .110 C8
Glades The HP1 . . . . .123 E4
Gladeside AL4 . . . . .128 D6
Gladesmere Ct WD2 . . . . .154 B2
Gladeway The EN9 . . . . . .163 D6
Gladsmuir Rd EN5 . . . . . . .171 E5
Gladstone Ave LU1 . . . . . .63 C7
Gladstone Ct SG2 . . . . . . .69 A8
Gladstone Pl EN5 . . . . . . .171 D5
Gladstone Rd
Dane End SG12 . . . . .71 F8
Hoddesdon EN11 . . . . . . .135 B7
Ware SG12 . . . . .93 C2
Watford WD1 . . . . .167 C6
Glaisdale LU4 . . . . .44 C5
Glamis Ct Cheshunt EN7 . . .148 A2
Hemel Hempstead HP2 . . . .105 A3
Glean Wlk AL10 . . . . . . .130 A2
Gleave Cl AL1 . . . . .128 B4
Glebe Ave SG15 . . . . .11 A3
Glebe Cl Essendon AL9 . . .131 F6
Hemel Hempstead HP3 . . . .138 C7
Hertford SG14 . . . . .113 D8
Pitstone LU7 . . . . .80 D5
Watton at Stone SG14 . . . .70 D3
Glebe Cotts AL9 . . . . .131 F6
Glebe La
Bishop's Stortford CM23 . . .77 B8
Hatfield AL10 . . . . .130 C6
Watton at Stone SG14 . . . .70 E3
Glebe Ho AL9 . . . . .131 F6
Glebe La EN5 . . . . .171 A3
Glebe Rd Hertford SG14 . . .113 D8
Letchworth SG6 . . . . .23 B8
Welwyn AL6 . . . . .89 B5
Glebe The Harlow CM20 . . .117 C1
Kings Langley WD4 . . . . . .139 A2
Stevenage SG2 . . . . .51 B6
Watford WD2 . . . . .154 D6
Glebelands CM20 . . . . . . .117 F3
Gleed Ave WD2 . . . . .168 C1
Glemsford Cl LU4 . . . . .44 B6
Glemsford Dr AL5 . . . . . . .86 C2
Glen Cres WD3 . . . . .165 C5
Glen Faba Rd CM19 . . . . . .135 F6
Glen The
Caddington LU1 . . . . .62 E3
Hemel Hempstead HP2 . . . .124 F8
Northwood HA6 . . . . .174 D3
Glen Way WD1 . . . . .153 E1
Glenblower Cl AL4 . . . . . . .128 D3
Glencoe Rd WD2 . . . . . . .168 A3
Glendale HP1 . . . . .124 B3
Glendale Wlk EN8 . . . . . . .148 E1
Glendean Ct EN3 . . . . . . .162 F3
Gleneagles Cl WD1 . . . . . .175 D6
Gleneagles Dr LU2 . . . . . . .45 E6
Glenester Cl EN11 . . . . . . .115 B1
Glenferrie Rd AL1 . . . . . . .128 A3
Glenfield HP2 . . . . .124 E6

Glenfield Ct SG14 . . . . . . .112 F7
Glenfield Rd LU3 . . . . .45 C6
Glengall Pl AL1 . . . . .141 E8
Glenhaven Ave WD6 . . . . . .170 A6
Glenlyn Ave AL1 . . . . .128 B2
Glenmire Terr SG12 . . . . . .115 D4
Glenmore Gdns WD5 . . . . .154 A7
Glenshee Cl HA6 . . . . .174 C4
Glenview Gdns HP1 . . . . . .124 B3
Glenview Rd HP1 . . . . .124 B3
Glenville Ave EN2 . . . . . . .161 D1
Glenwood
Hoddesdon EN10 . . . . . . .134 F4
Welwyn Garden City AL7 . . .111 D5
Glenwood Cl SG2 . . . . . . .51 C2
Glevum Cl AL3 . . . . .126 F1
Globe Cl AL5 . . . . .86 B1
Globe Cres CM23 . . . . . . .58 D6
Globe Ct Hertford SG14 . . .113 C8
Hoddesdon EN10 . . . . . . .148 E8
Gloucester Ave EN8 . . . . . .162 E6
Gloucester Cl SG1 . . . . . . .36 E2
Gloucester Rd
Enfield EN2 . . . . .161 C1
 Luton LU1 . . . . .63 F6
Glover Cl EN7 . . . . .147 F4
Glovers Cl SG13 . . . . .113 C4
Glovers Ct SG5 . . . . .21 F1
Glynde The SG2 . . . . .69 B8
Goat La EN1 . . . . .161 F1
Gobions Way EN6 . . . . . . .145 B3
Goblins Gn AL7 . . . . .110 D5
Goddard End SG2 . . . . . . .69 C8
Goddards Cl SG13 . . . . . . .132 C4
Gode Twr HP3 . . . . .138 F6
Godfrey Cl SG2 . . . . .51 B3
Godfreys Cl LU1 . . . . .63 B6
Godfreys Ct LU1 . . . . .63 B6
Godfries Cl AL6 . . . . .90 E3
Godsafe CM17 . . . . .118 E4
Godwin Cl E4 . . . . .163 C1
Goff's La EN7 . . . . .147 E2
Goff's Oak Ave EN7 . . . . . .147 C3
Goffs Cres EN7 . . . . .147 C2
Goffs La EN7 . . . . .148 A2
Goffs Oak
Jun Mix Sch EN7 . . . . . . .147 B3
Goffs Sch EN7 . . . . .148 A2
Gold Cl EN10 . . . . .134 E3
Gold Crest Cl LU4 . . . . . . .44 A5
Golda Cl EN5 . . . . .171 D3
Goldcrest Way WD2 . . . . . .168 C1
Goldcroft HP3 . . . . .125 A1
Golden Dell AL7 . . . . .110 F2
Goldfield Inf Sch HP23 . . . .99 F3
Goldfield Rd HP23 . . . . . . .99 F3
Goldfinch Way WD6 . . . . . .170 A5
Goldings CM23 . . . . .77 B8
Goldings Cres AL10 . . . . . .130 B6
Goldings Ho AL10 . . . . . . .130 B6
Goldings La SG12 . . . . . . .92 A2
Goldington Cl EN11 . . . . . .114 F1
Goldon SG6 . . . . .23 C4
Goldsmith Way AL3 . . . . . .127 C4
Goldstone Cl SG12 . . . . . .93 D2
Golf Cl WD2 . . . . .167 D6
Golf Club Rd AL9 . . . . . . .145 A6
Golf Ride EN2 . . . . .161 A4
Gombards AL3 . . . . .127 D4
Gomer Cl SG4 . . . . .67 E2
Gonnerston AL3 . . . . .127 B4
Gonville Ave WD3 . . . . . . .166 B3
Gonville Cres SG2 . . . . . . .51 C2
Goodey Meade SG2 . . . . . .52 F2
Goodliffe Pk CM23 . . . . . . .59 B2
Goodrich Cl WD2 . . . . . . .154 A4
Goodwin Ct EN8 . . . . .148 E3
Goodwin Ho WD1 . . . . . . .166 E3
Goodwin Stile CM23 . . . . . .76 D5
Goodwins Mead LU7 . . . . . .80 A7
Goodwood Ave
Enfield EN3 . . . . .162 C2
Watford WD2 . . . . .153 E3
Goodwood Cl EN11 . . . . . .135 A4
Goodwood Par WD1 . . . . . .153 E3
Goodwood Path WD6 . . . . .170 A4
Goodwood Rd SG8 . . . . . . .7 F6
Goodyers Ave WD7 . . . . . .155 F5
Goose Acre Botley HP5 . . . .136 A1
Cheddington LU7 . . . . .80 A7
Goose La CM22 . . . . .98 E2
Gooseacre AL7 . . . . .110 F4
Gooseberry Hill LU3 . . . . . .45 B7
Goosecroft HP1 . . . . .123 F4
Goosefields WD3 . . . . . . .165 C3
Goral Mead WD3 . . . . . . .165 D1
Gordian Way SG2 . . . . . . .37 C1
Gordon Ave HA7 . . . . .176 F4
Gordon Cl AL1 . . . . .128 B2
Gordon Ct SG3 . . . . .69 A5
Gordon Ho EN9 . . . . .163 A5
Gordon Rd EN9 . . . . .163 A5
Gordon St LU1 . . . . .63 D7
Gordon Way EN5 . . . . .171 F5
Gordon's Wlk AL5 . . . . . . .107 C8
Gore La SG11 . . . . .73 D3
Gorelands La HP8 . . . . . . .172 A4
Gorham Dr AL1 . . . . .141 E8
Gorhambury AL3 . . . . .126 C4
Gorle Cl WD2 . . . . .154 A4
Gorleston Cl SG1 . . . . .36 A1
Gorse Cl AL10 . . . . .129 F2
Gorse Cnr AL3 . . . . .127 D5
Gorselands AL5 . . . . .107 B7
Gorst Cl SG6 . . . . .22 E5

Gosford Ho WD1 . . . . .166 E3
Gosforth La WD1 . . . . . .175 B7
Gosforth Path WD1 . . . . .175 A7
Goshawk Cl LU4 . . . . .44 A4
Goslett Ct WD2 . . . . .168 A4
Gosling Ave SG5 . . . . .33 C2
Gosling Ski Ctr AL8 . . . . .110 C4
Gosling Sports Pk AL8 . . . .110 C4
Gosmore SG1 . . . . .36 C2
Gosmore Ley Cl SG4 . . . . .34 F3
Gosmore Rd SG4 . . . . .34 F5
Gossamers The WD2 . . . . .154 E4
Gosselin Ho SG14 . . . . . . .113 D8
Gosselin Rd SG14 . . . . . .113 C8
Gossoms Ryde HP4 . . . . . .122 A5
Gothic Mede Lower Sch
SG15 . . . . .11 A5
Gothic Way SG15 . . . . .11 B5
Gould Cl AL9 . . . . .144 B7
Government Row EN3 . . . . .163 A2
Gower Field EN6 . . . . .158 A7
Gower Rd SG8 . . . . .7 C7
Gowers The CM20 . . . . . . .118 B2
Grace Ave WD7 . . . . .156 E6
Grace Cl WD6 . . . . .170 D8
Grace Gdns CM23 . . . . . . .76 F4
Grace Way SG1 . . . . .50 E7
Graces Maltings HP23 . . . .100 A3
Graemesdyke Rd HP4 . . . .122 A4
Grafton Cl AL4 . . . . .128 D2
Grafton Pl SG11 . . . . .55 F1
Graham Ave EN10 . . . . . .134 E2
Graham Cl AL1 . . . . .127 D1
Graham Gdns LU3 . . . . . . .45 C4
Graham Rd HA3 . . . . .176 E1
Grailands CM23 . . . . .76 B8
Grammar School Wlk
SG5 . . . . .34 E7
Grampian Way LU3 . . . . . .44 C8
Granaries The EN9 . . . . . .163 E5
Granary Cl AL4 . . . . .108 D8
Granary Ct CM21 . . . . . . .97 E2
Granary La AL5 . . . . .86 C1
Granary The Roydon CM19 116 B1
Stanstead Abbotts SG12 . . .115 C3
Granby Ave AL5 . . . . .86 D2
Granby Ct AL5 . . . . .86 D2
Granby Rd Luton LU4 . . . . .44 E2
Stevenage SG1 . . . . .36 C2
Granchester Ct WD1 . . . . .167 B6
Grandfield Ave WD1 . . . . .167 A8
Grange Ave Barnet N20 . . .171 E2
Luton LU4 . . . . .44 D4
Grange Bottom SG8 . . . . . .7 E5
Grange Cl
Hemel Hempstead HP2 . . . .125 A2
Hertford SG14 . . . . .113 B6
Hitchin SG4 . . . . .35 A4
Markyate AL3 . . . . .83 D6
Watford WD1 . . . . .167 A8
Grange Court Rd AL5 . . . .107 C6
Grange Ct Hertford SG14 . .113 C7
Letchworth SG6 . . . . .12 A1
Waltham Abbey EN9 . . . . .163 C5
Grange Dr SG5 . . . . .11 F5
Grange Gdns SG12 . . . . . .114 E8
Grange Hill AL6 . . . . .89 C6
Grange Jun Sch SG6 . . . . .12 A2
Grange La AL2 . . . . .168 D8
Grange Pk CM23 . . . . .58 F1
Grange Rd
Bishop's Stortford CM23 . . .77 A7
Borehamwood WD6 . . . . . .169 F4
Letchworth SG6 . . . . .22 F8
Pitstone LU7 . . . . .80 D5
Tring HP23 . . . . .100 C3
Watford WD2 . . . . .167 F4
Wilstone HP23 . . . . .79 D1
Grange Rise SG4 . . . . .67 F1
Grange St AL3 . . . . .127 D4
Grange The
Abbots Langley WD5 . . . . .153 E8
Bishop's Stortford CM23 . . .58 F1
Hoddesdon EN11 . . . . .135 A5
Rickmansworth WD3 . . . . .165 D2
Grange Wlk CM23 . . . . . . .77 A7
Grangedale Cl HA6 . . . . . .174 E2
Grangeside CM23 . . . . . . .59 A2
Grangewood EN6 . . . . . . .145 E4
Grangewood Inf Sch
EN8 . . . . .148 D1
Gransden Cl LU3 . . . . .45 A7
Grant Gdns AL5 . . . . .86 B2
Grantham Ct SG8 . . . . .7 B8
Grantham Gdns SG12 . . . .93 E2
Grantham Gn WD6 . . . . . .170 C4
Grantham Rd LU4 . . . . . . .45 B1
Granville Ct AL1 . . . . .127 F3
Granville Dene HP3 . . . . . .137 A4
Granville Gdns EN11 . . . . .115 A2
Granville Rd Barnet EN5 . .171 D6
Berkhamsted HP4 . . . . . . .121 E6
Hitchin SG4 . . . . .22 C1
Luton LU1 . . . . .63 B8
St Albans AL1 . . . . .127 F3
Watford WD1 . . . . .167 C5
Grasmere SG1 . . . . .37 C3
Grasmere Ave
Harpenden AL5 . . . . .86 C1
Luton LU3 . . . . .45 B7
Grasmere Cl
Hemel Hempstead HP3 . . . .125 B1
Watford WD2 . . . . .154 B7
Grasmere Rd Luton LU3 . . .45 C7
St Albans AL1 . . . . .128 B1

Grasmere Rd continued
Ware SG12 . . . . .93 E3
Grass Mdws SG2 . . . . .51 D7
Grass Warren AL6 . . . . . . .90 E1
Grassington Cl AL2 . . . . . .141 A1
Grassy SG1 . . . . .124 A4
Gravel Dr HP23 . . . . .99 B3
Gravel La HP1 . . . . .124 A3
Gravel Path
Berkhamsted HP4 . . . . . . .122 E5
Hemel Hempstead HP1 . . . .124 A3
Graveley Ave WD6 . . . . . .170 C4
Graveley Cl SG1 . . . . .36 C2
Graveley Dell AL7 . . . . . . .111 B5
Graveley La SG4 . . . . .36 B5
Graveley Prim Sch SG4 . . .36 B4
Graveley Rd Graveley SG1 . .36 B3
Great Wymondley SG4 . . . .35 F6
Gravelhill Terr HP1 . . . . . .124 A2
Gravelly La SG11 . . . . .55 F8
Gravely Ct HP2 . . . . .125 C2
Gray's La SG1 . . . . .34 D7
Grayling Ct HP4 . . . . .121 F6
Graylings The WD5 . . . . . .153 D6
Grays Cl SG8 . . . . .7 C8
Grays Ct CM23 . . . . .76 E8
Graysfield AL7 . . . . .111 A3
Grazings The HP2 . . . . . . .124 F5
Great Ashby Way SG1 . . . .37 B3
Great Braitch La AL10 . . . .109 F1
Great Break AL7 . . . . .111 B5
Great Cambridge Rd
Cheshunt EN8 . . . . .148 D4
Enfield EN1 . . . . .162 C6
Great Conduit AL7 . . . . . .111 C7
Great Dell AL8 . . . . .89 D1
Great Eastern Cl CM23 . . .77 A6
Great Elms Rd HP3 . . . . . .138 F7
Great Gaddesden Sch
HP1 . . . . .103 D3
Great Ganett AL7 . . . . . . .111 C4
Great Gn SG5 . . . . .20 D7
Great Groves EN7 . . . . . . .147 E3
Great Hadham Rd CM23 . . .76 C5
Great Heart HP2 . . . . .124 E5
Great Heath AL10 . . . . . . .130 B8
Great Innings N SG14 . . . .70 D4
Great Innings S SG14 . . . .70 D3
Great Lawne SG3 . . . . .69 D2
Great Ley AL7 . . . . .110 E4
Great Mdw EN10 . . . . . . .135 A1
Great Molewood SG14 . . . .92 B1
Great North Rd
Barnet EN5 . . . . .171 E6
Brookmans Park AL9,EN6 . .145 B5
Hatfield AL9 . . . . .130 C5
Oaklands AL6 . . . . .89 E7
Radwell SG7 . . . . .12 D4
Welwyn Garden City AL8 . .110 A7
Great Palmers HP2 . . . . . .124 F8
Great Pk WD4 . . . . .139 A1
Great Plumtree CM20 . . . .117 F2
Great Rd HP2 . . . . .124 F4
Great Slades EN6 . . . . . . .158 F6
Great Stockwood Rd
EN7 . . . . .147 D5
Great Sturgess Rd HP1 . . .123 F3
Great Whites Rd HP3 . . . . .124 F1
Great Wood Ctry Pk EN6 .146 B5
Greatfield Cl AL5 . . . . .85 C4
Greatham Rd WD2 . . . . . .167 D6
Green Acres Lilley LU2 . . . .32 D2
Stevenage SG2 . . . . .51 C1
Welwyn Garden City AL7 . .110 F3
Green Bushes LU4 . . . . . . .44 D6
Green Cl
Brookmans Park AL9 . . . . .144 E5
Cheshunt EN8 . . . . .162 E6
Luton LU4 . . . . .44 C5
Stevenage SG2 . . . . .50 F2
Green Croft AL10 . . . . . . .130 A8
Green Ct 6 LU4 . . . . .44 C5
Green Dell Way HP3 . . . . .125 C3
Green Drift SG8 . . . . .7 C7
Green Edge WD2 . . . . . . .154 A4
Green End AL6 . . . . .89 B4
Green End Gdns HP1 . . . . .124 A2
Green End La HP1 . . . . . . .123 F3
Green End Rd HP1 . . . . . . .124 A2
Green Hill Cl SG11 . . . . . . .55 F7
Green La Ashwell SG7 . . . . .4 C5
Bovingdon HP3 . . . . .137 A3
Braughing SG11 . . . . .55 F7
Croxley Green WD3 . . . . . .165 F4
Hemel Hempstead HP2 . . . .125 D4
Hitchin SG4 . . . . .22 B1
Hoddesdon EN10 . . . . .149 B8
Kensworth Common LU6 . . .82 E8
Latimer HP5 . . . . .150 C6
Letchworth SG6 . . . . .23 C4
Luton LU2 . . . . .46 C4
Markyate AL3 . . . . .83 F5
Northwood HA6 . . . . .174 E3
Pitstone LU7 . . . . .80 E5
St Albans, New Greens AL3 127 D7
St Albans, Sopwell AL1 . . .142 A7
Watford WD1 . . . . .167 C5
Welwyn Garden City AL7 . .111 D5
Green Lane Cl AL5 . . . . . .107 E8
Green Lanes AL10 . . . . . . .109 F2
Green Lanes Prim Sch
AL10 . . . . .109 F1
Green Leys Cotts SG11 . . . .55 F1
Green Mdw EN6 . . . . .145 A1
Green Milverton LU3 . . . . .45 A7
Green Oaks LU2 . . . . .45 F3
Green Path HP22 . . . . .99 D4

Green St
Chorleywood WD3 . . . . . . .164 C6
Royston SG8 . . . . .7 D8
Shenley WD7 . . . . .157 A3
Stevenage SG1 . . . . .50 C7
Green The
Bishop's Stortford CM23 . . .76 F4
Cheddington LU7 . . . . .80 A7
Cheshunt EN8 . . . . .148 C3
Codicote SG4 . . . . .67 F1
Kimpton SG4 . . . . .66 D1
Knebworth SG3 . . . . .68 C5
Luton LU4 . . . . .44 C5
Newnham SG7 . . . . .12 E7
Peters Green LU2 . . . . .65 C3
Pitstone LU7 . . . . .80 D4
Potten End HP4 . . . . .123 B6
Royston SG8 . . . . .7 D6
Sarratt WD3 . . . . .152 A3
Stotfold SG5 . . . . .11 F7
Waltham Abbey EN9 . . . . .163 C5
Ware SG12 . . . . .93 D3
Welwyn AL6 . . . . .89 B5
Welwyn Garden City AL7 . .111 A4
Green Vale AL7 . . . . .111 A5
Green View Cl HP3 . . . . . .137 A2
Green Way Gdns HA3 . . . .176 E1
Green Way The HA3 . . . . .176 E2
Greenacre Cl EN5 . . . . . . .158 F1
Greenacres Bushey WD2 . .176 D8
Hemel Hempstead HP2 . . . .125 D2
Pitstone LU7 . . . . .80 C4
Greenall Cl EN8 . . . . .148 C1
Greenbank EN8 . . . . .148 B3
Greenbank Rd WD1 . . . . .153 D3
Greenbury Cl Barley SG8 . . .8 F1
Chorleywood WD3 . . . . . . .164 C5
Greencoates SG13 . . . . . . .113 E5
Greene Field Rd HP4 . . . . .122 C4
Greene Wlk HP4 . . . . .122 D3
Greenes Ct HP4 . . . . .122 C5
Greenfield Hatfield AL9 . . .130 D8
Royston SG8 . . . . .7 B7
Welwyn Garden City AL8 . .89 D1
Greenfield Ave
Ickleford SG5 . . . . .21 D4
South Oxhey WD1 . . . . . . .175 E8
Greenfield La SG5 . . . . . . .21 E4
Greenfield Rd SG1 . . . . . . .50 E7
Greenfield St EN9 . . . . . . .163 C5
Greenfields Cuffley EN6 . .146 E1
Stansted Mountfitchet CM24 .59 E7
Greenfields
Jun Mix Inf Sch WD1 . . . .175 C5
Greengate LU3 . . . . .44 C8
Greenheys Cl HA6 . . . . . . .174 E2
Greenhill Ave LU2 . . . . . . .45 E3
Greenhill Cres WD1 . . . . . .166 E3
Greenhill Ct HP1 . . . . .124 B2
Greenhill Pk CM23 . . . . . . .76 D5
Greenhills SG12 . . . . .93 C3
Greenhills Cl WD3 . . . . . . .165 B4
Greenland Rd EN5 . . . . . .171 C3
Greenlane Ind Est SG6 . . .23 C7
Greenleas EN9 . . . . .163 C5
Greenriggs LU2 . . . . .46 F2
Greenside WD6 . . . . .157 A1
Greenside Dr SG5 . . . . . . .34 D8
Greenside Pk LU2 . . . . . . .45 E3
Greenside Sch SG2 . . . . . .51 B2
Greensleeves Cl AL4 . . . . .128 C2
Greenstead CM21 . . . . . . .97 E1
Greensward WD2 . . . . . . .168 B3
Greenway
Berkhamsted HP4 . . . . . . .122 A4
Bishop's Stortford CM23 . . .77 C6
Harpenden AL5 . . . . .107 E8
Hemel Hempstead HP2 . . . .125 B3
Letchworth SG6 . . . . .23 A4
Pinner HA5 . . . . .175 B1
Walkern SG2 . . . . .52 B8
Greenway Fst Sch HP4 . . .121 F4
Greenway The
Enfield EN3 . . . . .162 D4
Potters Bar EN6 . . . . .159 A6
Rickmansworth WD3 . . . . .165 A4
Tring HP23 . . . . .99 F5
Greenways
Abbots Langley WD5 . . . . .153 E7
Buntingford SG9 . . . . .40 D8
Goff's Oak EN7 . . . . .147 B2
Hertford SG14 . . . . .113 B6
Luton LU2 . . . . .46 B5
Stevenage SG1 . . . . .50 E6
Greenwich Ct AL1 . . . . . . .128 A2
Greenwood Ave EN7 . . . . .162 B8
Greenwood Cl EN7 . . . . . .162 B8
Greenwood Dr WD2 . . . . .154 B5
Greenwood Gdns WD7 . . .156 E6
Greenwood Park L Ctr
AL2 . . . . .141 B6
Greenyard EN9 . . . . .163 C6
Greer Rd HA3 . . . . .176 C2
Gregories Cl LU3 . . . . .45 C1
Gregory Ave EN6 . . . . . . .159 C6
Gregory Mews EN9 . . . . . .163 B7
Gregson Rd WD6 . . . . . . .170 C8
Grenadier Cl AL4 . . . . . . .128 C2
Grenadine Way HP23 . . . .100 A5
Greneway Sch The SG8 . . .7 D7
Grenfell Cl WD6 . . . . .170 C8
Grenville Ave EN10 . . . . . .134 F2
Grenville Cl EN8 . . . . .162 D7
Grenville Ct WD3 . . . . . . .164 C5
Grenville Way SG2 . . . . . . .51 A1
Gresford Cl AL4 . . . . .128 D3
Gresham Cl LU2 . . . . .64 D7

Gresham Ct HP4 . . . . .122 B3
Gresley Cl AL8 . . . . .110 E8
Gresley Ct Enfield EN1 . . .162 C4
Potters Bar EN6 . . . . .145 C1
Gresley Way SG2 . . . . .51 D5
Greville Cl AL3 . . . . .144 C7
Grey House The 4 WD1 . .167 A7
Greycaine Rd WD2 . . . . . .154 D2
Greydells Rd SG1 . . . . .50 E6
Greyfriars SG12 . . . . .93 B3
Greyfriars La AL5 . . . . . . .107 A7
Greyhound La EN6 . . . . . . .158 A6
Greystoke Cl HP4 . . . . . . .122 A3
Griffiths Way AL1 . . . . . . .127 C1
Grimaldi Ave AL1 . . . . .45 A3
Grimsdyke Cres EN5 . . . . .171 C6
Grimsdyke Fst & Mid Sch
HA5 . . . . .175 F4
Grimsdyke Rd Pinner HA5 .175 E3
Wigginton HP23 . . . . .100 D1
Grimston Rd AL1 . . . . .127 F2
Grimstone Rd SG4 . . . . . . .35 E4
Grimthorpe Cl AL3 . . . . . .127 D6
Grindcobbe Cl AL1 . . . . . .141 D8
Grinstead La CM22 . . . . . .98 C6
Groom Rd EN10 . . . . .148 F5
Grooms Cotts HP5 . . . . . . .136 B5
Groomsby Dr LU7 . . . . .80 E5
Grosvenor Ave WD4 . . . . .139 C3
Grosvenor Cl CM23 . . . . . .76 D4
Grosvenor Ct WD3 . . . . . .166 A5
Grosvenor Ho 4 CM23 . . .77 B8
Grosvenor Rd Baldock SG7 .12 F1
Borehamwood WD6 . . . . . .170 B6
Hoddesdon EN10 . . . . .134 F3
Luton LU3 . . . . .45 B5
Moor Park HA6 . . . . .174 F5
St Albans AL1 . . . . .127 C2
Watford WD1 . . . . .167 C6
Grosvenor Rd W SG7 . . . . .12 F1
Grosvenor Terr HP1 . . . . .124 A2
Grotto The SG12 . . . . .114 D8
Ground La AL10 . . . . .130 B7
Grove Ave AL5 . . . . .107 D7
Grove Cotts WD2 . . . . . . .168 A3
Grove Cres WD3 . . . . .166 A5
Grove Ct Arlesey SG15 . . . .11 A8
Barnet EN5 . . . . .171 F6
Waltham Abbey EN9 . . . . .163 B6
Grove End LU1 . . . . .63 B5
Grove Farm Pk HA6 . . . . .174 D5
Grove Gdns Enfield EN3 . .162 D1
Tring HP23 . . . . .100 B5
Grove Hall Rd WD2 . . . . . .167 E5
Grove Hill CM24 . . . . .59 E7
Grove Ho Bushey WD2 . . .167 F3
Cheshunt EN8 . . . . .148 B1
Hitchin SG4 . . . . .22 A2
Grove Inf Sch The AL5 . . .107 D7
Grove Jun Sch The AL5 . . .107 D7
Grove La HP5 . . . . .136 B5
Grove Lea AL10 . . . . .130 A2
Grove Mdw AL7 . . . . .111 C6
Grove Mill La WD1 . . . . . .153 C1
Grove Mead AL10 . . . . . . .129 F5
Grove Park Rd LU1 . . . . . . .63 B3
Grove Path EN7 . . . . .162 A8
Grove Pk HP23 . . . . .100 C5
Grove Pl
18 Bishop's Stortford CM23 .76 F7
Welham Green AL9 . . . . . .144 C7
Grove Rd
Borehamwood WD6 . . . . . .170 A8
Harpenden AL5 . . . . .107 D7
Hemel Hempstead HP1 . . . .124 A1
Hitchin SG4 . . . . .21 F1
Luton LU1 . . . . .63 D7
Northwood HA6 . . . . .174 D5
Rickmansworth WD3 . . . . .173 A8
Slip End LU1 . . . . .63 B2
St Albans AL1 . . . . .127 D4
Stevenage SG1 . . . . .50 D7
Tring HP23 . . . . .100 C5
Ware SG12 . . . . .93 F2
Grove Rd W EN3 . . . . . . .162 C2
Grove Road Prim Sch
HP23 . . . . .100 C5
Grove The
Brookmans Park AL9 . . . . .145 A4
Great Hallingbury CM22 . . .77 A4
Latimer HP5 . . . . .150 D3
Little Hadham SG11 . . . . . .75 D4
Luton LU1 . . . . .63 B5
Potters Bar EN6 . . . . .159 C7
Radlett WD7 . . . . .156 A5
Tring HP23 . . . . .100 C5
Grove Way WD3 . . . . .164 B4
Grove Wlk SG14 . . . . .113 C8
Grovebury Gdns AL2 . . . . .141 C4
Grovedale Cl EN7 . . . . . . .147 F1
Groveland Way SG5 . . . . . .12 A5
Grovelands
Chiswellgreen AL2 . . . . . . .141 B4
Hemel Hempstead HP2 . . . .125 C6
Grovelands Ave SG4 . . . . . .22 C2
Grover Cl HP2 . . . . .124 D4
Grover Rd WD1 . . . . .167 D3
Grovewood Cl WD3 . . . . . .164 B4
Grubbs La AL9 . . . . .145 C8
Grubs La AL9 . . . . .131 A1
Gryphon Ind Est AL3 . . . .127 F8
Guardian Ind Est LU1 . . . .63 C8
Guernsey Cl LU4 . . . . .44 A3
Guernsey Ho Enfield EN3 .162 D1
Watford WD1 . . . . .167 A3
Guessens Ct AL8 . . . . .110 C6
Guessens Gr AL8 . . . . .110 C6

Guessens Rd AL8 . . . . .110 C6
Guessens Wlk AL8 . . . . . . .110 C7
Guilden Morden Prim Sch
SG8 . . . . .1 D1
Guildford Cl SG1 . . . . .36 C2
Guildford Rd AL1 . . . . .128 B2
Guildford St LU1 . . . . .63 F7
Guildhouse The WD3 . . . . .166 B3
Guilfords The CM17 . . . . . .118 C5
Guinevere Gdns EN8 . . . . .162 E8
Gulland Cl WD2 . . . . .168 C4
Gullbrook HP1 . . . . .124 C5
Gullet Wood Rd WD2 . . . .154 A4
Gulphs The SG13 . . . . . . .113 C5
Gun La SG3 . . . . .68 F4
Gun Meadow Ave SG3 . . . .69 A4
Gun Rd SG3 . . . . .69 A4
Gun Road Gdns SG3 . . . . . .68 F4
Gunnels Wood Ind Est
SG1 . . . . .50 D3
Gunnels Wood Rd SG1 . . . .50 B4
Gunner Dr EN3 . . . . .163 A2
Gurney Court Rd AL1 . . . .127 F5
Gurney's La SG5 . . . . .21 B7
Gwent Cl WD2 . . . . .154 D5
Gwynfa Cl AL6 . . . . .89 D7
Gwynne Cl HP23 . . . . .100 A5
Gwynns Wlk SG13 . . . . . .113 C6
Gyfford Wlk EN7 . . . . .162 B8
Gypsy Cl SG12 . . . . .114 F4
Gypsy La
Abbots Langley WD4 . . . . .153 D5
Great Amwell SG12 . . . . . .114 F4
Welwyn Garden City AL7 . .110 F1

H

Haberdashers' Aske's
Girls Sch WD6 . . . . .169 B5
Haberdashers' Aske's
Prep Sch The WD6 . . . . .169 B6
Hackforth Cl WD6 . . . . . . .171 B4
Hackney Cl WD6 . . . . .170 D4
Haddenham Ct HP2 . . . . . .105 B1
Haddestoke Gate EN8 . . . .148 F5
Haddon Cl
Borehamwood WD6 . . . . . .170 A6
Hemel Hempstead HP3 . . . .125 A2
Stevenage SG2 . . . . .69 C7
Haddon Ct 20 AL5 . . . . . . .86 B1
Haddon Rd
Chorleywood WD3 . . . . . . .164 C4
Luton LU2 . . . . .63 C4
Hadham Ct SG1 . . . . .76 E8
Hadham Gr CM23 . . . . . . .76 C8
Hadham Ho CM23 . . . . . . .76 D8
Hadham Rd
Bishop's Stortford CM23 . . .76 D8
Little Hadham SG11 . . . . . .57 F1
Standon SG11 . . . . .55 F1
Hadland Cl HP3 . . . . .137 A5
Hadleigh SG6 . . . . .23 B4
Hadleigh Ct
Hoddesdon EN10 . . . . .134 F1
Wheathampstead AL5 . . . .107 E6
Hadley Cl WD6 . . . . .169 F3
Hadley Ct LU3 . . . . .45 D1
Hadley Gn EN5 . . . . .171 F7
Hadley Gn W EN5 . . . . . . .171 F7
Hadley Gr EN5 . . . . .171 E7
Hadley Green Rd EN5 . . . .171 F7
Hadley Highstone EN5 . . . .171 F8
Hadley Rd
Enfield EN4,EN2 . . . . .160 C1
Hadley Wood EN2,EN4 . . .160 D1
Hadley Ridge EN5 . . . . . . .171 F6
Hadley Wood
Jun Mix Inf Sch EN4 . . . .159 C1
Hadley Wood Sta EN4 . . . .159 C1
Hadlow Down Cl LU3 . . . . .45 A5
Hadrain Cl AL3 . . . . .127 A1
Hadrian Way SG7 . . . . . . .23 D7
Hadrians Wlk SG1 . . . . . . .51 C8
Hadwell Cl SG2 . . . . .51 A3
Hagdell Rd LU1 . . . . .63 C5
Hagden La WD1 . . . . .167 A4
Haggerston Rd WD6 . . . . .156 E1
Hagsdell Rd SG13 . . . . . . .113 D5
Haig Cl AL1 . . . . .128 B2
Haig Ho AL1 . . . . .128 B2
Hailey Ave EN11 . . . . .115 A2
Hailey Hall Sch SG13 . . . .114 F2
Hailey La SG13 . . . . .114 F2
Haileybury Coll SG13 . . . .114 D2
Haines Way WD2 . . . . . . .154 A5
Haldens AL7 . . . . .89 F1
Haldens Ho 3 AL7 . . . . . .89 F1
Hale La SG13 . . . . .113 C5
Hale La HP22 . . . . .119 A3
Hale Rd SG13 . . . . .113 C5
Hales Mdw AL5 . . . . .86 A2
Hales Park Cl HP2 . . . . . . .125 C4
Hales Pk HP2 . . . . .125 C4
Haleswood Rd HP2 . . . . . .125 B4
Half Acres SG4 . . . . .34 D6
Half Acres CM23 . . . . .76 F8
Half Moon Cotts CM21 . . . .97 B1
Half Moon La LU7 . . . . . . .80 C8
Half Moon Mdw HP2 . . . . .125 C8
Half Moon Mews 5 AL1 . .127 D3
Halface La SG9 . . . . .29 A1
Halfhide La EN8 . . . . .148 D5
Halfhides EN9 . . . . .163 D6
Halfway La LU4 . . . . .44 D1
Halifax Rd WD3 . . . . .164 C2
Halifax Way AL7 . . . . .111 E6
Hall Cl WD3 . . . . .165 A1

Hall Cotts SG9 . . . . .29 A1
Hall Dr UB9 . . . . .173 C2
Hall Gdns AL4 . . . . .143 D8
Hall Gr AL7 . . . . .111 B4
Hall Heath Cl AL1 . . . . .128 B5
Hall La Great Chishill SG8 . . .9 F2
 Great Hormead SG9 . . . . . .29 A1
 Kimpton SG4 . . . . .87 C8
 Woolmer Green SG3 . . . . .69 A2
Hall Mead SG6 . . . . .22 D6
Hall Park Gate HP4 . . . . . .122 E3
Hall Park Hill HP4 . . . . . .122 E3
Hall Pk HP4 . . . . .122 E3
Hall Place Cl AL1 . . . . . . .127 E4
Hall Place Gdns AL1 . . . . .127 E4
Hall Rd HP2 . . . . .125 B5
Hallam Cl WD1 . . . . .167 C7
Hallam Gdns HA5 . . . . . . .175 E3
Halland Way HA6 . . . . . . .174 D4
Halleys Ridge SG14 . . . . . .113 A5
Halliday Cl WD7 . . . . . . .156 E7
Halling Hill HP20 . . . . . . .117 F2
Hallingbury Cl CM22 . . . . . .77 B1
Hallingbury Rd
 Bishop's Stortford CM22 . . .77 B4
 Sawbridgeworth CM21 . . . .98 A4
Hallmores EN10 . . . . .135 A4
Hallowell Rd HA6 . . . . . . .174 E3
Hallowes Cres WD1 . . . . . .175 A7
Halls Cl AL6 . . . . .89 C4
Hallside Rd EN1 . . . . .161 F1
Hallwicks Rd LU2 . . . . . . .46 B3
Hallworth Dr SG5 . . . . . . .11 E6
Hallworth Ho SG5 . . . . . . .11 E6
Halsey Dr
 Hemel Hempstead HP1 . . . .123 F5
 Hitchin SG4 . . . . .35 B7
Halsey Pk AL2 . . . . .142 F4
Halsey Pl WD2 . . . . .154 B1
Halsey Rd WD1 . . . . .167 B6
Halstead Hill EN7 . . . . . . .147 E1
Halter Cl WD6 . . . . .170 D4
Haltside AL10 . . . . .129 E4
Halwick Cl HP1 . . . . .124 B1
Halyard Cl LU3 . . . . .45 B6
Hamberlins La HP4 . . . . . .121 C7
Hamble Ct WD1 . . . . .167 A5
Hamblings Cl WD7 . . . . . .156 D6
Hambridge Way SG5 . . . . . .20 D4
Hambro Cl LU2 . . . . .85 F7
Hamburgh Ct EN8 . . . . . . .148 D3
Hamels Dr SG13 . . . . . . .114 B7
Hamer Cl HP3 . . . . .137 A3
Hamer Ct LU2 . . . . .45 D8
Hamilton Ave EN11 . . . . . .135 A8
Hamilton Cl
 Bricket Wood AL2 . . . . . .155 A8
 Dagnall HP4 . . . . .81 C5
 Ridge EN6 . . . . .158 A6
Hamilton Ct 8 AL10 . . . . .130 B3
Hamilton Mead HP3 . . . . . .137 A4
Hamilton Rd
 Abbots Langley WD4 . . . . .153 C6
 Berkhamsted HP4 . . . . . .122 B4
 South Oxhey WD1 . . . . . .175 B7
 St Albans AL1 . . . . .128 A4
Hamilton St WD1 . . . . . . .167 C4
Hamlet The HP4 . . . . .123 A7
Hammarskjold Rd CM20 . . . .117 D2
Hammer La HP2 . . . . .124 F4
Hammerdell SG6 . . . . .22 D7
Hammers Gate AL2 . . . . . .141 A5
Hammond Cl
 Hammond Street EN7 . . . . .147 F5
 Stevenage SG1 . . . . .50 D6
Hammond Ct LU1 . . . . .63 C1
Hammond Jun Mix Inf
 Sch The HP2 . . . . .124 F6
Hammonds Hill AL5 . . . . . .106 F4
Hammonds La AL10 . . . . . .109 B3
Hammondstreet Rd EN7 . . . .147 D5
Hammondswick AL5 . . . . . .106 F4
Hamonte SG6 . . . . .23 C4
Hampden SG4 . . . . .66 C1
Hampden Cl SG6 . . . . .23 B8
Hampden Cres EN7 . . . . . .162 B8
Hampden Hill SG12 . . . . . . .93 F2
Hampden Hill Cl SG12 . . . . .93 F2
Hampden Pl AL2 . . . . .141 E2
Hampden Rd Harrow HA3 . .176 C1
 Hitchin SG4 . . . . .22 C1
Hampden Way SG14 . . . . . .153 E3
Hampermill La WD1 . . . . . .167 A1
Hampton Cl SG2 . . . . .69 C2
Hampton Gdns CM21 . . . . .118 C7
Hampton Rd LU4 . . . . .63 B8
Hamstel Rd CM20 . . . . . . .117 C1
Hamsworth Ct SG14 . . . . . .112 F7
Hanaper Dr SG8 . . . . .93 D1
Hanbury Cl Cheshunt EN8 . .148 E2
 Ware SG12 . . . . .93 D1
Hanbury Cotts AL9 . . . . . .131 E6
Hanbury Dr SG12 . . . . .93 C6
Hanbury Mews SG12 . . . . . .93 C5
Hancock Ct WD6 . . . . . . .170 C8
Hancock Dr LU2 . . . . .45 E5
Hancroft Rd HP3 . . . . . . .124 F1
Hand La CM21 . . . . .97 C1
Handa Cl HP3 . . . . .139 B8
Handcross Rd LU2 . . . . . . .46 D2
Handside Cl AL8 . . . . .110 C6
Handside Gn AL8 . . . . . . .110 C7
Handside La AL8 . . . . .110 C6
Handsworth Way WD1 . . . . .175 A7
Hangar Ruding WD1 . . . . . .175 F7
Hanger Cl HP1 . . . . .124 B2
Hangmans La AL6 . . . . . . .89 F8
Hanover Cl SG2 . . . . .50 F1

Hanover Ct
 Croxley Green WD3 . . . . . .166 A4
 Hoddesdon EN11 . . . . . . .135 A7
 Luton LU4 . . . . .44 D5
 Waltham Abbey EN9 . . . . .163 C6
Hanover Gdns WD5 . . . . . .139 F1
Hanover Gn HP1 . . . . .124 A1
Hanover Wlk AL10 . . . . . . .129 F2
Hanscombe End Rd SG5 . . . .19 C2
Hanselin Cl HA7 . . . . . . .176 F5
Hanswick Cl LU2 . . . . .46 B2
Hanworth Rd LU2 . . . . .45 D7
Hanyards End EN6 . . . . . . .146 E3
Hanyards La EN6 . . . . . . .146 D3
Happy Valley Ind Pk
 WD4 . . . . .139 B3
Harbell Cl SG13 . . . . .114 B6
Harborne Cl WD1 . . . . . . .175 C5
Harbury Dell LU3 . . . . . . .45 B7
Harcourt Rd Bushey WD2 . . .168 C4
 Tring HP23 . . . . .100 C4
Harcourt St LU1 . . . . .63 E5
Hardenwick Ct 4 AL5 . . . . .86 A2
Harding Cl Luton LU3 . . . . .44 E7
 Redbourn AL3 . . . . .106 B5
 Watford WD2 . . . . .154 C6
Harding Ct AL5 . . . . .86 A4
Harding Par 8 AL5 . . . . . . .86 B1
Hardings AL7 . . . . .111 C7
Hardingstone Ct EN8 . . . . .162 F5
Hardwick Cl SG2 . . . . .69 C7
Hardwick Gn LU3 . . . . . . .45 B7
Hardwick Pl AL2 . . . . . . .142 D4
Hardy Cl Barnet EN5 . . . . . .171 E4
 Hitchin SG4 . . . . .35 C7
Hardy Dr SG8 . . . . .7 D8
Hardy Rd HP2 . . . . .124 F4
Hare Cres WD2 . . . . .154 A7
Hare La AL10 . . . . .130 B3
Hare Street Rd SG9 . . . . . .41 B8
Harebell Cl AL7 . . . . .110 E3
Harebreaks The WD2 . . . . .154 B2
Harefield Harlow CM20 . . . .118 A1
 Stevenage SG2 . . . . .51 C3
Harefield Ct LU1 . . . . .62 F8
Harefield Hospl UB9 . . . . . .173 C3
Harefield Inf Sch UB9 . . . . .173 C2
Harefield Jun Sch UB9 . . . . .173 C2
Harefield Pl AL4 . . . . .128 C6
Harefield Rd Luton LU1 . . . .62 F8
 Rickmansworth WD3 . . . . .173 D7
Harepark Cl HP1 . . . . .123 F4
Harewood WD3 . . . . .165 C4
Harewood Ct HA3 . . . . . . .176 E2
Harewood Rd WD1 . . . . . .175 B7
Harford Dr WD1 . . . . .166 E8
Harforde Ct SG13 . . . . . . .114 A6
Hargrave Ct CM24 . . . . . . .59 E6
Hargreaves Ave EN7 . . . . . .162 B8
Hargreaves Cl EN7 . . . . . .162 B8
Hargreaves Rd SG8 . . . . . .7 D5
Harkett Cl HA3 . . . . .176 F1
Harkness EN7 . . . . .148 B2
Harkness Ct SG4 . . . . .22 B1
Harkness Way SG4 . . . . . . .22 C2
Harlech Rd WD5 . . . . .154 A8
Harlequin The WD1 . . . . . .167 C5
Harlesden Rd AL1 . . . . . . .128 A3
Harlestone Cl LU3 . . . . . . .31 A1
Harley Ct AL4 . . . . .128 D7
Harlings The SG13 . . . . . . .114 C2
Harlow Coll CM20 . . . . . . .117 D1
Harlow Ct HP2 . . . . .125 A7
Harlow Mill Sta CM20 . . . . .118 C5
Harlow Rd Roydon CM19 . . .116 C1
 Sawbridgeworth CM21 . . . .118 C8
Harlow Sports Ctr CM20 . . .117 D2
Harlow Stad
 (Greyhounds) CM19 . . . .116 C1
Harlow Town Sta CM20 . . . .117 D3
Harlowbury
 Cty Prim Sch CM17 . . . . .118 D4
Harlton Ct SG9 . . . . .163 F5
Harmer Dell AL6 . . . . .89 F4
Harmer Green La AL6 . . . . .90 B5
Harmony Cl AL10 . . . . . . .130 A7
Harmsworth Way N20 . . . . .171 F1
Harness Way AL4 . . . . . . .128 D6
Harold Cres EN9 . . . . . . .163 C7
Harpenden Central Sta
 AL5 . . . . .86 B1
Harpenden Hospl
 (private) AL5 . . . . .86 A4
Harpenden La AL3 . . . . . . .106 B6
Harpenden Memorial
 Hospl AL5 . . . . .86 B2
Harpenden Prep Sch AL5 . . .85 F2
Harpenden Rd AL5,AL4 . . . .108 B8
Harpenden Rise AL5 . . . . . .85 F3
Harper Ct SG1 . . . . .50 F5
Harper La WD7,AL2 . . . . . .156 B8
Harperbury Hospl WD7 . . . .156 C5
Harps Hill AL3 . . . . .83 E5
Harpsfield Broadway
 AL10 . . . . .129 F6
Harptree Way AL1 . . . . . . .128 A5
Harriet Walker
 Way WD3 . . . . .164 F2
Harriet Way WD2 . . . . . . .168 B2
Harrington Cl 8 CM23 . . . . .77 A7
Harrington Ct SG13 . . . . . .114 C3
Harris Ho 14 WD1 . . . . . . .166 F3
Harris La Great Offley SG5 . .33 D2
 Shenley WD7 . . . . .157 A6
Harris Rd WD2 . . . . .154 A4
Harris's La SG12 . . . . .93 C1
Harrison Cl Hitchin SG4 . . . .34 F7
 Northwood HA6 . . . . . . .174 C4

Harrison Wlk EN8 . . . . . . .148 D1
Harrisons CM23 . . . . .59 D2
Harrogate Rd WD1 . . . . . .175 D7
Harrow Coll, Adult
 Learners Ctr HA5 . . . . . .176 A3
Harrow Coll, Harrow
 Weald Campus HA3 . . . . .176 E4
Harrow Ct SG1 . . . . .50 E5
Harrow View HA2 . . . . . . .176 C1
Harrow Way WD1 . . . . . . .175 E6
Harrow Weald Pk HA3 . . . . .176 D4
Harrow Yd HP23 . . . . . . .100 A3
Harrowden Ct LU2 . . . . . . .64 C8
Harrowden Rd LU2 . . . . . . .64 C8
Harrowdene SG2 . . . . .51 C4
Harry Scott Ct LU4 . . . . . . .44 C6
Harston Dr EN3 . . . . .163 A1
Hart Hill Dr LU2 . . . . .63 F8
Hart Hill La LU2 . . . . .63 F8
Hart Hill Prim Sch LU2 . . . . .63 F8
Hart La LU2 . . . . .64 A8
Hart Lodge EN5 . . . . .171 E6
Hart Rd Harlow CM17 . . . . .118 C6
 St Albans AL1 . . . . .127 D2
Hart Wlk LU2 . . . . .46 A1
Hartfield Ave LU2 . . . . . . .176 A1
Hartfield Cl WD6 . . . . . . .170 A4
Hartfield Ct 6 SG12 . . . . . .93 D2
Hartforde Rd WD6 . . . . . . .170 B8
Harthall La SG14 . . . . . . .113 D6
Hartham La SG14 . . . . . . .113 C6
Hartham Villas SG14 . . . . . .113 C6
Hartland Ct SG5 . . . . .34 D7
Hartland Rd EN8 . . . . .148 D1
Hartley Rd LU2 . . . . .63 F8
Hartmoor Mews EN3 . . . . .162 D2
Harts Cl WD2 . . . . .168 A8
Hartsbourne Ave WD2 . . . . .176 D8
Hartsbourne Cl WD2 . . . . . .176 D8
Hartsbourne Ctry Club
 WD2 . . . . .176 C8
Hartsbourne Pk WD2 . . . . .176 E8
Hartsbourne Prim Sch
 WD2 . . . . .176 D8
Hartsbourne Way HP2 . . . . .125 C2
Hartsfield Jun Mix Inf Sch
 SG7 . . . . .12 F1
Hartsfield Rd LU2 . . . . . . .46 B2
Hartspring La WD2 . . . . . .168 A8
Hartswood Gn WD2 . . . . . .176 D8
Hartwell Gdns AL5 . . . . . . .85 E1
Hartwood 3 LU2 . . . . .63 F8
Harvest Cl LU4 . . . . .44 A3
Harvest Ct Oaklands AL6 . . . .89 E7
 St Albans AL4 . . . . .128 D7
Harvest End WD2 . . . . . . .154 D3
Harvest La SG2 . . . . .51 D7
Harvest Mead AL10 . . . . . .130 B7
Harvest Rd WD2 . . . . .168 B5
Harvey Rd
 Croxley Green WD3 . . . . . .166 A3
 London Colney AL2 . . . . . .142 C5
 Stevenage SG2 . . . . .51 B6
Harvey Road Prim Sch
 WD3 . . . . .166 A3
Harvey's Hill LU2 . . . . . . .45 F5
Harveyfields EN9 . . . . . . .163 C5
Harveys Cotts SG12 . . . . . .75 F8
Harwood Cl Tewin AL6 . . . . .90 E2
 Welwyn Garden City AL8 . . .89 E1
Harwood Hill AL8 . . . . .89 E1
Harwood Hill Jun Mix Inf
 Sch AL8 . . . . .89 E2
Harwoods Rd WD1 . . . . . . .167 A5
Hasedines Rd HP1 . . . . . . .124 A4
Haseldine Mdws AL10 . . . . .129 F4
Haseldine Rd AL2 . . . . . . .142 D5
Haselfoot SG6 . . . . .22 E6
Haskeston Dr LU4 . . . . . . .44 B6
Haslemere CM23 . . . . .77 A4
Haslemere Est The EN11 . . .135 D6
Haslemere Ind Est AL7 . . . .110 F7
Haslewood Ave EN11 . . . . .135 A6
Haslewood Jun Sch
 EN11 . . . . .135 B6
Haslingden Cl AL5 . . . . . . .85 D3
Hastings Cl SG1 . . . . .50 A8
Hastings St LU1 . . . . .63 D6
Hastings Way
 Croxley Green WD3 . . . . . .166 C5
 Watford WD2 . . . . .167 E5
Hastoe La HP23 . . . . .100 A2
Hatch End High Sch
 HA3 . . . . .176 B2
Hatch End Sta HA5 . . . . . .176 A3
Hatch Gn CM22 . . . . .98 B8
Hatch La SG4 . . . . .24 A3
Hatching Green Cl AL5 . . . .107 A6
Hatfield Aerodrome
 AL10 . . . . .129 D6
Hatfield Ave AL10 . . . . . . .129 E8
Hatfield Bsns Ctr AL10 . . . .129 D8
Hatfield Cres HP2 . . . . . . .124 F7
Hatfield House & Gdns
 AL9 . . . . .130 D5
Hatfield Rd Essendon AL9 . . .111 E1
 Potters Bar EN6 . . . . . . .159 C8
 St Albans AL1,AL4 . . . . . .128 C3
 Watford WD2 . . . . .167 B8
Hatfield Sta AL9 . . . . .130 C6
Hatfield Tunnel AL10 . . . . .129 F6
Hathaway Cl LU4 . . . . .44 B1
Hatherleigh Gdns EN6 . . . . .159 C1
Hatters La WD1 . . . . .166 D3
Hatters Way LU1 . . . . .63 B8
Hatton Rd EN8 . . . . .148 D2

Havelock Rd
 Kings Langley WD4 . . . . . .138 F3
 Luton LU2 . . . . .45 E1
Havelock Rise LU2 . . . . . . .45 E1
Haven Cl AL10 . . . . .129 F6
Haven The SG5 . . . . .11 F6
Havenfield WD4 . . . . .152 B8
Havens Par CM23 . . . . .76 F5
Haverdale LU4 . . . . .44 C4
Havers Inf Sch The CM23 . . .76 E5
Havers La CM23 . . . . .76 E5
Haward Rd EN11 . . . . . . .135 C8
Hawbush Cl SG13 . . . . .89 B5
Hawbush Rd AL6 . . . . .89 B5
Hawes Cl HA6 . . . . .174 F3
Hawes La E4 . . . . .163 C1
Haweswater Dr WD2 . . . . .154 C6
Hawfield Gdns AL2 . . . . . .141 D5
Hawkesworth Cl HA6 . . . . .174 E3
Hawkfield SG6 . . . . .22 E8
Hawkfields LU2 . . . . .45 E6
Hawkins Cl WD6 . . . . . . .170 C7
Hawkins Hall La SG3 . . . . . .69 E2
Hawkins Way HP3 . . . . . . .137 A5
Hawkshead Ct EN8 . . . . . .162 F5
Hawkshead La AL9 . . . . . . .144 D3
Hawkshead Rd EN6 . . . . . .145 B2
Hawkshill Al1 . . . . .128 A2
Hawkshill Dr HP3 . . . . . . .137 F8
Hawksmead Ct EN3 . . . . . .162 D3
Hawksmoor WD7 . . . . . . .157 A6
Hawksmoor Sch WD6 . . . . .170 C8
Hawkwell Dr HP23 . . . . . .100 C4
Hawridge Cl HP5 . . . . . . .120 F1
Hawridge Vale HP5 . . . . . .120 F1
Hawsley Rd AL5 . . . . .107 A5
Hawthorn Ave LU2 . . . . . . .46 B4
Hawthorn Cl
 Abbots Langley WD5 . . . . .154 A7
 Harpenden AL5 . . . . . . .107 D7
 Hertford SG14 . . . . .113 C4
 Hitchin SG5 . . . . .34 E6
 Royston SG8 . . . . .7 F7
 Watford WD1 . . . . .153 F1
Hawthorn Cres LU1 . . . . . .62 E3
Hawthorn Gr EN2 . . . . . . .161 D1
Hawthorn Hill SG6 . . . . . . .22 F7
Hawthorn La HP1 . . . . . . .123 F4
Hawthorn Rd EN11 . . . . . .135 B8
Hawthorn Rise CM23 . . . . . .76 F3
Hawthorn Way
 Chiswellgreen AL2 . . . . . .141 A7
 Royston SG8 . . . . .7 F7
Hawthorne Ave EN7 . . . . . .162 B8
Hawthorne Cl EN7 . . . . . . .162 B8
Hawthorne Rd HA6 . . . . . .175 A1
Hawthorne Rd WD7 . . . . . .156 A5
Hawthornes AL8 . . . . . . .110 D8
Hawthorns The
 Berkhamsted HP4 . . . . . .122 A5
 Hemel Hempstead HP3 . . . .137 F7
 Maple Cross WD3 . . . . . .172 D5
 Stevenage SG1 . . . . .51 A4
 Ware SG12 . . . . .93 C3
Hawtrees WD7 . . . . .155 F4
Hay Cl WD6 . . . . .170 C7
Hay La AL5 . . . . .86 A1
Haybourn Mead HP1 . . . . .124 B2
Haycroft
 Bishop's Stortford CM23 . . .77 C7
 Luton LU2 . . . . .45 E6
Haycroft Rd SG1 . . . . .50 E7
Haydock SG8 . . . . .7 F6
Haydon Hill Ho WD2 . . . . .167 F2
Haydon Rd WD1 . . . . .167 E3
Hayes Cl LU2 . . . . .46 C5
Hayes Hill Farm EN9 . . . . .149 C3
Hayes Wlk EN10 . . . . . . .148 F6
Hayfield SG2 . . . . .51 D7
Hayfield Cl WD2 . . . . . . .168 B5
Haygarth SG3 . . . . .69 A4
Hayhurst Rd LU4 . . . . .44 B1
Hayley Bell Gdns CM23 . . . .76 F3
Hayley Comm SG2 . . . . . . .51 C3
Hayling Dr LU2 . . . . .46 D3
Hayling Rd WD1 . . . . .175 B8
Haymeads AL8 . . . . .89 E1
Haymeads La CM23 . . . . . .77 C6
Haymoor SG6 . . . . .22 E7
Haynes Cl AL7 . . . . .111 A5
Haynes Mead HP4 . . . . . . .122 A6
Haysman Cl SG6 . . . . .23 B7
Hayton Cl LU3 . . . . .31 B2
Haywood Cl HA5 . . . . . . .175 D1
Haywood Ct EN9 . . . . . . .163 F5
Haywood La SG8 . . . . .16 A6
Haywood Pk WD3 . . . . . . .164 F4
Haywoods Dr HP3 . . . . . . .137 F8
Haywoods La SG8 . . . . . . .7 E7
Hazel Cl
 Hammond Street EN7 . . . . .147 E5
 Welwyn AL6 . . . . .89 E3
Hazel Ct SG4 . . . . .35 A7
Hazel Gdns CM21 . . . . .97 F1
Hazel Gr Hatfield AL10 . . . .129 F2
 Stotfold SG5 . . . . .11 C5
 Watford WD2 . . . . .154 B4
 Welwyn Garden City AL7 . . .111 C7
Hazel Grove Ho AL10 . . . . .129 F3
Hazel Mead EN5 . . . . .171 A4
Hazel Rd
 Berkhamsted HP4 . . . . . .122 D3
 Chiswellgreen AL2 . . . . . .141 B3
Hazel Tree Rd WD2 . . . . . .154 B4
Hazelbury Ave WD5 . . . . . .153 C7
Hazelbury Cres LU1 . . . . . .63 C8

Hazelbury Ct LU1 . . . . . . .63 C8
Hazelcroft HA5 . . . . .176 B4
Hazeldell LU4 . . . . .70 D3
Hazeldell Link HP1 . . . . . .123 E2
Hazeldell Rd HP1 . . . . . . .123 F2
Hazeldene EN8 . . . . .162 E7
Hazelend Rd CM23 . . . . . . .59 B4
Hazelgrove Prim Sch
 AL4 . . . . .129 F2
Hazelmere Rd
 St Albans AL4 . . . . .128 C6
 Stevenage SG4 . . . . .69 A8
Hazels The AL6 . . . . .90 E2
Hazelwood Cl Hitchin SG5 . .34 F8
 Luton LU2 . . . . .46 B4
Hazelwood Dr
 Pinner HA5 . . . . .175 E4
 St Albans AL4 . . . . .128 C4
Hazelwood La WD5 . . . . . .153 D7
Hazelwood Rd WD3 . . . . . .166 C3
Hazely HP23 . . . . .100 C4
Heacham Cl LU4 . . . . .44 B4
Head Ct CM24 . . . . .59 D7
Headingley Cl
 Hammond Street EN7 . . . . .147 F5
 Shenley WD7 . . . . .156 E7
 Stevenage SG1 . . . . .50 E7
Headstone La HA2,HA3 . . . .176 B2
Headstone Lane Sta
 HA3 . . . . .176 B2
Healey Rd HA3 . . . . .176 F3
Health Farm La AL1,AL3 . . . .127 E5
Healy Ct EN5 . . . . .171 D3
Heath Ave Royston SG8 . . . .7 C3
 St Albans AL3 . . . . .127 D5
Heath Brow HP1 . . . . .124 C1
Heath Cl Harpenden AL5 . . .107 C7
 Hemel Hempstead HP1 . . . .124 C2
 Luton LU1 . . . . .63 B6
 Potters Bar EN6 . . . . . . .145 B1
Heath Ct SG14 . . . . .112 F7
Heath Dr Potters Bar EN6 . .145 A1
 Ware SG12 . . . . .93 C3
Heath Farm Ct WD1 . . . . .153 D2
Heath Hall SG7 . . . . .23 F7
Heath Hill SG4 . . . . .67 D1
Heath La Codicote SG4 . . . .67 F1
 Hemel Hempstead HP1 . . . .124 C2
 Hertford Heath SG13 . . . . .114 C2
Heath Lodge WD2 . . . . . . .168 D1
Heath Mount Sch SG14 . . . .71 B2
Heath Rd
 Breachwood Green SG4 . . . .47 D1
 Oaklands AL6 . . . . .68 F1
 Potters Bar EN6 . . . . . . .145 B1
 St Albans AL1 . . . . .127 E5
 Watford WD1 . . . . .167 E3
Heath Row CM23 . . . . .59 B1
Heath The
 Breachwood Green SG4 . . . .47 D2
 Radlett WD7 . . . . .156 A6
Heathbourne Rd
 WD2,HA7 . . . . .168 F1
Heathbrow Rd AL6 . . . . . . .89 F4
Heathcote Ave AL10 . . . . . .130 A7
Heathcote Sch SG2 . . . . . . .51 A2
Heathcroft AL7 . . . . .111 C6
Heathdene Manor WD1 . . . .166 F8
Heather Cl
 Abbots Langley WD5 . . . . .154 A7
 Bishop's Stortford CM23 . . .76 D6
Heather Rd AL8 . . . . .110 C4
Heather Rise WD2 . . . . . . .167 F7
Heather Way Harrow HA7 . . .176 F5
 Hemel Hempstead HP2 . . . .124 D4
 Potters Bar EN6 . . . . . . .158 F7
Heathermere SG6 . . . . . . .11 F1
Heathfield SG8 . . . . .7 B6
Heathfield Cl
 Caddington LU1 . . . . . . .62 F3
 Potters Bar EN6 . . . . . . .145 B1
Heathfield Ct AL1 . . . . . . .127 E4
Heathfield Lower Sch
 LU1 . . . . .62 E4
Heathfield Rd Hitchin SG5 . .21 F1
 Luton LU1 . . . . .45 C4
 Watford WD2 . . . . .167 F5
Heathgate SG13 . . . . .114 B2
Heathlands AL6 . . . . .68 F1
Heathlands Dr AL3 . . . . . .127 E5
Heathlands Sch AL3 . . . . . .127 E6
Heathside
 Colney Heath AL4 . . . . . .143 B8
 St Albans AL1 . . . . .127 C6
Heathside Cl HA6 . . . . . . .174 D5
Heathside Rd HA6 . . . . . . .174 D6
Heathview AL5 . . . . .107 B8
Heaton Ct EN8 . . . . .148 D2
Heaton Dell LU2 . . . . .46 E1
Heay Fields AL7 . . . . .111 C7
Hebden Cl LU4 . . . . .44 B4
Heckford Cl WD1 . . . . . . .166 C3
Hedge Row HP1 . . . . .124 A5
Hedgebrooms AL7 . . . . . . .111 C7
Hedgerow Cl SG2 . . . . .51 D8
Hedgerow La EN5 . . . . . . .171 A4
Hedgerow The LU4 . . . . . . .44 D6
Hedgerow Wlk EN8 . . . . . .148 D5
Hedgerows CM21 . . . . .97 F2
Hedgerows The SG2 . . . . . .51 D8
Hedges Cl AL10 . . . . .130 B4
Hedgeside HP4 . . . . .123 A7
Hedgeside Rd HA6 . . . . . . .174 C5
Hedley Cl HP22 . . . . .99 A4
Hedley Rd AL1 . . . . .128 B3

Hedley Rise LU2 . . . .**46** F2
Hedworth Ave EN8 . . . . . .**162** D6
Heights The
Hemel Hempstead HP2 . .**124** F6
Luton LU3 . . . .**44** E5
Helena Cl EN4 . . . .**159** D1
Helena Pl 5 HP2 . . . .**124** D5
Helens Gate EN8 . . . . . .**148** F5
Hellards Rd SG1 . . . .**50** D7
Hellebore Ct SG1 . . . .**51** B8
Helmsley Cl LU4 . . . .**44** C5
Helston Cl HA5 . . . .**175** F3
Helston Gr HP2 . . . .**124** D8
Helston Pl WD5 . . . .**153** F7
Hemel Hempstead
General Hospl HP2 . . . . .**124** D3
Hemel Hempstead Rd
Great Gaddesden HP4 . . . .**81** F1
Hemel
Hempstead HP2,HP3 . . . .**125** E1
Redbourn AL3 . . . .**105** E2
St Albans HP3,AL2,AL3 . .**126** D1
Hemel Hempstead Sch
HP1 . . . .**124** C2
Hemel Hempstead Sta
HP3 . . . .**138** A8
Hemingford Dr LU2 . . . . . .**45** D6
Hemingford Rd WD1 . . . .**153** E3
Hemming Way WD2 . . . . .**154** A4
Hemmings The HP4 . . . . .**121** F3
Hemp La HP23 . . . .**100** F1
Hempstall AL7 . . . .**111** B4
Hempstead La HP4 . . . . . .**123** C6
Hempstead Rd
Abbots Langley WD4 . . . .**139** A3
Bovingdon HP3 . . . .**137** B5
Watford WD1 . . . .**153** E2
Henbury Way WD1 . . . . . .**175** D7
Henderson Cl AL3 . . . . . .**127** C7
Henderson Rd EN9 . . . . . .**163** C7
Hendon Wood La NW1 . . .**171** A1
Henge Way LU3 . . . .**44** E7
Henlow Ind Est SG16 . . . . .**10** B4
Henry Cl EN2 . . . .**161** E1
Henry St
Hemel Hempstead HP3 . . .**138** D7
Tring HP23 . . . .**100** A3
Hensley Cl Hitchin SG4 . . .**35** B6
Welwyn AL6 . . . .**89** C6
Henstead Pl LU2 . . . .**46** D1
Herald Cl CM23 . . . .**76** D6
Herbert St HP2 . . . .**124** D4
Hereford Rd LU4 . . . .**44** A3
Hereward Cl EN9 . . . .**163** C7
Herga Ct WD1 . . . .**167** A7
Heritage Cl AL3 . . . .**127** D3
Herkomer Cl WD2 . . . . . .**168** B3
Herkomer Rd WD2 . . . . . .**168** A3
Herm Ho EN3 . . . .**162** D1
Hermitage Ct
Potters Bar EN6 . . . .**159** C6
Stansted Mountfitchet CM24 .**59** D7
Hermitage Rd SG5 . . . . . .**34** F7
Herne Ct WD2 . . . .**168** C2
Herne Rd Bushey WD2 . . . .**168** B3
Stevenage SG1 . . . .**36** B1
Herneshaw AL10 . . . .**129** F3
Herns La AL7 . . . .**111** B8
Herns Way AL7 . . . .**111** A7
Heron Cl
Hemel Hempstead HP3 . . .**138** F6
Rickmansworth WD3 . . . .**173** D8
Sawbridgeworth CM21 . . . .**97** D1
Heron Ct CM23 . . . .**77** A7
Heron Dr Luton LU2 . . . . . .**45** E6
Stansted Abbotts SG12 . . .**115** C3
Heron Trad Est LU3 . . . . . .**44** C7
Heron Way Hatfield AL10 . .**130** A3
Stotfold SG5 . . . .**11** E6
Heron Wlk HA6 . . . .**174** E6
Heronfield EN6 . . . .**145** C1
Herongate Rd EN8 . . . . . .**148** E4
Herons Elm HP4 . . . .**121** E7
Herons Way AL1 . . . .**142** B8
Herons Wood CM20 . . . . .**117** B2
Heronsgate Rd WD3 . . . . .**164** B3
Heronslea WD2 . . . .**154** C3
Heronswood EN9 . . . .**163** E5
Heronswood Pl AL7 . . . . .**111** A5
Heronswood Rd AL7 . . . . .**111** A5
Hertford Castle SG14 . . . .**113** C5
Hertford Cty Hospl
SG14 . . . .**113** B6
Hertford East Sta SG13 . .**113** E6
Hertford Heath
Jun Mix Inf Sch SG13 . . .**114** C4
Hertford Mews EN6 . . . . .**159** C8
Hertford Mus SG14 . . . . .**113** D6
Hertford North Sta
SG14 . . . .**113** B6
Hertford Rd
Enfield EN3 . . . .**162** D3
Great Amwell SG12 . . . . .**114** F4
Hatfield AL9 . . . .**111** B1
Hoddesdon EN11 . . . . . .**134** E8
Stevenage SG2 . . . .**69** B7
Tewin AL6 . . . .**90** F2
Welwyn AL6 . . . .**89** D3
Hertford Regional Coll
Cheshunt EN10 . . . .**148** F6
Ware SG12 . . . .**114** D8
Hertfordshire Bsns Ctr
AL2 . . . .**142** D5
Hertfordshire & Essex
High Sch CM23 . . . .**77** B7

Hertingfordbury Cowper
Prim Sch SG14 . . . .**112** C4
Hertingfordbury Rd
Hertford SG14 . . . .**113** B5
Hertingfordbury SG14 . . .**112** F4
Herts & Essex Comm
Hospl CM23 . . . .**77** B6
Herts & Essex High Sch
CM23 . . . .**77** B6
Hertsmere Ind Pk WD6 . .**170** D6
Hertswood Ct 1 EN5 . . .**171** E5
Hester Ho CM20 . . . .**117** C2
Heswall Ct 5 LU1 . . . .**63** F6
Heswall Gn WD1 . . . .**175** A7
Hetchleys HP1 . . . .**124** A6
Hewins Cl EN9 . . . .**163** E7
Hewitt Cl AL4 . . . .**108** D7
Hewlett Rd LU3 . . . .**44** A5
Hexton Cty Prim Sch SG5 .**19** A1
Hexton Rd
Great Offley SG5 . . . .**33** E8
Lilley LU2 . . . .**32** C4
Heybridge Ct SG14 . . . . .**112** F7
Heydon Rd SG8 . . . .**9** E3
Heydons Cl AL3 . . . .**127** D5
Heyford End AL2 . . . .**141** C3
Heyford Rd WD7 . . . .**155** F2
Heyford Way AL10 . . . . .**130** C7
Heysham Dr WD1 . . . . . .**175** D5
Heywood Dr LU2 . . . .**45** F2
Hibbert Ave WD2 . . . . . .**154** D1
Hibbert Rd HA3 . . . .**176** F1
Hibbert St LU1 . . . .**63** E6
Hibbert Street
Almshouses** 18 LU1 . . . .**63** E6
Hibberts Ct SG6 . . . .**22** E7
Hickling Cl LU2 . . . .**46** D1
Hickling Way AL5 . . . .**86** C3
Hickman Cl EN10 . . . . . .**134** D3
Hickman Ct LU3 . . . .**44** D8
Hicks Rd AL3 . . . .**83** F6
Hidalgo Ct HP2 . . . .**124** F6
Hideaway The WD5 . . . . .**153** F8
Hides The CM20 . . . .**117** D1
Higgins Rd
Hammond Street EN7 . . . .**147** D4
Hammond Street EN7 . . . .**147** D5
High Acres WD5 . . . .**153** D7
High Ash Rd AL4 . . . .**108** C2
High Ave SG6 . . . .**22** E4
High Barnet Sta EN5 . . . .**171** F5
High Beech Rd LU3 . . . . . .**44** D7
High Beeches
Jun Mix Inf Sch AL5 . . . . .**86** D1
High Canons WD6 . . . . . .**157** D2
High Cl WD3 . . . .**165** C4
High Cross WD2 . . . .**155** D2
High Dane SG4 . . . .**22** A2
High Dells AL10 . . . .**129** F4
High Elms AL5 . . . .**107** A6
High Elms Cl HA6 . . . . . .**174** D4
High Elms La
Abbots Langley WD2,WD5 . .**154** C8
Benington SG2 . . . .**52** F1
High Firs WD7 . . . .**156** A4
High Firs Cres AL5 . . . . . .**107** D8
High Gr AL8 . . . .**110** C7
High House Est CM17 . . .**118** F4
High La CM24 . . . .**59** F8
High Mead LU3 . . . .**45** A3
High Meads AL1 . . . .**108** C8
High Oak Rd SG12 . . . .**93** E3
High Oaks Enfield EN2 . . .**160** F1
St Albans AL3 . . . .**127** D7
High Oaks Rd AL8 . . . . . .**110** B7
High Pastures CM22 . . . . .**98** D1
High Plash SG1 . . . .**50** E5
High Point 1 LU1 . . . .**63** D6
High Rd Bushey WD2 . . . .**168** D1
Essendon AL9 . . . .**131** E5
Harrow HA3 . . . .**176** E3
Hoddesdon EN10 . . . . . .**134** F4
Shillington SG5 . . . .**19** E8
Stapleford SG14 . . . .**92** A2
Watford WD2 . . . .**154** A7
High Ridge Cuffley EN6 . .**146** E4
Harpenden AL5 . . . .**85** E3
Luton LU2 . . . .**46** C1
High Ridge Rd HP3 . . . . .**138** D7
High Road Broxbourne
EN10 . . . .**134** F1
High Road Turnford
EN10 . . . .**148** E6
High Road Wormley
EN10 . . . .**148** F8
High St
Abbots Langley WD5 . . . .**139** F1
Abbots Langley,
Bedmond WD5 . . . .**139** F4
Arlesey SG15 . . . .**11** A5
Ashwell SG7 . . . .**4** D4
Baldock SG7 . . . .**23** F8
Barkway SG8 . . . .**17** C3
Barley SG8 . . . .**8** F2
Barnet EN5 . . . .**171** F5
Berkhamsted HP4 . . . . . .**122** B4
Berkhamsted,
Northchurch HP4 . . . . . .**121** E6
Bishop's Stortford CM23 . . .**76** F7
Bovingdon HP3 . . . .**137** A4
Buntingford SG9 . . . .**40** E8
Bushey WD2 . . . .**168** A3
Cheddington LU7 . . . .**80** A7
Cheshunt EN8 . . . .**148** D2
Cheshunt,
Theabald's Grove Sta EN8 . .**162** D7
Cheshunt,
Waltham Cross EN8 . . . .**162** E5

High St continued
Codicote SG4 . . . .**67** F1
Colney Heath AL4 . . . . . .**129** B1
Elstree WD6 . . . .**169** D3
Eyeworth SG19 . . . .**1** A8
Flamstead AL3 . . . .**84** B2
Graveley SG4 . . . .**36** C4
Great Offley SG5 . . . .**33** C3
Guilden Morden SG8 . . . . . .**1** F4
Harefield UB9 . . . .**173** C1
Harlow CM17 . . . .**118** D4
Harpenden AL5 . . . .**86** A1
Harrow HA3 . . . .**176** E1
Hemel
Hempstead HP1,HP3 . . . .**124** D4
Hinxworth SG7 . . . .**3** D6
Hitchin SG5 . . . .**34** E7
Hitchin, Gosmore SG4 . . . .**34** F3
Hoddesdon EN11 . . . . . .**135** A5
Hunsdon SG12 . . . .**95** D1
Kimpton SG4 . . . .**66** C1
Kings Langley WD4 . . . . .**139** A2
London Colney AL2 . . . . .**142** D5
Luton LU4 . . . .**44** C4
Markyate AL3 . . . .**83** E5
Much Hadham SG10 . . . . .**74** F3
Northwood HA6 . . . .**174** F2
Pirton SG5 . . . .**20** D4
Pitstone LU7 . . . .**80** E5
Potters Bar EN6 . . . .**159** C7
Redbourn AL3 . . . .**106** B5
Reed SG8 . . . .**16** E5
Rickmansworth WD3 . . . .**165** E1
Roydon CM19 . . . .**116** B1
Royston SG8 . . . .**7** D6
Sandridge AL4 . . . .**108** C2
St Albans AL3 . . . .**127** D3
Standon SG11 . . . .**55** F1
Standon, Puckeridge SG11 . .**55** A7
Stanstead Abbotts SG12 . .**115** C4
Stevenage SG1 . . . .**50** C7
Stotfold SG5 . . . .**11** F6
Tring HP23 . . . .**100** A3
Walkern SG2 . . . .**38** B1
Ware SG12 . . . .**93** D1
Watford WD1 . . . .**167** B6
Watford WD1 . . . .**167** C5
Watton at Stone SG14 . . . .**70** E3
Welwyn AL6 . . . .**89** C5
Wheathampstead AL4 . . . .**87** D1
Whitwell SG4 . . . .**66** F7
Widford SG12 . . . .**95** E5
High Street Gn HP2 . . . . .**125** A5
High Town Rd LU2 . . . . . .**45** F1
High Tree Cl CM21 . . . . . .**97** D1
High View Birchanger CM23 .**59** D3
Chorleywood WD3 . . . . .**165** A5
Hatfield AL10 . . . .**130** A2
Hitchin SG5 . . . .**34** D7
Markyate AL3 . . . .**83** E5
Watford WD1 . . . .**166** F3
High View Cl HA3 . . . . . .**176** E3
High Wickfield AL7 . . . . .**111** C5
High Wood Cl LU1 . . . .**62** F7
High Wood Rd EN11 . . . .**114** F1
High Wych
CE Prim Sch CM21 . . . . . .**97** A1
High Wych La CM21 . . . . .**97** A2
High Wych Rd
Gilston CM21 . . . .**117** F7
High Wych CM21 . . . .**97** B1
High Wych Way HP2 . . . .**105** A1
Higham Dr LU2 . . . .**46** D1
Highbanks Rd HA5 . . . . .**176** B4
Highbarns HP3 . . . .**139** A6
Highbridge Ct EN9 . . . . .**163** B6
Highbridge Ho EN9 . . . . .**163** B6
Highbridge Ret Pk EN9 . .**163** B5
Highbridge St EN9 . . . . .**163** B6
Highbury Ho (North
Herts Rural Music Sch)
SG4 . . . .**35** A7
Highbury Inf Sch SG4 . . . .**34** F6
Highbury Rd Hitchin SG4 . .**35** A7
Luton LU3 . . . .**45** C1
Highbush Rd SG5 . . . .**11** E5
Highclere Ct AL1 . . . .**127** E4
Highclere Dr HP3 . . . . . .**139** B7
Highcroft 2 SG2 . . . .**50** F1
Highcroft Rd HP3 . . . . . .**138** B6
Highfield Bushey WD2 . . .**176** E8
Kings Langley WD4 . . . . .**138** E3
Letchworth SG6 . . . .**22** E4
Sawbridgeworth CM21 . . . .**97** E3
South Oxhey WD1 . . . . . .**175** F7
Watford WD2 . . . .**153** F5
Highfield Ave
Bishop's Stortford CM23 . . .**77** C6
Harpenden AL5 . . . .**107** C8
Highfield Cl HA6 . . . .**174** E2
Highfield Cres HA6 . . . . .**174** E2
Highfield Ct SG1 . . . .**50** F7
Highfield Dr EN10 . . . . . .**134** E2
Highfield La
Colney Heath AL1 . . . . . .**142** E8
Hemel Hempstead HP2 . . .**124** F5
Highfield Oval AL5 . . . . . .**86** A4
Highfield Park Dr AL4 . . .**142** C8
Highfield Rd
Berkhamsted HP4 . . . . . .**122** D4
Hammond Street EN7 . . . .**147** E5
Hertford SG13 . . . .**113** D4
Luton LU4 . . . .**45** B1
Northwood HA6 . . . .**174** E2
Sandridge AL4 . . . .**108** B1
Tring HP23 . . . .**99** E3
Watford WD2 . . . .**167** E4
Wigginton HP23 . . . .**100** D1

Highfield Sch The SG6 . . . .**22** D4
Highfield Way WD3 . . . . .**165** B3
Highfields Cuffley EN6 . . .**146** E3
Radlett WD7 . . . .**157** F4
Highfields Cl LU5 . . . .**44** A3
Highfield Way EN6 . . . . . .**159** B7
Highgate Gr CM21 . . . . . .**97** D2
Highgrove Ct EN8 . . . . . .**162** D5
Highland Dr Bushey WD2 .**168** C2
Hemel Hempstead HP3 . . .**125** B3
Highland Rd
Bishop's Stortford CM23 . . .**76** F3
Lower Nazeing EN9 . . . . .**135** E1
Northwood HA6 . . . .**175** A1
Highlands Hatfield AL9 . . .**130** C8
Royston SG8 . . . .**7** E6
Watford WD1 . . . .**167** C1
Highlands The
Potters Bar EN6 . . . .**145** C1
Rickmansworth WD3 . . . .**165** B2
Highmead CM24 . . . .**59** E8
Highmill SG12 . . . .**93** D3
Highmoor AL5 . . . .**86** A4
Highover Cl LU2 . . . .**46** B1
Highover
Jun Mix Inf Sch SG4 . . . . .**22** C1
Highover Rd SG6 . . . .**22** D5
Highover Way SG4 . . . . . .**22** B1
Highview Cl EN6 . . . .**159** C6
Highview Gdns
Potters Bar EN6 . . . .**159** C6
St Albans AL4 . . . .**128** C8
Highway The HA7 . . . . . .**176** E2
Highwood Ave WD2 . . . . .**167** F8
Highwood Prim Sch
WD2 . . . .**167** E8
Highwoodhall La HP3 . . .**139** C7
Hilbury AL10 . . . .**129** F4
Hilfield La WD2 . . . .**168** D6
Hilfield La S WD2 . . . . . .**168** F3
Hill Cl Barnet EN5 . . . . . .**171** C4
Harpenden AL5 . . . .**86** C4
Luton LU3 . . . .**45** C7
Hill Comm HP3 . . . .**139** A8
Hill Crest Potters Bar EN6 .**159** C5
Whitwell SG4 . . . .**66** E6
Hill Crest Lodge WD6 . . .**169** F5
Hill Croft LU4 . . . .**44** C6
Hill Ct HP4 . . . .**122** D5
Hill Dyke Rd AL4 . . . .**108** E2
Hill End La AL4 . . . .**128** C2
Hill End Rd UB9 . . . .**173** C3
Hill Farm Ave WD2 . . . . .**154** A6
Hill Farm Cl WD2 . . . . . .**154** A6
Hill Farm La
Ayot St Lawrence AL6 . . . .**88** C5
Redbourn AL3 . . . .**106** C1
Hill Ho SG13 . . . .**113** C5
Hill House Ave HA7 . . . . .**176** F3
Hill Ley AL10 . . . .**129** F5
Hill Leys EN6 . . . .**146** E3
Hill Mead HP4 . . . .**122** A3
Hill Milford AL5 . . . .**86** D3
Hill Pickford AL5 . . . .**86** D4
Hill Rd Codicote SG4 . . . . .**67** E1
Northwood HA6 . . . .**174** D4
Hill Rise Cuffley EN6 . . . .**146** E3
Luton LU3 . . . .**44** D7
Potters Bar EN6 . . . .**159** C5
Rickmansworth WD3 . . . .**165** B2
Hill Side LU7 . . . .**79** F7
Hill St AL3 . . . .**127** C3
Hill The Harlow CM17 . . .**118** C4
Wheathampstead AL4 . . .**108** D8
Hill Top SG7 . . . .**23** E7
Hill View
Berkhamsted HP4 . . . . . .**122** A6
Buckland SG9 . . . .**27** D8
Whitwell SG4 . . . .**66** E6
Hillary Cl LU3 . . . .**44** D7
Hillary Cres LU1 . . . .**63** C6
Hillary Rd HP2 . . . .**125** A4
Hillary Rise SG5 . . . .**11** B5
Hillborough Inf Sch LU1 . .**63** C6
Hillborough Jun Sch LU1 . .**63** D6
Hillborough Rd LU1 . . . . . .**63** D6
Hillbrow SG6 . . . .**22** D5
Hillcrest Baldock SG7 . . . .**23** F7
Barnet EN5 . . . .**171** B5
Hatfield AL10 . . . .**130** A5
St Albans AL3 . . . .**127** B1
Stevenage SG1 . . . .**50** F5
Hillcrest Ave LU2 . . . .**45** C8
Hillcrest Rd WD7 . . . . . .**157** A6
Hillcroft Cres WD1 . . . . .**175** B8
Hilldown Rd HP1 . . . .**124** A4
Hille Bsns Ctr WD2 . . . . .**167** B8
Hillfield AL10 . . . .**130** C4
Hillfield Ave SG4 . . . .**22** A2
Hillfield Ct HP2 . . . .**124** E3
Hillfield Rd HP2 . . . .**124** D4
Hillgate SG4 . . . .**22** A3
Hillhouse EN9 . . . .**163** F6
Hilliard Rd HA6 . . . .**174** F2
Hillingdon Rd WD2 . . . . .**154** B5
Hillmead SG1 . . . .**51** A6
Hillmead
Jun Mix Inf Sch CM23 . . . .**59** C1
Hillpath SG6 . . . .**23** B6
Hillrise Ave WD2 . . . .**154** D2
Hills La HA6 . . . .**174** E2
Hillsborough Gn WD1 . . .**175** A4
Hillshott SG6 . . . .**23** A6
Hillshott Inf Sch SG6 . . . .**23** A6
Hillside Codicote SG4 . . . . .**67** F1
Hatfield AL10 . . . .**130** A5
Hoddesdon EN11 . . . . . .**134** F1

Hillside continued
Royston SG8 . . . .**7** D5
Stevenage SG1 . . . .**50** F5
Ware SG12 . . . .**114** D8
Welwyn Garden City AL7 . .**111** B3
Hillside Ave
Bishop's Stortford CM23 . . .**77** A4
Borehamwood WD6 . . . .**170** B1
Cheshunt EN8 . . . .**162** D8
Hillside Cl WD5 . . . .**153** E7
Hillside Cotts
Birchanger CM23 . . . .**59** C3
Wareside SG12 . . . .**94** F4
Hillside Cres
Cheshunt EN8 . . . .**162** D8
Enfield EN2 . . . .**161** D1
Northwood HA6 . . . .**175** A2
Stanstead Abbotts SG12 . .**115** B4
Watford WD1 . . . .**167** D3
Hillside Ct EN8 . . . .**162** D8
Hillside End CM23 . . . . . .**59** C3
Hillside Gdns Barnet EN5 .**171** E5
Berkhamsted HP4 . . . . . .**122** D3
Northwood HA6 . . . .**175** B2
Hillside Jun & Inf Schs
HA6 . . . .**175** A3
Hillside La SG12 . . . .**115** A5
Hillside Mans EN5 . . . . . .**171** F5
Hillside Rd
Chorleywood WD3 . . . . .**164** C4
Harpenden AL5 . . . .**85** F3
Luton LU3 . . . .**45** D1
Northwood HA6,HA5 . . . .**175** B3
Radlett WD7 . . . .**156** B4
St Albans AL1 . . . .**127** E4
Watford WD2 . . . .**167** E4
Hillside Rise HA6 . . . . . .**175** A3
Hillside Sch The WD6 . . .**170** C5
Hillside Terr SG13 . . . . . .**113** C4
Hillside Way AL6 . . . .**90** A8
Hilltop AL3 . . . .**105** F4
Hilltop Cl EN7 . . . .**147** F5
Hilltop Cotts SG5 . . . .**33** C3
Hilltop Ct LU1 . . . .**63** C7
Hilltop Rd
Abbots Langley WD4 . . . .**139** A4
Berkhamsted HP4 . . . . . .**122** C3
Hillview Cl HA5 . . . .**175** F4
Hillview Cres LU2 . . . .**45** C8
Hillview Gdns EN8 . . . . .**148** E4
Hillview Rd HA5 . . . .**175** F4
Hilly Fields AL7 . . . .**111** C7
Hilmay Dr HP1 . . . .**124** C2
Hilton Cl SG1 . . . .**50** B7
Himalayan Way WD1 . . .**166** F3
Hindhead Gn WD1 . . . . .**175** C5
Hine Ho AL4 . . . .**128** C2
Hine Way SG5 . . . .**21** C1
Hinxworth Rd Ashwell SG7 . .**4** B4
Hinxworth SG7 . . . .**3** C1
Hipkins CM23 . . . .**76** E4
Hitchen Cl HP1 . . . .**123** F4
Hitchin Boys Sch SG5 . . . .**34** E8
Hitchin British Schools
Mus SG5 . . . .**34** F6
Hitchin Bsns Ctr The SG4 .**22** A3
Hitchin Girls Sch SG4 . . . .**34** F7
Hitchin Hill SG4 . . . .**34** F5
Hitchin Hospl SG5 . . . . . .**34** D8
Hitchin Mus SG5 . . . .**34** E7
Hitchin Rd Arlesey SG15 . .**11** A2
Great Wymondley SG4 . . . .**35** D6
Henlow SG16 . . . .**10** C6
Hexton SG5 . . . .**19** E1
Hitchin SG4 . . . .**34** F3
Kimpton SG4 . . . .**66** D2
Letchworth SG6 . . . .**22** E3
Luton LU2 . . . .**46** A4
Pirton SG5 . . . .**20** E2
Stevenage SG1 . . . .**36** B1
Stotfold SG5 . . . .**11** E5
Weston SG4 . . . .**24** B1
Hitchin Road
Ind & Bsns Ctr SG5 . . . . .**11** A3
Hitchin Road Ind Est LU2 . .**45** F1
Hitchin St SG7 . . . .**23** E8
Hitchin Sta SG4 . . . .**35** A8
Hitchwood La SG4 . . . . . .**49** A4
Hither Field SG12 . . . .**93** E3
Hitherbaulk AL7 . . . .**110** E4
Hitherfield La AL5 . . . . . .**86** A2
Hitherway AL8 . . . .**89** D2
Hitherwell Dr HA3 . . . . . .**176** D2
Hive Cl WD2 . . . .**176** D8
Hive Rd WD2 . . . .**176** D8
Hobart Wlk AL3 . . . .**127** F7
Hobbs Cl Cheshunt EN8 . . .**148** D2
St Albans AL4 . . . .**128** E2
Hobbs Cross Rd CM17 . . .**118** F3
Hobbs Ct SG1 . . . .**51** A8
Hobbs Hayes SG8 . . . .**16** E5
Hobbs Hill Rd HP3 . . . . .**138** F8
Hobbs Hill Wood
Prim Sch HP3 . . . .**125** B1
Hobbs Way AL8 . . . .**110** C5
Hobby Horse Cl EN7 . . . .**147** F5
Hobletts Inf Sch HP2 . . . .**125** A4
Hobletts Jun Sch HP2 . . .**125** A4
Hobletts Rd HP2 . . . .**124** F4
Hobsons Cl EN11 . . . . . .**114** F1
Hobsons Wlk HP23 . . . . . .**99** F5
Hobtoe Rd CM20 . . . . . .**117** A1
Hockerill SG14 . . . .**70** E3
Hockerill Anglo-European
Sch CM23 . . . .**77** B7
Hockerill Ct 7 CM23 . . . .**77** A7
Hockerill St CM23 . . . . . .**77** A7

Hocklands AL7 . . . . .111 C7
Hockwell Ring LU4 . . . . . . .44 C4
Hoddesdon Bsns Ctr
EN11 . . . . .135 A6
Hoddesdon Ind Ctr
EN11 . . . . .135 C7
Hoddesdon Rd SG12 . . . . . .115 C3
Hodges Way WD1 . . . . . .167 A3
Hodings Rd CM20 . . . . . . .117 C2
Hodwell SG7 . . . . .4 D4
Hoe La Enfield EN1,EN3 . .162 B1
Lower Nazeing EN9 . . . . . .135 C1
Ware SG12 . . . . .114 D7
Hoe The WD1 . . . . .175 D8
Hoecroft EN9 . . . . .135 F1
Hoecroft Ct EN3 . . . . .162 C1
Hoestock Rd CM21 . . . . . . .97 D2
Hog Hall La HP4 . . . . .81 A5
Hog La HP5 . . . . .121 D2
Hogarth Ct WD2 . . . . .168 B2
Hogg End La AL3 . . . . . . .126 C6
Hogg La WD6 . . . . .169 A5
Hogsdell La SG13 . . . . . . .114 B4
Holbeck La EN7 . . . . .147 F5
Holbein Gate HA6 . . . . . . .174 E5
Holborn Cl AL4 . . . . .128 D8
Holbrook Cl EN1 . . . . .162 A1
Holcroft Rd AL5 . . . . .86 D3
Holdbrook EN7 . . . . .35 B7
Holdbrook Sch EN8 . . . . .162 F5
Holdbrook South EN8 . . .162 F5
Holden Cl Hertford SG13 . .113 E7
Hitchin SG4 . . . . .35 C7
Holders La SG2 . . . . .51 E5
Holdings The AL9 . . . . . . .130 D7
Holecroft EN9 . . . . .163 E5
Holford Way LU3 . . . . .31 B1
Holgate Dr LU4 . . . . .44 B3
Holkham Cl LU4 . . . . .44 A4
Holland Ct LU3 . . . . .45 C2
Holland Gdns WD2 . . . . . .154 C4
Holland Rd LU3 . . . . .45 B2
Holland's Croft SG12 . . . . .95 D1
Holliday St HP4 . . . . .122 D4
Hollier Ct AL10 . . . . .130 B6
Holliers Way AL10 . . . . . .130 A5
Hollies Cl SG8 . . . . .7 E6
Hollies The
Bovingdon HP3 . . . . .137 A2
St Albans AL3 . . . . .127 C4
St Albans, Townsend AL3 .127 C5
Watford WD1 . . . . .166 F5
Wigginton HP23 . . . . . . .100 D1
Hollies Way EN6 . . . . .159 C8
Hollow La SG4 . . . . .34 F7
Holloway La WD3 . . . . . . .151 C2
Holloway The HP22 . . . . . . .99 C4
Holloways La AL9 . . . . . . .144 D7
Holly Cl AL10 . . . . .129 F4
Holly Copse SG1 . . . . .50 F4
Holly Croft SG14 . . . . . . .113 A7
Holly Dell SG13 . . . . .113 C4
Holly Dr Berkhamsted HP4 .122 D3
Potters Bar EN6 . . . . .159 B6
Holly Farm Cl LU1 . . . . . . .62 E3
Holly Gr HA5 . . . . .175 E2
Holly Grove Rd SG14 . . . . .91 C3
Holly Hall Ct AL6 . . . . .89 C5
Holly Hedges La HP3 . . . . .151 C8
Holly Ind Est WD2 . . . . . .167 C8
Holly La AL5 . . . . .86 E6
Holly Leys SG2 . . . . .69 C8
Holly Rd Enfield EN3 . . . . .162 D3
Woolmer Green SG3 . . . . .69 B1
Holly Shaws SG2 . . . . .51 B1
Holly St LU1 . . . . .63 E6
Holly Street Trad Est [12]
LU1 .63 E6
Holly Tree Ct HP2 . . . . . . .125 B3
Welwyn Garden City AL8 . .89 C2
Holly Wlk Harpenden AL5 . .86 D1
Hollybush Ave AL2 . . . . . .141 A7
Hollybush Cl Harrow HA3 .176 E2
Oaklands AL6 . . . . .89 E8
Potten End HP4 . . . . .123 D7
Watford WD1 . . . . .167 C2
Hollybush Hill SG5 . . . . . . .32 F1
Hollybush Ho AL7 . . . . . . .110 E4
Hollybush La
Datchworth SG3 . . . . .69 C3
Flamstead AL3 . . . . .84 B3
Harpenden AL5 . . . . .86 A3
Hemel Hempstead HP1 . .123 F4
Welwyn Garden City AL7 . .110 E3
Whitwell SG4 . . . . .66 B8
Hollybush Prim Sch
SG14 . . . . .113 A6
Hollybush Rd LU2 . . . . .46 C1
Hollybush Way EN7 . . . . . .148 A3
Hollycross Rd SG12 . . . . . .115 B7
Hollyfield Hatfield AL10 . . .130 B4
Tring HP23 . . . . .100 C5
Hollyfield Cl HP23 . . . . . .100 C5
Hollyfields EN10 . . . . .148 E5
Hollygrove WD2 . . . . .168 D2
Hollyhock Cl HP1 . . . . . . .123 E4
Hollytree Cl HP5 . . . . .150 B8
Hollytree Ho WD1 . . . . . . .153 E3
Hollywood Dr WD6 . . . . . .170 A5
Holmbrook Ave LU3 . . . . . .45 C5
Holmbury Cl WD2 . . . . . . .176 E8
Holmdale SG6 . . . . .23 B5
Holmdale Cl WD6 . . . . . . .169 F7
Holme Cl Cheshunt EN8 . . .162 E8
Hatfield AL10 . . . . .129 F8
Holme Lea WD2 . . . . .154 C5
Holme Pk WD6 . . . . .169 F7

Holme Pl HP2 . . . . .125 C4
Holme Rd AL10 . . . . .129 F8
Holme Way HA7 . . . . .176 F4
Holmes Ct AL3 . . . . .127 C4
Holmesdale EN8 . . . . .162 D4
Holmfield Cl LU1 . . . . .63 D5
Holmscroft Rd LU3 . . . . . . .44 F6
Holmshill La WD6 . . . . . . .157 F2
Holmside Rise WD1 . . . . . .175 B7
Holmwood Rd EN3 . . . . . .162 D3
Holroyd Cres SG7 . . . . .23 F7
Holt Cl WD6 . . . . .169 F5
Holt Ho EN8 . . . . .148 B3
Holt The
Hemel Hempstead HP2 . .124 E2
Welwyn Garden City AL7 . .111 D5
Holts Mdw AL7 . . . . .111 C4
Holtsmere Cl Luton LU2 . . .46 D1
Watford WD2 . . . . .154 C4
Holtsmere End Inf Sch
HP2 . . . . .125 B8
Holtsmere End Jun Sch
HP2 . . . . .125 B8
Holwell SG1 . . . . .36 C2
Holwell Hyde AL7 . . . . . . .111 C4
Holwell Hyde La AL7 . . . . .111 C3
Holwell Jun Mix Inf Sch
AL7 . . . . .110 F5
Holwell La AL9 . . . . .131 E8
Holwell Rd Holwell SG5 . . .21 C7
Pirton SG5 . . . . .20 E6
Welwyn Garden City AL7 . .110 E3
Holy Cross Hill EN10 . . . . .148 A8
Holy Family
RC Prim Sch AL7 . . . . . . .90 A1
Holy Rood RC Inf Sch
WD1 . . . . .153 D3
Holy Rood
RC Jun Mix Sch WD1 . . .153 D3
Holy Trinity CE Prim Sch
Cheshunt EN8 . . . . .162 D7
Northwood HA6 . . . . .174 C4
Holyfield Hall Farm EN9 . .149 C4
Holyfield Rd EN9 . . . . .149 D2
Holyrood Cres AL1 . . . . . .141 D7
Holyrood Ct WD1 . . . . . . .167 B5
Holywell Cl LU6 . . . . .82 C6
Holywell Ct LU3 . . . . .45 B4
Holywell Hill AL1 . . . . . . .127 D2
Holywell Jun Mix Inf Sch
WD1 . . . . .166 F3
Holywell Rd Studham LU6 . .82 D4
Watford WD1 . . . . .167 A4
Home Cl Cheshunt EN10 . .148 F7
Luton LU4 . . . . .44 C4
Stotfold SG5 . . . . .11 F7
Home Farm Ct SG11 . . . . .55 D3
Home Farm Ind Pk SG12 .115 F5
Home Farm Rd
Berkhamsted HP4 . . . . . .121 D7
Rickmansworth WD3 . . . .174 A6
Home Field EN5 . . . . .171 F4
Home Ley AL7 . . . . .110 E6
Home Mdw AL7 . . . . .110 F6
Home Park Ind Est WD4 . .139 B1
Home Park Mill Link Rd
WD4 . . . . .139 B1
Home Way WD3 . . . . .164 F1
Homedale Dr LU4 . . . . .44 D2
Homedell Ho AL5 . . . . .85 E3
Homefield Bovingdon HP3 .137 B3
Hinxworth SG7 . . . . .3 D6
Potten End HP4 . . . . .123 B7
Homefield La SG4 . . . . . . .49 F2
Homefield Rd
Bushey WD2 . . . . .168 A4
Chorleywood WD3 . . . . . .164 D5
Hemel Hempstead HP2 . .125 A4
Radlett WD7 . . . . .155 F2
Ware SG12 . . . . .93 E2
Homeleigh Ct EN8 . . . . . .148 B1
Homeleigh St EN8 . . . . . .148 B1
Homepark Cotts WD4 . . . .139 B1
Homerfield AL8 . . . . .110 C7
Homerswood
Jun & Inf Sch AL8 . . . . . . .89 D2
Homerswood La AL6 . . . . . .89 A2
Homerton Rd LU3 . . . . .45 A6
Homestead Cl AL2 . . . . . .141 C4
Homestead Ct AL7 . . . . . .110 F4
Homestead La AL7 . . . . . .110 F4
Homestead Moat SG1 . . . . .50 E4
Homestead Rd
Hatfield AL10 . . . . .130 B8
Rickmansworth WD3 . . . .165 D2
Homestead Way LU1 . . . . . .63 C5
Homewood Ave EN6 . . . . .146 E4
Homewood Ct EN8 . . . . . .148 B1
Homewood Wood SG6 . . .164 F5
Homewood Ind Sch AL2 . .141 B3
Homewood La EN6 . . . . . .146 C4
Honey Brook EN9 . . . . . . .163 E6
Honey La
Brent Pelham CB11 . . . . . . .30 F3
Buntingford SG9 . . . . .40 E8
[5] Hertford SG14 . . . . . . .113 D6
Waltham Abbey EN9 . . . . .163 E5
Honeybourne CM23 . . . . . .76 E4
Honeycroft AL8 . . . . .110 C5
Honeycroft Dr AL4 . . . . . .142 C8
Honeycross Rd HP1 . . . . . .123 E2
Honeygate LU2 . . . . .45 E4
Honeymead AL6 . . . . .89 F3
Honeymeade CM21 . . . . . .118 C7
Honeysuckle
Bishop's Stortford CM23 . . .76 C6
Hertford SG13 . . . . .114 A6

Honeysuckle Gdns AL10 . .130 B4
Honeyway SG7 . . . . .7 E6
Honeywood Cl EN6 . . . . . .159 D6
Honilands Inf Sch EN1 . . .162 B3
Honilands Jun Sch EN1 . . .162 B3
Honours Mead HP3 . . . . . .137 A4
Hoo Cotts SG5 . . . . .33 D1
Hoo Farm Cotts SG5 . . . . . .33 D1
Hoo St LU1 . . . . .63 E5
Hoo The CM17 . . . . .118 C5
Hook Gate EN1 . . . . .162 B3
Hook La Northaw EN6 . . . .159 F7
Northaw EN6 . . . . .160 A8
Hoops La SG8 . . . . .15 F6
Hope Gn WD2 . . . . .154 A6
Hopewell Rd SG7 . . . . .23 D8
Hopground Cl AL1 . . . . . . .128 A1
Hopkins Cres AL4 . . . . . . .108 B1
Hopkins Yd AL1 . . . . .127 E2
Hoppit Rd EN9 . . . . .163 B7
Hopton Rd SG1 . . . . .50 A8
Hopwood Rise AL7 . . . . . .111 D8
Horace Brightman Cl LU3 .45 A7
Horace Gay Gdns SG6 . . . .22 E6
Horbeam Cl WD6 . . . . .170 A8
Hordle Gdns AL1 . . . . .127 F2
Hormead CE Prim Sch
SG9 . . . . .41 F8
Horn Hill LU2 . . . . .66 E6
Hornbeam Cl SG14 . . . . . .113 B7
Hornbeam Ct SG4 . . . . .35 E5
Hornbeam La AL9 . . . . . . .131 E2
Hornbeam Spring SG3 . . . .68 F4
Hornbeam Way EN7 . . . . .147 F6
Hornbeams
Bricket Wood AL2 . . . . . .140 F1
Welwyn Garden City AL7 . .111 B5
Hornbeams Ave EN1 . . . . .162 C4
Hornbeams The
Harlow CM20 . . . . .117 C2
Stevenage SG2 . . . . .51 B4
Hornets The WD1 . . . . . . .167 A6
Hornhill Rd WD3 . . . . .172 D5
Horns Cl SG13 . . . . .113 C4
Horns Mill Rd SG13 . . . . .113 C3
Horns Rd SG13 . . . . .113 C5
Hornsby Cl LU2 . . . . .46 C1
Hornsfield AL7 . . . . .111 C7
Horrocks Cl SG12 . . . . .93 D3
Horse Cross SG11 . . . . .56 D3
Horse Hill HP5 . . . . .150 D7
Horsecroft Rd HP1 . . . . . .124 A1
Horselers HP3 . . . . .139 A8
Horsemans Dr AL2 . . . . . .141 B6
Horseshoe Cl SG12 . . . . . .115 D4
Horseshoe Hill SG9 . . . . . .42 A8
Horseshoe La Barnet N20 .171 D1
Great Hormead SG9 . . . . .42 A8
Watford WD2 . . . . .154 C7
Horseshoe The HP3 . . . . . .125 C1
Horseshoes Cl LU7 . . . . . . .80 A7
Horsham AL5 . . . . .86 E6
Horsleys WD3 . . . . .172 D5
Horton Gdns HP2 . . . . . . .105 A1
Horwood Cl WD3 . . . . . . .165 A2
Horwood Ct WD2 . . . . . . .154 E2
Hospital Rd SG15 . . . . .11 A4
Houghton Mews [11] LU1 . .63 D6
Housden Cl AL4 . . . . .108 E7
House La Arlesey SG15 . . . .11 A7
Sandridge AL4 . . . . .108 C1
St Albans AL4 . . . . .128 D7
Housefield Way AL4 . . . . .142 C8
Housewood End HP1 . . . . .124 B6
Housman Ave AL4 . . . . .2 C1
How Field AL5 . . . . .85 E3
How Wood AL2 . . . . .141 B3
How Wood Prim Sch
AL2 . . . . .141 C4
How Wood Sta AL2 . . . . . .141 C3
Howard Agne Cl HP3 . . . .137 A4
Howard Cl Bushey WD2 . . .168 E2
Luton LU4 . . . . .45 A4
St Albans AL1 . . . . .128 C1
Stotfold SG5 . . . . .11 E5
Waltham Abbey EN9 . . . . .163 D5
Watford WD2 . . . . .154 A4
Howard Ctr Enfield EN1 . .161 E1
Letchworth SG6 . . . . .23 B4
Howard Ctr The AL8 . . . . .110 D6
Howard Dr
Borehamwood WD6 . . . . .170 D5
Letchworth SG6 . . . . .23 B3
Howard Gate SG6 . . . . .23 B4
Howard Way Barnet EN5 . .171 D4
Harlow CM20 . . . . .117 F2
Howards Cl HA5 . . . . .175 B1
Howards Dr HP1 . . . . .124 A5
Howards Wood SG6 . . . . . .23 B3
Howardsgate AL8 . . . . . . .110 D6
Howe Cl WD7 . . . . .156 E7
Howe Dell AL10 . . . . .130 B5
Howe Dell Prim Sch
AL10 . . . . .130 B5
Howe Green House Sch
CM22 . . . . .77 D2
Howe Rd HP3 . . . . .125 A1
Howell Hill LU7 . . . . .61 D5
Howfield Gn EN11 . . . . . .115 A1
Howicks Gn AL7 . . . . .111 A3
Howland Garth AL1 . . . . . .141 C7
Howlands AL7 . . . . .111 B3
Howton Pl WD2 . . . . .168 D1
Hoylake Cl LU1 . . . . .63 F5
Hoylake Gdns WD1 . . . . . .175 D6
Hubbards Rd WD3 . . . . . .164 D4
Huckleberry Cl LU3 . . . . . . .45 A8

Hudnall La HP4 . . . . .102 E7
Watford WD2 . . . . .153 F3
Hudson Cl St Albans AL1 . .141 D8
Watford WD2 . . . . .153 F3
Hudson Rd SG2 . . . . .51 B7
Huggins La AL9 . . . . .144 C5
Hugh Villas CM23 . . . . .77 A5
Hughenden Rd AL4 . . . . . .128 C6
Hull Cl EN7 . . . . .147 D5
Hull La SG7 . . . . .55 E7
Humberstone Cl LU4 . . . . . .44 E2
Humberstone Rd LU4 . . . . .44 E2
Humphrey Talbot
Ave LU6 . . . . .81 F7
Hunsdon AL7 . . . . .111 D5
Hunsdon
Jun Mix Inf Sch SG12 . . .95 D1
Hunsdon Rd
Stanstead Abbotts SG12 . .115 E5
Widford SG12 . . . . .95 C5
Hunsdon Road
Cotts SG12 . . . . .115 C5
Hunston Cl LU4 . . . . .44 B5
Hunt Cl AL4 . . . . .128 D6
Hunter Cl
Borehamwood WD6 . . . . .170 C4
Potters Bar EN6 . . . . .159 C4
Hunter Wlk EN6 . . . . .170 C4
Hunter's La WD2 . . . . .153 A4
Huntercrombe Gdns
WD1 . . . . .175 C5
Hunters Cl Bovingdon HP3 .137 A2
Stevenage SG2 . . . . .51 D7
Stotfold SG5 . . . . .11 E5
Tring HP23 . . . . .100 B5
Hunters Gate WD2 . . . . . .154 A6
Hunters Oak HP2 . . . . .125 B8
Hunters Pk HP4 . . . . .122 E5
Hunters Reach EN7 . . . . . .147 F6
Hunters Ride AL2 . . . . . . .155 A8
Hunters Way Royston SG8 . .7 E6
Welwyn Garden City AL7 . .110 F3
Hunting Gate
Hemel Hempstead HP2 . .124 E7
Hitchin SG4 . . . . .22 A3
Hunting Hall LU2 . . . . .64 C8
Huntingdon Cl EN10 . . . . .148 E7
Huntingdon Rd SG1 . . . . . .50 B8
Hunton Bridge Hill WD4 . .153 C6
Hunts Cl LU2 . . . . .63 C6
Huntsman Cl SG13 . . . . . . .55 D3
Huntsmans Cl HP4 . . . . . . .81 C5
Huntsmill Rd HP1 . . . . . . .123 E2
Hurlock Way LU4 . . . . .44 C5
Hurricane Way WD5 . . . . .154 A4
Hurst Cl Baldock SG7 . . . . .13 A1
Bishop's Stortford CM23 . . .76 E7
Welwyn Garden City AL7 . .111 C5
Hurst Dr EN8 . . . . .162 D5
Hurst Drive Prim Sch
EN8 . . . . .162 D5
Hurst Pl HA6 . . . . .174 E8
Hurst Way LU3 . . . . .44 F5
Hurstlings AL7 . . . . .111 B5
Hutchings Lo WD3 . . . . . .165 E1
Hutton Cl SG14 . . . . .113 A6
Hutton Gdns HA3 . . . . . . .176 C3
Hutton La HA3 . . . . .176 D3
Hutton Wlk HA3 . . . . .176 C3
Hyatt Ind Est SG1 . . . . .50 A5
Hyburn Cl
Bricket Wood AL2 . . . . . .140 F1
Hemel Hempstead HP3 . .125 D2
Hyde Ave Potters Bar EN6 .159 B6
Stotfold SG5 . . . . .11 E5
Hyde Cl Barnet EN5 . . . . . .171 F6
Harpenden AL5 . . . . .86 A4
Hyde Gn E SG2 . . . . .51 B3
Hyde Gn N SG2 . . . . .51 B3
Hyde Gn S SG2 . . . . .51 B3
Hyde Ho [5] LU2 . . . . .63 F8
Hyde La
Abbots Langley HP3 . . . . .139 D5
Bovingdon HP3 . . . . .137 A3
Park Street AL2 . . . . .141 D3
Peters Green LU2 . . . . . . .65 C2
Hyde Mdws HP3 . . . . .137 A4
Hyde Mead EN9 . . . . .149 E8
Hyde Mead Ho EN9 . . . . .149 E8
Hyde Rd Caddington LU1 . .62 F4
Watford WD1 . . . . .167 A4
Hyde The Stevenage SG2 . .51 C3
Ware SG12 . . . . .93 B2
Hyde Valley AL7 . . . . .110 E6
Hyde View Rd AL5 . . . . . . .86 B4
Hyde Way AL7 . . . . .110 E6
Hydean Way SG2 . . . . .51 B3
Hyperion Ct HP2 . . . . .124 F6
Hyver Hill NW7 . . . . .170 D2

Icknield Walk Fst Sch SG8 . .7 E7
Icknield Way Baldock SG7 . .12 E1
Letchworth SG6 . . . . .22 E6
Luton LU3 . . . . .45 B7
Tring HP23 . . . . .99 E4
Icknield Way E SG7 . . . . . .12 F1
Icknield Wlk SG8 . . . . .7 F7
Idenbury Ct LU1 . . . . .63 C7
Ilex Cl HP4 . . . . .122 B4
Ilford Cl LU2 . . . . .46 D3
Ilkley Rd WD1 . . . . .175 D5
Imberfield LU4 . . . . .44 C3
Immanuel Coll WD2 . . . . .168 E2
Imperial Way WD2 . . . . . .167 C8
Indells AL10 . . . . .129 F4
Ingleheim Ct SG1 . . . . .50 D7
Ingersoll Rd EN3 . . . . .162 C1
Ingleheim EN6 . . . . .145 A1
Ingles AL8 . . . . .89 C3
Ingleside Dr SG1 . . . . .36 B1
Ingram Gdns LU2 . . . . .45 D7
Inkerman Rd AL1 . . . . .127 C4
Inkerman St LU1 . . . . .63 D7
Inn's Cl SG1 . . . . .50 D6
Innes Ct HP3 . . . . .138 D8
Innova Way Enfield EN3 . .162 A1
Holdbrook EN3 . . . . .163 A3
Inskip Cres SG1 . . . . .50 E5
Iona Cl SG1 . . . . .36 F2
Iredale View SG7 . . . . .100 A5
Irene Stebbings Ho AL4 . .128 C4
Iron Dr SG14 . . . . .114 B7
Irving Cl CM23 . . . . .76 D4
Irving Cres LU7 . . . . .80 A8
Isabelle Cl EN7 . . . . .147 C2
Isenburg Way HP2 . . . . . .124 D8
Isherwood Cl SG8 . . . . .7 C8
Islay Ho [4] WD1 . . . . . . .166 F3
Islington Way SG1 . . . . .36 F2
Italstyle Bldg The CM20 . .118 C6
Iveagh Cl HA6 . . . . .174 B2
Iveagh Ct HP2 . . . . .124 D4
Ivel Ct SG6 . . . . .23 C4
Ivel Rd SG1 . . . . .50 C7
Ivel Way Baldock SG7 . . . . .24 A6
Stotfold SG5 . . . . .11 E5
Ives Rd SG14 . . . . .113 B7
Ivinghoe Cl St Albans AL4 .128 C7
Watford WD1 . . . . .154 D4
Ivinghoe Rd Bushey WD2 . .168 D2
Rickmansworth WD3 . . . .165 A2
Ivory Cl AL4 . . . . .128 C1
Ivory Ct HP3 . . . . .138 E8
Ivy Ct LU1 . . . . .63 B8
Ivy Ho WD1 . . . . .167 D3
Ivy House La HP4 . . . . . . .122 E4
Ivy Lea WD3 . . . . .165 A1
Ivy Rd LU1 . . . . .63 C8
Ivy Terr EN11 . . . . .135 C8
Ivybridge EN10 . . . . .135 A4

J Ct CM20 . . . . .117 F1
Jackdaw Cl SG2 . . . . .51 D4
Jackdaws AL7 . . . . .111 C6
Jackets La HA6 . . . . .174 B3
Jacketts Field WD5 . . . . . .153 F8
Jackman's Pl SG6 . . . . .23 B5
Jacks La UB9 . . . . .173 A1
Jackson Sq [10] CM23 . . . . .76 F7
Jackson St SG7 . . . . .12 E1
Jackson's La SG8 . . . . .16 E5
Jacksons Dr EN7 . . . . .148 A3
Jacobs Ladder SG1 . . . . . .130 C5
James Bedford Cl HA5 . . .175 C1
James Cl WD2 . . . . .167 E4
James Cl Luton LU4 . . . . . . .44 B2
[14] Luton, New Town LU1 . .63 E6
James Foster Ho SG5 . . . . .21 E1
James Lee Sq EN3 . . . . . .163 A1
James Marshall
Commercial Ctr AL5 . . . . .86 A1
James Way SG1 . . . . .50 C7
Jameson St AL1 . . . . .127 F4
Jameson Rd AL5 . . . . .86 B3
Jane Cl HP2 . . . . .125 B8
Jansel Ho LU2 . . . . .46 B4
Jarden SG6 . . . . .23 C4
Jarman Cl HP3 . . . . .124 E1
Jarman Way
Hemel Hempstead HP2 . .124 F2
Royston SG8 . . . . .7 B7
Jarvis Cl EN5 . . . . .171 D4
Jarvis Cleys EN7 . . . . .147 F5
Jasmin Cl
Bishop's Stortford CM23 . . .76 C6
Northwood HA6 . . . . .174 F2
Jasmin Way HP1 . . . . .123 E4
Jasmine Dr SG13 . . . . .114 A6
Jasmine Gdns AL10 . . . . . .130 A7
Jasons Hill HP5 . . . . .136 B2
Jasper Cl EN3 . . . . .162 C1
Jay Cl SG6 . . . . .22 E8
Jaywood LU2 . . . . .46 F3
Jeans Cl CM23 . . . . .76 E7
Jeans Way LU5 . . . . .44 A1
Jeffrey Cl SG8 . . . . .7 C8
Jefferies Rd SG12 . . . . .93 E1
Jellicoe Gdns HA7 . . . . . . .176 F4
Jellicoe Rd WD1 . . . . .167 A3
Jenkins Ave AL2 . . . . .140 E1

Jenkins La
Bishop's Stortford CM22 ....77 C5
St Leonards HP23 ....119 E3
Jenning Wood AL6 ....89 F7
Jennings Cl SG1 ....50 E3
Jennings Rd AL1 ....128 A4
Jennings Way
Barnet EN5 ....171 C6
Hemel Hempstead HP3 ....124 A4
Jenningscroft Ct SG13 ...114 A4
Jepps La SG8 ....7 D6
Jerome Dr AL3 ....127 A1
Jersey Cl EN11 ....135 A7
Jersey Ho Enfield EN3 ...162 D1
 🖲 Watford WD1 ....166 F3
Jersey La St Albans,
Marshalswick AL4 ....128 B5
St Albans, Sandridge AL4 .128 A4
Jersey Rd LU4 ....44 A3
Jervis Ave EN3 ....162 E4
Jervis Rd CM23 ....76 F6
Jessop Rd SG1 ....37 A1
Jeve Cl SG7 ....13 A1
Jewell Ct WD2 ....154 D5
Jill Grey Pl SG4 ....34 C6
Jillifer Rd LU4 ....44 A2
Jim Desormeaux Bglws
CM20 ....117 E2
Jinnings The AL7 ....111 B3
Jocelyns CM17 ....118 C4
Jocketts Hill HP1 ....123 F3
Jocketts Rd HP1 ....123 F2
Jodies Ct AL4 ....128 C5
Joel St HA6 ....175 A1
John Barker Pl SG5 ....21 C1
John Ct EN11 ....115 A1
John Eliot Cl EN9 ....135 E2
John F Kennedy Sch
HP1 ....123 F4
John Henry Newman
RC Sch SG1 ....36 B1
John Lamb Ct HA3 ....176 C1
John Penrose Sch UB9 ...173 D2
John St Luton LU1 ....63 E7
Royston SG8 ....7 D6
John Tate Rd SG13 ....113 F6
John Warner Sch EN11 ...115 B1
Johnby Cl EN3 ....162 E2
Johns La HP5 ....121 E1
Johns Rd CM23 ....59 A1
Johnson Ct HP3 ....124 E1
Joiner's Close HP5 ....136 B1
Joint The SG8 ....16 E6
Jones Rd EN7 ....147 B1
Jonquil Cl AL7 ....111 B4
Jordan Cl WD2 ....153 F4
Jordan's Way AL2 ....140 F1
Jordans AL7 ....111 C4
Jordans Way WD3 ....165 A1
Joslyn Cl EN3 ....163 A1
Jowitt Ho 🖲 SG1 ....50 E6
Joyce Ct EN3 ....163 D5
Jubilee Ave
London Colney AL2 ....142 D5
Ware SG12 ....93 F2
Jubilee Cl HA5 ....175 C1
Jubilee Cotts
Aspenden SG9 ....40 D5
Great Hormead SG9 ....42 A8
Jubilee Cres SG15 ....11 A2
Jubilee Ct Harpenden AL5 .86 C3
Hatfield AL10 ....130 B8
Waltham Abbey EN9 ....163 F6
Jubilee Memorial Ave
SG1 ....50 D8
Jubilee Rd Letchworth SG6 .23 D7
Stevenage SG1 ....50 B8
Watford WD2 ....154 A1
Jubilee St LU2 ....45 F1
Jubilee Trad Ctr SG6 .....23 D7
Judge St WD2 ....154 B1
Judge's Hill EN6 ....145 F2
Julia Ct LU3 ....45 B4
Julia Gate SG2 ....51 C8
Julian's Ct SG1 ....50 C8
Julian's Rd SG1 ....50 B8
Julie Ho EN11 ....135 C8
Julius Gdns LU3 ....44 F7
Junction Cotts AL8 ....110 D7
Juniper Ave AL2 ....155 A8
Juniper Cl Barnet EN5 ....171 D4
Cheshunt EN10 ....148 F6
Luton LU4 ....44 E2
Juniper Ct HA3 ....176 F2
Juniper Gate WD3 ....173 D8
Juniper Gdns Oaklands AL6 .89 E7
Shenley WD7 ....156 E6
Juniper Gn HP1 ....123 E3
Juniper Gr WD1 ....154 A1
Juniper Ho EN10 ....148 F6
Jupiter Dr HP2 ....124 F5
Jupiter Drive
Jun Mix Inf Sch HP2 ......124 F5
Juxon Ho HA3 ....176 B2

K

Kardwell Cl SG4 ....35 A6
Karen Ho SG16 ....10 A4
Katemon Ct SG12 ....115 D4
Katescroft AL7 ....110 E2
Katherine Cl HP3 ....138 E8
Katherine Pl WD5 ....154 A7
Katrine Sq HP2 ....124 E7

Keats Cl
Hemel Hempstead HP2 ....105 B1
Royston SG8 ....7 C8
Stevenage SG2 ....51 C7
Keats Ho 🖲 AL5 ....86 B1
Keats Way SG4 ....35 C7
Keble Terr WD5 ....153 F7
Kecksy's CM21 ....97 F4
Keeble Cl LU2 ....46 E1
Keele Cl WD1 ....167 C7
Keepers Cl
Cheddington LU7 ....80 A7
Luton LU2 ....46 C2
Keiths Rd HP3 ....125 A2
Keiths Wood SG3 ....68 F5
Kelbys AL7 ....111 C7
Keller Cl SG2 ....51 B4
Kelling Cl LU2 ....45 C8
Kelly Cl WD6 ....170 D7
Kelman Cl EN8 ....162 D8
Kelmscott Cl WD1 ....167 A4
Kelmscott Cres WD1 .....167 A4
Kelshall Ct WD2 ....154 E3
Kelshall St SG8 ....15 E5
Kelvin Cl LU1 ....63 E6
Kelvin Cres HA3 ....176 E3
Kemble Cl HP6 ....159 D6
Kemp Pl WD2 ....168 A3
Kempe Cl AL1 ....141 C7
Kempe Rd EN1 ....162 C3
Kemprow WD2 ....155 D3
Kempsey Cl LU2 ....46 D2
Ken Davies Ct AL3 ....127 F7
Kendal Cl LU3 ....44 D7
Kendale HP3 ....125 B2
Kendale Rd 🖲 Hitchin SG4 .34 F6
Luton LU4 ....44 B2
Kendall Cl AL7 ....110 F2
Kendall Ct WD6 ....170 C8
Kendals LU7 ....155 E3
Kenerne Dr EN5 ....171 E4
Kenford Cl WD2 ....154 B7
Kenilworth Cl
Borehamwood WD6 ....170 C6
Hemel Hempstead HP2 ....124 E2
Stevenage SG2 ....69 C7
Kenilworth Cres EN1 .....161 E1
Kenilworth Ct WD1 ......167 A8
Kenilworth Dr
Borehamwood WD6 ....170 D6
Croxley Green WD3 ....166 B5
Kenilworth Fst Sch WD6 .170 D6
Kenilworth Gdns WD1 ...175 C5
Kenilworth Rd LU1 ....63 C8
Kennedy Ave EN11 ......134 F6
Kennedy Cl Cheshunt EN8 .148 E3
Pinner HA5 ....175 F4
Kennedy Rd SG12 ....71 E7
Kennel La AL5 ....85 A5
Kennelwood La AL10 ....130 B6
Kennesbourne Ct AL5 .....85 F1
Kenneth Rd LU2 ....46 A1
Kenning Rd EN11 ....135 B8
Kennington Rd LU3 ....45 B8
Kensington Ave WD1 ....166 F5
Kensington Cl AL1 ....128 A1
Kensington Ct EN1 ....161 E1
Kensington Way WD6 ....170 D6
Kensworth Lower Sch
LU6 ....82 F8
Kensworth Rd LU6 ....82 D4
Kent Cl WD6 ....157 D1
Kent Cres CM23 ....76 E4
Kent Pl SG5 ....34 D8
Kent Rd LU1 ....62 F8
Kent's La SG11 ....55 E2
Kentish La AL9 ....145 C7
Kenton Gdns AL1 ....127 F2
Kenton La HA3 ....176 F3
Kents Ave HP3 ....138 D7
Kenwood Dr WD3 ....172 F8
Kenworth Cl EN8 ....162 D6
Kerdistone Cl EN6 ....145 B1
Kernow Ct LU2 ....46 A1
Kerr Cl SG3 ....68 F5
Kerri Cl EN5 ....171 C5
Kerril Croft CM20 ....117 A1
Kershaw Cl LU3 ....45 A8
Kershaw's Hill SG4 ....34 F6
Kessingland Ave SG1 ......36 A1
Keston Mews WD1 ....167 B7
Kestrel Cl
Berkhamsted HP4 ....122 C3
Stevenage SG2 ....51 D2
Watford WD2 ....154 E5
Kestrel Ct 🖲 SG12 ....93 C3
Kestrel Gdns CM23 ....76 C6
Kestrel Rd AL10 ....130 A4
Kestrel Way Luton LU4 ....44 A5
Welwyn Garden City AL7 ..110 F8
Kestrel Wlk SG6 ....23 B3
Kestrels The AL2 ....154 E8
Keswick Cl AL1 ....128 B1
Keswick Dr EN3 ....162 C3
Kettering Rd EN3 ....162 D2
Kettle Green Rd SG10 .....74 E2
Ketton Cl LU2 ....64 A7
Ketton Ct LU2 ....64 A7
Kewferry Dr HA6 ....174 C5
Kewferry Rd HA6 ....174 C5
Keyfield Terr AL1 ....127 D2
Keymer Cl LU2 ....46 C3
Keynton Cl SG14 ....112 F7
Keysers Rd EN10 ....135 B1
Kibes La SG12 ....93 E1
Kidner Cl LU2 ....45 E5
Kilbride Ct HP2 ....124 F7

Kilby Cl WD2 ....154 D4
Kildonan Cl WD1 ....166 F8
Kilfillan Gdns HP4 ....122 A4
Kilfillan Pk HP4 ....122 A4
Killigrew Inf Sch AL2 ....141 B6
Killigrew Jun Sch AL2 ....141 B6
Kilmarnock Dr LU2 ....45 E5
Kilmarnock Rd WD1 .....175 D6
Kiln Ave HP6 ....150 C1
Kiln Ground HP3 ....125 A1
Kiln House Cl SG12 ....93 E2
Kiln House Yd SG8 ....7 C6
Kiln La HP5 ....150 B8
Kiln Way HA6 ....174 E4
Kilncroft HP3 ....125 B1
Kilnfield AL7 ....89 F1
Kilsmore La EN8 ....148 D2
Kilvinton Dr EN2 ....161 D1
Kilworth Cl AL7 ....111 B4
Kimberley SG6 ....11 F2
Kimberley Cl CM23 ....77 A5
Kimberley Rd AL3 ....127 D4
Kimble Cl WD1 ....166 E2
Kimble Cres WD2 ....168 C2
Kimblewick WD1 ....167 E1
Kimbolton Cres SG2 ....69 A7
Kimbolton Gn WD6 ......170 C5
Kimps Way HP3 ....139 A8
Kimpton Bottom SG4 .....86 E7
Kimpton Cl HP2 ....125 B8
Kimpton Pl WD2 ....154 D5
Kimpton Prim Sch SG4 ...66 C1
Kimpton Rd
Ayot St Peter AL6 ....89 A6
Codicote SG4 ....67 B1
Kimpton SG4,AL4 ....87 C7
Luton LU1,LU2 ....64 A6
Peters Green LU2,SG4 ......65 E2
Kimptons Cl EN6 ....158 D7
Kimptons Mead EN6 .....158 D7
Kinderscout HP3 ....125 A1
Kindersley Cl AL6 ....89 C6
Kindersley Way WD5 ....153 D8
Kinetic Cres EN3 ....162 F3
King Arthur Ct EN8 ......162 E8
King Charles Rd WD7 ....156 F7
King Edward Rd
Cheshunt EN8 ....162 E6
Shenley WD7 ....156 F6
Watford WD1 ....167 A5
King Edward St HP3 .....138 D7
King Edward's Rd SG12 ...93 E2
King George Ave WD2 ...168 B3
King George Cl SG1 ....50 E6
King George Rd
Waltham Abbey EN9 ....163 C5
Ware SG12 ....93 D3
King George's Way SG4 ...66 E6
King Georges Ave WD1 ..166 F5
King Georges Cl SG5 ......21 D1
King Harold Ct EN9 ......163 C6
King Harold Sch EN9 .....163 C6
King Harry La AL3 ....127 B1
King Harry St HP2 ....124 D2
King Henry Ct LU3 ....45 B2
King Henry's Mews EN3 .163 A2
King James Ave EN6 .....146 E2
King James Way SG6 ......7 D6
King St
Bishop's Stortford CM23 ...76 F7
Luton LU1 ....63 E7
Markyate AL3 ....83 E5
Tring HP23 ....100 A3
Watford WD1 ....167 C5
King Street Mews
 🖲 CM23 ....76 F7
King's Cotts CM23 ....77 A6
King's La WD4 ....152 B8
King's Mews 🖲 HP2 ......124 D4
King's Rd Cheshunt EN8 ..162 E5
Hertford SG13 ....114 A7
Hitchin SG5 ....34 F8
London Colney AL2 ....142 C5
St Albans AL3 ....127 C3
King's Walden Rd SG5 ....33 D2
King's Wlk SG8 ....7 D5
Kingcroft Rd AL5 ....107 D7
Kingfisher Cl Harrow HA3 .176 F3
Northwood HA6 ....174 B2
Stanstead Abbotts SG12 ...115 C3
Wheathampstead AL4 ......87 D1
Kingfisher Ct SG4 ....35 A6
Kingfisher Dr HP3 ....138 F6
Kingfisher Lure
Kings Langley WD4 ....139 B2
Rickmansworth WD3 ......165 B5
Kingfisher Rise SG2 ....51 D2
Kingfisher Way CM23 .....77 A7
Kingham Rd SG12 ....94 E5
Kinghamway LU2 ....45 E1
Kings Ave
Hemel Hempstead HP3 ....138 F7
Watford WD1 ....167 A5
Kings Cl Chipperfield WD4 .152 B8
Northwood HA6 ....174 F4
 🖲 Watford WD1 ....167 C5
Kings Ct
Berkhamsted HP4 ....122 C5
Bishop's Stortford CM23 ...77 A8
Kings Farm Rd WD3 .....164 D3
Kings Field Cotts WD5 ...153 F8
Kings Hedges SG5 ....34 C8
Kings Langley Prim Sch
WD4 ....138 F3
Kings Langley Sch WD4 ..138 E3
Kings Langley Sta WD4 ..139 C1
Kings Mdw WD2 ....139 A3
Kings Oak WD3 ....166 A5

Kings Oak Private Hospl
The EN2 ....161 A1
Kings Park Ind Est WD4 .139 B3
Kings Rd Barnet EN5 .....171 C6
Berkhamsted HP4 ....122 B3
Stevenage SG1 ....50 D4
Kings Sch AL5 ....85 F4
Kings Walden Rise SG2 ...51 B8
Kingsbridge Rd CM23 .....77 A8
Kingsbury Ave AL3 ....127 C4
Kingsbury Water Mill Mus
AL3 ....127 B4
Kingscroft AL7 ....111 B7
Kingsdale Ho AL6 ....89 B3
Kingsdale Rd HP4 ....122 A3
Kingsdown SG4 ....35 B6
Kingsdown Ave LU2 ....45 D5
Kingsfield EN11 ....135 A8
Kingsfield Ct WD1 ....167 D2
Kingsfield Dr EN3 ....162 D4
Kingsfield Rd
Dane End SG12 ....71 E8
Watford WD1 ....167 D3
Kingsfield Way EN3 ......162 D4
Kingsgate AL3 ....127 B1
Kingshill Ave AL4 ....128 B6
Kingshill Ct 🖲 EN5 ......171 E5
Kingshill Inf Sch SG12 ....93 D3
Kingshill Way HP4 ....122 A2
Kingshott Sch SG4 ....35 B5
Kingsland Ct 🖲 LU1 ......63 F6
Kingsland Rd
Hemel Hempstead HP1 ....124 A1
Luton LU1 ....63 F6
Kingsland Way SG7 ....4 D4
Kingsley Ave
Borehamwood WD6 ....169 F7
Cheshunt EN8 ....148 C6
Kingsley Ct AL7 ....110 F2
Kingsley Rd LU3 ....45 C6
Kingsley Wlk HP23 ....100 A4
Kingsmead Cheshunt EN8 .148 D3
Cuffley EN6 ....146 E3
Sawbridgeworth CM21 .....97 E1
St Albans AL4 ....128 D6
Kingsmead Rd AL3 ....77 A8
Kingsmill Ct 🖲 AL10 ....130 B3
Kingston Pl HA3 ....176 F3
Kingston Rd LU2 ....45 F1
Kingston Vale SG8 ....7 E5
Kingsway Cuffley EN6 ....146 E1
Luton LU4 ....45 A1
Royston SG8 ....7 C8
Stotfold SG5 ....11 F7
Ware SG12 ....93 D3
Kingsway Gdns SG5 ....11 F7
Kingsway Ind Est LU1 .....63 A8
Kingsway Inf Sch WD2 ...154 A5
Kingsway Jun Sch WD2 ..154 A5
Kingsway North Orbital Rd
WD2 ....154 B5
Kingswell Ride EN6 ......146 E1
Kingswood Ave SG4 ....35 C8
Kingswood Rd WD2 ......154 B5
Kingwell Rd EN4 ....159 D1
Kinloch Ct 🖲 AL5 ....86 B1
Kinross Cl LU3 ....44 D8
Kinsbourne Cl AL5 ....85 C4
Kinsbourne Cres AL5 .....85 D4
Kinsbourne Green La AL5 .85 B3
Kintyre Ho 🖲 WD1 ......166 F3
Kipling Cl SG4 ....35 C7
Kipling Gr HP2 ....105 B1
Kipling Pl HA7 ....176 F4
Kipling Rd LU3 ....45 B6
Kipling The LU3 ....45 B6
Kipling Way AL5 ....86 B1
Kirby Cl HA6 ....174 F4
Kirby Dr LU3 ....45 A8
Kirkcaldy Gn WD1 ....175 C7
Kirkdale Ct 🖲 LU1 ....63 E6
Kirkdale Rd AL5 ....86 A2
Kirklands AL8 ....89 D2
Kirkwick Ave AL5 ....86 A1
Kit's La SG7 ....25 C8
Kitchener Cl AL1 ....128 B2
Kitcheners La SG2 ....38 D1
Kitching La St Ippolyts SG4 .49 F5
Stevenage SG1 ....50 A5
Kite Field HP4 ....121 E7
Kite Way SG6 ....22 B8
Kitsbury Rd HP4 ....122 B4
Kitsbury Terr HP4 ....122 B4
Kitson Way CM20 ....117 C1
Kitswell Rd WD7 ....156 A6
Kitswell Way WD7 ....155 F6
Kitt's End Rd EN5 ....158 E2
Kiwi Cl SG5 ....21 F1
Klondyke AL5 ....85 D4
Knap Cl SG6 ....23 D8
Knebworth Ct CM23 ......76 D6
Knebworth Ctry Pk SG3 ...68 C7
Knebworth Ho SG3 ....68 B6
Knebworth Path WD6 ....170 D5
Knebworth Prim Sch SG3 .69 A5
Knebworth Sta SG3 ....69 F5
Kneesworth House Hospl
SG8 ....2 C5
Kneesworth Rd SG8 ....2 F8
Kneesworth St SG8 ....7 C6
Knella Gn AL7 ....111 A6
Knella Road Workshops
AL7 ....111 A6
Knight St CM21 ....97 E2
Knight's Ct CM21 ....97 E2
Knights Cl
Bishop's Stortford CM23 ...76 C8
Buntingford SG9 ....40 E6

Knights Ct Bushey WD2 ..168 D1
Standon SG11 ....55 F1
Knights Field LU2 ....45 D5
Knights Orch
Hemel Hempstead HP1 ....123 F5
St Albans AL3 ....127 C3
Knights Templar Sch The
SG7 ....23 E8
Knights Templars Gn SG2 .51 C8
Knightsbridge Way HP2 ..124 E4
Knightsfield AL8 ....89 D2
Knightsfield Sch AL8 ......89 C3
Knoll Cres HA6 ....174 F2
Knoll Gn HP2 ....124 E5
Knoll Rise LU2 ....45 E4
Knoll The SG13 ....114 B7
Knolles Cres AL9 ....144 B7
Knolls Cl HP2 ....60 B3
Knowl Piece SG4 ....22 A3
Knowl Pk WD6 ....169 E4
Knowl Way WD6 ....169 F4
Knowle SG1 ....36 B1
Knowle Dr AL5 ....107 D7
Knowle Ho EN11 ....135 A5
Knowle The EN11 ....135 A5
Knutsford Sch WD2 ....154 D1
Knutsford Sch WD2 ....154 D1
Koh-I-Noor Ave WD2 ....168 A3
Kristiansand Way SG6 .....23 C8
Kymswell Rd SG2 ....51 C3
Kynance Cl LU2 ....46 A2
Kynaston Cl HA3 ....176 D3
Kynaston Wood HA3 .....176 D3
Kyrkeby SG6 ....23 C4
Kytes Dr WD2 ....154 D6

L

Laburnum Cl
Cheshunt EN8 ....162 D8
Luton LU3 ....45 C7
Laburnum Gr
Chiswellgreen AL2 ....141 B6
Luton LU3 ....45 B7
Laburnum Rd EN11 ....135 B8
Lachbury Cl LU1 ....63 A6
Lackmore Rd EN1 ....162 C4
Lacre Way SG6 ....23 C7
Ladbrooke Cl EN6 ....159 A7
Ladbrooke Dr EN6 ....159 A7
Ladbrooke
Jun Mix Inf Sch EN6 .....159 B7
Ladies Gr AL3 ....127 C5
Lady Gr AL7 ....110 E2
Lady Spencer's Gr AL1 ...127 C2
Lady Zia Wernher Sch LU2 46 B3
Lady's Cl WD1 ....167 C5
Ladygrove Cotts SG4 ......48 F5
Ladygrove Ct SG4 ....48 F5
Ladyhill LU4 ....44 B6
Ladymeadow HP3 ....138 D2
Ladyshot CM20 ....118 B1
Ladysmith Rd
Harrow HA3 ....176 E1
Pitstone LU7 ....80 E5
St Albans AL3 ....127 D4
Ladywalk WD3 ....172 E6
Ladywood Prospect CM21 .98 A1
Ladywood Cl WD3 ....165 C6
Ladywood Rd SG14 ....112 F6
Laidon Sq HP2 ....124 D7
Lake Dr WD2 ....176 D8
Lake Rd EN9 ....135 E2
Lake The WD2 ....168 D1
Lake View EN6 ....159 C6
Lake Villas SG9 ....43 B4
Lakeland Cl HA3 ....176 D4
Lakes Ct SG12 ....115 B4
Lakeside
Borehamwood WD6 ....170 A4
Tring HP23 ....100 A5
Lakeside Pl AL2 ....142 D4
Lakeside Rd EN8 ....148 C3
Lakeside Sch AL8 ....110 B4
Lalleford Rd LU2 ....46 D1
Lalsham Ho WD1 ....175 C7
Lamb Cl Hatfield AL10 ...130 B4
Watford WD2 ....154 C5
Lamb Ct AL4 ....108 E2
Lamb La AL3 ....106 B5
Lamb Mdw SG15 ....11 A3
Lambert Ct WD2 ....167 D5
Lambourn Chase WD7 ...155 F3
Lambourn Dr LU2 ....45 E6
Lambourn Gdns AL5 ......85 F3
Lambs Cl Cuffley EN6 ....146 F2
Dunstable LU5 ....44 A1
Lambs Gdns SG12 ....95 D4
Lambton Ave EN8 ....162 D6
Lamer La AL4 ....87 D3
Lamers Rd LU2 ....46 B2
Lammas Mead SG5 ....21 E2
Lammas Path SG2 ....51 B4
Lammas Rd
Cheddington LU7 ....80 A7
Watford WD1 ....167 C4
Watton at Stone SG14 .....70 D4
Lammas Way SG6 ....22 F8
Lammasmead EN10 ....148 F8
Lamorna Cl Luton LU3 .....44 F6
Radlett WD7 ....156 B5
Lampits EN11 ....135 B6
Lamsey Rd HP3 ....124 D1
Lancaster Ave
Hadley Wood EN4 ....159 D1
Hitchin SG5 ....34 E8
Luton LU2 ....45 C8

Lancaster Cl SG1 ....36 E2
Lancaster Dr HP3 ......136 F4
Lancaster Rd Hitchin SG5 ...34 E8
St Albans AL1 ....127 F5
Lancaster Way
  Abbots Langley WD5 ....153 F8
  Bishop's Stortford CM23 ...76 C8
  Welwyn Garden City AL6 ...89 C3
Lancing Ho 5 WD1 .....167 C7
Lancing Rd LU2 ....46 D3
Lancing Way WD3 ......166 B4
Landau Way EN10 ......148 A5
Landford Cl WD3 ....173 E8
Landmead Rd EN8 ......148 E2
Landridge Dr EN1 ......162 B1
Lands' End WD6 ....169 D3
Lane End
  Berkhamsted HP4 ......121 F4
  Hatfield AL10 ....129 F2
Lane Gdns WD2 ....168 E2
Lanefield Wlk AL8 ......110 C6
Lanercost Cl AL6 ....90 A7
Langbridge Cl SG4 .....35 A4
Langdale Ave AL5 ......86 D2
Langdale Ct 2 HP2 ....124 E6
Langdale Gdns EN3 ....162 D4
Langdon St HP23 ......100 A3
Langfield Cl EN9 ....135 C1
Langford Dr LU2 ....46 A3
Langham
  Luton LU2 ....45 D7
  St Albans AL4 ....128 C8
Langham Ho 8 LU1 ....63 D8
Langholme WD2 ....168 C1
Langland Ct SG4 ......174 D3
Langland Dr HA5 ......175 E3
Langleigh SG6 ....11 F1
Langley Ave HP3 ....138 F8
Langley Cres
  Kings Langley WD4 ....139 A1
  St Albans AL3 ....127 C5
Langley Ct EN7 ....147 C3
Langley Gn EN9 ....135 D1
Langley Gr AL1 ....108 C2
Langley Hill WD4 ......138 F2
Langley Hill Cl WD4 ...139 A2
Langley La
  Abbots Langley WD5 ...153 F7
  Langley SG4 ....49 E2
Langley Lodge La WD4 .153 A8
Langley Rd
  Abbots Langley WD5 ...153 F8
  Chipperfield WD4 .....138 B1
  Watford WD1 ....167 A8
Langley Row EN5 ......171 F8
Langley St LU1 ....63 E6
Langley Terrace Ind Pk
  LU1 ....63 E6
Langley Way WD1 .....166 F8
Langley Wharf WD4 ...139 A4
Langleybury La WD4 ..153 B4
Langleybury Sch WD4 .153 B5
Langmead Dr WD2 ....168 D1
Langstanton Ct HP2 ..105 D3
Langthorne Ave SG1 ...50 E6
Langton Gr HA6 ....174 C6
Langton Ho EN11 .....134 F6
Langton Rd Harrow HA3 ..176 C3
  Hoddesdon EN11 .....134 F6
Langwood 6 WD1 ....167 A8
Langwood Gdns WD1 .167 A8
Langworthy HA5 ......176 A4
Lankester Rd SG8 ......7 C5
Lannock SG6 ....23 D4
Lannock Hill SG4 ......23 E1
Lannock Jun Mix Inf
  Sch SG6 ....23 C4
Lanrick Copse HP4 ....122 E5
Lansdowne Cl WD4 ...154 D4
Lansdowne Ct EN10 ..135 A3
Lansdowne Rd LU3 ....45 D1
Lanterns La SG2 ....51 D5
Lanthony Ct SG15 .....11 A4
Laporte Way LU4 ......44 F1
Lapwing Cl HP2 ......124 E6
Lapwing Dell SG6 .....23 B3
Lapwing Rd LU4 ......44 A4
Lapwing Rise SG2 .....51 D3
Lapwing Way WD5 ...154 A8
Larch Ave
  Bricket Wood AL2 ....140 E1
  Hitchin SG4 ....35 A4
Larch Cl EN7 ....147 E4
Larch La AL6 ....89 C4
Larch Rise HP4 ....122 A5
Larches Ave EN1 ......162 C4
Larches The
  Berkhamsted HP4 ....121 D5
  Little Chalfont HP6 ...150 B1
  Luton LU2 ....45 D1
  Northwood HA6 .....174 C4
  St Albans AL4 ....128 D7
  Ware SG12 ....93 C4
  Watford WD2 ....167 E4
Larchwood CM23 .....76 D6
Lark Rise AL10 ....130 A3
Larken Cl WD2 ....168 C1
Larken Dr WD2 ....168 C1
Larkens Cl SG15 ......55 D3
Larkin Pl SG8 ....2 D1
Larkins Cl SG7 ....12 F1
Larkinson SG1 ....50 C7
Larks Ridge AL2 ......141 A4
Larksfield SG12 ......93 E3
Larksway CM23 ......76 C6
Larkspur Cl
  Bishop's Stortford CM23 ..76 D6
  Hemel Hempstead HP1 ..123 E4
Larkspur Gdns LU4 ...44 F2
Larksway CM23 ......76 C6

Larkswood Rise AL4 ....128 C8
Larmans Rd EN3 ......162 D3
Larsen Dr EN9 ....163 D5
Larwood Gr SG1 ......51 A8
Larwood Sch SG1 .....50 F7
Latchmore Bank
  Bishop's Stortford CM22 ..77 B2
  Little Hallingbury CM22 ..98 B8
Latchmore Cl SG4 .....34 F5
Latimer Cl
  Hemel Hempstead HP2 ..125 B8
  Pinner HA5 ....175 C2
  Watford WD1 ....166 E2
Latimer Ct EN8 ....162 F5
Welwyn Garden City AL7 ..111 B6
Latimer Rd
  Little Chalfont HP6 ...150 C2
  Luton LU1 ....63 E6
Latium Cl AL1 ....127 D2
Lattimore Rd
  St Albans AL1 ....127 E3
  Wheathampstead AL4 ..108 C8
Latton Hall Cl CM20 ..118 A1
Lauderdale Rd WD4 ..153 C6
Laughton Ct WD6 ....170 D7
Laundry La EN9 ......149 E6
Launton Cl LU3 ......31 B1
Laurance Haines Prim
  Sch WD1 ....167 A3
Laureate Way HP1 ...124 B5
Laurel Ave EN6 ......158 F7
Laurel Bank HP3 .....137 F8
Laurel Cl HP2 ....124 F4
Laurel Fields EN6 ....158 F8
Laurel Mews SG7 ....12 F1
Laurel Pk HA3 ....176 F3
Laurel Rd AL1 ....127 F3
Laurel Way SG5 ......21 E3
Laureldene SG10 ....74 F1
Laurels Cl AL3 ....141 B8
Laurels The Bushey WD2 ..176 E8
  Hammond Street EN7 ..147 E5
  Potten End HP4 ......123 C6
Laurelside Wlk LU5 ..44 A2
Laurino Pl WD2 ......176 C8
Lavender Cl
  Bishop's Stortford CM23 ..76 D6
  Hammond Street EN7 ..147 E5
  Harlow CM20 ....117 C1
  Luton LU2 ....45 E7
Lavender Ct SG7 .....12 E1
Lavender Gdns
  Enfield EN2 ....161 B1
  Harrow HA3 ....176 E4
Lavender Prim Sch EN2 ..161 B1
Lavender Rd EN2 .....161 D1
Lavender Way SG5 ...34 D7
Lavender Wlk HP2 ...124 D5
Lavinia Ave WD2 ....154 D5
Lavrock La WD3 .....165 F2
Law Hall La SG4 .....66 A4
Law Hall Lane Cotts SG4 ..66 A8
Lawford Ave WD3 ...164 C3
Lawford Cl
  Chorleywood WD3 ...164 C3
  Luton LU1 ....63 C7
Lawn Ave SG4 ....66 C1
Lawn Gdns LU1 .....63 D6
Lawn La HP3 ....138 D8
Lawn The CM20 .....118 B3
Lawn Vale HA5 ......175 E1
Lawns Cl SG5 ....33 C2
Lawns Ct SG8 ....7 E5
Lawns Dr The EN10 ..134 F2
Lawns The Harrow HA5 ..176 B3
  Hemel Hempstead HP1 ..123 E4
  Shenley WD7 ....156 E6
  St Albans AL3 ....127 C4
  Stevenage SG1 ......51 D4
  Welwyn Garden City AL8 ..89 D1
Lawrance Gdns EN8 ..148 D3
Lawrance Rd AL3 ....127 C7
Lawrence Ave
  Letchworth SG6 .....23 A4
  Sawbridgeworth CM21 ..97 E4
  Stanstead Abbotts SG12 ..115 C4
  Stevenage SG1 ......50 E7
Lawrence Cl SG14 ...112 E7
Lawrence Ct WD1 ...175 D7
Lawrence End Rd LU2 ..65 D4
Lawrence Moorings CM21 ..97 F2
Lawrie Ct HA3 ......176 F3
Laxton Cl LU2 ....46 E1
Laxton Gdns Baldock SG7 ..24 A7
  Shenley WD7 ....156 E2
Lay Brook AL4 ....128 A2
Layard Rd EN1 ......161 F1
Layham Dr LU2 ......46 E1
Layhill HP2 ....124 D5
Layston CE Fst Sch SG9 ..40 F8
Layston Mdw SG9 ...40 F6
Layston Pk SG8 .....7 D5
Lea Bank LU3 ....44 E6
Lea Bank Ct LU3 ....44 E6
Lea Bushes WD2 ....154 E4
Lea Cl
  Bishop's Stortford CM23 ..59 B1
  Bushey WD2 ....168 B4
Lea Ct AL5 ....86 A3
Lea Farm Jun Mix Sch
  WD2 ....154 D4
Lea Gr LU3 ....59 B1
Lea Manor High Sch LU3 ..44 F8
Lea Manor Recn Ctr LU3 ..44 F8
Lea Mount EN7 .....147 E3
Lea Prim Sch AL5 ...86 B4
Lea Rd Harpenden AL5 ..86 B3

Lea Rd continued
  Hoddesdon EN11 .....135 C8
  Holdbrook EN9 ......163 A5
  Luton LU1 ....63 F7
  Watford WD2 ....154 B1
Lea Road Ind Pk EN9 ..163 A5
Lea Valley High Sch EN3 ..162 C4
Lea Wlk AL5 ....86 C4
Leacroft AL5 ....86 D3
Leaders Cl HP22 .....60 B3
Leaf Cl HA6 ....174 D3
Leafield LU3 ....44 F4
Leaford Cres WD2 ...153 F2
Leaford Ct WD2 .....153 F2
Leaforis Rd AL7 .....148 A3
Leafy La HP23 ......99 E1
Leagrave High St LU4 ..44 C4
Leagrave Prim Sch LU4 ..44 C4
Leagrave Rd LU4 ....45 B2
Leagrave Sta LU4 ...44 C5
Leahoe Gdns SG13 ..113 C5
Lealands High Sch LU3 ..44 C8
Leamington Rd LU3 ..45 A7
Leander Gdns WD2 ..154 E2
Leas The Baldock SG7 ..23 E7
  Bushey WD2 ....167 F7
  Hemel Hempstead HP3 ..139 A7
Leasey Dell Dr AL4 ..87 A2
Leaside HP2 ....125 C2
Leaside Ct AL5 .....86 C3
Leaside Wlk 6 SG12 ..93 D1
Leat Cl CM21 ......97 F3
Leathersellers Cl EN5 ..171 E6
Leathwaite Cl LU3 ..45 A6
Leaves Spring SG2 ..51 A2
Leavesden Film Studios
  WD4 ....153 E5
Leavesden Green
  Jun Mix Inf Sch WD2 ..154 A5
Leavesden Rd WD2 ..154 B1
Leaview EN3 ......163 B6
Lebanon Cl WD1 ...153 D3
Lectern La AL1 ....141 E7
Leda Ave EN3 .....162 D1
Ledgemore La HP2 ..103 F5
Ledwell Rd LU1 ....62 F3
Lee Bridge Cnr LU2 ..85 F7
Lee Cl Hertford SG13 ..113 C4
  Stanstead Abbotts SG12 ..115 C4
Lee Farm Cl HP3 ...136 A1
Lee Valley Ctry Pk EN10 ..135 B2
Leeches Way LU7 ...80 A7
Leecroft Rd EN5 ....171 E5
Leefe Way EN6 .....146 D3
Leeming Rd WD6 ...169 F8
Lees Ave HA6 ......174 F4
Leeside Barnet EN5 ..171 E3
  Potters Bar EN6 ....159 D7
Leete Pl SG8 ......7 D7
Leeway Cl HA5 ....175 E1
Leggatts Cl WD2 ...153 F3
Leggatts Rise WD2 ..154 A4
Leggatts Way WD2 ..154 A3
Leggatts Wood
  Ave WD2 ....154 B3
Leggett Gr SG1 ....50 E8
Leghorn Cres LU4 ..44 A3
Legions Way CM23 ..77 A8
Legra Ave EN11 ....135 A6
Leicester Rd LU4 ...44 E1
Leigh Comm AL7 ...110 F4
Leigh Ct WD6 .....170 D7
Leigh Rodd WD1 ..175 F7
Leighton Buzzard Rd
  Great Gaddesden HP1 ..103 E2
  Hemel Hempstead HP1 ..124 C5
Leighton Ct EN8 ...148 A5
Leighton Rd Harrow HA3 ..176 D1
  Wingrave HP22 ....60 C3
Lemon Field Dr WD2 ..154 E6
Lemsford Ct WD6 ..170 C5
Lemsford La AL8 ...110 B4
Lemsford Rd
  Hatfield AL10 ......130 A6
  St Albans AL1 .....127 F4
Lemsford Springs
  (Nature Reserve) AL8 ..110 A5
Lemsford Village AL8 ..109 F5
Lennon Cl LU1 .....63 D7
Lennox Gn LU2 ....46 F2
Lensbury Cl EN8 ...148 E3
Leonard's Cl AL6 ..89 E8
Lesbury Cl LU2 ....46 E1
Leslie Cl SG2 ......51 C2
Letchfield HP5 ....150 B8
Letchmore Cl SG1 ..50 D6
Letchmore Inf Sch SG1 ..50 D7
Letchmore Rd
  Radlett WD7 ......156 A3
  Stevenage SG1 ....50 D7
Letchworth Bsns & Ret Pk
  SG6 ....23 C6
Letchworth Cl WD1 ..175 D5
Letchworth Gate SG6 ..23 B4
Letchworth La SG6 ..23 A3
Letchworth Mus & Art Gall
  SG6 ....22 F5
Letchworth Rd
  Baldock SG7 ......23 D7
  Luton LU2 ....45 A4
Letchworth Sta SG6 ..22 F6
Letter Box Row SG4 ..66 B4
Leven Cl Cheshunt EN8 ..162 D6
  South Oxhey WD1 ..175 D5
Leven Dr EN8 .....162 D6
Leven Way HP2 ...124 D7
Levenage La SG12 ..95 E3

Levendale LU4 ......44 C5
Leventhorpe Sch The
  CM21 ....97 E3
Leveret Cl WD2 ...154 A5
Leverstock Green
  CE Prim Sch HP2 ..125 D2
Leverstock Green Rd
  Hemel Hempstead HP2 ..125 B3
  Hemel
  Hempstead HP2,HP3 ..125 C2
Leverstock Green Way
  HP2,HP3 ....125 C3
Leverton Jun & Inf Sch
  The EN9 ....163 F5
Leverton Way EN9 ..163 C6
Lewes Way WD3 ...166 C5
Lewis Cl UB9 ......173 C1
Lewis Ho 3 WD1 ..166 F3
Lewis La SG15 ....11 A6
Lewsey Park Ct LU4 ..44 A4
Lewsey Rd LU4 ....44 B2
Lexington Cl WD6 ..169 F6
Lexington Ct EN6 ..158 D8
Lexington Way EN5 ..171 D5
Ley Hill Cty Prim Sch
  HP5 ....136 B1
Ley Hill Rd HP3 ...136 E2
Ley Ho AL7 ....111 C6
Ley Park Prim Sch EN10 ..134 F1
Ley Wlk AL7 ......111 C6
Leyburne Cl LU7 ..61 C8
Leyburne Rd LU3 ..45 B6
Leycroft Way AL5 ..107 E6
Leyden Rd SG1 ...50 D2
Leygreen Cl LU2 ..64 A8
Leyhill Dr LU1 ....63 B4
Leyland Ave AL1 ..127 C6
Leyland Ct EN8 ...148 C2
Leys Ave SG6 .....22 F6
Leys Cl UB9 ......173 D2
Leys Prim Sch The SG1 ..37 A2
Leys The St Albans AL4 ..128 D6
  Tring HP23 ....100 B4
Leysdown Ct LU1 ..111 D6
Leyton Gn AL5 ....86 A5
Leyton Rd AL5 ....86 A1
Liberty Cl SG13 ..113 C3
Library Rd LU1 ...63 E6
Lichfield Rd HA5 ..175 A1
Lichfield Way EN10 ..134 F1
Liddel Cl AL3 .....45 B3
Lidgate Cl LU4 ...44 B6
Lieutenant Ellis
  Way EN7,EN8 ....162 A7
Lighthorne Rise LU3 ..45 A7
Lightswood Cl EN7 ..147 D4
Lilac Ave EN1 ....162 C3
Lilac Cl EN7 .....162 B8
Lilac Gr LU3 .....44 C8
Lilac Rd EN11 ...135 B8
Lilac Way AL5 ...107 C6
Lilley Bottom LU2,SG4 ..47 C5
Lilley Bottom Rd SG4 ..48 B1
Lilleyhoo La LU2 ..32 C2
Lilliard Ct EN11 ..115 B2
Lilly La HP2 .....125 D2
Lime Ave Kimpton AL4 ..87 B7
  Luton LU4 ....44 C3
Lime Cl Aston SG2 ..51 D4
  Ware SG12 ....93 C2
  Watford WD1 .....167 D2
Lime Gr Barnet N20 ..171 C1
  Royston SG8 .....7 E8
Lime Tree PI AL1 ..127 E2
Lime Tree Wlk
  Bushey WD2 .....176 E8
  Enfield EN2 ......161 C1
  Rickmansworth WD3 ..165 B4
Lime Walk Prim Sch
  HP2 ....124 F1
Lime Wlk HP3 ...124 F1
Limedene Cl HA5 ..175 D2
Limekiln Cl SG5 ...7 E5
Limekiln La Baldock SG7 ..23 E7
  Stansted Mountfitchet CM24 ..59 C5
Limes Cres 4 CM23 ..77 A7
Limes Ct EN11 ...135 A6
Limes Rd EN8 ...162 E7
Limes The Arlesey SG15 ..11 A8
  Cheshunt EN10 ...148 F7
  Hitchin SG5 ......34 D6
  Luton LU1 ....63 E6
  St Albans AL1 ....127 E5
  Welwyn Garden City AL7 ..111 A4
Limetree Ave LU1 ..85 A7
Limetree Ct HA5 ..176 A3
Linacres LU4 .....44 D4
Linbridge Way LU2 ..46 C2
Linces Way AL7 ...111 B4
Lincoln Cl
  Bishop's Stortford CM23 ..76 D5
  Welwyn Garden City AL7 ..111 D6
Lincoln Ct
  Berkhamsted HP4 ..122 D4
  Borehamwood WD6 ..170 D4
Lincoln Dr
  Croxley Green WD3 ..166 C5
  South Oxhey WD1 ..175 C7
Lincoln Hill SG9 ..29 A5
Lincoln Mews AL3 ..127 C2
Lincoln Rd SG1 ...45 B1
  Stevenage SG1 ...37 B2
Lincoln Way WD3 ..166 B5
Lincoln's Cl AL4 ..128 D8

Lan-Lit 195

Lincot La SG4 ....67 C7
Lindbergh AL7 .....111 C6
Linden Cl EN7 .....148 B1
Linden Cres AL1 ...128 C3
Linden Ct Harpenden AL5 ..107 B8
  4 Luton LU2 .....63 F8
Linden Glade HP1 ..124 A2
Linden Lea WD2 ..154 A6
Linden Rd Luton LU4 ..44 E4
  Redbourn AL3 ...106 A6
Lindencroft SG6 ...12 A1
Lindens The
  Bishop's Stortford CM23 ..76 F6
  Hatfield AL10 ....129 F6
  Hemel Hempstead HP3 ..137 F8
  Stevenage SG1 ...50 E4
Lindfield Cl AL5 ...86 A4
Lindlings HP1 .....123 E2
Lindrick Ho WD1 ..175 C2
Lindsay Ave SG4 ..35 B5
Lindsay Cl SG8 ...2 C1
Lindsay Pl EN7 ...148 B1
Lindsey Cl CM23 ..58 F1
Lindsey Rd
  Bishop's Stortford CM23 ..58 F1
  Luton LU2 ....46 D1
Lindum Pl AL3 ...127 A1
Linfield Ct SG14 ..112 F7
Lingfield Cl HA6 ..174 E3
Lingfield Rd Royston SG8 ..7 F6
  Stevenage SG1 ...37 C1
Lingfield Way WD1 ..153 C1
Lingholm Way LU5 ..44 A8
Linington Ave HP5 ..136 A1
Lingmoor Dr WD2 ..154 C6
Link Cl AL10 ....130 B5
Link Dr AL10 ....130 B5
Link Rd
  Bishop's Stortford CM23 ..76 F8
  Borehamwood WD6 ..167 D7
  Oaklands AL6 ....89 C8
Link The SG6 ....12 A1
Link Way CM23 ..76 E6
Link Wlk AL10 ...130 B6
Linkfield AL7 ....110 E2
Links Ave SG13 ..114 B7
Links Bsns Ctr The CM23 ..77 C7
Links Dr
  Borehamwood WD6 ..169 F5
  Radlett WD7 .....155 F6
Links The Cheshunt EN8 ..148 D5
  Welwyn Garden City AL8 ..110 B8
Links View AL3 ..127 C5
Links Way
  Croxley Green WD3 ..166 C5
  Luton LU2 ....45 D8
Linksway HA6 ...174 C2
Linkway HA5 ....175 D2
Linkways E SG1 ..50 F5
Linkways W SG1 ..50 F5
Linley Dell LU2 ..46 D2
Linnet Cl Bushey WD2 ..168 C1
  Letchworth SG6 ..22 E8
  Luton LU4 ....44 A4
Linnet Rd WD5 ..154 A8
Linnet Wlk 1 AL10 ..130 A3
Linsey Cl HP3 ...139 A7
Linster Gr WD6 ..170 C4
Linton Cl SG4 ...35 C6
Linton Ave WD6 ..169 F7
Lintott Cl SG1 ...50 D6
Linwood CM21 ..97 E2
Linwood Rd
  Harpenden AL5 ..107 C7
  Ware SG12 ......93 F3
Lion Ct WD6 ....170 C8
Lion Yd SG4 ....66 D1
Liphook Rd WD1 ..175 D6
Lippitts Hill LU2 ..45 E5
Lismirrane Ind Pk WD6 ..169 B3
Lismore
  Hemel Hempstead HP3 ..125 C1
  Stevenage SG2 ..51 C1
Lister Ave SG4 ..34 F5
Lister Cl SG1 ...36 C2
Lister Hospl SG1 ..36 B2
Liston Cl LU4 ...44 B5
Little Acre AL3 ..127 D6
Little Acres SG12 ..114 D8
Little Berries LU3 ..44 E7
Little Bridge Rd HP4 ..122 D4
Little Burrow AL7 ..110 D4
Little Bushey La WD2 ..168 C5
Little Catherells HP1 ..123 F5
Little Chishill Rd SG8 ..18 C8
Little Church Rd LU2 ..46 B3
Little Dell AL8 ...110 D8
Little Furze Prim Sch
  WD1 ....175 B7
Little Gaddesden CE Sch
  HP4 ....102 C8
Little Ganett AL7 ..111 C4
Little Gr WD2 ...168 B5
Little Graylings WD5 ..153 E6
Little Green Jun Sch
  WD3 ....166 B6
Little Green La WD3 ..166 B6
Little Hadham Prim Sch
  SG11 ....57 C2
Little Hallingbury
  CE Prim Sch CM22 ..98 C7
Little Hardings AL7 ..111 C7
Little Hayes WD4 ..139 A2
Little Heath CM22 ..98 F3
Little Heath La HP4 ..123 B4

Little Heath Prim Sch EN6 145 C1
Little Heath Spinney AL3 127 E5
Little Henleys SG12 95 D1
Little Hill WD3 164 C3
Little Hoo HP23 99 F4
Little How Croft WD5 153 C8
Little Hyde SG2 51 B4
Little La Harpenden AL5 107 C6
Pirton SG5 20 D5
Little Lake AL7 111 B3
Little Larkins EN5 171 E3
Little Ley AL7 110 E3
Little Martins WD2 168 B4
Little Mead AL10 130 B8
Little Mimms 2 HP2 124 E4
Little Mollards HP22 60 A3
Little Moss La HA5 175 E1
Little Mundells AL7 110 F8
Little Munden CE Prim Sch SG12 71 E8
Little Orchard HP2 125 A5
Little Orchard Cl
Abbots Langley WD5 153 D7
Pinner HA5 175 E1
Little Oxhey La WD1 175 E6
Little Parndon Cty Jun & Inf Schs CM20 117 B1
Little Piper's Cl EN7 147 B2
Little Pk HP3 137 A3
Little Potters WD2 168 E2
Little Rd HP2 124 F4
Little Reddings Prim Sch WD2 168 B4
Little Ridge AL7 111 A6
Little Rivers AL7 111 A7
Little Stock Rd EN7 147 D5
Little Thistle AL7 111 C4
Little Tring Rd HP23 99 F6
Little Twye Rd
Cholesbury HP23 120 A3
St Leonards HP23 119 F3
Little Wade AL7 110 F3
Little Widbury SG12 93 F1
Little Widbury La SG12 93 F1
Little Windmill Hill WD4 151 F7
Little Wood Croft LU3 44 E7
Little Youngs AL8 110 C6
Littlebrook Gdns EN8 148 D1
Littlecote Pl HA5 175 E2
Littlefield Rd LU2 46 B2
Littlegreen La LU1 62 E3
Liverpool Rd Luton LU1 63 D7
St Albans AL1 127 E3
Watford WD1 167 B4
Livingstone Ct EN5 171 E7
Livingstone Link SG2 51 B8
Livingstone Wlk HP2 124 F7
Lloyd Way SG4 66 C1
Lloyd-Taylor Cl SG11 57 B2
Loates La WD1 167 C6
Loates Pasture CM24 59 D8
Local Board Rd WD1 167 D4
Locarno Ave LU4 44 C6
Lochinver House Sch EN6 145 B1
Lochnell Rd HP4 121 F6
Lock View CM21 97 F2
Lockers Park La HP1 124 B3
Locket Rd HA3 176 F1
Lockley Cres AL10 130 B7
Lockleys Dr AL6 89 C5
Lodge Ave WD6 169 F4
Lodge Cl SG14 113 C8
Lodge Cres EN8 162 D5
Lodge Ct
Abbots Langley HA0 154 A7
Ickleford SG5 21 E3
Lodge Dr Hatfield AL9 130 D8
Rickmansworth WD3 165 C5
Lodge End
Croxley Green WD3 166 D5
Radlett WD7 156 B5
Lodge Farm Jun Mix Inf Schs SG2 51 C7
Lodge Field AL7 89 E1
Lodge Gdns AL5 86 A2
Lodge La EN9 163 D4
Lodge The WD1 167 C7
Lodge Way SG2 51 A1
Loftus Cl LU4 44 B3
Logans EN5 171 D6
Loire Mews AL5 107 C7
Lombardy Cl HP2 125 D2
Lombardy Dr HP4 122 D3
Lombardy Way WD6 169 E7
Lomond Rd HP2 124 D7
Lomond Way SG1 37 C3
London Bible Coll HA6 174 D4
London Colney Jun Mix Inf Sch AL2 142 D6
London Luton Airport LU2 64 D7
London Rd
Aston Clinton HP22 99 A4
Baldock SG7 23 F6
Barkway SG8 17 D1
Barley SG8 8 F1
Berkhamsted HP4 122 E3
Bishop's Stortford CM23 77 A5
Buntingford SG9 40 F6
Bushey WD2 167 F3
Harlow CM17 118 C2
London Rd *continued*
Hemel Hempstead HP1,HP3 124 A1
Hertford SG13 113 E5
Hertford Heath SG13 114 B3
Hitchin SG4 34 F5
Knebworth SG3 69 A3
Langley SG4 49 D5
Luton LU1 84 F7
Luton, New Town LU1 63 E4
Markyate AL3 83 F5
Rickmansworth WD3 173 E8
Royston SG8 7 D5
Sawbridgeworth CM21 97 E2
Shenley WD7 157 A5
Stevenage SG1,SG2 50 D3
Stotfold SG5 3 A2
Tring HP23 100 C3
Ware SG12 114 E7
Welwyn AL6 89 C4
London Row SG15 11 A3
Londrina Ct HP4 122 D4
Londrina Terr HP4 122 D4
Long Acre CM17 118 B4
Long Arrotts HP1 124 B5
Long Barn Cl WD2 154 A7
Long Buftlers AL5 107 F8
Long Chaulden HP1 123 E3
Long Cl LU2 46 C3
Long Croft
Stansted Mountfitchet CM24 59 D8
Watford WD1 167 B2
Long Croft Dr EN8 163 A5
Long Croft Rd Luton LU1 63 D7
Maple Cross WD3 172 D5
Long Cutt AL3 106 A6
Long Elmes HA3 176 C2
Long Elms WD5 153 D6
Long Elms Cl WD5 153 D6
Long Fallow AL2 141 A4
Long Hale LU7 80 C3
Long Hyde SG2 51 B4
Long John HP3 124 F1
Long La Aston SG2 51 E5
Bovingdon HP3 150 F8
Chorleywood WD3 164 D2
Rickmansworth WD3 172 F8
Whitwell SG4 66 A7
Long Leaves SG2 51 A2
Long Ley Cheddington LU7 80 A7
Harlow CM20 117 F1
Welwyn Garden City AL7 111 C6
Long Marston CE Prim Sch HP23 79 B4
Long Marston Rd HP23 79 F2
Long Mdw
Bishop's Stortford CM23 76 D6
Markyate AL3 83 F5
Long Mimms 3 HP2 124 E4
Long Moor EN8 148 E2
Long Ridge SG2 51 D1
Long Spring AL3 127 F7
Long View HP4 122 A6
Longacres AL4 128 D3
Longbridge Cl HP23 100 A6
Longcliffe Path WD1 175 A7
Longcroft Ave AL5 85 F1
Longcroft Gdns AL8 110 D5
Longcroft Gn AL8 110 D5
Longcroft La
Bovingdon HP3 137 D5
Welwyn Garden City AL8 110 D5
Longcroft Rd SG1 50 E7
Longcrofts EN9 163 E5
Longdean Pk HP3 139 A7
Longdean Sch HP3 139 B8
Longfield HP3 125 B1
Longfield Ave EN3 162 C1
Longfield Ct SG6 22 D7
Longfield Dr LU4 44 D1
Longfield Gdns HP23 99 E3
Longfield La EN7 148 A4
Longfield Rd
Harpenden AL5 107 C7
Tring HP23 99 F3
Longfields SG2 51 C1
Longlands HP2 125 A3
Longlands Cl EN8 162 D7
Longlands Prim Sch EN10 148 F6
Longlands Rd AL7 110 F5
Longlees WD3 172 D5
Longmans SG11 55 F7
Longmans Cl WD1 166 C3
Longmead Buntingford SG9 40 D7
Hatfield AL10 130 B8
Letchworth SG6 22 E7
Woolmer Green SG3 69 A2
Longmeadow Dr SG5 21 F5
Longmeadow Gn SG2 51 C1
Longmeadow Jun & Inf Schs SG2 51 B1
Longmore Cl WD3 172 F6
Longmore Gdns AL7 110 F6
Longspring WD2 154 B2
Longwood Rd SG14 112 F8
Loning The EN3 162 C1
Lonsdale HP2 124 E6
Lonsdale Cl Luton LU3 45 B5
Pinner HA5 175 E2
Lonsdale Ct SG1 50 F7
Lonsdale Rd SG1 50 F7
Lonsdale Sch SG1 50 F7
Loom La WD7 156 A2
Loom Pl WD7 156 A3
Loop Rd EN9 163 B7
Lorane Ct WD1 167 A7
Lord Mead La AL6,SG4 88 C7
Lord St Hoddesdon EN11 134 D6
Watford WD1 167 C6
Lords Ave CM23 76 B7
Lords Cl WD7 156 E7
Lords Mdw AL3 106 A5
Lords Pl 12 LU2 45 D1
Lords Wood AL7 111 C6
Lordship Ctr SG6 23 A3
Lordship Farm Prim Sch SG6 23 A3
Lordship La SG6 23 B4
Lordship Rd EN7 148 B1
Loreto RC Girls Sch AL1 127 E3
Loring Rd HP4 122 C3
Lorne Rd HA3 176 F1
Lorraine Pk HA3 176 E3
Lorrimer Cl LU2 45 E6
Lothair Ct 3 AL10 130 A6
Lothair Rd LU2 46 A4
Loudwater Dr WD3 165 C5
Loudwater Ho WD3 165 C5
Loudwater Hts WD3 165 C6
Loudwater La WD3 165 E5
Loudwater Ridge WD3 165 C5
Louisa Cotts HP23 100 A3
Louise Wlk HP3 137 A3
Louvain Way WD2 154 B7
Lovatts WD3 166 A5
Love La
Abbots Langley WD5 139 F1
Ashwell SG7 4 A4
Kings Langley WD4 138 E3
Pinner HA5 175 E1
Lovel Cl HP1 124 A3
Lovell Cl SG4 35 A6
Lovell Rd EN1 162 B3
Lovering Rd EN7 147 C6
Low Hill Rd CM19 135 F6
Low Rd AL9 131 F8
Lowbell La AL2 142 E4
Lower Adeyfield Rd HP2 124 D4
Lower Barn HP3 138 F8
Lower Bourne Gdns SG12 93 C3
Lower Clabdens SG12 93 F1
Lower Cotts SG9 30 A2
Lower Dagnall St AL3 127 C3
Lower Derby Rd 4 WD1 167 C5
Lower Emms HP2 125 C8
Lower End HP22 60 B2
Lower Gower Rd SG8 7 D8
Lower Harpenden Rd LU1,LU2 64 C3
Lower Hatfield Rd SG13 112 F1
Lower High St WD1 167 D4
Lower Ickfield Way HP22 99 C7
Lower Icknield Way
Marsworth HP23 80 A1
Wilstone HP23 99 C7
Lower Innings SG5 34 D8
Lower Island Way EN9 163 B4
Lower King St SG8 7 D6
Lower Kings Rd HP4 122 C5
Lower Luton Rd AL5 86 C3
Lower Mardley Hill AL6 89 F8
Lower Mdw EN8 148 D4
Lower Paddock Rd WD1 167 E3
Lower Park Cres CM23 76 F5
Lower Paxton Rd AL1 127 E2
Lower Plantation WD3 165 C6
Lower Rd
Breachwood Green SG4 47 F1
Chorleywood WD3 164 D5
Great Amwell SG12 114 F6
Hemel Hempstead HP3 139 A5
Little Hallingbury CM22 98 C7
Lower Sales HP1 123 F2
Lower Sean SG2 51 A3
Lower Shott EN7 147 F5
Lower St CM24 59 F7
Lower Tail WD1 175 E7
Lower Tub WD2 168 D2
Lower Yott HP2 124 F2
Lowerfield AL7 111 A5
Lowes Cl SG1 37 C2
Lowestoft Rd WD2 167 B8
Loweswater Cl WD2 154 C6
Lowfield CM21 97 E1
Lowfield La EN11 135 A6
Lowgate La Dane End SG12 72 A8
Thundridge SG11 72 C5
Lowlands AL9 130 C8
Lowson Gr WD1 167 E2
Lowswood Cl HA6 174 C2
Lowther Cl WD6 169 F4
Loxley Rd HP4 121 F6
Lucan Rd EN5 171 E6
Lucas Gdns LU3 45 B8
Lucas La Ashwell SG7 4 E4
Hitchin SG5 34 D7
Lucerne Way LU3 45 C4
Lucks Hill HP1 123 E3
Ludgate HP23 99 F4
Ludlow Ave LU1 63 E4
Ludlow Mead WD1 175 B7
Ludlow Way WD3 166 C5
Ludwick Cl AL7 110 F4
Ludwick Gn AL7 110 F5
Ludwick Way AL7 110 F5
Luffenham Ho WD1 175 D7
Lukes La HP23 79 D3
Lukes Lea HP23 80 A1
Lullington Cl LU2 46 C3
Lullington Garth WD6 170 B4
Lulworth Ave EN7 147 B2
Lumbards AL7 90 A1
Lumen Rd SG8 7 D7
Lunardi Ct SG11 55 C3
Lundin Wlk WD1 175 D6
Lundy Ho WD1 166 F4
Luton Airport Parkway Sta LU1 64 B5
Luton Dr The LU1 64 B3
Luton & Dunstable Hospl LU4 44 C2
Luton & Dunstable Hospl (Faringdon Wing) LU4 44 C3
Luton Ind Coll LU1 63 E7
Luton La Harpenden AL3 85 B1
Redbourn AL3 106 A8
Luton Maternity Hospl LU4 44 C2
Luton Mus & Art Gall LU3 45 D2
Luton Rd Caddington LU1 63 A4
Cockernhoe LU2 46 E3
Dunstable LU5 44 A1
Great Offley SG5 33 B2
Harpenden AL5 85 D4
Kimpton SG4 66 B2
Luton LU4 44 A7
Markyate AL3 83 F7
Streatley LU3 31 A6
Luton Regional Sports Ctr LU2 46 A5
Luton Ret Pk LU1 64 A6
Luton Sixth Form Coll LU2 45 E4
Luton Sta LU2 63 E8
Luton Town FC LU1 63 C8
Luton Univ LU1 63 F7
Luton Univ, Putteridge Bury LU2 46 D6
Luton White Hill
Great Offley SG5 33 B2
Lilley LU2 46 F8
Luxembourg Cl LU3 44 D8
Luxford Pl CM21 97 F1
Luynes Rise SG9 40 E6
Lybury La AL3 105 F7
Lycaste Cl AL1 128 A2
Lych Gate WD2 154 D6
Lydekker Mews 1 AL5 86 A2
Lydia Ct AL9 144 C7
Lydia Mews AL9 144 C7
Lye Hill SG4 65 D7
Lye La AL2 141 A2
Lye The HP4 102 D6
Lygean Ave SG12 93 E1
Lygetun Dr LU3 44 F7
Lygrave SG2 69 C8
Lyle's Row SG4 34 F6
Lyles La AL8 110 E8
Lymans Rd SG15 11 A6
Lyme Ave HP4 121 D7
Lymington Ct WD2 154 A5
Lymington Rd SG1 50 B8
Lynbury Ct WD1 167 A6
Lynch Hill LU6 83 A8
Lynch The EN11 135 B6
Lyndale SG1 50 E4
Lyndhurst Ave HA5 175 B2
Lyndhurst Cl AL5 86 C2
Lyndhurst Dr AL5 86 C2
Lyndhurst Gdns HA5 175 B2
Lyndhurst Rd LU1 63 C7
Lyndhurst Sch WD6 169 F8
Lyndon Ave HA5 175 E4
Lyndon Mead AL4 108 C2
Lyne Way HP1 123 F5
Lyneham Rd LU2 46 C1
Lynn Cl HA3 176 D1
Lynsey Cl AL3 106 A6
Lynton Ave Arlesey SG15 11 A5
St Albans AL1 128 C2
Lynton Ct CM23 76 E4
Lynton Par EN8 148 D1
Lynwood Ave LU2 46 A3
Lynwood Dr HA6 174 F2
Lynwood Hts WD3 165 C4
Lyon Way AL4 129 A3
Lyrical Way HP1 124 B5
Lys Hill Gdns SG14 113 B8
Lysander Cl HP3 137 A4
Lysander Way
Abbots Langley WD5 154 A7
Welwyn Garden City AL7 111 D7
Lytham Ave WD1 175 D5
Lytton Ave Enfield EN3 162 E1
Letchworth SG6 22 F5
Lytton Fields SG3 68 F5
Lytton Gdns AL8 110 D6
Lytton Rd HA5 175 E3
Lytton Way SG1 50 C6
Lyttons Way EN11 115 A1

M

Mabbutt Cl AL2 140 E1
Mabey's Wlk CM21 97 B1
Macaulay Rd LU4 44 A2
Macdonnell Gdns WD2 153 F4
Macer's La EN10 148 F7
Macers Ct EN10 148 F7
Macfadyen Webb Ho SG6 23 A7
Macintosh Cl EN7 147 D5
Mackenzie Sq SG2 51 B3
Mackerel Hall SG8 7 B6
Maddesfield Ct WD7 156 E6
Maddles SG6 23 D4
Maddox Rd HP2 125 B3
Made Field SG1 50 F5
Madgeways Cl SG12 114 F5
Madgeways La SG12 114 F5
Magellan Cl SG2 51 D5
Magisters Lo WD3 166 A3
Magna Cl AL5 107 D6
Magnaville Rd
Bishop's Stortford CM23 76 E4
Bushey WD2 168 F2
Magnolia Ave WD5 154 A7
Magnolia Cl
Hertford SG13 114 A6
Park Street AL2 141 D5
Magpie Cl EN1 162 A1
Magpie Cres SG2 51 D4
Magpie Hall Rd WD2 176 E8
Magpie Wlk 2 AL10 130 A3
Magpies The LU2 45 E6
Maiden St SG4 24 C1
Maidenhall Inf Sch LU4 45 A2
Maidenhall Jun Sch LU4 45 A2
Maidenhall Rd LU4 45 A2
Maidenhead St 3 SG14 113 D6
Maidenhead Yd SG14 113 D6
Main Ave HA6 174 C7
Main Par WD3 164 C5
Main Rd SG14 91 D3
Main Rd N HP4 81 A6
Main Rd S HP4 81 D4
Maison Alfort HA3 176 E2
Maitland Rd CM24 59 E6
Malden Fields WD2 167 D4
Malden Ho WD1 175 C7
Malden Lodge 2 WD1 167 A7
Malden Rd
Borehamwood WD6 170 A6
Watford WD1 167 B7
Maldon Ct AL5 86 B2
Malham Cl LU4 44 F2
Malins Cl EN5 171 C4
Mall The AL2 141 C4
Mallard Gdns LU3 45 A5
Mallard Rd Royston SG8 7 C6
Stevenage SG2 51 D2
Watford WD5 154 A8
Mallard Way
Northwood HA6 174 C3
Watford WD2 154 E3
Mallards Ct WD1 175 F7
Mallards The HP3 138 F6
Mallion Ct EN9 163 F6
Mallories CM20 117 F2
Mallow The LU3 44 F3
Mallow Wlk
Goff's Oak EN7 147 D3
Royston SG8 7 E5
Malm Cl WD3 173 D8
Malmes Croft HP3 125 C1
Malmsdale AL8 89 D2
Maltby Dr EN1 162 B1
Malthouse Ct AL1 127 D2
Malthouse Gn LU2 46 F1
Malthouse La SG5 12 A7
Malthouse Pl WD7 156 A5
Malthouse The 18 SG14 113 D6
Malting Cotts SG9 40 D5
Malting La Aldbury HP23 101 D5
Braughing SG11 55 E7
Dagnall HP4 81 C5
Much Hadham SG10 74 F2
Malting Mead AL10 130 C6
Maltings Cl Baldock SG7 13 B1
Royston SG8 7 C7
Maltings Ct SG12 114 D8
Maltings Dr AL4 108 C8
Maltings Ind Est The SG12 115 D4
Maltings La SG8 9 E2
Maltings Orch SG5 20 D3
Maltings The
Abbots Langley WD4 153 C5
Hemel Hempstead HP2 124 D4
Letchworth SG6 12 C1
Royston SG8 7 C7
St Albans AL1 127 D3
Walkern SG2 52 B8
Malus Cl HP2 125 A4
Malvern Cl Hatfield AL10 129 F6
St Albans AL4 128 C7
Malvern Rd Enfield EN3 162 E2
Luton LU1 63 B7
Malvern Way
Croxley Green WD3 166 B4
Hemel Hempstead HP2 124 F6
Malvern Way Inf Sch WD3 166 C4
Malzeard Ct 17 LU3 45 D1
Malzeard Rd LU3 45 D1
Manan Cl HP3 125 C1
Manchester Cl SG1 36 F3
Manchester St LU1 63 E7
Mancroft Rd LU1 62 E2
Mandela Pl 4 WD2 167 D7
Mandelyns HP4 121 E7
Mandeville SG2 69 C8
Mandeville Cl
Hertford SG13 113 C3
Hoddesdon EN10 134 F3
Watford WD1 153 F1
Mandeville Dr AL1 141 D8
Mandeville Prim Sch
Sawbridgeworth CM21 97 D3
St Albans AL1 141 D8
Mandeville Rd
Enfield EN3 162 E3
Hertford SG13 113 C3
Potters Bar EN6 159 C7
Mandeville Rise AL8 110 D8
Mangrove Dr SG13 113 E4
Mangrove La SG13 113 E2
Mangrove Rd
Cockernhoe LU2 46 E4
Hertford SG13 113 E5
Luton LU2 46 C2

Manland Ave AL5 . . . . .86 C2
Manland Way AL5 . . . . . . .86 C3
Manley Rd HP2 . . . . .124 E4
Manly Dixon Dr EN3 . . . . .162 E2
Mannicotts AL8 . . . . .110 B6
Manning Ct WD1 . . . . . . .167 D3
Manor Ave HP3 . . . . .138 D8
Manor Cl Barnet EN5 . . . . .171 E5
 Berkhamsted HP4 . . . . . .122 C4
 Hatfield AL10 . . . . .129 F8
 Hertford SG14 . . . . .113 D8
 Ickleford SG5 . . . . .21 E3
 Letchworth SG6 . . . . .22 F3
Manor Cotts
 Chorleywood WD3 . . . . . .164 B3
 Northwood HA6 . . . . . . .174 F2
Manor Cres SG4 . . . . .35 B6
Manor Ct Caddington LU1 . .62 F4
 Cheshunt EN8 . . . . .162 D8
 Enfield EN1 . . . . .162 B3
 Potters Bar EN6 . . . . . . .158 F7
 Waltham Abbey EN9 . . . .163 D6
Manor Dr AL2 . . . . .141 A4
Manor Farm Cl LU4 . . . . . .44 C3
Manor Farm La LU7 . . . . . .61 C8
Manor Farm Rd EN8 . . . . .162 B4
Manor Fields
 Jun Mix Inf Sch CM23 . . . .76 D5
Manor House Dr HA6 . . . .174 B3
Manor House Gdns
 WD5 . . . . .153 D8
Manor Links CM23 . . . . . . .77 C7
Manor Lodge Sch WD7 . . .143 C1
Manor Par AL10 . . . . .129 F8
Manor Pound Rd LU7 . . . . .80 A7
Manor Rd Barnet EN5 . . . .171 E5
 Bishop's Stortford CM23 . . .77 A7
 Caddington LU1 . . . . .62 F2
 Cheddington LU7 . . . . . . .79 F7
 Harlow CM17 . . . . .118 C5
 Hatfield AL10 . . . . .129 F8
 Hoddesdon EN11 . . . . . .135 A4
 Lea Valley AL4 . . . . .86 F2
 London Colney AL2 . . . . .142 C5
 Luton LU1 . . . . .63 F6
 Potters Bar EN6 . . . . . . .159 A8
 St Albans AL1 . . . . .127 E4
 Stansted Mountfitchet CM24 .59 E5
 Tring HP23 . . . . .100 A4
 Waltham Abbey EN9 . . . .163 D6
 Watford WD1 . . . . .167 B8
Manor St HP4 . . . . .122 D4
Manor View SG2 . . . . .51 B1
Manor Way
 Borehamwood WD6 . . . . .170 C6
 Cheshunt EN8 . . . . .148 E1
 Croxley Green WD3 . . . . .166 B5
 Knebworth SG3 . . . . .68 C5
 Letchworth SG6 . . . . .22 F3
 Potters Bar EN6 . . . . . . .145 A1
Manorcroft Par 6 EN8 . . .148 D1
Manorside EN5 . . . . .171 E5
Manorville Rd HP3 . . . . . .138 C7
Mansard Cl HP23 . . . . . . .100 A3
Mansards The AL1 . . . . . .127 F4
Manscroft Rd HP1 . . . . . .124 D8
Mansdale Rd AL3 . . . . . . .105 F4
Manse Ct AL3 . . . . .83 F5
Mansfield CM21 . . . . .97 A1
Mansfield Ct SG14 . . . . . .113 C8
Mansfield Gdns SG14 . . . .113 C8
Mansfield Rd Baldock SG7 . .23 E8
 Luton LU4 . . . . .45 B1
Mansion Dr HP23 . . . . . . .100 B3
Manston Cl EN8 . . . . .148 C1
Manston Dr CM23 . . . . . . .59 B1
Manston Way AL4 . . . . . .128 D2
Manton Dr LU2 . . . . .45 D3
Manton Rd Hitchin SG4 . . . .35 B6
 Holdbrook EN3 . . . . .163 A2
Manx Ct LU4 . . . . .45 A2
Maple Ave
 Bishop's Stortford CM23 . . .76 D8
 St Albans AL3 . . . . .127 C7
Maple Cl
 Bishop's Stortford CM23 . . .76 D8
 Bushey WD2 . . . . .167 E7
 Hatfield AL10 . . . . .130 A4
Maple Cotts AL5 . . . . . . .107 B5
Maple Cross
 Jun Mix Inf Sch WD3 . . . .172 E5
Maple Ct 15 Luton LU1 . . . .63 D6
 5 Pinner HA5 . . . . .175 C1
 Stansted Abbotts SG12 . . .115 D3
 Watford WD2 . . . . .154 D3
Maple Flats AL5 . . . . .86 A3
Maple Gn HP1 . . . . .123 F4
Maple Gr
 Bishop's Stortford CM23 . . .76 D8
 Watford WD1 . . . . .167 A8
 Welwyn Garden City AL7 . . .89 F1
Maple Leaf Cl WD5 . . . . .154 A7
Maple Lodge Cl WD3 . . . .172 E6
Maple Rd AL5 . . . . .85 F1
Maple Rd E LU4 . . . . .63 B8
Maple Rd W LU4 . . . . .63 B8
Maple River Ind Est
 CM20 . . . . .118 B6
Maple Sch AL1 . . . . .127 E4
Maple Spring CM23 . . . . . .76 D8
Maple Way
 Kensworth Common LU6 . . .82 E8
 Royston SG8 . . . . .7 E8
Maplecroft La EN9 . . . . . .135 E2
Maplefield AL2 . . . . .141 C2
Mapleleaf Villas EN8 . . . .148 D4
Maples Ct 1 SG5 . . . . .34 E7

Maples The
 Goff's Oak EN7 . . . . .147 E3
 Hitchin SG4 . . . . .34 F6
Maplethorpe Ct SG12 . . . . .93 C1
Mapleton Cres EN3 . . . . . .162 C1
Maplewood SG12 . . . . .93 C3
Maran Ave AL6 . . . . .89 C4
Marbury Pl LU3 . . . . .44 F4
Marchmont Green HP2 . . .124 D5
Marconi Way AL4 . . . . . . .128 D3
Marcus Cl 1 SG1 . . . . .51 C8
Mardle Cl LU1 . . . . .62 E2
Mardley Ave AL6 . . . . .90 A8
Mardley Dell AL6 . . . . .68 F1
Mardley Hts AL6 . . . . .69 A1
Mardley Wood AL6 . . . . . .68 F1
Mardleybury Ct SG3 . . . . . .69 A1
Mardleybury Rd SG3 . . . . . .69 B1
Mardon 6 HA5 . . . . .175 F3
Mardyke Rd CM20 . . . . . .118 A2
Marford Rd
 Hatfield AL4,AL6 . . . . . . .109 C7
 Wheathampstead AL4 . . . .108 E8
Margaret Ave AL3 . . . . . .127 D5
Margaret Cl
 Abbots Langley WD5 . . . . .153 F7
 Potters Bar EN6 . . . . . . .159 C6
 Waltham Abbey EN9 . . . .163 D6
Margaret Wix Prim Sch
 AL3 . . . . .127 C7
Margeholes WD1 . . . . . . .175 E8
Margery Wood AL7 . . . . . .90 A1
Margrave Gdns 4 CM23 . . .76 E5
Marguerite Way CM23 . . . .76 C6
Marian Gdns WD2 . . . . . .154 B6
Maricas Ave HA3 . . . . . . .176 D2
Marigold Pl CM17 . . . . . . .118 B4
Marina Gdns EN8 . . . . . . .148 C1
Mariner Way 2 HP2 . . . . .125 A2
Marion Cl WD2 . . . . .167 F8
Marion Wlk 4 HP2 . . . . . .124 F6
Mark Hall Comp Sch
 CM17 . . . . .118 C3
Mark Hall Cycle Mus &
 Gdns CM20 . . . . .118 B3
Mark Hall Moors CM20 . . .118 B3
Mark Rd HP2 . . . . .125 B5
Markab Rd HA6 . . . . .175 A5
Markeston Gn WD1 . . . . . .175 D6
Market Hill Buntingford SG9 .40 E7
 Royston SG8 . . . . .7 D5
 Royston SG8 . . . . .7 D6
Market Ho CM20 . . . . . . .117 D1
Market Oak La HP3 . . . . . .139 A7
Market Pl Hatfield AL10 . . .130 B7
 6 Hertford SG14 . . . . . . .113 D6
 Hitchin SG5 . . . . .34 E7
 St Albans AL3 . . . . .127 D4
 Stevenage SG1 . . . . .50 D5
 Watford WD1 . . . . .167 C5
Market Sq
 6 Bishop's Stortford CM23 .76 F7
 Luton LU1 . . . . .63 B6
 Stevenage SG1 . . . . .50 D5
 Waltham Abbey EN9 . . . .163 C6
Market St
 7 Bishop's Stortford CM23 .76 F7
 Harlow CM17 . . . . .118 C4
 Hertford SG14 . . . . .113 D6
 Watford WD1 . . . . .167 B5
Markfield Cl LU3 . . . . .45 C7
Markham Cl WD6 . . . . . . .169 F4
Markham Rd
 Hammond Street EN7 . . . .147 C6
 Luton LU3 . . . . .45 C8
Markyate Jun Mix Inf Sch
 AL3 . . . . .83 D6
Markyate Rd LU1 . . . . .63 D1
Marlborough Cl
 Bishop's Stortford CM23 . . .76 F5
 Oaklands AL6 . . . . .89 C4
 Weston SG4 . . . . .37 B8
Marlborough Gate AL1 . . .127 E3
Marlborough Ho HP4 . . . .122 B3
Marlborough Rd
 Luton LU3 . . . . .45 D1
 St Albans AL1 . . . . .127 E3
 Stevenage SG2 . . . . .51 C5
 Watford WD1 . . . . .167 B5
Marlborough Rise HP2 . . .124 E6
Marlborough Sch AL1 . . . .141 E8
Marle Gdns EN9 . . . . . . .163 C7
Marley Ct EN10 . . . . .148 F8
Marley Rd AL7 . . . . .111 A4
Marlin Cl HP4 . . . . .121 F5
Marlin Copse HP4 . . . . . .122 A3
Marlin Hill HP23 . . . . . . .120 A8
Marlin Sq WD5 . . . . .153 F8
Marlins Cl WD3 . . . . .164 E4
Marlins Mdw WD1 . . . . . .166 D3
Marlins The HA6 . . . . . . .174 F5
Marlins Turn HP1 . . . . . . .124 B6
Marlowe Cl SG2 . . . . .51 C8
Marlowes HP1 . . . . .124 D3
Marnham Rise HP1 . . . . . .124 A5
Marquis Cl
 Bishop's Stortford CM23 . . .76 B7
 Harpenden AL5 . . . . .86 D2
Marquis Ct 9 LU2 . . . . . . .45 D1
Marquis La AL5 . . . . .86 D2
Marrilyne Ave EN3 . . . . . .162 F1
Marriott Rd Barnet EN5 . . .171 D6
 Luton LU3 . . . . .45 B6
Marriott Terr WD3 . . . . . .164 F5
Marriotts CM17 . . . . .118 C5
Marriotts Sch SG2 . . . . . . .51 A6
Marriotts Way HP3 . . . . . .124 D1
Marryat Rd EN1 . . . . .162 B4

Marschefield SG5 . . . . . . .11 E6
Marsden Cl AL8 . . . . .110 B4
Marsden Gn AL8 . . . . . . .110 B4
Marsden Rd AL8 . . . . . . .110 C5
Marsh Cl EN8 . . . . .162 F6
Marsh Hill EN9 . . . . .149 E4
Marsh Ho LU3 . . . . .44 F4
Marsh La Harlow CM17 . . .118 C5
 Stanstead Abbotts SG12 . . .115 D4
 Ware SG12 . . . . .114 E8
Marsh Rd LU3 . . . . .44 F4
Marshal's Dr AL1 . . . . . . .128 A6
Marshall Ave AL3 . . . . . . .127 F6
Marshall Rd LU2 . . . . .46 C2
Marshall's La SG12,SG11 . .72 C2
Marshalls Heath La
 AL4,AL5 . . . . .87 A4
Marshalls Way AL4 . . . . . .86 F2
Marshals Ct AL1 . . . . .128 B5
Marshalswick La AL1 . . . .128 B6
Marshbarns CM23 . . . . . . .76 C8
Marshcroft Dr EN8 . . . . . .148 F1
Marshcroft La HP23 . . . . .100 D6
Marshe Cl EN6 . . . . .159 D7
Marshgate SG1 . . . . .50 D5
Marshgate Dr SG13 . . . . .113 E7
Marshgate Ind Pk SG13 . . .113 E7
Marshmoor Cres AL9 . . . .130 D1
Marshmoor La AL9 . . . . . .144 D8
Marsom Gr LU3 . . . . .45 B8
Marston Cl HP3 . . . . .125 A2
Marston Ct AL3 . . . . .127 C7
Marston Dr HP23 . . . . .79 B4
Marston Gdns LU2 . . . . . . .45 D4
Marston Rd EN11 . . . . . . .135 B7
Marsworth Ave HA5 . . . . .175 D1
Marsworth CE Fst Sch
 HP23 . . . . .80 A2
Marsworth Cl WD1 . . . . . .166 E2
Marsworth Rd LU7 . . . . . . .80 D4
Marten Gate AL4 . . . . . . .128 A7
Marthorne Cres HA3 . . . . .176 D1
Martian Ave HP2 . . . . . . .124 F6
Martin Cl AL10 . . . . .130 A3
Martin Way SG2 . . . . .22 D5
Martindale Prim Sch
 HP1 . . . . .123 F4
Martindale Rd HP1 . . . . . .123 F4
Martindales The LU2 . . . . .63 F7
Martinfield AL7 . . . . .110 F7
Martinfield Bsns Ctr AL7 . .110 F7
Martingale Rd SG8 . . . . . . .7 E6
Martini Dr EN3 . . . . .163 A2
Martins Cl WD7 . . . . .155 E3
Martins Dr Cheshunt EN8 . .148 E3
 Hertford SG13 . . . . .114 B6
Martins Way SG1 . . . . .36 E1
Martins Wlk WD6 . . . . . .170 A5
Martins Wood Prim Sch
 SG1 . . . . .37 B1
Martlesham AL7 . . . . .111 E6
Martyr Cl AL1 . . . . .141 D7
Marwood Cl WD4 . . . . . . .138 F2
Mary Brash Ct LU2 . . . . . .46 C3
Mary Cross Cl HP23 . . . . .100 D1
Mary Exton
 Jun Mix Inf Sch SG4 . . . . .35 C7
Mary McArthur Pl CM24 . . .59 E8
Mary Park Gdns CM23 . . . .76 E4
Mary Proud Ct AL6 . . . . . .89 E7
Maryland AL10 . . . . .129 F5
Marymead Ct SG2 . . . . . . .69 A8
Marymead Dr SG2 . . . . . . .69 A8
Marymead Ind Est SG2 . . . .69 B8
Maryport Rd LU4 . . . . .45 A2
Masefield Ave
 Borehamwood WD6 . . . . .170 B4
 Stanmore HA7 . . . . .176 F5
Masefield Ct AL5 . . . . .86 B4
Masefield Rd AL5 . . . . .86 B4
Masefield Way SG8 . . . . . . .2 D1
Maslen Rd AL4 . . . . .128 C1
Mason Cl WD6 . . . . .170 D7
Mason Way EN9 . . . . .163 F6
Masons Ct CM23 . . . . .76 E7
Masons Rd Enfield EN1 . . .162 C3
 Hemel Hempstead HP2 . . .125 B4
Masterman Wharf
 12 Bishop's Stortford,
 Hockerill CM23 . . . . .77 A7
 12 Bishop's Stortford,
 New Town CM23 . . . . . . .76 F7
Masters Cl LU1 . . . . .63 B5
Matching La CM23 . . . . . . .76 D8
Mathams Dr CM23 . . . . . . .76 D5
Mathews Cl SG1 . . . . .36 D1
Matlock Cres Luton LU4 . . . .44 F7
 South Oxhey WD1 . . . . . .175 C7
Matthew Gate SG4 . . . . . . .35 A5
Mattocke Rd SG5 . . . . . . .21 C1
Maud Jane's Cl LU7 . . . . . .80 E5
Maude Cres WD2 . . . . . . .154 B1
Maulden Cl LU2 . . . . .46 C1
Maxted Cl HP2 . . . . .125 C5
Maxted Cnr HP2 . . . . .125 B6
Maxted Rd HP2 . . . . .125 C6
Maxwell Cl WD3 . . . . . . .173 A8
Maxwell Rd
 Borehamwood WD6 . . . . .170 B6
 Northwood HA6 . . . . . . .174 E3
 St Albans AL1 . . . . .128 B2
 Stevenage SG1 . . . . .50 B5
Maxwell Rise AL1 . . . . . . .167 E2
Maxwell's Path SG5 . . . . . .34 D8
May Cl AL3 . . . . .127 D5
May Cotts WD1 . . . . .167 C4
May Gdns WD6 . . . . .169 D3

May St Great Chishill SG8 . . .9 E2
 Luton LU1 . . . . .63 E6
Maybury Ave EN8 . . . . . . .148 B3
Maybury Cl EN1 . . . . .162 B1
Maycock Gr HA6 . . . . .174 F4
Maycroft Letchworth SG6 . . .12 A1
 Pinner HA5 . . . . .175 B1
Maycroft Rd EN7 . . . . . . .147 C5
Maydencroft La SG4 . . . . . .34 E3
Maydwell Lodge WD6 . . . .169 F7
Mayes Cl CM23 . . . . .77 D8
Mayfair Cl AL4 . . . . .128 C8
Mayfare WD3 . . . . .166 D4
Mayfield
 Waltham Abbey EN9 . . . .163 D5
 Welwyn Garden City AL8 . . .89 C2
Mayfield Cl Harlow CM17 . .118 F4
 Harpenden AL5 . . . . .85 E3
Mayfield Inf Sch EN8 . . . .148 E4
Mayfield Pk CM23 . . . . . . .76 D3
Mayfield Rd LU2 . . . . .46 B4
Mayflower Ave HP2 . . . . .124 D3
Mayflower Cl
 Codicote SG4 . . . . .67 F1
 Hertingfordbury SG14 . . . .112 C4
 Lower Nazeing EN9 . . . . .149 E8
Mayflower Gdns CM23 . . . .76 B6
Mayflower Rd AL2 . . . . . .141 B4
Mayhill Rd EN5 . . . . .171 E4
Maylands Ave HP2 . . . . . .125 B5
Maylands Ind Est HP2 . . . .125 B4
Maylands Rd WD1 . . . . . .175 C6
Mayles Cl SG1 . . . . .50 B7
Maylin Cl SG4 . . . . .35 C5
Maylins Dr CM21 . . . . .97 D2
Maynard Ct
 Holdbrook EN3 . . . . .163 A1
 Waltham Abbey EN9 . . . .163 F5
Maynard Dr AL1 . . . . .141 D8
Maynard Pl EN6 . . . . .146 E2
Maynard Rd HP2 . . . . . . .124 D2
Mayne Ave Luton LU4 . . . . .44 C4
 St Albans AL3 . . . . .127 A2
Mayo Cl EN8 . . . . .148 C3
Mayo Gdns HP1 . . . . .124 B2
Mays La EN5 . . . . .171 D3
Mayshades Cl SG3 . . . . . . .69 A2
Maythorne Cl WD1 . . . . . .166 E5
Maytree Cres WD2 . . . . . .153 F3
Maytree La HA7 . . . . .176 F5
Maytrees Hitchin SG4 . . . . .35 A6
 Radlett WD7 . . . . .156 A2
Maze Green Hts CM23 . . . .76 C7
Maze Green Rd CM23 . . . . .76 D7
Mazoe Cl CM23 . . . . .76 F5
Mazoe Rd CM23 . . . . .76 F5
Mc Gredy EN7 . . . . .148 B2
McAdam Cl EN11 . . . . . . .135 A8
McDonald Ct AL10 . . . . . .130 A3
McKellar Cl WD2 . . . . . . .176 C8
McKenzie Rd EN10 . . . . . .135 A3
Mead Bsns Ctr SG13 . . . . .113 E7
Mead Cl Harrow HA3 . . . . .176 D2
 Stevenage SG1 . . . . .50 F6
Mead Ct EN9 . . . . .163 B5
Mead Ho AL10 . . . . .130 B8
Mead La SG13 . . . . .113 E7
Mead Park Ind Est CM20 . .117 F4
Mead Pl WD3 . . . . .165 B1
Mead Rd WD7 . . . . .157 A6
Mead The Cheshunt EN8 . .148 C2
 Hitchin SG5 . . . . .21 F2
 Hoddesdon EN10 . . . . . .135 B2
 South Oxhey WD1 . . . . . .175 E7
Mead View WD2 . . . . .43 E6
Mead Way WD2 . . . . .167 F2
Meadgate Rd EN9 . . . . . .135 C3
Meadow Cl Barnet EN5 . . .171 F3
 Bricket Wood AL2 . . . . . .141 A2
 Datchworth SG3 . . . . .69 D1
 Enfield EN3 . . . . .162 E1
 Hertford SG13 . . . . .113 F7
 London Colney AL2 . . . . .142 D4
 St Albans AL4 . . . . .128 C6
 Tring HP23 . . . . .100 A4
 Welham Green AL9 . . . . .144 D7
Meadow Croft
 Caddington LU1 . . . . .62 F4
 Hatfield AL10 . . . . .129 F5
Meadow Dell AL10 . . . . . .129 F5
Meadow Gn AL8 . . . . .110 C6
Meadow La LU7 . . . . .80 E3
Meadow Rd
 Berkhamsted HP4 . . . . . .122 B6
 Borehamwood WD6 . . . . .168 B4
 Bushey WD2 . . . . .139 A7
 Hemel Hempstead HP3 . . .139 A7
 Luton LU3 . . . . .45 B4
 Watford WD2 . . . . .154 B5
Meadow The
 Hertford Heath SG13 . . . .114 E2
 Welwyn Garden City AL7 . .111 C6
Meadow View SG9 . . . . . . .40 F6
Meadow Way
 Abbots Langley WD5 . . . . .139 F4
 Caddington LU1 . . . . .62 E4
 Codicote SG4 . . . . .67 E1
 Great Offley SG5 . . . . . . .33 C3
 Hitchin SG5 . . . . .34 D6
 Kings Langley WD4 . . . . .139 A1
 Letchworth SG6 . . . . .22 F6
 Potters Bar EN6 . . . . . . .159 A5
 Rickmansworth WD3 . . . .165 C2
 Sawbridgeworth CM21 . . . .98 A1
 Stevenage SG1 . . . . .50 F5
 Stotfold SG5 . . . . .11 D4
 Therfield SG8 . . . . .16 A6
Meadow Way The HA3 . . .176 E2

Man–Mer 197

Meadow Wlk
 Harpenden AL5 . . . . .107 C8
 Standon SG11 . . . . .55 E2
Meadow Wood Sch
 WD2 . . . . .168 C4
Meadowbank Hitchin SG4 . . .22 B1
 Kings Langley WD4 . . . . .139 A1
 Watford WD1 . . . . .167 C2
Meadowbanks EN5 . . . . . .171 A4
Meadowbrook HP23 . . . . .100 B6
Meadowcroft
 Berkhamsted HP4 . . . . . .121 D7
 Bushey WD2 . . . . .168 B3
 St Albans AL1 . . . . .142 A8
 Stansted Mountfitchet CM24 .59 E7
Meadowcross EN9 . . . . . .163 C6
Meadowlands CM23 . . . . . .59 A2
Meadows The
 Bishop's Stortford CM23 . . .76 E5
 Breachwood Green SG4 . . . .47 E1
 Hemel Hempstead HP1 . . .123 E4
 Sawbridgeworth CM21 . . . .98 A2
Meadowsweet Cl CM23 . . . .76 C6
Meads La AL4 . . . . .87 C1
Meads Prim Sch The LU3 . .45 A6
Meads The
 Berkhamsted HP4 . . . . . .121 F6
 Bricket Wood AL2 . . . . . .140 F2
 Letchworth SG6 . . . . .22 E6
 Luton LU3 . . . . .45 A6
 Stansted Mountfitchet CM24 .59 F5
Meadview Rd SG12 . . . . . .114 D8
Meadway Barnet EN5 . . . .171 F5
 Berkhamsted HP4 . . . . . .122 E5
 Colney Heath AL4 . . . . . .143 D8
 Enfield EN3 . . . . .162 D3
 Harpenden AL5 . . . . .107 E8
 Hoddesdon EN11 . . . . . .135 A4
 Knebworth SG3 . . . . .68 F4
 Stevenage SG1 . . . . .50 A6
 Welwyn Garden City AL7 . .110 F4
Meadway Cl HA5 . . . . . . .176 B4
Meadway The EN6 . . . . . .146 F2
Meautys AL3 . . . . .127 A1
Medalls Link SG2 . . . . .51 A3
Medalls Path SG2 . . . . .51 A3
Medcalf Rd EN3 . . . . .162 F2
Medina Rd LU4 . . . . .45 A1
Medlows AL5 . . . . .85 E2
Medow Mead WD7 . . . . . .155 F6
Medway Cl WD2 . . . . .154 C5
Medway Rd HP2 . . . . .124 F8
Medwick Mews HP2 . . . . .125 B8
Mees Cl LU3 . . . . .31 A1
Meeting Alley WD1 . . . . . .167 C5
Meeting House La
 Baldock SG7 . . . . .12 E1
 Buntingford SG9 . . . . .40 F7
Megg La WD4 . . . . .138 B1
Melbourn Cl SG5 . . . . .11 F6
Melbourn Rd SG8 . . . . .7 D7
Melbourn St SG8 . . . . .7 D6
Melbourne Cl AL3 . . . . . . .127 F7
Melbourne Ct AL8 . . . . . . .110 B5
Melbourne Rd WD2 . . . . . .168 B3
Melford Cl 3 LU2 . . . . .46 D1
Melings The HP2 . . . . .125 B8
Melne Rd SG2 . . . . .69 B8
Melrose Ave
 Borehamwood WD6 . . . . .170 B4
 Potters Bar EN6 . . . . . . .159 B7
Melrose Ct EN8 . . . . .148 C2
Melrose Pl WD1 . . . . .153 F1
Melson Sq 8 LU1 . . . . .63 E7
Melson St LU1 . . . . .63 E7
Melsted Rd HP1 . . . . .124 B3
Melvern Cl SG2 . . . . .69 B7
Melvyn Cl EN7 . . . . .147 B3
Memorial Rd LU3 . . . . .44 F4
Memorial Way WD1 . . . . . .167 A6
Mendip Cl AL4 . . . . .128 C8
Mendip Rd WD2 . . . . .168 C3
Mendip Way
 Hemel Hempstead HP2 . . .124 E6
 Luton LU3 . . . . .44 C8
Mendlesham AL7 . . . . . . .111 E6
Mentley La E SG11 . . . . . . .54 E4
Mentley La S SG11 . . . . . . .55 D4
Mentley La W SG11 . . . . . .55 C4
Mentmore LU7 . . . . .61 C4
Mentmore Cross Rds LU7 . .60 F6
Mentmore Rd
 Cheddington LU7 . . . . . . .79 F2
 St Albans AL1 . . . . .127 E1
Mentmore Sch AL3 . . . . . .127 D6
Mentmore View HP23 . . . . .99 F5
Mepham Cres HA3 . . . . . .176 C3
Mepham Gdns HA3 . . . . . .176 C3
Mercer Pl HA5 . . . . .175 C1
Mercers HP2 . . . . .124 E6
Mercers Ave CM23 . . . . . . .76 B4
Mercers Row AL1 . . . . . . .127 C1
Merchant Dr SG13 . . . . . .113 F7
Merchant Taylors' Sch
 HA6 . . . . .166 E1
Merchants Wlk SG7 . . . . . .13 B1
Mercia Rd SG7 . . . . .24 A8
Mercury Wlk 1 HP2 . . . . .124 F6
Mereden Ct AL1 . . . . .141 C8
Meredith Cl HA5 . . . . . . .175 D3
Meredith Rd SG1 . . . . .51 A8
Merefield CM21 . . . . .97 C1
Meriden Ho 3 EN5 . . . . . .171 E5
Meriden Prim Sch WD2 . . .154 D3
Meriden Way WD2 . . . . . .154 E2

Meridian Sch The SG8 . . . . .7 E7
Meridian Way SG12 . . . . . .115 B5
Merle Ave UB9 . . . . .173 C1
Merlin Ctr The AL4 . . . . .128 F3
Merling Croft HP4 . . . . .121 E7
Mermaid Cl SG4 . . . . .35 B7
Merrill Pl 2 CM23 . . . . .76 E5
Merritt Wlk AL9 . . . . .144 B8
Merrow Dr HP1 . . . . .123 E4
Merrows Cl HA6 . . . . .174 C4
Merry Hill Inf Sch WD2 . . . .168 B2
Merry Hill Mount WD2 . . . .168 B1
Merry Hill Rd WD2 . . . . . . .168 B1
Merryfield WD1 . . . . .154 A1
Merryfield Cl WD6 . . . . . . .169 F7
Merryfields AL4 . . . . .128 E3
Mersey Pl
 Hemel Hempstead HP2 . . . .124 F8
 1 Luton LU1 . . . . .63 D7
Merton Rd Enfield EN2 . . . .161 D1
 Watford WD1 . . . . .167 B5
Meryfield Fst Sch WD6 . . . .169 F8
Metford Cres EN3 . . . . .163 A1
Metro Ctr
 Moor Park WD1 . . . . .166 D2
 St Albans AL4 . . . . .127 F7
Metropolitan Station App
 WD1 . . . . .166 F5
Meux Cl EN7 . . . . .162 A8
Mews The
 Bishop's Stortford CM22 . . . .77 A3
 3 Harpenden AL5 . . . . .86 B1
 Letchworth SG6 . . . . .12 C1
 Sawbridgeworth CM21 . . . . .97 E3
 St Albans AL1 . . . . .128 B2
 Stansted Mountfitchet CM24 .59 F7
Meyer Rd EN1 . . . . .162 A1
Meyrick Ave LU1 . . . . .63 C6
Meyrick Ct LU1 . . . . .63 D6
Mezen Cl HA4 . . . . .174 D5
Michaels Rd CM23 . . . . .59 C4
Micklefield Rd HP2 . . . . . . .125 C3
Micklefield Way WD6 . . . . .156 E1
Micklem Dr HP1 . . . . .123 F4
Micklem Sch The HP1 . . . . .124 A4
Midcot Way HP4 . . . . .121 F6
Middle Drift SG8 . . . . .7 C6
Middle Furlong WD2 . . . . . .168 B5
Middle La HP3 . . . . .137 A1
Middle Ope WD2 . . . . .154 B2
Middle Rd
 Berkhamsted HP4 . . . . .122 B4
 Waltham Abbey EN9 . . . . . .163 B7
Middle Row
 5 Bishop's Stortford CM23 .76 F6
 1 Stevenage SG1 . . . . .50 C7
Middle St EN9 . . . . .149 F8
Middle Way WD2 . . . . .154 B2
Middle Way The HA3 . . . . . .176 F1
Middlefield
 Hatfield AL10 . . . . .130 A6
 Welwyn Garden City AL7 . . .110 E3
Middlefield Ave EN11 . . . . .135 A8
Middlefield Cl
 Hoddesdon EN11 . . . . .135 A8
 St Albans AL4 . . . . .128 C6
Middlefield La SG16 . . . . . . .10 C7
Middlefield Rd EN11 . . . . . .135 A8
Middlefields SG6 . . . . .11 F1
Middlefields Ct SG6 . . . . . . .11 F1
Middlehill HP1 . . . . .123 E3
Middleknights Hill HP1 . . . .124 A6
Middlesborough Cl SG1 . . . . .36 F2
Middleton Mid Sch SG12 114 D7
Middleton Rd Luton LU2 . . . .46 D4
 Rickmansworth WD3 . . . . . .165 A1
Midhurst SG6 . . . . .22 F8
Midhurst Gdns LU3 . . . . .45 C4
Midland Cotts SG4 . . . . .22 C4
Midland Rd
 Hemel Hempstead HP2 . . . .124 D3
 Luton LU1 . . . . .63 E8
Milbourne Ct 1 WD1 . . . . .167 A2
Milburn Cl LU3 . . . . .31 B7
Mildmay Rd SG1 . . . . .37 B1
Mildred Ave
 Borehamwood WD6 . . . . . .170 B5
 Watford WD1 . . . . .167 A5
Mile Cl EN9 . . . . .163 C6
Mile House Cl AL1 . . . . .142 A8
Mile House La AL1 . . . . .142 A8
Milestone Cl SG1 . . . . .51 D4
Milestone Rd Hitchin SG5 . . .21 D2
 Knebworth SG3 . . . . .69 A5
Milford Cl AL4 . . . . .128 D7
Milford Hill AL5 . . . . .86 D4
Milksey La SG4 . . . . .36 C5
Mill Bridge Barnet EN5 . . . .171 F3
 Hertford SG14 . . . . .113 C6
Mill Cl Buntingford SG9 . . . . .40 E7
 Hatfield AL8 . . . . .110 A5
 Hemel Hempstead,
 Nash Mills HP3 . . . . .139 A6
 Hemel Hempstead,
 Piccotts End HP1 . . . . .124 B7
 Stotfold SG5 . . . . .12 A6
 Ware SG12 . . . . .93 D1
 Wingrave HP22 . . . . .60 A3
Mill Cnr EN5 . . . . .171 F8
Mill End SG11 . . . . .55 F2
Mill Farm Cl HA5 . . . . .175 C1
Mill Field CM17 . . . . .118 C4
Mill Gdns HP23 . . . . .100 A4
Mill Green La AL9 . . . . .110 E1

Mill Green Mus & Mill
 AL9 . . . . .130 E8
Mill Green Rd AL7 . . . . .110 E5
Mill Hill Farnham CM23 . . . .58 E5
 Royston SG8 . . . . .7 E4
 Stansted Mountfitchet CM24 .59 E6
Mill La Albury SG11 . . . . .57 C6
 Arlesey SG15 . . . . .10 F4
 Cheshunt EN8 . . . . .148 E3
 Flamstead AL3 . . . . .84 A1
 Harlow CM17 . . . . .118 E4
 Hatfield Heath CM22 . . . . . .98 F3
 Hexton SG5 . . . . .19 C3
 Hitchin SG4 . . . . .34 F3
 Hoddesdon EN10 . . . . .135 A2
 Kings Langley WD4 . . . . . . .139 A2
 Meesden SG9 . . . . .30 A5
 Sawbridgeworth CM21 . . . . .97 F3
 Stotfold SG5 . . . . .12 A6
 Therfield SG8 . . . . .15 F8
 Watton at Stone SG12 . . . . .71 A6
 Welwyn AL6 . . . . .89 C5
 Weston SG4 . . . . .24 C1
 Wingrave HP22 . . . . .60 C2
Mill Lane Cl EN10 . . . . .134 F2
Mill Mead Sch SG14 . . . . . .113 C6
Mill Race SG12 . . . . .115 D4
 Royston SG8 . . . . .7 D7
 St Ippolyts SG4 . . . . .35 A3
Mill Side CM24 . . . . .59 E6
Mill St Ashwell SG7 . . . . .4 D4
 Berkhamsted HP4 . . . . .122 C4
 Bishop's Stortford CM23 . . . .77 A5
 Hemel Hempstead HP3 . . . .138 D8
 Luton LU1 . . . . .63 D8
Mill View AL2 . . . . .141 D4
Mill View Rd HP23 . . . . .99 F4
Mill Way Bushey WD2 . . . . .167 E8
 Rickmansworth WD3 . . . . . .164 F1
Millacres 1 SG12 . . . . .93 E1
Milland Ct WD6 . . . . .170 D8
Millard Way SG4 . . . . .22 C1
Millbank HP3 . . . . .138 D7
Millbridge Mews 2
 SG14 . . . . .113 C6
Millbrook Rd WD2 . . . . .167 F8
Millbrook Sch EN8 . . . . . . .148 D2
Millcrest Rd EN7 . . . . .147 B3
Millcroft CM23 . . . . .59 A1
Miller Cl HA5 . . . . .175 C1
Millers Cl CM23 . . . . .76 C5
Millers Ct SG14 . . . . .113 D5
Millers La SG12 . . . . .115 C4
Millers Rise AL1 . . . . .127 E2
Millers View SG10 . . . . .74 E1
Millfield Berkhamsted HP4 .122 D5
 Thundridge SG12 . . . . .93 E8
 Welwyn Garden City AL7 . . .111 C7
Millfield Ho WD1 . . . . .166 D3
Millfield La Caddington LU1 . .62 D2
 Hitchin SG4 . . . . .34 F4
 Little Hadham SG11 . . . . . . .75 D8
Millfield Rd LU3 . . . . .45 B3
Millfield Way LU1 . . . . .62 D3
Millfield Wlk HP3 . . . . .139 A8
Millfields
 Sawbridgeworth CM21 . . . . .97 F3
 Stansted Mountfitchet CM24 .59 E6
Millhoo Ct EN9 . . . . .163 F5
Millhouse La WD5 . . . . .140 A4
Millhurst Mews CM17 . . . . .118 A4
Milliners Ct AL1 . . . . .127 E3
Milliners Way
 Bishop's Stortford CM23 . . . .76 C4
 Luton LU3 . . . . .45 C1
Millmead Way SG14 . . . . . .113 B6
Millside CM23 . . . . .77 A5
Millstream Cl
 Hertford SG14 . . . . .113 B6
 Hitchin SG4 . . . . .22 A1
Millthorne Cl WD3 . . . . .165 F4
Millwards AL10 . . . . .130 B2
Millway SG4 . . . . .47 D2
Millwood Ct SG5 . . . . .11 F6
Milne Cl SG6 . . . . .23 B3
Milne Field HA5 . . . . .176 A3
Milner Cl WD2 . . . . .154 B6
Milner Ct Bushey WD2 . . . . .168 B3
 Luton LU2 . . . . .63 E8
Milneway UB9 . . . . .173 B2
Milton Ave EN5 . . . . .171 F4
Milton Cl SG8 . . . . .2 C1
Milton Ct
 Hammond Street EN7 . . . . .147 F5
 12 Harpenden AL5 . . . . . . .86 B1
 Hemel Hempstead HP2 . . . .105 B1
 Waltham Abbey EN9 . . . . . .163 C5
Milton Dene HP2 . . . . .125 B8
Milton Dr WD6 . . . . .170 B8
Milton Rd Harpenden AL5 . . .86 B1
 Luton LU1 . . . . .63 C6
 Ware SG12 . . . . .93 D2
Milton St
 Waltham Abbey EN9 . . . . . .163 C5
 Watford WD2 . . . . .167 B8
Milton View SG4 . . . . .35 C7
Milverton Gn LU3 . . . . .45 A7
Mimms Hall Rd EN6 . . . . . .158 D7
Mimms La WD7 . . . . .157 C6
Mimram Cl SG4 . . . . .66 E7
Mimram Pl AL6 . . . . .89 C5
Mimram Rd
 Hertford SG14 . . . . .113 B5
 Welwyn AL6 . . . . .89 C5
Mimram Wlk AL6 . . . . .89 C5
Minchen Rd CM20 . . . . .118 A1
Minehead Way SG1 . . . . .50 A7

Minerva Cl 3 SG1 . . . . .51 C8
Minerva Dr WD2 . . . . .153 E3
Minims The LU10 . . . . .130 A7
Minorca Way LU4 . . . . .44 A3
Minsden Rd SG2 . . . . .51 D3
Minster Cl AL10 . . . . .130 A3
Minster Ho AL10 . . . . .130 A3
Minster Rd SG8 . . . . .7 C8
Minstrel Cl HP1 . . . . .124 B4
Minstrel Ct HA3 . . . . .176 E1
Miss Joans Ride HP4,LU6 . . .81 E7
Missden Dr HP3 . . . . .125 C1
Missenden Ho WD1 . . . . . . .166 E2
Mistletoe Cl LU3 . . . . .64 C8
Mistletoe Hill LU2 . . . . .64 C8
Mistley Rd CM20 . . . . .118 A2
Miswell La HP23 . . . . .99 F3
Mitchell Cl
 Abbots Langley WD5 . . . . . .154 A7
 Bovingdon HP3 . . . . .136 F4
 St Albans AL1 . . . . .141 D4
Mitre Bldgs CM20 . . . . .117 C1
Mitre Ct 17 SG14 . . . . .113 D6
Mitre Gdns CM23 . . . . .77 A4
Mixes Hill Cl LU2 . . . . .46 A4
Mixes Hill Rd LU2 . . . . .45 F4
Mixies The SG5 . . . . .11 E6
Moakes The LU3 . . . . .44 E7
Moat Cl WD2 . . . . .168 B4
Moat La Luton LU3 . . . . .45 B4
 Wingrave HP22 . . . . .60 B2
Moat The SG11 . . . . .55 D3
Moatfield Rd WD2 . . . . .168 B4
Moatside SG9 . . . . .29 B7
Moatview Ct WD2 . . . . .168 B4
Moatwood Gn AL7 . . . . .110 E5
Mobbsbury Way SG2 . . . . . . .51 C7
Mobley Gn LU2 . . . . .46 B3
Moffats Cl AL9 . . . . .145 A5
Moffats La AL9 . . . . .144 F5
Moira Cl LU3 . . . . .44 D7
Moles La SG9 . . . . .28 A3
Molescroft AL5 . . . . .85 D4
Molesworth EN11 . . . . .115 A2
Molewood Rd SG14 . . . . . . .113 B7
Mollison Ave EN3 . . . . .163 A4
Molteno Rd WD1 . . . . .167 A8
Momples Rd CM20 . . . . . . .118 B1
Monarch Hall LU2 . . . . .64 C8
Monarch's Way EN8 . . . . . .162 E6
Monastery Cl AL3 . . . . .127 C3
Money Hill Par WD3 . . . . . .165 C1
Money Hill Rd WD3 . . . . . . .165 C1
Money Hole La AL6 . . . . . . .111 E7
Moneyhill Ct WD3 . . . . .165 B1
Monica Cl WD2 . . . . .167 D7
Monkhams Hall EN9 . . . . . .149 C2
Monklands SG6 . . . . .22 D6
Monks Cl Hoddesdon EN10 135 A3
 Letchworth SG6 . . . . .22 C6
 Redbourn AL3 . . . . .106 B5
 St Albans AL1 . . . . .127 E1
Monks Horton Way AL1 . . .128 A4
Monks Rise AL8 . . . . .89 D2
Monks Row 7 SG12 . . . . . . .93 D2
Monks View SG2 . . . . .50 F2
Monks Wlk SG9 . . . . .40 E7
Monks Walk Fst Sch SG2 . . .40 E7
Monks Walk Sch AL8 . . . . . .89 C3
Monksmead Sch WD6 . . . . .170 C5
Monkswick Rd CM20 . . . . . .117 F1
Monkswood AL8 . . . . .89 C2
Monkswood Ave EN9 . . . . . .163 D6
Monkswood Dr CM23 . . . . . .76 D6
Monkswood Gdns WD6 . . . .170 D5
Monkswood Ret Pk SG1 . . . .50 E3
Monkswood Way SG1 . . . . . .50 E3
Monmouth Rd WD1 . . . . . . .167 B6
Monro Gdns HA3 . . . . .176 E3
Mons Ave SG7 . . . . .23 F6
Mons Cl AL5 . . . . .107 D6
Monson Rd EN10 . . . . .134 F3
Montacute Rd WD2 . . . . . . .168 E2
Montague Ave LU4 . . . . .44 C6
Montague Hall Pl WD2 . . . .168 A3
Montague Rd HP4 . . . . .122 B4
Montayne Rd EN8 . . . . .162 D7
Montesole Ct 6 HA5 . . . . . .175 C1
Montfitchet Wlk SG2 . . . . . .51 D7
Montgomerie Cl HP4 . . . . . .122 A6
Montgomery Ave HP2 . . . . .125 A4
Montgomery Dr EN8 . . . . . .148 E3
Monton Cl LU3 . . . . .44 F6
Montrose Ave LU3 . . . . .45 C3
Montrose Rd HA3 . . . . .176 F1
Monument Pl AL3 . . . . .127 D4
Moon La EN5 . . . . .171 F6
Moor End Rd HP1 . . . . .124 C2
Moor Hall La CM23 . . . . .76 B3
Moor Hall Rd CM17 . . . . . . .118 C4
Moor La Moor Park WD3 . . .174 A8
 Sarratt WD3 . . . . .151 E3
Moor Lane Crossing
 WD1 . . . . .166 C2
Moor Mill La AL2 . . . . .141 E2
Moor Park Rd HA6 . . . . .174 D4
Moor Park Sta HA6 . . . . . . .174 D7
Moor Pk Ind Ctr WD1 . . . . .166 C2
Moor St LU1 . . . . .63 C8
Moor View WD1 . . . . .167 A3
Moore Rd HP4 . . . . .121 F6
Moorend AL7 . . . . .111 A3
Moorfields SG9 . . . . .41 E8
Moorhead Cl SG5 . . . . .34 D6
Moorhurst Ave EN7 . . . . . . .147 B2
Moorings The CM23 . . . . . . .77 A5

Moorland Gdns LU2 . . . . . . .63 D8
Moorland Rd
 Harpenden AL5 . . . . .86 B4
 Hemel Hempstead HP1 . . . .124 A1
Moorlands
 Park Street AL2 . . . . .141 E3
 Welwyn Garden City AL7 . . .111 A3
Moorlands Prep Sch AL7 . . .111 A3
Moormead Hill SG5 . . . . .34 D6
Moors Ley SG2 . . . . .38 C7
Moors The AL7 . . . . .111 A7
Moors Wlk AL7 . . . . .111 C6
Moorside
 Hemel Hempstead HP3 . . . .138 B8
 Welwyn Garden City AL7 . . .111 A3
Moortown Rd WD1 . . . . .175 C6
Moorymead Cl SG14 . . . . . . .70 D3
Moran Cl AL2 . . . . .154 F8
Morecambe Cl SG1 . . . . .50 B7
Morefields HP23 . . . . .100 A6
Moremead WD1 . . . . .163 D6
Moreton Ave AL5 . . . . .85 D6
Moreton Cl EN7 . . . . .148 B4
Moreton End Cl AL5 . . . . . . .85 F2
Moreton End La AL5 . . . . . . .85 F2
Moreton Pk LU2 . . . . .46 A2
Moreton Pl AL5 . . . . .85 F2
Moreton Rd N LU2 . . . . .46 A2
Moreton Rd S LU2 . . . . .46 A2
Morgan Cl
 Northwood HA6 . . . . .174 F4
 Stevenage SG1 . . . . .36 D1
Morgan Gdns WD2 . . . . . . .155 B2
Morgan's Rd SG13 . . . . .113 D4
Morgan's Wlk SG13 . . . . . . .113 D3
Morgans CM23 . . . . .113 D4
Morgans Jun Mix Inf
 Sch SG13 . . . . .113 D4
Morland Way EN8 . . . . .148 E3
Morley Gr CM20 . . . . .117 C2
Morley Hill EN2 . . . . .161 D1
Morley La SG13 . . . . .73 F5
Morning Rd EN6 . . . . .90 A4
Mornington AL6 . . . . .90 A4
Mornington Rd WD7 . . . . . .156 B5
Morpeth Ave WD6 . . . . .156 F1
Morpeth Cl 3 HP2 . . . . .124 E2
Morrell Cl LU3 . . . . .45 A7
Morrell Ct AL7 . . . . .110 F7
Morris Cl Henlow SG16 . . . . .10 C5
 Luton LU3 . . . . .44 E8
Morris Ct Holdbrook EN3 . . .163 A4
 Waltham Abbey EN9 . . . . . .163 F5
Morris Way AL2 . . . . .142 D5
Morrison Ct 5 EN5 . . . . . . .171 E5
Morriston Cl WD1 . . . . .175 C5
Morse Cl UB9 . . . . .173 C1
Mortain Dr HP4 . . . . .121 F6
Mortimer Cl Bushey WD2 . . .168 B3
 Luton LU2 . . . . .63 A7
Mortimer Gate EN8 . . . . . . .148 F4
Mortimer Hill HP23 . . . . . . .100 B4
Mortimer Rd SG8 . . . . .7 E7
Mortimer Rise HP23 . . . . . .100 B4
Morton Cl LU7 . . . . .80 C4
Morton St SG8 . . . . .7 D7
Morven Cl EN6 . . . . .159 C8
Mosquito Aircraft Mus
 AL2 . . . . .143 B2
Moss Bury Prim Sch SG1 . . .50 E7
Moss Cl Pinner HA5 . . . . . . .175 F1
 Rickmansworth WD3 . . . . . .173 D8
Moss Gn AL7 . . . . .110 E4
Moss La HA5 . . . . .175 E1
Moss Rd WD2 . . . . .154 B5
Moss Side AL2 . . . . .140 F1
Moss Way SG5 . . . . .21 C1
Mossbank Ave LU2 . . . . .64 C8
Mossdale Ct 3 LU4 . . . . . . .44 C5
Mossendew Cl UB9 . . . . . . .173 C2
Mossman Dr LU1 . . . . .62 E4
Mostyn Rd Bushey WD2 . . . .168 C4
 Luton LU3 . . . . .44 E4
Mott St E4 . . . . .163 D1
Motts Cl SG14 . . . . .70 D4
Moulton Rise LU2 . . . . .63 F8
Mount Cl HP1 . . . . .123 F3
Mount Dr Park Street AL2 . .141 D6
 Stansted Mountfitchet CM24 .59 E6
Mount Garrison SG4 . . . . . . .34 F7
Mount Grace Rd Luton LU2 46 C6
 Potters Bar EN6 . . . . .159 B8
Mount Grace Sch EN6 . . . . .159 B8
Mount Pleasant
 Harefield UB9 . . . . .173 A2
 Hitchin SG5 . . . . .34 D6
 St Albans AL3 . . . . .127 C3
Mount Pleasant Cl AL9 . . . .130 D8
Mount Pleasant Flats SG1 . .50 E8
Mount Pleasant La
 Bricket Wood AL2 . . . . .140 E1
 Hatfield AL9 . . . . .130 C8
Mount Pleasant Lane
 Jun Mix Inf Sch AL2 . . . .140 E1
Mount Pleasant Rd
 Hertford Heath SG13 . . . . .114 C4
 Luton LU2 . . . . .44 E6
Mount Rd Hertford SG14 . . .113 A5
 Wheathampstead AL4 . . . . . .87 D1
Mount The Barley SG8 . . . . . .8 F1
 Hammond Street EN7 . . . . .147 D5
 4 Luton LU2 . . . . .63 D8
 Potters Bar EN6 . . . . .145 A4
 Rickmansworth WD3 . . . . . .165 C3
Mount Vernon &
 Watford Hospl HA6 . . . . .174 B4
Mount View Enfield EN2 . . .160 F1

Mount View continued
 London Colney AL2 . . . . . .142 F4
 Rickmansworth WD3 . . . . . .165 B1
Mount Way AL7 . . . . .110 F3
Mountbatten Cl AL1 . . . . . . .142 B8
Mounteagle SG8 . . . . .7 D5
Mountfield Rd
 Hemel Hempstead HP2 . . . .124 D3
 Luton LU2 . . . . .45 E2
Mountfitchet Castle &
 Norman Village CM24 . . . .59 F6
Mountfitchet High Sch
 The CM24 . . . . .59 F4
Mountfitchet Rd CM24 . . . . .59 E5
Mountjoy SG8 . . . . .22 C1
Mountside HA7 . . . . .176 F2
Mountsorrel SG13 . . . . .113 F6
Mountview HA6 . . . . .174 F4
Mountview Rd EN7 . . . . . . .147 E5
Mountway EN6 . . . . .145 A1
Mountway Cl AL7 . . . . .110 F3
Mowat Ind Est WD2 . . . . . .154 C1
Mowbray Cres SG5 . . . . .11 F7
Mowbray Gdns SG4 . . . . . . .35 A5
Mowbray Rd CM20 . . . . . . .118 A3
Moxes Wood LU3 . . . . .44 E7
Moxom Ave EN8 . . . . .148 E1
Moxon St EN5 . . . . .171 F6
Mozart Cl SG1 . . . . .50 C5
Muddy La SG6 . . . . .22 F3
Muirfield LU2 . . . . .45 E6
Muirfield Cl WD1 . . . . .175 C5
Muirfield Gn WD1 . . . . .175 C6
Muirfield Rd WD1 . . . . .175 B6
Muirhead Way SG3 . . . . .68 F5
Mulberry Cl
 Cheshunt EN10 . . . . .148 F7
 Chiswellgreen AL2 . . . . . . .141 B3
 Luton LU1 . . . . .63 B7
 Stotfold SG5 . . . . .11 F5
 Tring HP23 . . . . .100 A5
 Watford WD1 . . . . .153 C3
Mulberry Ct CM23 . . . . .77 A5
Mulberry Gdns WD7 . . . . . .156 E6
Mulberry Gn CM17 . . . . . . .118 D4
Mulberry Terr CM17 . . . . . .118 B4
Mulberry Way SG5 . . . . .21 D2
Mull Ho WD1 . . . . .166 F3
Mullion Cl Harrow HA3 . . . .176 F1
 Luton LU2 . . . . .46 B5
Mullion Wlk WD1 . . . . .175 C6
Mullway SG6 . . . . .22 C6
Mundells
 Hammond Street EN7 . . . . .148 A4
 Welwyn Garden City AL7 . . .111 A8
Mundells Ct AL7 . . . . .110 F8
Munden Gr WD2 . . . . .154 D1
Munden Rd SG12 . . . . .71 E7
Munden View WD2 . . . . . . .154 D3
Mundesley Cl
 South Oxhey WD1 . . . . . . .175 C6
 Stevenage SG1 . . . . .36 B1
Mungo-Park Cl WD2 . . . . . .176 C8
Munro Rd WD2 . . . . .168 C4
Muntings The SG2 . . . . .51 A3
Munts Mdw SG4 . . . . .24 C1
Murchison Rd EN11 . . . . . . .115 C4
Muriel Ave WD1 . . . . .167 C4
Murray Cres HA5 . . . . .175 D2
Murray Rd
 Berkhamsted HP4 . . . . .122 C6
 Northwood HA6 . . . . .174 E3
Murrell La SG5 . . . . .12 A5
Murton Ct AL1 . . . . .127 C4
Museum Ct HP23 . . . . .100 A3
Museum of St Albans
 AL1 . . . . .127 E3
Musgrave Cl EN7 . . . . .147 F4
Musk Hill HP1 . . . . .123 E2
Muskalls Cl EN7 . . . . .148 A4
Muskham Rd CM20 . . . . . . .118 B3
Musleigh Manor SG12 . . . . .93 F3
Musley Hill SG12 . . . . .93 E2
Musley Inf Sch SG12 . . . . . .93 E2
Musley La SG12 . . . . .93 E2
Mussons Path LU2 . . . . .45 E1
Muswell Cl LU3 . . . . .45 B6
Mutchetts Cl WD2 . . . . .154 E6
Mutford Croft 2 LU2 . . . . .46 D1
Mutton La EN6 . . . . .158 E8
Myddelton Ave EN1 . . . . . . .161 C1
Myddelton House Gdns
 EN2 . . . . .162 A3
Myddelton Path EN7 . . . . . .162 B8
Myddleton Rd SG12 . . . . . .114 D8
Myers Cl WD7 . . . . .156 E7
Myles Ct EN7 . . . . .147 C2
Mylne Cl EN8 . . . . .148 C4
Mylne Ct EN11 . . . . .115 A1
Mymms Dr AL9 . . . . .145 B4
Myrtle Cotts WD3 . . . . .152 A3
Myrtle Gr EN2 . . . . .161 D1
Myrtleside Cl HA6 . . . . .174 D3
Myson Way CM23 . . . . .77 B7

N

Nails La 15 CM23 . . . . .76 C3
Nairn Cl AL5 . . . . .107 D6
Nairn Gn WD1 . . . . .175 A7
Nan Aires HP22 . . . . .60 A3
Nancy Downs WD1 . . . . . . .167 C3
Nap The WD4 . . . . .139 A2
Napier Cl AL2 . . . . .142 D6
Napier Ct Cheshunt EN8 . . .148 B3
 Luton LU1 . . . . .63 D7
Napier Dr WD2 . . . . .167 E5

Napier Hall LU2 . . . . .64 C8
Napier Rd LU1 . . . . .63 D7
Nappsbury Rd LU4 . . . . . .44 D5
Napsbury Ave AL2 . . . . . .142 C5
Napsbury La AL1 . . . . . . .142 A7
Nascot PI WD1 . . . . .167 B7
Nascot Rd WD1 . . . . .167 B7
Nascot St WD1 . . . . .167 B7
Nascot Wood Inf Sch
  WD1 . . . . .154 A1
Nascot Wood Jun Sch
  WD1 . . . . .154 A1
Nascot Wood Rd WD1 . .153 F1
Naseby Rd LU1 . . . . .63 B7
Nash Cl
  Borehamwood WD6 . . . . .169 F5
  Stevenage SG2 . . . . .51 B6
  Welham Green AL9 . . . . .144 D8
Nash Gn HP3 . . . . .138 F6
Nash Mills CE Prim Sch
  HP3 . . . . .138 F6
Nash Mills La HP3 . . . . .138 F5
Nash Rd SG8 . . . . .7 D5
Nathaniel Wlk HP23 . . . .100 A5
Nathans Cl AL6 . . . . .89 C6
Nayland Cl LU2 . . . . .46 E1
Nazeing Cty Prim Sch
  EN9 . . . . .149 E8
Nazeing New Rd EN10 . .135 B2
Nazeing Rd EN9 . . . . . . .135 D1
Nazeingbury Cl EN9 . . . .135 D1
Nazeingbury Par EN9 . . .135 D1
Neach Cl SG1 . . . . .37 C3
Neal Cl HA6 . . . . .175 A2
Neal Ct Hertford SG14 . . .113 C6
  Waltham Abbey EN9 . . . .163 F6
Neal St WD1 . . . . .167 C4
Neaole Cl WD6 . . . . .170 C8
Necton Rd AL4 . . . . .108 E8
Needham Rd LU4 . . . . .44 B6
Neild Way WD3 . . . . .164 F2
Nell Gwynn Cl WD7 . . . .156 E7
Nelson Ave AL1 . . . . .142 B8
Nelson Rd
  Bishop's Stortford CM23 . . .77 A5
  Dagnall HP4 . . . . .81 C5
Nelson St SG14 . . . . .113 B7
Nene Rd SG16 . . . . .10 B4
Neptune Ct WD6 . . . . . . .170 A6
Neptune Dr HP2 . . . . . . .124 E5
Neptune Gate SG2 . . . . . .51 B8
Neston Rd WD2 . . . . .154 C2
Nether St SG12 . . . . .95 E4
Netherby Cl HP3 . . . . . . .100 C6
Nethercott Cl LU2 . . . . . . .46 C1
Nethercott Villas WD1 . .167 C4
Netherfield Ct SG12 . . . .115 D3
Netherfield La SG12 . . . .115 E3
Netherfield Rd AL5 . . . . .107 B4
Netherhall Rd CM19 . . . .135 F5
Netherstones SG5 . . . . . . .11 F1
Netherway AL3 . . . . .141 A8
Netley Dell SG6 . . . . .23 B3
Netteswell Cross CM20 . .117 C2
Netteswell Orch CM20 . .117 D1
Netteswell Rd CM20 . . . .117 F3
Netteswell Twr CM20 . . .117 D1
Nettlecroft
  Hemel Hempstead HP1 . . .124 B2
  Welwyn Garden City AL7 .111 B7
Nettleden Rd
  Little Gaddesden HP4 . . .102 E4
  Nettleden HP1 . . . . .103 C1
  Potten End HP4 . . . . . . .123 B8
Nevell's Gn SG6 . . . . .22 F6
Nevells Rd SG6 . . . . .22 F6
Nevil Cl HA6 . . . . .174 D5
Nevill Gr WD2 . . . . .167 B8
Neville Cl EN6 . . . . .158 F8
Neville Rd LU3 . . . . .45 A5
Neville Road Pas LU3 . . . .45 A5
Neville's Ct SG6 . . . . .23 B7
New Barn La CM22 . . . . . .77 D1
New Barnes Ave AL1 . . . .142 A8
New Barns La SG10 . . . . . .74 E4
New Bedford Rd LU3 . . . .45 D3
New Briars Prim Sch
  AL10 . . . . .130 A5
New Cl SG3 . . . . .68 F6
New Cotts
  Brookmans Park AL9 . . . .144 D3
  Cheshunt EN8 . . . . .162 C5
  Whitwell SG4 . . . . .66 A7
New Ct SG4 . . . . .69 A2
New England Cl SG4 . . . .34 F4
New England St AL3 . . . .127 C3
New Farm La HA6 . . . . . .174 E2
New Ford La EN8 . . . . . . .162 F5
New Ford Rds EN8 . . . . .162 F5
New Forge PI AL3 . . . . . .106 B5
New Greens Ave AL3 . . . .127 D7
New House Pk AL1 . . . . .142 B7
New Inn Rd SG7 . . . . .3 D5
New Kent Rd AL1 . . . . . . .127 D3
New Mill Terr HP23 . . . . .100 B6
New Par WD3 . . . . .164 C5
New Park Dr HP2 . . . . . . .125 B3
New Park La SG2 . . . . .51 F2
New Park Rd
  Harefield UB9 . . . . .173 C2
  Newgate Street SG13 . . .146 D7
New PI AL4 . . . . .89 B4
New Rd Berkhamsted HP4 .122 D6
  Chipperfield WD4 . . . . . .137 F1
  Croxley Green WD3 . . . . .166 A4
  Elstree WD6 . . . . .169 D3
  Great Chishill SG8 . . . . . . .9 D6

New Rd continued
  Harlow CM17 . . . . .118 D4
  Hatfield AL8 . . . . .110 A3
  Hertford SG14 . . . . .113 D8
  Hoddesdon EN10 . . . . . .135 A4
  Little Hadham SG11 . . . . .75 A7
  Lower Stondon SG17 . . . . .10 A7
  Radlett WD7 . . . . .155 E2
  Radlett,
  Letchmore Heath WD7 . . .168 E8
  Ridge EN6 . . . . .158 A6
  Sarratt WD3 . . . . .151 F1
  Shenley WD7 . . . . .157 A5
  Tring HP23 . . . . .100 B6
  Ware SG12 . . . . .93 D1
  Watford WD1 . . . . .167 C5
  Welwyn AL6 . . . . .89 F3
  Woolmer Green SG3 . . . . .69 B3
New Town SG4 . . . . .67 F1
New Town Rd 9 LU1 . . . .63 E6
New Town St LU1 . . . . . . .63 E6
New Wood AL7 . . . . .111 C7
Newark Cl SG8 . . . . .7 C8
Newark Gn WD6 . . . . . . .170 D6
Newark Rd LU4 . . . . .45 A2
Newberries Ave WD7 . . .156 B4
Newberries Prim Sch
  WD7 . . . . .156 C4
Newbiggin Path WD1 . . .175 C6
Newbold Rd LU3 . . . . .45 B7
Newbolt Cl SG8 . . . . .7 D8
Newbolt Rd HA7 . . . . . . .176 F5
Newbury Ave EN3 . . . . . .162 F2
Newbury Cl
  Bishop's Stortford CM23 . . .76 E8
  Luton LU4 . . . . .44 E2
  Stevenage SG1 . . . . .36 D1
Newcastle Cl SG1 . . . . . . .36 F2
Newcombe Rd LU1 . . . . . .63 C7
Newcome Path WD7 . . . .157 A5
Newcome Rd WD7 . . . . . .157 A5
Newdigate Gn UB9 . . . . .173 D2
Newdigate Rd UB9 . . . . .173 C2
Newdigate Rd E UB9 . . .173 D2
Newell La SG2 . . . . .38 D7
Newell Rd HP3 . . . . .138 E8
Newell Rise HP3 . . . . . . .138 E8
Newells SG6 . . . . .23 D4
Newells Hedge LU7 . . . . .80 D5
Newfield La HP2 . . . . . . .124 F3
Newfield Way AL4 . . . . .128 D1
Newfields AL8 . . . . .110 B5
Newford Cl HP2 . . . . .125 B4
Newgate SG2 . . . . .51 A4
Newgate Cl AL4 . . . . .128 D6
Newgate St SG13 . . . . . . .146 D7
Newgate Street Village
  SG13 . . . . .146 E6
Newgatestreet Rd EN7 . .147 B4
Newground Rd HP23 . . . .101 B3
Newhall Cl HP3 . . . . .137 A4
Newhall Ct EN9 . . . . .163 F6
Newhouse Cres WD2 . . . .154 B6
Newhouse Rd HP3 . . . . . .137 A4
Newland Cl Pinner HA5 . .175 F4
  St Albans AL1 . . . . .142 A8
Newlands Hatfield AL9 . .130 C7
  Letchworth SG6 . . . . .23 A3
Newlands Ave WD7 . . . . .155 F5
Newlands Cl E SG4 . . . . . .34 F4
Newlands Cl W SG4 . . . . .34 F4
Newlands La SG4 . . . . . . .34 F4
Newlands PI EN5 . . . . . . .171 D4
Newlands Rd
  Hemel Hempstead HP1 . . .123 E3
  Luton LU1 . . . . .63 C3
Newlands Way EN6 . . . . .145 B1
Newlands Wlk WD2 . . . .154 D6
Newlyn Cl
  Bricket Wood AL2 . . . . . .140 E1
  Stevenage SG1 . . . . .50 A6
Newlyn Rd EN5 . . . . .171 F5
Newman Ave SG8 . . . . .7 F6
Newmans Cl SG14 . . . . . . .70 D3
Newmans Dr AL5 . . . . . . .85 F2
Newmarket Rd Royston SG8 .7 F6
  Royston SG8 . . . . .7 F6
Newnham Cl LU2 . . . . . . .46 D1
Newnham Par 5 EN8 . . . .148 D1
Newnham Rd SG7 . . . . . . .12 E6
Newnham Way SG7 . . . . . .4 B2
Newport Cl EN3 . . . . .162 E2
Newport Mead WD1 . . . .175 D6
Newports CM21 . . . . .97 C1
Newquay Gdns WD1 . . . .175 B8
Newstead AL10 . . . . .129 F2
Newstead Ho UB9 . . . . . .173 C1
Newteswell Dr EN9 . . . . .163 D7
Newton Cl Harpenden AL5 .107 D6
  Hoddesdon EN11 . . . . . .115 B2
Newton Cres WD6 . . . . . .170 C5
Newton Dr CM21 . . . . . . .97 D1
Newton Rd Harrow HA3 . .176 E1
Newtondale LU4 . . . . .44 C5
Newtons Way SG4 . . . . . . .34 F6
Newtown Rd CM23 . . . . . .76 F6

Niagara Cl EN8 . . . . .148 D2
Nicholas Breakspear
  RC Sch AL4 . . . . .128 E2
Nicholas St St Albans AL3 .127 D7
  Watford WD2 . . . . .154 B2
Nicholas La SG14 . . . . . . .113 D6
Nicholas PI SG1 . . . . .36 D1
Nicholas Rd WD6 . . . . . . .169 F4
Nicholas Way
  Hemel Hempstead HP2 . . .124 F5
  Northwood HA6 . . . . . . .174 C2
Nicholls Cl AL3 . . . . .105 F5
Nichols Cl LU2 . . . . .46 C2
Nicholson Court Ind Ctr
  EN11 . . . . .135 B6
Nicholson Dr WD2 . . . . . .176 C8
Nicola Cl HA3 . . . . .176 D1
Nicoll Way WD6 . . . . . . .170 D5
Nidderdale HP2 . . . . .124 F6
Nightingale Ave SG8 . . . . .2 A5
Nightingale Cl Luton LU2 . .46 C4
  Radlett WD7 . . . . .155 F3
  Watford WD5 . . . . .154 A8
Nightingale Ct
  Hertford SG14 . . . . .113 C6
  Hitchin SG5 . . . . .35 A8
  Luton LU3 . . . . .63 C8
  Rickmansworth WD3 . . . .165 C2
Nightingale La AL1,AL4 . .142 C7
Nightingale Lodge HP4 . .122 B4
Nightingale PI WD3 . . . . .165 D2
Nightingale Rd
  Bushey WD2 . . . . .168 A4
  Hammond Street EN7 . . .147 C6
  Hitchin SG5 . . . . .34 F8
  Rickmansworth WD3 . . . .165 C2
Nightingale Terr SG15 . . . .11 A3
Nightingale Way SG7 . . . .23 F6
Nightingale Wlk
  Hemel Hempstead HP2 . . .105 C4
  Stevenage SG2 . . . . .51 C5
Nightingales EN9 . . . . . . .163 E5
Nimbus Way SG4 . . . . . . .35 C7
Nimmo Dr WD2 . . . . .168 D2
Nimrod Cl AL4 . . . . .128 C5
Ninefields EN9 . . . . .163 F6
Ninesprings Way SG4 . . . .35 B6
Ninfield Cl LU2 . . . . .46 C3
Ninian Rd HP2 . . . . .124 E8
Ninning's La AL6 . . . . .68 D2
Ninth Ave LU3 . . . . .44 D7
Niton Cl EN5 . . . . .171 D3
Niven Cl WD6 . . . . .170 C8
Nobel Sch SG2 . . . . .51 C7
Nobel Villas EN9 . . . . . . .163 D5
Nobles The CM23 . . . . . . .76 D6
Nodes Dr SG2 . . . . .51 A1
Noke La AL2 . . . . .140 E4
Noke Shot AL5 . . . . .86 C4
Noke Side AL2 . . . . .141 A4
Noke The SG2 . . . . .69 B8
Nokes The HP1 . . . . .124 A5
Nokeside SG2 . . . . .69 B8
Nook The SG2 . . . . .115 B4
Norbury Ave WD1 . . . . . .167 C7
Norfolk Ave SG8 . . . . .7 F6
Norfolk Ct 4 EN5 . . . . . .171 E5
Norfolk Gdns WD6 . . . . .170 D5
Norfolk Rd
  Buntingford SG9 . . . . .40 E8
  Luton LU2 . . . . .64 A7
  Rickmansworth WD3 . . . .165 C1
Norfolk Way CM23 . . . . . .76 F5
Normady Ct HP1 . . . . . . .124 D4
Norman Ave CM23 . . . . . .76 D6
Norman Cl CM23 . . . . . . .76 D6
Norman Cres HA5 . . . . . .175 C2
Norman Ct
  Potters Bar EN6 . . . . . . .145 C1
  Stansted Mountfitchet CM24 .59 E4
  Stevenage SG1 . . . . .36 F1
Norman Rd Luton LU3 . . . .45 B2
  Welwyn AL6 . . . . .89 B3
Norman's La SG8 . . . . .7 D5
Norman's Way CM24 . . . .59 E7
Normandy Ave EN5 . . . . .171 F5
Normandy Dr HP4 . . . . . .122 B6
Normandy Rd AL3 . . . . . .127 C3
Normandy Way EN11 . . .135 D8
Normans Cl SG6 . . . . .11 F1
Normans La AL6 . . . . .68 E2
Normansfield Cl WD2 . . .168 B2
Norris Cl CM23 . . . . .77 C7
Norris Gr EN10 . . . . .134 E3
Norris La EN11 . . . . .135 A7
Norris Rd EN11 . . . . .135 A6
Norris Rise EN11 . . . . . . .134 F7
North App Moor Park HA6 .174 C8
  Watford WD2 . . . . .154 A5
North Ave Letchworth SG6 . .23 B8
  Shenley WD7 . . . . .156 E7
North Barn EN10 . . . . . . .135 B1
North Cl Barnet EN5 . . . .171 C4
  Chiswellgreen AL2 . . . . .141 B6
  Royston SG8 . . . . .7 C7
North Comm AL3 . . . . . .106 A5
North Common Rd AL3 . .106 A4
North Ct AL3 . . . . .83 E5
North Dr St Albans AL4 . .128 E5
  Thundridge SG12 . . . . . . .72 E1
North Drift Way LU1 . . . .63 B6
North Gate CM20 . . . . . .117 C1
North Hertfordshire Coll
  SG6 . . . . .22 F5
North Hertfordshire Coll
  (Hitchin Ctr) SG4 . . . . . .35 B8
North Hertfordshire Coll
  (Stevenage Ctr) SG1 . . .50 D4

North Herts Ed Support
  Ctr SG6 . . . . .22 D3
North Hill WD3 . . . . .164 E6
North Luton Ind Est LU4 .44 B7
North Orbital Rd
  Bricket Wood AL2 . . . . . .140 E2
  Chiswellgreen AL2 . . . . .141 B5
  Colney Heath AL4 . . . . . .129 C2
  London Colney AL1,AL2,AL4 142 D6
  Park Street AL2 . . . . .141 E6
  Watford WD2 . . . . .154 A7
North Orbital Trad Est
  AL1 . . . . .142 A7
North PI Harlow CM20 . . .118 B5
  Hitchin SG5 . . . . .21 D1
  Waltham Abbey EN9 . . . .163 B6
North Rd Baldock SG7 . . . .12 E2
  Berkhamsted HP4 . . . . . .122 B4
  Cheshunt EN8 . . . . .162 E6
  Chorleywood WD3 . . . . . .164 D4
  Hertford SG14 . . . . .113 A7
  Hertford SG14 . . . . .113 C6
  Hoddesdon EN11 . . . . . .135 A7
  Stevenage SG5 . . . . .36 C2
North Ride AL6 . . . . .89 C6
North Riding AL2 . . . . . . .141 A1
North Road Ave SG14 . . .113 A7
North Road Gdns SG14 . .113 B6
North St
  4 Bishop's Stortford CM23 .76 F7
  Lower Nazeing EN9 . . . . .135 E1
  Luton, Hart Hill LU2 . . . . .45 E1
  Luton, High Town LU2 . . . .63 E8
North Terr 5 CM23 . . . . . .76 F7
North View Cotts SG12 . . .95 D4
North Western Ave
  Abbots Langley WD2 . . . .153 D4
  Stanmore WD6 . . . . .169 A2
  Watford WD2 . . . . .154 C3
Northaw CE Sch EN6 . . .146 A1
Northaw Cl HP2 . . . . .125 B8
Northaw Pk EN6 . . . . . . .159 F7
Northaw Rd E EN6 . . . . .146 E1
Northaw Rd W EN6 . . . . .160 C8
Northbridge Rd HP4 . . . .122 A6
Northbridge Way HP1 . . .124 A3
Northbrook Dr HA6 . . . . .174 E3
Northbrook Rd EN5 . . . . .171 E3
Northchiffe Dr N20 . . . . .171 F1
Northcote 1 HA5 . . . . . . .175 C1
Northcotts AL9 . . . . .130 C6
Northcourt WD3 . . . . .165 A1
Northdown Rd AL10 . . . . .130 A2
Northend HP3 . . . . .125 C1
Northern Ave SG16 . . . . . .10 C3
Northern Ho SG4 . . . . . . .35 B7
Northfield Braughing SG11 .55 F7
  Hatfield AL10 . . . . .130 B8
  Standon SG11 . . . . .55 E2
Northfield Gdns WD2 . . .154 C6
Northfield Rd
  Aldbury HP23 . . . . .100 F7
  Borehamwood WD6 . . . . .170 B8
  Cheshunt EN8 . . . . .162 E7
  Guilden Morden SG7 . . . . .1 C2
  Harpenden AL5 . . . . .86 C4
  Sawbridgeworth CM21 . . .97 E4
Northfields AL9 . . . . .11 F1
Northfields Inf Sch SG6 . .11 F1
Northgate HA6 . . . . .174 C3
Northgate End CM23 . . . .76 E8
Northgate Ho EN8 . . . . . .148 D2
Northgate Jun Mix Inf
  Sch CM23 . . . . .76 E8
Northgate Path WD6 . . . .169 F8
Northlands EN6 . . . . .159 D8
Northolt Ave CM23 . . . . . .59 B1
Northridge Way HP1 . . . .124 A3
Northside AL4 . . . . .108 B1
Northumberland
  Ave EN1 . . . . .162 B1
Northview Rd LU2 . . . . . . .45 F2
Northway
  Rickmansworth WD3 . . . .165 D2
  1 Welwyn Garden City AL7 .89 F1
Northwell Dr LU3 . . . . .44 F4
Northwick Rd WD1 . . . . .175 C6
Northwood AL7 . . . . .111 C6
Northwood Cl EN7 . . . . . .147 F4
Northwood Coll HA6 . . . .174 D3
Northwood Comp Sch
  HA6 . . . . .175 B2
Northwood Hills Cir
  HA6 . . . . .175 A2
Northwood Hills Sta
  HA6 . . . . .175 A1
Northwood & Pinner
  District Hospl HA6 . . . .175 A2
Northwood Prep Boys
  Sch WD3 . . . . .174 C8
Northwood Rd UB9 . . . . .173 E3
Northwood Sta HA6 . . . .174 E1
Northwood Way
  Harefield UB9 . . . . .173 D2
  Northwood HA6 . . . . . . .175 A3
Norton Bury La SG6 . . . . .12 C2
Norton Cl WD6 . . . . .170 A8
Norton Cres SG7 . . . . .23 E8
Norton Gn SG1 . . . . .50 B3
Norton Green Rd SG1 . . . .50 C4
Norton Mill La SG6 . . . . . .12 C1
Norton Rd Letchworth SG6 .12 C2
  Luton LU3 . . . . .44 F4
  Stevenage SG1 . . . . .50 D4
  Stotfold SG5 . . . . .12 A4
Norton Road Prim Sch
  LU3 . . . . .44 F4
Norton Sch SG6 . . . . .23 A8

Norton Way N SG6 . . . . . .23 A7
Norton Way S SG6 . . . . . .23 A5
Nortonstreet La SG4 . . . . .67 B7
Norvic Rd HP23 . . . . .80 A1
Norwich Cl SG1 . . . . .37 B1
Norwich Way WD3 . . . . .166 B5
Norwood Cl SG14 . . . . . .112 F7
Norwood Cl EN8 . . . . . . .148 E1
Norwood Rd WD3 . . . . . .164 C1
Nottingham Cl WD2 . . . .154 A6
Nottingham Rd WD3 . . . .164 C1
Novello Way WD6 . . . . . .170 D8
Nugent's Pk HA5 . . . . . . .175 F2
Nugents Ct HA5 . . . . .175 E2
Nun's Cl SG5 . . . . .34 E7
Nunfield WD4 . . . . .152 B8
Nunnery Cl AL1 . . . . .127 E1
Nunnery La LU3 . . . . .45 B5
Nunnery Stables AL1 . . . .127 D1
Nuns La AL1 . . . . .141 E8
Nunsbury Dr EN10 . . . . . .148 E6
Nunsbury Drive Cotts
  EN10 . . . . .148 E6
Nup End Cl HP22 . . . . . . .60 B3
Nup End La HP22 . . . . . . .60 B3
Nupton Dr EN5 . . . . .171 C3
Nurseries Rd AL4 . . . . . . .108 E7
Nursery Cl
  Bishop's Stortford CM23 . .76 F6
  Stevenage SG2 . . . . .69 A8
Nursery Cotts SG1 . . . . . .50 A6
Nursery Fields CM21 . . . .97 D2
Nursery Gdns
  Goff's Oak EN7 . . . . .147 D3
  Tring HP23 . . . . .100 B4
  Ware SG12 . . . . .93 E1
  Welwyn Garden City AL7 . .89 E1
Nursery Hill AL7 . . . . .89 E1
Nursery Par LU3 . . . . .44 E5
Nursery Rd
  Bishop's Stortford CM23 . .76 F6
  Cheshunt EN10 . . . . . . .148 F6
  Hoddesdon EN11 . . . . . .115 B1
  Lower Nazeing EN9 . . . . .135 D2
  Luton LU3 . . . . .44 F5
Nut Gr AL8 . . . . .89 D1
Nut Slip SG9 . . . . .40 E6
Nutcroft SG3 . . . . .69 D2
Nutfield AL7 . . . . .90 A1
Nuthampstead Rd SG8 . . .17 E2
Nutleigh Gr SG5 . . . . .21 D1
Nuttfield Cl WD3 . . . . . . .166 B3
Nye Way HP3 . . . . .137 A3
Nymans Cl LU2 . . . . .46 D3

O

Oak Ave Bricket Wood AL2 .141 A1
  Enfield EN2 . . . . .160 F1
Oak Cl
  Hemel Hempstead HP3 . . .138 F7
  Waltham Abbey EN9 . . . .163 D5
Oak Ct HA6 . . . . .174 D4
Oak Dr Berkhamsted HP4 .122 D3
  Sawbridgeworth CM21 . . .118 C8
Oak End SG9 . . . . .40 D7
Oak Farm WD6 . . . . .170 C4
Oak Glade HA6 . . . . .174 B2
Oak Gn WD5 . . . . .153 E7
Oak Gr Hatfield AL10 . . . .129 F5
  Hertford SG13 . . . . .113 E4
Oak Green Way WD5 . . .153 E7
Oak Hall CM23 . . . . .76 E8
Oak La Cholesbury HP23 . .120 B2
  Cuffley EN6 . . . . .146 F3
  Graveley SG4 . . . . .36 C4
Oak Piece AL6 . . . . .89 E7
Oak Piece Ct AL6 . . . . . . .89 E7
Oak Rd Luton LU4 . . . . . . .63 C8
  Woolmer Green SG3 . . . . .69 C8
Oak St
  Bishop's Stortford CM23 . .76 F6
  Hemel Hempstead HP3 . . .138 F7
Oak Tree Cl
  Abbots Langley WD5 . . . .153 D7
  Benington SG2 . . . . .52 F4
  Hatfield AL10 . . . . .130 A6
  Hertford Heath SG13 . . . .114 C3
Oak Tree Ct Elstree WD6 .169 D3
  Oaklands AL6 . . . . .89 E8
Oak Way AL5 . . . . .107 A5
Oak Wood HP4 . . . . .121 F3
Oakbank WD7 . . . . .156 B3
Oakcroft Cl HA5 . . . . .175 B1
Oakdale AL8 . . . . .89 D1
Oakdale Ave HA6 . . . . . . .175 A1
Oakdale Cl WD1 . . . . .175 C6
Oakdale Rd WD1 . . . . . . .175 C6
Oakdene EN8 . . . . .148 E1
Oakdene Cl HA5 . . . . .175 E1
Oakdene Rd
  Hemel Hempstead HP3 . . .138 F7
  Watford WD2 . . . . .154 B3
Oakdene Way AL1 . . . . . .128 C3
Oaken Gr AL7 . . . . .110 E3
Oakfield WD3 . . . . .165 A2
Oakfield Ave SG4 . . . . . . .35 B5
Oakfield Cl EN6 . . . . .158 F8
Oakfield Rd AL5 . . . . .107 A5
Oakfields SG2 . . . . .51 C1
Oakfields Ave SG3 . . . . . .69 A6
Oakfields Cl SG2 . . . . .51 C1
Oakfields Rd SG3 . . . . . . .69 A6
Oakhill SG6 . . . . .23 D4
Oakhill Ave HA5 . . . . .175 E1

Oakhill Cl WD3 . . . .**172** E6
Oakhill Dr AL6 . . . .**89** A6
Oakhill Rd WD3 . . . .**172** D6
Oakhurst Ave AL5 . . . .**107** A5
Oakhurst Pl WD1 . . . .**166** F5
Oakhurst Rd EN3 . . . .**162** D3
Oakington AL7 . . . .**111** D6
Oakland's Coll AL4 . . . . . .**128** C1
Oaklands HP4 . . . .**122** A4
Oaklands Ave
  Brookmans Park AL9 . . . . .**144** E4
  Watford WD1 . . . .**167** B1
Oaklands Cl CM23 . . . .**59** B2
Oaklands Coll AL1 . . . .**127** E3
**Oaklands Coll (Boreham
  Wood Campus)** WD6 . . . .**170** C7
**Oaklands Coll (Lemsford
  Lane Campus)** AL8 . . . . .**110** B4
**Oaklands Coll (Welwyn
  Garden City Campus)**
  AL8 . . . .**110** D7
Oaklands Ct WD1 . . . .**167** A8
Oaklands Dr CM23 . . . .**59** B2
Oaklands Gate HA6 . . . . . .**174** E4
Oaklands Gr EN10 . . . .**148** E7
**Oaklands (Herts Coll of
  Agriculture &
  Horticulture)** AL4 . . . . . .**128** E4
Oaklands La Barnet EN5 . .**171** B5
  St Albans AL4 . . . .**128** F5
Oaklands Pk SG2 . . . .**59** B2
Oaklands Rd Barnet EN7 . .**171** F2
  Hammond Street EN7 . . . .**147** E5
Oaklands Rise AL6 . . . .**89** F7
Oaklands Sch AL6 . . . .**89** E7
Oaklawn HP23 . . . .**100** A3
Oaklea AL6 . . . .**89** E7
Oaklea Cl AL6 . . . .**89** E8
Oaklea Wood AL6 . . . .**89** E7
Oakleigh Dr WD3 . . . .**166** C3
Oakleigh Rd HA5 . . . .**175** F4
Oakley Cl LU4 . . . .**44** D4
Oakley Ct SG8 . . . .**7** D7
Oakley Rd Harpenden AL5 . .**107** D7
  Luton LU4 . . . .**44** E3
Oakmeade Barnet EN5 . . . .**171** D5
  Pinner HA5 . . . .**176** A4
Oakmere Ave EN6 . . . .**159** C6
Oakmere Cl EN6 . . . .**159** D8
Oakmere La EN6 . . . .**159** C7
Oakmere Prim Sch EN6 . . .**159** D7
Oakridge AL2 . . . .**140** F2
Oakridge Ave WD7 . . . .**155** F6
Oakridge La WD2 . . . .**155** E5
Oakroyd Ave EN6 . . . .**158** F6
Oakroyd Cl EN6 . . . .**158** F6
Oaks Cl Hitchin SG4 . . . . . .**34** F5
  Radlett WD7 . . . .**155** F4
Oaks Cross SG2 . . . .**51** B1
Oaks Ret Pk CM20 . . . .**117** F3
Oaks The
  Berkhamsted HP4 . . . .**122** A4
  Slip End LU1 . . . .**63** C1
  Watford WD1 . . . .**167** C1
Oaktree Cl CM23 . . . .**76** F7
Oaktree Garth AL7 . . . .**110** E5
Oakview Cl
  Cheshunt EN7 . . . .**148** B3
  Harpenden AL5 . . . .**106** F5
Oakway LU6 . . . .**82** B7
Oakwell Cl SG2 . . . .**69** D7
Oakwell Dr EN6 . . . .**160** B7
Oakwood EN9 . . . .**163** E5
Oakwood Ave WD6 . . . .**170** B5
Oakwood Cl SG2 . . . .**51** C2
Oakwood Dr Luton LU3 . . . . .**44** C8
  St Albans AL4 . . . .**128** C4
Oakwood Est CM20 . . . .**118** B4
Oakwood Prim Sch AL4 . .**128** C4
Oakwood Rd
  Bricket Wood AL2 . . . .**140** F2
  Pinner HA5 . . . .**175** B1
Oban Terr LU1 . . . .**63** B8
Oberon Cl WD6 . . . .**170** C8
Obrey Way CM23 . . . .**76** C3
Occupation Rd WD1 . . . . . .**167** B4
Octagan The SG12 . . . .**93** D2
Octavia Ct WD2 . . . .**167** C7
Oddy Hill Tring HP23 . . . . . .**100** C3
  Wigginton HP23 . . . .**100** C2
Odessey Rd WD6 . . . .**170** B8
Offa Rd AL3 . . . .**127** C3
Offas Way AL4 . . . .**108** D8
Offerton Ho WD1 . . . .**175** C7
Offley Cross SG5 . . . .**34** B5
Offley Endowed Prim Sch
  SG5 . . . .**33** C3
Offley Hill SG5 . . . .**33** C3
Offley Rd SG5 . . . .**34** D6
Ogard Rd EN11 . . . .**135** C8
Okeford Cl HP23 . . . .**99** F4
Okeford Dr HP23 . . . .**99** F4
Okeley La HP23 . . . .**99** E3
Old Bakery SG5 . . . .**34** E7
Old Barn La WD3 . . . .**165** E4
Old Bedford Rd Luton LU2 . .**45** E4
  Luton, Warden Hill LU2 . . .**45** D6
Old Bell Cl CM24 . . . .**59** D6
Old Bourne Way SG1 . . . . . .**37** A3
Old Brewery Cl SG5 . . . .**11** F7
Old Brewery Pl SG4 . . . .**66** D1
Old Chantry La SG4 . . . .**35** F2
Old Charlton Rd SG5 . . . . . .**34** E6
Old Church La SG12 . . . .**93** E7
Old Coach Rd The SG14 . .**112** C4

Old Common The SG9 . . . . .**43** B4
Old Crabtree La HP2 . . . . .**124** E2
Old Cross SG14 . . . .**113** C6
Old Dean HP3 . . . .**137** A4
Old Dr The AL8 . . . .**110** B5
Old Farm LU7 . . . .**80** D4
Old Fishery La
  Hemel Hempstead HP1 . . .**123** F1
  Hemel Hempstead HP1 . . .**137** F8
Old Fold Cl EN5 . . . .**171** F8
Old Fold La EN5 . . . .**171** F8
Old Fold View EN5 . . . .**171** C6
Old Forge Cl
  Abbots Langley WD5 . . . . .**154** A6
  Welwyn Garden City AL7 . . .**89** F2
Old Forge Rd EN1 . . . .**161** F1
Old French Horn La AL10 **130** B6
Old Gannon Cl HA6 . . . . . .**174** C5
Old Garden Ct AL3 . . . .**127** C3
Old Hale Way SG5 . . . .**21** E2
Old Hall Cl HA5 . . . .**175** E2
Old Hall Dr HA5 . . . .**175** E2
Old Harpenden Rd AL3 . . .**127** E6
Old Hat Factory The ❶
  LU2 . . . .**45** D1
Old Herns La AL7 . . . .**111** C8
Old Hertford Rd AL9 . . . . .**130** C7
Old Highway EN11 . . . .**135** C8
Old House Ct HP2 . . . .**124** F3
Old House La
  Lower Nazeing EN9 . . . . . .**149** F8
  Sarratt WD4 . . . .**152** F4
Old House Rd HP2 . . . .**124** F3
Old Knebworth La
  SG3,SG2 . . . .**68** D8
Old La SG3 . . . .**69** B5
Old Leys AL10 . . . .**130** A2
Old London Rd
  Hertford SG13 . . . .**113** E6
  St Albans AL1 . . . .**127** E2
Old Maltings The ❷ CM23 . .**77** A7
Old Maple HP2 . . . .**104** F1
Old Meadow Cl HP4 . . . . . .**122** A2
Old Mill Gdns HP4 . . . .**122** B4
Old Mill La CM22 . . . .**98** B6
Old Mill Rd WD4 . . . .**153** C5
Old Nazeing Rd EN10 . . . .**135** C1
Old North Rd
  Kneesworth SG8 . . . .**2** A5
  Royston SG8 . . . .**7** C8
Old Oak AL1 . . . .**141** E8
Old Oak Cl SG15 . . . .**11** A8
Old Oak Gdns HP4 . . . .**121** E2
Old Oaks EN9 . . . .**163** E7
Old Orch Luton LU1 . . . .**63** D5
  Park Street AL2 . . . .**141** D5
Old Orchard Cl EN4 . . . . . .**159** D1
Old Orchard Mews HP4 . .**122** C3
Old Park Rd SG5 . . . .**34** E7
Old Parkbury La AL2 . . . . .**141** F1
Old Parkway Sch AL8 . . . .**110** C5
Old Priory Pk AL1 . . . .**127** E2
Old Rd CM17 . . . .**118** D5
Old Rectory Cl AL5 . . . .**86** A2
Old Rectory Dr AL10 . . . . .**130** B5
Old Rectory Gdns AL4 . . . .**108** D8
Old Redding HA3 . . . .**176** C6
Old River La CM23 . . . .**76** F7
Old School Cl SG4 . . . .**67** F1
Old School Gn SG2 . . . .**52** E5
Old School Orch SG14 . . . . .**70** E3
Old School Wlk
  Arlesey SG15 . . . .**11** A4
  Slip End LU1 . . . .**63** C1
Old Shire La
  Chalfont St Peter WD3 . . .**172** B6
  Chorleywood WD3 . . . . . .**164** A2
Old Sopwell Gdns AL1 . . .**127** E1
Old Uxbridge Rd WD3 . . . .**172** E3
Old Vicarage Gdns AL3 . . . .**83** D6
Old Walled Garden The
  SG1 . . . .**36** C1
Old Watford Rd AL2 . . . . . .**140** E2
Old Watling St AL3 . . . .**84** B3
Old's App WD1 . . . .**166** C1
Old's Cl WD1 . . . .**166** B1
Olden Mead SG6 . . . .**23** B3
Oldfield Cl EN8 . . . .**148** E3
Oldfield Ct AL1 . . . .**127** E3
Oldfield Dr EN8 . . . .**148** E3
Oldfield Farm Rd
  Henlow SG16 . . . .**10** B4
  Henlow SG16 . . . .**10** C4
Oldfield Rd
  Hemel Hempstead HP1 . . .**123** E2
  London Colney AL2 . . . . . .**142** D6
Oldfield Rise SG4 . . . .**66** E7
Oldhall Ct SG4 . . . .**66** E7
Oldhall St SG14 . . . .**113** D6
Oldhouse Croft CM20 . . . .**117** E2
Oldings Cnr AL2 . . . .**110** B1
Oldpark Ride EN7 . . . .**161** D2
Oldwood AL6 . . . .**89** D7
Olive Taylor Ct HP2 . . . . . .**124** F7
Oliver Cl
  Hemel Hempstead HP3 . . .**138** E7
  Park Street AL2 . . . .**141** D4
Oliver Ct SG12 . . . .**92** E4
Oliver Rd HP3 . . . .**138** E7
Oliver Rise HP3 . . . .**138** E7
Oliver's La SG5 . . . .**11** F7
Olivers Cl HP4 . . . .**123** C7
Olivia Gdns UB9 . . . .**173** C1
Olleberrie La WD3 . . . .**151** D7
Olwen Mews HA5 . . . .**175** D1
Olyard Ct LU1 . . . .**63** B6
Olympus Rd SG16 . . . .**10** B4
Omega Ct ❹ SG12 . . . .**93** D1

Omega Maltings ❷ SG12 . .**93** E1
On-The-Hill WD1 . . . .**175** E8
Onslow Cl AL10 . . . .**130** B5
Onslow Rd LU4 . . . .**44** D5
Onslow St Audrey's Sch
  AL10 . . . .**130** B5
Opening The SG4 . . . .**88** F8
Openshaw Way SG6 . . . . . .**23** A6
Oram Pl HP3 . . . .**138** D8
Orbital Cres WD2 . . . .**153** F4
Orchard Ave
  Berkhamsted HP4 . . . .**122** A4
  Harpenden AL5 . . . .**85** F1
  Watford WD2 . . . .**154** B8
Orchard Cl
  Borehamwood WD6 . . . . .**169** F6
  Bushey WD2 . . . .**168** D1
  Chorleywood WD3 . . . . . .**164** D5
  Cuffley EN6 . . . .**146** E3
  Hemel Hempstead HP2 . . .**124** F5
  Kneesworth SG8 . . . .**2** A5
  Letchworth SG6 . . . .**22** F8
  Little Berkhamsted SG13 . .**132** C4
  Radlett WD7 . . . .**155** E3
  St Albans AL1 . . . .**127** F2
  St Ippolyts SG4 . . . .**34** F3
  Stanstead Abbotts SG12 . .**115** C4
  Ware SG12 . . . .**93** D2
  Watford WD1 . . . .**166** F7
  Wingrave HP22 . . . .**60** B3
Orchard Cres SG1 . . . .**50** C7
Orchard Croft CM20 . . . . .**118** A2
Orchard Ct HP9 . . . .**137** A4
Orchard Dr
  Chiswellgreen AL2 . . . . . .**141** B5
  Chorleywood WD3 . . . . . .**164** D5
  Watford WD1 . . . .**166** F8
Orchard Gdns EN9 . . . .**163** C5
Orchard House La AL1 . . . .**127** D2
Orchard Lea CM21 . . . .**97** C1
Orchard Mead AL10 . . . . . .**129** F5
**Orchard On The Green
  The** WD3 . . . .**166** F8
Orchard Prim Sch WD2 . .**153** F3
Orchard Rd Baldock SG7 . . .**12** E1
  Barnet EN5 . . . .**171** F5
  Bishop's Stortford CM23 . . .**59** B1
  Hitchin SG4 . . . .**22** B1
  Royston SG8 . . . .**7** B7
  Stevenage SG1 . . . .**50** C7
  Tewin AL6 . . . .**90** C5
  Welwyn AL6 . . . .**89** C5
Orchard Sq SG10 . . . .**148** F7
Orchard St
  Hemel Hempstead HP3 . . .**138** D8
  St Albans AL3 . . . .**127** C2
Orchard The Baldock SG7 . .**23** F8
  Codicote SG4 . . . .**67** F1
  Hertford SG14 . . . .**92** C1
  Kings Langley WD4 . . . . . .**139** A2
  Tonwell SG12 . . . .**92** E7
  Welwyn Garden City AL8 . .**110** D8
Orchard Way
  Bovingdon HP3 . . . .**137** A3
  Breachwood Green SG4 . . .**47** E1
  Brookmans Park EN6 . . . . .**145** B2
  Goff's Oak EN7 . . . .**147** B3
  Knebworth SG3 . . . .**68** E5
  Letchworth SG6 . . . .**22** F8
  Lower Stondon SG16 . . . . .**10** B3
  Luton LU4 . . . .**44** C4
  Pitstone LU7 . . . .**80** E5
  Rickmansworth WD3 . . . .**165** A2
  Royston SG8 . . . .**7** C8
Orchards The
  Sawbridgeworth CM21 . . . .**97** E3
  Slip End LU1 . . . .**63** C2
  Tring HP23 . . . .**99** F3
Orchid Ho AL1 . . . .**127** F3
Ordelmere SG6 . . . .**11** F1
Ordnance Rd EN3 . . . .**162** E2
Oregon Way LU3 . . . .**45** A8
Organ Hall Rd WD6 . . . . . .**169** E8
Orient Cl AL1 . . . .**127** E1
Orient Ctr The WD2 . . . . .**154** D2
Oriole Cl WD5 . . . .**154** A8
Oriole Way CM23 . . . .**76** C6
Orion Way HA6 . . . .**175** A6
Orkney Ho WD1 . . . .**166** F1
Orlando Cl SG4 . . . .**35** A6
Ormesby Dr EN6 . . . .**158** D7
Ormonde Rd HA6 . . . .**174** D6
Ormsby Cl LU1 . . . .**63** E5
Ormskirk Rd WD1 . . . .**175** D5
Oronsay HP3 . . . .**125** B1
Orphanage Rd WD1 . . . . . .**167** C7
Orpington Cl LU4 . . . .**44** A3
Orton Cl AL4 . . . .**128** A7
Orwell Ct ❺ WD2 . . . .**167** D7
Orwell View SG7 . . . .**13** B1
Osborn Way AL8 . . . .**110** D6
Osborne Cl EN8 . . . .**63** F6
Osborne Gdns EN6 . . . .**145** B1
Osborne Rd Cheshunt EN8 .**148** A4
  Hoddesdon EN10 . . . .**135** A4
  Luton LU1 . . . .**63** F6
  Potters Bar EN6 . . . .**145** B1
  Watford WD2 . . . .**154** C1
Osborne Way HP23 . . . . . .**100** D1
Osbourne Ave WD4 . . . . . .**138** F3
Osbourne Gdns ❺ CM23 . . .**76** E5
Osmington Pl HP23 . . . .**99** F4
Osprey Cl WD2 . . . .**154** E5
Osprey Gdns SG2 . . . .**51** D6
Osprey Ho ❸ SG12 . . . .**93** C3
Osprey Wlk LU4 . . . .**44** A5
Oster St AL3 . . . .**127** C4
Osterley Cl SG2 . . . .**69** C7

Ostler Cl CM23 . . . .**76** C4
Oswald Rd AL1 . . . .**127** E2
Otley Way WD1 . . . .**175** C7
Otter Cl AL10 . . . .**130** B4
Otter Gdns AL10 . . . .**130** B4
Otterspool La WD2 . . . . . .**154** E1
Otterspool Way WD2 . . . .**154** F1
Otterton Cl AL5 . . . .**85** F3
Ottoman Terr WD1 . . . . . .**167** C6
Ottway Wlk AL6 . . . .**89** C4
Otway Gdns WD2 . . . .**168** C2
Otways Cl EN6 . . . .**159** B6
Oudle La SG10 . . . .**74** F2
Oughton Cl SG5 . . . .**34** C8
Oughton Head Way SG5 . . .**34** D8
**Oughtonhead Jun & Inf
  Schs** SG5 . . . .**21** C1
Oughtonhead Jun Sch
  SG5 . . . .**34** C8
Oughtonhead La SG5 . . . . .**34** C8
Oulton Cres EN6 . . . .**158** D7
Oulton Rise AL5 . . . .**86** C5
Oulton Way WD1 . . . .**175** F6
Oundle Ave WD2 . . . .**168** C3
Oundle Ct SG2 . . . .**69** C8
Oundle Path SG2 . . . .**69** C8
Oundle The SG2 . . . .**69** C8
**Our Lady's Jun Mix Inf
  Sch** AL7 . . . .**110** E4
**Our Lady's RC Jun Mix
  Inf Sch** SG5 . . . .**21** E2
Ousden Cl EN8 . . . .**148** E1
Ousden Dr EN8 . . . .**148** E1
Ouseley Cl LU4 . . . .**44** D3
Oval The Cheshunt EN10 . .**148** E7
  Henlow SG16 . . . .**10** C3
  Stevenage SG1 . . . .**37** A1
Overfield Rd LU2 . . . .**46** C1
Overlord Cl EN10 . . . .**134** E3
Overstone Rd
  Harpenden AL5 . . . .**86** C1
  Luton LU4 . . . .**44** D1
Overstream WD3 . . . .**165** B5
Overtrees AL5 . . . .**85** F3
Oving Cl LU2 . . . .**46** D2
Owen Dr SG8 . . . .**2** D1
Owen Jones Cl SG16 . . . . . .**10** C5
Owens Way WD3 . . . .**166** A5
Owles La SG9 . . . .**41** A6
Ox La AL5 . . . .**86** B3
Oxcroft CM23 . . . .**76** F3
Oxen Rd LU2 . . . .**45** F1
Oxendon Dr EN11 . . . .**135** A5
Oxfield Cl HP4 . . . .**122** A3
Oxford Ave AL1 . . . .**128** C2
Oxford Cl Cheshunt EN8 . .**148** D2
  Kneesworth SG8 . . . .**2** A7
  Moor Park HA6 . . . .**174** D6
Oxford Rd
  Breachwood Green SG4 . . .**47** E1
  ❷ Luton LU1 . . . .**63** E6
Oxford St WD1 . . . .**167** B4
Oxhey Ave WD1 . . . .**167** D2
Oxhey Dr WD1 . . . .**175** B7
Oxhey Inf Sch WD2 . . . . . .**167** E4
Oxhey La Pinner HA5 . . . . .**176** A5
  South Oxhey WD1 . . . .**175** F7
  Watford WD1 . . . .**167** D2
Oxhey Rd WD1 . . . .**167** D2
Oxhey Ridge Cl HA6 . . . . .**175** B5
Oxhey Wood Prim Sch
  WD1 . . . .**175** C7
Oxlease Dr AL10 . . . .**130** B4
Oxleys Rd SG2 . . . .**51** B3
Oxleys The CM17 . . . .**118** E4
Oysterfields AL3 . . . .**127** C4

P

Pacatian Way SG1 . . . .**51** C8
Packhorse Cl AL4 . . . .**128** C6
Packhorse La EN6 . . . .**157** D8
Paddick Cl EN11 . . . .**134** F7
Paddock Cl Hunsdon SG12 . .**95** D1
  Letchworth SG6 . . . .**23** A5
  Watford WD1 . . . .**167** E3
Paddock Ho AL7 . . . .**111** B6
Paddock Rd SG9 . . . .**40** E8
Paddock The
  Bishop's Stortford CM23 . . .**76** D3
  Hatfield AL10 . . . .**130** A6
  Hitchin SG4 . . . .**35** A5
  Hoddesdon EN10 . . . .**135** A3
Paddock Wood AL5 . . . . . .**107** E7
Paddocks Cl SG2 . . . .**51** B4
Paddocks The
  Chorleywood WD3 . . . . . .**164** F5
  Codicote SG4 . . . .**68** A1
  Hertford Heath SG13 . . . .**114** B3
  Kimpton AL4 . . . .**87** B6
  Stevenage SG2 . . . .**51** B3
  Welwyn Garden City AL7 . .**111** B7
Padgate Ho WD1 . . . .**175** C7
Page Cl SG7 . . . .**23** F6
Page Hill SG12 . . . .**93** C2
Page Rd SG13 . . . .**114** A6
Pageant Rd AL1 . . . .**127** D2
Pages Cl CM23 . . . .**76** D5
Pages Croft HP4 . . . .**122** A6
Paget Cotts SG12 . . . .**71** C7
Paignton Cl LU4 . . . .**44** D4
Paine's La HA5 . . . .**175** E1
Paines Orch LU7 . . . .**80** A8
Painters La EN3 . . . .**162** E4
Palace Cl WD4 . . . .**139** A1
Palace Gdns
  Bishop's Stortford CM23 . . .**76** E5
  Royston SG8 . . . .**7** C4

Palfrey Cl AL3 . . . .**127** D5
Pallas Rd HP2 . . . .**124** F5
Palmer Ave WD2 . . . .**168** B4
Palmer Cl AL4 . . . .**113** C8
Palmer Ct SG12 . . . .**92** E4
Palmer Gdns EN5 . . . .**171** D4
Palmer Rd SG14 . . . .**113** C6
Palmers Gr EN9 . . . .**135** F1
Palmers La ❽ CM23 . . . .**76** F7
Palmers Rd WD6 . . . .**170** B8
Palmers Way EN8 . . . .**148** E2
Palmerston Cl AL8 . . . .**110** C6
Palmerston Ct SG2 . . . .**51** B7
Pamela Ave HP3 . . . .**138** C3
Pams La SG4 . . . .**66** D1
Pancake La HP2 . . . .**125** D2
Pankhurst Cres SG2 . . . . . .**51** C5
Pankhurst Pl WD1 . . . .**167** C6
Panshanger Dr AL7 . . . . . .**111** C6
Panshanger Prim Sch
  AL7 . . . .**111** A7
Pantiles The WD2 . . . .**168** D1
Panxworth Rd ❶ HP3 . . . .**124** D1
Paper Mill La SG11 . . . .**55** E1
Parade The Hatfield AL10 .**130** C7
  Letchworth SG6 . . . .**11** F1
  Luton LU3 . . . .**44** C7
  South Oxhey WD1 . . . .**175** D7
  South Oxhey,
  Carpenders Park WD1 . . .**175** E7
  Watford WD1 . . . .**167** B6
Paradise HP2 . . . .**124** D2
Paradise Cl EN7 . . . .**148** B3
Paradise Rd EN9 . . . .**163** C5
Paradise Wildlife Park
  EN10 . . . .**133** F2
Paramount Ind Est WD2 .**154** C1
Parish Cl WD2 . . . .**154** C1
Parishes Mead SG2 . . . .**51** D4
Park Ave
  Bishop's Stortford CM23 . . .**76** F3
  Bushey WD2 . . . .**167** E2
  Luton LU3 . . . .**44** C7
  Potters Bar EN6 . . . .**159** D6
  Radlett WD7 . . . .**156** B6
  Rickmansworth WD3 . . . .**165** A5
  St Albans AL1 . . . .**128** A3
  Watford WD1 . . . .**167** A5
Park Ave N AL5 . . . .**85** F1
Park Ave S AL5 . . . .**85** F1
Park Avenue Trad Est
  LU3 . . . .**44** C7
Park Cl Baldock SG7 . . . . . .**23** F7
  Brookmans Park AL9 . . . . .**145** A5
  Bushey WD2 . . . .**167** D6
  Harrow HA3 . . . .**176** E2
  Hatfield AL9 . . . .**130** C6
  Markyate AL3 . . . .**83** D5
  Rickmansworth WD3 . . . .**174** B6
  Stevenage SG2 . . . .**51** B1
Park Cres Baldock SG7 . . . .**23** F7
  Borehamwood WD6 . . . . .**169** F6
  Harrow HA3 . . . .**176** E2
Park Ct Harlow CM20 . . . . .**117** D2
  Letchworth SG6 . . . .**23** A6
  Luton LU2 . . . .**45** D1
Park Dr Baldock SG7 . . . . . .**23** E7
  Letchworth SG6 . . . .**23** A6
  Potters Bar EN6 . . . .**159** D8
  Standon SG11 . . . .**55** D3
  Stanmore HA3 . . . .**176** E4
Park Farm Cl SG16 . . . .**10** D8
Park Farm Ind Est
  Buntingford SG9 . . . .**40** D8
  Nuthampstead SG8 . . . . . .**18** C2
Park Farm Ind Pk SG8 . . . .**18** F2
Park Farm La SG8 . . . .**18** C2
Park Gate SG4 . . . .**34** F6
Park Gdns SG7 . . . .**23** E7
Park Hill Harlow CM17 . . . .**118** B4
  Harpenden AL5 . . . .**85** F2
Park Hill Rd HP1 . . . .**124** B3
Park Ho Berkhamsted HP4 .**122** B5
  Welwyn Garden City AL8 . .**110** D7
Park Ind Est AL2 . . . .**141** E4
Park La
  Bishop's Stortford CM23 . . .**76** F4
  Cheshunt EN7 . . . .**162** D6
  Colney Heath AL4 . . . .**129** C1
  Hammond Street EN7 . . . .**148** A4
  Harefield UB9 . . . .**173** B2
  Harlow CM20 . . . .**117** D2
  Hemel Hempstead HP2 . . .**124** D2
  Hoddesdon EN10 . . . .**134** F3
  Kimpton SG4 . . . .**66** C1
  Knebworth SG3 . . . .**68** D5
  Standon SG11 . . . .**55** D3
Park Lane Paradise EN7 . .**148** A6
Park Lodge WD2 . . . .**154** D5
Park Mansions HA6 . . . . . .**174** C7
Park Mdw AL9 . . . .**130** C6
Park Mead CM20 . . . .**117** B1
Park Mews AL9 . . . .**130** C6
Park Mount AL5 . . . .**85** F2
Park Nook Gdns EN2 . . . .**161** D2
Park Pl Harefield UB9 . . . . .**173** C2
  Park Street AL2 . . . .**141** D4
  Stevenage SG1 . . . .**50** D5
**Park Place
  Chambers** SG1 . . . .**50** D5
Park Rd Barnet EN5 . . . . . .**171** F5
  Bushey WD2 . . . .**168** A3
  Cheshunt EN8 . . . .**162** D6
  Enfield EN3 . . . .**162** D1
  Hemel Hempstead HP1 . . .**124** C1
  Hertford SG13 . . . .**113** E6
  Hoddesdon EN11 . . . .**135** A6
  Northaw EN6 . . . .**146** A1
  Radlett WD7 . . . .**156** A4

Park Rd continued
Rickmansworth WD3 . . . . . .**165** E2
Stansted Mountfitchet CM24 .**59** E6
Tring HP23 . . . .**100** A3
Ware SG12 . . . .**93** B2
Watford WD1 . . . .**167** B8
Park Rise
Berkhamsted HP4 . . . .**121** E6
Harpenden AL5 . . . .**85** E3
Harrow HA3 . . . .**176** E2
Park Rise Cl AL5 . . . .**85** E3
Park Sq LU1 . . . .**63** E7
Park St Baldock SG7 . . . .**23** E8
Berkhamsted HP4 . . . .**122** B5
Hatfield AL9 . . . .**130** C6
Hitchin SG4 . . . .**34** E6
Luton LU1 . . . .**63** F6
Park Street AL2 . . . .**141** D5
Tring HP23 . . . .**100** A3
Park St W LU1 . . . .**63** E7
Park Street La AL2 . . . .**141** D5
Park Street Sch AL2 . . . .**141** D4
Park Terr Enfield EN3 . . . . .**162** E1
2 Luton LU1 . . . .**63** F6
Much Hadham SG10 . . . .**74** F3
Park The Redbourn AL3 . . .**106** B5
St Albans AL1 . . . .**128** A5
Park Viaduct LU1 . . . .**63** E6
Park View
Great Hormead SG9 . . . .**42** A7
Hatfield AL9 . . . .**130** C7
Hoddesdon EN11 . . . .**135** A5
Pinner HA5 . . . .**175** F2
Potters Bar EN6 . . . .**159** C6
Stevenage SG2 . . . .**51** B1
Park View Cl Luton LU3 . . . .**44** D6
St Albans AL1 . . . .**128** A2
Park View Ct HP4 . . . .**122** B4
Park View Dr AL3 . . . .**83** D6
Park View Rd
Berkhamsted HP4 . . . .**122** B4
Pinner HA5 . . . .**175** B3
Park Way Hitchin SG5 . . . . . .**34** E6
Rickmansworth WD3 . . . . . .**165** C1
Parker Ave SG14 . . . .**113** D8
Parker Cl SG6 . . . .**22** E4
Parker St WD2 . . . .**167** B8
Parker's Field SG2 . . . .**51** C4
Parkfield
Chorleywood WD3 . . . .**164** F5
Letchworth SG6 . . . .**23** D4
Parkfield Ave HA2 . . . .**176** C1
Parkfield Cres
Harrow HA2 . . . .**176** C1
Kimpton SG4 . . . .**66** D1
Parkfield Ho HA2 . . . .**176** C1
Parkfield Rd AL3 . . . .**83** D5
Parkfields AL8 . . . .**110** D6
Parkgate Inf Sch WD2 . . . . .**154** C2
Parkgate Jun Sch WD2 . . . . .**154** C2
Parkgate Rd WD2 . . . .**154** C2
Parkhurst Rd SG14 . . . .**113** C2
Parkinson Cl AL4 . . . .**108** D8
Parkland Cl EN11 . . . .**115** B1
Parkland Dr LU1 . . . .**63** D5
Parklands Bushey WD2 . . . .**168** C3
Hemel Hempstead HP1 . . . .**123** F5
Royston SG8 . . . .**7** E6
Waltham Abbey EN9 . . . . . .**163** D7
Parklands Cl EN4 . . . .**159** D1
Parklands Dr AL3 . . . .**127** A2
Parkmead 6 LU1 . . . .**63** F6
Parkside
Potters Bar EN6 . . . .**159** C7
Watford WD1 . . . .**167** C3
Welwyn AL6 . . . .**89** C5
Wyddial SG9 . . . .**27** D2
Parkside Comm Sch
WD6 . . . .**156** F1
Parkside Ct EN7 . . . .**148** B3
Parkside Dr WD1 . . . .**166** F7
Parkside Rd HA6 . . . .**174** F5
Parkview Ho WD1 . . . .**167** D3
Parkway
Sawbridgeworth CM21 . . . . .**97** F1
Stevenage SG2 . . . .**51** A1
Welwyn Garden City AL8 . . .**110** C6
Parkway Cl AL8 . . . .**110** C6
Parkway Ct AL1 . . . .**142** B8
Parkway Gdns AL8 . . . . . .**110** D5
Parkwood Cl EN10 . . . .**134** F4
Parkwood Dr HP1 . . . .**123** F3
Parliament Sq SG14 . . . . . .**113** C6
Parmiter's Sch WD2 . . . . . .**154** C8
Parndon Mill La CM20 . . . .**117** B3
Parnel Rd SG12 . . . .**93** F2
Parnell Cl HA8 . . . .**139** F1
Parr Cres HP2 . . . .**125** B8
Parrott's HP23 . . . .**120** A4
Parrotts Cl WD3 . . . .**166** A4
Parrotts Field EN11 . . . . . .**135** B7
Parson's Cl AL3 . . . .**84** B1
Parsonage Cl
Abbots Langley WD5 . . . . . .**139** E1
Tring HP23 . . . .**100** A4
Parsonage Farm
Rickmansworth WD3 . . . . . .**165** C2
Wingrave HP22 . . . .**60** B3
Parsonage Farm Trad Est
CM24 . . . .**59** F3
Parsonage La Albury SG11 .**57** A4
Bishop's Stortford CM23 . . . .**77** C8
Spellbrook CM21 . . . .**97** C6
Stansted Mountfitchet CM24 .**59** F4
Welham Green AL9 . . . .**144** B8
Parsonage Pl HP23 . . . .**100** A3
Parsonage Rd
Rickmansworth WD3 . . . . . .**165** D2

Parsonage Rd continued
Welham Green AL9 . . . .**144** B8
Parsons Green Est SG1 . . . . .**37** C2
Parthia SG8 . . . .**7** E6
Partridge Cl Barnet EN5 . . .**171** C3
Bushey WD2 . . . .**168** C1
Luton LU4 . . . .**44** A5
Partridge Hill SG7 . . . .**4** C3
Partridge Rd AL3 . . . .**127** D7
Parva Cl AL5 . . . .**107** D6
Parvills EN9 . . . .**163** D7
Pascal Way SG6 . . . .**23** B8
Pasfield EN9 . . . .**163** D6
Passfield Cotts SG11 . . . .**72** F1
Passingham Ave SG4 . . . . . .**35** A6
Paston Rd HP2 . . . .**124** E5
Pasture Cl WD2 . . . .**168** C2
Pasture La SG4 . . . .**65** E8
Pasture Rd SG6 . . . .**22** E3
Pastures Ct LU4 . . . .**44** A3
Pastures The Barnet N20 . . .**171** F1
Chiswellgreen AL2 . . . .**141** A7
Hatfield AL10 . . . .**130** B4
Hemel Hempstead HP1 . . . .**123** E4
Stevenage SG2 . . . .**51** D8
Ware SG12 . . . .**93** C3
Watford WD1 . . . .**167** C2
Welwyn Garden City AL7 . . .**111** B4
Pastures Way LU4 . . . .**44** A4
Pat Larner Ho AL1 . . . .**127** D2
Paternoster Cl EN9 . . . . . .**163** F6
Paternoster Hill EN9 . . . . .**163** F7
Pathway The Radlett WD7 .**155** F3
Watford WD1 . . . .**167** D1
Patmore Cl CM23 . . . .**76** C8
Patmore Heath (Nature
Reserve) SG11 . . . .**57** D8
Patmore Link Rd SG12 . . . .**125** C2
Patmore Rd EN9 . . . .**163** E5
Patricia Gdns CM23 . . . .**76** E5
Patrick Gr EN9 . . . .**163** B6
Paul's Gn EN8 . . . .**162** E6
Pauls La EN11 . . . .**135** A6
Paxton Rd
Berkhamsted HP4 . . . .**122** D4
St Albans AL1 . . . .**127** C2
Payne End SG9 . . . .**15** B1
Payne's Pk SG5 . . . .**34** E7
Paynes Cl SG6 . . . .**12** A1
Paynes La EN9 . . . .**149** C7
Paynesfield Rd WD2 . . . . . .**168** F2
Pea La HP4 . . . .**121** D7
Peabody Ct EN3 . . . .**163** A2
Peace Cl EN7 . . . .**148** B2
Peace Dr WD1 . . . .**167** A6
Peace Gr AL6 . . . .**90** A7
Peace Prospect WD1 . . . . .**167** A6
Peach Cl LU1 . . . .**63** F6
Peacock Wlk WD5 . . . .**154** A8
Peacocks Cl HP4 . . . .**121** F6
Peakes La EN7 . . . .**147** F4
Peakes Pl AL1 . . . .**127** F3
Peakes Way EN7 . . . .**147** F4
Pear Tree Cl SG16 . . . .**10** B3
Pear Tree Dell SG6 . . . .**23** B3
Pear Tree Wlk EN7 . . . .**147** E5
Pearl Ct EN11 . . . .**135** A6
Pearman Dr SG12 . . . .**71** E7
Pearsall SG6 . . . .**23** B5
Pearson Ave SG13 . . . .**113** C4
Pearson Cl SG13 . . . .**113** C4
Peartree Cl
Hemel Hempstead HP1 . . . .**124** A4
Welwyn Garden City AL7 . . .**110** E6
Peartree Ct Watford WD2 . .**154** D3
Welwyn Garden City AL7 . . .**110** E5
Peartree Farm AL7 . . . .**110** E6
Peartree La AL7 . . . .**110** E6
Peartree Prim Sch AL7 . . . .**110** E5
Peartree Rd
Hemel Hempstead HP1 . . . .**124** A4
Luton LU2 . . . .**46** C4
Peartree Spring Inf Sch
SG2 . . . .**51** B3
Peartree Spring Jun Sch
SG2 . . . .**51** B3
Peartree Way SG2 . . . .**51** A3
Peascroft Rd HP3 . . . .**125** B1
Peasecroft SG9 . . . .**39** C7
Peasmead SG9 . . . .**40** E6
Pebbles The SG7 . . . .**12** C4
Peck's Hill EN9 . . . .**135** E2
Peckworth Ind Est SG16 . . .**10** A4
Pedlars La SG16 . . . .**15** E7
Pedley Hill HP4,LU6 . . . .**82** C1
Peel Cres SG14 . . . .**113** C8
Peel Pl 7 LU1 . . . .**63** D7
Peel St 6 LU1 . . . .**63** D7
Peerglow Ctr SG12 . . . .**114** E8
Peerglow Ind Est WD1 . . . .**166** B1
Peg's La SG13 . . . .**113** D5
Pegmire La WD2 . . . .**168** C8
Pegs La SG12 . . . .**95** D5
Pegsdon Cl LU3 . . . .**45** B7
Pegsdon Way SG5 . . . .**19** E1
Pelham Ct
Hemel Hempstead HP2 . . . .**125** C3
Welwyn Garden City AL7 . . .**111** C5
Pelham Rd SG13 . . . .**55** F7
Pelhams The WD2 . . . .**154** D4
Pelican Way SG6 . . . .**11** F1
Pemberton Cl AL1 . . . .**141** D8
Pembridge Chase HP3 . . . .**137** A3
Pembridge La EN10 . . . . . .**133** E2
Pembridge Rd HP3 . . . .**137** A3
Pembroke Ave
Enfield EN1 . . . .**162** E1

Pembroke Ave continued
Luton LU4 . . . .**44** F3
Pembroke Cl EN10 . . . .**148** E8
Pembroke Dr EN7 . . . .**147** B2
Pembroke Rd Baldock SG7 . .**23** F8
Moor Park HA6 . . . .**174** C7
Pemsel Ct HP3 . . . .**124** E1
Penda Cl LU3 . . . .**44** F7
Pendennis Ct AL5 . . . .**107** D7
Penfold Cl SG7 . . . .**24** A7
Penfold Trad Est WD2 . . . .**167** C8
Pengelly Cl EN7 . . . .**148** B1
Penhill LU3 . . . .**44** E6
Penhill Ct LU3 . . . .**44** E6
Penman Cl AL2 . . . .**141** A4
Penn Cl WD3 . . . .**164** D3
Penn Ho Moor Park HA6 . . .**174** C7
South Oxhey WD1 . . . .**175** C7
Penn Pl WD3 . . . .**165** D2
Penn Rd
Chiswellgreen AL2 . . . .**141** C4
Rickmansworth WD3 . . . . . .**165** A1
Stevenage SG1 . . . .**50** D6
Penn Way
Chorleywood WD3 . . . .**164** D3
Letchworth SG6 . . . .**23** B3
Pennard Ho WD1 . . . .**175** D7
Penne Cl WD7 . . . .**156** A5
Pennine Ave LU3 . . . .**44** D8
Pennine Way HP2 . . . .**125** A7
Penningtons CM23 . . . .**76** C5
Penny Croft AL5 . . . .**107** A4
Penny Ct WD1 . . . .**167** B7
Pennyfathers La AL6 . . . . . .**90** B4
Pennymead CM20 . . . .**118** A1
Penrose Ave WD1 . . . .**175** E8
Penrose Ct HP2 . . . .**124** E7
Penscroft Gdns WD6 . . . . .**170** D5
Penrose CM17 . . . .**118** C3
Penshurst Cl AL5 . . . .**85** D4
Penshurst Rd EN6 . . . .**159** D7
Pentland Ho WD1 . . . .**175** D7
Pentland Rd WD2 . . . .**168** C3
Pentley Cl AL8 . . . .**89** D1
Penton Dr EN8 . . . .**148** D2
Pentrich Ave EN1 . . . .**162** A1
Penzance Cl UB9 . . . .**173** D1
Peplins Cl AL9 . . . .**144** E5
Peplins Way AL9 . . . .**144** E5
Peppard Cl AL3 . . . .**106** A6
Pepper Ct SG7 . . . .**23** F8
Pepper Hill SG4 . . . .**114** F4
Peppercorn Wlk SG4 . . . . . .**35** B7
Peppett's Gn HP5 . . . .**120** D1
Pepsal End SG2 . . . .**69** B8
Pepsal End Rd LU1 . . . .**84** C7
Pepys Cres EN5 . . . .**171** C4
Pepys Way SG7 . . . .**23** E8
Percheron Dr LU4 . . . .**44** A3
Percheron Rd WD6 . . . . . .**170** D3
Percival Ct EN8 . . . .**148** E1
Percival Way LU2 . . . .**64** C7
Percy Rd WD1 . . . .**167** B5
Peregrine Cl
Bishop's Stortford CM23 . . . .**76** D6
Watford WD2 . . . .**154** E5
Peregrine Ho 1 SG12 . . . . .**93** C3
Peregrine Rd LU4 . . . .**44** A4
Perham Way AL2 . . . .**142** D6
Perivale Gdns WD2 . . . . . .**154** B5
Periwinkle Cl SG6 . . . .**17** C5
Periwinkle La SG5 . . . .**21** F1
Permain Cl WD7 . . . .**156** E6
Perowne Way SG11 . . . .**55** E3
Perram Cl EN10 . . . .**148** E5
Perriors Cl EN7 . . . .**148** A4
Perry Dr SG8 . . . .**7** E7
Perry Gn HP2 . . . .**105** A1
Perry Hill EN9 . . . .**149** F8
Perry Mead WD2 . . . .**168** C3
Perrymead LU2 . . . .**46** F2
Pescot Hill HP1 . . . .**124** B5
Petard Cl LU4 . . . .**44** A2
Peter Kirk Sch CM24 . . . .**59** F6
Peter's Pl HP4 . . . .**121** E6
Peterlee Ct 2 HP2 . . . .**124** F7
Peters Ave AL2 . . . .**142** C5
Peters Way SG3 . . . .**68** F6
Peters Wood Hill SG12 . . .**114** E7
Petersfield AL3 . . . .**127** E7
Pettys Cl EN8 . . . .**148** D3
Petunia Ct LU3 . . . .**45** C1
Petworth Cl SG2 . . . .**69** C7
Pevensey Cl LU2 . . . .**46** D4
Pewterers Ave CM23 . . . . . .**76** C4
Pheasant Cl
Berkhamsted HP4 . . . .**122** C3
Tring HP23 . . . .**100** B6
Pheasants Way WD3 . . . . . .**165** B2
Phillimore Ct WD7 . . . .**155** E3
Phillimore La WD7 . . . .**155** E3
Phillipers WD2 . . . .**154** E4
Phillips Ave SG8 . . . .**7** C8
Phipps Hatch La EN2 . . . . .**161** C1
Phoenix Cl HA6 . . . .**174** F6
Phoenix Ct EN3 . . . .**162** C1
Phyllis Courtnage Ho
HP2 . . . .**124** D5
Piccotts End HP1 . . . .**124** C6
Piccotts End La HP2 . . . . . .**124** D7
Piccotts End Rd HP1 . . . . .**124** B7
Pick Hill EN9 . . . .**163** F7
Pickets Cl WD2 . . . .**168** E1
Picketts AL8 . . . .**89** D1
Pickford Hill AL5 . . . .**86** C3

Pickford Rd AL3 . . . .**83** C3
Pickname Cnr SG8 . . . .**9** A2
Pickname Rd SG8 . . . .**9** A2
Pie Cnr AL3 . . . .**84** B1
Pie Gdn AL3 . . . .**84** C1
Pierian Spring HP1 . . . .**124** B5
Pietley Hill AL3 . . . .**84** A1
Pig La CM22 . . . .**77** A3
Pigeonwick AL5 . . . .**86** B3
Piggotts La LU4 . . . .**44** D4
Piggotts Way CM23 . . . .**76** E5
Piggottshill La AL5 . . . .**107** D8
Pightle Cl SG8 . . . .**7** D7
Pike End SG1 . . . .**50** D6
Pilgrim Cl
Chiswellgreen AL2 . . . .**141** C4
Watford WD2 . . . .**154** D6
Pilgrims Row SG9 . . . .**40** F3
Pilgrims Way SG1 . . . .**37** B2
Piltdown Rd WD1 . . . .**175** D6
Pin Green Ind Est SG1 . . . . .**37** C2
Pin Green
Jun Mix Inf Sch SG1 . . . . . .**50** F6
Pinchfield WD3 . . . .**172** D5
Pindar Rd EN11 . . . .**135** C7
Pine Cl Berkhamsted HP4 . .**122** B4
Cheshunt EN8 . . . .**148** D3
Northwood HA6 . . . .**174** E4
Pine Crest AL6 . . . .**89** E8
Pine Gr Barnet N20 . . . .**171** F1
Bishop's Stortford CM23 . . . .**77** B6
Bricket Wood AL2 . . . .**140** F1
Brookmans Park AL9 . . . . . .**145** B6
Bushey WD2 . . . .**167** F8
Pine Ridge AL1 . . . .**142** A8
Pine Tree Cl HP2 . . . .**124** D4
Pine Wlk HP4 . . . .**121** D7
Pinecroft HP3 . . . .**138** F7
Pinecroft Cres EN5 . . . . . .**171** E5
Pinehill Hospl SG4 . . . .**35** C1
Pinehurst Cl WD5 . . . .**153** E7
Pinelands CM23 . . . .**58** F1
Pineridge Ct EN5 . . . .**171** D5
Pines Ave EN1 . . . .**162** B3
Pines Hill CM24 . . . .**59** D5
Pines Jun Mix Inf Sch
The SG13 . . . .**114** B7
Pines The
Borehamwood WD6 . . . . . .**169** F7
Hemel Hempstead HP3 . . . .**137** F7
Pinetree Ho WD2 . . . .**154** E3
Pinewood AL7 . . . .**110** E4
Pinewood Ave HA5 . . . . . .**176** B4
Pinewood Cl
Borehamwood WD6 . . . . . .**170** D7
Pinner HA5 . . . .**176** B4
St Albans AL4 . . . .**128** C3
Watford WD1 . . . .**167** A8
Pinewood Dr EN6 . . . .**158** F8
Pinewood Gdns
Hemel Hempstead HP1 . . . .**124** B3
5 Hemel Hempstead HP2 . .**124** E2
Pinewood Sch SG12 . . . . . .**114** D7
Pinewoods 4 SG2 . . . .**50** F1
Pinfold Rd WD2 . . . .**167** F7
Pinfold Dell 4 LU2 . . . .**46** D1
Pinnacles EN9 . . . .**163** E5
Pinnate Pl AL7 . . . .**110** E2
Pinner Gn HA5 . . . .**175** C1
Pinner Hill HA5 . . . .**175** B3
Pinner Hill Rd HA5 . . . .**175** C1
Pinner Park Ave HA2 . . . .**176** C1
Pinner Park Gdns HA2 . . .**176** C1
Pinner Rd Northwood HA6 .**175** A1
Watford WD1 . . . .**167** E2
Pinner Wood
Fst & Mid Schs HA5 . . . . .**175** C2
Pinnocks SG7 . . . .**23** F7
Pinnocks La SG7 . . . .**23** F8
Pinto Cl WD6 . . . .**170** D3
Pioneer Way WD1 . . . .**166** F3
Pipers Ave AL5 . . . .**107** D7
Pipers Cl AL3 . . . .**106** A6
Pipers Hill HP1 . . . .**103** D3
Pipers La
Caddington AL3,LU1 . . . .**62** F1
Wheathampstead AL5 . . . . .**107** F7
Pippens AL8 . . . .**89** E1
Pippin Cl WD7 . . . .**156** E6
Pirton Cl
Hemel Hempstead HP2 . . . .**124** F4
Hitchin SG5 . . . .**34** C8
St Albans AL4 . . . .**128** C8
Pirton Cross SG5 . . . .**34** A7
Pirton Hill Inf Sch LU4 . . . . .**44** B6
Pirton Hill Jun Sch LU4 . . . . .**44** B6
Pirton Jun Mix Inf Sch
SG5 . . . .**20** D4
Pirton Rd Hitchin SG5 . . . . .**34** C6
Holwell SG5 . . . .**21** A7
Luton LU4 . . . .**44** D5
Pishiobury Dr CM21 . . . . . .**118** D8
Pitsfield AL3 . . . .**89** D1
Pitsford Terr LU2 . . . .**46** A1
Pitstone Cl AL4 . . . .**128** C8
Pitstone Windmill LU7 . . . . .**80** F4
Pitt Cl SG2 . . . .**51** B3
Pitt Dr AL4 . . . .**142** C8
Pittman's Field CM20 . . . .**117** C1
Pix Cl SG5 . . . .**11** A8
Pix Farm La HP1 . . . .**123** C2
Pix Rd Letchworth SG6 . . . . .**23** A6
Stotfold SG5 . . . .**11** E5
Pixies Hill Inf Sch HP1 . . . .**123** F2
Pixies Hill Cres HP1 . . . . . .**123** F2

Pixmore Ind Est SG6 . . . . . .**23** A6
Pixmore Jun Sch SG6 . . . . . .**23** A5
Pixmore Way SG6 . . . .**23** A5
Plaistow Way SG8 . . . .**9** E8
Plaiters Cl LU7 . . . .**100** B4
Plaitford Cl WD3 . . . .**173** E8
Plantagenet Pl EN9 . . . . . .**163** B6
Plantation Rd LU3 . . . .**44** D7
Plantation Wlk HP1 . . . . . .**124** A6
Plash Dr SG1 . . . .**50** E5
Plashes Cl SG11 . . . .**55** D2
Plashets CM22 . . . .**98** A1
Platt Cl LU4 . . . .**44** D4
Plaw Hatch Cl CM23 . . . . . .**77** B8
Plaw Hatch Cnr CM23 . . . . .**77** D8
Playford Sq LU4 . . . .**44** D5
Pleasance The AL5 . . . .**85** D4
Pleasant Pl WD3 . . . .**172** E3
Pleasant Rd LU2 . . . .**76** E8
Pleasant Rise AL9 . . . .**130** C8
Plewes Cl LU6 . . . .**82** E8
Plough Hill EN6 . . . .**146** E2
Plough La Harefield UB9 . . .**173** C4
King's Walden SG4 . . . .**48** A5
Potten End HP4 . . . .**123** B7
Sarratt WD3 . . . .**151** F6
Ploughmans Cl CM23 . . . . . .**76** C5
Ploughmans End AL7 . . . . .**111** C5
Plover Cl HP4 . . . .**122** C3
Plum Tree Rd SG16 . . . .**10** B2
Plummers La LU2 . . . .**65** C2
Plumpton Cl LU2 . . . .**46** D3
Plumpton Rd EN11 . . . .**135** C8
Pluto Rise HP2 . . . .**124** F5
Plymouth Cl LU2 . . . .**46** B1
Poets Cl HP1 . . . .**124** B4
Poets Ct AL5 . . . .**86** B1
Poets Gate EN7 . . . .**147** E3
Poets Gn LU4 . . . .**44** A2
Polayn Garth AL8 . . . .**110** C7
Polegate LU2 . . . .**46** D2
Polehanger La HP1 . . . .**123** E5
Poles Hill WD3 . . . .**151** E6
Poles La Thundridge SG12 . . .**93** C6
Ware SG12 . . . .**93** C3
Poles Pk SG12 . . . .**93** C6
Police Row SG8 . . . .**15** F7
Police Station La WD2 . . . .**168** B2
Pollard Gdns SG1 . . . .**50** F8
Pollards WD3 . . . .**172** D5
Pollards Cl EN7 . . . .**147** C2
Pollards Way SG5 . . . .**20** D4
Pollicott Cl AL4 . . . .**128** C8
Pollywick Rd HP23 . . . .**100** D1
Polzeath Cl LU2 . . . .**64** C8
Pomeroy Cres WD2 . . . . . .**154** B3
Pomeroy Gr LU2 . . . .**45** E6
Pomfret Ave LU2 . . . .**45** F1
Pond Cl Harefield UB9 . . . .**173** C1
Luton LU4 . . . .**44** B5
Stevenage SG1 . . . .**50** C7
Tring HP23 . . . .**100** A4
Pond Croft Hatfield AL10 . .**129** F5
Welwyn Garden City AL7 . . .**110** E5
Pond Field AL7 . . . .**90** A1
Pond La Baldock SG7 . . . .**23** E8
Little Gaddesden HP4 . . . . .**102** E7
Pond Lodge **67** F1
Pond Rd HP3 . . . .**139** A6
Pondcroft Rd SG3 . . . .**69** A4
Pondfield Cres AL4 . . . . . .**128** B7
Pondside SG4 . . . .**36** C4
Pondsmeade AL3 . . . .**106** B5
Pondwick Rd AL5 . . . .**85** E2
Pondwicks Cl AL1 . . . .**127** C2
Pondwicks Rd LU1 . . . .**63** F7
Ponsbourne Park
Cotts SG13 . . . .**146** F8
Ponsbourne St Mary's
CE Sch SG13 . . . .**146** E7
Pooleys La LU4 . . . .**144** C8
Pope Paul RC Prim Sch
EN6 . . . .**158** F6
Pope's Rd WD5 . . . .**153** E8
Popes Cl LU3 . . . .**45** D1
Popes La WD2 . . . .**154** B1
Popes Row SG12 . . . .**93** D3
Popis Gdns SG12 . . . .**93** E2
Poplar Ave Hatfield AL4 . . .**129** C5
Luton LU3 . . . .**45** C8
Poplar Cl Hitchin SG4 . . . . . .**35** B6
Pinner HA5 . . . .**175** D2
Royston SG8 . . . .**7** E7
Thundridge SG11 . . . .**72** F2
Poplar Dr SG8 . . . .**7** E7
Poplar Rd LU6 . . . .**82** E8
Poplar Shaw EN9 . . . .**163** F6
Poplar View SG14 . . . .**92** E4
Poplars AL7 . . . .**111** B7
Poplars Cl Hatfield AL10 . . .**129** B7
Luton LU3 . . . .**46** B3
Watford WD2 . . . .**154** B1
Poplars The Arlesey SG15 . .**11** A8
Great Hallingbury CM22 . . . .**77** F4
Hammond Street EN7 . . . . .**147** E5
Harefield UB9 . . . .**173** C2
Hemel Hempstead HP1 . . . .**124** B2
Ickleford SG5 . . . .**21** F5
St Albans AL1 . . . .**142** B7
Popple Way SG1 . . . .**50** D8
Poppy Cl HP1 . . . .**123** E4
Poppy Mead SG1 . . . .**50** F4
Poppy Wlk EN7 . . . .**147** D3
Poppyfields AL7 . . . .**111** C5
Porlock Dr LU2 . . . .**46** C1

Port Hill SG14 . . . . .113 C7
Port La CM22 . . . . .77 B2
Port Vale SG14 . . . . .113 C6
Porters Cl SG9 . . . . .40 E8
Porters Hill AL5 . . . . .86 C4
Porters Park Dr WD7 . . . .156 E7
Porters Wood AL3 . . . . . . .127 F7
Portland Ct LU4 . . . . .45 A1
Portland Dr Cheshunt EN7 .162 A8
Enfield EN2 . . . . .161 E1
Portland Hts HA6 . . . . . . .174 F6
Portland Ind Est SG15 . . . . .11 A3
Portland Pl
17 Bishop's Stortford CM23 . . .76 F7
Hertford Heath SG13 . . . . . .114 C4
Portland Rd
Bishop's Stortford CM23 . . .76 F7
Luton LU4 . . . . .45 A1
Portland St AL3 . . . . .127 C4
Portman Cl Hitchin SG5 . . . .21 D2
St Albans AL4 . . . . .128 C7
Portman Ho AL3 . . . . .127 D6
Portmill La SG5 . . . . .34 F7
Post Office Cotts CM22 . . . .98 C8
Post Office Rd CM20 . . . . .117 D1
Post Office Row SG4 . . . . . .24 B1
Post Wood Rd SG12 . . . . .114 E7
Postfield AL7 . . . . .90 A1
Postwood Gn SG13 . . . . . .114 C3
Potash La HP23 . . . . .79 A5
Potten End CE First Sch
HP4 . . . . .123 B6
Potten End Hill HP1 . . . . . .123 E8
Potter St
Bishop's Stortford CM23 . . .76 F7
Pinner HA5 . . . . .175 B2
Potter Street Hill HA5 . . . .175 B3
Potters Bar Hospl EN6 . . . .159 C5
Potters Bar Sta EN6 . . . . .158 F7
Potters Field AL5 . . . . .127 C2
Potters Heights Cl HA5 . . .175 B8
Potters La
Borehamwood WD6 . . . . . .170 C8
Stevenage SG1 . . . . .50 B4
Potters Mews WD6 . . . . . .169 D3
Potterscrouch La
AL2,AL3 . . . . .140 E7
Pottersheath Rd AL6 . . . . .68 D1
Pottery Cl LU3 . . . . .44 F7
Potton Rd SG8 . . . . .1 F6
Pouchen End La HP1 . . . . .123 D3
Poulteney Rd CM24 . . . . . . .59 E8
Poultney Cl WD7 . . . . .156 F7
Pound Ave SG1 . . . . .50 D6
Pound Cl
Lower Nazeing EN9 . . . . . .149 E8
Sandridge AL4 . . . . .108 C2
Pound Field WD2 . . . . . . .153 F4
Pound Gn SG8 . . . . .1 F5
Pound La WD7 . . . . .156 F6
Poundwell AL7 . . . . .111 A5
Powdermill La EN9 . . . . . .163 B6
Powdermill Mews EN9 . . . .163 B6
Powdermill Way EN9 . . . . .163 B6
Power Ct LU1 . . . . .63 F7
Power Dr EN3 . . . . .162 F3
Powis Ct Bushey WD2 . . . .168 D1
Potters Bar EN6 . . . . .159 C5
Powys Ct WD6 . . . . .170 D6
Poynders Hill HP2 . . . . . . .125 C3
Poynders Mdw SG4 . . . . . . .88 F8
Poynings Cl AL5 . . . . .107 F8
Poynters Rd LU5 . . . . .44 A1
Prae Cl AL3 . . . . .127 B3
Prae Wood Prim Sch
AL3 . . . . .127 A1
Praetorian Ct AL1 . . . . . . .141 C8
Prebendal Dr LU1 . . . . .63 B2
Precinct The EN10 . . . . . . .134 F3
Premier Ct EN3 . . . . .162 D1
Prentice Way LU2 . . . . .64 D7
Prescott Rd EN8 . . . . .148 E4
Presdales Dr SG12 . . . . . . .114 E8
Presdales Sch SG12 . . . . .114 D7
Presentation Ct LU1 . . . . . .63 F6
President Way LU2 . . . . .64 D8
Prestatyn Cl SG1 . . . . .50 B8
Preston Gdns Enfield EN3 .162 E2
Luton LU2 . . . . .45 A1
Preston Path LU2 . . . . .45 F2
Preston Prim Sch SG4 . . . . .48 D6
Preston Rd Preston SG4 . . .48 E7
St Ippolyts SG4 . . . . .34 F1
Prestwick Cl LU2 . . . . .45 E5
Prestwick Dr CM23 . . . . . . .59 B1
Prestwick Rd WD1 . . . . . . .175 D6
Pretoria Rd WD1 . . . . .167 A5
Pretty Cnr HA6 . . . . .175 A5
Priestleys LU1 . . . . .63 A7
Primary Way SG15 . . . . .11 A4
Primett Rd SG1 . . . . .50 C7
Primley La CM22 . . . . .98 C1
Primrose Cl Arlesey SG15 . . .11 A4
Bishop's Stortford CM23 . . .76 C6
Hatfield AL10 . . . . .130 B4
Primrose Cotts WD7 . . . . . .156 A4
Primrose Ct SG1 . . . . .50 D7
Primrose Dr SG13 . . . . . . .114 B6
Primrose Gdns WD2 . . . . .168 B2
Primrose Hill WD4 . . . . . . .139 B3
Primrose Hill Rd SG1 . . . . .50 D7
Primrose La SG15 . . . . .11 A4
Primrose Path EN7 . . . . . .162 A8
Primrose View SG8 . . . . .7 C6
Prince Andrew's Cl SG8 . . . .7 D5

Prince Edward St HP4 . . . .122 C4
Prince of Wales
Inf & Jun Sch EN3 . . . . . .162 F2
Prince Pk HP1 . . . . .124 A2
Prince St WD1 . . . . .167 C6
Prince Way LU2 . . . . .64 D8
Prince's St SG5 . . . . .11 F7
Princes Ave Enfield EN3 . . .162 E4
Watford WD1 . . . . .167 A5
Princes Cl HP4 . . . . .122 A6
Princes Ct CM23 . . . . .76 C7
Princes Gate
Bishop's Stortford CM23 . . .76 C7
Harlow CM20 . . . . .117 E3
Princes Mews SG8 . . . . .7 C6
Princes Pl **18** LU2 . . . . .45 D1
Princes St SG12 . . . . .93 D2
Princess Alexandra
Hospl CM20 . . . . .117 C1
Princess Diana Dr AL4 . . .128 D2
Princess Helena Coll
SG4 . . . . .48 E6
Princess St LU1 . . . . .63 D7
Printers Way CM20 . . . . . .118 A5
Priors **9** CM23 . . . . .77 A7
Priors Cl SG13 . . . . .114 B3
Priors Ct CM22 . . . . .98 A2
Priors Hill SG5 . . . . .20 C4
Priors Wood Prim Sch
SG12 . . . . .94 A3
Priors Wood Rd SG13 . . . .114 C3
Priory Ave CM17 . . . . .118 C5
Priory Cl Barnet N20 . . . . .171 F2
Cheshunt EN8 . . . . .148 E7
Hoddesdon EN11 . . . . .135 A5
Royston SG8 . . . . .7 E6
Stanmore HA7 . . . . .176 F7
Priory Ct
Berkhamsted HP4 . . . . . . .122 C4
Bishop's Stortford CM23 . . .76 F7
Bushey WD2 . . . . .168 C1
Hitchin SG4 . . . . .34 F5
St Albans AL1 . . . . .127 E2
Priory Dell SG1 . . . . .50 F5
Priory Dr Stanmore HA7 . .176 F7
Stansted Mountfitchet CM24 .59 E5
Priory End SG4 . . . . .34 F5
Priory Gate EN8 . . . . .148 F4
Priory Gdns
Berkhamsted HP4 . . . . . . .122 C4
Luton LU2 . . . . .45 D4
Priory La
Great Wymondley SG4 . . . .35 F4
Royston SG8 . . . . .7 D6
Priory Lo WD3 . . . . .165 D2
Priory Orch AL3 . . . . .84 B2
Priory Sch The SG5 . . . . . . .21 E2
Priory St Hertford SG14 . . .113 D6
Ware SG12 . . . . .93 C1
Priory View Bushey WD2 . .168 E2
Little Wymondley SG4 . . . . .35 F4
Priory Way SG4 . . . . .34 F4
Priory Wharf **10** SG14 . . . .113 D6
Priory Wlk AL1 . . . . .141 E8
Proctor Way LU2 . . . . .64 C7
Proctors Way CM23 . . . . . . .77 A4
Progress Way LU4 . . . . .44 B7
Progression Ctr HP2 . . . . .125 A6
Prospect La AL5 . . . . .107 A4
Prospect Pl AL6 . . . . .89 C5
Prospect Rd
Cheshunt EN8 . . . . .148 C2
St Albans AL1 . . . . .127 D1
Prospect Way LU2 . . . . .64 C7
Protea Way SG6 . . . . .23 B6
Providence Gr SG1 . . . . . . .50 E8
Providence Way SG7 . . . . . .23 F7
Provost Way LU2 . . . . .64 C8
Prowse Ave WD2 . . . . .176 C8
Pryor Cl WD5 . . . . .153 F7
Pryor Rd SG7 . . . . .23 F6
Pryor Way SG6 . . . . .23 D5
Pryors Cl CM23 . . . . .77 A6
Pryors Ct SG7 . . . . .12 F1
Puddephat's La AL3 . . . . . .104 D7
Pudding La Barley SG8 . . . . .9 A4
Hemel Hempstead HP1 . . .124 A5
Puddingstone Dr AL4 . . . .128 C1
Pudgell The SG8 . . . . .9 E2
Pulham Ave EN10 . . . . .134 E3
Pullar Memorial
Jun Mix Inf Sch SG11 . . . .72 E2
Puller Rd Barnet EN5 . . . . .171 E7
Hemel Hempstead HP1 . . .124 A2
Pulleys Cl HP1 . . . . .123 F4
Pulleys La HP1 . . . . .123 F4
Pullman Dr SG4 . . . . .35 B7
Pulter's Way SG4 . . . . .35 A6
Pump Hill SG9 . . . . .30 A2
Punch Bowl La AL3 . . . . . .126 B8
Purbeck Ho **8** WD1 . . . . .166 F3
Purbrock Ave WD2 . . . . . .154 C3
Purcell Cl
Datchworth AL6 . . . . .90 E6
Radlett WD6 . . . . .169 D8
Purcell Ct SG1 . . . . .50 C8
Purcell Sch of Music
WD2 . . . . .168 A7
Purkiss Rd SG13 . . . . .113 C3
Purley Ctr LU3 . . . . .44 E7
Purlings Rd WD2 . . . . .168 B4
Pursley Gdns WD6 . . . . . . .157 A1
Purway Cl LU3 . . . . .44 E7
Purwell La SG4 . . . . .35 C8
Purwell Prim Sch SG4 . . . .35 D8
Putney Rd EN3 . . . . .162 D3
Puttenham Cl WD1 . . . . . .175 D8

Putteridge High Sch LU2 . .46 C5
Putteridge Inf Sch LU2 . . .46 C5
Putteridge Jun Sch LU2 . . .46 C5
Putteridge Par LU2 . . . . . . .46 B4
Putteridge Rd LU2 . . . . .46 C4
Putteridge Recn Ctr LU2 . .46 C5
Putterills The AL5 . . . . .86 A1
Putters Croft HP2 . . . . .124 F8
Puttocks Cl AL9 . . . . .144 C8
Puttocks Dr AL9 . . . . .144 C8
Pye Cnr CM20 . . . . .117 D5
Pyghtle Ct LU2 . . . . .63 A7
Pyghtle The
Buntingford SG9 . . . . .40 D7
Luton LU1 . . . . .63 A7
Pyms Cl SG6 . . . . .23 B8
Pynchbek CM23 . . . . .76 E3
Pynchon Paddocks
CM22 . . . . .98 D7
Pynefield WD3 . . . . .164 F2
Pytchley Cl LU2 . . . . .45 E5

Q

Quadrangle The AL8 . . . . .110 C7
Quadrant The
Letchworth SG6 . . . . .22 F6
Royston SG8 . . . . .7 C8
St Albans AL4 . . . . .128 B6
Stevenage SG1 . . . . .50 D4
Quaker La EN9 . . . . .163 C5
Quaker Rd SG12 . . . . .93 E3
Quakers La EN6 . . . . .159 B8
Quantock Cl Luton LU3 . . . .45 B8
St Albans AL4 . . . . .128 C7
Quantock Rise LU3 . . . . . . .31 B1
Quantocks HP2 . . . . .124 F6
Quarmass Cl HP1 . . . . .124 A4
Quarmass Rd HP1 . . . . . . .124 A4
Queen Anne's Cl SG1 . . . .51 B8
Queen Elizabeth Ct EN5 . .171 F5
Queen Elizabeth II Hospl
AL7 . . . . .111 A2
Queen Elizabeth's Boys
Sch EN5 . . . . .171 D6
Queen Elizabeth's Girls
Sch EN5 . . . . .171 F5
Queen Hoo La AL6 . . . . . . .90 F6
Queen Mary's Ave WD1 . .166 E5
Queen St
Chipperfield WD4 . . . . .152 A7
Hitchin SG4,SG5 . . . . .34 F7
Pitstone LU7 . . . . .80 D4
St Albans AL3 . . . . .127 C3
Stotfold SG5 . . . . .12 A3
Tring HP23 . . . . .100 A3
Queen Victoria Memorial
Hospl AL6 . . . . .89 B4
Queen's Cl CM21 . . . . .97 F4
Queen's Ct
Aspenden SG9 . . . . .40 D5
Hertford SG13 . . . . .113 D5
St Albans AL1 . . . . .128 B3
Queen's Dr EN8 . . . . .163 A5
Queen's Dr The WD3 . . . . .165 A3
Queen's Pl WD1 . . . . .167 C6
Queen's Rd
Cheshunt EN8 . . . . .162 E6
Harpenden AL5 . . . . .107 B7
Hertford SG13 . . . . .113 D5
Watford WD1 . . . . .167 C6
Queen's Sq The HP2 . . . . .124 F4
Queens Ave WD1 . . . . .166 F5
Queens Cl **4** Luton LU1 . . .63 E6
Stansted Mountfitchet CM24 .59 E8
Queens Cres
Bishop's Stortford CM23 . . .76 E5
St Albans AL4 . . . . .128 B6
Queens Ct **14** Luton LU2 . . .45 D1
Watford WD1 . . . . .167 C6
Queens Dr WD5 . . . . .153 F7
Queens Head Wlk EN10 . .148 E8
Queens Rd Barnet EN5 . . . .171 E7
Berkhamsted HP4 . . . . . . .122 A5
Royston SG8 . . . . .7 D7
Ware SG12 . . . . .93 F2
Queens' Sch WD2 . . . . . . .168 A6
Queens Way
Cheshunt EN8 . . . . .162 F5
Shenley WD7 . . . . .156 F7
Queensgate EN8 . . . . .162 F5
Queensgate Ctr CM20 . . . .117 F4
Queensway
1 Hatfield AL10 . . . . .130 A6
Hemel Hempstead HP1,
HP2 . . . . .124 E4
Royston SG8 . . . . .7 D7
Stevenage SG1 . . . . .50 D5
Queenswood Cres WD2 . . .154 A6
Queenswood Dr SG4 . . . . . .22 C1
Queenswood Sch AL9 . . . .145 D3
Quendell Wlk HP2 . . . . . . .124 E3
Quendon Dr EN9 . . . . .163 D6
Quickbeams AL7 . . . . .90 A1
Quickley La WD3 . . . . .164 C4
Quickley Rise WD3 . . . . . .164 C3
Quickly Brow WD3 . . . . . . .164 B3
Quickmoor La WD4 . . . . . .152 C6
Quickswood LU3 . . . . .45 A7
Quickwood Cl WD3 . . . . . .165 A3
Quills SG6 . . . . .23 D4
Quilter Cl LU3 . . . . .44 F4
Quinces Croft HP1 . . . . . . .124 A5
Quincey Rd SG12 . . . . .93 C4
Quinn Ct SG11 . . . . .55 F7
Quinn Way SG6 . . . . .23 C5
Quinta Dr EN5 . . . . .171 C4

R

Raans Rd HP6 . . . . .150 A1
Raban Cl SG2 . . . . .51 C1
Raban Ct SG7 . . . . .12 F1
Rabley Heath Rd AL6 . . . . .68 B2
Rackman Dr AL3 . . . . .45 C5
Radburn Prim Sch SG6 . . . .23 C5
Radburn Way SG6 . . . . .23 C4
Radcliffe Rd SG5 . . . . .35 A8
Radlett Inf Sch WD7 . . . . .156 B3
Radlett La WD7 . . . . .156 E6
Radlett Park Rd WD7 . . . .156 A4
Radlett Rd
London Colney AL2 . . . . . .141 E2
Watford WD1,WD2 . . . . . .167 D7
Radlett Sta WD7 . . . . .156 A4
Radnor Ct HA3 . . . . .176 F2
Radstone Pl LU2 . . . . .46 E1
Radwell La SG7 . . . . .12 C4
Raebarn Gdns EN5 . . . . . .171 B4
Raffin Cl SG3 . . . . .69 E3
Raffin Green La SG3 . . . . . .69 F4
Raffin Pk SG3 . . . . .69 E3
Ragged Hall La AL2 . . . . . .140 E7
Raglan Ave EN5 . . . . .162 D5
Raglan Gdns WD1 . . . . . . .167 B1
Raglan Ho HP4 . . . . .122 A4
Rags La EN7 . . . . .147 C4
Railway Pl SG13 . . . . .113 E6
Railway Rd EN8 . . . . .162 F6
Railway St SG13,SG14 . . .113 D6
Railway Terr WD4 . . . . . . .139 A4
Rainbow Cl AL3 . . . . .105 F6
Rainbow Ct WD1 . . . . .167 C3
Rainer Cl EN8 . . . . .148 D2
Rainsford Rd CM24 . . . . . . .59 E8
Raleigh Cres SG2 . . . . .51 B8
Raleigh Gr LU4 . . . . .44 D1
Rally The SG15 . . . . .11 A7
Ralph Sadleir Sch SG11 . . .55 E3
Ralston Way WD1 . . . . . . .175 D8
Ram Gorse CM20 . . . . .117 A6
Ramblers Way AL7 . . . . . . .111 C5
Rambling Way HP4 . . . . . . .123 C6
Ramerick Gdns SG15 . . . . . .11 A1
Ramney Dr EN3 . . . . .162 E2
Ramparts The AL3 . . . . . . .127 B2
Ramridge Inf Sch LU2 . . . . .46 B2
Ramridge Jun Sch LU2 . . . .46 B2
Ramridge Rd LU2 . . . . .46 A2
Ramryge Ct AL1 . . . . .127 D1
Ramsay Cl EN10 . . . . .134 E2
Ramsbury Rd AL1 . . . . .127 E2
Ramsdell SG1 . . . . .50 F5
Ramsey Cl
Brookmans Park AL9 . . . . .145 D4
St Albans AL1 . . . . .128 A1
Ramsey Lodge Ct AL1 . . . .127 E4
Ramson Rise HP1 . . . . .123 E2
Rand's Cl SG2 . . . . .21 B7
Rand's Cotts SG5 . . . . .21 B7
Rand's Mdw SG5 . . . . .21 B7
Randalls Ride HP2 . . . . . . .124 C5
Randalls Wlk AL2 . . . . .140 F1
Randals Hill SG2 . . . . .51 C3
Randolph Ct HA5 . . . . .176 A3
Randon Cl HA2 . . . . .176 B1
Ranelagh Rd HP2 . . . . .125 B3
Ranleigh Wlk AL5 . . . . .107 D6
Ranock Cl LU3 . . . . .44 D8
Ranskill Rd WD6 . . . . .170 A8
Ransom Cl SG4 . . . . .34 F4
Ransome Cl WD1 . . . . .167 C2
Rant Ave
Hemel Hempstead HP3 . . .125 A1
Hemel Hempstead HP3 . . .125 A1
Ranulf Cl CM17 . . . . .118 C6
Ranworth Ave
Hoddesdon EN11 . . . . .115 B2
Stevenage SG2 . . . . .69 C7
Ranworth Cl **2** HP3 . . . . .124 D1
Raphael Ct WD7 . . . . .156 E7
Raphael Dr WD7 . . . . .167 D7
Rapper Ct LU3 . . . . .63 D8
Rasehill Cl WD3 . . . . .165 A4
Rathlin HP3 . . . . .139 B8
Ratty's La EN11 . . . . .135 D6
Raven Cl WD3 . . . . .165 D2
Raven Ct AL10 . . . . .130 A4
Ravenbank Rd LU2 . . . . . . .46 C5
Ravenfield Rd AL7 . . . . . . .110 F6
Ravenhill Way LU4 . . . . . . .44 B4
Ravens La HP4 . . . . .122 D4
Ravens Wharf HP4 . . . . . . .122 D4
Ravenscroft
Harpenden AL5 . . . . .107 D6
Hoddesdon EN10 . . . . .134 F3
Watford WD2 . . . . .154 A4
Ravenscroft Pk EN5 . . . . . .171 D5
Ravenscroft Sch N20 . . . . .171 F2
Ravensdell HP1 . . . . .123 F4
Ravensthorpe LU2 . . . . .46 B4
Ravenswood Pk HA6 . . . . .175 A4
Rawdon Dr EN11 . . . . .135 A5
Ray's Hill HP5 . . . . .120 C2
Rayburn Rd HP1 . . . . .124 A5
Raydon Rd EN8 . . . . .162 D7
Rayfield AL8 . . . . .89 D1
Rayleigh Ho WD5 . . . . . . .153 F7
Raymer Cl AL1 . . . . .127 E4
Raymond Cl WD5 . . . . . . .153 D7
Raymond Cotts SG5 . . . . . .21 E4
Raymond Ct EN6 . . . . .159 C5
Raymonds Cl AL7 . . . . . . .110 E4
Raymonds Plain AL7 . . . . .110 E4
Raynham Rd CM23 . . . . . . .77 B8

Raynham St SG13 . . . . . . .113 E6
Raynham Way LU2 . . . . . . .46 D1
Raynsford Rd SG12 . . . . . .93 E1
Raynton Rd EN3 . . . . .162 D2
Readings The WD3 . . . . . .164 C5
Recreation Ground CM24 .59 E6
Rectory Cl
Bishop's Stortford CM23 . . .76 D3
Essendon AL9 . . . . .131 F6
Hunsdon SG12 . . . . .116 C8
Rectory Gdns AL10 . . . . . .130 B5
Rectory La
Berkhamsted HP4 . . . . . . .122 C4
Farnham CM23 . . . . .58 D6
Kings Langley WD4 . . . . . .139 A3
Lilley LU2 . . . . .32 D2
Rickmansworth WD3 . . . . .165 D1
Shenley WD7,AL2 . . . . . . .157 B7
Stevenage SG1 . . . . .36 C1
Watton at Stone SG14 . . . . .70 D3
Welwyn SG3 . . . . .69 C2
Rectory Rd
Rickmansworth WD3 . . . . .165 D2
Welwyn Garden City AL8 . . .89 D3
Rectory Wood CM20 . . . . .117 C1
Red House Cl SG12 . . . . . .114 E8
Red Lion Cl WD2 . . . . .155 C2
Red Lion Cotts SG5 . . . . . .33 D2
Red Lion La **5** CM23 . . . . .77 A7
Red Lion La
Hemel Hempstead HP3 . . .139 A5
Sarratt WD3 . . . . .152 A4
Red Lodge WD6 . . . . .169 F6
Red Lodge Gdns HP4 . . . .122 A3
Red Rails LU1 . . . . .63 C5
Red Rails Ct LU1 . . . . .63 C5
Red Rd WD6 . . . . .169 F6
Redan Rd SG12 . . . . .93 E3
Redbourn Ind Est AL3 . . . .106 B5
Redbourn Inf Sch AL3 . . . .106 C4
Redbourn Jun Sch AL3 . . .106 A6
Redbourn La AL3,AL5 . . . .106 C4
Redbourn Rd
Hemel Hempstead HP2 . . .125 B8
St Albans AL3 . . . . .126 E7
Redbourn Recn Ctr AL3 . .106 A7
Redbournbury La AL3 . . . .106 D2
Redbournbury Water
Mill AL3 . . . . .106 E2
Redbrick Row CM22 . . . . . .98 B8
Redcar Dr SG1 . . . . .50 A6
Redding Ho WD1 . . . . .166 E3
Redding La AL3 . . . . .105 F8
Reddings
Hemel Hempstead HP3 . . .125 A1
Welwyn Garden City AL8 . .110 C7
Reddings Ave WD2 . . . . . .168 B4
Reddings Cty Prim Sch
The HP3 . . . . .125 A1
Reddings The WD6 . . . . . .169 F6
Redferns Cl LU1 . . . . .63 A6
Redferns Ct LU1 . . . . .63 A6
Redgrave Gdns LU3 . . . . . .44 F7
Redhall Cl AL10 . . . . .129 F1
Redhall Dr AL10 . . . . .129 F1
Redhall La
Colney Heath AL4 . . . . . . .129 E1
Sarratt WD3 . . . . .165 E8
Redheath Cl WD2 . . . . . . .153 F4
Redhill Rd SG5 . . . . .34 D8
Redhoods Way E SG6 . . . . .22 E7
Redhoods Way W SG6 . . . .22 E6
Redhouse The EN10 . . . . . .134 F1
Redlands Rd EN3 . . . . .162 E1
Redmire Cl LU4 . . . . .44 B6
Redoubt Cl SG4 . . . . .22 A1
Redricks La CM21 . . . . . . .118 A6
Redvers Cl CM23 . . . . .59 A2
Redwell Ct EN8 . . . . .162 F5
Redwing Cl SG2 . . . . .51 D4
Redwing Gr WD5 . . . . .154 A8
Redwood Cl WD1 . . . . . . .175 D6
Redwood Dr
Hemel Hempstead HP3 . . .124 E1
Luton LU3 . . . . .44 C8
Redwood Rise WD6 . . . . . .157 B2
Redwood Way EN5 . . . . . .171 D4
Redwoods Hertford AL8 . . .113 C7
Welwyn Garden City AL8 . . .89 D3
Reed Cl AL2 . . . . .142 E4
Reed Fst Sch SG8 . . . . .16 E5
Reed Pl AL5 . . . . .85 F3
Reedham Cl AL2 . . . . .141 A2
Reedings Jun Sch CM21 . . .97 E3
Reedings Way CM21 . . . . . .97 F4
Reeds Cres WD1 . . . . .167 C5
Reeds The AL7 . . . . .110 D5
Reedsdale LU2 . . . . .46 F2
Reeves Ave LU3 . . . . .45 B4
Reeves Pightle SG8 . . . . . . .9 F3
Regal Cl SG11 . . . . .55 E2
Regal Ct **4** SG5 . . . . .34 F8
Regal Way WD2 . . . . .154 C1
Regency Ct CM23 . . . . .76 E7
Regency Ct
Hemel Hempstead HP2 . . .124 D1
Hoddesdon EN10 . . . . .148 F8
Regent Cl
Kings Langley WD4 . . . . . .139 A3
St Albans AL4 . . . . .128 C7
Welwyn Garden City AL7 . .110 E5
Regent Ct SG5 . . . . .11 F7
Regent Gate EN8 . . . . .162 E5
Regent St Luton LU1 . . . . . .63 E7
Stotfold SG5 . . . . .11 F7
Watford WD2 . . . . .154 B1
Regents Cl WD7 . . . . .156 A5
Regina Cl EN5 . . . . .171 D6

Reginald Rd HA6 . . . . .174 F3
Reginald St LU2 . . . . .45 E1
Rendlesham Ave WD7 . . . .155 F2
Rendlesham Cl SG12 . . . . . .93 B2
Rendlesham Rd EN2 . . . . . .161 B1
Rendlesham Way WD3 . . . .164 C3
Rennie Ct EN3 . . . . .163 A1
Rennison Cl EN7 . . . . .147 F4
Renshaw Cl LU2 . . . . .46 E2
Repton Cl LU3 . . . . .44 F6
Repton Gn AL3 . . . . .127 D6
Repton Way WD3 . . . . . . .166 A4
Reson Way HP1 . . . . .124 B2
Reston Cl WD6 . . . . .157 B1
Reston Path LU2 . . . . .46 E2
Retford Cl WD6 . . . . .157 A1
Retreat The WD5 . . . . .153 C8
Revels Cl SG14 . . . . .113 D8
Revels Rd SG14 . . . . .113 D8
Reynard Copse CM23 . . . . .58 F1
Reynard Way SG13 . . . . . .114 B6
Reynard's Way AL2 . . . . . .140 F2
Reynards Rd AL6 . . . . .89 C7
Reynolds Cl 11 F1
Reynolds Cl HP1 . . . . .124 A4
Reynolds Cres AL4 . . . . . . .128 B8
Rhee Spring SG7 . . . . .13 B1
Rhodes Ave CM23 . . . . . . .76 F5
Rhodes Memorial Mus &
  Commonwealth Ctr
  CM23 . . . . .77 A6
Rhodes Way WD2 . . . . . . .167 D8
Rhymes HP1 . . . . .124 B5
Rib Cl SG11 . . . . .55 E2
Rib Vale SG14 . . . . .92 D1
Ribbledale AL2 . . . . .142 F4
Ribblesdale HP2 . . . . .124 E6
Ribocon Way LU4 . . . . .44 B7
Ribston Ct WD7 . . . . .156 D6
Rice Cl HP2 . . . . .124 F4
Richard Ct EN5 . . . . .171 E6
Richard Hale Sch SG13 . . .113 D5
Richard Stagg Cl AL1 . . . .128 C1
Richard Wittington
  Jun Mix Inf Sch SG13 . . .113 D5
Richards Cl Bushey WD2 . .168 D2
  Luton LU1 . . . . .63 B6
Richards Ct LU1 . . . . .63 B5
Richardson Cl AL2 . . . . . . .142 E4
Richardson Cres EN7 . . . . .147 B6
Richardson Pl AL4 . . . . . . .129 B1
Richfield Rd WD2 . . . . . . .168 C2
Richmond Cl
  Bishop's Stortford CM23 . . .76 C1
  Cheshunt EN8 . . . . .148 C2
  Ware SG12 . . . . .93 B3
Richmond Ct
  4 Hatfield AL10 . . . . . . .130 B3
  Hoddesdon EN10 . . . . . . .134 F3
  Luton LU2 . . . . .45 F1
  Potters Bar EN6 . . . . .159 C8
Richmond Dr WD1 . . . . . .166 E7
Richmond Gdns HA3 . . . . .176 F3
Richmond Hill LU2 . . . . . . .45 F2
Richmond Hill Sch LU2 . . .45 E2
Richmond Rd EN6 . . . . . . .159 C8
Richmond Way WD3 . . . . .166 C5
Richmond Wlk AL4 . . . . . .128 D7
Rickfield Cl AL10 . . . . .130 A3
Rickmansworth La SL9 . . .172 A5
Rickmansworth Park
  Jun Mix Inf Sch WD3 . . .165 E2
Rickmansworth Rd
  Chorleywood WD3 . . . . . .164 F6
  Harefield UB9 . . . . .173 D3
  Northwood HA6 . . . . .174 D3
  Pinner HA5 . . . . .175 C1
  Watford WD1 . . . . .166 E5
Rickmansworth Sch
  WD3 . . . . .165 E1
Rickmansworth Sta
  WD3 . . . . .165 D2
Rickyard Cl LU2 . . . . .46 B1
Rickyard Mdw AL3 . . . . . .106 A5
Rickyard The Ashwell SG7 . .4 D3
  Letchworth SG6 . . . . .12 C1
Riddell Gdns SG7 . . . . .23 F8
Riddy Hill Cl SG4 . . . . .35 A6
Riddy La Hitchin SG4 . . . . .35 A6
  Luton LU3 . . . . .45 C5
Riddy The SG4 . . . . .88 F8
Ridge Ave Harpenden AL5 . .85 E4
  Letchworth SG6 . . . . .23 A6
Ridge Ct LU2 . . . . .46 A1
Ridge La WD1 . . . . .153 F2
Ridge Lea HP1 . . . . .123 F2
Ridge Rd SG6 . . . . .23 A6
Ridge St WD2 . . . . .154 B1
Ridge The Barnet EN5 . . . .171 F4
  Letchworth SG6 . . . . .23 A6
  Northwood HA6 . . . . .174 F3
Ridge View HP23 . . . . . . .100 C5
Ridge Way WD3 . . . . .165 B2
Ridgedown AL3 . . . . .106 A5
Ridgefield WD1 . . . . .153 E2
Ridgehurst Ave WD2 . . . . .153 F5
Ridgeview Cl EN5 . . . . . . .171 D3
Ridgeway
  Berkhamsted HP4 . . . . . .121 F4
  Harpenden AL5 . . . . .85 E4
  Kensworth Common LU6 . . .82 E8
  Little Hadham SG11 . . . . . .57 B1
  Stevenage SG1 . . . . .50 F5
  Welwyn Garden City AL7 . .111 B6
Ridgeway HP3 . . . . .138 F5
Ridgeway Ct HA5 . . . . . . .176 A3
Ridgeway The
  Codicote SG4 . . . . .67 F1

Ridgeway The continued
  Cuffley EN6 . . . . .146 A4
  Hadley Wood EN2,EN4 . . .160 D3
  Hertford SG14 . . . . .112 F7
  Hitchin SG5 . . . . .34 D6
  Radlett WD7 . . . . .155 F2
  St Albans AL4 . . . . .128 C7
  Ware SG12 . . . . .93 C3
  Watford WD1 . . . . .153 E2
Ridgewood Dr AL5 . . . . . . .85 E4
Ridgewood Gdns AL5 . . . . .85 E4
Ridgmont Rd AL1 . . . . . . .127 E2
Ridgway Rd LU2 . . . . .45 F1
Ridings The
  Bishop's Stortford CM23 . . .76 D4
  Hertford SG14 . . . . .113 A5
  Latimer HP5 . . . . .150 D3
  Luton LU3 . . . . .45 C1
  Markyate AL3 . . . . .83 E6
  Stevenage SG2 . . . . .51 B3
Ridler Rd EN1 . . . . .161 E1
Ridlins End SG2 . . . . .51 C2
Rigby Pl EN3 . . . . .163 A2
Rigery La SG11 . . . . .72 F6
Riley Rd EN3 . . . . .162 C1
Ringmer Ct LU2 . . . . .46 C3
Ringshall Dr HP4 . . . . .102 C8
Ringshall Rd HP4 . . . . .81 B3
Ringtale Pl SG7 . . . . .13 B1
Ringway Rd AL2 . . . . .141 C4
Ringwood Rd LU2 . . . . .45 D7
Ripley Rd Enfield EN2 . . . .161 C1
  Luton LU4 . . . . .44 E5
Ripley Way Cheshunt EN7 .148 B1
  Hemel Hempstead HP1 . . .123 E4
Ripon Rd SG1 . . . . .37 A2
Ripon Way
  Borehamwood WD6 . . . . .170 D4
  St Albans AL4 . . . . .128 D7
Rise Cotts SG12 . . . . .95 D2
Rise The Baldock SG7 . . . . .23 E7
  Borehamwood WD6 . . . . .169 F4
  Park Street AL2 . . . . .141 D6
Risdale Cl HP3 . . . . .138 E8
Risedale Hill HP3 . . . . .138 E8
Risedale Rd HP3 . . . . .138 E8
Rising Hill Cl HA6 . . . . . . .174 C4
Risingholme Cl
  Bushey WD2 . . . . .168 B2
  Harrow HA3 . . . . .176 E2
Risingholme Rd HA3 . . . . .176 E1
Ritcroft Cl HP3 . . . . .125 B2
Ritcroft Dr HP3 . . . . .125 B2
Ritcroft St HP3 . . . . .125 B2
Ritz Ct EN6 . . . . .159 A8
Rivenhall End AL7 . . . . . . .111 C6
River Ave EN11 . . . . .135 B7
River Cl EN8 . . . . .163 A5
River Ct Ickleford SG5 . . . . .21 F4
  Sacombe SG14 . . . . .92 E4
  Sawbridgeworth CM21 . . . .97 F3
River Gn SG9 . . . . .40 E8
River Hill AL3 . . . . .84 B2
River Lee Ctry Pk EN9 . . . .149 B1
River Mead SG5 . . . . .21 C2
River Meads SG12 . . . . . . .115 C4
River Pk HP1 . . . . .124 A1
River St SG12 . . . . .93 E1
River View AL7 . . . . .89 F2
River Way Harlow CM20 . .118 B5
  Luton LU3 . . . . .44 E5
Riverbanks AL5 . . . . .86 C4
Riverfield La CM21 . . . . . . .97 E3
Riverford Cl AL5 . . . . .86 B4
Rivermill CM20 . . . . .117 C2
Rivermill Cl SG8 . . . . .7 C7
Rivers Hospl The CM21 . . . .97 C1
Riversend Rd HP3 . . . . . . .138 C8
Rivershill SG14 . . . . .70 E3
Riverside
  Bishop's Stortford CM23 . . .76 F7
  Buntingford SG9 . . . . .40 E7
  London Colney AL2 . . . . .142 E4
  Welwyn AL6 . . . . .89 B5
Riverside Ave EN10 . . . . . .135 A1
Riverside Cl
  Kings Langley WD4 . . . . .139 B2
  St Albans AL1 . . . . .127 E1
Riverside Cotts SG12 . . . .115 C4
Riverside Ct Harlow CM20 .118 C6
  St Albans AL1 . . . . .127 E1
Riverside Dr WD3 . . . . . . .165 D1
Riverside Est AL5 . . . . .86 C4
Riverside Gdns HP4 . . . . . .122 A5
Riverside Mews
  Hoddesdon EN10 . . . . . . .148 E8
  10 Ware SG12 . . . . .93 D1
Riverside Path EN8 . . . . . .148 C2
Riverside Rd Luton LU3 . . .45 A5
  St Albans AL1 . . . . .127 E2
  Watford WD1 . . . . .167 B3
Riverside Wlk **16** CM23 . . .76 F7
Rivermead EN11 . . . . .135 A5
Riversmead SG14 . . . . . . .113 B5
Rivett Cl SG7 . . . . .13 A1
Roan Wlk SG8 . . . . .7 E6
Roaring Meg Ret & L Pk
  SG1 . . . . .50 E3
Robbery Bottom La AL6 . . .90 A8
Robbs Cl HP1 . . . . .124 A5
Robe End HP1 . . . . .123 F5
Robert Allen Ct **11** LU1 . . .63 E6
Robert Ave AL1 . . . . .141 C7
Robert Cl EN6 . . . . .158 E6
Robert Humbert Ho SG6 . .23 A5
Robert Saunders Ct SG6 . .22 E4
Robert Tebbutt Ct SG5 . . .34 E6

Robert Wallace Cl CM23 . . .58 F1
Roberts Cl EN8 . . . . .148 E1
Roberts La SL9 . . . . .172 B5
Roberts Rd WD1 . . . . .167 C4
Roberts Way AL10 . . . . . . .129 F3
Roberts Wood Dr SL9 . . . .172 A5
Robertson Cl EN10 . . . . . .148 E5
Robeson Way WD6 . . . . . .170 C8
Robin Cl SG12 . . . . .115 C3
Robin Cl AL5 . . . . .86 B4
Robin Hill HP4 . . . . .122 C3
Robin Hood Dr
  Bushey WD2 . . . . .167 F8
  Harrow HA3 . . . . .176 F3
Robin Hood La AL10 . . . . .130 A6
Robin Hood Mdw HP2 . . . .124 F8
Robin Mead AL7 . . . . .90 A1
Robin Way EN6 . . . . .146 E3
Robina Cl HA6 . . . . .174 F2
Robins Cl AL2 . . . . .142 E4
Robins Nest Hill SG13 . . . .132 C6
Robins Rd HP3 . . . . .125 A1
Robins Way AL10 . . . . .129 F2
Robinsfield HP1 . . . . .124 A3
Robinson Ave EN7 . . . . . . .147 B3
Robinson Cl CM23 . . . . . . .76 F5
Robinson Cres WD2 . . . . . .168 C1
Robinsway EN9 . . . . .163 E5
Robinswood LU2 . . . . .45 E5
Robsons Cl EN8 . . . . .148 C2
Rochdale Ct **6** LU1 . . . . . .63 E6
Rochester Ave LU2 . . . . . . .46 C4
Rochester Dr WD2 . . . . . . .154 C4
Rochester Way
  Croxley Green WD3 . . . . .166 B5
  Royston SG8 . . . . .7 D8
Rochford Ave EN9 . . . . . . .163 D5
Rochford Cl
  Cheshunt EN10 . . . . .148 E5
  Stansted Mountfitchet CM24 .59 E5
Rochford Dr LU2 . . . . .46 E2
Rochford Ho EN9 . . . . .163 D6
Rochford Rd CM23 . . . . . . .59 C1
Rock Rd SG8 . . . . .7 C8
Rockfield Ave LU2 . . . . .93 D3
Rockingham Gate WD2 . . .168 C3
Rockingham Way SG1 . . . . .50 E4
Rockleigh SG14 . . . . .113 C6
Rockley Rd LU1 . . . . .63 A7
Rockliffe Ave WD4 . . . . . . .139 A1
Rockways EN5 . . . . .170 F3
Rodeheath LU4 . . . . .44 D3
Roden Cl CM17 . . . . .118 F4
Rodgers Cl WD6 . . . . .169 D3
Rodings The EN5 . . . . .171 E5
Rodney Ave AL1 . . . . .128 A1
Rodney Cres EN11 . . . . . . .135 A8
Roe Cl SG5 . . . . .11 E5
Roe End La AL3 . . . . .83 B4
Roe Green Cl AL10 . . . . . .129 F4
Roe Green Ctr AL10 . . . . .129 F4
Roe Green La AL10 . . . . . .129 F5
Roe Hill AL10 . . . . .129 F4
Roebuck Cl Hertford SG13 .114 A6
  Luton LU1 . . . . .63 B6
Roebuck Ct **1** SG2 . . . . . .50 F1
Roebuck Gate SG2 . . . . . . .50 F1
Roebuck Jun & Inf Schs
  SG2 . . . . .50 F2
Roebuck Ret Pk SG1 . . . . . .50 E2
Roecroft Lower Sch SG5 . .11 F6
Roedean Ave EN3 . . . . . . .162 C4
Roedean Cl LU2 . . . . .46 D3
Roedean Ho **3** WD1 . . . . .167 C7
Roefields Cl HP3 . . . . .138 A7
Roehyde Way AL10 . . . . . .129 E4
Roestock Gdns AL4 . . . . . .129 E1
Roestock La AL4 . . . . .129 E1
Rofant Rd HA6 . . . . .174 E4
Rogate Rd LU2 . . . . .46 C5
Roger de Clare CE Fst Sch
  SG11 . . . . .55 E2
Rogers Ruff HA6 . . . . .174 C2
Rokewood Mews **3** SG12 .93 D2
Roland St AL1 . . . . .128 B2
Rolleston Cl SG12 . . . . .93 C3
Rollswood AL7 . . . . .110 E3
Rollswood Rd AL6 . . . . . . .89 B8
Rollys SG7 . . . . .4 D4
Roman Gdns
  Kings Langley WD4 . . . . .139 B1
  Letchworth SG6 . . . . .22 E6
Roman La SG7 . . . . .24 A8
Roman Mews **7** EN11 . . . .135 A7
Roman La LU4 . . . . .44 E3
Roman Rise SG9 . . . . .97 D2
Roman St **8** EN11 . . . . . .135 A7
Roman Vale CM21 . . . . . . .117 D3
Roman Way Markyate AL3 . .83 E6
  Standon SG11 . . . . .55 D3
  Welwyn AL6 . . . . .89 C6
Roman Way Fst Sch SG8 . . .7 C8
Romans End AL3 . . . . .127 C1
Romany Cl SG6 . . . . .22 C6
Romany Ct HP2 . . . . .124 E6
Romeland Elstree WD6 . . .169 D3
  St Albans AL3 . . . . .127 C3
  Waltham Abbey EN9 . . . .163 C6
Romeland Hill AL3 . . . . . .127 C3
Romilly Dr WD1 . . . . .175 F6
Rondini Ave LU3 . . . . .45 B3
Rook Tree Cl SG5 . . . . .12 A6
Rook Tree La SG5 . . . . .12 A6
Rookery Ct CM20 . . . . . . .117 B2
Rookery The Hatfield AL9 .144 D8
  Stansted Mountfitchet CM24 .59 E8
Rookery Yd SG1 . . . . .50 C7

Rookes Cl SG6 . . . . .23 B3
Rooks Cl AL8 . . . . .110 D5
Rooks Hill
  Rickmansworth WD3 . . . .165 D5
  Welwyn Garden City AL8 .110 C5
Rooks Nest La SG8 . . . . . . .16 A5
Rookwood Dr SG2 . . . . . . .51 B1
Rosary Ct EN6 . . . . .145 B1
Rosary Gdns WD2 . . . . . . .168 E2
Rose Acre AL3 . . . . .105 F6
Rose Cl AL10 . . . . .130 A8
Rose Cotts Arlesey SG15 . . .11 A6
  Meesden SG9 . . . . .30 A5
  Wyddial SG9 . . . . .28 A3
Rose Ct
  Hammond Street EN7 . . . .148 A4
  St Albans AL4 . . . . .128 C5
Rose Gdns WD1 . . . . .167 A4
Rose La Essendon AL9 . . . .131 C5
  Wheathampstead AL4 . . . .87 C2
Rose Lawn WD2 . . . . .168 C1
Rose Mdw SG11 . . . . .41 E4
Rose Mead EN6 . . . . .145 C1
Rose Vale EN11 . . . . .135 A6
Rose Wlk Royston SG8 . . . . .7 C5
  St Albans AL4 . . . . .128 C5
Rose Wlk The WD7 . . . . . .156 B3
Rose Wood Cl LU2 . . . . . . .45 F3
Roseacre Gdns AL7 . . . . . .111 D6
Roseacres CM21 . . . . .97 D3
Rosebank EN9 . . . . .163 E6
Roseberry Ct WD1 . . . . . . .167 A8
Rosebery CM23 . . . . .77 C6
Rosebery Ave AL5 . . . . . . .85 F1
Rosebery Mews LU7 . . . . . .61 D4
Rosebery Rd WD2 . . . . . . .168 B2
Rosebery Way HP23 . . . . .100 B5
Rosebriar Wlk WD2 . . . . . .153 F3
Rosecroft Ct HA6 . . . . . . .174 C4
Rosecroft Dr WD1 . . . . . . .153 E3
Rosecroft La AL6 . . . . .90 A8
Rosedale AL7 . . . . .89 F2
Rosedale Ave EN7 . . . . . . .147 F2
Rosedale Cl
  Bricket Wood AL2 . . . . . .140 E1
  Luton LU3 . . . . .44 C7
Rosedale Way EN7 . . . . . . .148 A3
Roseheath HP1 . . . . .123 E4
Rosehill HP4 . . . . .122 B4
Rosehill Cl EN11 . . . . .134 F6
Rosehill Ct HP1 . . . . .124 A1
Rosehill Gdns WD3 . . . . . .153 C7
Rosehill Hospl SG6 . . . . . . .22 D2
Roselands Prim Sch
  EN11 . . . . .114 F1
Roseley Cotts CM20 . . . . .117 B4
Rosemary Ct CM17 . . . . . .118 C4
Rosemont Cl SG6 . . . . .22 E6
Rosewood Ct HP1 . . . . . . .123 E4
Rosewood Dr EN2 . . . . . . .161 A4
Roslyn Cl EN10 . . . . .134 F2
Ross Cl Luton LU1 . . . . . . .63 B6
  Stanmore HA3 . . . . .176 C3
Ross Cres WD2 . . . . .154 A4
Ross Ct SG2 . . . . .51 B7
Ross Haven Pl HA6 . . . . . .174 F6
Ross Way HA6 . . . . .174 F6
Rossfold Rd LU3 . . . . .44 D8
Rossgate HP1 . . . . .124 A5
Rossgate Prim Sch HP1 . .124 A5
Rossington Ave WD6 . . . . .156 E1
Rossington Cl EN1 . . . . . . .162 B1
Rossiter Fields EN5 . . . . . .171 F3
Rosslyn Cres LU3 . . . . .45 C5
Rosslyn Rd WD1 . . . . .167 B6
Rossway LU1 . . . . .63 B1
Rossway Dr WD2 . . . . . . .168 D4
Rossway La HP4 . . . . .121 A7
Roswell Cl EN8 . . . . .148 E1
Rothamsted Ave AL5 . . . . .86 A1
Rothamsted Ct AL5 . . . . . .86 A1
Rothamsted
  Experimental Sta AL5 . .107 A8
Rother Cl WD2 . . . . .154 C4
Rother Field LU2 . . . . .46 D3
Rotheram Ave LU1 . . . . . . .63 B5
Rotherfield Rd EN3 . . . . . .162 D2
Rothesay Cl HP4 . . . . .122 A4
Rothesay Rd LU1 . . . . .63 D7
Roughdown Ave HP3 . . . . .138 A8
Roughdown Rd HP3 . . . . . .138 A8
Roughdown Villas
  Rd HP3 . . . . .138 A8
Roughs The HA6 . . . . .174 E7
Roughwood Cl WD1 . . . . . .153 E1
Round Diamond Prim Sch
  SG1 . . . . .51 B8
Roundabout Ho HA6 . . . . .175 A2
Roundabout La AL6 . . . . . .89 F8
Roundcroft EN7 . . . . .147 D5
Roundfield Ave AL5 . . . . . .86 D3
Roundhaye SG13 . . . . .55 D3
Roundhedge Way EN2 . . . .160 F1
Roundhills EN9 . . . . .163 E4
Roundings The SG13 . . . . .114 C2
Roundmoor Dr EN8 . . . . . .148 E2
Roundway The WD1 . . . . .166 F2
Roundwood HP3 . . . . .138 C4
Roundwood Cl
  Hitchin SG4 . . . . .22 C6
  Oaklands AL6 . . . . .89 D8
Roundwood Dr AL8 . . . . . .110 C2
Roundwood Gdns AL5 . . . . .85 E2
Roundwood La AL5 . . . . . .85 D3
Roundwood Park
  Sch AL5 . . . . .85 E2
Roundwood Pk AL5 . . . . . .85 E3

Roundwood Prim Sch
  AL5 . . . . .85 E2
Rounton Rd EN9 . . . . .163 E6
Rousebarn La WD3 . . . . . .166 C7
Rowan Cl
  Bricket Wood AL2 . . . . . .155 A8
  Harrow HA7 . . . . .176 F4
  Luton LU1 . . . . .63 B7
  Shenley WD7 . . . . .156 E6
  St Albans AL4 . . . . .128 E3
  Weston SG4 . . . . .37 B8
Rowan Cres
  Letchworth SG6 . . . . .22 E7
  Stevenage SG1 . . . . .50 E7
Rowan Dr EN10 . . . . .148 F6
Rowan Gr SG4 . . . . .35 A4
Rowan Way AL5 . . . . .107 C8
Rowan Wlk **2** AL10 . . . . .130 A2
Rowans AL7 . . . . .90 A1
Rowans Prim Sch The
  AL7 . . . . .90 A1
Rowans The Baldock SG7 . .23 E7
  Hemel Hempstead HP1 . . .124 A3
  Hoddesdon EN10 . . . . . . .134 F4
Rowcroft HP1 . . . . .123 E2
Rowelfield LU2 . . . . .46 C1
Rowington Cl LU2 . . . . .46 C2
Rowland Pl HA6 . . . . .174 E3
Rowland Rd SG1 . . . . .50 F4
Rowland Way SG6 . . . . . . .22 F6
Rowlands Ave HA5 . . . . . .176 B4
Rowlands Cl EN8 . . . . .148 D1
Rowlands Ct **3** EN8 . . . . .148 D1
Rowlatt Cl AL1 . . . . .127 E4
Rowlatt Dr AL3 . . . . .127 A1
Rowley Cl WD1 . . . . .167 E3
Rowley Gdns EN8 . . . . . . .148 D3
Rowley Green Rd EN5 . . . .171 A4
Rowley La Barnet EN5 . . . .170 F5
  Borehamwood WD6 . . . . .170 D7
Rowley Wlk HP2 . . . . .125 C8
Rowley's Rd SG13 . . . . . . .113 F7
Rowney Gdns CM21 . . . . .118 C8
Rowney La SG12 . . . . .72 B5
Rowney Wood CM21 . . . . .97 C1
Rows The CM20 . . . . .117 C1
Roxley Cotts SG6 . . . . .23 B2
Roy Rd HA6 . . . . .174 F3
Royal Ave EN8 . . . . .162 E6
Royal Ct HP3 . . . . .138 E8
Royal Masonic Sch WD3 . .165 D4
Royal National
  Orthopaedic Hospl HA7 .169 B1
Royal Oak Cl SG9 . . . . .27 D5
Royal Oak Gdns **6** CM23 . .76 F6
Royal Oak La SG5 . . . . .20 D4
Royal Rd AL1 . . . . .128 B3
Royal Veterinary Coll
  AL9 . . . . .144 D3
Royce Cl EN10 . . . . .134 F2
Roydon Cl LU4 . . . . .44 A4
Roydon Ct HP2 . . . . .105 A1
Roydon Lodge Chalet
  Est CM19 . . . . .116 C1
Roydon Mill CM19 . . . . . .116 E1
Roydon Rd Harlow CM19 . .116 E1
  Stanstead Abbotts SG12 . .115 F4
Roydon Sta CM19 . . . . . . .116 B2
Royse Gr SG8 . . . . .7 D4
Roysia Mid Sch SG8 . . . . . .7 D8
Royston Cl SG14 . . . . .113 B6
Royston & District Mus
  SG8 . . . . .7 C6
Royston Gr HA5 . . . . .176 A4
Royston Hospl SG8 . . . . . . .7 D4
Royston Park Rd HA5 . . . .176 A5
Royston Rd Baldock SG7 . .23 D2
  Barkway SG8 . . . . .17 C5
  Barley SG8 . . . . .8 F3
  St Albans AL1 . . . . .128 B2
Royston Sta SG8 . . . . .7 C7
Rucklers La WD4 . . . . .138 C4
Ruckles Cl SG1 . . . . .50 E5
Rudd Cl SG2 . . . . .51 B3
Rudham Gr SG6 . . . . .23 C3
Rudolf Steiner Sch WD4 . .138 E2
Rudolph Rd WD2 . . . . .168 A3
Rudyard Cl LU4 . . . . .44 D3
Rue de St Lawrence
  EN9 . . . . .163 C5
Rueley Dell Rd LU2 . . . . . .32 C2
Rufford Cl WD1 . . . . .153 F2
Rugby Way WD3 . . . . .166 B4
Ruins The AL3 . . . . .106 B5
Rumballs Cl HP3 . . . . .139 A8
Rumballs Rd HP3 . . . . .139 A8
Rumbold Rd EN11 . . . . . . .135 C8
Rumsley EN7 . . . . .148 A4
Runcie Cl AL4 . . . . .128 C4
Runcorn Cres HP2 . . . . . . .124 F7
Rundells SG6 . . . . .23 B4
Runfold Ave LU3 . . . . .45 A5
Runham Cl LU4 . . . . .44 A4
Runham Rd HP3 . . . . .124 E1
Runley Rd LU1 . . . . .62 F2
Runnalow SG6 . . . . .22 E7
Runsley AL7 . . . . .90 A1
Rural Bygones Mus LU7 . . .80 D4
Ruscombe Dr AL2 . . . . . . .141 C5
Rush Cl SG12 . . . . .115 C4
Rushall Gn LU2 . . . . .46 C2
Rushby Mead SG6 . . . . . . .23 A5
Rushby Pl SG6 . . . . .23 A5
Rushby Wlk SG6 . . . . .23 A6
Rushden Rd SG9 . . . . .26 A8

Rushen Dr SG13 . . . .**114** C3
Rushendon Furlong LU7 . .**80** E5
Rushes Ct CM23 . . . .**77** A5
Rushfield Potters Bar EN6 .**158** E6
Sawbridgeworth CM21 . . . . .**97** E2
Rushfield Rd SG12 . . . .**93** F3
Rushleigh Ave EN8 . . . .**148** D1
Rushleigh Gn CM23 . . . .**76** D4
Rushmere La HP5 . . . .**136** B3
Rushmoor Cl WD3 . . . .**173** D8
Rushmore Cl LU1 . . . .**62** E4
Rushton Ave WD2 . . . .**154** A4
Rushton Ct EN8 . . . .**148** D2
Ruskin Ave EN9 . . . .**163** E5
Ruskin Cl EN7 . . . .**147** E5
Ruskin La SG4 . . . .**35** C7
Rusper Gn LU2 . . . .**46** D3
Russell Ave AL3 . . . .**127** D3
Russell Cl
  Kensworth Common LU6 . . .**82** E8
  Moor Park HA6 . . . .**174** C5
  Stevenage SG2 . . . .**51** B2
Russell Cres WD2 . . . .**153** F4
Russell Ct AL2 . . . .**141** A1
Russell La WD1 . . . .**153** D3
Russell Pl HP3 . . . .**138** B8
Russell Rd Enfield EN1 . . . .**161** F1
  Moor Park HA6 . . . .**174** C6
Russell Rise LU1 . . . .**63** D6
Russell Sch The WD3 . . . . .**164** B5
Russell St Hertford SG14 . .**113** C6
  Luton LU1 . . . .**63** D6
Russell Way WD1 . . . .**167** B2
Russell's Ride EN8 . . . .**162** E8
Russellcroft Rd AL8 . . . . . .**110** C7
Russet Ct EN7 . . . .**147** E5
Russet Dr Shenley WD7 . . .**156** E7
  St Albans AL4 . . . .**128** C2
Russett Ho AL7 . . . .**111** D6
Russett Wood AL7 . . . .**111** D5
Rutherford Cl
  Borehamwood WD6 . . . . . .**170** C7
  Stevenage SG1 . . . .**50** B6
Rutherford Way WD2 . . . .**168** E1
Ruthin Cl LU1 . . . .**63** D5
Ruthven Ave EN8 . . . .**162** D6
Rutland Cres LU2 . . . .**64** A7
Rutland Ct LU2 . . . .**64** A7
Rutland Hall LU2 . . . .**64** A7
Rutland Pl WD2 . . . .**168** D1
Rutts The WD2 . . . .**168** D1
Ryall Cl AL2 . . . .**140** E2
Ryan Way WD2 . . . .**167** C8
Ryans Ct LU2 . . . .**45** F1
Rydal Ct WD2 . . . .**154** B7
Rydal Mount EN6 . . . .**158** E6
Rydal Way LU3 . . . .**44** F5
Ryde Sch The AL9 . . . .**130** C8
Ryde The AL9 . . . .**130** C8
Ryder Ave SG5 . . . .**21** D3
Ryder Cl Bovingdon HP3 . . .**137** A4
  Bushey WD2 . . . .**168** B3
  Hertford SG13 . . . .**114** B7
Ryder Seed Mews AL1 . . . .**127** D2
Ryder Way SG5 . . . .**21** D3
Ryders Ave AL4 . . . .**129** E3
Rye Cl AL5 . . . .**86** B4
Rye Gdns SG7 . . . .**13** B1
Rye Hill Harpenden AL5 . . . .**86** B4
  2 Luton LU2 . . . .**45** D1
Rye House Gatehouse
  EN11 . . . .**135** D8
Rye House Sta EN11 . . . . .**135** C8
Rye Mead Cotts EN11 . . . .**135** C8
Rye Rd EN11 . . . .**135** C8
Rye St CM23 . . . .**58** F1
Ryecroft Hatfield AL10 . . . .**129** F3
  Stevenage SG1 . . . .**50** E7
Ryecroft Cl HP2 . . . .**125** C2
Ryecroft Cres EN5 . . . .**171** B4
Ryecroft Ct AL4 . . . .**128** F3
Ryecroft Way LU2 . . . .**46** A4
Ryefeld Cl EN11 . . . .**115** B2
Ryefield LU3 . . . .**31** A1
Ryefield Cres HA6 . . . .**175** A1
Ryelands AL7 . . . .**110** F3
Ryelands Prim Sch EN11 .**135** B7
Rylands Heath LU2 . . . .**46** F2
Ryley Cl SG16 . . . .**10** B5
Ryman Ct WD3 . . . .**164** C3
Rymill Ct HP3 . . . .**137** A3
Ryton Cl LU1 . . . .**63** B6

S

Saberton Cl AL3 . . . .**105** F4
Sabine Ho WD5 . . . .**153** F7
Sacombe Gn LU3 . . . .**31** B1
Sacombe Green Rd SG12 . .**71** E4
Sacombe Pound SG12 . . . . .**71** E3
Sacombe Rd
  Hemel Hempstead HP1 . . . .**123** F5
  Hertford SG14 . . . .**92** C1
  Stapleford SG14 . . . .**92** B4
Sacombs Ash La SG10 . . . . .**96** E7
Sacred Heart High Sch
  HA3 . . . .**176** E1
Sacred Heart Inf Sch
  LU2 . . . .**46** A3
Sacred Heart Jun Sch
  Luton LU2 . . . .**46** A3
  St Albans AL3 . . . .**127** B1
Sacred Heart
  RC Prim Sch SG12 . . . .**93** D1

Sacred Heart
  RC Prim Sch The WD2 . . .**167** F3
Saddlers Cl Baldock SG7 . .**23** E8
  Barnet EN5 . . . .**171** B4
  Bishop's Stortford CM23 . . .**76** C4
  Borehamwood WD6 . . . . . .**170** D3
  Pinner HA5 . . . .**176** A4
Saddlers Path WD6 . . . . . .**170** D4
Saddlers Pl SG8 . . . .**7** C7
Saddlers Wlk WD4 . . . .**139** A2
Sadleir Rd AL1 . . . .**127** E1
Sadler Cl EN7 . . . .**147** C6
Sadlers Way SG14 . . . .**113** A6
Saffron Cl Arlesey SG15 . . .**11** A7
  Hoddesdon EN11 . . . .**134** F7
  Luton LU2 . . . .**45** D7
Saffron Green Fst Sch
  WD6 . . . .**170** C5
Saffron Hill SG6 . . . .**22** E6
Saffron La HP1 . . . .**124** B4
Saffron Mdw SG11 . . . .**55** E2
Saffron St SG8 . . . .**7** F5
Sainfoin End HP2 . . . .**125** A5
St Adrian's
  RC Prim Sch AL1 . . . .**141** C8
St Agnell's Farm Mews
  HP2 . . . .**105** A1
St Agnells Ct HP2 . . . .**125** A7
St Agnells La HP2 . . . .**125** A8
St Alban & St Stephen
  RC Inf Sch AL1 . . . .**127** F2
St Alban & St Stephen
  RC Jun Sch AL1 . . . .**128** A3
St Alban's Cath AL3 . . . . .**127** D3
St Albans City Hospl
  AL3 . . . .**127** C5
St Albans City Sta AL1 . . .**127** F3
St Albans Dr SG1 . . . .**36** E1
St Albans Girls' Sch
  AL3 . . . .**127** E7
St Albans High Sch for
  Girls AL1 . . . .**127** E4
St Albans Hill HP3 . . . .**124** F1
St Albans La WD5 . . . .**140** A5
St Albans Link SG1 . . . .**36** E1
St Albans Music Sch
  AL3 . . . .**127** D4
St Albans
  RC Prim Sch CM20 . . . . . .**117** F2
St Albans Rd Barnet EN5 . .**171** E7
  Codicote SG4 . . . .**88** F7
  Harpenden AL5 . . . .**107** B6
  Hemel
  Hempstead HP2,HP3 . . . . .**124** E2
  Potters Bar EN5 . . . .**158** C3
  Redbourn AL3 . . . .**106** C3
  Ridge EN6 . . . .**157** F8
St Albans Rd
  Sandridge AL4 . . . .**108** B1
  St Albans AL4 . . . .**128** A8
  Watford WD1,WD2 . . . . . .**154** B2
St Albans Rd E AL10 . . . . .**130** B6
St Albans Rd W AL4 . . . . .**129** D5
St Albans Sch AL3 . . . .**127** C3
St Albert the Great
  RC Prim Sch HP3 . . . .**125** A2
St Aldates Ct AL3 . . . .**45** B3
St Andrew St SG14 . . . . . .**113** C6
St Andrew's Ave AL5 . . . . .**85** F1
St Andrew's CE Prim Sch
  Hertford SG14 . . . .**112** F7
  Hitchin SG4 . . . .**35** A7
St Andrew's Cl LU1 . . . .**63** B1
St Andrew's Ho CM20 . . . .**117** F2
St Andrew's Pl **2** SG4 . . . .**34** F6
St Andrew's Rd HP3 . . . . .**138** D7
St Andrews CE Prim Sch
  Much Hadham SG10 . . . . . .**74** F2
  Stanstead Abbotts SG12 . .**115** D4
St Andrews Dr SG1 . . . .**36** F2
St Andrews Mews
  1 Hertford SG14 . . . .**113** C6
  Luton LU3 . . . .**45** A4
St Andrews Rd WD1 . . . . .**175** D7
St Andrews Terr WD1 . . . .**175** C5
St Andrews Wlk LU1 . . . . . .**63** C1
St Ann's Rd LU1 . . . .**63** F7
St Anna Rd EN5 . . . .**171** D4
St Anne's Cl EN7 . . . .**148** A3
St Anne's Ct **7** SG5 . . . .**34** F8
St Anne's Pk EN10 . . . .**135** A4
St Anne's Rd Hitchin SG5 . .**34** F8
  London Colney AL2 . . . . . .**142** D4
St Annes Cl WD1 . . . .**175** C6
St Anthonys Ave HP3 . . . .**125** B1
St Anthonys RC Prim Sch
  WD1 . . . .**166** B4
St Audreys Cl AL10 . . . . . .**130** B2
St Audreys Gn AL7 . . . . . .**110** F5
St Augusta Ct AL3 . . . .**127** D5
St Augustine Ave LU3 . . . . .**45** C3
St Augustine Cl **1** SG5 . . .**34** F8
St Augustine's
  RC Prim Sch LU1 . . . .**135** B6
St Augustines Cl EN10 . . . .**134** F3
St Augustines Dr EN10 . . . .**134** F3
St Barnabas Ct
  Harrow HA3 . . . .**176** C2
  Hemel Hempstead HP2 . . .**125** A3
St Bartholomew's
  CE Prim Sch HP23 . . . . . .**100** D1
St Barts Cl AL4 . . . .**128** D2
St Bernadette's
  RC Prim Sch AL2 . . . .**142** D4
St Bernard's Cl LU3 . . . .**45** C3
St Bernard's Rd AL3 . . . . .**127** E4
St Brelades Pl AL4 . . . .**128** D7

St Catharine's Rd EN10 . .**135** A4
St Catherine of Siena
  RC Jun Mix Inf Sch
  WD2 . . . .**154** D6
St Catherine's CE Prim Sch
  SG12 . . . .**93** B2
St Catherines Ave LU3 . . . .**45** B3
St Catherines Ct CM23 . . . .**76** E7
St Christopher Sch SG6 . . .**22** F3
St Clement Danes Sch
  WD3 . . . .**164** D7
St Clement's CE Jun Sch
  EN8 . . . .**148** E4
St Clements Ct EN9 . . . . . .**163** C6
St Columba's Coll AL3 . . . .**127** C1
St Cross Ct EN11 . . . .**135** A4
St Cross RC Prim Sch
  EN11 . . . .**135** A4
St Cuthbert Mayne
  RC Jun Sch HP1 . . . .**124** B4
St Cuthberts Gdns **1**
  HA5 . . . .**175** F3
St Cuthberts Rd EN11 . . . .**115** C1
St David's St HP2 . . . .**125** D2
St David's Dr EN10 . . . . . .**134** F4
St Davids Cl SG1 . . . .**36** F2
St Dominic RC Prim Sch
  AL5 . . . .**107** B8
St Dunstan's Rd SG12 . . . .**116** D8
St Edmund's Coll SG11 . . . .**73** A8
St Edmund's Way CM17 . .**118** C4
St Edmunds HP4 . . . .**122** C3
St Edmunds Wlk AL4 . . . . .**128** D2
St Edward's Coll N20 . . . . .**171** B1
St Elizabeth's Sch &
  Home SG13 . . . .**96** C6
St Elmo Ct SG4 . . . .**34** F5
St Ethelbert Ave LU3 . . . . .**45** C4
St Etheldreda's Dr AL10 . .**130** C5
St Evroul Ct **5** SG12 . . . . . .**93** D2
St Faiths Cl SG8 . . . .**22** B1
St Francis Cl
  Buntingford SG9 . . . .**40** F6
  Potters Bar EN6 . . . .**159** C5
  Watford WD1 . . . .**167** B1
St Francis' Coll SG6 . . . . . .**22** E4
St Francis de Sales
  Ind Prim Sch HP23 . . . . . .**99** F3
St George's CE Inf Sch
  EN3 . . . .**162** D3
St George's Dr WD1 . . . . .**175** E6
St George's Rd
  Enfield EN1 . . . .**161** F1
  Hemel Hempstead HP3 . . .**138** C7
  Watford WD2 . . . .**154** B1
St George's Sch AL5 . . . . . .**86** B2
St George's Way SG1 . . . . .**50** D5
St Giles' Ave EN6 . . . .**158** B7
St Giles'
  CE Prim Sch EN6 . . . .**158** A7
St Giles Rd SG4 . . . .**67** F2
St Helen's
  CE Prim Sch AL4 . . . .**108** D8
St Helen's Cl AL4 . . . .**108** D8
St Helen's Sch HA6 . . . . . .**174** E4
St Heliers Rd AL4 . . . .**128** B8
St Hilda's Sch
  Bushey WD2 . . . .**168** B2
  Harpenden AL5 . . . .**85** F2
St Ignatius Coll EN1 . . . . . .**162** B2
St Ippolyts
  CE Prim Sch SG4 . . . .**35** B3
St Ives Ct Luton LU3 . . . . . .**45** B3
  Welwyn AL6 . . . .**89** F3
St James Ctr CM20 . . . . . .**118** A4
St James Rd AL5 . . . .**86** B4
St James' Rd LU3 . . . .**45** B3
St James Rd WD1 . . . .**167** B4
St James Way CM23 . . . . . .**76** C3
St James's Ct AL5 . . . .**86** B3
St James's Rd EN7 . . . .**147** D3
St Joan of Arc
  RC Sch WD3 . . . .**165** E2
St John Cl LU1 . . . .**63** B5
St John Fisher RC
  Jun Mix Inf Sch AL4 . . . . .**128** C6
St John The Baptist
  CE Prim Sch SG12 . . . . . .**115** A5
St John's Ave CM17 . . . . . .**118** D4
St John's CE Prim Sch
  Hatfield AL8 . . . .**109** F5
  Welwyn Garden City AL6 . . .**89** F2
St John's Cl EN6 . . . .**159** C6
St John's Cres CM24 . . . . . .**59** E7
St John's Ct
  Harpenden AL5 . . . .**107** C7
  10 Hertford SG13 . . . .**113** D6
St John's La CM24 . . . .**59** E7
St John's Prim Sch EN2 .**161** B2
St John's
  RC Jun Mix Inf Sch SG7 . .**23** F7
St John's
  RC Prim Sch WD3 . . . . . .**165** B1
St John's Rd
  Arlesey SG15 . . . .**11** A4
  Harpenden AL5 . . . .**107** C7
  Hemel Hempstead HP1 . . .**124** B1
  Hitchin SG4 . . . .**35** A4
  Stansted Mountfitchet CM24 .**59** E7
  Watford WD1 . . . .**167** B7
St John's St SG13 . . . .**113** D6
St John's Terr EN2 . . . .**161** D2
St John's Well Ct HP4 . . . .**122** B5
St John's Well La HP4 . . . .**122** B5
St Johns SG11 . . . .**55** E3
St Johns CE Inf Sch
  WD7 . . . .**155** F4
St Johns Cl AL6 . . . .**89** C6

St Johns Ct Luton LU1 . . . . .**63** B5
  St Albans AL1 . . . .**128** B5
St Johns La SG12 . . . .**115** A6
St Johns Wlk CM17 . . . . . .**118** C4
St Joseph's Cl LU3 . . . .**45** A4
St Joseph's Inf Sch LU3 . . .**45** A4
St Joseph's Jun Sch LU3 . .**45** A4
St Joseph's RC
  Jun Mix Inf Sch CM23 . . . .**76** E6
St Joseph's RC Prim Sch
  Hertford SG14 . . . .**113** A7
  South Oxhey WD1 . . . .**175** C7
St Joseph's RC Sch EN8 .**162** E6
St Joseph's Sch SG14 . . . .**113** A4
St Joseph's Wlk AL5 . . . . .**107** A8
St Julian's Rd AL1 . . . .**127** D1
St Katharines Cl SG5 . . . . . .**21** D3
St Katherine's Way HP4 . .**121** F7
St Laurence Dr EN10 . . . . .**148** F8
St Lawrence
  CE Jun Sch EN9 . . . .**163** F6
St Lawrence Cl
  Abbots Langley HP3 . . . . .**139** E1
  Bovingdon HP3 . . . .**137** A4
St Lawrence Way AL2 . . . .**140** F1
St Lawrences Ave LU3 . . . . .**45** C3
St Leonard's Ct AL4 . . . . . .**108** C1
St Leonard's Rd SG14 . . . .**113** D8
St Leonards Cl
  Hertford SG14 . . . .**113** E8
  Watford WD2 . . . .**167** E5
St Leonards Cres AL4 . . . .**108** C1
St Leonards Rd EN9 . . . . . .**149** D6
St Luke's Ave EN2 . . . .**161** D1
St Luke's Cl LU3 . . . .**44** E2
St Luke's Sch AL3 . . . .**106** A6
St Magnus Ct HP4 . . . .**125** C1
St Margaret Clitheroe
  RC Prim Sch SG2 . . . .**50** F2
St Margaret of Scotland
  Inf Sch LU1 . . . .**63** B5
St Margaret of Scotland
  Jun Sch LU1 . . . .**63** B5
St Margaret's HP4 . . . .**122** C3
St Margaret's Rd SG12 . . .**115** B2
St Margaret's Sch WD2 . .**168** A2
St Margarets Ct LU2 . . . . . .**50** F2
St Margarets Cl LU3 . . . . . .**31** A6
St Margarets Sta SG12 . . .**115** C4
St Margarets Way HP2 . . .**125** D3
St Mark's Cl SG5 . . . .**21** D1
St Marks Cl AL4 . . . .**129** B1
St Martha's Jun Sch SG7 . .**171** E5
St Martin de Porres
  RC Inf Sch LU2 . . . .**44** A4
St Martin de Porres
  RC Jun Sch LU2 . . . .**44** A4
St Martin's Ave LU2 . . . . . .**45** F2
St Martin's Rd SG3 . . . .**69** A5
St Martin's Sch HA6 . . . . .**174** D5
St Martins Cl
  Harpenden AL5 . . . .**86** C4
  South Oxhey WD1 . . . .**175** C6
St Mary's Ave
  Berkhamsted UB2 . . . .**121** D6
  Moor Park HA6 . . . .**174** C6
  Stotfold SG5 . . . .**11** F6
St Mary's CE Fst Sch
  HP4 . . . .**121** E6
St Mary's CE High Sch
  EN7 . . . .**148** B1
St Mary's
  CE Jun Mix Inf Sch AL9 .**144** B8
St Mary's CE Jun Sch
  SG12 . . . .**93** D3
St Mary's
  CE Prim Sch CM24 . . . . . .**59** E7
St Mary's Cl
  Letchworth SG6 . . . .**22** F2
  Pirton SG5 . . . .**20** D4
  Redbourn AL3 . . . .**106** A4
St Mary's Ct
  4 Hemel Hempstead HP2 .**124** D4
  Potters Bar EN6 . . . .**159** B7
  Welwyn AL6 . . . .**89** C4
St Mary's Ctyd **3** SG12 . .**93** D1
St Mary's Dr CM24 . . . .**59** F5
St Mary's Inf Sch SG7 . . . .**23** E6
St Mary's Jun Mix Sch
  SG7 . . . .**23** E6
St Mary's La SG14 . . . .**112** F3
St Mary's Prim Sch AL6 . .**89** B4
St Mary's RC Prim Sch
  SG8 . . . .**7** D7
St Mary's RC Sch CM23 . . .**76** E7
St Mary's Rd
  Cheshunt EN8 . . . .**148** C2
  Hemel Hempstead HP2 . . .**124** D4
  Luton LU1 . . . .**63** F7
  Standon SG11 . . . .**55** D2
  Watford WD1 . . . .**167** B5
St Mary's Rise SG4 . . . .**47** D3
St Mary's (Stotfold)
  Lower Sch SG5 . . . .**12** A6
St Mary's Way SG7 . . . .**23** E6
St Marys SG2 . . . .**51** E2
St Marys Rd AL6 . . . .**89** C5
St Marys Wlk AL4 . . . .**128** B7
St Matthew's Inf Sch LU2 .**45** E1
St Matthews Cl Luton LU2 .**63** E8
  Watford WD1 . . . .**167** D3
St Meryl
  Jun Mix Inf Sch WD1 . . . .**175** E7
St Michael's CE Prim Sch
  Bishop's Stortford CM23 . . .**76** E7
  St Albans AL3 . . . .**127** B3

St Michael's Cres LU3 . . . . .**45** D3
St Michael's Ct AL3 . . . . . .**127** B3
St Michael's Mount SG4 . .**35** A8
St Michael's RC Sch
  WD2 . . . .**154** D3
St Michael's Rd EN10 . . . .**135** A3
St Michael's St AL3 . . . . . .**127** B3
St Michaels Ave HP3 . . . . .**125** B1
St Michaels Cl
  Harlow CM20 . . . .**117** E1
  Harpenden AL5 . . . .**107** D7
St Michaels Ct SG1 . . . .**51** B8
St Michaels Dr WD2 . . . . .**154** B6
St Michaels Rd SG4 . . . .**35** B7
St Michaels View AL10 . . .**130** B7
St Michaels Way EN6 . . . .**145** B1
St Mildreds Ave LU3 . . . . . .**45** C3
St Monicas Ave LU3 . . . . . .**45** B3
St Neots Cl WD6 . . . .**157** A1
St Nicholas Ave AL5 . . . . . .**86** A1
St Nicholas
  CE Jun Mix Inf Sch
  Harpenden AL5 . . . .**86** A1
  Letchworth SG6 . . . .**12** C1
St Nicholas CE Prim Sch
  SG2 . . . .**50** F4
St Nicholas Cl WD6 . . . . . .**169** D3
St Nicholas Cl AL5 . . . .**85** F3
St Nicholas Elstree
  CE Prim Sch WD6 . . . . . .**169** D3
St Nicholas House Sch
  HP3 . . . .**139** B6
St Nicholas Mount HP1 . .**123** F3
St Nicholas Sch CM17 . . . .**118** F3
St Ninian's Ct **7** LU2 . . . . . .**63** D8
St Olam's Cl LU3 . . . .**45** B6
St Olives SG5 . . . .**11** E6
St Pancras Ho SG8 . . . .**2** D1
St Paul's CE Inf Sch
  EN11 . . . .**135** B6
St Paul's CE Prim Sch
  WD4 . . . .**152** A8
St Paul's Gdns LU1 . . . .**63** E5
St Paul's Rd
  Hemel Hempstead HP2 . . .**124** E4
  Luton LU1 . . . .**63** E5
St Paul's Walden SG4 . . . . .**49** A1
St Paul's Walden Prim Sch
  SG4 . . . .**66** D2
St Pauls CE Prim Sch
  WD4 . . . .**153** C5
St Pauls Ct **3** SG2 . . . .**50** F1
St Pauls Pl AL1 . . . .**128** A3
St Pauls RC Prim Sch
  EN7 . . . .**148** B4
St Pauls Way
  Waltham Abbey EN9 . . . . .**163** D6
  Watford WD2 . . . .**167** C7
St Peter's Ave SG15 . . . . . .**11** A7
St Peter's Cl
  WD3 . . . .**165** B1
St Peter's Cl Barnet EN5 . .**171** B4
  Bushey WD2 . . . .**168** D1
  Rickmansworth WD3 . . . . .**165** B1
  St Albans AL1 . . . .**127** D4
St Peter's Rd AL1 . . . .**127** E4
St Peter's Sch AL1 . . . .**127** D4
St Peter's St AL1 . . . .**127** D4
St Peters Cl Hatfield AL10 .**130** A6
  London Colney AL2 . . . . . .**142** C5
St Peters Hill HP23 . . . . . .**100** A4
St Peters Rd LU1 . . . .**63** B7
St Peters Way WD3 . . . . . .**164** B5
St Philip Howard
  RC Prim Sch AL10 . . . . . .**130** B5
St Raphaels Ct AL1 . . . . . .**127** E4
St Ronans Cl EN4 . . . .**159** D1
St Rose's Inf Sch HP1 . . . .**124** A1
St Saviors View AL1 . . . . .**127** E4
St Saviour's Cres LU1 . . . . .**63** D6
St Stephen's Ave AL3 . . . . .**141** B8
St Stephen's Cl AL3 . . . . . .**141** B8
St Stephen's Hill AL1 . . . . .**127** C1
St Stephen's Rd EN3 . . . . .**162** D2
St Stephens Rd EN5 . . . . .**171** D4
St Teresa's
  Fst & Mid RC Sch HA3 . .**176** C2
St Teresa's
  RC Prim Sch WD6 . . . . . .**170** B7
St Thomas' Dr HA5 . . . . . .**175** E2
St Thomas More
  RC Jun Mix Inf Sch SG6 . .**22** C4
St Thomas More
  RC Prim Sch HP4 . . . .**122** A4
St Thomas of Canterbury
  RC Prim Sch SG11 . . . .**55** C3
St Thomas Pl AL4 . . . .**108** D8
St Thomas's Rd LU2 . . . . . .**46** A4
St Vincent de Paul
  RC Prim Sch SG1 . . . .**51** A6
St Vincent Dr AL1 . . . .**128** A1
St Vincent Gdns LU4 . . . . .**44** D3
St Vincent's Way EN6 . . . .**159** C6
St Winifreds Ave LU3 . . . . .**45** C3
Sale Dr SG7 . . . .**13** A1
Salisbury Ave
  Harpenden AL5 . . . .**86** A1
  St Albans AL1 . . . .**128** A4
Salisbury Cl
  Bishop's Stortford CM23 . . .**76** C4
  Potters Bar EN6 . . . .**159** C7
Salisbury Cres EN8 . . . . . .**162** D7
Salisbury Gdns AL7 . . . . . .**110** F5
Salisbury Ho AL1 . . . .**127** D4
Salisbury Inf Sch AL10 . . .**130** B7
Salisbury Rd Baldock SG7 . .**12** F1
  Barnet EN5 . . . .**171** E6

Salisbury Rd continued
Enfield EN3 . . . . .162 F2
Harpenden AL5 . . . . .86 D3
Hoddesdon EN11 . . . . . . .135 C8
Luton LU1 . . . . .63 D6
Stevenage SG1 . . . . .37 A2
Watford WD2 . . . . .154 C1
Welwyn Garden City AL7 . .111 A5
Salisbury Sq Hatfield AL9 .130 C6
7 Hertford SG14 . . . . . . .113 D6
Sally Deards La AL6 . . . . . .68 B3
Salmon Cl AL7 . . . . .90 A1
Salmons Cl SG12 . . . . .93 D4
Saltdean Cl LU2 . . . . .46 D4
Salter's Cl HP4 . . . . .121 F6
Salters CM23 . . . . .76 C4
Salters WD3 . . . . .165 E1
Salters Gdns WD1 . . . . . .167 A8
Saltfield Cres LU4 . . . . . . .44 C4
Salusbury La SG5 . . . . . . .33 C2
Salvatorian Coll HA3 . . . .176 E1
Salwey Cres EN10 . . . . . .134 F3
Samian Gate AL3 . . . . . . .126 F1
Sampson Ave EN5 . . . . . .171 D4
Samuel Lucas
 Jun Mix Inf Sch SG5 . . . .34 D7
Sancroft Rd HA3 . . . . . . .176 F1
Sanctuary Cl UB9 . . . . . . .173 C3
Sandalls Spring HP1 . . . . .123 F5
Sandalwood Cl LU3 . . . . . .45 B7
Sanday Cl HP3 . . . . .125 B1
Sandbrook La HP23 . . . . . .79 C1
Sandell Cl LU2 . . . . .45 F2
Sanderling Cl SG6 . . . . . . .22 E8
Sanders Cl
 Hemel Hempstead HP3 . . .138 F7
 London Colney AL2 . . . . . .142 D4
Sanders Rd HP3 . . . . .139 A7
Sandfield Rd AL1 . . . . . . .128 A3
Sandgate Rd LU4 . . . . .44 D2
Sandhurst Ct AL5 . . . . . . .107 D6
Sandifield AL10 . . . . .130 B2
Sandle Rd CM23 . . . . .77 A7
Sandmere Cl HP2 . . . . . . .125 A4
Sandon Cl HP23 . . . . .99 F4
Sandon Jun Mix Inf Sch
 SG9 . . . . .15 C1
Sandon Rd EN8 . . . . .148 C1
Sandover Cl SG4 . . . . .35 B6
Sandown Rd
 Stevenage SG1 . . . . .37 C1
 Watford WD2 . . . . .154 C1
Sandown Road Ind Est
 WD2 . . . . .154 C2
Sandpit Hill Cotts HP23 . .120 B3
Sandpit La AL1,AL4 . . . . . .128 C5
Sandpit Rd AL7 . . . . .110 E4
Sandridge Cl HP2 . . . . . . .105 A1
Sandridge Ct AL4 . . . . . . .128 D7
Sandridge Rd AL1 . . . . . . .127 F5
Sandridge Sch AL4 . . . . . .108 D1
Sandridgebury La
 Sandridge AL3,AL4 . . . . . .108 A2
 St Albans AL3 . . . . .127 E8
Sandringham Cres AL4 . . .128 C8
Sandringham Gdns **6**
 CM23 . . . . .76 E5
Sandringham Rd
 Potters Bar EN6 . . . . .145 B1
 Watford WD2 . . . . .154 C2
Sandringham Sch AL4 . . . .128 B7
Sandringham Way EN8 . . .162 D5
Sandy Cl SG5 . . . . .113 B6
Sandy Gr SG4 . . . . .34 F6
Sandy La Bushey WD2 . . . .168 C6
 Moor Park HA6 . . . . .175 A5
Sandy Lodge HA6 . . . . . . .174 E8
Sandy Lodge Ct HA6 . . . . .174 E5
Sandy Lodge La HA6 . . . . .174 E8
Sandy Lodge Rd WD3 . . . .174 C8
Sandy Lodge Way HA6 . . .174 E4
Sandycroft Rd HP6 . . . . . .150 C1
Sanfoin Rd LU4 . . . . .44 A4
Sanfoine Cl SG4 . . . . .35 C8
Santers La EN6 . . . . .158 E6
Santingfield N LU1 . . . . . . .63 B6
Santingfield S LU1 . . . . . . .63 B6
Sappers Cl CM21 . . . . .97 F2
Saracen Est HP2 . . . . .125 B5
Saracens Head HP2 . . . . .125 A4
Sark Ho Enfield EN3 . . . . .162 D1
 10 Watford WD1 . . . . . .166 F3
Sarratt Ave HP2 . . . . .125 A8
Sarratt Jun Mix Inf Sch
 WD3 . . . . .152 A3
Sarratt La
 Rickmansworth WD3 . . . . .165 C6
 Sarratt WD3 . . . . .165 D8
Sarratt Rd WD3 . . . . .165 C8
Sarum Pl HP2 . . . . .124 E7
Sarum Rd LU3 . . . . .44 F4
Satinwood Ct **1** HP3 . . . .124 E1
Saturn Way HP2 . . . . .124 F6
Saucey Ave AL5 . . . . .86 B3
Saucey Wood AL5 . . . . . . .86 E4
Saucey Wood La AL5 . . . . .86 E6
Saunders Cl
 Cheshunt EN8 . . . . .148 D4
 Letchworth SG6 . . . . .23 C7
Savanna Cl WD1 . . . . .166 F5
Savill Cl EN7 . . . . .147 C6
Savoy Cl UB9 . . . . .173 D1
Sawbridgeworth Rd
 Hatfield Heath CM22 . . . . . .98 E3
 Little Hallingbury CM22 . . . .98 B6
Sawbridgeworth Sta
 CM21 . . . . .98 A3
Sawells EN10 . . . . .134 F2

Sawtry Cl LU3 . . . . .45 A6
Sawtry Way WD6 . . . . . . .157 A1
Sawyers Cl SG6 . . . . .11 F8
Sawyers Way HP2 . . . . . . .124 F3
Sax Ho SG6 . . . . .11 E1
Saxon Ave SG5 . . . . .11 F8
Saxon Cl Harpenden AL5 . . .86 C4
 Letchworth SG6 . . . . .11 F1
Saxon Ct WD6 . . . . .169 E8
Saxon Ct Luton LU3 . . . . . .45 C2
 Welwyn AL6 . . . . .89 B3
 Wheathampstead AL4 . . . .108 C7
Saxon Way Baldock SG7 . . .13 B1
 Waltham Abbey EN9 . . . . .163 C6
Saxtead Cl LU4 . . . . .46 D1
Sayer Way SG3 . . . . .68 F4
Sayers Gdns HP4 . . . . . . .122 A6
Sayesbury Ave CM21 . . . . .97 E3
Sayesbury Rd CM21 . . . . . .97 E2
Saywell Rd LU2 . . . . .46 B1
Scammell Way WD1 . . . . .166 F3
Scarborough Ave SG1 . . . . .50 B7
Scatterdells La WD4 . . . . .138 A2
Scholar's Hill SG12 . . . . . . .95 A4
Scholars Ct AL4 . . . . .143 C8
Scholars Mews AL8 . . . . .110 D8
Scholars The WD1 . . . . . . .167 C4
Scholars Wlk **4** AL10 . . . .130 A2
School Cl Essendon AL9 . . .131 F6
 Stevenage SG2 . . . . .51 B3
School Gdns HP4 . . . . .123 B6
School La Ardeley SG2 . . . .38 D3
 Aston SG2 . . . . .51 E2
 Barley SG8 . . . . .9 A1
 Bricket Wood AL2 . . . . . . .155 A4
 Bushey WD2 . . . . .168 B2
 Essendon AL9 . . . . .131 F6
 Great Offley SG5 . . . . .33 C3
 Harlow CM20 . . . . .117 E2
 Hatfield AL10 . . . . .130 C6
 Luton LU4 . . . . .44 D4
 Preston SG4 . . . . .48 E5
 Tewin AL6 . . . . .90 E2
 Watton at Stone SG14 . . . . .70 E3
 Welwyn AL6 . . . . .89 B4
 Weston SG4 . . . . .24 C1
School Mead WD5 . . . . . .153 D7
School Rd EN6 . . . . .145 C1
School Row HP1 . . . . .123 F2
School Wlk SG6 . . . . .23 B6
Schoolfields SG6 . . . . .23 C5
Schubert Rd WD6 . . . . . . .169 D3
Scot Gr HA5 . . . . .175 D3
Scotfield Cl LU2 . . . . .46 D3
Scots Hill WD3 . . . . .165 F3
Scots Hill Cl WD3 . . . . . . .165 F3
Scotscraig WD7 . . . . .155 F4
Scott Ave SG12 . . . . .115 B4
Scott Cl SG8 . . . . .2 D1
Scott Rd
 Bishop's Stortford CM23 . . .76 E6
 Luton LU3 . . . . .44 C7
 Stevenage SG2 . . . . .51 B6
Scott's Grotto SG12 . . . . .114 D8
Scott's Rd SG12 . . . . .114 D8
Scotts Cl SG12 . . . . .114 D8
Scotts Mill La WD3 . . . . . .165 F3
Scotts View AL8 . . . . .110 C5
Scottswood Cl WD2 . . . . .167 E7
Scottswood Rd WD2 . . . . .167 E7
Scratchwood Nature
 Trail NW7 . . . . .170 D2
Scriveners Cl HP2 . . . . . . .124 E3
Scrubbits Sq WD7 . . . . . .156 A4
Scrubbits Park Rd WD7 . . .156 A4
Seabrook LU4 . . . . .44 B3
Seabrook Rd WD5 . . . . . . .139 D4
Seacroft Gdns WD1 . . . . .175 D7
Seaford Cl LU2 . . . . .46 C3
Seaforth Dr EN8 . . . . .162 A4
Seal Cl LU4 . . . . .44 D3
Seaman Cl AL2 . . . . .141 D4
Searches La WD5 . . . . . . .140 C4
Seaton Rd
 Hemel Hempstead HP3 . . .124 E1
 London Colney AL2 . . . . . .142 D5
 Luton LU4 . . . . .44 F3
Sebright Rd Barnet EN5 . . .171 E6
 Hemel Hempstead HP1 . . .124 A1
 Markyate AL3 . . . . .83 E5
Sebright Sch AL3 . . . . .83 C4
Secker Cres HA3 . . . . .176 C2
Second Ave
 Letchworth SG6 . . . . .23 C6
 Watford WD2 . . . . .154 D4
Sedbury Cl LU3 . . . . .45 A6
Sedge Gn EN9 . . . . .135 E3
Sedgewick Ct HP2 . . . . . . .105 B1
Sedgwick Rd LU4 . . . . .44 B7
Sedley Cl EN1 . . . . .162 B1
Seebohm Cl SG5 . . . . .21 C1
Seeleys CM17 . . . . .118 C4
Sefton Ave HA3 . . . . .176 D2
Sefton Cl AL1 . . . . .127 F4
Sefton Rd SG1 . . . . .37 B1
Selbourne Rd LU4 . . . . .45 A2
Selby Ave AL3 . . . . .127 D3
Selden Hill HP2 . . . . .124 D2
Sele Mill SG14 . . . . .113 B6
Sele Rd SG14 . . . . .113 B6
Sele Sch The SG14 . . . . . .112 F6
Selina Cl LU3 . . . . .44 C7
Sell Cl EN7 . . . . .147 B5
Sellers Cl WD6 . . . . .170 A8
Sells Rd SG12 . . . . .93 F2
Sellwood Dr EN5 . . . . .171 D4
Selsey Dr LU2 . . . . .46 D4

Selwyn Ave AL10 . . . . . . .129 E4
Selwyn Cres AL10 . . . . . . .129 E5
Selwyn Dr AL10 . . . . .129 E5
Sempill Rd HP3 . . . . .124 E1
Senate Pl SG1 . . . . .37 B3
Sentis Ct HA6 . . . . .174 F4
Service Industry Bays
 CM20 . . . . .117 F2
Service Rd The EN6 . . . . . .159 A7
Seven Acres HA6 . . . . .175 A4
Sevenoaks Ct HA6 . . . . . .174 C3
Severalls The LU2 . . . . .46 B3
Severn Dr EN1 . . . . .162 A1
Severn Way WD2 . . . . . . .154 C5
Severnmead HP2 . . . . .124 E6
Severnvale AL2 . . . . .142 F4
Sewardstone Rd EN9 . . . .163 D3
Sewardstone St EN9 . . . . .163 C5
Sewell Cl AL4 . . . . .128 E3
Sewell Harris Cl CM20 . . .117 F1
Sewells AL8 . . . . .89 E2
Sexton Cl EN7 . . . . .147 B6
Seymour Ave LU1 . . . . .63 F5
Seymour Cl HA5 . . . . .175 F2
Seymour Cres HP2 . . . . . .124 E3
Seymour Ct HP4 . . . . .121 E6
Seymour Mews CM21 . . . .118 E7
Seymour Rd
 Berkhamsted HP4 . . . . . . .121 E6
 Luton LU1 . . . . .63 F5
 St Albans AL3 . . . . .127 E5
Shackledell SG2 . . . . .50 F2
Shacklegate La SG4 . . . . . .66 E5
Shackleton Spring SG2 . . . .51 A3
Shackleton Way
 Abbots Langley WD5 . . . . .154 A7
 Welwyn Garden City AL7 . .111 D6
Shady Bush Cl WD2 . . . . . .168 C2
Shady La WD1 . . . . .167 B3
Shaftenhoe End Rd
 Barley SG8 . . . . .9 A1
 Nuthampstead SG8 . . . . . . .18 B8
Shaftesbury Ct
 Croxley Green WD3 . . . . . .166 C4
 Stevenage SG1 . . . . .50 E4
Shaftesbury Ind Ctr SG6 . .23 B7
Shaftesbury Quay **9**
 SG14 . . . . .113 D6
Shaftesbury Rd Luton LU4 . .45 B1
 Watford WD1 . . . . .167 C6
Shaftesbury Sch HA3 . . . .176 B2
Shaftesbury Way
 Abbots Langley WD4 . . . . .139 C3
 Royston SG8 . . . . .7 E5
Shakespeare SG8 . . . . .7 D8
Shakespeare Ind Est
 WD2 . . . . .154 A1
Shakespeare Rd
 Harpenden AL5 . . . . .86 C1
 Luton LU4 . . . . .44 B2
Shakespeare St WD2 . . . . .154 B1
Shalcross Dr EN8 . . . . . . .148 F1
Shallcross Cres **6** AL10 . .130 A2
Shambrook Rd EN7 . . . . . .147 B6
Shangani Rd CM23 . . . . . . .76 F5
Shanklin Cl
 Goff's Oak EN7 . . . . .147 F2
 Luton LU3 . . . . .45 A7
Shanklin Gdns WD1 . . . . .175 C6
Shantock Hall La HP3 . . . .136 F1
Shantock La HP3 . . . . .136 E1
Sharmans Cl AL6 . . . . .89 F4
Sharose Ct AL3 . . . . .83 E5
Sharpcroft **1** HP2 . . . . . .124 D5
Sharpenhoe Rd LU3 . . . . . .31 A5
Sharpes La HP1 . . . . .123 B1
Sharples Gn LU3 . . . . .45 B8
Sharps Way Hitchin SG4 . . .22 A1
 Hitchin SG4 . . . . .35 A8
Shaw Cl Bushey WD2 . . . . .176 E8
 Cheshunt EN8 . . . . .148 C3
Shaw's Corner AL6 . . . . . . .88 A6
Shaws The AL7 . . . . .111 C5
Shearers The CM23 . . . . . .76 C4
Sheares Hoppit SG12 . . . . .95 D2
Shearwater Cl SG2 . . . . . . .51 D4
Sheepcot Dr WD2 . . . . . . .154 C5
Sheepcot La WD2 . . . . . . .154 B6
Sheepcote LU7 . . . . .111 A3
Sheepcote La AL4 . . . . .87 F1
Sheepcote Rd HP2 . . . . . . .124 F3
Sheepcroft Hill SG2 . . . . . .51 D3
Sheephouse Rd HP3 . . . . .124 F1
Sheering CE Prim Sch
 CM22 . . . . .98 D1
Sheering Dr CM17 . . . . . . .118 E4
Sheering Lower Rd CM21 . .98 A2
Sheering Mill La CM21 . . . .97 F2
Sheering Rd CM17 . . . . . . .118 E4
Sheethanger La HP3 . . . . .138 A7
Shefton Rise HA6 . . . . .175 A3
Sheldon Cl EN7 . . . . .147 E5
Shelford Rd EN5 . . . . .171 C3
Shelley Cl Hitchin SG4 . . . .35 C7
 Moor Park HA6 . . . . .174 F5
 Royston SG8 . . . . .2 D1
Shelley Ct Cheshunt EN7 . .148 A3
 16 Harpenden AL5 . . . . .86 B1
 Waltham Abbey EN9 . . . . .163 F6
Shelley La UB9 . . . . .173 A3
Shelley Rd LU4 . . . . .44 B2
Shelton Way LU3 . . . . .46 A3

Shendish Edge HP3 . . . . . .138 F6
Shenley Ct HP2 . . . . .125 B8
Shenley Hill WD7 . . . . . . .156 B4
Shenley La AL2 . . . . .142 C4
Shenley Prim Sch WD7 . . .156 F5
Shenley Rd
 Borehamwood WD6 . . . . . .170 B6
 Hemel Hempstead HP2 . . .105 B1
 Radlett WD7 . . . . .156 C4
Shenleybury WD7,AL2 . . . .156 E8
Shenleybury Cotts WD7 . .156 E8
Shenleybury Villas WD7 . .156 E8
Shenstone Hill HP4 . . . . . .122 E5
Shenval Ho CM20 . . . . . . .118 A4
Shephall Gn SG2 . . . . .51 B2
Shephall Green Inf Sch
 SG2 . . . . .51 B2
Shephall View SG1 . . . . . . .51 B5
Shephall Way SG2 . . . . .51 C3
Shepherd Cl SG8 . . . . .7 C4
Shepherd Inf Sch WD3 . . .165 A1
Shepherd Jun Mix Inf Sch
 WD3 . . . . .165 A1
Shepherd's La WD3 . . . . . .164 E2
Shepherd's Row AL3 . . . . .106 B5
Shepherds Cl CM23 . . . . . .76 C4
Shepherds Gn HP1 . . . . . . .123 E2
Shepherds La SG1 . . . . .50 A6
Shepherds Mead SG5 . . . . .21 F2
Shepherds Rd WD1 . . . . . .166 F5
Shepherds Way
 Brookmans Park AL9 . . . . .145 D4
 Harpenden AL5 . . . . .85 D4
 Rickmansworth WD3 . . . . .165 B2
Shepherds Wlk WD2 . . . . .176 B3
Shepley Mews EN3 . . . . . .163 A2
Sheppard Cl EN1 . . . . .162 B1
Sheppards Cl AL3 . . . . . . .127 E6
Shepperton Cl WD6 . . . . . .170 D8
Sheppey's La WD5 . . . . . . .139 E3
Sheraton Cl WD6 . . . . .169 F4
Sheraton Ho WD3 . . . . . . .164 C5
Sheraton Mews WD1 . . . . .166 E5
Sherborne Ave LU2 . . . . . .45 D4
Sherborne Cotts WD1 . . . .167 C4
Sherborne Pl HA6 . . . . . . .174 D4
Sherborne Way WD3 . . . . .166 B5
Sherbourne Cl HP2 . . . . . .124 E2
Sherd Cl LU3 . . . . .44 F7
Sheredes Cty Prim Sch
 EN11 . . . . .134 F4
Sheredes Dr EN11 . . . . . . .134 F4
Sheredes Sch EN11 . . . . . .134 F5
Sherfield Ave WD3 . . . . . .173 E6
Sheridan Cl HP1 . . . . .124 B2
Sheridan Rd Luton LU3 . . . .45 C2
 Watford WD7 . . . . .167 D2
Sheriden Wlk EN10 . . . . . .134 F3
Sheriff Way WD2 . . . . .154 A5
Sheringham Ave SG1 . . . . .36 B1
Sheringham Cl LU2 . . . . . . .45 C7
Sherington Ave HA5 . . . . .176 A3
Sherland Ct WD7 . . . . .156 A4
Shernbroke Rd EN9 . . . . . .163 F5
Sherrards Mews AL8 . . . . .89 D4
Sherrardspark Rd AL8 . . . .110 D8
Sherrardswood Sch AL6 . . .89 D4
Sherwood SG6 . . . . .22 F8
Sherwood Ave
 Potters Bar EN6 . . . . .158 A6
 St Albans AL4 . . . . .128 B6
Sherwood Ct **20** CM23 . . . .76 F7
Sherwood Ho HA2 . . . . . . .153 F8
Sherwood Rd **1** HP2 . . . .124 F7
Sherwood Rd LU4 . . . . .45 A2
Sherwoods Rd WD1 . . . . .167 E2
Sherwoods Rise AL5 . . . . .107 D8
Shetland Cl WD6 . . . . .170 D3
Shetland Ho **18** WD1 . . . .166 F3
Shillington Rd SG5 . . . . . . .20 B5
Shillitoe Ave EN6 . . . . . . .158 E7
Shingle Cl LU3 . . . . .45 A8
Shire Cl EN10 . . . . .148 F5
Shire La
 Chalfont St Peter WD3 . . . .172 C4
 Chorleywood WD3 . . . . . .164 C4
 Maple Cross WD3 . . . . . . .172 B5
 Tring WD3 . . . . .120 B4
Shiremeade WD6 . . . . .169 F4
Shires The Luton LU2 . . . . .45 D1
 Royston SG8 . . . . .7 E6
Shirley Cl Cheshunt EN8 . . .148 C2
 Hoddesdon EN10 . . . . . . .148 F1
 Stevenage SG2 . . . . .51 C8
Shirley Rd
 Abbots Langley WD5 . . . . .153 F7
 Luton LU1 . . . . .63 C8
 St Albans AL1 . . . . .127 F2
Shooters End HP4 . . . . . . .121 F4
Shootersway La HP4 . . . . .121 F4
Shootersway Pk HP4 . . . . .121 F3
Shoplands AL8 . . . . .89 D2
Shoreham Cl SG1 . . . . .50 A8
Short Hale LU7 . . . . .80 C3
Short La Aston SG2 . . . . . . .51 E4
 Bricket Wood AL2 . . . . . . .140 E2
Shortcroft CM23 . . . . .77 D7
Shortlands Gn AL7 . . . . . .110 F5
Shortlands Pl CM23 . . . . . .76 F8
Shortmead Dr EN8 . . . . . .162 B8
Shothanger Way HP3 . . . . .137 D6
Shott La SG6 . . . . .23 A5
Shottfield Cl AL3 . . . . .106 A4
Shrub Hill Rd HP1 . . . . . . .123 F2
Shrubbery Gr SG3 . . . . .7 D4
Shrubbery The HP1 . . . . . .123 E4
Shrublands AL9 . . . . .145 B3

Sal–Smi 205

Shrublands Ave HP4 . . . . .122 A4
Shrublands Rd HP4 . . . . . .122 A4
Shrublands The EN6 . . . . .158 E6
Shugars Gn CM23 . . . . . . .100 B5
Sibley Ave AL5 . . . . .107 E7
Sibley Cl LU2 . . . . .46 B3
Sibthorpe Rd AL9 . . . . . . .144 D7
Siccut Rd SG4 . . . . .35 E4
Sicklefield Cl EN7 . . . . . . .147 F5
Siddons Rd SG2 . . . . .51 C6
Sidford Cl HP1 . . . . .123 F3
Sidings The Hatfield AL10 . .129 E4
 Hemel Hempstead HP2 . . .124 D3
 Hoddesdon EN10 . . . . . . .135 A1
Sidmouth Cl WD1 . . . . . . .175 B8
Sidney Terr CM23 . . . . .76 F6
Silam Rd SG1 . . . . .50 E5
Silecroft Rd LU2 . . . . .64 B8
Silk Mill Ct WD1 . . . . .167 B2
Silk Mill Rd Redbourn AL3 .106 B4
 Watford WD1 . . . . .167 B2
Silk Mill Way HP23 . . . . . .100 A5
Silkin Ct SG2 . . . . .51 D3
Silver Cl HA3 . . . . .176 D3
Silver Ct SG5 . . . . .34 F8
Silver Dell WD2 . . . . .153 F4
Silver Hill WD3 . . . . .157 B3
Silver St Anstey SG9 . . . . . .29 A5
 Ashwell SG7 . . . . .4 D4
 Goff's Oak EN7 . . . . .147 D1
 Guilden Morden SG8 . . . . . .1 F4
 Luton LU1 . . . . .63 E7
 Stansted Mountfitchet CM24 .59 D6
 Waltham Abbey EN9 . . . . .163 C6
Silver Trees AL2 . . . . .140 C4
Silverbirch Ave SG5 . . . . . .11 F8
Silverdale Rd WD2 . . . . . .167 E4
Silverfield EN10 . . . . .134 F1
Silverthorn Dr HP3 . . . . . .139 B7
Silverwood Cl HA6 . . . . . . .174 C2
Simmonds Rise HP3 . . . . . .124 D1
Simon Balle Sch SG13 . . . .113 E5
Simon Dean HP3 . . . . .137 A4
Simpson Cl LU4 . . . . .44 D2
Simpson Dr SG7 . . . . .23 F8
Simpsons Ct SG7 . . . . .23 F8
Sinderby Cl WD6 . . . . .169 E8
Sinfield Cl SG1 . . . . .51 A5
Singlets La AL3 . . . . .84 C2
Sir Frederic Osborn Sch
 AL7 . . . . .111 B7
Sir Herbert Janes Village
 The LU4 . . . . .44 D4
Sir James Altham Pool
 WD1 . . . . .175 E5
Sir John Lawes Sch AL5 . . .86 C3
Sir John Newsom Sch
 AL7 . . . . .110 E3
Sir Peter's Way HP4 . . . . . .81 E6
Sirita Cl HA3 . . . . .176 D1
Sirus Rd HA6 . . . . .175 A5
Sish Cl SG1 . . . . .50 D6
Sish La SG1 . . . . .50 D6
Siskin Cl
 Borehamwood WD6 . . . . . .170 A5
 Watford WD2 . . . . .167 E5
Sisson Cl SG2 . . . . .51 C2
Sitwell Gr HA7 . . . . .176 F5
Six Acres HP3 . . . . .139 A8
Six Hills Way SG1,SG2 . . . .50 C4
Sixth Ave Letchworth SG6 . .23 C4
 Watford WD2 . . . . .154 D4
Skegness Rd SG1 . . . . .50 A8
Skegsbury La SG4 . . . . .65 F1
Skelton Cl LU3 . . . . .31 F5
Skidmore Way WD3 . . . . .165 E1
Skimpans Cl AL9 . . . . .144 D7
Skimpot Rd LU4 . . . . .44 A1
Skinners St CM23 . . . . .76 C4
Skipton Cl SG2 . . . . .68 F8
Skua Cl LU4 . . . . .44 F5
Skye Ho **11** WD1 . . . . . . .166 F3
Skylark Cnr SG2 . . . . .51 D3
Skys Wood Rd AL4 . . . . . .128 B7
Skyswood Prim Sch AL4 . .128 C6
Slade Cl WD7 . . . . .156 A4
Sleaford Gn WD1 . . . . .175 D7
Sleapcross Gdns AL4 . . . . .129 C2
Sleaps Hyde SG2 . . . . .51 C1
Sleapshyde La AL4 . . . . . . .129 C2
Sleddale HP2 . . . . .124 D4
Sleets End HP1 . . . . .124 B5
Slimmons Dr AL4 . . . . .128 A4
Slip End Lower Sch LU1 . . .63 B1
Slip La SG3,AL6 . . . . .68 C4
Slipe La EN10 . . . . .148 F1
Slipe The LU7 . . . . .80 A7
Slippers Hill HP2 . . . . .124 D4
Sloan Ct SG1 . . . . .50 F6
Sloansway AL7 . . . . .90 A1
Slowmans AL2 . . . . .141 C3
Slype The AL5,AL4 . . . . . . .87 B5
Small Acre HP1 . . . . .123 F4
Smallcroft AL7 . . . . .111 B7
Smallford La AL4 . . . . .129 B2
Smallwood Cl AL4 . . . . . . .108 E7
Smarts Gn EN7 . . . . .147 F5
Smeaton Cl EN9 . . . . .163 E1
Smeaton Rd EN3 . . . . .163 F3
Smith St WD1 . . . . .167 C5
Smith's End La Barley SG8 . .17 F8
 Nuthampstead SG8 . . . . . . .18 A8
Smithfield HP2 . . . . .124 D5
Smiths La EN7 . . . . .147 D5
Smiths Lane Mall **5** LU1 . .63 E7

Smiths Sq **6** LU1 . . . . .63 E7
Smithy The SG11 . . . . .57 B2
Smug Oak Bsns Ctr AL2 .141 B1
Smug Oak La AL2 . . . . .141 D1
Snailswell La SG5 . . . . .21 E5
Snatchup AL3 . . . . .106 A5
Snells Mead SG9 . . . . .40 F7
Snipe The SG4 . . . . .24 B1
Snowdrop Cl CM23 . . . . . . .76 C6
Snowford Cl **1** LU3 . . . . . .45 A7
Snowley Par CM23 . . . . .59 B1
Soham Rd EN3 . . . . .162 F2
Solar Ct WD1 . . . . .166 F4
Solar Way EN3 . . . . .162 F2
Solesbridge Cl WD3 . . . . . .164 F6
Solesbridge La WD3 . . . . . .165 B7
Sollershott E SG6 . . . . .22 F4
Sollershott Hall SG6 . . . . . .22 F4
Sollershott W SG6 . . . . .22 E4
Solomon's Hill WD3 . . . . . .165 D2
Solway HP2 . . . . .124 F5
Solway Rd N LU3 . . . . .45 A4
Solway Rd S LU3 . . . . .45 A3
Somerby Cl EN10 . . . . .135 A2
Someries Inf Sch LU2 . . . . .46 C3
Someries Jun Sch LU2 . . . . .46 C3
Someries Rd
  Harpenden AL5 . . . . .86 C4
  Hemel Hempstead HP1 . . .123 F5
Somers Rd AL9 . . . . .144 C7
Somers Sq AL9 . . . . .144 C8
Somers Way WD2 . . . . .168 C2
Somersby Cl LU1 . . . . .63 E5
Somerset Ave LU2 . . . . .46 A1
Somerset Rd EN3 . . . . .163 A1
Somersham AL7 . . . . .111 D6
Sonia Cl WD1 . . . . .167 C2
Soothouse Spring AL3 . . . . .127 F7
Soper Mews EN3 . . . . .163 A1
Sopers Rd EN6 . . . . .146 F2
Sopwell La AL1 . . . . .127 D2
Sorrel Cl Luton LU3 . . . . . . .45 B8
  Royston SG8 . . . . .7 F5
Sorrel Garth SG4 . . . . .35 A6
Sotheron Rd WD1 . . . . .167 C6
Souberie Ave SG6 . . . . .22 F5
Souldern St WD1 . . . . .167 B4
South App HA6 . . . . .174 D7
South Bank Rd HP4 . . . . . . .121 F6
South Block CM21 . . . . .97 F2
South Charlton Mead La
  EN11 . . . . .135 D5
South Cl Baldock SG7 . . . . .23 F7
  Barnet EN5 . . . . .171 F6
  Chiswellgreen AL2 . . . . . .141 B6
  Pinner HA5 . . . . .175 D2
  Royston SG8 . . . . .7 B7
South Cottage Dr WD3 . . . .164 F4
South Cottage Gdns
  WD3 . . . . .164 F4
South Dr Cuffley EN6 . . . . .146 E1
  St Albans AL4 . . . . .128 E4
South Drift Way LU1 . . . . . .63 B5
South Hill Cl SG4 . . . . .35 A6
South Hill Prim Sch HP1 . .124 C2
South Hill Rd HP1 . . . . .124 C3
South Ley AL7 . . . . .110 E3
South Ley Ct AL7 . . . . .110 E3
South Luton High Sch
  LU1 . . . . .63 F5
South Ordnance Rd EN3 .163 A2
South Par EN9 . . . . .163 C6
South Park Ave WD3 . . . . . .164 F4
South Park Gdns HP4 . . . . .122 B5
South Pl Harlow CM20 . . . .118 A4
  Hitchin SG5 . . . . .34 D8
South Rd Baldock SG7 . . . .24 A7
  Bishop's Stortford CM23 . .77 A5
  Chorleywood WD3 . . . . . .164 C4
  Harlow CM20 . . . . .118 A4
  Luton LU1 . . . . .63 D6
  Standon SG11 . . . . .55 D2
South Riding AL2 . . . . .141 A1
South St
  Bishop's Stortford CM23 . . .76 F6
  Hertford SG14 . . . . .113 D6
  Stanstead Abbotts SG12 . .115 C4
South Street Commercial
  Ctr **1** CM23 . . . . .76 F6
South View SG6 . . . . .22 F5
South View Rd HA5 . . . . . .175 B4
South Way
  Abbots Langley WD5 . . . .153 E6
  Hatfield AL10 . . . . .130 B2
  Waltham Abbey EN9 . . . .163 C3
South Weald Dr EN9 . . . . .163 D6
Southacre Way HA5 . . . . . .175 C2
Southall Cl SG12 . . . . .93 D2
Southbrook CM21 . . . . .97 E1
Southbrook Rd **2** EN8 . .148 D3
Southdown Ct AL10 . . . . . .130 A2
Southdown Ho AL5 . . . . . .107 C8
Southdown Ind Est AL5 . .107 C7
Southdown Rd
  Harpenden AL5 . . . . .107 B8
  Hatfield AL10 . . . . .130 A2
Southend Cl SG1 . . . . .50 D7
Southern Ave SG16 . . . . . . .10 C3
Southern Rise LU2 . . . . .85 F7
Southern Terr EN11 . . . . . .115 B1
Southern Way
  Letchworth SG6 . . . . .22 E8
  Studham LU6 . . . . .82 C4
Southernwood Cl HP2 . .125 A4
Southerton Way WD7 . .156 E6

Southfield Barnet EN5 . . . . .171 D3
  Braughing SG11 . . . . .55 F7
  Welwyn Garden City AL7 . .110 D4
Southfield Ave WD2 . . . . . .154 C1
Southfield Rd
  Cheshunt EN8 . . . . .162 E7
  Hoddesdon EN11 . . . . . . .135 A7
Southfield Sch AL10 . . . . . .130 B1
Southfield Way AL4 . . . . . .128 D6
Southfields Letchworth SG6 . .11 F1
  Standon SG11 . . . . .55 E2
Southgate SG1 . . . . .50 D4
Southgate Cotts WD3 . . . . .165 E2
Southgate Ct **5** AL5 . . . .86 A2
Southgate Ho **1** EN8 . . .148 D1
Southgate Rd EN6 . . . . .159 C6
Southlynn Ho **2** LU2 . . . .63 F8
Southmead Cres EN8 . . . . .148 F1
Southmill Rd CM23 . . . . . . .77 A5
Southmill Trad Ctr CM23 . . .77 A6
Southsea Ave WD1 . . . . . . .167 A5
Southsea Rd SG1 . . . . .50 B8
Southside SG9 . . . . .28 A3
Southview Cl EN7 . . . . .147 E5
Southview Rd AL5 . . . . .86 D3
Southwark Cl SG1 . . . . .37 B2
Southwold Cl SG1 . . . . .50 A6
Southwold Rd WD2 . . . . . . .154 C2
Sovereign St WD1 . . . . .167 A5
Sovereign Pk HP2 . . . . .125 B5
Sowerby Ave LU2 . . . . .46 C3
Sparhawke SG6 . . . . .12 A1
Sparrow Cl LU4 . . . . .44 A4
Sparrow Dr SG2 . . . . .51 D4
Sparrows Herne WD2 . . . . .168 C2
Sparrows Way WD2 . . . . . . .168 C1
Sparrowswick Ride AL3 . . .127 C8
Spayne Cl LU3 . . . . .45 B8
Spear Cl LU3 . . . . .44 E6
Speedwell Cl LU3 . . . . .45 A8
Speke Cl SG2 . . . . .51 D5
Spellbrook La E CM22 . . . .97 F8
Spellbrook La W CM22 . . . .97 E7
Spellbrook Prim Sch
  CM23 . . . . .97 F7
Spellbrooke **5** SG5 . . . . .34 D8
Spencer Ave EN7 . . . . .147 E5
Spencer Cl CM24 . . . . .59 E6
Spencer Gate AL1 . . . . .127 E5
Spencer Ho SG5 . . . . .11 F6
Spencer Jun Sch AL3 . . . . .127 E6
Spencer Mews AL1 . . . . . . .127 E4
Spencer Pl AL4 . . . . .108 C2
Spencer Rd Harrow HA3 . . .176 E1
  Luton LU3 . . . . .45 C2
Spencer St Hertford SG13 . .113 E1
  St Albans AL3 . . . . .127 D3
Spencer Way HP1 . . . . .124 A6
Spencer Wlk WD3 . . . . .165 C4
Spenser St SG8 . . . . .2 D1
Spenser Rd AL5 . . . . .86 C1
Sperberry Hill SG4 . . . . .35 B2
Sphere Ind Est The AL1 . . .128 A2
Spicer St AL3 . . . . .127 C3
Spicersfield EN7 . . . . .148 A4
Spindle Berry Cl AL6 . . . . . .90 A7
Spinney Ct CM21 . . . . .97 E2
Spinney Jun & Inf Schs
  The CM20 . . . . .118 A1
Spinney La AL6 . . . . .68 E3
Spinney Rd LU3 . . . . .44 D7
Spinney St SG13 . . . . .114 A6
Spinney The Baldock SG7 . .23 E7
  Berkhamsted HP4 . . . . . . .121 F3
  Cheshunt EN7 . . . . .148 B1
  Harpenden AL5 . . . . .85 E3
  Hertford SG13 . . . . .113 F6
  Hoddesdon EN10 . . . . . . .134 F4
  Potters Bar EN6 . . . . .159 D8
  Stanstead Mountfitchet CM24 . .59 E6
  Stevenage SG2 . . . . .51 B7
  Watford WD1 . . . . .167 A8
  Welwyn Garden City AL7 . .110 E5
Spinneys Dr AL3 . . . . .127 B1
Spires The SG15 . . . . .171 E6
Spittlesea Rd LU2 . . . . .64 C7
Spooners Dr AL2 . . . . .141 C4
Spratts La LU6 . . . . .82 F8
Spreckley Cl SG16 . . . . .10 B5
Spring Cl Barnet EN5 . . . . .171 D4
  Borehamwood WD6 . . . . .170 A8
  Harefield UB9 . . . . .173 D2
  Latimer HP5 . . . . .150 D3
Spring Court Rd EN2 . . . . .161 A1
Spring Crofts WD2 . . . . . . .168 A4
Spring Dr SG2 . . . . .69 B8
Spring Field Rd HP4 . . . . . .122 A6
Spring Gdns WD2 . . . . .154 C3
Spring Glen AL10 . . . . .129 F4
Spring Hills CM20 . . . . .117 B1
Spring La Cottered SG9 . . . .39 C5
  Hemel Hempstead HP1 . . .124 A4
Spring Mews CM21 . . . . . . .97 E2
Spring Pl **5** LU1 . . . . .63 D6
Spring Rd Harpenden AL5 . .85 A4
  Letchworth SG6 . . . . .22 E4
  Letchworth SG6 . . . . .22 E6
Spring View Rd SG12 . . . . .114 C8
Spring Way HP2 . . . . .125 C5
Spring Wlk EN10 . . . . .134 C2
Springfield WD2 . . . . .168 D1
Springfield Cl
  Croxley Green WD3 . . . . .166 B4
  Northaw EN6 . . . . .159 E8
Springfield Cres AL5 . . . . . .86 B5
Springfield Ct
  Bishop's Stortford CM23 . . .76 E8
  Rickmansworth WD3 . . . .165 B1

Springfield Rd
  Cheshunt EN8 . . . . .162 E7
  Hemel Hempstead HP2 . . .124 F4
  Luton LU3 . . . . .45 C6
  St Albans, Smallford AL4 . .129 B3
  St Albans, The Camp AL1 . .128 A2
  Watford WD2 . . . . .154 B6
Springfields
  Hoddesdon EN10 . . . . . . .134 F4
  Waltham Abbey EN9 . . . .163 E5
  Welwyn Garden City AL8 . .110 B4
Springfield Ho AL8 . . . . . . .110 C4
Springhall Ct CM21 . . . . . . .97 E2
Springhall La CM21 . . . . . . .97 E1
Springhall Rd CM21 . . . . . . .97 E2
Springhead SG7 . . . . .4 D4
Springle La SG13 . . . . .114 F2
Springmead
  Jun Mix Inf Sch AL7 . . . .111 C7
Springs Cotts EN10 . . . . . .148 E7
Springs The
  Cheshunt EN10 . . . . .148 E6
  Hertford SG13 . . . . .113 F7
Springshott SG6 . . . . .22 E5
Springwell Ave WD3 . . . . . .173 A8
Springwell La WD3 . . . . . . .173 A6
Springwood EN7 . . . . .148 A5
Springwood Cl UB9 . . . . . . .173 D2
Springwood Wlk AL4 . . . . .128 D6
Spruce Way AL2 . . . . .141 B4
Spur Cl WD5 . . . . .153 D6
Spur The
  3 Cheshunt EN8 . . . . .148 D3
  Stevenage SG1 . . . . .50 E4
Spurcroft LU3 . . . . .31 C1
Spurrs Cl SG4 . . . . .35 B7
Square The Braughing SG11 . .55 F7
  Buckland SG9 . . . . .27 D5
  Hemel Hempstead HP1 . . .124 C3
  Hoddesdon EN10 . . . . . . .148 E8
  Much Hadham SG10 . . . . .74 F3
  Redbourn AL3 . . . . .105 F6
  Sawbridgeworth CM21 . . . .97 E2
  Watford WD2 . . . . .154 B2
Squires Cl CM23 . . . . .76 C8
Squires Ct EN11 . . . . .135 A5
Squires Ride HP2 . . . . .104 F1
Squirrel Chase HP1 . . . . . . .123 E4
Squirrels Cl **2** CM23 . . . .76 F8
Squirrels The
  Bushey WD2 . . . . .168 D3
  Hertford SG13 . . . . .114 B6
  Welwyn Garden City AL7 . .111 C5
Stable Ct AL1 . . . . .127 E5
Stable Mews AL1 . . . . .127 E4
Stacey Ct **9** CM23 . . . . . .76 F6
Stackfield CM20 . . . . .118 A3
Stacklands AL8 . . . . .110 B4
Staddles CM22 . . . . .98 B8
Stadium Est The LU4 . . . . . .44 B1
Stadium Way CM19 . . . . . .116 F1
Stafford Cl EN10 . . . . .148 B2
Stafford Ct EN10 . . . . .135 A3
Stafford Ct EN10 . . . . .135 A3
Stafford Ho
  Bishop's Stortford CM23 . . .76 F5
  Hoddesdon EN10 . . . . . . .135 A3
Stafford Rd HA3 . . . . .176 C3
Staffords CM17 . . . . .118 E4
Stag Ct WD3 . . . . .164 C5
Stag Green Ave AL9 . . . . . .130 C7
Stag La Berkhamsted HP4 . .122 B5
  Chorleywood WD3 . . . . . .164 C3
Stagg Hill EN4 . . . . .159 E3
Stainer Rd
  Borehamwood WD6 . . . . .156 D1
  Radlett WD6 . . . . .169 D8
Stains Cl EN8 . . . . .148 F3
Stake Piece Rd SG8 . . . . . . .7 C5
Stakers Cl AL5 . . . . .86 B1
Stamford Ave SG8 . . . . .7 D7
Stamford Cl Harrow HA3 . . .176 E3
  Potters Bar EN6 . . . . .159 D7
Stamford Ct SG8 . . . . .7 D7
Stamford Rd WD1 . . . . .167 B7
Stamford Yd SG8 . . . . .7 C6
Stanborough Ave WD6 . . . .157 B1
Stanborough Cl AL8 . . . . . .110 C5
Stanborough Gn AL8 . . . . . .110 C4
Stanborough La AL8 . . . . . .110 C4
Stanborough Prim Sch
  WD2 . . . . .154 C4
Stanborough Rd AL8 . . . . . .110 C4
Stanborough Sch
  Watford WD2 . . . . .154 B4
  Welwyn Garden City AL8 . .110 B4
Stanbury Ave WD1 . . . . . . .153 E2
Standalone Farm SG6 . . . . .22 D7
Standard Rd EN3 . . . . .162 E2
Standfield WD5 . . . . .139 E1
Standhill Cl SG4 . . . . .34 F6
Standhill Rd SG4 . . . . .34 F6
Standon Bsns Pk SG11 . . . .55 E1
Standon Cl SG11 . . . . .55 F1
Standon Hill SG11 . . . . .55 D2
Standon Rd SG11 . . . . .56 E3
Standring Rise HP3 . . . . . . .138 B8
Stane Cl SG1 . . . . .50 D7
Stane Field SG6 . . . . .23 B3
Stane St SG7 . . . . .13 A1
Stanelow Cres SG11 . . . . . . .55 D2
Stanfields Ct CM20 . . . . . . .117 E1
Stanford Rd LU2 . . . . .46 A1
Stangate Cres WD6 . . . . . .170 E4
Stanhope Ave HA3 . . . . .176 D2
Stanhope Rd Barnet EN5 . .171 D3
  Cheshunt EN8 . . . . .162 E6
  St Albans AL1 . . . . .127 F3

Stanier Rise HP4 . . . . .121 F7
Stanley Ave AL2 . . . . .141 A6
Stanley Dr AL10 . . . . .130 B3
Stanley Gdns
  Borehamwood WD6 . . . . .169 E8
  Tring HP23 . . . . .99 F3
Stanley Livingstone Ct
  LU1 . . . . .63 D6
Stanley Rd Hertford SG13 . .113 E5
  Northwood HA6 . . . . .175 A2
  Stevenage SG2 . . . . .51 B7
  Streatley LU3 . . . . .31 A5
  Watford WD1 . . . . .167 C5
Stanley St LU1 . . . . .63 D6
Stanmore Chase AL4 . . . . .128 D2
Stanmore Cres LU3 . . . . . . .45 C8
Stanmore Rd
  Stevenage SG2 . . . . .50 D7
  Watford WD2 . . . . .167 B8
Stanmount Rd AL2 . . . . . . .141 A6
Stannington Path WD6 . . . .170 A8
Stanstead Dr EN11 . . . . . . .135 B8
Stanstead Rd
  Hertford SG13 . . . . .114 A6
  Hertford Heath SG13 . . . .114 D5
  Hoddesdon EN11 . . . . . . .115 B1
Stansted Hill SG5 . . . . .75 A1
Stansted Mountfitchet Sta
  . . . . .59 E6
Stansted Rd
  Birchanger CM23 . . . . . . .59 C4
  Bishop's Stortford CM23 . .59 B2
Stanton Cl AL4 . . . . .128 D7
Stanton Rd LU4 . . . . .44 C1
Stantons CM20 . . . . .117 B1
Staplefield Cl HA5 . . . . .175 E3
Stapleford AL7 . . . . .111 D6
Stapleford
  Jun Mix Inf Sch SG14 . . . .92 A6
Stapleford Rd LU2 . . . . .46 C4
Stapleton Cl EN6 . . . . .159 D8
Stapleton Rd WD6 . . . . . . .157 A4
Stapley Rd AL3 . . . . .127 D4
Staplyton Rd EN5 . . . . .171 E6
Star Holme Ct SG12 . . . . . .93 E1
Star St SG12 . . . . .93 E1
Starkey Cl EN7 . . . . .147 C6
Starlight Way AL4 . . . . .128 C1
Starling La EN6 . . . . .146 F3
Startpoint LU1 . . . . .63 C7
Stately Cl LU3 . . . . .45 D1
Statham Cl LU3 . . . . .31 B1
Station App Cheshunt EN8 .162 E5
  Chorleywood WD3 . . . . . .164 D5
  Harlow CM20 . . . . .118 C5
  Harpenden AL5 . . . . .86 B1
  Hitchin SG4 . . . . .35 A8
  Kings Langley WD4 . . . . .139 A6
  Knebworth SG3 . . . . .68 F5
  Northwood HA6 . . . . .174 E3
  Radlett WD7 . . . . .156 A4
  South Oxhey WD1 . . . . . .175 D7
Station Cl
  Brookmans Park AL9 . . . .144 E5
  Potters Bar EN6 . . . . .158 F8
Station Ct **15** SG12 . . . . .93 D1
Station Footpath WD4 . . . .139 B1
Station Mews EN6 . . . . .159 A8
Station Par SG6 . . . . .22 F6
Station Pl SG6 . . . . .22 F6
Station Rd Aldbury HP23 . . .101 B5
  Arlesey SG15 . . . . .11 A4
  Ashwell SG7 . . . . .4 F4
  Baldock SG7 . . . . .12 F1
  Berkhamsted HP4 . . . . . . .122 D4
  Bishop's Stortford CM23 . .77 A7
  Borehamwood WD6 . . . . .170 A5
  Braughing SG11 . . . . .55 E5
  Bricket Wood AL2 . . . . . .155 A8
  Brookmans Park AL9 . . . .144 D6
  Buntingford SG9 . . . . .40 E7
  Cheddington LU7 . . . . . . .79 F8
  Cuffley EN6 . . . . .146 F2
  Harlow CM17 . . . . .118 C4
  Harpenden AL5 . . . . .86 C2
  Hemel Hempstead HP1 . . .124 C1
  Hertingfordbury SG14 . . . .112 B3
  Hoddesdon EN10 . . . . . . .135 A3
  Holdbrook EN9 . . . . .163 A5
  Kings Langley WD4 . . . . .139 B1
  Knebworth SG3 . . . . .69 A5
  Letchworth SG6 . . . . .22 F6
  Long Marston HP23 . . . . .79 B4
  Lower Stondon SG16 . . . .10 A4
  Luton, High Town LU1 . . .63 E8
  Luton, Leagrave LU4 . . . . .44 E5
  Much Hadham SG10 . . . . .74 E1
  Pitstone LU7 . . . . .80 E5
  Radlett WD7 . . . . .156 A4
  Rickmansworth WD3 . . . .165 D2
  Sawbridgeworth CM21 . . . .97 F3
  St Albans AL4 . . . . .129 B3
  Standon SG11 . . . . .55 E2
  Stanstead Abbotts SG12 . .115 C4
  Stansted Mountfitchet CM24 . .59 E6
  Steeple Morden SG7,SG8 . .5 C5
  Tring HP23 . . . . .100 D4
  Ware SG12 . . . . .93 E1
  Watford WD1 . . . . .167 B7
  Watton at Stone SG14 . . . .70 D3
  Welwyn AL6 . . . . .89 E3
  Wheathampstead AL4 . . . .87 D1
Station Terr Hitchin SG4 . . . .35 A8
  Park Street AL2 . . . . .141 D5
Station Way SG6 . . . . .22 E6
Staveley Rd LU4 . . . . .44 C1
Steeplands WD2 . . . . .168 B2
Steeple View CM23 . . . . . . .76 F8

Sten Cl EN3 . . . . .163 A2
Stephens Cl LU2 . . . . .46 A3
Stephens Gdns LU2 . . . . . . .46 A2
Stephens Way AL3 . . . . . . .105 F5
Stephenson Cl SG8 . . . . . . .7 B7
Stephenson Way WD2 . . . .167 D2
Stepnells HP23 . . . . .80 A1
Stepping Stones The
  LU3 . . . . .44 E5
Sterling Ave EN8 . . . . .162 D5
Sterling Rd EN2 . . . . .161 D1
Stevenage Cres WD6 . . . . .169 E8
Stevenage Mus SG1 . . . . . .50 E5
Stevenage Rd Hitchin SG4 . .34 F5
  Knebworth SG2,SG3 . . . . .68 F7
  Little Wymondley SG4 . . . .35 E3
  Little Wymondley,
    Titmore Green SG4 . . . . .35 E2
  St Ippolyts SG4 . . . . .35 C2
  Walkern SG2 . . . . .51 E8
Stevenage Rise HP2 . . . . . .124 F7
Stevenage Sta SG1 . . . . . . .50 C5
Stevens Gn SG2 . . . . .168 C1
Steward Cl EN8 . . . . .148 E1
Stewart Cl WD5 . . . . .154 A7
Stewart Rd AL5 . . . . .86 B2
Stewarts The CM23 . . . . . . .76 E6
Stirling Bsns Pk EN8 . . . . .162 F5
Stirling Cl Hitchin SG4 . . . . .35 C7
  Stevenage SG2 . . . . .69 D7
Stirling Cnr EN5 . . . . .170 D3
Stirling Ho WD6 . . . . .170 C5
Stirling Way
  Borehamwood WD6 . . . . .170 D4
  Watford WD5 . . . . .154 A7
  Welwyn Garden City AL7 . .111 E6
Stoat Cl SG13 . . . . .114 A6
Stobarts Cl SG3 . . . . .68 F6
Stock Bank SG8 . . . . .8 D1
Stockbreach Cl AL10 . . . . . .130 A6
Stockbreach Rd AL10 . . . . .130 A6
Stockens Dell SG3 . . . . .68 F4
Stockens Gn SG3 . . . . .68 F4
Stockers Farm Rd WD3 . . .173 D8
Stockfield Ave EN11 . . . . . .135 B8
Stockholm Way LU3 . . . . . . .44 E8
Stocking Hill SG9 . . . . .39 B8
Stocking La SG8 . . . . .18 C1
Stockings La SG13 . . . . . . .132 C6
Stockingstone Rd LU2 . . . . .45 E3
Stockmen Field CM23 . . . . .76 C5
Stockport Rd WD3 . . . . . . .164 C2
Stocks Mdw HP2 . . . . .125 A4
Stocks Rd HP23 . . . . .101 D7
Stockwell Cl EN7 . . . . .148 E3
Stockwell La EN7 . . . . .148 B3
Stockwood Craft Mus &
  Gdns LU1 . . . . .63 D4
Stockwood Cres LU1 . . . . . .63 D6
Stockwood Ct **16** LU1 . . .63 D6
Stockwood Pk LU1 . . . . .63 D3
Stone Cross CM20 . . . . . . .117 D1
Stonecroft SG3 . . . . .68 F5
Stonecross AL1 . . . . .127 E4
Stonecross Rd AL10 . . . . . .130 B7
Stonehill
  Jun Mix Inf Sch SG6 . . . . .11 E1
Stonehills AL8 . . . . .110 D7
Stonelea Rd HP3 . . . . .138 F8
Stoneleigh CM21 . . . . .97 D3
Stoneleigh Ave EN1 . . . . . .162 B1
Stoneleigh Cl
  Cheshunt EN8 . . . . .162 D6
  Luton LU3 . . . . .45 B7
Stoneleigh Dr EN11 . . . . . .115 B1
Stoneley SG6 . . . . .11 F1
Stonemason Cl AL5 . . . . . . .86 A3
Stonemead AL8 . . . . .89 D3
Stonesdale LU4 . . . . .44 C4
Stoneways Cl LU4 . . . . .44 C6
Stoney Cl HP4 . . . . .121 F6
Stoney Comm CM24 . . . . . .59 E5
Stoney Common Rd CM24 . .59 D5
Stoney Croft HP23 . . . . . . .101 C5
Stoney La Bovingdon HP3 . .137 C5
  Chipperfield HP3 . . . . . . .137 E1
  Hemel Hempstead HP1 . . .137 B8
Stoney Pl CM24 . . . . .59 E5
Stoneycroft
  Hemel Hempstead HP1 . . .124 A3
  Welwyn Garden City AL7 . .111 A4
Stoneyfield Dr CM24 . . . . . .59 E6
Stoneygate Rd LU4 . . . . . . .44 D3
Stonnells Cl SG6 . . . . .22 F8
Stony Croft SG1 . . . . .50 E6
Stony Hills SG14 . . . . .92 C7
Stony La Chenies HP5,HP6 .150 E1
  Great Offley LU2,SG4 . . . .47 C4
Stonyshotts EN9 . . . . .163 E6
Stookslade HP22 . . . . .60 A3
Stopsley High Sch LU2 . . . .45 F4
Stopsley Inf Sch LU2 . . . . .46 A4
Stopsley Jun Sch LU2 . . . . .46 A4
Stopsley Way LU2 . . . . .46 A3
Storehouse La SG4 . . . . .34 F6
Storey Ct WD2 . . . . .168 B4
Storey St HP3 . . . . .138 D7
Stormont Rd SG5 . . . . .21 F1
Stormont Sch EN6 . . . . . . .159 D8
Stornoway HP3 . . . . .125 B1
Stort Lodge CM23 . . . . .76 D8
Stort Mill CM20 . . . . .118 B6
Stort Rd CM23 . . . . .76 F6
Stort Valley Ind Pk CM23 . .59 B2
Stortford Hall Ind Pk
  CM23 . . . . .77 B7
Stortford Hall Pk CM23 . . . .77 B8
Stortford Hall Rd **3** CM23 . .77 B8

Stortford Rd
Hatfield Heath CM22 . . . . . .**98** E4
Hoddesdon EN11 . . . .**135** C7
Little Hadham SG11 . . . .**57** C2
Standon SG11 . . . .**55** F2
Stotfold Rd SG5 . . . .**11** F6
Stotfold Rd Arlesey SG15 . .**11** C7
Hinxworth SG7 . . . .**3** C1
Hitchin SG6 . . . .**22** C4
Letchworth SG6 . . . .**11** D1
Stow The CM20 . . . .**117** F2
Stox Mead HA3 . . . .**176** C2
Strafford Cl EN6 . . . .**159** A7
Strafford SG3 . . . .**69** A5
Strafford Gate EN6 . . . . . .**159** A7
Strafford Rd EN5 . . . .**171** E6
Straits The EN9 . . . .**163** B7
Strandburgh Pl HP3 . . . . .**125** B1
Strangers Way LU4 . . . .**44** C4
Strangeways WD1 . . . .**153** E3
Stratford Dr EN10 . . . .**134** E4
Stratford Rd WD6 . . . .**170** A7
Stratford Lodge WD1 . . . .**167** B8
Stratford Rd Luton LU4 . . . .**45** B1
Watford WD1 . . . .**167** A7
Stratford Way
Bricket Wood AL2 . . . .**140** F2
Hemel Hempstead HP3 . . . .**138** B8
Watford WD1 . . . .**167** A7
Strathmore Ave
Hitchin SG5 . . . .**21** F1
Luton LU1 . . . .**63** F5
Strathmore Ct SG5 . . . .**21** F1
Strathmore Inf Sch SG5 . . .**21** E2
Strathmore SG4 . . . .**66** E6
Strathmore Wlk LU1 . . . . . .**63** F6
Stratton Ave EN2 . . . .**161** D2
Stratton Gdns LU2 . . . .**45** D4
Straw Plait SG15 . . . .**10** F4
Strawberry Field
8 Hatfield AL10 . . . .**130** A2
Luton LU3 . . . .**44** E7
Strawberry Fields SG12 . . .**93** B2
Strawfields AL7 . . . .**111** B7
Strawmead AL10 . . . .**130** B7
Strawplaiters Cl SG3 . . . . . .**69** A2
Straws Hadley Ct HP22 . . . .**60** B2
Strayfield Rd EN2 . . . .**161** B2
Stream Woods
Jun Mix Inf Sch AL10 . . . .**130** B4
Street The Braughing SG11 . .**55** F7
Chipperfield WD4 . . . .**152** A8
Dane End SG11 . . . .**53** F3
Furneux Pelham SG9 . . . . . .**43** A4
Sheering CM22 . . . .**98** E1
Wallington SG7 . . . .**25** C8
Stretton Way WD6 . . . . . .**156** E1
Stringers La SG2 . . . .**51** E2
Stripling Way WD1 . . . . . .**167** A3
Stroma Cl HP3 . . . .**125** C1
Stronnell Cl LU2 . . . .**46** B3
Stronsay HP3 . . . .**125** C1
Stroud Wood Bsns Ctr
AL2 . . . .**141** E4
Stuart Ct WD6 . . . .**169** D3
Stuart Dr Hitchin SG4 . . . . . .**35** B7
Royston SG8 . . . .**7** D8
Stuart Ho EN9 . . . .**163** F6
Stuart Rd AL6 . . . .**89** B3
Stuart St LU1 . . . .**63** D7
Stuart Way EN7 . . . .**162** B8
Stuarts Cl **8** HP3 . . . . . .**124** D1
Stud Gn WD2 . . . .**154** B7
Studham La Dagnall HP4 . . .**81** D4
Whipsnade LU6 . . . .**82** A7
Studham Lower Sch LU6 . .**82** B4
Studio Way WD6 . . . .**170** C8
Studios The WD2 . . . .**168** A3
Studlands Rise SG8 . . . .**7** E6
Studlands Rise Fst Sch
SG8 . . . .**7** E5
Studley Rd LU3 . . . .**45** D1
Sturgeon's Rd SG4 . . . .**22** B2
Sturla Cl SG14 . . . .**113** B7
Sturlas Way EN8 . . . .**162** D6
Sturmer Cl AL4 . . . .**128** C2
Sturrock Way SG4 . . . .**35** C6
Stylemans La CM22 . . . .**77** B5
Styles Cl LU2 . . . .**46** C2
Such Cl SG6 . . . .**23** B7
Sudbury Ct AL1 . . . .**127** C2
Sudbury Rd LU4 . . . .**44** B6
Suffolk Cl
Borehamwood WD6 . . . . . .**170** D4
London Colney AL2 . . . .**142** C6
Luton LU4 . . . .**44** A3
Suffolk Rd
Potters Bar EN6 . . . .**158** E7
Royston SG8 . . . .**7** E6
Sugar La HP1 . . . .**123** B1
Sulgrave Cres HP23 . . . . .**100** C5
Sullivan Cres UB9 . . . .**173** D1
Sullivan Way WD6 . . . . . .**169** C3
Summer Ct HP2 . . . .**124** D5
Summer Dale AL8 . . . .**89** D4
Summer Gr WD6 . . . .**169** D3
Summer Hill WD6 . . . .**170** A4
Summer St LU1 . . . .**63** C1
Summer Wlk AL3 . . . .**83** E5
Summercroft
Jun & Inf Schs CM23 . . . . .**77** C8
Summerfield AL10 . . . .**130** A2
Summerfield Cl AL2 . . . . .**142** C5
Summerfield Rd Luton LU1 . .**62** F8
Watford WD2 . . . .**154** A4
Summerhill Ct AL1 . . . . . .**127** F4
Summerhouse La
Harefield UB9 . . . .**173** A3

Summerhouse La *continued*
Radlett WD2 . . . .**168** C8
Summerhouse Way WD5 .**139** F1
Summers Rd LU2 . . . .**46** C1
Summers Way AL2 . . . . . .**142** E4
Summersland Rd AL4 . . . .**128** C7
Summerswood Fst Sch
WD6 . . . .**170** B5
Summerswood La WD6 . . .**157** E4
Summit Rd EN6 . . . .**144** E1
Sumpter Yd AL1 . . . .**127** D3
Sun Hill SG8 . . . .**7** C5
Sun La AL5 . . . .**86** A2
Sun Sq **2** HP1 . . . .**124** D4
Sun St Baldock SG7 . . . .**23** E8
Hitchin SG5 . . . .**34** E6
Sawbridgeworth CM21 . . . . .**97** F1
Waltham Abbey EN9 . . . . . .**163** C6
Sunbury Ct **2** EN5 . . . . . .**171** E5
Sunderland Ave AL1 . . . . .**128** A4
Sundew Rd HP1 . . . .**123** E2
Sundon Park Jun Sch
LU3 . . . .**44** C8
Sundon Park Rd LU3 . . . . . .**44** C7
Sunmead Rd HP2 . . . .**124** D5
Sunningdale CM23 . . . .**76** E6
Luton LU2 . . . .**45** F3
Sunningdale Mews AL7 . . . .**89** F2
Sunny Bank LU7 . . . .**79** F7
Sunny Bank Prim Sch
EN6 . . . .**159** A5
Sunny Hill SG9 . . . .**40** F7
Sunnybank Rd EN6 . . . . . .**159** A6
Sunnydell AL2 . . . .**141** B5
Sunnyfield AL9 . . . .**130** D8
Sunnyhill Rd
Hemel Hempstead HP1 . . . .**124** B3
Maple Cross WD3 . . . .**172** D4
Sunnyside
Lower Nazeing EN9 . . . . . .**135** F1
Stansted Mountfitchet CM24 .**59** E6
Sunnyside Rd SG4 . . . .**35** A5
Sunridge Ave LU2 . . . .**45** E2
Sunrise Cres HP3 . . . .**138** F8
Sunset Dr LU2 . . . .**45** F3
Sunset View EN5 . . . .**171** E7
Surrey Pl HP23 . . . .**100** A3
Surrey St LU1 . . . .**63** E6
Surrey Street Prim Sch
LU1 . . . .**63** F6
Sursham Ct AL3 . . . .**83** E5
Sussex Cl EN11 . . . .**135** A7
Sussex Pl LU2 . . . .**46** D2
Sussex Rd WD2 . . . .**154** A1
Sutcliffe Cl Bushey WD2 . . .**168** C5
Stevenage SG1 . . . .**51** A8
Sutherland Ave EN6 . . . . .**146** D3
Sutherland Cl EN5 . . . . . .**171** E5
Sutherland Ct
Moor Park WD1 . . . .**166** C2
Welwyn Garden City AL7 . . .**110** F7
Sutherland Pl LU1 . . . .**63** D5
Sutherland Way EN6 . . . . .**146** E3
Sutton Acres CM22 . . . .**98** D7
Sutton Cl Hoddesdon EN10 .**134** E4
Tring HP23 . . . .**100** B6
Sutton Cres EN5 . . . .**171** D4
Sutton Gdns LU3 . . . .**44** D6
Sutton Path WD6 . . . .**170** A4
Sutton Rd St Albans AL1 . . .**128** B3
Watford WD1 . . . .**167** C6
Swallow Cl Bushey WD2 . . .**168** C1
Luton LU4 . . . .**44** A4
Rickmansworth WD3 . . . . . .**165** C2
Swallow Ct Hertford SG14 .**113** C6
Welwyn Garden City AL7 . . .**110** F6
Swallow End AL7 . . . .**110** F6
Swallow Gdns AL10 . . . . . .**130** A3
Swallow Oaks WD5 . . . . . .**153** F7
Swallowdale La HP2 . . . . .**125** B6
Swallowfields AL7 . . . .**110** F6
Swallows CM17 . . . .**118** C4
Swallows The AL7 . . . .**89** F2
Swan Cl WD3 . . . .**165** D2
Swan Ct
2 Bishop's Stortford CM23 . .**76** F6
Chorleywood WD3 . . . .**164** C5
Swan La SG8 . . . .**1** F4
Swan Mead
Hemel Hempstead HP3 . . . .**138** F6
Luton LU4 . . . .**44** B4
Swan & Pike Rd EN3 . . . . .**163** A1
Swan St SG7 . . . .**4** D4
Swanfield Rd EN8 . . . .**162** E6
Swangley's La SG3 . . . .**69** B4
Swanhill AL7 . . . .**90** A1
Swanland Rd EN6 . . . .**144** B3
Swanley Bar La EN6 . . . . .**145** B3
Swanley Cres EN6 . . . .**145** B2
Swanley Ct WD2 . . . .**154** C2
Swannells Wood LU6 . . . . .**82** C4
Swans Cl AL4 . . . .**128** C2
Swans Ct EN8 . . . .**162** E6
Swanstand SG6 . . . .**23** D4
Swanston Grange LU4 . . . . .**44** B2
Swanston Path WD1 . . . . .**175** D7
Swasedale Rd LU3 . . . .**45** A6
Sweet Briar
Bishop's Stortford CM23 . . . .**76** B6
Welwyn Garden City AL7 . . .**111** A5
Sweetbriar Cl HP1 . . . .**124** A6
Sweyns Mead SG2 . . . .**51** C7
Swift Cl Letchworth SG6 . . . .**22** E8
Royston SG8 . . . .**2** D1
Stansted Abbotts SG12 . . . .**115** C3
Swiftfields AL7 . . . .**111** A7
Swifts Green Cl LU2 . . . . . .**46** B5

Swifts Green Rd LU2 . . . . . .**46** B5
Swinburne Ave SG5 . . . . . .**21** C1
Swinburne Cl SG5 . . . .**21** C1
Swing Gate Fst Sch HP4 .**122** D3
Swing Gate La HP4 . . . . . .**122** D2
Swingate SG1 . . . .**50** D5
Swinnell Cl SG8 . . . .**2** B5
Swiss Ave WD1 . . . .**166** E6
Swiss Cl WD1 . . . .**166** E6
Sword Cl EN10 . . . .**134** D3
Sworders Yd **8** CM23 . . . . .**76** F7
Sycamore Ave AL10 . . . . . .**130** A4
Sycamore Cl Bushey WD2 . .**167** E7
Hammond Street EN7 . . . . . .**147** F4
Hitchin SG4 . . . .**35** A4
Watford WD2 . . . .**154** B4
Sycamore Dr
Park Street AL2 . . . .**141** D4
Tring HP23 . . . .**100** B4
Sycamore Rd WD3 . . . .**166** D4
Sycamore Rise HP4 . . . . . .**122** D3
Sycamores The
Baldock SG7 . . . .**23** E8
Bishop's Stortford CM23 . . . .**77** B6
Hemel Hempstead HP3 . . . .**137** F8
Radlett WD7 . . . .**156** B5
St Albans AL1 . . . .**127** D2
Sydney Rd WD1 . . . .**166** F4
Sylam Cl LU3 . . . .**44** E7
Sylvan Cl HP3 . . . .**125** A2
Sylvan Way AL7 . . . .**111** C5
Sylvandale AL7 . . . .**111** C5
Sylvia Ave HA5 . . . .**175** F4
Symonds Green La SG1 . . .**50** A6
Symonds Green Rd SG1 . . .**50** A6
Symonds Rd SG5 . . . .**34** D8

T

Tabbs Cl SG6 . . . .**23** B7
Tacitus Cl **2** SG1 . . . .**51** C8
Tailors CM23 . . . .**76** B5
Takeley Cl EN9 . . . .**163** D6
Talbot Ave WD1 . . . .**167** E2
Talbot Ct HP3 . . . .**124** D1
Talbot Rd Harrow HA3 . . . .**176** F1
Hatfield AL10 . . . .**130** A8
Luton LU2 . . . .**45** F2
Rickmansworth WD3 . . . . . .**165** L1
Talbot St Hertford SG13 . . .**113** E6
Hitchin SG5 . . . .**34** C8
Talbot Way SG6 . . . .**12** B1
Talisman St SG4 . . . .**35** C6
Tall Trees Hitchin SG4 . . . . .**35** A4
Royston SG8 . . . .**7** E6
Tallack Cl HA3 . . . .**176** E3
Tallents Cres AL5 . . . .**86** D3
Tallis Way WD6 . . . .**169** E8
Tamar Cl SG1 . . . .**37** A3
Tamar Gn HP2 . . . .**124** F8
Tamarisk Cl AL3 . . . .**127** D7
Tameton Cl LU2 . . . .**46** F2
Tamworth Rd SG13 . . . . . .**113** F7
Tancred Rd LU2 . . . .**46** A4
Tanfield Cl EN7 . . . .**148** A4
Tanfield Gn LU2 . . . .**46** E1
Tanglewood
Harpenden AL5 . . . .**85** F2
Welwyn AL6 . . . .**90** A7
Tanglewood Cl HA7 . . . . . .**176** E8
Tanner Ho WD1 . . . .**167** B2
Tanners Cl AL3 . . . .**127** C4
Tanners Cres SG13 . . . . . .**113** C4
Tanners Hill WD5 . . . .**154** A8
Tanners Way SG12 . . . . . .**116** D8
Tanners Wood Cl WD5 . . . .**153** E7
Tanners Wood
Jun Mix Inf Sch WD5 . . . .**153** E7
Tanners Wood La WD5 . . .**153** E7
Tannery Cl SG8 . . . .**7** C6
Tannery Drift SG8 . . . .**7** C6
Tannery Drift Sch SG8 . . . . .**7** C6
Tannery The SG9 . . . .**40** E7
Tannery Yd SG4 . . . .**66** F6
Tannsfield Dr **1** HP2 . . . . .**124** F5
Tannsmore Cl **2** HP2 . . . .**124** F5
Tansycroft AL7 . . . .**111** B7
Tanworth Cl HA6 . . . .**174** C4
Tanworth Gdns HA5 . . . . .**175** C1
Tany's Dell CM20 . . . .**118** A3
Tany's Dell
Cty Prim Sch CM20 . . . . . .**118** A3
Tanyard La AL6,SG4 . . . .**88** B8
Tapster St EN5 . . . .**171** F6
Taransay HP3 . . . .**125** B1
Tarlings CM20 . . . .**117** F3
Tarpan Way EN10 . . . .**148** F6
Tarrant SG1 . . . .**36** B1
Tarrant Dr AL5 . . . .**107** D7
Tassell Hall AL3 . . . .**105** F6
Tate Gdns WD2 . . . .**168** A2
Tatlers La SG2 . . . .**51** E4
Tatsfield Ave EN9 . . . .**149** D8
Tattershall Dr HP2 . . . . . .**105** B1
Tattle Hill SG14 . . . .**91** E2
Tattlers Hill HP22 . . . .**60** B3
Tauber Rd WD6 . . . .**169** F5
Taunton Rd LU2 . . . .**46** B1
Taverners HP2 . . . .**124** E5
Taverners Way EN11 . . . . .**135** A6
Tavistock Ave AL1 . . . .**141** D8
Tavistock Cl
Potters Bar EN6 . . . .**159** D8
St Albans AL1 . . . .**141** D8
Tavistock Cres LU1 . . . .**63** E5
Tavistock Rd WD2 . . . .**167** D8

Tavistock St LU1 . . . .**63** E6
Taylor Cl Harefield UB9 . . . .**173** C1
St Albans AL4 . . . .**128** A8
Taylor St LU2 . . . .**63** F8
Taylor Trad Est SG13 . . . .**114** B7
Taylor's Hill SG4 . . . .**34** F6
Taylor's La EN5 . . . .**171** E5
Taylors Ave EN11 . . . .**135** A5
Taywood Cl SG2 . . . .**51** B2
Teal Dr HA6 . . . .**174** C3
Teal Ho WD2 . . . .**154** E3
Teasdale Cl SG8 . . . .**2** D1
Teasel Cl SG8 . . . .**7** B5
Tedder Ave SG16 . . . .**10** B5
Tedder Rd HP2 . . . .**125** A4
Tee Side SG13 . . . .**114** B7
Teesdale
Hemel Hempstead HP2 . . . .**124** E6
Luton LU4 . . . .**44** C5
Telford Ave SG2 . . . .**51** B6
Telford Cl WD2 . . . .**154** D4
Telford Ct Hatfield AL10 . . .**129** F3
St Albans AL1 . . . .**127** E2
Telford Rd AL2 . . . .**142** C4
Telford Way LU1 . . . .**63** D8
Telmere Ind Est **18** LU1 . . .**63** E6
Telscombe Way LU2 . . . . . .**46** C3
Temperance St AL3 . . . . . .**127** C3
Tempest Ave EN6 . . . .**159** D7
Templar Ave SG7 . . . .**23** F6
Templars Dr HA3 . . . .**176** D4
Templars La SG4 . . . .**48** D6
Temple Bank CM20 . . . . . .**118** B5
Temple Cl Cheshunt EN7 . . .**162** A8
Luton LU2 . . . .**45** E5
Preston SG5 . . . .**34** B4
Watford WD1 . . . .**166** F7
Temple Ct Baldock SG7 . . . .**23** F6
Hertford SG14 . . . .**92** D1
Temple Fields SG14 . . . . . .**92** D1
Temple Gdns
Letchworth SG6 . . . .**23** C8
Moor Park WD3 . . . .**174** B6
Temple La SG12 . . . .**92** F1
Temple Mead
Hemel Hempstead HP2 . . . .**124** D5
Roydon CM19 . . . .**116** B1
Temple View AL3 . . . .**127** C5
Templefields Ent Ctr
CM20 . . . .**118** A3
Templepan La WD3 . . . . . .**152** E2
Templewood AL8 . . . .**89** D1
Templewood
Jun Mix Inf Sch AL8 . . . . .**110** D8
Tempsford HP2 . . . .**111** D6
Tempsford Ave WD6 . . . . .**170** D5
Temsford Cl HA2 . . . .**176** C1
Tenby Dr LU4 . . . .**44** A3
Tenby Mews LU4 . . . .**44** E3
Tene The SG7 . . . .**23** F8
Tennand Cl EN7 . . . .**147** F2
Tennison Ave WD6 . . . .**170** B4
Tennyson Ave
Hitchin SG4 . . . .**35** C7
Waltham Abbey EN9 . . . . . .**163** E5
Tennyson Cl SG8 . . . .**2** E1
Tennyson Ho LU1 . . . .**63** E5
Tennyson Rd
Chiswellgreen AL2 . . . .**141** B5
Harpenden AL5 . . . .**86** A2
Luton LU1 . . . .**63** E5
Tennyson Road Prim Sch
LU1 . . . .**63** E5
Tenterfield Ho AL6 . . . .**89** C4
Tenth Ave LU3 . . . .**44** C7
Tenzing Gr LU1 . . . .**63** C6
Tenzing Rd HP2 . . . .**125** A3
Teresa Gdns EN8 . . . .**162** D5
Terminus St CM20 . . . .**117** D1
Terrace Gdns WD1 . . . . . .**167** B7
Terrace The
Essendon AL9 . . . .**131** C6
Redbourn AL3 . . . .**106** A5
Tring HP23 . . . .**100** A3
Tethys Rd HP2 . . . .**124** F6
Tewin Cl St Albans AL4 . . . .**128** C7
Tewin AL6 . . . .**90** C5
Tewin Ct AL7 . . . .**110** F7
Tewin Hill AL6 . . . .**90** C5
Tewin Rd
Hemel Hempstead HP2 . . . .**125** C3
Welwyn Garden City AL7 . . .**110** F7
Thackeray Cl SG8 . . . .**2** D1
Thames Ave HP2 . . . .**124** F8
Thames Ct LU3 . . . .**45** B3
Thames Tallis
Cty Inf Sch The EN9 . . . . .**163** F6
Thamesdale AL2 . . . .**142** F4
Thanet Ho **1** WD1 . . . . . .**166** F3
Thatchers Croft HP2 . . . . .**124** E7
Thatchers End SG4 . . . .**35** D8
Thatchers The CM23 . . . . . .**76** C5
Thaxted Cl LU2 . . . .**46** F2
Thaxted Way EN9 . . . .**163** D6
Thaynesfield EN6 . . . .**159** D8
The Riverside Club
(Tennis Ctr) HA6 . . . .**174** B3
Theabald's Grove Sta
EN8 . . . .**162** D7
Thelby Cl LU3 . . . .**44** F6
Thele Ave SG12 . . . .**115** D4
Thele Est SG12 . . . .**115** D4
Theleway Cl EN11 . . . .**115** B1
Thellusson Way WD3 . . . .**165** A2
Thelusson Ct WD7 . . . .**156** A3
Theobald Bsns Ctr SG4 . . . .**22** A3

Sto–Thr 207

Theobald Cres HA3 . . . . . .**176** C2
Theobald St
Borehamwood WD6 . . . . . .**169** F7
Radlett WD7 . . . .**156** D2
Theobald's Pk
Cheshunt EN8 . . . .**162** B7
Cheshunt EN8 . . . .**162** D7
Theobald's Rd EN6 . . . . . .**146** F1
Theobalds Cl EN6 . . . .**146** F1
Theobalds Park Coll
EN7 . . . .**162** A6
Theobalds Park Rd EN2 . .**161** B3
Therfield Fst Sch SG8 . . . . .**15** F7
Therfield Heath Nature
Reserve SG8 . . . .**7** B5
Therfield Rd AL3 . . . .**127** D6
Thetford Gdns LU2 . . . .**45** E6
Thieves' La SG14 . . . .**112** F7
Third Ave Letchworth SG6 . . .**23** C7
Luton LU3 . . . .**44** D7
Watford WD2 . . . .**154** D4
Thirlestane AL1 . . . .**127** F4
Thirlestone Rd LU4 . . . .**44** D1
Thirlmere SG1 . . . .**37** C2
Thirlmere Dr AL1 . . . .**128** B1
Thirlmere Gdns HA6 . . . . .**174** C4
Thirsk Rd WD6 . . . .**157** A1
Thirston Path WD6 . . . . . .**170** A7
Thistle Cl HP1 . . . .**123** E2
Thistle Gr AL7 . . . .**111** C3
Thistle Rd LU1 . . . .**63** F7
Thistlecroft HP1 . . . .**124** B2
Thistles The HP1 . . . .**124** B4
Thistley La SG4 . . . .**34** F1
Thomas Alleyne Sch The
SG1 . . . .**50** C8
Thomas Coram
CE Mid Sch The HP4 . . . .**122** D2
Thomas Ct HP4 . . . .**121** F5
Thomas Heskin Ct **11**
CM23 . . . .**77** A7
Thomas Rochford Way
EN8 . . . .**148** F4
Thomas Watson
Cottage Homes The
EN5 . . . .**171** E4
Thomas Way SG8 . . . .**2** D1
Thompson Way WD3 . . . . .**165** A1
Thompsons Cl
Goff's Oak EN7 . . . .**147** F2
Harpenden AL5 . . . .**86** A1
Thompsons Mdw SG8 . . . . .**1** F4
Thorley Ctr CM23 . . . .**76** D4
Thorley High CM23 . . . .**76** F2
Thorley Hill CM23 . . . .**76** F5
Thorley Hill
Jun Mix Inf Sch CM23 . . . .**76** F4
Thorley La Bishop's Stortford,
Thorley CM23 . . . .**76** D3
Bishop's Stortford,
Thorley Houses CM23 . . . .**76** B4
Bishop's Stortford,
Thorley Street CM23 . . . . .**76** F3
Thorley Park Rd CM23 . . . .**76** F4
Thorn Ave WD2 . . . .**168** C1
Thorn Gr CM23 . . . .**77** B6
Thorn Grove
Jun Mix Inf Sch CM23 . . . .**77** B6
Thorn Tree Dr HP23 . . . . . .**99** F4
Thornage Cl LU2 . . . .**45** D7
Thornbera Cl CM23 . . . .**76** F4
Thornbera Gdns CM23 . . . .**76** F4
Thornbera Rd CM23 . . . . . .**76** F4
Thornbury AL5 . . . .**86** D1
Thornbury Cl
Hoddesdon EN11 . . . .**115** B2
Stevenage SG2 . . . .**69** A8
Thornbury Gdns WD6 . . . .**170** C5
Thorncroft HP2 . . . .**125** B1
Thorndyke Ct HA5 . . . .**175** F3
Thorne Cl HP1 . . . .**124** B1
Thorne Ho AL1 . . . .**127** E4
Thorne Way HP22 . . . .**99** B4
Thorneycroft Dr EN3 . . . . .**163** A2
Thornfield Rd Luton LU4 . . .**44** F2
Moor Park HA6 . . . .**174** C6
Thornton Gr HA5 . . . .**176** A4
Thornton Rd Barnet EN5 . .**171** E6
Potters Bar EN6 . . . .**145** C1
Thornton St
Hertford SG14 . . . .**113** D4
St Albans AL1 . . . .**127** C4
Thorntondale **5** LU4 . . . . .**44** C5
Thorpe Cres WD1 . . . .**167** C2
Thorpe Rd AL1 . . . .**127** D2
Thorpefield Cl AL4 . . . . . .**128** D6
Thrales Cl LU3 . . . .**44** E7
Three Cherrytrees La
HP2 . . . .**125** B7
Three Close La HP4 . . . . . .**122** C4
Three Closes SG5 . . . .**20** C4
Three Corners HP3 . . . . . .**125** A1
Three Houses La SG4 . . . . .**67** D5
Three Rivers Mus of
Local History WD3 . . . . . .**165** E2
Three Stiles SG2 . . . .**52** E4
Three Valleys Way WD2 . .**167** E4
Tremhall Ave CM23 . . . .**77** F8
Thresher Cl CM23 . . . .**76** C5
Thricknells Cl LU3 . . . .**44** E7
Thrift Farm La HP4 . . . . . .**170** C7
Thristers Cl SG6 . . . .**23** B7
Throcking La SG9 . . . .**27** C1
Thrums WD2 . . . .**154** B2

Thrush Ave AL10 . . . .**130** A3
Thrush Gn WD3 . . . .**165** C2
Thrush La EN6 . . . .**146** F3
Thumbswood AL7 . . . .**111** A3
Thumbswood Inf Sch
 AL7 . . . .**111** A5
Thumpers HP2 . . . .**124** E5
Thunder Hall **1** SG12 . . . . .**93** D2
Thundercourt SG12 . . . .**93** D2
Thundridge Cl AL7 . . . .**111** B5
Thurgood Rd EN11 . . . .**135** A8
Thurlow Cl SG1 . . . .**36** D2
Thurnall Ave SG8 . . . .**7** D5
Thurnall Cl SG8 . . . .**23** F8
Tibbles Cl WD2 . . . .**154** E4
Tibbs Hill Rd WD5 . . . .**139** F1
Tiberius Rd LU3 . . . .**44** F6
Tichborne WD3 . . . .**172** D5
Tile Kiln Cl HP3 . . . .**125** B2
Tile Kiln Cres HP3 . . . .**125** B2
Tile Kiln La HP3 . . . .**125** B2
Tilecroft AL8 . . . .**89** D1
Tilehouse Cl WD6 . . . .**169** F6
Tilehouse La UB9 . . . .**172** E2
Tilehouse St SG5 . . . .**34** E6
Tilekiln Cl EN7 . . . .**147** F2
Tilgate LU2 . . . .**46** D3
Tillers Link SG2 . . . .**51** A2
Tillotson Rd HA3 . . . .**176** B3
Tilsworth Wlk AL4 . . . .**128** C8
Timber Orch SG14 . . . .**92** A2
Timber Ridge WD3 . . . .**165** D5
Timbercroft AL7 . . . .**89** F1
Timbers Cl AL5 . . . .**85** F2
Times Cl SG5 . . . .**21** D2
Timplings Row HP1 . . . .**124** B5
Timworth Cl LU2 . . . .**46** D1
Tingeys Cl AL3 . . . .**106** A5
Tinkers La HP23 **2** **121** A6
Tinsley Cl LU1 . . . .**63** E5
Tintagel Cl
 Hemel Hempstead HP2 . . . .**124** D8
 Luton LU3 . . . .**45** B4
Tintern Cl Harpenden AL5 . . .**85** C4
 Stevenage SG2 . . . .**69** A7
Tinwell Mews WD6 . . . .**170** D4
Tippendell La AL2 . . . .**141** C5
Tippet Ct SG1 . . . .**50** D3
Titan Cl LU4 . . . .**44** F1
Titan Rd HP2 . . . .**124** F6
Titchfield Rd EN3 . . . .**162** E2
Tithe Barn Cl AL1 . . . .**141** C8
Tithe Cl SG4 . . . .**67** F1
Titian Ave WD6 . . . .**168** E2
Titmore Ct SG4 . . . .**35** E2
Titmus Cl SG1 . . . .**50** E6
Tiverton Ct AL5 . . . .**107** E6
Tiverton Rd EN6 . . . .**159** E8
Toddington Rd LU4 . . . .**44** C6
Toland Cl LU4 . . . .**44** C1
Tolcarne Dr HA5 . . . .**175** A1
Tollgate Cl WD3 . . . .**164** F5
Tollgate Rd
 Colney Heath AL4,AL9 . . . . .**143** E7
 Enfield EN3 . . . .**162** D4
 Welham Green AL4 . . . .**144** A6
Tollpit End HP1 . . . .**124** A6
Tollsworth Way SG11 . . . . . .**55** D3
Tolmers Ave EN6 . . . .**146** E3
Tolmers Gdns EN6 . . . .**146** F2
Tolmers Mews EN6 . . . .**146** E6
Tolmers Rd EN6 . . . .**146** E3
Tolpits Cl WD1 . . . .**166** F4
Tolpits La WD1 . . . .**166** E2
Tom's Hill WD3 . . . .**152** E3
Tomkins Cl WD6 . . . .**169** E8
Toms Croft HP2 . . . .**124** E2
Toms Field AL10 . . . .**129** E4
Toms Hill Rd HP23 . . . .**101** D5
Toms La WD4,WD5 . . . .**139** D3
Tomshill HP23 . . . .**101** D5
Tonwell St Mary's
 CE Prim Sch SG12 . . . .**92** E7
Tooke Cl HA5 . . . .**175** E2
Toorack Rd HA3 . . . .**176** D1
Tooveys Mill Cl WD4 . . . . . .**139** A2
Topstreet Way AL5 . . . .**107** C8
Torquay Cres SG1 . . . .**50** B7
Torquay Dr LU4 . . . .**44** D4
Torridge Wlk **2** HP2 . . . . . .**124** F8
Torrington Dr EN6 . . . .**159** D7
Torrington Rd HP4 . . . .**122** B4
Tortoiseshell Way HP4 . . . . .**121** F4
Torwood Cl HP4 . . . .**121** F4
Torworth Rd WD6 . . . .**157** A1
Tot La CM23 . . . .**59** D4
Totteridge Comm N20 . . . .**171** D1
Totteridge Pk N20 . . . .**171** C1
Totteridge Rd EN3 . . . .**162** D2
Totteridge Village N20 . . . .**171** F1
Totton Mews AL3 . . . .**106** B5
Totts La SG2 . . . .**38** C1
Toulmin Dr AL3 . . . .**127** C7
Tovey Cl AL2 . . . .**142** D5
Tower Cl
 Berkhamsted HP4 . . . .**122** A3
 Kneesworth SG8 . . . .**2** A5
 Little Wymondley SG4 . . . . .**35** F3
Tower Ct LU2 . . . .**46** A1
Tower Ctr **10** EN11 . . . .**135** A7
Tower Hill
 Chipperfield HP3,WD4 . . . . .**137** F1
 Much Hadham SG10 . . . .**74** F2
Tower Hill La AL4 . . . .**108** F4
Tower Hts EN11 . . . .**135** A6

Tower Prim Sch SG12 . . . . . .**93** E3
Tower Rd Codicote SG4 . . . . .**67** F2
 Luton LU2 . . . .**64** A8
 Ware SG12 . . . .**93** F2
Tower St SG14 . . . .**113** C8
Tower View SG4 . . . .**66** D6
Tower Way LU2 . . . .**64** A8
Towers Rd
 Hemel Hempstead HP2 . . . .**124** E4
 Pinner HA5 . . . .**175** E2
 Stevenage SG1 . . . .**50** D4
Towers The SG1 . . . .**50** D4
Town Ctr AL10 . . . .**130** A6
Town Farm
 Cheddington LU7 . . . .**80** A7
 Wheathampstead AL4 . . . . .**108** D8
Town Farm Cl SG8 . . . .**1** F4
Town Farm Cres SG11 . . . . . .**55** F2
Town Fields AL10 . . . .**130** A6
Town La SG2 . . . .**52** E4
Town Mead Rd EN9 . . . . . .**163** D5
Town Sq SG1 . . . .**50** D5
Town Rd SG8 . . . .**7** D5
Townfield WD3 . . . .**165** C2
Townley SG6 . . . .**23** D4
Townsend HP2 . . . .**124** D5
Townsend Ave AL1 . . . .**127** E4
Townsend CE Sch AL3 . . . . .**127** C4
Townsend Cl Barkway SG8 . . .**17** C3
 Harpenden AL5 . . . .**85** F1
Townsend Dr AL3 . . . .**127** D5
Townsend La AL5 . . . .**85** F1
Townsend Rd AL5 . . . .**86** A2
Townsend La AL5 . . . .**85** F1
Townshend St SG13 . . . . . .**113** E6
Townsley Cl LU1 . . . .**63** E6
Tracey Ct **15** LU1 . . . .**63** E6
Trafalgar Ave EN10 . . . . . .**134** F2
Trafford Cl Shenley WD7 . . .**156** F7
 Stevenage SG1 . . . .**36** E1
Traherne Cl **2** SG4 . . . .**34** F5
Trajan Gate SG1 . . . .**37** D1
Trapstyle Rd SG12 . . . .**93** A2
Travellers Cl AL9 . . . .**144** C8
Travellers La
 Hatfield AL9,AL10 . . . .**130** B2
 Welham Green AL9 . . . .**130** C1
Treacle La SG9 . . . .**25** F3
Treacy Cl WD2 . . . .**176** C8
Trebellan Dr HP2 . . . .**124** F4
Tree Cl HP3 . . . .**125** B1
Tree Ct WD6 . . . .**169** D3
Treehanger Cl HP23 . . . . . .**100** B4
Treetops AL6 . . . .**89** E7
Treetops Cl HA6 . . . .**174** D5
Trefoil Cl LU4 . . . .**44** A4
Trefusis Wlk WD1 . . . .**166** E8
Tremaine Gr HP2 . . . .**124** E7
Trent Cl Shenley WD7 . . . . .**156** F7
 Stevenage SG1 . . . .**50** E8
Trent Rd LU3 . . . .**45** B4
Tresco Rd HP4 . . . .**121** F5
Trescott Cl LU2 . . . .**46** E2
Tresilion Sq HP2 . . . .**125** A8
Treslian Sq **1** HP2 . . . .**124** F8
Trevalga Way HP2 . . . .**124** E7
Trevellance Way WD2 . . . . .**154** D6
Trevelyan Way HP4 . . . .**122** B6
Trevera Ct EN11 . . . .**135** A7
Trevero Ct EN8 . . . .**162** E6
Trevor Cl HA3 . . . .**176** F3
Trevor Rd SG4 . . . .**35** A8
Trevose Way WD1 . . . .**175** C7
Trewenna Dr EN6 . . . .**159** D7
Triangle The SG4 . . . .**34** F6
Trident Ave AL10 . . . .**129** E6
Trident Ind Est EN11 . . . . . .**135** C7
Trident Rd WD2 . . . .**153** F5
Triggs Way LU2 . . . .**46** E3
Trimley Cl LU4 . . . .**44** B5
Trinder Rd EN5 . . . .**171** C4
Tring Bsns Ctr HP23 . . . .**99** E4
Tring Ford Rd HP23 . . . . . .**100** A7
Tring Hill HP23 . . . .**99** C3
Tring Ho WD1 . . . .**166** E8
Tring Rd
 Berkhamsted HP4 . . . .**121** D7
 Long Marston HP23 . . . .**79** C3
 Wingrave HP22 . . . .**60** C1
Tring Sch HP23 . . . .**100** B4
Tring Sta HP23 . . . .**101** A5
Trinity Cl
 Bishop's Stortford CM23 . . . .**76** F6
 Northwood HA6 . . . .**174** E4
Trinity Gr SG14 . . . .**113** C8
Trinity Hall Cl WD2 . . . .**167** C6
Trinity La EN1 . . . .**162** E7
Trinity Mews HP2 . . . .**125** D2
Trinity Pl SG1 . . . .**50** D6
Trinity Rd
 Hertford Heath SG13 . . . . .**114** C3
 Luton LU3 . . . .**45** A4
 Stevenage SG1 . . . .**50** C6
 Stotfold SG5 . . . .**11** F7
 Ware SG12 . . . .**93** E2
Trinity St CM23 . . . .**76** E5
Trinity Way CM23 . . . .**76** F6
Trinity Wlk SG13 . . . .**114** C3
Tristram Rd SG4 . . . .**22** B2
Triton Way HP2 . . . .**124** F5
Trojan Terr CM21 . . . .**97** E3
Troon Gdns LU2 . . . .**45** E7
Trooper Rd HP23 . . . .**101** C5
Trotter's Gap SG12 . . . .**115** E4
Trotters Bottom EN5 . . . . . .**158** B2
Trotts Hill Prim Sch SG1 . . . .**36** F1
Trout Rise WD3 . . . .**165** B6

Troutstream Way WD3 . . . .**165** B5
Trouvere Pk HP1 . . . .**124** B5
Trowbridge Gdns LU2 . . . . . .**45** E3
Trowley Bottom AL3 . . . . . .**105** B8
Trowley Hill Rd AL3 . . . .**84** B1
Trowley Hts AL3 . . . .**84** B2
Trowley Rise WD5 . . . .**153** F8
Truemans Rd SG5 . . . .**21** D2
Trumper Rd SG1 . . . .**36** F1
Trumpington Dr AL1 . . . . . .**141** D8
Truncals LU1 . . . .**63** D5
Trundlers Way WD2 . . . . . .**168** E1
Truro Gdns LU3 . . . .**45** C5
Trust Cotts HP4 . . . .**81** A1
Trust Rd EN8 . . . .**162** E5
Tucker St WD1 . . . .**167** C4
Tucker's Row **4** CM23 . . . . .**76** F6
Tudor Ave Cheshunt EN7 . . .**162** B8
 Watford WD2 . . . .**154** D2
Tudor Cl Cheshunt EN7 . . . .**162** B8
 Hatfield AL10 . . . .**129** F2
 Hunsdon SG12 . . . .**116** D8
 Stevenage SG1 . . . .**36** C1
Tudor Cres EN2 . . . .**161** C1
Tudor Ct
 Borehamwood WD6 . . . . . .**169** E7
 Hitchin SG5 . . . .**34** D6
 Kneesworth SG8 . . . .**2** B4
 Rickmansworth WD3 . . . . . .**165** A1
 Sawbridgeworth CM21 . . . . .**97** E3
Tudor Dr WD2 . . . .**154** D2
Tudor Jun Mix Inf Sch
 HP3 . . . .**124** E1
Tudor Manor Gdns WD2 . . .**154** D7
Tudor Par HP3 . . . .**165** A2
Tudor Rd Harrow HA3 . . . . .**176** D1
 Luton LU3 . . . .**45** B2
 Pinner HA5 . . . .**175** C1
 St Albans AL3 . . . .**127** E7
 Welwyn AL6 . . . .**89** B3
 Wheathampstead AL4 . . . . .**108** E8
Tudor Rise EN10 . . . .**134** F2
Tudor Way Hertford SG14 . .**113** A7
 Rickmansworth WD3 . . . . . .**165** A2
 Waltham Abbey EN9 . . . . . .**163** D6
Tudor Wlk WD2 . . . .**154** D2
Tuffnells Way AL5 . . . .**85** D4
Tunfield Rd EN11 . . . .**115** B1
Tunnel Wood Cl WD1 . . . . .**153** F2
Tunnel Wood Rd WD1 . . . . .**153** F2
Tunnmeade CM20 . . . .**118** A1
Turf La SG4 . . . .**36** B4
Turkey St EN1,EN3 . . . .**162** C2
Turkey Street Sta EN3 . . . . .**162** C2
Turmore Dale AL8 . . . .**110** C5
Turn Braemar HP2 . . . .**105** B1
Turnberry Ct WD1 . . . .**175** C7
Turnberry Dr AL2 . . . .**140** E1
Turner Cl SG1 . . . .**36** C2
Turner Rd WD2 . . . .**168** C5
Turners Cl Bramfield SG14 . . .**91** C4
 Harpenden AL5 . . . .**86** C4
Turners Cres CM23 . . . .**76** C4
Turners Ct EN8 . . . .**162** D8
Turners Hill
 Cheshunt EN8 . . . .**148** D1
 Hemel Hempstead HP2 . . . .**124** E2
Turners Orch WD3 . . . .**164** D4
Turners Rd N LU2 . . . .**46** A2
Turners Rd S LU2 . . . .**46** A2
Turnford Sch EN8 . . . .**148** E3
Turnford Villas EN8 . . . .**148** F5
Turnpike Dr LU3 . . . .**31** C1
Turnpike Gn HP2 . . . .**124** F7
Turnpike La SG5 . . . .**21** E3
Turnstones The WD2 . . . . . .**154** E3
Turpin Cl EN3 . . . .**163** A2
Turpin's Ride SG8 . . . .**7** D5
Turpin's Rise SG2 . . . .**50** F1
Turpin's Way SG7 . . . .**23** F7
Turpins Chase AL6 . . . .**89** F7
Turpins Cl SG14 . . . .**112** F6
Turpins Ride AL6 . . . .**89** F7
Tuthill Ct SG8 . . . .**15** E7
Tuxford Cl WD6 . . . .**156** E1
Tweed Cl HP4 . . . .**122** B5
Twelve Acres AL7 . . . .**110** E4
Twelve Leys HP22 . . . .**60** B3
Twickenham Gdns HA3 . . . .**176** E3
Twigden Ct LU3 . . . .**44** E5
Twin Foxes SG3 . . . .**69** A1
Twinwoods SG1 . . . .**50** F4
Twist The HP23 . . . .**100** D2
Twitchell The SG7 . . . .**23** F8
Two Acres AL7 . . . .**110** F3
Two Beeches HP2 . . . .**124** F8
Two Dells La HP5 . . . .**136** A4
Two Oaks Dr AL6 . . . .**90** C6
Two Waters Prim Sch
 HP3 . . . .**138** D6
Two Waters Rd
 Hemel Hempstead HP3 . . . .**124** C1
 Hemel Hempstead HP3 . . . .**138** D8
Twyford Bsns Ctr The
 CM23 . . . .**77** A4
Twyford Bury La CM22 . . . . .**77** A4
Twyford Cl CM23 . . . .**77** A5
Twyford Dr LU2 . . . .**46** D1
Twyford Gdns CM23 . . . .**76** F4
Twyford Mill CM22 . . . .**77** A3
Twyford Rd
 Bishop's Stortford CM23 . . . .**77** A5
 St Albans AL4 . . . .**128** D7
Tye End SG2 . . . .**69** B8
Tyfield Cl EN8 . . . .**148** C1
Tylers AL5 . . . .**86** D1
Tylers Cl Buntingford SG9 . . .**40** D7
 Kings Langley WD4 . . . .**138** F3

Tylers Cswy SG13 . . . .**132** C1
Tylers Hill Rd HP5 . . . .**150** A8
Tylers Mead LU2 . . . .**45** E5
Tylers Way WD2 . . . .**168** E4
Tylers Wood AL6 . . . .**90** C6
Tylersfield WD5 . . . .**154** A8
Tynedale AL2 . . . .**142** F4
Tynemouth Dr EN1 . . . .**162** A1
Typleden Cl HP2 . . . .**124** D5
Tysoe Ave EN3 . . . .**162** F2
Tythe Rd LU4 . . . .**44** C6
Tyttenhanger Gn AL1 . . . . .**142** E8

U
Uckfield Rd EN3 . . . .**162** D2
Ufford Cl HA3 . . . .**176** B3
Ufford Rd HA3 . . . .**176** B3
Ullswater Cl SG1 . . . .**37** C2
Ullswater Rd HP3 . . . .**125** C1
Underacres Cl HP2 . . . .**125** A4
Underhill Jun & Inf Schs
 EN5 . . . .**171** E4
Underwood Rd SG1 . . . .**36** C2
Union Chapel Ho **1** LU1 . . .**63** E6
Union Gn HP2 . . . .**124** D4
Union St Barnet EN5 . . . . . .**171** E6
 Luton LU1 . . . .**63** E6
Union Terr SG9 . . . .**40** E7
Unity Rd EN3 . . . .**162** D2
University AL10 . . . .**168** A5
University of Hertfordshire
 AL10 . . . .**129** F3
University of Hertfordshire
(Hertford Campus)
 SG13 . . . .**113** E4
Unwin Cl SG6 . . . .**22** C5
Unwin Pl SG2 . . . .**51** C3
Unwin Rd SG2 . . . .**51** C3
Updale Cl EN6 . . . .**158** E6
Upland Dr AL9 . . . .**145** B6
Uplands Braughing SG11 . . .**55** F6
 Croxley Green WD3 . . . . . .**165** F3
 Luton LU3 . . . .**44** D8
 Stevenage SG2 . . . .**51** D7
 Ware SG12 . . . .**93** F2
 Welwyn Garden City AL8 . . .**89** C2
Uplands Ave SG4 . . . .**35** B6
Uplands Ct LU1 . . . .**63** E4
Uplands The
 Bricket Wood AL2 . . . .**140** E1
 Harpenden AL5 . . . .**107** A4
Upper Ashlyns Rd HP4 . . . .**122** B3
Upper Barn HP3 . . . .**138** F8
Upper Bourne End La
 HP1 . . . .**137** B8
Upper Clabdens SG12 . . . . . .**93** F2
Upper Culver Rd AL1 . . . . . .**127** F5
Upper Dagnall St AL3 . . . . .**127** D3
Upper George St LU1 . . . . . .**63** D7
Upper Gn AL6 . . . .**90** D3
Upper Green Rd AL6 . . . .**90** E3
Upper Hall Pk HP4 . . . .**122** E2
Upper Heath Rd AL1 . . . . . .**127** F5
Upper Highway WD5 . . . . . .**153** D6
Upper Hill Rise WD3 . . . . . .**165** B3
Upper Hitch WD1 . . . .**167** E1
Upper Icknield Way
 Aldbury LU7 . . . .**80** E1
 Aston Clinton HP22 . . . .**99** A3
 Tring HP23 . . . .**100** D8
Upper King St SG8 . . . .**7** D6
Upper Lattimore Rd
 AL1 . . . .**127** E3
Upper Marlborough Rd
 AL1 . . . .**127** E3
Upper Marsh La EN11 . . . . .**135** A5
Upper Maylins SG6 . . . .**23** C3
Upper Paddock Rd WD1 . . .**167** E3
Upper Pk CM20 . . . .**117** B1
Upper Sales HP1 . . . .**123** F2
Upper Sean SG2 . . . .**51** A3
Upper Shot AL7 . . . .**111** A7
Upper Shott EN7 . . . .**147** F5
Upper Station Rd WD7 . . . .**156** A4
Upper Tail WD1 . . . .**175** E7
Upper Tilehouse St SG5 . . . .**34** E7
Upperfield Rd AL7 . . . .**110** F5
Upperstone Cl SG5 . . . .**11** F6
Upshire Rd EN9 . . . .**163** F7
Upton Ave AL3 . . . .**127** D4
Upton Cl Luton LU2 . . . .**45** D9
 Park Street AL2 . . . .**141** D6
Upton Lodge Cl WD2 . . . . .**168** C2
Upton Rd WD1 . . . .**167** B6
Upwell Rd LU2 . . . .**46** B2
Uranus Rd HP2 . . . .**124** F5
Urban Rd CM23 . . . .**77** B7
Uxbridge Rd WD3 . . . .**173** A8
Uxbridge Rd
 (Harrow Weald) HA3 . . .**176** D3
Uxbridge Rd
 (Hatch End) HA5 . . . . . .**175** F3
Uxbridge Rd
 (Pinner) HA5 . . . .**175** D2
Uxbridge Rd
 (Stanmore) HA7 . . . .**176** F4

V
Vadis Cl LU3 . . . .**44** F7
Vale Ave WD6 . . . .**170** B4
Vale Cl AL5 . . . .**85** D4
Vale Ct AL4 . . . .**108** D7
Vale Ind Pk WD1 . . . .**166** C1
Vale Rd WD2 . . . .**167** E4

Valence Dr EN7 . . . .**148** A3
Valency Cl HA6 . . . .**174** F6
Valerian Way SG2 . . . .**51** D8
Valerie Cl AL1 . . . .**128** B3
Valerie Ct WD2 . . . .**168** C2
Valeside SG14 . . . .**113** A5
Vallance SG2 . . . .**51** B1
Vallans Cl SG12 . . . .**93** D3
Vallansgate SG2 . . . .**51** B1
Valley Cl Hertford SG13 . . . .**113** D5
 Pinner HA5 . . . .**175** B1
 Studham LU6 . . . .**82** B4
 Waltham Abbey EN9 . . . . . .**163** C7
 Ware SG12 . . . .**93** B2
 Whipsnade HP4 . . . .**81** E7
Valley Gn HP1 . . . .**105** B1
Valley Gn The AL8 . . . .**110** C7
Valley La AL3 . . . .**83** E1
Valley Rd
 Berkhamsted HP4 . . . .**121** F6
 Codicote SG4 . . . .**67** F1
 Letchworth SG6 . . . .**22** D7
 Rickmansworth WD3 . . . . . .**165** B3
 St Albans AL3 . . . .**127** F7
 Studham LU6 . . . .**82** B3
 Welwyn Garden City AL8 . . .**110** B6
Valley Rise Lea Valley AL4 . . .**86** F2
 Royston SG8 . . . .**7** E5
 Watford WD2 . . . .**154** B6
Valley Sch The SG2 . . . .**50** F2
Valley The SG4 . . . .**66** E7
Valley View Barnet EN5 . . . .**171** E3
 Goff's Oak EN7 . . . .**147** C3
Valley Way SG2 . . . .**51** A3
Valley Wlk WD3 . . . .**166** C4
Valleyside HP1 . . . .**123** F3
Valpy Cl HP3 . . . .**100** D1
Vanda Cres AL1 . . . .**127** C2
Vantorts Cl CM21 . . . .**97** E2
Vantorts Rd CM21 . . . .**97** E2
Vardon Rd SG1 . . . .**50** F8
Varna Ct LU3 . . . .**45** A3
Varney Cl
 Hammond Street EN7 . . . . .**148** A4
 Hemel Hempstead HP1 . . . .**123** F3
Varney Rd HP1 . . . .**123** F3
Vaughan Mead AL3 . . . .**106** A4
Vaughan Rd
 Harpenden AL5 . . . .**86** B1
 Stotfold SG5 . . . .**11** E7
Vauxhall Rd
 Hemel Hempstead HP2 . . . .**125** B3
 Luton LU1,LU2 . . . .**64** B5
Vauxhall Way LU2 . . . .**46** B1
Vega Cres HA6 . . . .**175** A5
Vega Rd WD2 . . . .**168** C2
Velizy Ave CM20 . . . .**117** D1
Venetia Rd LU2 . . . .**46** A4
Ventnor Gdns LU3 . . . .**45** A7
Ventura Pk AL2 . . . .**141** F2
Venus Hill HP3 . . . .**151** A8
Ver Rd Redbourn AL3 . . . . .**106** C6
 St Albans AL3 . . . .**127** C3
Vera Ct WD1 . . . .**167** D2
Vera La AL6 . . . .**90** B4
Verdure Cl WD2 . . . .**154** E7
Verity Way SG1 . . . .**51** B8
Veritys AL10 . . . .**130** A5
Verney Cl
 Berkhamsted HP4 . . . .**121** F5
 Tring HP23 . . . .**100** C5
Vernon Ave EN3 . . . .**162** E3
Vernon Ct CM23 . . . .**76** E4
Vernon Dr UB9 . . . .**173** C2
Vernon Rd Luton LU1 . . . . . .**63** C8
 Watford WD2 . . . .**167** E4
Vernon's Cl AL1 . . . .**127** E2
Veronica Ho AL7 . . . .**111** B4
Verulam Cl AL7 . . . .**110** F6
Verulam Gdns LU3 . . . .**44** F6
Verulam Rd Hitchin SG5 . . . .**34** F8
 St Albans AL3 . . . .**127** C4
Verulam Sch AL1 . . . .**128** A4
Verulam Rd AL3 . . . .**127** B3
Verulamium Mus AL3 . . . . .**127** B3
Verulamium Roman
 Town AL3 . . . .**127** A3
Verwood Rd HA2 . . . .**176** C1
Vespers Cl LU4 . . . .**44** A2
Vesta Ave AL1 . . . .**141** C8
Vestry Cl LU1 . . . .**63** D7
Veysey Cl HP1 . . . .**124** B1
Viaduct Cotts LU1 . . . .**85** F8
Viaduct Rd SG12 . . . .**114** E8
Viaduct Way AL7 . . . .**89** F2
Vian Ave EN3 . . . .**162** E4
Vicarage Cl Arlesey SG15 . . . .**11** A8
 18 Bishop's Stortford CM23 . .**76** F7
 Hemel Hempstead HP1 . . . .**124** C2
 Northaw EN6 . . . .**145** F1
 Shillington SG5 . . . .**19** F8
 St Albans AL1 . . . .**141** C8
 Standon SG11 . . . .**55** E2
Vicarage Cswy SG13 . . . . . .**114** B4
Vicarage Gdns
 Flamstead AL3 . . . .**84** B1
 Marsworth HP23 . . . .**80** A2
 Potten End HP4 . . . .**123** B7
Vicarage La
 Bovingdon HP3 . . . .**137** B4
 Kings Langley WD4 . . . .**138** F2
 Pitstone LU7 . . . .**80** F5
 Stapleford SG14 . . . .**92** B2
Vicarage Rd
 Buntingford SG9 . . . .**40** E8
 Marsworth HP23 . . . .**80** A2
 Pitstone LU7 . . . .**80** D3
 Potten End HP4 . . . .**123** A7
 Ware SG12 . . . .**93** E1

Vicarage Rd continued
Watford WD1 ....167 A4
Wigginton HP23 ....100 D1
Vicarage Road Prec
WD1 ....167 B5
Vicarage St LU1 ....63 F7
Vicarage Wood CM20 ....118 A1
Vicerons Pl CM23 ....76 D4
Victoria CE Fst Sch HP4 .122 C4
Victoria Cl
Rickmansworth WD3 ....165 D2
Stevenage SG1 ....50 D7
Victoria Cres SG8 ....7 D7
Victoria Ct WD1 ....167 C6
Victoria Dr SG5 ....12 A5
Victoria La EN5 ....171 F5
Victoria Pl HP2 ....124 D3
Victoria Rd
Berkhamsted HP4 ....122 C4
Bushey WD2 ....168 B1
7 Harpenden AL5 ....86 B1
Waltham Abbey EN9 ....163 C5
Watford WD2 ....154 B1
Victoria St Luton LU1 ....63 E6
St Albans AL1 ....127 E3
Victoria Way SG5 ....34 D8
Victors Way EN5 ....171 F6
Victory Ct SG8 ....7 E5
Victory Rd HP4 ....122 A5
View Point SG1 ....50 A5
View Rd EN6 ....159 C7
Vigors Croft AL10 ....129 F4
Villa Ct 5 LU2 ....63 D8
Villa Rd LU2 ....63 D8
Village Ct AL4 ....128 D7
Village St SG4 ....49 F1
Villiers Cl LU4 ....44 D3
Villiers Cres AL4 ....128 D6
Villiers Rd WD1 ....167 E3
Villiers St SG13 ....113 E6
Villiers-Sur-Marne Ave
CM23 ....76 D4
Vincent Ave SG6 ....23 C4
Vincent Cl EN8 ....148 E3
Vincent Ct HA6 ....174 F2
Vincent Rd LU4 ....44 D5
Vincenzo Cl AL9 ....144 C8
Vine Cl AL8 ....110 E8
Vine Gr CM20 ....117 E5
Vines The SG5 ....11 E6
Vineyard The Ware SG12 ....94 A2
Welwyn Garden City AL8 ....110 E8
Vineyards Rd EN6 ....146 B2
Vinters Ave SG1 ....50 F5
Violet Ave EN2 ....161 D1
Violet Way WD3 ....165 C5
Violets La SG9 ....43 B5
Virgil Dr EN10 ....148 F8
Virginia Cl LU2 ....45 F3
Viscount Cl LU3 ....45 A5
Viscount Ct 11 LU2 ....45 D1
Vivian Cl WD1 ....167 A1
Vivian Gdns WD1 ....167 A1
Vixen Dr SG13 ....114 A6
Vyse Cl EN5 ....171 C5

W

Wacketts EN7 ....148 A4
Waddesdon Cl LU2 ....46 D2
Waddeston Ct EN2 ....161 E1
Waddington Rd 1 AL3 ....127 D3
Wade The AL7 ....111 A3
Wades The AL10 ....130 A2
Wadesmill Rd
Tonwell SG14 ....92 D3
Ware SG12 ....93 D2
Wadham Rd WD5 ....153 F8
Wadhurst Ave LU3 ....45 C4
Wadley Cl 1 HP2 ....124 F2
Wadnall Way SG3 ....68 F3
Waggon Rd EN4 ....159 E2
Waggoners Yd 4 SG12 ....93 D2
Wagon Rd EN4 ....159 B2
Wagon Way WD3 ....165 C6
Wain Cl EN6 ....145 B2
Wakefield Wlk EN8 ....162 E8
Walcot Ave LU2 ....46 B1
Waldeck Rd LU3 ....63 C8
Waldegrave Pk AL5 ....86 D1
Walden End SG1 ....50 E4
Walden Pl AL8 ....110 D8
Walden Rd AL8 ....110 D8
Waleran Cl HA7 ....176 F4
Waleys Cl LU3 ....44 E8
Walfords Cl CM17 ....118 C3
Walk The EN6 ....159 B7
Walkern Prim Sch SG2 ....52 C5
Stevenage SG1 ....50 D8
Watton at Stone SG14 ....70 D5
Walkers Cl AL5 ....107 C7
Walkers' Ct SG7 ....23 F8
Walkers Rd AL5 ....107 B7
Wall Hall (Univ Campus)
WD2 ....155 B3
Wallace Way SG4 ....22 A2
Waller Ave LU4 ....44 F3
Waller Dr HA6 ....175 A2
Waller Street Mall 3 LU1 .63 E7
Waller's Cl SG8 ....9 F2
Wallers Way EN11 ....115 B1
Wallingford Wlk AL1 ....141 D8
Wallington Rd SG7 ....13 D1
Walnut Ave SG7 ....24 A7
Walnut Cl
Chiswellgreen AL2 ....141 B4

Walnut Cl continued
Hitchin SG4 ....35 A6
Luton LU2 ....46 B4
Much Hadham SG10 ....74 F2
Royston SG8 ....7 D6
Stotfold SG5 ....11 F6
Walnut Cotts CM21 ....97 E3
Walnut Ct
Welwyn Garden City AL7 ....110 E3
Wheathampstead AL4 ....108 D8
Walnut Dr CM23 ....76 D3
Walnut Gn WD2 ....167 F7
Walnut Gr
Hemel Hempstead HP2 ....124 D3
Welwyn Garden City AL7 ....110 E3
Walnut Ho AL7 ....110 F3
Walnut Tree Ave CM21 ....97 E4
Walnut Tree Cl Aston SG2 ....51 D5
Cheshunt EN8 ....162 D8
Hoddesdon EN11 ....135 A6
Walnut Tree Cres CM21 ....97 E3
Walnut Tree La SG8 ....58 E4
Walnut Tree Rd SG5 ....20 D3
Walnut Tree Wlk SG5 ....114 E6
Walnut Way SG5 ....21 E4
Walpole Cl HA5 ....176 A4
Walpole Ct SG2 ....69 C7
Walsh Cl SG5 ....34 D7
Walsham Cl SG2 ....69 C7
Walshford Way WD6 ....157 A1
Walsingham Cl
Hatfield AL10 ....129 F6
Luton LU2 ....45 D7
Walsingham Way AL2 ....142 C4
Walsworth Rd SG4 ....35 A8
Walter Rothschild
Zoological Mus The
HP23 ....100 A3
Walters Cl EN7 ....147 B6
Waltham Abbey EN9 ....163 C6
Waltham Cross Sta EN8 ....162 F5
Waltham Ct 46 C3
Waltham Gate EN8 ....148 F5
Waltham Gdns EN3 ....162 C2
Waltham Holy Cross
Cty Jun Sch EN9 ....163 D6
Waltham Rd 4 Hitchin SG4 ....34 F6
Waltham Abbey EN9 ....149 C5
Walton Cl EN11 ....135 C8
Walton Gdns EN9 ....163 B6
Walton Rd
Hoddesdon EN11 ....135 C8
Ware SG12 ....114 D8
Watford WD2 ....167 E5
Walton St AL1 ....127 F5
Walverns Cl WD1 ....167 C3
Wandon Cl LU2 ....46 C4
Wannions Cl HP5 ....136 A1
Wansbeck Cl SG1 ....37 A3
Wansford Pk WD6 ....170 E5
Warburton Cl HA3 ....176 D4
Ward Cl
Hammond Street EN7 ....148 A4
Ware SG12 ....93 C2
Ward Cres CM23 ....76 E6
Ward Hatch CM20 ....118 A3
Warden Hill Cl LU2 ....45 C8
Warden Hill Gdns LU2 ....45 C8
Warden Hill Inf Sch LU3 .45 C7
Warden Hill Jun Sch LU3 .45 C7
Warden Hill Rd LU2 ....45 C8
Wardown Cres LU2 ....45 E2
Wardown Ct LU3 ....45 D2
Ware Mus SG12 ....93 D1
Ware Park SG14 ....113 E8
Ware Rd Hertford SG13 ....113 E6
Hoddesdon EN11 ....115 A1
Tonwell SG14 ....92 D3
Watton at Stone SG14,SG12 ....71 C3
Widford SG12 ....95 D4
Ware Sta SG12 ....114 E8
Wareham's La SG12 ....113 C5
Warenford Way WD6 ....170 A8
Wareside HP2 ....105 A1
Wareside CE Prim Sch
SG12 ....94 E3
Wareside Cl AL7 ....111 B5
Warham Rd HA3 ....176 F1
Warmark Rd HP1 ....123 E5
Warminster Cl LU2 ....46 F1
Warneford Pl WD1 ....167 E3
Warner Rd SG12 ....114 D8
Warners Ave EN11 ....134 F4
Warners Cl SG2 ....51 C3
Warners End Rd HP1 ....124 B4
Warren Cl Hatfield AL10 ....130 B8
Letchworth SG6 ....22 D7
Warren Dale AL8 ....89 D1
Warren Dell Prim Sch
WD1 ....175 C7
Warren Dr The LU1 ....64 C1
Warren Gn AL10 ....130 B8
Warren Gr WD6 ....170 D5
Warren La Clothall SG7 ....24 D7
Cottered SG9 ....39 B6
Stanmore HA7 ....176 F8
Warren Park Rd SG14 ....113 D7
Warren Pl 14 SG14 ....113 D6
Warren Rd Bushey WD2 ....168 D1
Luton LU1 ....62 F8
St Albans AL1 ....141 C7
Warren Terr SG14 ....113 D8
Warren The
Harpenden AL5 ....107 A6
Radlett WD7 ....156 B6
Royston SG8 ....7 D5
Warren Way AL6 ....89 E4
Warrenfield Cl EN7 ....162 A8

Warrengate La EN6 ....158 C8
Warrengate Rd AL9 ....144 C4
Warrensgreen La SG4 ....37 D5
Warton Gn LU2 ....46 E2
Warwick Ave EN6 ....146 D4
Warwick Cl Bushey WD2 ....168 D2
Cuffley EN6 ....146 D4
Hertford SG13 ....113 C4
Warwick Ct
Chorleywood WD3 ....164 F6
Luton LU4 ....63 B8
Warwick Dr EN8 ....148 D3
Warwick Rd
Bishop's Stortford CM23 ....77 B6
Borehamwood WD6 ....170 D6
Enfield EN3 ....162 F2
St Albans AL1 ....127 F5
Stevenage SG2 ....51 C6
Warwick Rd E LU4 ....63 B8
Warwick Rd W LU4 ....63 B8
Warwick Way WD3 ....166 C5
Wash La Potters Bar,
Dancers Hill EN5 ....158 C4
Potters Bar,
South Mimms EN6 ....158 C5
Wash The
Furneux Pelham SG9 ....43 D5
Hertford SG14 ....113 D6
Washington Ave HP2 ....124 E8
Watchlytes AL7 ....111 C6
Watchlytes Sch AL7 ....111 C6
Watchmead AL7 ....111 A6
Water End HP1 ....103 F2
Water End Rd HP4 ....123 C7
Water Hall Farm SG4 ....66 F7
Water La
Abbots Langley WD4 ....139 B2
Berkhamsted HP4 ....122 C4
Bishop's Stortford CM23 ....76 F8
Bovingdon HP3 ....137 B1
Hitchin SG5 ....21 F1
Stansted Mountfitchet CM24 ....59 E6
Watford WD1 ....167 D5
Water Row 11 SG12 ....93 D1
Waterbeach AL7 ....111 D6
Watercress Cl SG2 ....51 D5
Watercress Rd EN7 ....147 D5
Waterdale SG13 ....113 C4
Waterdell La SG4 ....35 A2
Waterend La
Ayot St Peter AL4,AL6 ....88 E1
Redbourn AL3 ....106 B5
Waterfield
Chorleywood WD3 ....164 C2
Welwyn Garden City AL7 ....111 B7
Waterfields Way
WD1,D2 ....167 D5
Waterford Comm SG14 ....92 B2
Waterford Gn AL7 ....111 B6
Watergate The WD1 ....175 D8
Waterhouse Gate AL1 ....127 D3
Waterhouse St HP1 ....124 C2
Waterhouse The HP1 ....124 C3
Waterloo La SG5 ....21 A6
Waterlow Mews SG4 ....35 E3
Waterman Cl WD1 ....167 B3
Watermark Way SG13 ....113 F6
Watermead Rd LU3 ....44 F6
Watermill Ind Est SG9 ....40 E6
Waters Dr WD3 ....165 E1
Waters End SG5 ....11 E6
Waterside
Berkhamsted HP4 ....122 D4
Kings Langley WD4 ....139 A2
London Colney AL2 ....142 E4
Radlett WD7 ....156 B5
Stansted Mountfitchet CM24 ....59 E6
Welwyn Garden City AL7 ....90 B1
Waterside Ct WD4 ....139 B2
Waterside Ind Est EN11 ....135 D5
Waterside Pl CM22 ....98 A2
Waterslade Gn LU3 ....45 B6
Watersplash Ct AL7 ....142 F4
Watery La Flamstead AL3 ....84 E3
Hatfield AL10 ....129 E4
Marsworth HP23 ....79 F1
Watford Arches Ret Pk
WD1 ....167 D4
Watford By-Pass WD6 ....169 C2
Watford Coll (annex)
WD2 ....167 D6
Watford County Ct WD1 .167 C5
Watford Ent Ctr WD1 ....166 F2
Watford Field
Jun Mix Sch WD1 ....167 C4
Watford Field Rd WD1 .167 C4
Watford Football Gd
WD1 ....167 B4
Watford General Hospl
(Shrodells Wing) WD1 .167 B4
Watford Gram Sch for
Boys WD1 ....166 F5
Watford Gram Sch for
Girls WD1 ....167 B5
Watford Heath WD1 ....167 E3
Watford Heath Farm
WD1 ....167 D2
Watford High Street Sta
WD1 ....167 C5
Watford Junction Sta
WD1 ....167 C7
Watford Mus WD1 ....167 C5
Watford North Sta WD2 .154 C2
Watford Rd
Abbots Langley WD4 ....153 C6
Chiswellgreen AL2 ....141 A6

Watford Rd continued
Croxley Green WD3 ....166 B3
Elstree WD6 ....169 C3
Kings Langley WD4 ....139 A1
Moor Park HA6 ....175 A4
Radlett WD7 ....155 F4
Watford Sch of Music
WD1 ....154 A1
Watford Sta WD1 ....166 F6
Watling Cl 1 HP2 ....124 E6
Watling Ct WD6 ....169 D3
Watling Knoll WD7 ....155 F6
Watling St
Park Street AL2 ....141 D6
St Albans AL1 ....141 C8
Watling View AL1 ....141 C8
Watling View Sch AL1 ....141 D7
Watlington Rd CM17 ....118 D4
Watson Ave AL3 ....127 C6
Watson's Wlk AL1 ....127 E2
Watton at Stone
Prim Sch SG14 ....70 D3
Watton at Stone Sta SG14 .70 D3
Watton Ho SG14 ....70 F3
Watton Rd Knebworth SG3 .69 A5
Ware SG12 ....93 C2
Watton at Stone SG3,SG14 .70 B2
Watts Cl SG11 ....57 C2
Waulud Prim Sch LU3 ....44 E7
Waulud's Bank Dr LU3 ....44 E7
Wavell Cl EN8 ....148 E4
Wavell Ho AL1 ....128 A2
Waveney HP2 ....124 F8
Waveney Rd AL5 ....86 C3
Waverley Cl SG2 ....69 A8
Waverley Gdns HA6 ....175 A2
Waverley Rd AL3 ....127 D5
Waxwell Cl HA5 ....175 D1
Waxwell La HA5 ....175 D1
Wayfarers Pk HP4 ....121 F4
Wayletts Dr CM23 ....77 B7
Waynes Cl AL7 ....111 C6
Wayre St CM17 ....118 C4
Wayre The CM17 ....118 C4
Waysbrook SG6 ....23 B5
Wayside Chipperfield WD4 .138 B1
Potters Bar EN6 ....159 D6
Shenley WD7 ....156 D6
Wayside Ave WD2 ....168 D3
Wayside The HP3 ....125 C2
Waysmeet SG4 ....23 B4
Waytemore Rd CM23 ....76 E6
Waytemore Castle CM23 .77 A7
Weald Fst & Mid Sch
HA3 ....176 F3
Weald La HA3 ....176 F2
Weald Rise HA3 ....176 F2
Wealdwood Gdns HA5 ....176 B4
Weall Gn WD2 ....154 B7
Weardale Ct EN5 ....171 C4
Weatherby Rd LU4 ....44 D2
Weaver St CM23 ....76 C4
Weavers Rd HP23 ....99 E4
Weavers Way SG7 ....24 A8
Webb Cl SG6 ....23 C5
Webb Rise SG1 ....50 F7
Webber Cl WD6 ....169 D3
Wedgewood Cl HA6 ....174 C4
Wedgewood Pk SG1 ....37 C2
Wedgewood Rd SG4 ....35 B7
Wedgwood Ct SG1 ....37 C2
Wedgwood Gate SG1 ....37 B2
Wedgwood Way SG1 ....37 B2
Wedmore Rd SG4 ....35 A6
Wedon Way SG7 ....13 C4
Weedon Cl SG16 ....10 C5
Weighton Rd HA3 ....176 D2
Welbeck Cl WD6 ....170 A6
Welbeck Rd 3 LU2 ....63 E8
Welbeck Rise AL5 ....107 D6
Welbury Ave LU3 ....45 C7
Welch Pl HA5 ....175 C2
Welclose St AL3 ....127 C3
Welcote Dr HA6 ....174 D4
Weldon Cl LU2 ....46 E1
Welham Cl AL9 ....144 C7
Welham Ct AL9 ....144 C7
Welham Green Sta AL9 ....144 D8
Welham Manor AL9 ....144 C7
Welkin Gn HP2 ....125 C4
Well App EN5 ....171 C4
Well Croft HP1 ....124 B4
Well End Rd WD6 ....157 C1
Well Garth AL7 ....110 E5
Well Gn SG14 ....91 C4
Well La Harlow CM19 ....117 A1
Mentmore LU7 ....61 B8
Northaw EN6 ....145 E2
Well-Row SG13 ....132 F6
Wellands AL10 ....130 A7
Wellbrook Mews HP23 ....100 B4
Wellcroft LU7 ....80 F5
Wellcroft AL1 ....111 A4
Wellcroft Rd AL7 ....111 A4
Wellen Rise HP3 ....138 E8
Wellers Gr EN7 ....148 A3
Wellesley Ave HA6 ....174 F5
Wellesley Cres EN6 ....158 E6
Wellfield Ave LU3 ....44 C8
Wellfield Cl AL10 ....130 A6
Wellfield Ct SG1 ....37 B1
Wellfield Rd AL10 ....130 A7
Wellgate Rd LU4 ....44 D2
Wellhouse Cl LU1 ....63 A7
Wellhouse La EN5 ....171 D5
Wellingham Ave SG5 ....21 D1
Wellington Ave HA5 ....175 F2
Wellington Cl WD1 ....175 F7

Wellington Cotts SG11 ....73 B7
Wellington Ct 3 LU1 ....63 D6
Wellington Dr AL7 ....111 C6
Wellington Ho 1 WD1 ....167 C7
Wellington Pl
Cheshunt EN10 ....148 C8
Kneesworth SG8 ....2 B5
Wellington Rd
London Colney AL2 ....142 D5
Pinner HA5 ....175 F2
St Albans AL1 ....128 B2
Stevenage SG2 ....51 C5
Watford WD1 ....167 B7
Wellington St
Hertford SG14 ....113 B7
Luton LU1 ....63 D7
Wells Cl
Hammond Street EN7 ....147 C6
Harpenden AL5 ....85 E4
St Albans AL3 ....127 C4
Wells Yd 8 Ware SG12 ....93 D1
Wellside WD1 ....167 B6
Wellside Cl EN5 ....171 C5
Wellstones WD1 ....167 B5
Welsummer Way EN8 ....148 D3
Weltmore Rd LU3 ....44 F6
Welwyn By Pass Rd AL6 .89 C5
Welwyn Campus Liby
(Tourist Information)
AL8 ....110 D3
Welwyn Ct HP2 ....124 F7
Welwyn Garden City Sta
AL8 ....110 D6
Welwyn Hall Gdns AL6 ....89 C5
Welwyn North Sta AL6 ....89 D1
Welwyn Rd SG14 ....112 F7
Wendover Cl
Harpenden AL5 ....86 D1
St Albans AL4 ....128 C8
Wendover Ct AL6 ....89 C5
Wendover Dr AL6 ....89 C5
Wendover Ho WD1 ....166 E2
Wendover Way
Bushey WD2 ....168 C3
Luton LU2 ....45 F3
Wengeo La SG12 ....93 B2
Wenham Ct SG2 ....52 B8
Wenlock Jun Sch LU2 ....64 B8
Wenlock St LU2 ....63 E8
Wensley Cl AL5 ....107 D6
Wensleydale
Hemel Hempstead HP2 ....124 F6
Luton LU2 ....45 E1
Wensum Way WD3 ....165 D5
Wentbridge Path WD6 ....157 A1
Wentworth Ave
Borehamwood WD6 ....169 F4
Luton LU4 ....44 C4
Wentworth Cl
Potters Bar EN6 ....159 A8
Watford WD1 ....153 F1
Wentworth Cotts EN10 ....134 E1
Wentworth Ct EN5 ....171 E6
Wentworth Dr CM23 ....76 D6
Wentworth Rd
Barnet EN5 ....171 D6
Hertford SG13 ....113 C3
Wenwell Cl HP22 ....99 A3
Wesley Cl Arlesey SG15 ....11 A4
Goff's Oak EN7 ....147 C3
Wesley Rd AL3 ....83 E5
Wessex Cl EN5 ....171 D5
Wessex Dr HA5 ....175 E3
West Alley 3 SG5 ....34 E2
West Ave Baldock SG7 ....23 C4
Chiswellgreen AL2 ....141 B6
West Burrowfield AL7 ....110 D4
West Chantry HA3 ....176 B2
West Cl Barnet EN5 ....171 B4
Hitchin SG4 ....22 B1
Hoddesdon EN11 ....135 A8
Stevenage SG1 ....50 F5
West Comm
Harpenden AL5 ....107 B6
Redbourn AL3 ....106 A4
West Common Cl AL5 ....107 B5
West Common Gr AL5 ....107 B5
West Common Way AL5 .107 A5
West Ct CM21 ....97 E3
West Dene HP2 ....104 A8
West Dr Arlesey SG15 ....11 A4
Stanmore HA3 ....176 D4
Watford WD2 ....154 B3
West Drive Gdns HA3 ....176 D4
West End SG7 ....4 C3
West End La Barnet EN5 ....171 D5
Essendon AL9 ....131 C5
West End Rd
Brickendon EN7 ....147 F8
Cheddington LU7 ....79 F7
West Herts Coll
Cassio Campus WD1 ..154 C4
Leggatts Campus WD2 .154 A3
West Herts Coll
Watford Campus WD1 .167 A6
West Herts Coll
Watford Campus Sch of
Art & Design WD2 ....154 C4
West Hill SG5 ....34 D7
West Hill Rd
Hoddesdon EN11 ....134 F8
Luton LU1 ....63 E5
West Hyde La SL9 ....172 A4

West La Great Offley SG5 . . . . .**33** C2
Pirton SG5 . . . .**20** D5
West Lieth HP23 . . . .**99** F1
West Lodge Cotts LU2 . . . . .**46** D5
West Mead AL7 . . . .**111** B3
West Pas HP23 . . . .**100** A3
West Rd Berkhamsted HP4 .**122** A5
  Bishop's Stortford CM23 . . .**76** E6
  Harlow CM20 . . . .**118** A4
  Sawbridgeworth CM21 . . . . .**97** C3
  Stansted Mountfitchet CM24 .**59** E6
West Reach SG2 . . . .**50** F2
West Riding
  Bricket Wood AL2 . . . .**140** F1
  Tewin AL6 . . . .**90** D5
West Side EN10 . . . .**148** E6
West Sq CM20 . . . .**117** C1
West St Hertford SG13 . . . . .**113** C5
  Lilley LU2 . . . .**32** D1
  Ware SG12 . . . .**93** D1
  Watford WD1 . . . .**167** B7
West Valley Rd HP3 . . . . . .**138** D7
West View Hatfield AL10 . . .**130** A7
  Letchworth SG6 . . . .**22** E5
West View Gdns WD6 . . . . .**169** D3
West View Rd AL3 . . . .**127** D4
West Way Harpenden AL5 . . .**86** C2
  Rickmansworth WD3 . . . . . .**165** B1
West Ways HA6 . . . .**175** A1
Westall Cl SG13 . . . .**113** C5
Westall Mews SG13 . . . .**113** C5
Westbourne Mews AL1 . . . .**127** D3
Westbourne Rd LU4 . . . .**45** B1
Westbrook Cl SG8 . . . .**5** B8
Westbrook Hay
  Ed Trust Ltd HP3 . . . .**137** D7
Westbury EN8 . . . .**148** D1
Westbury Cl SG5 . . . .**34** D8
Westbury Gdns LU2 . . . .**45** E3
Westbury
  Jun Mix Inf Sch SG6 . . . . . .**22** E5
Westbury Pl SG6 . . . .**22** E5
Westbury Rd
  Moor Park HA6 . . . .**174** E7
  Watford WD1 . . . .**167** B4
Westbush Cl EN11 . . . .**114** F1
Westcott AL7 . . . .**111** D7
Westcroft CE EN3 . . . .**162** C1
Westell Cl SG7 . . . .**24** A8
Westerdale
  Hemel Hempstead HP2 . . . .**124** E6
  Luton LU4 . . . .**44** B5
Western Ave SG16 . . . .**10** B3
Western Cl SG6 . . . .**11** E1
Western House Hospl
  SG12 . . . .**93** E2
Western Rd
  Lower Nazeing EN9 . . . . . .**135** E1
  Luton LU1 . . . .**63** D6
  Tring HP23 . . . .**99** F3
Western Terr EN11 . . . .**115** B1
Western Way SG6 . . . .**11** E1
Westfield
  Welham Green AL9 . . . .**144** F8
  Welwyn Garden City AL7 . . .**111** A7
Westfield Ave
  Harpenden AL5 . . . .**86** A3
  Watford WD2 . . . .**154** D1
Westfield Cl
  Bishop's Stortford CM23 . . .**76** E8
  Cheshunt EN8 . . . .**162** F8
  Hitchin SG5 . . . .**34** D7
Westfield Ct AL4 . . . .**128** D6
Westfield Dr AL5 . . . .**86** B4
Westfield Fst Sch HP4 . . . .**121** F5
Westfield
  Jun Mix Inf Sch EN11 . . . .**134** F7
Westfield La SG5 . . . .**34** D7
Westfield Pk HA5 . . . .**175** F3
Westfield Pl AL5 . . . .**86** B4
Westfield Rd
  Berkhamsted HP4 . . . .**121** F5
  Bishop's Stortford CM23 . . .**76** E8
  Harpenden AL5 . . . .**86** B4
  Hertford SG14 . . . .**113** C8
  Hoddesdon EN11 . . . .**134** F7
  Pitstone LU7 . . . .**80** C3
Westfield Sch WD1 . . . .**166** F3
Westfield Wlk EN8 . . . .**162** F8
Westfields AL3 . . . .**141** A8
Westgate SG1 . . . .**50** D5
Westgate Ct EN3 . . . .**162** D4
Westholm SG6 . . . .**23** A8
Westholme SG6 . . . .**22** F8
Westland Dr AL9 . . . .**144** E4
Westland Rd WD1 . . . .**167** B7
Westlea Ave WD2 . . . .**154** E4
Westlea Cl EN10 . . . .**148** F8
Westlea Rd EN10 . . . .**148** F8
Westlecote Gdns LU2 . . . . .**45** D4
Westly Wood AL7 . . . .**111** A4
Westmeade Cl EN7 . . . .**148** B2
Westmill La Hitchin SG5 . . . .**21** C2
  Ickleford SG5 . . . .**21** C3
Westmill Lawns SG5 . . . . . .**21** D1
Westmill Rd Hitchin SG5 . . . .**21** D1
  Thundridge SG12 . . . .**93** A3
Westminster Ct AL1 . . . . . .**127** C1
Westminster Ho CE WD1 .**167** C7
Westmorland Ave LU3 . . . . .**44** F5
Weston Ave SG8 . . . .**7** C2
Weston Cl EN6 . . . .**158** F7
Weston
  Jun Mix Inf Sch SG4 . . . . . .**24** C1
Weston Rd Stevenage SG1 . . .**36** E1

Weston Rd continued
  Stevenage SG1 . . . .**37** A3
Weston Way SG7 . . . .**23** E7
Westray HP3 . . . .**125** C1
Westridge Cl HP1 . . . .**123** F3
Westron Gdns HP23 . . . . . .**100** B4
Westview Ct WD6 . . . .**169** D3
Westview Rise HP2 . . . .**124** D4
Westway LU2 . . . .**46** C4
Westwick Cl HP2 . . . .**125** D2
Westwick Pl WD2 . . . .**154** C5
Westwick Row CM21 . . . . . .**125** E2
Westwood Ave SG4 . . . .**35** A6
Westwood Cl EN6 . . . .**145** A1
Wetherby Cl SG1 . . . .**51** C8
Wetherby Rd
  Borehamwood WD6 . . . . . .**169** E8
  Enfield EN1 . . . .**161** C1
Wetherfield CM24 . . . .**59** D7
Wetherly Cl WD1 . . . .**118** F4
Wetherne Link LU4 . . . .**44** C5
Wexham LU3 . . . .**44** E8
Weybourne Cl AL5 . . . .**86** D2
Weybourne Dr LU2 . . . .**45** C7
Weymouth St HP3 . . . .**138** D7
Weyver Ct AL1 . . . .**127** E4
Whaley Rd EN6 . . . .**159** C6
Wharf La
  Berkhamsted HP4 . . . .**121** C8
  Rickmansworth WD3 . . . . . .**165** E1
Wharf Rd
  12 Bishop's Stortford CM23 . .**76** F6
  Hemel Hempstead HP1 . . . .**124** B1
  Hoddesdon EN10 . . . .**148** F8
Wharf Row HP22 . . . .**99** B4
Wharfdale CE LU4 . . . .**44** C5
Wharfedale HP2 . . . .**124** E6
Wheat Cl AL4 . . . .**128** A7
Wheat Croft CM23 . . . .**76** E4
Wheat Hill SG6 . . . .**22** F8
Wheatbarn AL7 . . . .**111** B7
Wheatcotes SG3 . . . .**69** C1
Wheatcroft EN7 . . . .**148** B3
Wheatcroft Prim Sch
  SG13 . . . .**114** A7
Wheatfield Hatfield AL10 . . .**130** B6
  Hemel Hempstead HP2 . . . .**124** D5
Wheatfield Ave AL5 . . . . . .**107** A5
Wheatfield Cl SG8 . . . .**7** E6
Wheatfield Rd AL5 . . . .**107** A4
Wheatfields CM17 . . . .**118** D6
Wheatfields Inf Sch AL4 .**128** B7
Wheatfields
  Jun Mix Sch AL4 . . . .**128** B7
Wheathampstead Rd
  Harpenden AL5 . . . .**107** E8
  Wheathampstead AL5,AL4 .**108** A8
Wheathampstead Sch
  AL4 . . . .**108** C7
Wheatlands SG2 . . . .**51** C7
Wheatley Cl
  Sawbridgeworth CM21 . . . . .**97** C1
  Welwyn Garden City AL7 . . .**111** A4
Wheatley Rd AL7 . . . .**111** A4
Wheatleys AL4 . . . .**128** C5
Wheatlock Mead AL3 . . . . .**106** A5
Wheatsheaf Dr SG12 . . . . . .**93** B3
Wheatsheaf Rd SG12 . . . . . .**95** D1
Wheelers Cl EN9 . . . .**135** F1
Wheelers La HP3 . . . .**124** E1
Wheelright Cl WD2 . . . . . .**168** B3
Wheelwrights Cl CM23 . . . .**76** C4
Whempstead La SG12 . . . . .**71** B6
Whempstead Rd SG12 . . . . .**71** B7
Whetstone Cl AL6 . . . .**89** E8
Whinbush Gr SG5 . . . .**34** F8
Whinbush Rd SG5 . . . .**34** F8
Whippendell Hill WD4 . . . .**138** C1
Whippendell Rd WD1 . . . . .**166** F4
Whipperley Ct LU1 . . . .**63** C5
Whipperley Inf Sch LU1 . . .**63** A6
Whipperley Ring LU1 . . . . .**63** A6
Whipperley Way LU1 . . . . . .**63** C5
Whipsnade Wildlife
  Animal Park LU6 . . . .**81** E7
Whisper Wood WD3 . . . . . .**165** B6
Whisperwood Cl HA3 . . . . .**176** E3
Whit Hern Ct EN8 . . . .**148** C1
Whitby Rd LU3 . . . .**45** C1
White Bear CM24 . . . .**59** E8
White Craig Cl HA5 . . . . . .**176** A5
White Crofts SG5 . . . .**11** F6
White Gate Gdns HA3 . . . .**176** F3
White Hart Cl SG9 . . . .**40** E8
White Hart Ct HP2 . . . .**125** A2
White Hart Dr HP2 . . . .**124** F2
White Hart Rd HP2 . . . .**125** A2
White Hart St HP11 . . . . . .**138** D7
White Hedge Dr AL3 . . . . .**127** C5
White Hill
  Ashley Green HP5 . . . .**136** C7
  Flamstead AL3 . . . .**105** B8
  Hemel Hempstead HP1 . . . .**123** F2
  Rickmansworth WD3 . . . . . .**174** A4
  Walkern SG2 . . . .**38** C2
  Welwyn AL6 . . . .**89** A3
White Ho The CE EN8 . . . .**148** D3
White Horse La
  London Colney AL2 . . . .**142** E5
  Welwyn AL6 . . . .**90** C7
White House Cl SG14 . . . . . .**70** E3
White House The SG6 . . . . .**23** B5
White La SG4 . . . .**49** C7
White Orchards N20 . . . . .**171** F1
White Post Field CM21 . . . .**97** D2
White Shack La WD3 . . . . .**152** F2
White Stubbs La
  EN10,SG13 . . . .**133** C2

White Way The SG2 . . . .**51** C7
Whitebarns SG9 . . . .**43** A5
Whitebarns La SG9 . . . .**43** A6
Whitebeam Cl EN7 . . . .**147** E5
Whitebeams
  Chiswellgreen AL2 . . . .**141** C3
  Hatfield AL10 . . . .**130** A2
Whitebroom Rd HP1 . . . . . .**123** E5
Whitechurch Cl LU2 . . . .**46** D2
Whitechurch Gdns SG6 . . .**23** C3
Whitecroft AL1 . . . .**142** B8
Whitecroft Rd LU2 . . . .**64** A8
Whitefield Ave LU3 . . . .**44** C7
Whitefield Ho AL10 . . . . . .**130** C7
Whitefield Inf Sch LU3 . . . .**44** E8
Whitefield Jun Sch LU3 . . .**44** E8
Whitefields Rd EN8 . . . . . .**148** C3
Whitefriars HA3 . . . .**176** E1
Whitefriars Dr HA3 . . . . . .**176** E1
Whitefriars
  Fst & Mid Sch HA3 . . . . . .**176** E1
Whitefriars Teaching Sch
  HA3 . . . .**176** D1
Whitefriars Trad Est
  HA3 . . . .**176** D1
Whitegale Cl SG4 . . . .**35** A6
Whitegates Cl WD3 . . . . . .**166** A5
Whitehall Cl EN9 . . . .**135** C1
Whitehall Coll CM23 . . . .**58** E1
Whitehall La CM23 . . . .**58** F1
Whitehall Rd CM23 . . . .**58** E1
Whitehands CE EN11 . . . . .**134** F6
Whitehart Cross HP3 . . . . .**136** F3
Whitehicks SG6 . . . .**12** A1
Whitehill HP4 . . . .**122** D5
Whitehill Ave LU1 . . . .**63** D5
Whitehill Cotts AL6 . . . .**89** A3
Whitehill Ct HP4 . . . .**122** D5
Whitehill Jun Sch SG4 . . . . .**35** A5
Whitehorse Cl SG8 . . . .**17** D4
Whitehorse St SG7 . . . .**23** F8
Whitehorse Vale LU3 . . . . . .**31** A1
Whitehouse Ave WD6 . . . . .**170** B5
Whitehouse La WD5 . . . . . .**140** C4
Whitehurst Ave SG5 . . . .**21** F1
Whitelands Ave WD3 . . . . .**164** C5
Whiteleaf Rd HP3 . . . .**138** C8
Whiteley Cl SG12 . . . .**71** E7
Whiteley La SG9 . . . .**27** C8
Whitesmead Rd SG1 . . . .**50** E7
Whitestone Wlk HP1 . . . . .**124** A6
Whitethorn AL7 . . . .**111** B5
Whitethorn La SG6 . . . .**23** A4
Whitethorn Way LU1 . . . . . .**63** A6
Whitewaits CM20 . . . .**117** E1
Whiteway SG6 . . . .**23** C4
Whitewaybottom La
  LU2,SG4 . . . .**66** A3
Whitewebbs La EN2 . . . . . .**161** F4
Whitewebbs Mus of
  Transport EN2 . . . .**161** B4
Whitewebbs Park
  Ctry Pk EN2 . . . .**161** D4
Whitewood Rd HP4 . . . .**122** A4
Whitfield Way WD3 . . . . . .**164** F1
Whitings Cl AL5 . . . .**86** D4
Whitings Hill
  Jun Mix & Inf Sch EN5 . . .**171** C4
Whitings Hill Rd EN5 . . . . .**171** C4
Whitlars Dr WD4 . . . .**138** F3
Whitley Cl WD5 . . . .**154** A7
Whitley Ct EN11 . . . .**135** B8
Whitley Gn LU2 . . . .**46** D2
Whitley Rd EN11 . . . .**135** B8
Whitmores Wood HP2 . . . .**125** B4
Whitney Dr SG1 . . . .**36** C1
Whittingham Cl LU2 . . . .**46** F1
Whittingstall Rd EN11 . . . .**135** C8
Whittington La SG1 . . . .**50** E4
Whittington Way CM23 . . . .**76** F3
Whittle Cl SG16 . . . .**10** B4
Whittlesea Cl HA3 . . . .**176** B1
Whittlesea Path HA3 . . . . . .**176** C2
Whittlesea Rd HA3 . . . .**176** C2
Whittlesea Sch HA3 . . . . . .**176** C3
Whitworth Jones Ave
  SG16 . . . .**10** C5
Whitworth Rd SG1 . . . .**37** B3
Whomerley Rd SG1 . . . .**50** E4
Whydale Rd SG8 . . . .**7** E5
Whytingham Rd HP23 . . . .**100** C4
Wick Ave AL4 . . . .**108** D8
Wick Hill LU6 . . . .**82** F8
Wick Rd HP23 . . . .**120** D8
Wick The SG14 . . . .**92** C1
Wicken Fields SG12 . . . .**93** C3
Wickets End WD7 . . . .**156** E6
Wickets The LU2 . . . .**45** E1
Wickfield SG3 . . . .**69** A2
Wickfield Cl SG3 . . . .**69** A2
Wickham Cl UB9 . . . .**173** D2
Wickham Rd HA3 . . . .**176** D1
Wickham Way SG11 . . . .**55** E3
Wickhams Wharf SG12 . . . . .**93** E1
Wicklands Rd SG12 . . . . . .**116** D8
Wickmere Cl LU2 . . . .**45** C7
Wickstead Ave LU4 . . . .**44** E4
Wickwood Ct AL1 . . . .**128** B5
Widbury Gdns SG12 . . . .**93** F1
Widbury Hill SG12 . . . .**93** F1
Widford
  Jun Mix Inf Sch SG12 . . . .**95** D4
Widford Rd Hunsdon SG12 . .**95** D2
  Much Hadham SG10 . . . .**95** F7

Widford Rd continued
  Welwyn Garden City AL7 . .**111** B6
Widford Terr HP2 . . . .**105** A1
Widgeon Way WD2 . . . .**154** E2
Widmore Dr HP2 . . . .**125** A5
Wieland Rd HA6 . . . .**175** A3
Wiggenhall Rd WD1 . . . . . .**167** C4
Wiggington Bottom
  HP23 . . . .**120** E8
Wight Ho WD1 . . . .**166** F4
Wigmore La LU2 . . . .**46** E1
Wigmore Park Ctr LU2 . . . .**46** E1
Wigmore Pl LU2 . . . .**46** E1
Wigmore Prim Sch LU2 . . . .**46** E2
Wigmores N AL8 . . . .**110** D7
Wigram Way SG2 . . . .**51** B3
Wilbury Cl SG6 . . . .**22** C7
Wilbury Hills Rd SG6 . . . . . .**22** C7
Wilbury Jun Sch SG6 . . . . . .**22** D6
Wilbury Lodge EN5 . . . . . .**171** D5
Wilbury Rd SG6 . . . .**22** E8
Wilbury Way SG4 . . . .**22** A3
Wilcot Ave WD1 . . . .**167** E2
Wilcot Cl WD1 . . . .**167** E2
Wilcox Cl WD6 . . . .**170** C8
Wild Cherry Dr LU1 . . . .**63** D5
Wild March Ct EN8 . . . . . .**162** E2
Wild Oaks Cl HA6 . . . .**174** F4
Wilderness The HP4 . . . . . .**122** C4
Wildhill rd AL9 . . . .**131** B2
Wildwood HA6 . . . .**174** D4
Wildwood Ave AL2 . . . .**140** F1
Wildwood Ct WD3 . . . .**164** F5
Wildwood La SG1 . . . .**50** E3
Wilford Cl HA6 . . . .**174** D3
Wilga Rd AL6 . . . .**89** B5
Wilkin's Green La AL4 . . . .**129** C4
Wilkins Gr AL8 . . . .**110** D5
Wilkinson Cl EN7 . . . .**147** C6
Wilkinson Ct LU3 . . . .**45** A7
Willenhall LU3 . . . .**45** A7
William Austin Inf Sch
  LU3 . . . .**45** C4
William Austin Jun Sch
  LU3 . . . .**45** C4
William Covell Cl EN2 . . . .**160** F1
William Ct HP3 . . . .**138** D7
William Pl SG2 . . . .**51** A3
William Ransom
  Prim Sch The SG4 . . . .**35** B7
William St
  Berkhamsted HP4 . . . .**122** D4
  Luton LU2 . . . .**45** E1
  Markyate AL3 . . . .**83** E5
  Watford WD2 . . . .**167** D6
William Sutton Ct LU2 . . . .**46** B5
Williams Way WD7 . . . .**156** C4
Williamson St CE LU1 . . . . .**63** E7
Williamson Way WD3 . . . . .**165** A1
Willian Church Rd SG6 . . . .**23** A2
Willian Rd
  Great Wymondley SG4 . . . . .**35** F7
  Hitchin SG4 . . . .**22** E1
Willian Way Baldock SG7 . . .**23** E6
  Letchworth SG6 . . . .**23** A3
Willingham Cl EN9 . . . .**163** D7
Williton Rd LU2 . . . .**46** C2
Willoughby Cl EN10 . . . . . .**134** E2
Willoughby Rd AL5 . . . .**86** B4
Willoughby Way SG4 . . . . . .**35** A6
Willow Cl
  Bishop's Stortford CM23 . . .**76** E8
  Great Hormead SG9 . . . . . .**42** A8
  Hammond Street EN7 . . . . .**147** E5
  Reed SG8 . . . .**16** D5
Willow Corner SG13 . . . . . .**132** F5
Willow Cres AL1 . . . .**128** C3
Willow Ct Harrow HA3 . . . .**176** F2
  Luton LU3 . . . .**44** E5
Willow Dean HA5 . . . .**175** D1
Willow Dene WD2 . . . .**168** E2
Willow Dr EN5 . . . .**171** E5
Willow Edge WD4 . . . .**139** A2
Willow End HA6 . . . .**175** A4
Willow Gn WD6 . . . .**170** D4
Willow Gr AL8 . . . .**89** D3
Willow La Hitchin SG5 . . . . .**34** D6
  Watford WD1 . . . .**167** A4
Willow Mead CM21 . . . .**97** E2
Willow Path EN9 . . . .**163** E5
Willow Springs CM23 . . . . .**76** D8
Willow Tree Way SG5 . . . . .**21** F2
Willow Way
  Chiswellgreen AL2 . . . .**141** A4
  Harpenden AL5 . . . .**86** C4
  Hatfield AL10 . . . .**129** F2
  Hemel Hempstead HP1 . . . .**124** B5
  Luton LU3 . . . .**44** E5
  Potters Bar EN6 . . . .**159** B6
  Radlett WD7 . . . .**155** E3
Willow Wlk AL6 . . . .**89** C8
Willowby Ct AL2 . . . .**142** D5
Willowdene EN8 . . . .**148** E4
Willowfield Lower Sch
  LU1 . . . .**62** F4
Willowgate Trad Est LU3 . .**44** B8
Willowmead SG14 . . . .**113** B5
Willows Cl HA5 . . . .**175** C1
Willows Link
  Stevenage SG2 . . . .**51** A1
  Stevenage SG2 . . . .**69** A8
Willows The
  Buntingford SG9 . . . .**40** D8
  Hemel Hempstead HP2 . . . .**125** B5
  Hitchin SG4 . . . .**35** A5
  Rickmansworth WD3 . . . . . .**173** A8
  St Albans AL1 . . . .**142** B7
  Stevenage SG2 . . . .**51** A1

Willows The continued
  Watford WD1 . . . .**167** B2
Willowside AL2 . . . .**142** E4
Willowside Way SG8 . . . .**7** C8
Willowtree Lo HA6 . . . .**174** F5
Wilsden Ave LU1 . . . .**63** C6
Wilshere Ave AL1 . . . .**127** C1
Wilshere Cres SG4 . . . .**35** C8
Wilshere Rd AL6 . . . .**89** A5
Wilshere-Dacre Jun Sch
  SG5 . . . .**34** E8
Wilsmere Dr HA3 . . . .**176** E3
Wilson Cl
  Bishop's Stortford CM23 . . .**76** F5
  Stevenage SG1 . . . .**36** D1
Wilsons La SG7 . . . .**4** C4
Wilstone Dr AL4 . . . .**128** C8
Wilton Cl CM23 . . . .**77** B7
Wilton Cres SG13 . . . .**113** C4
Wilton Ct WD1 . . . .**167** C6
Wilton Rd SG5 . . . .**21** C1
Wilton Way SG13 . . . .**113** C4
Wiltshire Rd SG2 . . . .**51** A4
Wimborne Cl CM21 . . . .**97** D2
Wimborne Gr WD1 . . . .**153** E2
Wimborne Rd LU1 . . . .**63** C8
Wimple Rd LU4 . . . .**44** A2
Winch Cl SG4 . . . .**88** F8
Winch St LU2 . . . .**45** F1
Winchdells HP3 . . . .**139** A8
Winchester Cl
  Bishop's Stortford CM23 . . .**76** D4
  Stevenage SG1 . . . .**37** D2
Winchester Ho AL3 . . . . . .**127** C2
Winchester Rd HA6 . . . . . .**174** F1
Winchester Way WD3 . . . .**166** B4
Winchfield Way WD3 . . . . .**165** C2
Windermere Ave AL1 . . . . .**128** B1
Windermere Cl
  Chorleywood WD3 . . . .**164** F5
  Hemel Hempstead HP3 . . . .**125** C2
Windermere Cres LU3 . . . . .**44** F5
Windermere Ct CE WD1 . .**167** A4
Windermere
  Jun Mix Inf Sch AL1 . . . . .**128** B1
Windhill
  Bishop's Stortford CM23 . . .**76** F4
  Welwyn Garden City AL7 . . .**111** A7
Windhill Old Rd CM23 . . . . .**76** F3
Winding Hill SG10 . . . .**75** A4
Winding Shot HP1 . . . .**124** A4
Winding Shott SG14 . . . .**91** C4
Windmill Ave AL4 . . . .**128** C7
Windmill Cl Barkway SG8 . . .**17** C5
  Pitstone LU7 . . . .**80** F5
  Waltham Abbey EN9 . . . . . .**163** E6
Windmill Dr WD3 . . . .**165** F3
Windmill Field SG12 . . . . . .**114** D8
Windmill Fields CM17 . . . .**118** C4
Windmill Hill
  Buntingford SG9 . . . .**40** F6
  Chipperfield WD4 . . . .**151** F7
  Hitchin SG4 . . . .**34** F7
Windmill La Barnet EN5 . . .**170** F3
  Bushey WD2 . . . .**168** E1
  Cheshunt EN8 . . . .**148** E1
Windmill Rd
  Breachwood Green SG4 . . . .**47** D2
  Hemel Hempstead HP2 . . . .**124** F2
  Luton LU1 . . . .**63** F6
  Markyate AL3 . . . .**84** B6
Windmill St WD2 . . . .**168** E1
Windmill Way
  Much Hadham SG10 . . . .**74** E1
  Tring HP23 . . . .**99** F4
Windmills SG12 . . . .**71** E8
Windmore Ave EN6 . . . . . .**158** C4
Windridge Cl AL3 . . . .**127** A1
Winds End Cl HP2 . . . .**125** A5
Windsor Cl
  Borehamwood WD6 . . . . . .**170** A8
  Bovingdon HP3 . . . .**137** A3
  Cheshunt EN7 . . . .**148** A1
  Hemel Hempstead HP3 . . . .**124** C4
  Northwood HA6 . . . .**175** A1
  Stevenage SG2 . . . .**69** B2
  Welwyn AL6 . . . .**89** B3
Windsor Ct Bushey WD2 . . .**168** C2
  Kings Langley WD4 . . . . . .**139** B2
  10 Luton LU1 . . . .**63** D6
  St Albans AL1 . . . .**128** A2
Windsor Gdns CM23 . . . . . .**76** C7
Windsor Rd Barnet EN5 . . .**171** E3
  Enfield EN3 . . . .**162** D3
  Harrow HA3 . . . .**176** D2
  Pitstone LU7 . . . .**80** C3
  Royston SG8 . . . .**7** F6
  Watford WD2 . . . .**154** C1
  Welwyn AL6 . . . .**89** B3
Windsor St LU1 . . . .**63** D6
Windsor Way WD3 . . . .**165** A1
Windsor Wlk CE LU1 . . . . . .**63** D6
Windsor Wood EN9 . . . . . .**163** E6
Windward Cl EN3 . . . .**162** D4
Windy Rise SG12 . . . .**71** F7
Winford Dr EN10 . . . .**134** F1
Wingate Cl LU4 . . . .**44** F2
Wingate Gdns AL6 . . . .**89** B5
Wingate Rd LU4 . . . .**44** F2
Wingate Way AL1 . . . .**128** A2
Wingrave CE Comb Sch
  HP22 . . . .**60** A3
Wingrave Rd Tring HP23 . .**100** B6
  Wilstone HP23 . . . .**79** D1
Winifred Ho
  (Conv Hospl for Children)
  EN5 . . . .**170** F3
Winifred Rd HP3 . . . .**138** D7

Winkfield Cl LU4 ....44 B1
Winnington Rd EN3 ....162 C2
Winsdon Ct **1** LU1 ......63 D6
Winsdon Rd LU1 ....63 D6
Winslow Cl LU3 ....45 C4
Winslow Rd HP2 ....60 B3
Winston Churchill Way
EN8 ....162 E8
Winston Cl Harrow HA3 ..176 F4
Hitchin SG5 ....34 D7
Winston Ct HA3 ....176 B3
Winston Gdns HP4 ....121 F4
Winston Way EN6 .....159 A6
Winstre Rd WD6 ......170 A8
Winters La SG2 ....38 C1
Winterscroft Rd EN11 .134 F7
Winton App WD3 ......166 C4
Winton Cl Letchworth SG6 .23 D8
Luton LU2 ....45 D6
Winton Cres WD3 .....166 B4
Winton Dr Cheshunt EN8 .148 E2
Croxley Green WD3 ...166 C4
Winton Rd SG12 ....93 F1
Wisden Rd SG1 ....36 F1
Wiseman Cl LU2 ....45 E7
Wisemans Gdns CM21 ..97 C1
Wistlea Cres AL4 .....129 E1
Wistow Rd LU3 ....45 A6
Witchford AL7 ....111 D6
Withy Cl LU4 ....44 B4
Withy Pl AL2 ....141 C3
Witney Cl HA5 ....175 F4
Witsend SG13 ....113 E1
Witter Ave SG5 ....21 E4
Wiveton Cl LU2 ....45 D7
Woburn Ave CM23 ......76 C7
Woburn Cl Bushey WD2 .168 C3
Stevenage SG2 ....69 C7
Woburn Ct LU4 ....44 D5
Wodecroft Rd LU3 .....45 B6
Wodson Park
Sports & L Ctr SG12 ..93 D4
Wolfsburg Ct **4** LU4 ...44 C5
Wolsey Ave EN7 ......147 F2
Wolsey Bsns Pk WD1 ..166 D2
Wolsey Mansions HA6 .174 C7
Wolsey Rd
Hemel Hempstead HP2 .124 D2
Moor Park HA6 ......174 F7
Wolston Ct LU1 ....63 C7
Wolves Mere SG3 ....69 A2
Wolvescroft SG3 ....69 A2
Wood Cl AL10 ....130 B5
Wood Comm AL10 .....130 B8
Wood Cres HP3 ....124 E1
Wood Dr SG2 ....51 B2
Wood End AL2 ....141 C2
Wood End Cl HP2 .....125 C4
Wood End Hill AL5 .....85 D4
Wood End
Jun Mix Inf Sch AL5 ..85 D3
Wood End La AL3 .....104 E8
Wood End Rd AL5 ......85 D3
Wood Farm Rd HP2 ...124 E2
Wood Green Cl LU2 ....46 B5
Wood Green Rd LU2 ...46 C5
Wood Green Way EN8 .162 E8
Wood House La EN10 ..134 A2
Wood La Birchanger CM23 .59 E2
Hemel Hempstead HP2 .124 D2
Meesden SG9 ....30 A6
Wood Lane End HP2 ...125 B4
Wood St Barnet EN5 ..171 D5
Luton LU1 ....63 F6
Wood Vale AL10 ......130 B5
Wood View Cuffley EN6 .146 E4
Hemel Hempstead HP1 .124 B5
Woodacre Dr EN8 ......90 A8
Woodbine Gr EN2 .....161 D1
Woodbridge Cl LU4 ....44 E4
Woodbrook Gdns EN9 .163 E6
Woodbury Hill LU2 .....45 E2
Woodcock Hill
Rickmansworth WD3 ..173 E4
Sandridge AL4 ....108 E1

Woodcock Rd Luton LU1 ..63 A7
Stevenage SG2 ....51 D2
Woodcote Cl EN8 ......148 C1
Woodcote Ho **1** SG4 ....34 F7
Woodcroft SG5 ....34 E6
Woodcroft Ave SG12 ..115 E4
Woodfall Ave EN5 ....171 F4
Woodfield Ave HA6 ...174 E6
Woodfield Cl CM24 .....59 E6
Woodfield Dr HP3 ....125 D1
Woodfield Gdns HP3 ..125 D1
Woodfield La AL9 .....145 E8
Woodfield Rd
Radlett WD7 ....156 A3
Stevenage SG2 ....36 C1
Welwyn Garden City AL7 .110 F6
Woodfield Rise WD2 ..168 D2
Woodfield Sch HP3 ...125 C1
Woodfield Terr CM24 ..59 E6
Woodfield Way AL4 ...128 C6
Woodfields
Stansted Mountfitchet CM24 .59 E6
2 Watford WD1 ......167 C5
Woodford Cres HA5 ..175 B1
Woodford Rd WD1 ....167 C7
Woodforde Cl SG7 ......4 E4
Woodgate WD2 ....154 B6
Woodgate Ave EN6 ...160 B7
Woodgate Cres HA6 ..175 A4
Woodgrange Ct EN11 .135 A5
Woodhall Ave HA5 ...175 E2
Woodhall Cl SG14 ....113 C8
Woodhall Ct AL7 .....110 E5
Woodhall Dr HA5 ....175 E2
Woodhall Gate HA5 ..175 D2
Woodhall Ho AL7 ....110 F4
Woodhall La
Hemel Hempstead HP2 .124 E4
Shenley WD7 ....156 F4
South Oxhey WD1 ...175 E2
Welwyn Garden City AL7 .110 E4
Woodhall Sch WD1 ...175 E6
Woodham Way SG12 ..115 C4
Woodhouse Eaves HA6 .175 A5
Woodhurst Ave WD2 ..154 D4
Woodland Ave
Hemel Hempstead HP1 .124 B2
Luton LU3 ....45 B2
Woodland Cl
Hemel Hempstead HP1 .124 B2
Tring HP23 ....99 F2
Woodland Dr
St Albans AL4 ....128 C4
Watford WD1 ....166 F8
Woodland La WD3 ....164 D6
Woodland Mount SG13 .113 F6
Woodland Pl
Chorleywood WD3 ...164 F5
Hemel Hempstead HP1 .124 B2
Woodland Rd
Hertford Heath SG13 .114 C3
Maple Cross WD3 ....172 D5
Woodland Rise
Studham LU6 ....82 B7
Welwyn Garden City AL8 .110 C8
Woodland Way
Abbots Langley WD5 .139 F4
Baldock SG7 ....23 F6
Goff's Oak EN7 ......147 B3
Stevenage SG2 ....51 A1
Welwyn AL6 ....90 A7
Woodlands
Bishop's Stortford CM23 ..77 C8
Brookmans Park AL9 .145 B4
Caddington LU1 ....62 E3
Chiswellgreen AL2 ...141 C4
Harpenden AL5 ....85 E3
Radlett WD7 ....156 A5
Royston SG8 ....7 B6
Woodlands Ave HP4 ..122 D3
Woodlands Cl
Borehamwood WD6 ..170 B5
Hoddesdon EN11 ....135 A5

Woodlands Dr
Abbots Langley WD4 ..139 C3
Harrow HA7 ....176 F4
Hoddesdon EN11 ....135 A4
Woodlands Inf Sch WD6 .170 A8
Woodlands Meade SG4 ..37 B8
Woodlands Rd
Abbots Langley HP3 ..139 A4
Enfield EN2 ....161 D1
Hertford SG13 ....113 F6
Thundridge SG12 .....93 D6
Watford WD2 ....167 E4
Woodlea AL2 ....141 A6
Woodlea Gr HA6 .....174 C4
Woodley Rd SG12 ......93 F2
Woodleys CM20 ......118 A1
Woodman Rd **4** HP3 ..124 E1
Woodmere LU3 ....31 A1
Woodmere Ave WD2 ..154 E1
Woodmill Mews EN11 .135 B8
Woodpecker Cl
Bishop's Stortford CM23 ..76 C6
Bushey WD2 ....168 C1
Harrow HA3 ....176 F2
Hatfield AL10 ....129 F2
Woodridge Way HA6 ..174 E4
Woodridings Ave HA5 .175 F2
Woodridings Cl HA5 ..175 F3
Woods Ave AL10 .....130 B4
Woods Pl HP23 ....100 A3
Woods The Radlett WD7 .156 B5
South Oxhey WD1 ...175 A5
Woodside
Bishop's Stortford CM23 ..77 D8
Borehamwood WD6 ..169 F5
Cheshunt EN7 ....162 A8
Hertford Heath SG13 .114 C2
Watford WD2 ....154 A3
Woodside Farm &
Wildfowl Park LU1 ...84 A8
Woodside Ho AL8 ....110 C7
Woodside Ind Pk SG6 ..23 B7
Woodside La AL9 .....131 A1
Woodside Prim Sch EN7 .147 B2
Woodside Rd
Abbots Langley WD5 .154 B8
Bricket Wood AL2 ...140 F2
Welwyn AL6 ....89 F3
Woodside LU1 ....63 B3
Woodstock SG3 ....68 F3
Woodstock Cl SG13 ..114 B4
Woodstock Rd
Bushey WD2 ....168 F2
Hoddesdon EN10 ....134 E4
Woodstock Rd N AL1 .128 B4
Woodstock Rd S AL1 .128 B3
Woodvale EN8 ....162 C4
Woodville Court Mews
WD1 ....167 A7
Woodville Ct WD1 ...167 A7
Woodville Pl SG14 ...113 B8
Woodward Gdns HA7 .176 F3
Woodwaye WD1 .....167 C2
Woodwicks WD3 .....172 D5
Woolenwick Inf Sch SG1 .50 B6
Woolenwick Jun Mix Sch
SG1 ....50 B6
Woolgrove Ct SG4 .....22 B1
Woolgrove Rd SG4 ....22 B1
Woolgrove Sch SG6 ...23 D5
Woollam Cres AL3 ...127 C7
Woollams AL3 ....106 A4
Woollard St EN9 .....163 C5
Woolmans Cl EN10 ..134 F1
Woolmer Cl WD6 .....157 A1
Woolmer Dr HP2 .....125 C3
Woolmer Green
Jun Mix Inf Sch SG3 ..69 A1
Woolmerdine Ct WD2 .167 D6
Woolmers La SG14 ...112 B2
Woolners Way SG1 ....50 C6
Woolston Ave SG6 .....23 A4
Wootton Cl LU3 ....45 B7
Wootton Dr HP2 .....124 F8

Worboys Ct SG8 ....1 F5
Worcester Ct AL1 .....128 A2
Worcester Rd AL10 ...129 F6
Worcesters Ave EN1 ..162 A1
Worcesters Prim Sch
EN1 ....161 F1
Wordsworth Cl SG8 .....2 D1
Wordsworth Rd
Harpenden AL5 ....86 A3
Luton LU4 ....44 A2
Works Rd SG6 ....23 C7
Worley Rd AL3 ....127 D4
Wormley Ct EN10 ....148 F7
Wormley Lodge Cl EN10 .148 F8
Wormley Prim Sch EN10 .148 E8
Worsdell Way SG4 .....35 B4
Worsted La SG9 ....41 E7
Wortham Rd SG8 ....7 A5
Wortham Way SG2 .....51 B3
Wraglins The CM23 .....77 B5
Wratten Cl SG5 ....34 E6
Wratten Rd E SG5 .....34 E6
Wratten Rd W SG5 ....34 E6
Wrayfields SG5 ....12 B8
Wraysbury Cl LU4 .....44 D3
Wren Cl Kimpton SG4 ..66 B1
Luton LU2 ....46 C6
Stevenage SG2 ....51 B6
Wren Cres WD2 ....168 C1
Wren Wood AL7 .....111 B7
Wrenbrook Rd CM23 ..76 F6
Wrensfield HP1 ....124 B3
Wrestlers Cl AL10 ....130 C7
Wrexham Terr SG8 .....7 D7
Wright Cl AL4 ....108 E7
Wright's Bldgs WD1 ..167 B7
Wright's Green La CM22 .98 D8
Wrights Green La CM22 .98 D7
Wrights Mdw SG2 .....52 B8
Wrights Orch SG2 .....51 E2
Wrotham Park EN5 ...158 E3
Wrotham Rd EN5 ....171 E7
Wroxham Ave HP3 ...124 D1
Wroxham Gdns
Crews Hill EN2 ......161 B4
Potters Bar EN6 ....158 D8
Wroxham Sch The EN6 .158 D8
Wroxham Way AL5 .....86 C3
Wulfrath Way SG12 ...93 C3
Wulstan Pk EN6 .....159 D7
Wulwards Cl LU1 ......63 B6
Wulwards Cl LU1 ......63 B6
Wyatt Cl Bushey WD2 .168 E2
Ickleford SG5 ....21 D4
Wyatt's Cl SG3 ....165 A6
Wyatt's Rd WD3 .....165 A6
Wyburn Ave EN5 .....171 F6
Wych Elm CM20 .....117 C1
Wych Elm La AL6,SG3 ..68 F2
Wych Elms AL2 ......141 B3
Wychdell SG2 ....69 C8
Wychford Dr CM21 ....97 C1
Wychwood Ave LU2 ...45 E3
Wychwood Way HA6 ..174 F3
Wycklond Cl SG5 ......11 E6
Wycliffe Cl LU3 ....45 C6
Wycliffe Ct WD5 .....153 E7
Wycombe Way Luton LU3 .45 C8
St Albans AL4 ....128 B6
Wyddial Gn AL7 .....111 B6
Wyddial Rd SG9 ....40 E8
Wye The HP2 ....125 A4
Wyedale AL2 ....142 F4
Wykeham Rise N20 ...171 E4
Wyken Cl LU3 ....45 A7
Wyldwood Cl CM17 ..118 C6
Wyllyotts Cl EN6 ....158 F7
Wyllyotts Pl EN6 ....158 F7
Wylo Dr EN5 ....171 A4
Wymondley Cl SG4 ....35 A7
Wymondley
Jun Mix Inf Sch SG4 ..35 E4
Wymondley Rd Hitchin SG4 .35 B6
Letchworth SG6 ......23 A1
Wynches Farm Dr AL4 .128 D3

Wynchgate HA3 ......176 E3
Wynchlands Cres AL4 .128 D3
Wynd Arc The SG6 ....22 F6
Wynd The SG6 ....22 F6
Wyndham Rd LU4 .....44 C2
Wyndhams End AL7 ..110 F2
Wynlie Gdns HA5 ....175 B1
Wynn Cl SG7 ....13 A1
Wyrley Dell SG6 ....23 A3
Wysells Ct SG6 ....22 D7
Wyton AL7 ....111 D6
Wyvern Cl LU4 ....44 E3

Y

Yardley SG6 ....23 C4
Yardley Ave LU7 ....80 D4
Yardley Ct **14** AL5 .....86 B1
Yarmouth Rd
Stevenage SG1 ....50 A7
Watford WD2 ....154 C1
Yately Cl LU2 ....45 D7
Ye Cnr WD1 ....167 E3
Yearling Cl SG12 .....114 F7
Yeatman Ho WD2 ....154 B3
Yeats Cl SG8 ....2 D1
Yeomanry Dr SG7 .....13 A1
Yeomans Ave AL5 .....85 D3
Yeomans Cl CM23 .....76 D6
Yeomans Dr SG2 ......51 E2
Yeomans Ride HP2 ...105 A1
Yeovil Cl EN7 ....147 E4
Yeovil Rd LU2 ....46 B2
Yew Cl EN7 ....147 E4
Yew Gr AL7 ....111 C5
Yew Tree Cl Botley HP5 .136 A1
Pitstone LU7 ....80 E5
Yew Tree Ct HP1 ....124 A1
Yew Tree Dr HP3 ....137 B3
Yew Tree Pl CM23 .....76 F8
Yew Wlk EN11 ....135 A5
Yewlands
Hoddesdon EN11 ....135 A5
Sawbridgeworth CM21 .97 E1
Yewlands Dr EN11 ...135 A5
Yewns Ave EN1 ......162 B3
Yewstone Ct WD1 ...167 A6
Yewtree End AL2 ....141 B4
York Cl WD4 ....139 A2
York Cres WD6 ......170 D7
York Ho AL3 ....127 E3
York Mead Prim Sch
WD3 ....166 A4
York Rd Cheshunt EN8 .162 E6
Hitchin SG5 ....34 E8
Northwood HA6 .....175 A1
St Albans AL1 ....127 F4
Stevenage SG1 ....36 F1
Watford WD1 ....167 C4
York St LU2 ....63 F8
York Terr EN2 ....161 C1
York Way
Hemel Hempstead HP2 .124 E2
Royston SG8 ....7 B8
Welwyn Garden City AL6 .89 C3
Yorke Gate WD1 .....167 A7
Yorke Rd WD3 ....166 A3
Youngfield Rd HP1 ..123 F4
Youngs Rise AL8 ....110 C6
Youngsbury La SG12 ..93 E8
Yule Cl AL2 ....140 F1

Z

Zambesi Rd CM23 ......76 F5

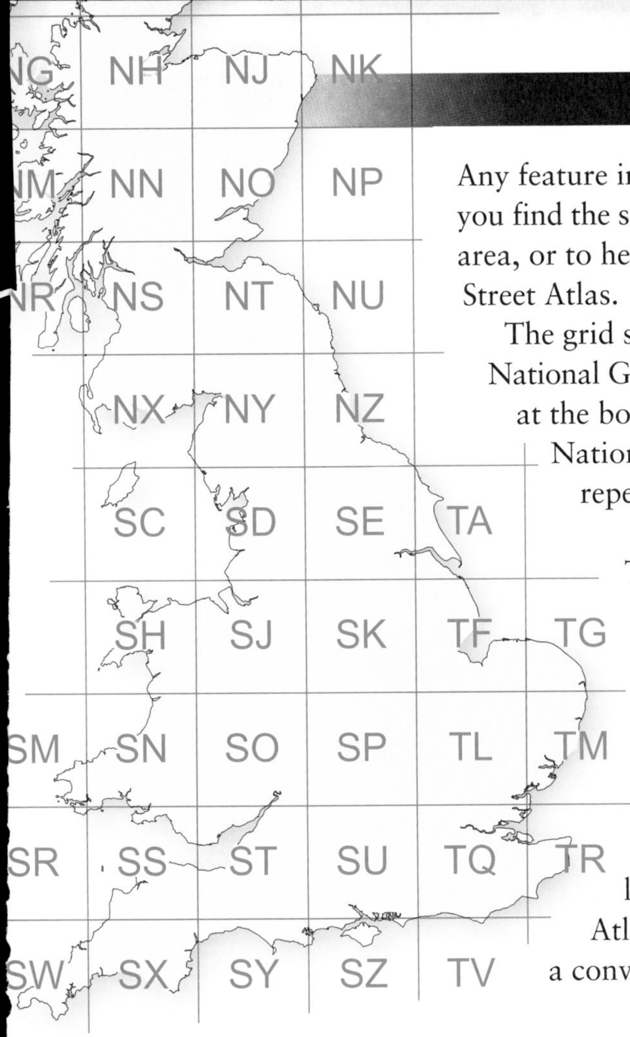

Any feature in this atlas can be given a unique reference to help you find the same feature on other Ordnance Survey maps of the area, or to help someone else locate you if they do not have a Street Atlas.

The grid squares in this atlas match the Ordnance Survey National Grid and are at 500 metre intervals. The small figures at the bottom and sides of every other grid line are the National Grid kilometre values (**00** to **99** km) and are repeated across the country every 100 km (see left).

To give a unique National Grid reference you need to locate where in the country you are. The country is divided into 100 km squares with each square given a unique two-letter reference. Use the administrative map to determine in which 100 km square a particular page of this atlas falls.

The bold letters and numbers between each grid line (**A** to **F**, **1** to **8**) are for use within a specific Street Atlas only, and when used with the page number, are a convenient way of referencing these grid squares.

Example   The railway bridge over DARLEY GREEN RD in grid square B1

Step 1: Identify the two-letter reference, in this example the page is in **SP**

Step 2: Identify the 1 km square in which the railway bridge falls. Use the figures in the southwest corner of this square: Eastings **17**, Northings **74**. This gives a unique reference: **SP 17 74**, accurate to 1 km.

Step 3: To give a more precise reference accurate to 100 m you need to estimate how many tenths along and how many tenths up this 1 km square the feature is (to help with this the 1 km square is divided into four 500 m squares). This makes the bridge about **8** tenths along and about **1** tenth up from the southwest corner.

This gives a unique reference: **SP 178 741**, accurate to 100 m.

Eastings (read from left to right along the bottom) come before Northings (read from bottom to top). If you have trouble remembering say to yourself "Along the hall, THEN up the stairs"!

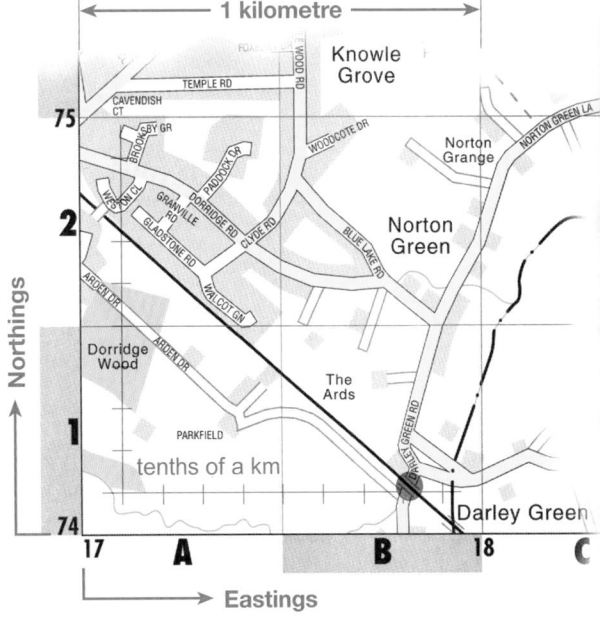

Addresses

Name and Address	Telephone	Page	Grid reference

 **Ordnance Survey**

 **MOTORING ATLAS**
Britain

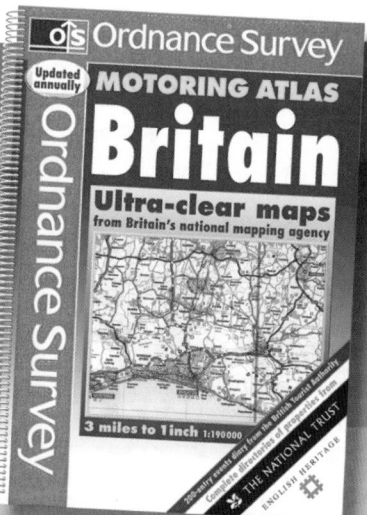

The best-selling *OS Motoring Atlas Britain* uses unrivalled and up-to-date mapping from the Ordnance Survey digital database. The exceptionally clear mapping is at a large scale of 3 miles to 1 inch (Orkney/Shetland Islands at 5 miles to 1 inch).

A special feature of the atlas is its wealth of tourist and leisure information. It contains comprehensive directories, including descriptions and location details, of the properties of the National Trust in England and Wales, the National Trust for Scotland, English Heritage and Historic Scotland. There is also a useful diary of British Tourist Authority Events listing more than 300 days out around Britain during the year.

Available from all good bookshops or direct from the publisher:
Tel: 01933 443863

The atlas includes:

◆ **112 pages of fully updated mapping**
◆ **45 city and town plans**
◆ **8 extra-detailed city approach maps**
◆ **route-planning maps**
◆ **restricted motorway junctions**
◆ **local radio information**
◆ **distances chart**
◆ **county boundaries map**
◆ **multi-language legend**

Street Atlases from Philip's

Philip's publish an extensive range of regional and local street atlases which are ideal for motoring, business and leisure use. They are widely used by the emergency services and local authorities throughout Britain.

Key features include:

◆ Superb county-wide mapping at an extra-large scale of 3½ inches to 1 mile, or 2½ inches to 1 mile in pocket editions

◆ Complete urban and rural coverage, detailing every named street in town and country

◆ Each atlas available in three handy formats – hardback, spiral, pocket paperback

'The mapping is very clear... great in scope and value'
★★★★ BEST BUY   **AUTO EXPRESS**

1 Bedfordshire
2 Berkshire
3 Birmingham and West Midlands
4 Bristol and Bath
5 Buckinghamshire
6 Cambridgeshire
7 Cardiff, Swansea and The Valleys
8 Cheshire
9 County Durham and Teesside
10 Derbyshire
11 Edinburgh and East Central Scotland
12 North Essex
13 South Essex
14 Glasgow and West Central Scotland
15 North Hampshire
16 South Hampshire
17 Hertfordshire
18 East Kent
19 West Kent
20 Lancashire
21 Leicestershire and Rutland
22 London
23 Greater Manchester
24 Merseyside
25 Northamptonshire
26 Nottinghamshire
27 Oxfordshire
28 Staffordshire
29 Surrey
30 East Sussex
31 West Sussex
32 Tyne and Wear and Northumberland
33 Warwickshire
34 East Yorkshire and Northern Lincolnshire
35 South Yorkshire
36 West Yorkshire

How to order

The Philip's range of street atlases is available from good retailers or directly from the publisher by phoning 01933 443863